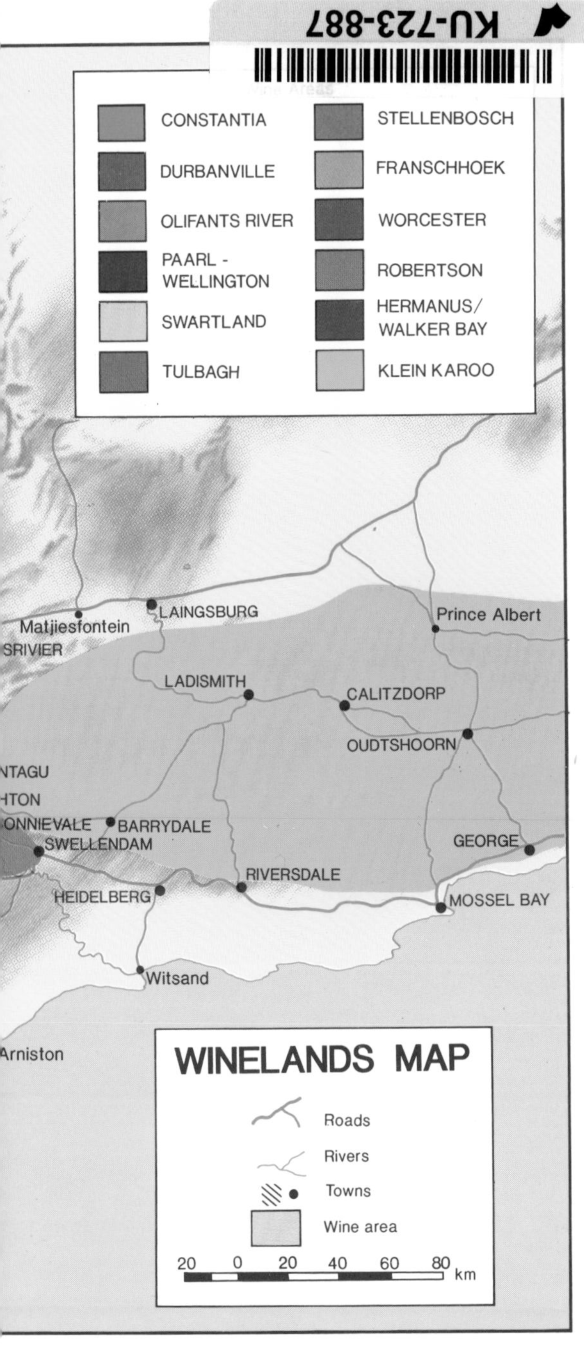

CONSTANTIA
STELLENBOSCH
DURBANVILLE
FRANSCHHOEK
OLIFANTS RIVER
WORCESTER
PAARL - WELLINGTON
ROBERTSON
SWARTLAND
HERMANUS/ WALKER BAY
TULBAGH
KLEIN KAROO
LAINGSBURG
Matjiesfontein
Prince Albert
LADISMITH
CALITZDORP
OUDTSHOORN
BARRYDALE
SWELLENDAM
GEORGE
RIVERSDALE
HEIDELBERG
MOSSEL BAY
Witsand
WINELANDS MAP
Roads
Rivers
Towns
Wine area
20 0 20 40 60 80 km

JOHN PLATTER

SOUTH AFRICAN WINES 1999

Cellars • Vineyards • Winemakers
Wine Country Restaurants

PUBLISHER
Andrew McDowall

CONSULTING EDITOR
Erica Platter

EDITOR
Philip van Zyl

Associates

Michael Fridjhon
Colin Frith
Dave Hughes
David Johnson
Angela Lloyd
Tony Mossop
Jabulani Ntshangase
John Platter
Dave Swingler
Irina von Holdt

Co-ordinator and Sales
Alison Worrall

Maps
Frits Beneke, Angela Lloyd

Photographer
Dennis Gordon

Published by

The Platter Wine Guide SA (Pty) Ltd
A wholly owned subsidiary of Creda Communications (Pty) Ltd
Eliot Avenue
Epping Industria
7475
E-mail: info@creda.co.za
Tel. No.: (021) 547321 Fax No.: (021) 548118

TO USE THE GUIDE

Wines are entered under the name of the producer, estate, co-operative winery or brand name of a merchant. These are listed alphabetically. Entries feature some or all of the following information: producer's name, address, phone/fax number, e-mail address, website; wine colour and style; grape variety (or varieties), vintage detail, area of origin, recent awards and star-ratings as below. For brevity, only ★★★ or higher are indicated (note: no half stars).

Ratings

★★★★★	**Superlative. A Cape classic.**
★★★★	**Excellent. Fine international standard.**
★★★	**Very good/promising. Stands out from the crowd.**
◀	**Good value.**
☺	**Super-quaffer. Exceptionally drinkable and well priced.**

Subjective choices in a SA wine context. See also "Seeing Stars".

Symbols & Abbreviations

Veritas	SA National Bottled Wine Show
VVG	Veritas Double Gold Medal
VG	Veritas Gold Medal
SAA	Selection (First & Business Class)
WINE	★★★★ stars in S.A. WINE Magazine
CIWG	Cape Independent Winemakers Guild
IWSC	International Wine & Spirit Competition
WO	Wine of Origin
[bottle]	Bottles own wine on property
[glass]	Visiting hours, tasting details
[knife & fork]	Restaurant/refreshments
MCC	Méthode Cap Classique; sparkling by méthode champenoise
NLH	Noble Late Harvest
SLH	Special Late Harvest
NV	Non-vintage
Malo	Malolactic fermentation
gms/l	Grams per litre
% alc.	Percentage of alcohol by volume.

ISBN 0-9583898-5-3.

CONTENTS

Foreword

It's the little guys mostly and often the new ones who are setting the pace in Cape wine. It's an uplifting story, a mouthfilling, delicious one and, as they say in Burgundy—with a raised eyebrow, France being the land of sub-texts—it's a good idea to know the person who makes the wine if you "want to drink the best".

At the top end of this sentiment there would be the craftsmen and women—and cheerful, uncommercial nutters—trying to worry the individuality of their vineyards into a bottle. At the other, could they be inferring there are low lifers who fake labels or pay workers extortionist wages and fidget with additives? All can change the taste of wine.

So in Burgundy it is not enough and anyway a generalisation to understand that Aloxe-Corton is thought by habitués to be the St. Tropez of the Côte d'Or, the most "open and relaxed" wine of the region. To make an informed choice you should know, *within* Aloxe, your seemingly casual but scrupulous winemaker from the idle, corner-cutting one—and no country escapes its rogues (nor its commercial Blue Nuns). And worse.

Wine is neither dull nor simple.

The Cape may not be as complex yet as Burgundy but we're headed there. And personalities matter—at least as much as *terroir,* the great, all-encompassing French word meaning climate, soil and aspect—and probably including quality defining ingredients like natural yeast strains. But the winemaker is part of a wine's *terroir* too!

How enjoyable and thirst-making to be able to say as you twirl a bottle: "The woman who produces this jumps out of aeroplanes for fun and has a weakness for Italian skiing instructors." You cannot make great wine without passion—and nor should we drink it without it.

Passion there certainly is now in the Cape. A few years ago, we talked of a stampede into the unknown—and it's still thudding along. In wine's varied and delightful 7 000-year odyssey out from Mesopotamia, has there ever been such a refreshing facelift?

Of course there has, but let's romanticise and revel for a while in our own little renaissance. One minute it seemed the wine industry's governing fathers still had all their crazed quota and area restrictions and pricing privileges in place, a farrago of nonsense consonant with the old South Africa. Now people of all races are allowed to grow anything, anywhere, sell at prices they think the market will stand; and unions, farm owners, MPs, consumers, sociologists and all-comers are "interfacing" in the reassuringly unsettling way of a democracy. We no longer have to adjust our minds; there *was* a fault in reality after all.

There's fresh air and a combustible vitality and some chaos as the wine revival blazes forward. Even the most carefree wine drinker—"I know what I like, ha, ha, and don't give me that stuff about an impertinent little wine"—has noticed a new elegance starting to creep into the latest vintages. The harder-nosed among us of course acknowledge the renewal still remains more in the promise than in the drinking—that the Cape at its best still needs to bow to Australia and California, that with few exceptions we don't reach the very top notes yet—and that our productivity in international terms needs much improvement.

But there is much newness everywhere and it can't go nowhere. Just consider:

We have new regions opening up fast in this post-quota new age, from Bredasdorp in the east to heaven knows where in the dry west. Some disappointments? Inevitable, but surprises galore too in the next decade.

We have new investors both local and foreign, with unbridled minds and chequebooks and cool ideas. They mean new wines, tastes, prices and sure, some gimmickry and puffery. But again, more surprises.

We have new winemakers, and older ones with fresh attitudes, again both domestic and international, brimming with curiosity and experiment. They've moved on from the sterile, fruit-versus-Cape "tradition" debate about styles. Ripe grapes, fine tannins and elegant balance are the general aims now, even if they're still achieved too infrequently. The contentions that more fruit in wine would threaten longevity and destroy the Cape's wine identity were always Irish arguments. But there's plenty of unfinished work: the Cape has yet to produce dry whites which last and improve with any certainty. And there still is no more than a small handful of really world-class producers. But at least more and more are scrabbling toward the most difficult summits in wine—establishing a credible, inimitable, alluring difference between this one and the next.

We have "new" grape varieties—viognier, mourvèdre, nebbiolo and others, coming on stream, again broadening choice, prompting new fashions, creating excitement; still too few and being planted too slowly perhaps, compared with California for example, but we're on our way. South Africa's skewed ratios of grape variety plantings will take time to reverse, but there's no burying of heads in the sand any more. ("We have only about 20% of classic, internationally-in-demand big-five varieties—cabernet sauvignon, merlot, shiraz, chardonnay, sauvignon blanc—to 80% bulk and brandy sorts, almost the converse of our competitors".) But perhaps there's also an opportunity here—to leapfrog international trends by quickly achieving a richer mix of both the accepted big-selling classics and the rare and new. It is a sight easier to grub palomino for carmenere than it is to pull cabernet for roussanne. We should be sending mission after mission to ferret out likely prospects all over the globe, for example among the 500 little-known varieties in and around Moldavia, surely a fabulous treasury of "discovery" wines.

And we have new export markets and consumers, the most powerful catalysts of all. They mean bolder, more critical foreign wine buyers—and wine critics, unfettered by the incestuousness and links among producers and too many domestic wine writers (this one included sometimes, I'm afraid). The lines between critics and the trade have been far too blurred. And until the industry moderates its foaming equation of criticism with treason, so long as it believes the duty of the wine writer is to promote wine rather than to comment, advise and entertain consumers, it will continue to see anodyne and blurred images of itself. The South African wine renaissance could still be derailed by three huge and urgent problems—one viticultural, two political. First, unless something is done radically and speedily to overcome the shortage of planting material, improve the availability of new clones and varieties and make virus-resistant rootstocks generally obtainable, the industry will remain critically handicapped against international competition. The industry is too faction-ridden for this to be left to private players, the government must step in, especially to fix up enabling legislation. It should declare war on the whole insidious viticultural virus scourge, which has been at the root of the Cape's wine quality problems for decades.

Second, world-class competitiveness will elude South African wine for as long as farming ownership and the farm working community remain so starkly demarcated racially and remuneratively. Yes, of course it's impossible to right skewed historic legacies overnight. Yes, wages and conditions are doubtless sometimes as bad or even worse elsewhere. But South Africa has its unique, inescapable history and will stand scrutinised, exposed on a separate (apartheid?) stage for decades yet. In fact though, this could be turned to advantage if exploited sincerely not cynically, with demonstrable, racially inclusive partnerships and new deals. Each becomes a Mandela miracle story that improves the taste of the wine. Again, it's mostly small-scale and private producers who are taking morale-boosting initiatives. There are plenty of details in the following pages.

But there remains a less uplifting side. In mid-1998, a Wine Workers' Conference in Stellenbosch heard that in one long-established wine region of the Cape, average wages were R120 a week (about UK£10 or US$16, at prevailing exchange rates). "Not much evidence of gain sharing," said the laconic researcher, Dr. Joachim Ewert of Stellenbosch University, noting a tenfold increase in exports in the previous five years. "My prediction is that conflict will arise," he said.

"These are explosively unconscionable wages," said ANC MP Sue van der Merwe, an activist in winelands affairs. "And we're already nearly five years into the New South Africa. We have the sense that international buyers do not want wine which is made from the sweat of someone living in a hovel."

It's not solely the wine industry's duty in these exceptional South Africa times to respond to one of the colossal acts of moral generosity this century. But wine is an especially symbolic, national and cultural asset and has mirrored society at every stage in the past 340 years. And every Cape wine today on a table abroad is an ambassador. Wine is as important in its way as soccer, rugby and all those other high-profile pursuits that define—or can defile—the new patriotism.

Which, thirdly, brings us to South Africa's extraordinary violence and crime. They threaten to drag the miracle into the mire, and with them much else. Quo vadis then the grand African Renaissance—and with it our proud little wine revival?

Ultimately, as people look back in a decade or two, the heros and heroines of these stirring times will be the small-time folk with heads down and focused (on world-class wine quality in this case), using their wits and all the intuitive wisdom and indestructible wit of people of the soil. Serge Hochar made wine—and distinctive wine too, Chateau Musar's spicy blend of Cabernet Sauvignon and Cinsault—near the Bekaar Valley outside Beirut for all 20 vintages of the war in Lebanon. The pages that follow celebrate that indomitable spirit of great winemaking everywhere. Perhaps Serge should be the Nederburg Auction's next guest of honour to explain how to produce finesse under fire in wine appellations with the most testing of *terroirs*. We shall always need good wine, to freshen our feelings, for friends, for life, for fun—and to brace ourselves for the challenges of making the new reality work.

John Platter

SEEING STARS (AND "SMILEYS")

The purpose of this guide, as always, is to enlighten, inform, amuse—yes, there's a smile in every glass, or have we forgotten?—to encourage, inspire and advise, as best we can, given the necessary subjectivity of such an undertaking.

Our aim, first and foremost, is to offer a bulletin-board—a vinous gazette, if you like—of developments, trends, incidents, appointments (disappointments too) across the winelands, from Malmesbury to Marondera. But also: to be an escort, pathfinder and even, on occasion, loyal catechist and conscience. Which is why we present not just raw (green?) facts—dissections, snippets, sound-bites—but opinion (often fresh, sometimes piquant but, we like to believe, never astringent) of ten seasoned tasters, all with international experience, along with suggestions and pronouncements about wine-intrinsics—balance (or lack of), longevity, readiness. These are offered not to praise or damn, but to assist visitors to cellars, wine-store customers, wine-students and others in their explorations and purchases.

From the 1997 edition we chose to not judge wines on a strictly comparative basis. That decision—after 16 years of ranking entries by means of stars—was not taken lightly, nor in haste. In wine (we noted at the time), as in all matters of personal taste, there are neither fixed absolutes nor unfailingly exact measures. To imply, by way of hierarchical star-ratings that numeric accuracy is attainable (desirable?) was, we felt, inappropriate. Instead, we opted for an altogether less judgemental approach of highlighting what we consider are each range's strengths and/or idiosyncrasies, and flagging these with one or two "bunches", as distinct from "stars". "Pleasure," (we wrote), "the irreproachable, often indefinable yardstick of the French, is the main criterion." For watchers of top form, we collated results of recent and major wine contest results, plus our own best-of-bunch selections.

However, we polled a great many consumers (and producers, people in the trade, media mavens, academics *et al*) informally over the past year and the vote was overwhelmingly in favour of the previous star-ratings—precisely because these are more concise and, furthermore, enable users to easily pick out gems (quality and value-wise) among the swelling profusion of Cape wine labels.

While our own views remain unchanged, we do not wish to dictate to consumers who, first and foremost, are the users of this guide. Thus, for this edition, we have revived the familiar star-rating system with these key amendments:

- only 3, 4 and 5 stars have been awarded on the usual ascending scale of quality (see *To use the guide*); wines below 3 stars have been tasted and described but not rated.
- no half-stars have been awarded, mainly to avoid academic hair-splitting
- well-priced quaffing wines have been identified by the ☺ indicator in the entries and collated separately (see *Super-quaffers*)

It is worth noting that our tasters were confronted with an excruciating task: like the first-team coach who must choose among a dazzling, equally-admired array of talent, they had to make exquisitely nuanced judgements on many occasions, particularly when tasting potential 5-star wines. No doubt the assessments will provoke rumblings of displeasure—but hopefully roars of approval too. We do not pretend, nor have we ever presumed to be the arbiters of taste. Our own judgements are personal—obviously—and, wherever possible, counter-weighted by other tastings and opinions. Again, users of the guide will decide whether or not the approach followed here needs revisiting. In any event we encourage readers to consider the star-ratings in conjunction with the tasting notes. Together these provide a better indicator of breed than either in isolation.

A SELECTION OF WELL-PRICED QUAFFERS

These super-quaffing wines are indicated thus: ☺ in the A-Z section and collated here for easy reference:

WHITES

Backsberg Bin 215 Chenin Blanc 97 **(Makro)**
Bellingham Sauvenay 98
Berg & Brook Chardonnay 97
Bloupunt Chardonnay (unwooded) 97/98
Bon Courage Gewürztraminer 98
Bovlei Gewürztraminer 97
Brampton Sauvignon Blanc 98 **(Rustenberg)**
Cape Chamonix Blanc NV
Clairvaux Rhine Riesling 98

Craighall Chardonnay-Sauvignon Blanc 97 **(Gilbeys)**
De Wet Cape Riesling 98
De Wet Chardonnay 98
Dewetshof Chardonnay Bon Vallon 98
Du Toitskloof Chenin Blanc 98
Eersterivier Muscat d'Alexandrie 98
Excelsior Sauvignon Blanc 98
Fort Simon Wooded Chenin Blanc 98
Franschhoek Misty NV **(Makro)**
Franschhoek Vineyards Chardonnay-Chenin Barrel Fermented 97
Goede Hoop Sauvignon Blanc 98
Goedverwacht Colombard 98
Goudini Chenin Blanc 98
Hartenberg Bin 6 NV
Jordan Chameleon Chardonnay-Sauvignon Blanc
Kleinbosch Bushvine Dry Muscat 98 **(Cape Wine Cellars)**
Koelenhof Koelenhoffer 98
KWV Steen
Laibach Chardonnay-Sauvignon Blanc 98
Landskroon Pinot Blanc-Chenin Blanc 97
Leidersburg Chardonnay 98 **(Stellenbosch Wines Direct)**
Long Mountain Sémillon-Chardonnay
Longridge Capelands Chardonnay 98
Longridge Capelands Classic Cape White 98
Lutzville Sauvignon Blanc 98
McGregor Colombard-Chardonnay 98
Morgenhof Blanc de M 98
Nederburg Elegance
Oddbins Sauvignon Blanc-Chardonnay Bin 61 98 **(Shoprite Checkers)**
Oscar's Reserve Chenin Blanc 98 **(Wine Warehouse)**
Oscar's Reserve Sauvignon Blanc 98 **(Wine Warehouse)**
Perdeberg Chardonnay-Sauvignon Blanc 98
Perdeberg Chenin Blanc Semi-Sweet 98
Pick 'n Pay Chardonnay-Sauvignon Blanc 98
Romansrivier Ceres Colombard Off-dry 98
Romansrivier Ceres Vin Blanc 98
Rooiberg Colombard 98
Ruitersvlei Sauvignon Blanc-Chenin 98
Simonsig Chenin Blanc
Swartland Riesling 98
Vaughan Johnson Good Everyday Cape White
Vaughan Johnson Seriously Good Plonk (white)
Vaughan Johnson Sunday Best (white)
Vlottenburg Chenin Blanc 98 off-dry
Vredendal Goiya Kgeisje 98
Weltevrede Rhine Riesling 98
Woolworths Blanc de Blanc (Vin de Cuvée)
Woolworths Fernão Pires 97
Zonnebloem Blanc de Blanc 98

REDS
Avontuur Avon Rouge NV
Babbling Brook Ruby Cabernet 97 **(Makro)**
Barrydale Tinta Barocca/Ruby Cabernet 98
Berg & Brook Ruby Cabernet
Boschendal Pavillon Rouge 98
Botha Dassie's Rood 97
Cape Bay Mellow Red 98

Clos Malverne Devonet 97
De Wet Droë Rooi NV
Douglas Green St. Raphael NV
Goudini Ruby Cabernet 98
Goue Vallei Chianti 98
Groot Constantia Rood NV
Hartenberg Bin 3 NV
Hartenberg Bin 9 NV
Kleine Zalze Gamay Noir 98
KWV Cinsaut 97
Longridge Capelands Merlot 98
Longridge Capelands Ruby Cabernet 98
McGregor Village Red 97
Merwespont/Agulhas Cabernet Sauvignon 97
Nuy Rouge de Nuy 97
Paddagang Paddajolyt 98
Pick 'n Pay Dry Red NV
Riebeek Dry Red 98
Robertson Cabernet Sauvignon Reserve 97
Robertson "Wide River" Ruby Cabernet 98
Romansrivier De Kijker Pinotage 97
Romansrivier Vino Rood 97
Ruitersvlei Cinsaut-Cabernet Sauvignon 97
Rust en Vrede Tinta Barocca 97
Simonsig Adelberg
Sinnya Cabernet-Merlot 97
Spier Cellars Unwooded Cabernet Sauvignon 97
Spruitdrift Cabernet Sauvignon-Merlot 97
Swartland Dry Red NV
Tassenberg NV **(SFW)**
Twin Oaks Dry Red 97 **(Stellenbosch Wines Direct)**
Twin Oaks Ruby Cabernet 97 **(Stellenbosch Wines Direct)**
Van Loveren River Red 98
Vaughan Johnson Captain's Claret
Vaughan Johnson Good Everyday Cape Red
Vlottenburg Rouge NV
Wellington Cabernet Sauvignon 96
Wellington Pinotage 97
Windmeul Merry Mill Red 98
Woolworths Maison Rouge (Vin de Cuvée)
Woolworths Selected Cape Red
Zevenwacht Zevenrood NV

BLANC DE NOIR/ROSÉ
De Wet Blanc de Noir 98
Villiersdorp Overberg Rosé 98

SPARKLING
Domein Doornkraal Tickled Pink Sparking Wine NV
Roodezandt Sparkling Wine Demi Sec NV
Van Loveren Papillon Brut NV

EXPORT ONLY
Arniston Bay Chenin Blanc-Chardonnay 98 **(Vinfruco)**
Benguela Current Chardonnay 97 **(Berg & Brook)**
Cheetah Valley Chardonnay 97 **(Berg & Brook)**
Cullinan View Chardonnay 98 **(Vinimark)**
Sainsbury Cinsaut-Pinotage 97 **(Vinfruco)**
Signature Cinsaut 97 **(IWS)**

LEADING CAPE WINES

Top tasting performers 96-98							
GV	General Vintage rating; not confined to 1 year						
	SAA Trophy Winner						
WINE★	WINE 5 Stars						
N.B.	Some wineries do not enter SAA or Veritas etc.						
	This is not a comprehensive list						
		Veritas	WINE	SAA	Platter		
	Year	2 gold	4-stars	Selctns	98 Ed.	GV	5-stars
RED BLENDS							
Backsberg Kln B/toren	92			SAA			
Bertrams R Fuller Res	90	VVG					
B'wachting Christine	93						
B'wachting Christine	92	VVG		SAA			
B'wachting Christine	91						
B'wachting Christine	90						
B'wachting Christine	89					GV	
Cordoba Crescendo	95		WINE				★★★★★
Douglas Gr. Cab/Shiraz	95	VVG					
Glen Carlou Gr Classique	95		WINE				
Grangehurst Cab/Mer	95		WINE			GV	★★★★★
Grangehurst Cab/Mer	94			SAA			
Grangehurst Cab/Mer Res	93						
Kanonkop Paul Sauer	95		WINE				★★★★★
Kanonkop Paul Sauer	94		WINE				
KWV Roodeberg	95	VVG					
KWV Cath Cellars Trip.	94			SAA			
L'Avenir L'Ami Simon	96	VVG		SAA			
Le Bonheur Prima	95		WINE				
Le Bonheur Prima	92			SAA			
Lievland DVB	94						
L'Ormarins Optima	94						
Meerlust Rubicon	94						
Meerlust Rubicon	91					GV	
Morgenhof	95						
Nederburg Edelrood	93	VVG					
N'hof Lord N'ling Res	93			SAA			
Neil Ellis Cab/Mer	95						
Rozendal	95		WINE				
Rozendal	94		WINE				
Rustenberg Peter Barlow	96						★★★★★
Rust en Vrede Estate	94			SAA			
Rust en Vrede Estate	93	VVG		SAA			
Simonsig Tiara	95	VVG		SAA			
Simonsig F. Malan Res	95						
Stellenzicht	94		WINE				
Thelema Cab/Mer	93						
Thelema Cab/Mer	91					GV	
Veenwouden Classic	95					GV	★★★★★
Veenwouden Classic	94	VVG					
Vergenoegd Res	95		WINE				
Villiera Cru Monro	95	VVG					

Top tasting performers 96-98							
		Veritas	WINE	SAA	Platter		
	Year	2 gold	4-stars	Selctns	98 Ed.	GV	5-stars
Villiera Cru Monro	94			SAA			
Warwick Trilogy	95				🍇🍇		
Zevenwacht Cab/Merlot	96			SAA			
CABERNET SAUVIGNON							
Alto	95		WINE				
Backsberg	94			SAA			
Bellingham	95	VVG					
Blaauwklippen	94			SAA			
Brampton	95		WINE	SAA	🍇🍇		
B'wachting	92	VVG		SAA	🍇🍇	GV	
B'wachting	91				🍇🍇		
Delheim	96				🍇🍇		
Delheim	95			SAA	🍇🍇		
Delheim	94			SAA			
De Trafford	95		WINE				
Douglas Green	93		WINE				
Eikendal Reserve	94				🍇🍇		
Fairview	95			SAA			
Grangehurst CIWG	95		WINE★				
Haute Provence	96	VVG					
Haute Provence	95		WINE				
Jordan	93		WINE				
Kaapzicht Cape View	95	VVG					
Kaapzicht Cape View	94	VVG					
Kanonkop	95		WINE				
Kanonkop	94		WINE				
Klein Constantia	93	VVG	WINE				
KWV Cath. Cellars	95	VVG		SAA			
KWV Cath. Cellars	94	VVG		SAA	🍇🍇		
KWV Cath. Cellars	93			SAA			
Laborie Estate	95		WINE				
Lanzerac	95		WINE				
L'Avenir	94	VVG					
Le Bonheur	95		WINE				
Le Riche Res	97						★★★★★
Meerlust	93		WINE				
Mont Rochelle	96	VVG					
Moreson	95	VVG					
Morgenhof	94		WINE				
Nederburg Res	91			SAA			
Nederburg PB163	86	VVG					
Neil Ellis	95				🍇🍇		
Neil Ellis	94		WINE				
Overgaauw	93		WINE				
Plaisir de Merle	95			SAA	🍇🍇		
Plaisir de Merle	94			SAA	🍇🍇	GV	
Plaisir de Merle	93				🍇🍇		
Ruitersvlei	96	VVG					
Saxenburg PC	95		WINE	SAA	🍇🍇		
Saxenburg PC	92			SAA	🍇🍇		

Top tasting performers 96-98

		Veritas	WINE	SAA	Platter		
	Year	2 gold	4-stars	Selctns	98 Ed.	GV	5-stars
Saxenburg PC	91	VVG					
Simonsig	92	VVG					
Simonsig	90	VVG					
Stellenryck	92	VVG					
Stellenryck	91	VVG	WINE				
Stellenzicht	94	VVG		SAA			
Stellenzicht	91			SAA			
Swartland	94		WINE				
Thelema	95						*****
Thelema	94		WINE	SAA	🍇🍇		
Thelema	93			SAA	🍇🍇		
Thelema	92				🍇🍇	GV	
Uitkyk	92	VVG					
Vergenoegd	95		WINE				
Vlottenburg	94		WINE				
Warwick	94	VVG	WINE				
PINOT NOIR							
B/F Galpin Peak	97						*****
Cabrière	97				🍇🍇		
Cabrière	94				🍇🍇		
Glen Carlou	96		WINE				
Ham. Russell Ashbourne	96		WINE		🍇🍇		
Hamilton Russell	97						*****
Hamilton Russell	96		WINE				
Hamilton Russell	95				🍇🍇	GV	
WhaleHaven	96		WINE				
MERLOT							
Backsberg	94		WINE				
Backsberg	93		WINE				
Bellingham	95	VVG					
Bloemendal	96	VVG					
Boschendal	95		WINE				
Delheim	96	VVG					
Eikendal	96				🍇🍇		
Fairview Res	93			SAA	🍇🍇		
Fleur du Cap	95	VVG					
Grangehurst	94		WINE				
Hartenberg	95	VVG		SAA	🍇🍇		
Jordan	95	VVG					
KWV Cath Cellars	95			SAA	🍇🍇		
Lanzerac	95		WINE				
Le Moutonne	91		WINE				
Louisvale	94		WINE				
Môreson	95	VVG					
Morgenhof	95				🍇🍇		
Morgenhof	94	VVG			🍇🍇		
Overgaauw	95		WINE				
Overgaauw	94		WINE				
Plaisir de Merle	95			SAA	🍇🍇		
Saxenburg PC	95				🍇🍇		

Top tasting performers 96-98							
		Veritas	WINE	SAA	Platter		
	Year	2 gold	4-stars	Selctns	98 Ed.	GV	5-stars
Saxenburg PC	94	VVG			🍇🍇		
Stellenzicht	95	VVG		SAA			
Thelema	94		WINE	SAA	🍇🍇		
Thelema	92			SAA	🍇🍇	GV	
Veenwouden	95		WINE		🍇🍇		
Veenwouden	94				🍇🍇		
Vergelegen	95				🍇🍇		
Warwick	95			SAA			
Warwick	94			SAA			
CABERNET FRANC							
Avontuur	96		WINE				
Bellingham	96			SAA			
Bellingham	95	VVG					
Bellingham Premium	95				🍇🍇		
Warwick	95		WINE	SAA	🍇🍇		
Warwick	94		WINE*				
PINOTAGE							
Altydgedacht	95		WINE				
Beaumont	95		WINE				
Bellingham Premium	96	VVG					
Beyerskloof	96			SAA			
Beyerskloof	95		WINE				
Bredell	96		WINE				
Diemersdal	93			SAA			
Fairview Cyril Back	95			SAA	🍇🍇		
Grangehurst	96				🍇🍇		
Grangehurst	95		WINE		🍇🍇	GV	
Hidden Valley	96		WINE				
Jacobsdal	95			SAA	🍇🍇		
Kaapzicht	96	VVG	WINE				
Kanonkop CIWG Res	95		WINE		🍇🍇		
Kanonkop	95				🍇🍇		
Kanonkop	94				🍇🍇		
Kanonkop	93				🍇🍇		
Kanonkop	92				🍇🍇	GV	
KWV Cath. Cellars	95			SAA			
KWV Cath. Cellars	94			SAA			
Laborie	95			SAA			
Lanzerac	95		WINE				
L'Avenir	96	VVG	WINE				
L'Avenir CIWG	96		WINE		🍇🍇		
Oak Village	95			SAA			
Perdeberg Reserve	97	VVG					
Saxenburg PC	96		WINE				
Saxenburg PC	95		WINE	SAA			
Southern Right	95			SAA			
Swartland Reserve	96	VVG					
Uiterwyk (Single Vineyard)	96		WINE				*****
Uiterwyk	95	VVG					
Vlottenburg	95		WINE				

Top tasting performers 96-98							
		Veritas	WINE	SAA	Platter		
	Year	2 gold	4-stars	Selctns	98 Ed.	GV	5-stars
Warwick	95	VVG			🍇🍇		
Zonnebloem	94			SAA			
SHIRAZ							
Backsberg	93		WINE				
Bellingham	95			SAA			
Blaauwklippen	95		WINE				
Blaauwklippen	93			SAA			
Boschendal	94		WINE				
Bovlei	93		WINE				
Bredell's	96		WINE				
Fairview	95			SAA			
Fairview	93				🍇🍇	GV	
Hartenberg	95	VVG		SAA	🍇🍇		
Hartenberg	93			SAA			
Klein Constantia	94			SAA			
La Motte	94				🍇🍇	GV	
Middelvlei	97				🍇🍇		
Rust en Vrede	94		WINE		🍇🍇		
Saxenburg PC	95		WINE	SAA	🍇🍇		
Saxenburg PC	93				🍇🍇	GV	
Simonsig	94			SAA			
Simonsvlei	95			SAA			
Slaley	97		WINE				
Stellenzicht	96	VVG		SAA	🍇🍇		
Stellenzicht	95				🍇🍇		
Stellenzicht	94				🍇🍇	GV	
Swartland	97		WINE				
Swartland	96	VVG					
Zandvliet	92	VVG					
CHARDONNAY							
Backsberg	95			SAA			
Boland	97			SAA			
Bon Courage Reserve	97			SAA			
Bon Courage	96			SAA			
Bouchard Finlayson	96				🍇🍇	GV	
Bouchard Finlayson	95				🍇🍇		
Bouchard Finlayson	93		WINE				
B'wachting	96			SAA	🍇🍇		
Constantia Uitsig	97		WINE				
Delaire	97		WINE				
Delheim	97			SAA			
De Wetshof Bateleur	95			SAA			
De Wetshof d'Honneur	95			SAA			
Eikendal	97	VVG					
Eikendal	96		WINE		🍇🍇		
Eikendal	94				🍇🍇	GV	
Fairview	96				🍇🍇	GV	
Fairview	95		WINE		🍇🍇		
Glen Carlou	97		WINE				
Glen Carlou Res.	96				🍇🍇		

Top tasting performers 96-98							
		Veritas	WINE	SAA	Platter		
	Year	2 gold	4-stars	Selctns	98 Ed.	GV	5-stars
Glen Carlou	96		WINE		🍇🍇		
Glen Carlou Res/Reg	94,95				🍇🍇	GV	
Groot Constantia Res	95		WINE				
Ham Russell Ashbourne 96			WINE		🍇🍇		
Hamilton Russell	96		WINE		🍇🍇		
Hamilton Russell	95		WINE		🍇🍇	GV	
Hoopenburg	93		WINE				
Jordan	96		WINE	SAA	🍇🍇		
Jordan	95	VVG	WINE	SAA	🍇🍇		
Jordan	94				🍇🍇	GV	
Klein Constantia	93		WINE				
KWV Cath. Cellars	95			SAA			
Longridge	97				🍇🍇		
Longridge	96				🍇🍇		
Louisvale	96				🍇🍇		
Louisvale	95		WINE		🍇🍇		
Meerlust	96				🍇🍇	GV	
Meerlust	95				🍇🍇		
Mont Rochelle	96		WINE				
Mulderbosch	94			SAA			
Mulderbosch	93		WINE				
Pick 'n Pay (Backsberg)	95		WINE				
Saxenburg	95		WINE	SAA			
Simonsig	96		WINE	SAA	🍇🍇		
Simonsig	95			SAA			
Slaley Sentinel	96		WINE				
Stellenryck	95	VVG					
Stellenzicht	97		WINE				
Stellenzicht	96		WINE	SAA			
Stellenzicht	95	VVG	WINE				
Thelema Res	97						★★★★★
Thelema	97		WINE				
Thelema	96			SAA	🍇🍇		
Thelema	95		WINE	🍾 SAA	🍇🍇		
Thelema	94				🍇🍇		
Thelema Res	93		WINE		🍇🍇	GV	
Thelema	93		WINE			GV	
Vergelegen Res	97		WINE				
Vergelegen Res	96			🍾 SAA	🍇🍇		
Vergelegen Res	95		WINE	SAA			
Zandvliet	97		WINE				
Zandvliet	95		WINE				
Zevenwacht	96	VVG		SAA			
SAUVIGNON BLANC							
Bloemendal	97		WINE				
Bon Courage Oaked Res	97	VVG					
Brampton	97			SAA	🍇🍇		
Brampton	96			SAA			
B'wachting	96				🍇🍇		
B'wachting	95				🍇🍇		

Top tasting performers 96-98							
		Veritas	WINE	SAA	Platter		
	Year	2 gold	4-stars	Selctns	98 Ed.	GV	5-stars
B'wachting	94		WINE	SAA	🍇🍇	GV	
Groot Constantia	96			SAA			
Haute Provence	97			SAA			
Jordan Blanc Fumé	97		WINE				
Jordan Blanc Fumé	96		WINE	SAA			
Kaapzicht	97		WINE				
Ken Forrester Bl Fume	94		WINE				
Klein Constantia	97	VVG		SAA	🍇🍇		
Klein Constantia	96	VVG	WINE	SAAx2 ★	🍇🍇		
Klein Constantia	95				🍇🍇	GV	
Klein Constantia	86		WINE★				
KWV Cath. Cellars	95			SAA			
La Petite Ferme B Fumé	96	VVG					
Le Bonheur	96			SAA			
Mulderbosch	97		WINE		🍇🍇		
Mulderbosch	96		WINE	SAA	🍇🍇		
Mulderbosch	94				🍇🍇	GV	
Mulderbosch Barrel F.	95			SAA			
Mulderbosch Barrel F.	94		WINE				
Neil Ellis Groenkloof	97		WINE		🍇🍇		
Nitida	95	VVG					
Plaisir de Merle	96			SAA			
Plaisir de Merle	95			SAA			
Rooiberg	94		WINE				
Saxenburg PC	97				🍇🍇		
Saxenburg PC	96		WINE		🍇🍇		
Saxenburg PC	95				🍇🍇	GV	
Simonsig	97		WINE				
Southern Right	96			SAA			
Spier IV Spears	96			SAA			
Springfield Sp. Cuvée	96	VVG					
Steenberg	97	VVG	WINE	SAA	🍇🍇		
Stellenzicht	97		WINE		🍇🍇		
Stellenzicht	96	VVG			🍇🍇		
Stellenzicht	95				🍇🍇	GV	
Thelema	97				🍇🍇		
Thelema	96			SAA	🍇🍇		
Thelema	95				🍇🍇		
Thelema	94		WINE		🍇🍇	GV	
Vergelegen Schaapenberg	98						★★★★★
Vergelegen	97			SAA			
Vergelegen	96			SAA			
Vergelegen Reserve	96	VVG					
Villiera Blanc Fumé	97		WINE	SAA			
Villiera	97	VVG	WINE	SAA			
Villiera Bush Vine	97	VVG	WINE	SAA	🍇🍇		
Welmoed Reserve	97		WINE				
Welmoed	96	VVG					
WHITE BLENDS							
Bon Courage Col/Chard	96	VVG					

Top tasting performers 96-98							
		Veritas	WINE	SAA	Platter		
	Year	2 gold	4-stars	Selctns	98 Ed.	GV	5-stars
B'wachting Buiten Blanc	97			SAA			
L'Avenir Vin d'Erstelle	96	VVG					
Louisvale SB/Chard	96			SAA			
Rheboksklоof GVBlanc	96			SAA			
Stellenzicht S/B. Sémillon	96	VVG					
Stellenzicht Fragrance	96	VVG					
Stellenzicht Heerenblanc	97			SAA			
V'gelegen Vin de Florence	96			SAA			
Zonnebloem Sémillon S/B	96			SAA			
RHINE RIESLING							
Bon Courage	96			SAA			
Groot Constantia	96	VVG	WINE				
Klein Constantia	96			SAA			
Lievland (Woolworths)	96	VVG					
L'Ormarins	96		WINE				
Rooiberg	94	VVG					
Simonsig (Dry)	96	VVG	WINE	SAA			
GEWÜRZTRAMINER							
Delheim	94			SAA			
Groot Constantia	97			SAA			
Nederburg	96			SAA			
Neethlingshof	97			SAA			
CHENIN BLANC							
Cederberg	97			SAA			
Charles Back Barrel F.	94		WINE				
Glen Carlou Peter Devereux	95		WINE				
Hartenberg Barrel-ferm	97		WINE				
Haute Provence	97		WINE				
Ken Forrester	95		WINE				
KWV Steen	96	VVG					
Laibach wooded	97		WINE				
L'Avenir	97		WINE				
Morgenhof Bin 210	96		WINE				
M'bosch Steen op Hout	97		WINE				
M'bosch Steen op Hout	96			SAA			
Savanha Barrel-ferm	97		WINE				
Stellenzicht	96		WINE	SAA			
Villiera	96		WINE	SAA			
SÉMILLON							
Delheim	97			SAA			
Klein Constantia	97						
Landau du Val	95		WINE				
Stellenzicht	97		WINE				
Stonybrook	97		WINE				
DESSERTS							
B'wachting Noblesse	95		WINE				
Klein Constantia Constance	94						*****
Klein Constantia Constance	93		WINE				
Klein Constantia Constance	92					GV	
L'Avenir Vin de Meurveur	97		WINE				

Top tasting performers 96-98							
		Veritas	WINE	SAA	Platter		
	Year	2 gold	4-stars	Selctns	98 Ed.	GV	5-stars
Lievland Nat Sweet	94	VVG					
Morgenhof	93		WINE				
Nederburg Eminence	96		WINE				
Nederburg Eminence	95	VVG					
Nederburg Private B S354	92	VVG					
Neethlingshof Weisser R	97	VVG			🍇🍇		★★★★★
Neethlingshof Weisser R	93				🍇🍇	GV	
Neethlingshof Weisser R	91		WINE		🍇🍇		
Simonsig Bukettraube	96		WINE				
Spier IV Spears	96	VVG					
Stellenzicht Weisser-R	96	VVG	WINE		🍇🍇	GV	
MÉTHODE CAP CLASSIQUE							
Bon Courage Brut Res	NV		WINE				
Graham Beck Bl de Blancs	92		WINE	🍾SAA	🍇🍇		
Graham Beck Bl de Blancs	91		WINE				
Graham Beck RD	91				🍇🍇		
JC Le Roux Chardonnay	90		WINE				
JC Le Roux Pinot Noir	89		WINE				
Laborie	92	VVG	WINE				
Longridge	94		WINE				
Mystery Reserve Brut	92		WINE				
Pongrácz	NV		WINE				
Villiera Gr Cuvée Brut	NV		WINE	🍾SAA			
FORTIFIED DESSERTS							
Bakenskop White M'del	91		WINE				
Boland White Muscadel	96	VVG					
Bon Courage Red M'del	94		WINE				
Du Toitskloof H'poot	92	VVG					
KWV Red Muscadel	75		WINE				
KWV White Jerepigo	79	VVG					
Landzicht White M'del	NV		WINE				
Nuy Wit Muskadel	96		WINE★				
Nuy Wit Muskadel	95				🍇🍇		
Nuy Wit Muskadel	93	VVG			🍇🍇		
Nuy Wit Muskadel	92				🍇🍇	GV	
Nuy Rooi Muskadel	96		WINE				
Nuy Rooi Muskadel	93	VVG					
Nuy Rooi Muskadel	92	VVG					
Rooiberg Wit Muskadel	94	VVG					
Rooiberg Wit Muskadel	93	VVG					
Rooiberg Jerepigo	95	VVG					
Rooiberg Jerepigo	94	VVG					
Rooiberg Jerepigo	93	VVG					
S'vlei Premier Muscadel	95		WINE				
Slanghoek Hanepoot	95	VVG					
"PORTS"							
Boplaas Vintage Res.	96		WINE				
Boplaas VR Touriga Nac	95		WINE	🍾SAA	🍇🍇		
Boplaas VR Touriga Nac	94		WINE		🍇🍇		
Boplaas Vintage Res	94			SAA			

Top tasting performers 96-98							
		Veritas	WINE	SAA	Platter		
	Year	2 gold	4-stars	Selctns	98 Ed.	GV	5-stars
Bredell Cape Vint. Res.	95		WINE		🍇🍇	GV	★★★★★
Bredell Cape Vint. Res.	94		WINE		🍇🍇		
Bredell Cape Vintage	93				🍇🍇	GV	
Die Krans Vintage Res	95		WINE		🍇🍇		
KWV Red	79	VVG					
KWV Wynoes	86	VVG					
Landskroon	95		WINE				
Landskroon	94			SAA			
Monis VO Tawny	NV	VVG		🍷SAA	🍇🍇		
Overgaauw VR Touriga N	93		WINE		🍇🍇		
Overgaauw	88				🍇🍇		
Rooiberg LBV	92	VVG					
Rustenberg Vintage	90	VVG					
Vergenoegd	94		WINE				

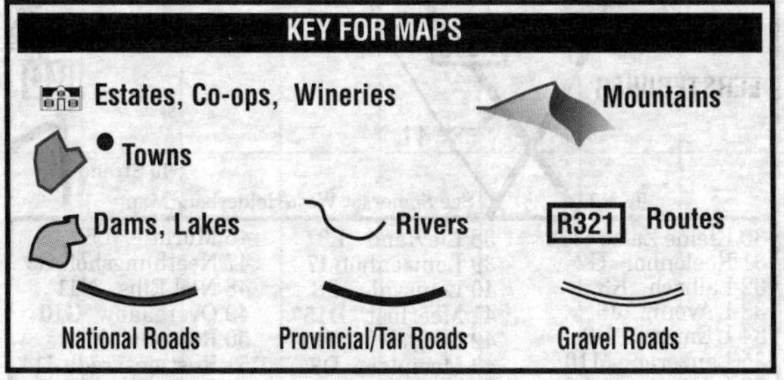

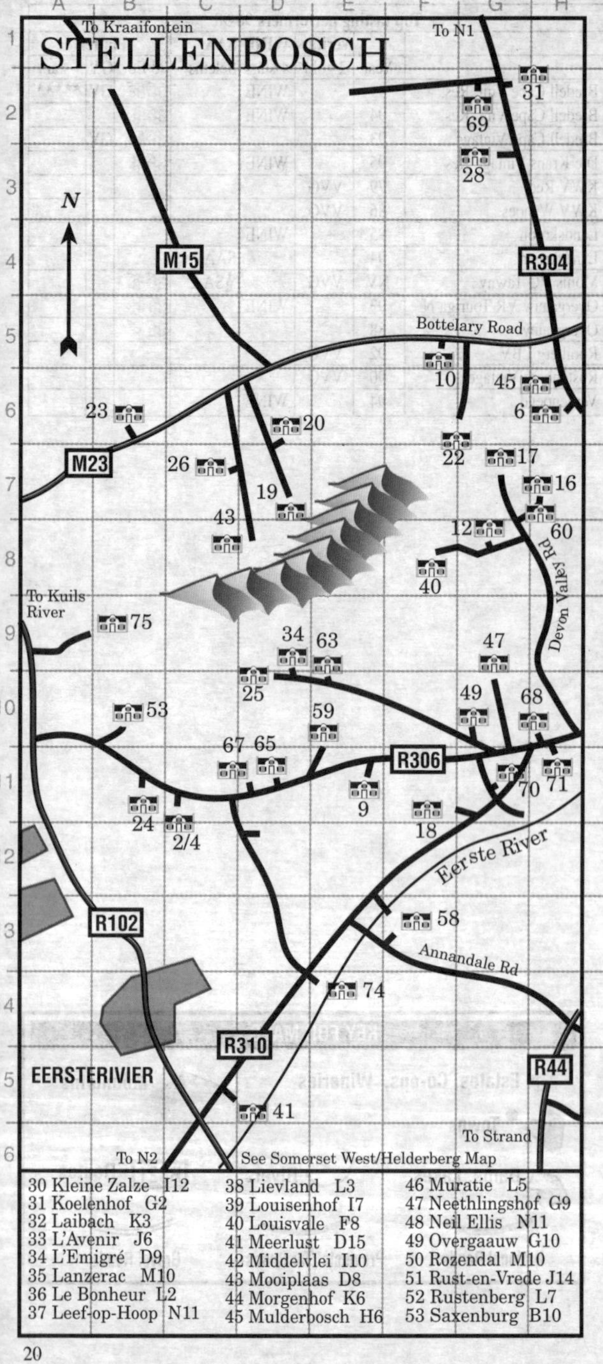
STELLENBOSCH
A B C D E F G H
1 2 3 4 5 6 7 8 9 10 11 12 13 14 15 16
To Kraaifontein
To N1
N
M15
R304
M23
R306
R102
R310
R44
Bottelary Road
Devon Valley Rd
Eerste River
Annandale Rd
To Kuils River
EERSTERIVIER
To N2
See Somerset West/Helderberg Map
To Strand
31
69
28
10
45
6
23
20
22
17
16
26
19
43
12
60
40
75
34
63
47
25
49
68
53
59
67
65
70
71
9
24
2/4
18
58
74
41
30 Kleine Zalze I12
31 Koelenhof G2
32 Laibach K3
33 L'Avenir J6
34 L'Emigré D9
35 Lanzerac M10
36 Le Bonheur L2
37 Leef-op-Hoop N11
38 Lievland L3
39 Louisenhof I7
40 Louisvale F8
41 Meerlust D15
42 Middelvlei I10
43 Mooiplaas D8
44 Morgenhof K6
45 Mulderbosch H6
46 Muratie L5
47 Neethlingshof G9
48 Neil Ellis N11
49 Overgaauw G10
50 Rozendal M10
51 Rust-en-Vrede J14
52 Rustenberg L7
53 Saxenburg B10

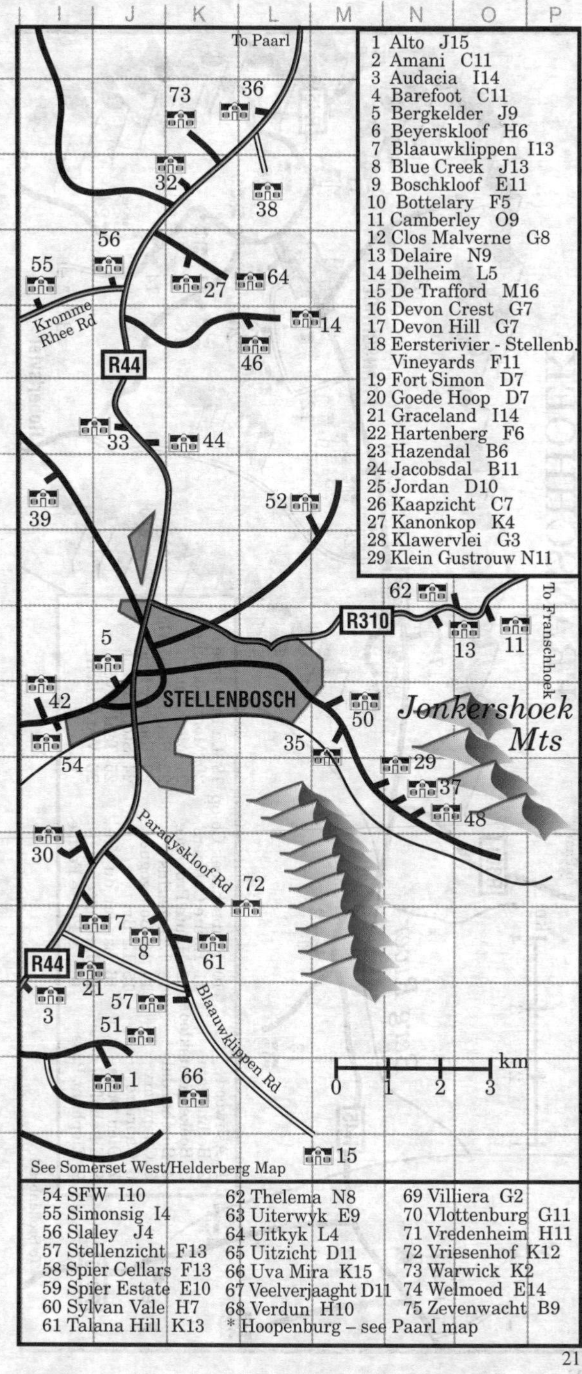
I J K L M N O P
To Paarl
1 Alto J15
2 Amani C11
3 Audacia I14
4 Barefoot C11
5 Bergkelder J9
6 Beyerskloof H6
7 Blaauwklippen I13
8 Blue Creek J13
9 Boschkloof E11
10 Bottelary F5
11 Camberley O9
12 Clos Malverne G8
13 Delaire N9
14 Delheim L5
15 De Trafford M16
16 Devon Crest G7
17 Devon Hill G7
18 Eersterivier - Stellenb. Vineyards F11
19 Fort Simon D7
20 Goede Hoop D7
21 Graceland I14
22 Hartenberg F6
23 Hazendal B6
24 Jacobsdal B11
25 Jordan D10
26 Kaapzicht C7
27 Kanonkop K4
28 Klawervlei G3
29 Klein Gustrouw N11
Kromme Rhee Rd
R44
R310
To Franschhoek
STELLENBOSCH
Jonkershoek Mts
Paradyskloof Rd
Blaauwklippen Rd
km
0 1 2 3
See Somerset West/Helderberg Map
54 SFW I10
55 Simonsig I4
56 Slaley J4
57 Stellenzicht F13
58 Spier Cellars F13
59 Spier Estate E10
60 Sylvan Vale H7
61 Talana Hill K13
62 Thelema N8
63 Uiterwyk E9
64 Uitkyk L4
65 Uitzicht D11
66 Uva Mira K15
67 Veelverjaaght D11
68 Verdun H10
* Hoopenburg – see Paarl map
69 Villiera G2
70 Vlottenburg G11
71 Vredenheim H11
72 Vriesenhof K12
73 Warwick K2
74 Welmoed E14
75 Zevenwacht B9

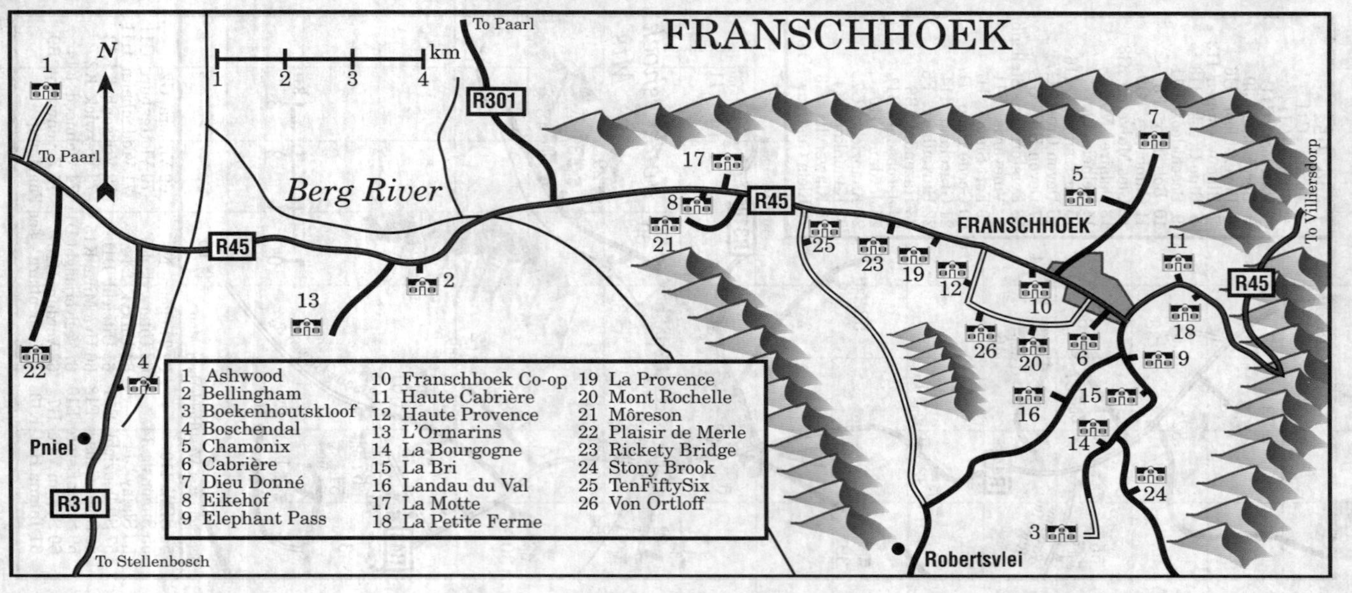
FRANSCHHOEK
N
1 2 3 4 km
To Paarl
R301
To Paarl
Berg River
R45
R45
R45
R310
Pniel
To Stellenbosch
FRANSCHHOEK
To Villiersdorp
Robertsvlei
1 Ashwood
2 Bellingham
3 Boekenhoutskloof
4 Boschendal
5 Chamonix
6 Cabrière
7 Dieu Donné
8 Eikehof
9 Elephant Pass
10 Franschhoek Co-op
11 Haute Cabrière
12 Haute Provence
13 L'Ormarins
14 La Bourgogne
15 La Bri
16 Landau du Val
17 La Motte
18 La Petite Ferme
19 La Provence
20 Mont Rochelle
21 Môreson
22 Plaisir de Merle
23 Rickety Bridge
24 Stony Brook
25 TenFiftySix
26 Von Ortloff

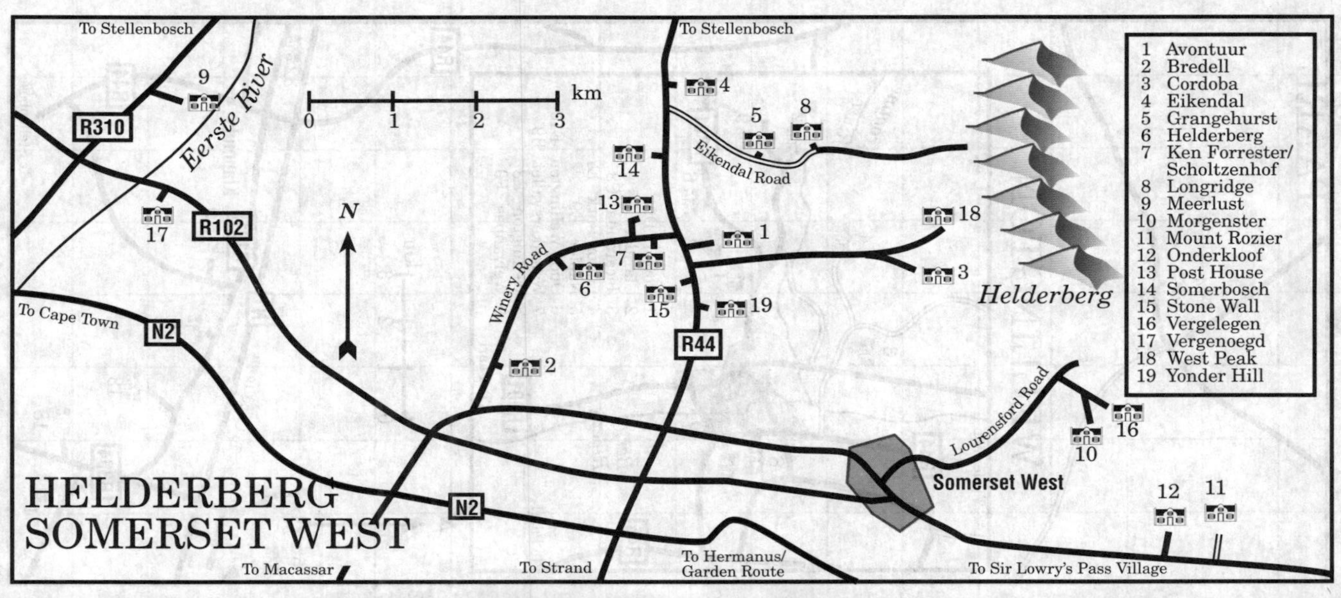
HELDERBERG
SOMERSET WEST
1 Avontuur
2 Bredell
3 Cordoba
4 Eikendal
5 Grangehurst
6 Helderberg
7 Ken Forrester/ Scholtzenhof
8 Longridge
9 Meerlust
10 Morgenster
11 Mount Rozier
12 Onderkloof
13 Post House
14 Somerbosch
15 Stone Wall
16 Vergelegen
17 Vergenoegd
18 West Peak
19 Yonder Hill
To Stellenbosch
To Stellenbosch
Eerste River
R310
R102
R44
N2
N2
km
0
1
2
3
N
Eikendal Road
Winery Road
Lourensford Road
Helderberg
Somerset West
To Cape Town
To Macassar
To Strand
To Hermanus/ Garden Route
To Sir Lowry's Pass Village

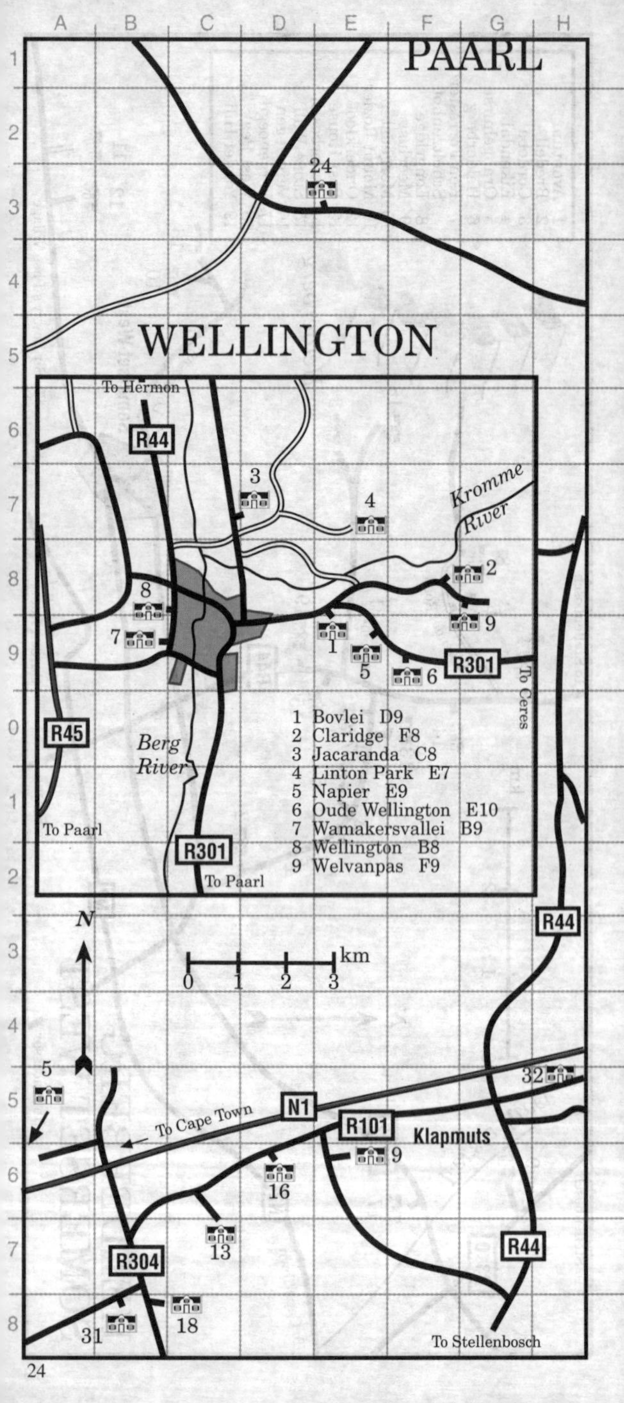

A
B
C
D
E
F
G
H
PAARL
24
WELLINGTON
To Hermon
R44
3
4
Kromme River
2
8
9
7
1
5
6
R301
To Ceres
R45
Berg River
1 Bovlei D9
2 Claridge F8
3 Jacaranda C8
4 Linton Park E7
5 Napier E9
6 Oude Wellington E10
7 Wamakersvallei B9
8 Wellington B8
9 Welvanpas F9
To Paarl
R301
To Paarl
N
0 1 2 3 km
R44
5
32
N1
To Cape Town
R101
Klapmuts
9
16
13
R304
R44
18
31
To Stellenbosch

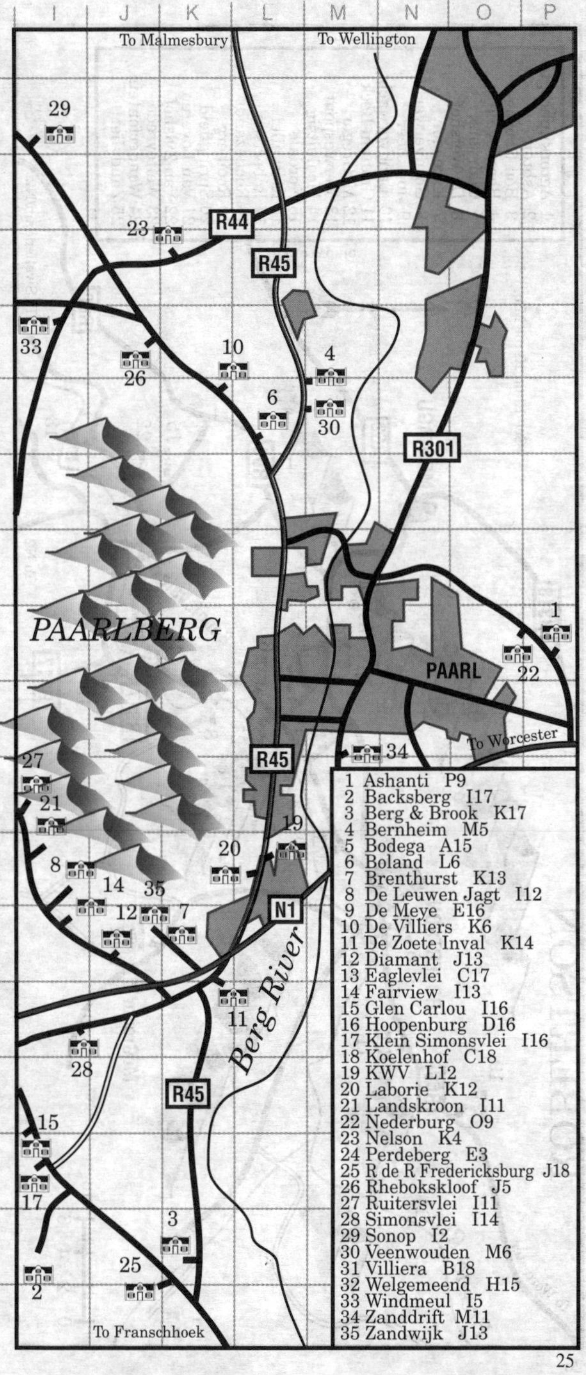

I
J
K
L
M
N
O
P
To Malmesbury
To Wellington
R44
R45
R301
PAARLBERG
PAARL
To Worcester
N1
Berg River
To Franschhoek
1 Ashanti P9
2 Backsberg I17
3 Berg & Brook K17
4 Bernheim M5
5 Bodega A15
6 Boland L6
7 Brenthurst K13
8 De Leuwen Jagt I12
9 De Meye E16
10 De Villiers K6
11 De Zoete Inval K14
12 Diamant J13
13 Eaglevlei C17
14 Fairview I13
15 Glen Carlou I16
16 Hoopenburg D16
17 Klein Simonsvlei I16
18 Koelenhof C18
19 KWV L12
20 Laborie K12
21 Landskroon I11
22 Nederburg O9
23 Nelson K4
24 Perdeberg E3
25 R de R Fredericksburg J18
26 Rheboksklooof J5
27 Ruitersvlei I11
28 Simonsvlei I14
29 Sonop I2
30 Veenwouden M6
31 Villiera B18
32 Welgemeend H15
33 Windmeul I5
34 Zanddrift M11
35 Zandwijk J13

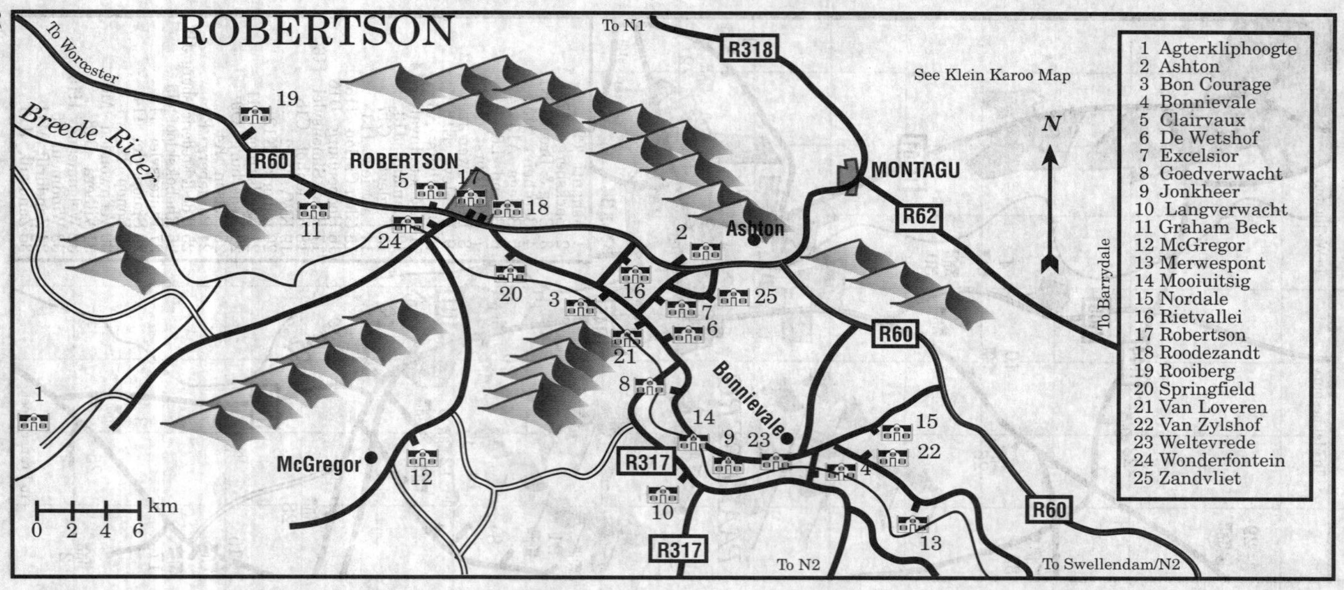
ROBERTSON
To Worcester
Breede River
To N1
R318
See Klein Karoo Map
N
MONTAGU
R62
To Barrydale
R60
ROBERTSON
Ashton
Bonnievale
McGregor
R317
To N2
To Swellendam/N2
km
0 2 4 6
1 Agterkliphoogte
2 Ashton
3 Bon Courage
4 Bonnievale
5 Clairvaux
6 De Wetshof
7 Excelsior
8 Goedverwacht
9 Jonkheer
10 Langverwacht
11 Graham Beck
12 McGregor
13 Merwespont
14 Mooiuitsig
15 Nordale
16 Rietvallei
17 Robertson
18 Roodezandt
19 Rooiberg
20 Springfield
21 Van Loveren
22 Van Zylshof
23 Weltevrede
24 Wonderfontein
25 Zandvliet

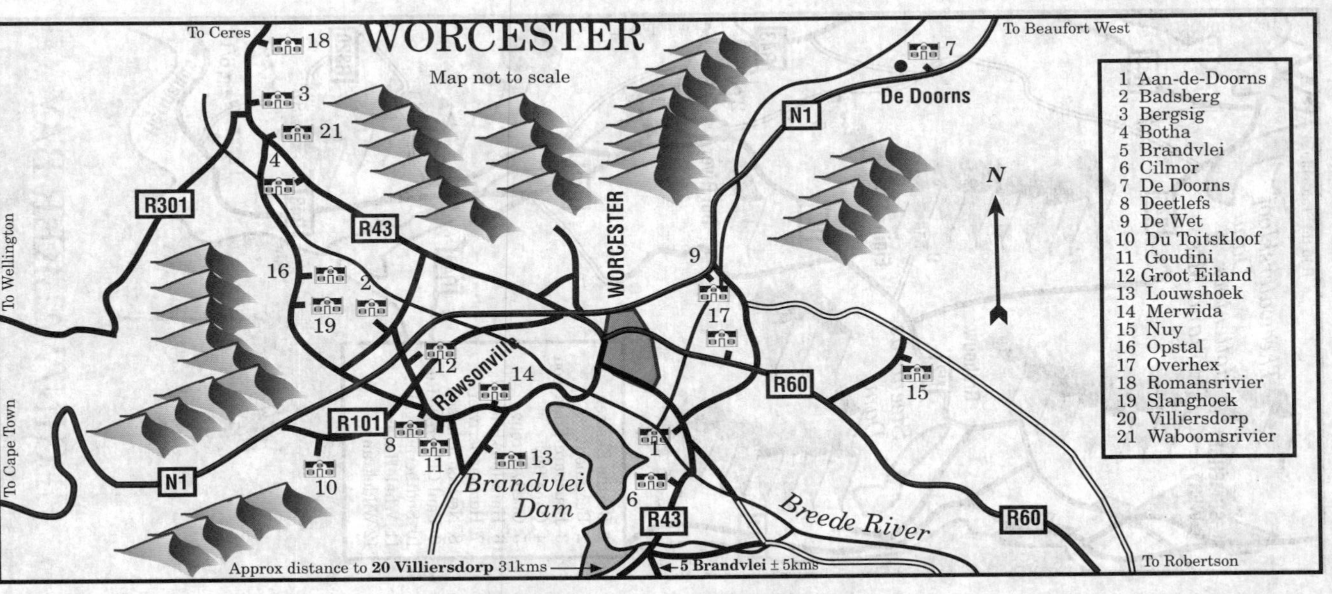

WORCESTER
Map not to scale
1 Aan-de-Doorns
2 Badsberg
3 Bergsig
4 Botha
5 Brandvlei
6 Cilmor
7 De Doorns
8 Deetlefs
9 De Wet
10 Du Toitskloof
11 Goudini
12 Groot Eiland
13 Louwshoek
14 Merwida
15 Nuy
16 Opstal
17 Overhex
18 Romansrivier
19 Slanghoek
20 Villiersdorp
21 Waboomsrivier
N
To Ceres
To Beaufort West
To Wellington
To Cape Town
To Robertson
De Doorns
WORCESTER
Rawsonville
Brandvlei Dam
Breede River
N1
R60
R43
R101
R301
Approx distance to 20 Villiersdorp 31kms
5 Brandvlei ± 5kms

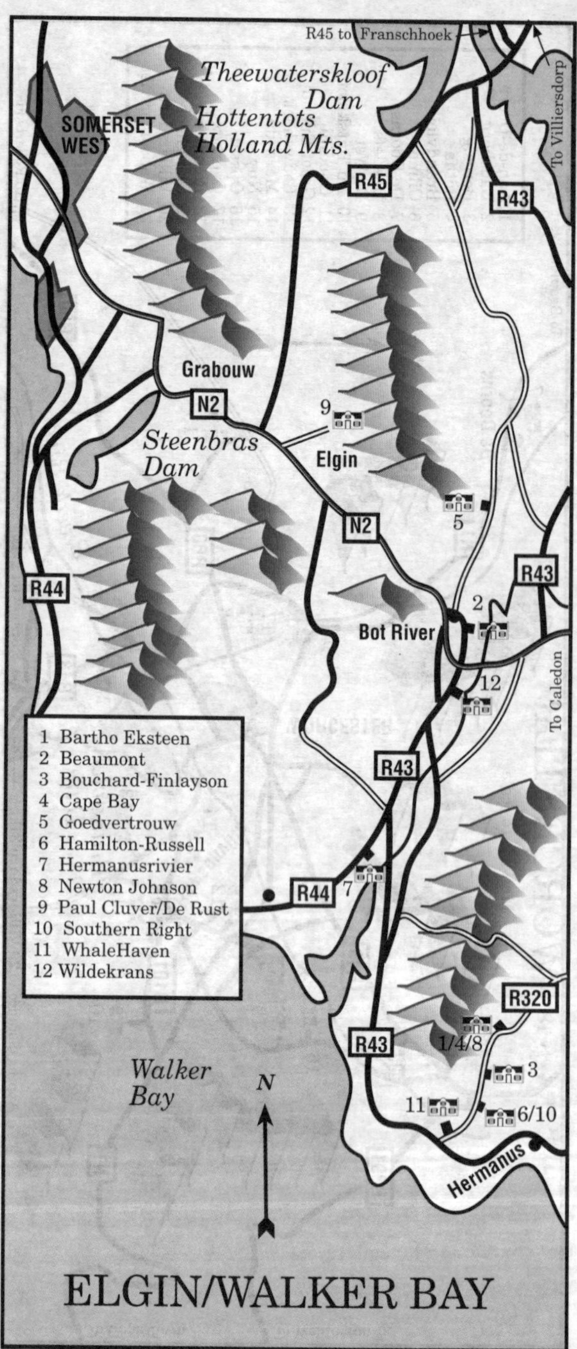
R45 to Franschhoek
Theewaterskloof Dam
To Villiersdorp
SOMERSET WEST
Hottentots Holland Mts.
R45
R43
Grabouw
N2
9
Steenbras Dam
Elgin
5
N2
R43
R44
2
Bot River
12
To Caledon
1 Bartho Eksteen
2 Beaumont
3 Bouchard-Finlayson
4 Cape Bay
5 Goedvertrouw
6 Hamilton-Russell
7 Hermanusrivier
8 Newton Johnson
9 Paul Cluver/De Rust
10 Southern Right
11 WhaleHaven
12 Wildekrans
R43
7
R44
R320
R43
1/4/8
3
11
6/10
Walker Bay
N
Hermanus
ELGIN/WALKER BAY

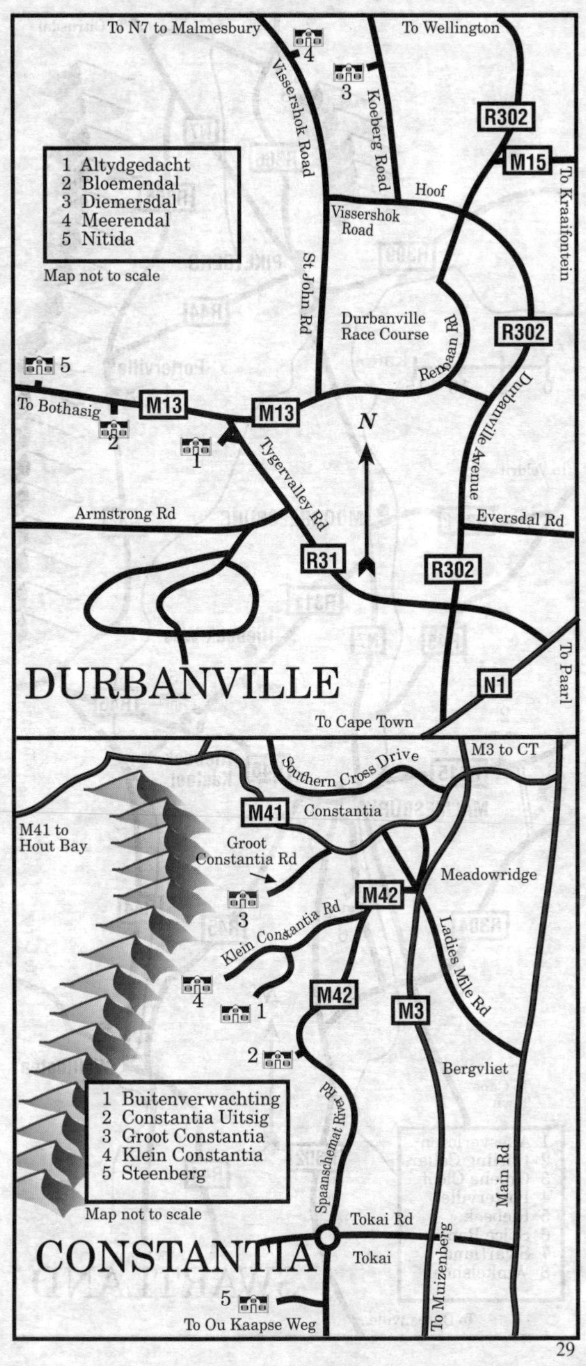

To N7 to Malmesbury
To Wellington
Vissershok Road
Koeberg Road
R302
M15
To Kraaifontein
1 Altydgedacht
2 Bloemendal
3 Diemersdal
4 Meerendal
5 Nitida
Map not to scale
Hoof
Vissershok Road
St John Rd
Durbanville Race Course
Rembaan Rd
R302
Durbanville Avenue
To Bothasig
M13
M13
Tygervalley Rd
N
Armstrong Rd
Eversdal Rd
R31
R302
DURBANVILLE
N1
To Paarl
To Cape Town
M3 to CT
Southern Cross Drive
M41
Constantia
M41 to Hout Bay
Groot Constantia Rd
Meadowridge
M42
Klein Constantia Rd
Ladies Mile Rd
M42
M3
Bergvliet
1 Buitenverwachting
2 Constantia Uitsig
3 Groot Constantia
4 Klein Constantia
5 Steenberg
Spaanschemat River Rd
Main Rd
Map not to scale
Tokai Rd
CONSTANTIA
Tokai
To Muizenberg
To Ou Kaapse Weg

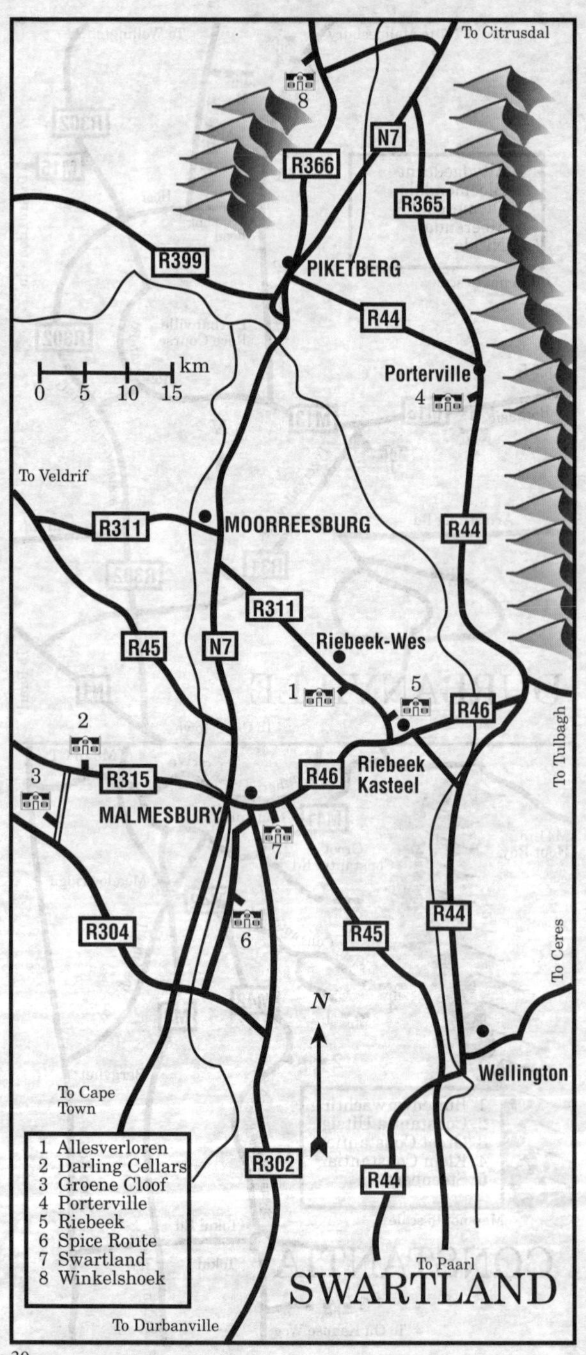
To Citrusdal
8
N7
R366
R365
R399
PIKETBERG
R44
Porterville
4
km
0 5 10 15
To Veldrif
MOORREESBURG
R311
R44
R311
R45
N7
Riebeek-Wes
1
5
R46
2
To Tulbagh
Riebeek
Kasteel
R46
3
R315
MALMESBURY
7
6
R304
R45
R44
To Ceres
N
Wellington
To Cape
Town
1 Allesverloren
2 Darling Cellars
3 Groene Cloof
4 Porterville
5 Riebeek
6 Spice Route
7 Swartland
8 Winkelshoek
R302
R44
To Paarl
SWARTLAND
To Durbanville

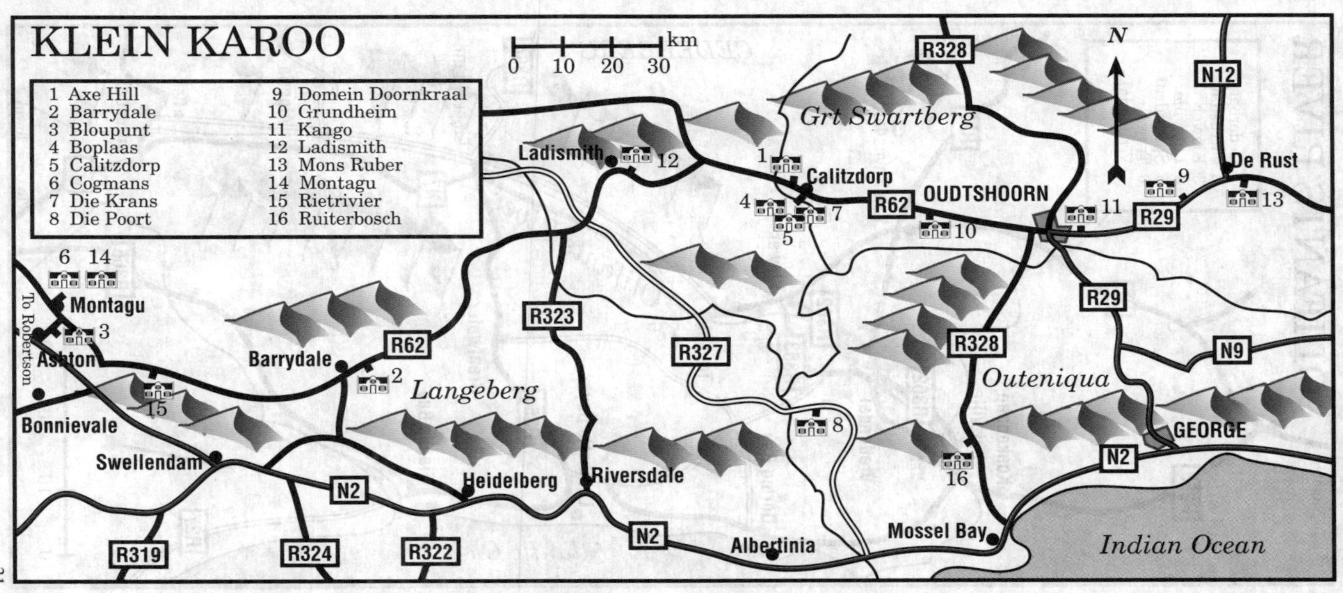

KLEIN KAROO
0 10 20 30 km
1 Axe Hill
2 Barrydale
3 Bloupunt
4 Boplaas
5 Calitzdorp
6 Cogmans
7 Die Krans
8 Die Poort
9 Domein Doornkraal
10 Grundheim
11 Kango
12 Ladismith
13 Mons Ruber
14 Montagu
15 Rietrivier
16 Ruiterbosch
N
R328
N12
Grt Swartberg
Ladismith
Calitzdorp
OUDTSHOORN
De Rust
R62
R29
Montagu
To Robertson
Ashton
Barrydale
R323
R327
R328
Outeniqua
N9
Langeberg
Bonnievale
Swellendam
Heidelberg
Riversdale
GEORGE
N2
Mossel Bay
Albertinia
Indian Ocean
R319
R324
R322

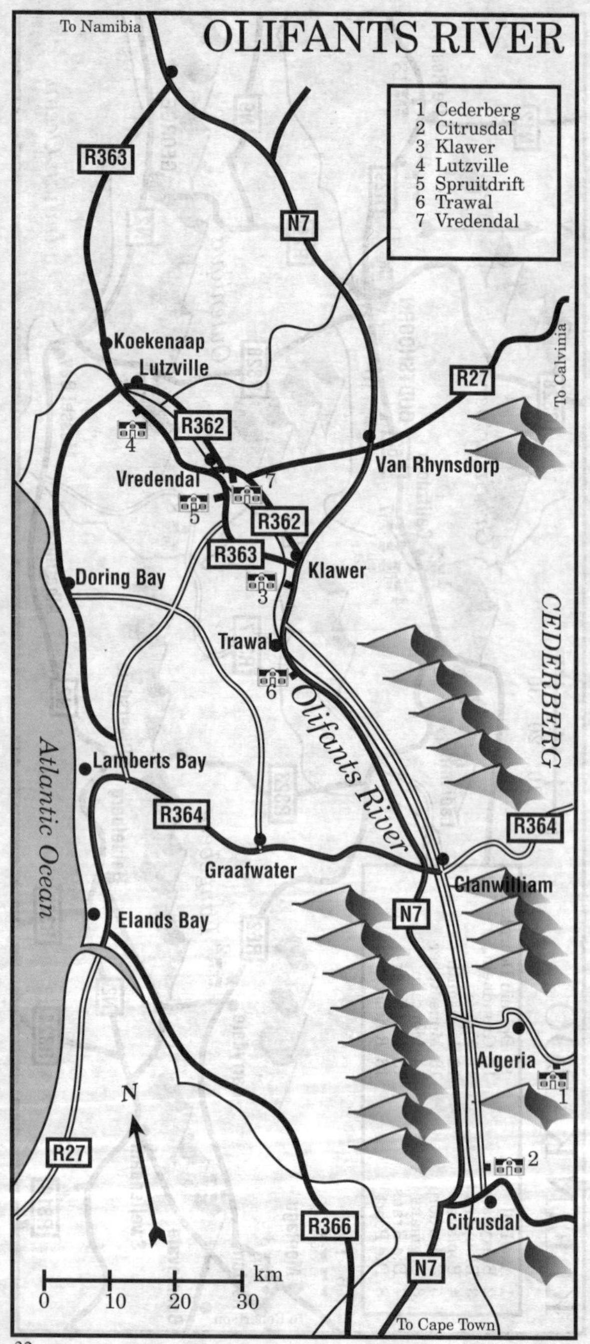
OLIFANTS RIVER
To Namibia
1 Cederberg
2 Citrusdal
3 Klawer
4 Lutzville
5 Spruitdrift
6 Trawal
7 Vredendal
R363
N7
Koekenaap
Lutzville
R27
To Calvinia
R362
Van Rhynsdorp
Vredendal
R362
R363
Klawer
Doring Bay
Trawal
Olifants River
CEDERBERG
Atlantic Ocean
Lamberts Bay
R364
R364
Graafwater
Clanwilliam
N7
Elands Bay
Algeria
N
R27
R366
Citrusdal
N7
km
0 10 20 30
To Cape Town

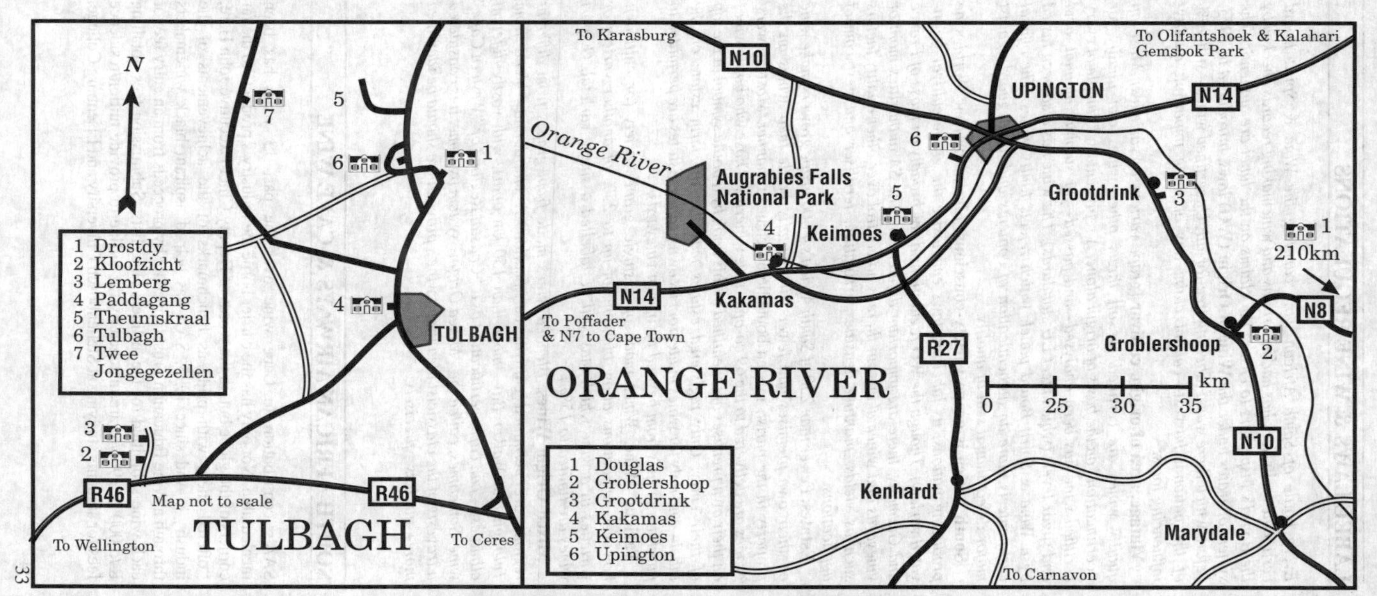
N
1 Drostdy
2 Kloofzicht
3 Lemberg
4 Paddagang
5 Theuniskraal
6 Tulbagh
7 Twee Jongegezellen
TULBAGH
R46
R46
Map not to scale
To Wellington
To Ceres
TULBAGH
To Karasburg
N10
To Olifantshoek & Kalahari Gemsbok Park
UPINGTON
N14
Orange River
Augrabies Falls National Park
Keimoes
Grootdrink
Kakamas
N14
210km
N8
To Poffader & N7 to Cape Town
R27
Groblershoop
ORANGE RIVER
km
0
25
30
35
N10
1 Douglas
2 Groblershoop
3 Grootdrink
4 Kakamas
5 Keimoes
6 Upington
Kenhardt
Marydale
To Carnavon

LABEL LAWS & WINE REGULATIONS

Every bottle of South African wine carrying the Wine & Spirit Board certificate on its neck has had its origins and winemaking records checked by the Board's inspectors to ensure the claims on the label are authentic. The system operates under the **Wine of Origin (WO)** *laws, introduced in 1973, before which there was a labelling free-for-all. Uncertified wines—still 90% of the national harvest—cannot claim any of three important quality-influencing facts:*

Vintage, area of origin, cultivar *(grape variety, or varieties). Most top quality wines are certified for all three, other wines can qualify for "certification" on the basis of origin alone. A representative sample of every certified wine has been analysed—and passed—for sulphur, alcohol, acid and sugar levels (which meet EU standards). The wine has also been tasted by a Wine & Spirit Board panel, which rejects faulty wines. The official certificate is more an authentication of contents and a safeguard against major defect than a seal of quality.*

South Africa is grape variety-conscious. *Like many New World wine producing nations, its labelling laws emphasise the grape cultivar (cultivated variety). Though the WO regulations draw broadly on those of France and Germany, there are important differences. The SA authorities monitor vineyards and winemaking but there is no control over other quality factors such as yields, planting densities, irrigation, fertiliser and pest control applications.*

Estates. *Fewer than 250 of South Africa's 4 600 grape growers make wine on their own premises and fewer still actually bottle their wines on the property in the purist,* mis en bouteille au château *manner. Most growers' grapes are delivered to the 69 co-operative wineries. Those who bottle wines on their own premises are identified in this book by a bottle symbol at the top of their entry. Only registered estates may use the term estate on the label—and only for wines made from its own grapes. Estates are permitted to purchase grapes from beyond their own vineyards.*

Varietal Wine. *Wines made of a single grape variety (or cultivar); however, regulations allow blending of up to 25% of another variety or varieties in a wine which may still be labelled a single varietal. (Export wines are limited to 15%.)*

Mixed Origin Wines. *Blended wines made from grapes from different regions are permitted cultivar certification. A chardonnay blend from Tulbagh and Walker Bay—more than 150 km apart, with vastly different climates — can carry certification as a "Coastal Region" or "Western Cape" wine. Sometimes, called the "Mixed Origin" system by some, it is considered a travesty of the classicist idea that a wine's provenance should be identified more—not less—precisely.*

SOUTH AFRICAN AIRWAYS & CAPE WINE

SAA's contribution to Cape wine over the past 13 years has been incalculable. Not only has the carrier borne the industry's products to the far corners of the globe but, in the words of Deputy Chief Executive John Hare, "offered them with pride as benchmarks of the achievements of the industry". And since 1995, SAA has helped aspirant black winemakers through a Wine Education Trust topped up by proceeds from an entry fee for each wine submitted for the airline's wine lists. Submission fees, totalling R75 000 in 1997/8, are matched by the airline to provide tuition/residence fees for students studying at Stellenbosch University and Elsenburg College.

For the annual SAA Selections, the airline flies five international judges to the Cape to help choose (with five local judges) the following year's onboard wine lists. The successful wines for the past two years are listed among other top scoring wines in the section: **Leading Wines, Top Performers.** SAA awards trophies each for the four best wines in their categories. These are listed below:

SAA TROPHY WINNERS

1997: 95 **KWV Cathedral Cellars Cabernet Sauvignon;** 96 **Vergelegen Chardonnay Res;** 92 **Graham Beck Blanc de Blancs;** 95 **Boplaas Touriga Naçional.**

1996: 92 **Thelema Merlot;** 95 **Thelema Chardonnay;** 92 **Simonsig MCC Kaapse Vonkel;** 91 **Landskroon Port.**

1995: 92 **KWV Cathedral Cellar Triptych Cabernet Sauvignon blend;** 93 **Thelema Chardonnay Res;** 86 **KWV Rooi Port, Pongrácz** NV.

1994: 89 **Buitenverwachting Grand Vin;** 93 **Mulderbosch Sauvignon Blanc;** NV **Villiera Vintage Tradition;** 90 **Landskroon Port.**

1993: 88 **Klein Constantia Cabernet Sauvignon;** 91 **Villiera Blanc Fumé;** 88 **Boplaas Vintage Port; Pongrácz** NV.

1992: 84 **Rustenberg Cabernet Sauvignon Reserve,** 86 **Klein Constantia Sauvignon Blanc,** 66 **KWV Late Bottled Vintage.**

1991: 75 **Nederburg Cabernet Sauvignon**; 89 **Buitenverwachting Chardonnay.**

DINERS CLUB WINEMAKER OF THE YEAR

SA winedom's single most coveted prize, awarded annually. Diners Club South Africa MD Hugh Peatling introduced the contest in 1981. Competing wines are judged by a panel of local experts headed by an eminent international authority. Focuses on a different category each year; these are announced far in advance, giving local producers enough time to experiment, fine-tune, even plant new vineyards. A major motivating force for Cape winemakers.

WINNERS:

1997 (Sauvignon Blanc): Jeff Grier (Villiera)
1996 (Cabernet Sauvignon): Gyles Webb (Thelema)
1995 (MCC): Nicky Krone (Twee Jonge Gezellen Estate)
1994 (Cabernet Sauvignon-based blends): Gyles Webb (Thelema)
1993 (Chardonnay): Danie de Wet (Dewetshof)
1992 (Merlot): Jean Daneel (Buitenverwachting)
1991 (Cape riesling): Wilhelm Linde (Nuy)
1990 (SLH): André Bruwer (Bon Courage)
1989 (Pinot noir): Peter Finlayson (Hamilton Russell)
1988 (Muscadel): Wilhelm Linde (Nuy)
1987 (Pinotage): Beyers Truter (Kanonkop)
1986 (Oak-matured white): Sydney Back (Backsberg)
1985 (Gewürztraminer): Günter Brözel (Nederburg)
1984 (Sauvignon blanc): Manie Rossouw (Eersterivier)
1983 (Rhine riesling): Günter Brözel (Nederburg)
1982 (Cabernet sauvignon): Walter Finlayson (Blaauwklippen)
1981 (Innovative wines): Walter Finlayson (Blaauwklippen)

Categories from 1998-2005, in order:

Shiraz, Cape-style red blends, port, chenin blanc, pinotage, brandy, innovative red blends, sémillon blends.

As a promoter of fine wine standards in SA, Diners Club runs an annual **Winelist of the Year** contest amongst more than 3 500 local restaurants, hotels and clubs.

1997 Winners:
Platinum Awards:
Cento (Kensington, Johannesburg), **Hotel Onduri** (Outjo), **Lake Pleasant Hotel** (Sedgefield), **Le Ballon Rouge** (Franschhoek), **Noupoort Guest Farm & Conference Centre** (Piketberg), **Redbourne Lodge** (Plettenberg Bay), **The Palm House Guest House** (Wynberg, Cape Town), **The Upper Crust Restaurant** (Cape Town), **Victoria Junction Hotel** (Green Point, Cape Town).
Merit Awards: (made for each province; we list only those in or around the Western Cape winelands):
96 Winery Road (Stellenbosch), **Au Jardin** (Cape Town), **Arlindo's Seafood Restaurant** (V & A Waterfront), **Aubergine Restaurant** (Cape Town), **Berties Moorings Restaurant** (Gordons Bay), **Black Marlin Restaurant** (Simon's Town), **Blue Danube Restaurant** (Tamboerskloof, Cape Town), **Constantia Uitsig** (Constantia), **Champers** (Cape Town), **De Oude Welgemoed** (Welgemoed), **Die Ou Pastorie** (Somerset West), **Flutes Restaurant & Wine Bar** (Cape Town), **Fujiyama** (Sea Point), **Grand Hotel & Restaurant** (Robertson), **Greyton Lodge** (Greyton), **Jonkerhuis Restaurant** (Stellenbosch), **Kelvin Grove Club** (Newlands, Cape Town), **Le Quartier Français** (Franschhoek), **Merlion Restaurant** (Cape Town), **The Cellars—Hohenhort Hotel** (Constantia), **The Old Mill Lodge** (McGregor), **The Overberger Country Hotel & Spa** (Caledon), **The Quay West Restaurant** (V & A Waterfront), **The Red Herring** (Noordhoek), **The Stellenbosch Hotel** (Stellenbosch), **Tuscany Beach Restaurant** (Camps Bay).

GRAPES—Red Wines

With a few identifying flavour associations

CABERNET SAUVIGNON

Flavour associations: Blackcurrant, but general blackberry, cassis-like, chocolate, ripe plum, grass, capsicum, minerals (inky), mint, liquorice; and from oak barrels, sweet spices, cinnamon, vanilla, cloves; from maturation, tobacco, lead pencils, violets, tea-leaves. Old style Cape versions also sometimes were: tarry, dried hay, rubbery, mixed dry herbs.

The world's most widely planted classic black grape for making grand, age-worthy red wine; fine and strong, at its best and ripest with blackcurrant fruit flavours and firm tannins for keeping, invariably matured in oak barrels by the world's top producers. The grape is best known for its dominance in the vineyards of Bordeaux where it is usually blended (mainly with merlot and cabernet franc). Cabernet, as it's generally known, is often associated with tough, tannic, mouth-drying puckeriness in youth, the kind of platform upon which to build a long future.

A certain, slight early hardness is entirely right—with quite pungent bell pepper aromas—provided it is not "green" or bitter or very unripe. A muted herby, grassy, nutty quality can be there too and a feature in many South African cabernets made from "old clone" vineyards. "New clone" vineyards, or those without the virus and often uneven ripening problems of some older ones, make wines with supple, fleshy ripe fruit qualities. **5,1% of SA vineyards.**

CABERNET FRANC

Flavour associations: Very similar to Cabernet Sauvignon generally though a shade less intense (including colour) and perhaps slightly more herbaceous, heathery.

Soon destined to be seen more as a stand-alone variety rather than in its traditional blending rôle of supporting its close relative, Cabernet Sauvignon. Slightly earlier to bud—and ripen—it generally produces wines slightly fleshier, lighter and less tannic than its senior, much more widely planted relation. A number of outstanding recent Cape examples show much individuality and promise. **Insignificant vineyard area.**

CINSAUT

Flavour associations: Gentle, watery sweetness, dried (out) nuts, bon-bons, jellybabies. (Rarely bottled on its own.)

(In France spelled Cinsault.) Formerly known as Hermitage in the Cape (hence pinotage from the pinot noir-hermitage cross). Usually bears too prolifically to produce top quality reds unless severely pruned. Most useful as a blend with harder wines to hasten drinkability. Appears to have transmitted its incipient sweetness to pinotage. Under normal conditions, unblended, produces light, ordinary reds. **4,1% of SA vineyards.**

GAMAY

Light, fragrant, cheerful short-lived reds (making the Beaujolais Nouveau in France). Earthier wine results from the vine in the Cape, with a bouquet all its own, a deep ruby colour at its best, and a youthful grapey fruitiness. **Insignificant vineyard area.**

MERLOT

Flavour associations: Minerals, spices, fruitcake, plums, blackberries, violets, plus oak infusions as for Cabernet above; with time, coffee, toffee.

Worldwide, the grape and red wine of the moment. Its fragrant perfumes and (usually) softer structure make it more "accessible" sooner than cabernet, more "restaurant ready". This is not always so, but it is probably a fair generalisation. In France, this rich variety often is critical in the clarets of Bordeaux, particularly in poorer vintages. There is a school which believes the Cape climate does not require merlot to improve cabernet. Now it is increasingly bottled as a "varietal" on its own. There have been some outstanding examples. Generally—but certainly not always—they have been slightly softer, showing earlier drinkability than cabernet. Sometimes even mistaken for cabernet, Cape merlot can show a minerally-fruity depth and, like cabernet, is at its best when oak-aged. **2,2% of SA vineyards.**

MOURVÈDRE

Flavour associations: Black pepper, black currant, laced with sweet-bitter spiciness and liquorice.

A "warm region" grape, dark and hard-skinned. Soon to make limited appearances in the Cape; already a "cult" variety in California, long-established in France—four centuries at least—in the Rhône, Provence and the Midi; also big in Spain, where it's thought to have its origins. One of its biggest New World homes has been Australia (where it's been known as Mataro) but usually as a junior blending partner. French Midi varietals—but often with a dash of Syrah—more carefully vinified and aged in oak have elevated Mourvèdre to a completely new status. **Insignificant vineyard area.**

PINOTAGE

Flavour associations: Sweets, bananas, cloves, pine, bon-bons; sometimes harsh acetones, paint.

No longer ignored as a serious quality grape for red wine—and virtually proclaimed the "national" grape of South Africa. A 1926 cross in South Africa, a mix of pinot noir and cinsault—at that time called "hermitage" here, and hence the name pinotage. Substantial, flavoursome, very individual, fruity, robust wine, specially when oak-matured—which it rarely was until recently. Typically showing boiled sweets, banana flavours. **3,9% of SA vineyards.**

PINOT NOIR

Flavour associations: When young, cranberry sauce, cherries, strawberries, roses; with time, compost, mushrooms, damp forest leaves underfoot, violets, spices, truffle, liquorice, civet.

Makes red wines of many fine scents and flavours in Burgundy; until recently unable to replicate quite this glory elsewhere. Successful pinots from the USA (specially Oregon but from California too) and increasingly elsewhere. Several new vineyards in South Africa are promising; making clean, lively, wines with fruity, sweet-cherry flavours, ripening over time into something akin to the organic, damp leafy depth of classical pinot. Until the early 1990s, virtually all Cape pinot noirs were made from a clone grown in Switzerland (designated BK5 in South Africa); new vineyards of Burgundian clones have come into production and are widening the spectrum of Cape pinot styles. **Insignificant SA vineyard area.**

RUBY CABERNET

Flavour associations: Cut grass, strawberries.

Cabernet sauvignon-carignan cross developed in California mid-20th century; prolific bearer for good but, until recently, ordinary drinking. **Insignificant SA vineyard area.**

SHIRAZ

Flavour associations: At first, peppery-spicy, blackberries; later, leather, spice (cocoa) fudge, gamey, tar and smoke. Also violets.

Also known as Syrah. Produces heavyish, savoury, deep wine, quicker to mature than cabernet, so sometimes blended with it. On its own can age with distinction; look for a smoky, perfumed, softish, chocolaty warmth. A number of good Cape shiraz wines started to appear from the late 1980s; before that they were often heavy, flat, sometimes tarry and clumsy. **1,3% of SA vineyards.**

TINTA BAROCCA

A Portuguese port-making grape, with immediately discernible earthiness, little elegance; can be useful as a blend. **Insignificant SA vineyard area.**

ZINFANDEL

A little-grown grape variety, popular in California as "Zin" where it is made into some fine reds. Hasn't caught on among Cape growers, but a few interesting examples, specially when well-oaked. **Insignificant vineyard area.**

GRAPES—White Wines

With a few identifying flavour associations

BUKETTRAUBE

Flavour associations: Soft peaches and pears.

Usually producing off-dry and dessert-style wines, with faint Muscat aroma. Often used in blending. Can make fine botrytis wine.

CHARDONNAY

Flavour associations: Citrus (lemons but also limes), pineapple, honey, buttery, melons, butterscotch, spices. Mature ones in bottle—buttered toast, toasted almonds, cloves, cinnamon, caramel. (Badly made ones: bitter, woody aftertaste.)

The grape of the great dry white wines of the world, the classics of Burgundy, including Chablis, the champagnes (including blanc de blancs) of Champagne. The grape responds to oak—preferably barrel-fermentation and ageing—which enhances its natural and otherwise often quite neutral qualities. Over-oaked woodiness in chardonnay has been a problem among Cape examples, where the grapey/lemony/lime freshness of the grape is buried under oak, which fattens but also hardens, weighs down the wine, detracting from its natural elegance. **4% of the SA vineyard area.**

CHENIN BLANC OR STEEN

Flavour associations: Guava, tropical fruit, when young (under 1 year) to general easy fruity softness; honeyed, nuts. Dry ones tend to an almondy staleness, a toasted almond quality can emerge in some sweet ones after several years in bottle.

The Cape's staple white grape. Wines are called by either name. A well-adapted, versatile South African variety, related to the Loire Valley's chenin blanc. Makes whites of many hues, through the entire range of sweetness, dryness, fruitiness, still or sparkling, and is the basis of many rosés. It is relatively trouble-free in the vineyard and a moderately heavy bearer. Its forté is in producing sweeter wines and botrytis desserts. Its dry wines, though attractively fresh and fruity in good years, are usually short-lived and eclipsed by more classic varieties. A few growers are now attempting to give Chenin a grander image, improving winery practices and reducing v'yd yields in the hope of infusing wines with more intensity, lasting power. Oak-fermenting and ageing is now practised by the growing band of Chenin "believers". **26,8% of SA vineyard area.**

COLOMBARD

Flavour associations: In good years (otherwise blandish acidity) tropical fruit scents, guava, fermentation yeast, doughy esters, fading rapidly in most, specially dry ones.

Has sometimes produced exciting, pleasantly fresh wines, suffused with guava, granadilla and fresh fermentation characters plus acidity for crispness, and, specially from the Breede River regions, with attractive fruity flavours. But they (especially the drier styles) are best drunk young. Colombard in France is used mainly for brandy, a rôle it still performs in South Africa. **10,9% of SA vineyard area.**

GEWÜRZTRAMINER

Flavour associations: Rose petals, ripe, soft apricots, spices, ginger, litchis (some muscat aromas), general springtime blossom, honeysuckle.

Makes spicy, boldly scented whites of character. Usually in sweeter style in the Cape, only a few dry examples in the style of Alsace. **Insignificant vineyard area.**

HANEPOOT—see Muscat below.

MUSCADEL

Flavour associations: Raisins, litchis, dried apricots, honey.

Used chiefly for dessert and fortified wines, giving distinctive, raisiny, muscaty bouquet. Both red and white varieties grown chiefly in Breede River and Klein Karoo districts. Member of the muscat family. Also known as Muscat de Frontignan the grapes responsible for the famous Constantia desserts of the 18th century, considered a much finer, more delicate grape—and wine—than the more common Muscat d'Alexandrie, or Hanepoot. **0,7% of SA vineyard area.**

MUSCAT D'ALEXANDRIE

Flavour associations: Grapes! Spices (gingery sometimes), roses, raisins, very ripe pineapple, cinnamon, apricot. When aged, in fortified wines: chocolates, nuts, sweet cloves, liquorice.

Also known in South Africa as Hanepoot and imparting an intense flowery bouquet and deep, strong, honeyed-muscaty flavour to its wines. Can be red or white, both also popular as a table grape. Probably still the country's most widely-grown dessert and fortified wine grape. Distinct raisiny character, but can be made into an adequate dry wine. **5,3% of SA vineyard area.** Other relatives are Muscat Ottonel, Morio Muscat.

RHINE RIESLING (also referred to as "true" or **Weisser** riesling)

Flavour associations: Apples, sugared lemons, limes, roses, peony, honeysuckle—when still youthful: petrol, kerosene (terpenes), oily, spices, biscuits when aged, often honeyed too, sp. when sweet.

Much more aromatic, spicier, more complex, more subtle, more scented than Cape or South African riesling. Can develop a terpene, resinous, oily character with a little age: in Europe, this is an accepted characteristic. **0,8% of SA vineyard area.**

RIESLING (Cape Riesling or S.A. Riesling)

Flavour associations: Dried hay, dull, thatch, grassy, thyme, geranium; sometimes rises above this in first flushes after fermentation.

Different to the Weisser or Rhine riesling, a shy bearer, can be steely. Now considered a relation to crouchen blanc, a French variety relegated to very vin ordinaire status and now hardly planted at all. From 1983 no Cape riesling could be exported to Europe bearing the name "riesling" on the label. Acquires bottle age dullness after about a year. **3,3% of SA vineyards.**

SAUVIGNON BLANC

Flavour associations: Three main forms—gooseberry, grass, nettles, capsicum, cat's pee; stony, flinty, peppery; and vegetal, asparagus (tinned). Those which have aged well: dried figs, mushrooms.

South African sauvignons are now turning heads in world tastings. The general climate of the Cape may be warm, but scores of individual microclimates are perfect for growing outstanding examples: bold, high-profile wines similar to showy New World sauvignons, and even the newer style French wines of the Graves, with a definite peppery gooseberry/grassiness; dry and arresting. Some are more flinty, austere; others show fig scents, still others display asparagus-like or capsicum flavours (mainly from riper harvests) and, in our view, less fascinating, clumsier as wines, and more obtrusive at table. **4,8% of SA vineyards.**

SÉMILLON

Flavour associations: Mown hay, pine, almond; after time, honey, lanolin.

(Pronounced semiyon) produces wines with body and keeping power. The best are elegant, compact and specially well suited to a wide variety of dishes; they are neither flowery nor spicy and do not compete aggressively for attention. However, several wines are called sémillon when the grapes, often known locally as groen or green, obviously are from vines that have undergone mutations. A number of recent Cape blends of sémillon and sauvignon blanc are outstanding. **1% of SA vineyards.**

VIOGNIER

Flavour associations: Blossom scents generally, then ripe, even faintly over-ripe peaches, pears, apricots, some honey, also sometimes when well-aged, intriguing burned rubber tyre whiffs among the decaying fruity scents. At best, full-bodied, lusciously textured.

Just beginning to make its first commercial appearances in 1998 in the Cape. A little over a decade ago when only 36 hectares were planted worldwide, Jancis Robinson wrote in her *Vines, Grapes, Wines,* "If we had the opportunity to taste Viognier grown on less than suitable land and made carelessly into wine, the grape might seem less of a star." She's been proved at least partly right by some wishy-washy examples made outside France. At least the Cape presents a good, warm, dry climate—which must be among the reasons why Viognier reaches its fabled allure in wines from the northern Rhône. **Insignificant vineyard area.**

THE WINE GROWING DISTRICTS OF SOUTH AFRICA

Below are the most important of the many officially declared "regions", "districts" and "wards"—nearly 50 in all. Consult the maps in this guide for the locations of individual cellars within each region.

Constantia is a southern suburb of Cape Town, on the south-eastern side of the Cape Peninsula pointing into the South Atlantic, cooled by the sea on two sides. It's a relatively cool area, with usefully slow summer ripening (average daily temperatures of 18-19° C) and wet winters with annual rainfall in excess of 1 000 mm.

Grape varieties which do well: Sauvignon Blanc, Cabernet Sauvignon, Chardonnay, Muscat de Frontignan (one of the muscats used by Hendrik Cloete for the legendary Constantia desserts of the 18th century, South Africa's most famous vinous export.)

Stellenbosch is a charming, spacious, oak-lined Afrikaans university town with many good restaurants and interesting museums. Surrounded by rugged grey-blue mountains and vineyards in almost every direction, it's regarded as the home of the Cape's finest red wines. But most estates and v'yds have white varieties too. A 45-minute drive from Cape Town. Also headquartered here is the Oenological and Viticultural Research Institute (OVRI), and the large wine wholesalers, Stellenbosch Farmers' Winery (SFW), Distillers and Gilbeys. Many soil types—from acidic decomposed granite to sandy alluvial tracts along the valley floors. Very diverse climates too, from very hot to relatively cool. Stellenbosch occupies 15% of the South African vineyard area.

Helderberg is the mountainside and coastal region bordering False Bay, between Cape Town and Stellenbosch—and usually considered part of the latter. A score of growers have "declared independence" now, claiming the elevations and maritime influences are distinctive. A number of the newest but suddenly leading wineries can be visited within a few minutes of a drive along the beaches. The area abounds in bed and breakfast stayovers, many with stunning vineyard and mountain views.

Paarl is the headquarters of the wine industry's controlling body, the Co-operative Wine Growers' Association (KWV) charged with "removing the annual surplus" of grape products for its 4 600 farmer-members. Its sprawling 19 ha. complex—making brandies, "ports", "sherries" and many liqueurs as well as red and white table wines—is said to be the biggest winery facility in the world. Paarl, meaning Pearl in Afrikaans, is a relatively warm region, large, spread out—like Stellenbosch—with wide valley floors and high mountains. The region is exactly on the same latitude south as Spain's sherry region is north, 33,4 degrees. Paarl accounts for about 20% of the country's vineyard area.

Worcester is an inland, warm, fertile region, producing mainly bulk wines—about 20% of the national crop, referred to locally as "Over the Mountain"; it is an hour's drive inland from Cape Town. Down to 250 mm annual rainfall in some parts here. Vineyards need heavy irrigation. Many co-operatives, a few estates.
Robertson is a hot, dry region but has excellent, lime-rich soils, needing few adjustments for ideal vine-growing pHs (unlike Stellenbosch). Mostly whites, including bold chardonnays, outstanding chenin blancs, colombards and muscadels (hitherto mostly indifferent reds and often very so-so sauvignons, which needs more research). V'yds require irrigation (only 400 mm annual rainfall). Most are clustered along the Breede River. Very friendly community. Robertson has 10% of the national v'yd area.
Olifants River/Orange River. Chiefly bulk grape producing region, featuring inland, mountain vineyards, farms along the Atlantic western seaboard, and irrigation schemes along the Orange River. The majority of growers supply large co-operatives with wine for distillation. South Africa's biggest single winery, the Vredendal Co-operative, processes nearly 50 000 tons of grapes here annually. The Orange River is the hottest, most northerly Cape growing area. Up to 50 tons/ha. harvested—5 times the national average, 7 times what is considered normal in Stellenbosch—along what are little more than river-beds—vines regularly flooded in winter by sprawling Orange River. The area supplies about 10% of South Africa's crop.
Klein Karoo. Inland ostrich farming region; but also some outstanding dessert wines, traditional muscadels—very reasonably priced. Parched region in summer, snow-topped mountains in winter. Under 200 mm rain most years! A few outstanding "modern style" "ports" from here too—the climate (if not the soil) has a few similarities with the Duoro in Portugal. The area covers 3,3% of the national v'yd area.
Walker Bay, Elgin (Overberg). Since the 1980s, a few enterprising growers have begun producing wine from this upland and cool coastal southerly region, offering a fresh dimension to Cape quality wines. Along the Garden Route on the N2 heading east, the visitor leaves the closely patterned winelands around Cape Town and moves up into the apple orchards around Elgin and then down into the open-spaced wheatlands, branching off to Hermanus. Scattered like lonely pins on the map are some pioneering cellars and farms, so far contributing a minuscule proportion of the annual grape crop, and none to its surplus.
Swartland/Tulbagh. Amongst the wheat lands just inland from the Atlantic West Coast, north-west of Cape Town, sprawling, hot and dry regions—accounting for about 12% of the national vineyard area. A long, usually very warm, dry summer enables farmers to minimise use of pesticides and many of them, growing vineyards on very deep, moisture-retaining soils, manage without irrigation. Low yields often afford excellent grape quality delivered both large co-operative cellars, and, around Tulbagh, smaller estates. More of these are being established in the Swartland—and the now very fashionable Darling area, which is even closer to the Atlantic.

Further inland, Tulbagh is one of the Cape's most charming and historic towns, tucked into a mountainous valley, and quite restored after a devastating earthquake some years ago.

AFRICAN LEGEND — See Sonop

See Sonop

AGUSTA Wines — See Haute Provence

ALLESVERLOREN ESTATE

Riebeek West — See Swartland map

By appointment only.
Owners/Winemakers: Danie and Fanie Malan
Production: 1 400 tons. **Vineyards:** 160 ha.
P.O. Box 23, Riebeek West 7306
Tel: 022-4612320/327 **Fax:** 022-4612444

After raving about the 1997 harvest ("Man, it was good! Best ever in volume, quality"), Fanie and Danie Malan are a shade less effusive about 1998. "Really light, maybe 40% down on average," they say, hastening to reassure Allesverloren's many fans "but the wines are exceptional. We're very optimistic." The Malans—Fanie's the owner, son Danie took over winemaking duties from him in 1990—are no strangers to seasonal variations: their family has lived on the farm below Kasteelberg at Riebeek West for well over a century. In recent years the father-and-son team replanted some older v'yds with shiraz, tinta barocca and touriga naçional. The latter—king of traditional Portuguese port varieties—features in the estate's flagship Late Bottled Vintage-style **Port** for the first time in 1998.

★★★★ **Cabernet Sauvignon 96** packed with potential. Bright mulberry colour, cassis/mulberry aromas that ring on palate, lots of chewy fruit, mouthfilling, substantial tannins in long finish. **94** (★★★) marginally less concentrated, still very good. **91** full of ripe blackcurrant-heather aromas, opulent palate, less strapping than usual (12,5% alc.). 13,8% in **89 VG, WINE★★★★**. 18 months Nevers oak.

★★★★ **Shiraz 95** as rich, concentrated as pvs., bit more elegant (despite 13,5% alc.). Blackcurrant, spice, pepper scents; ripe mouthful, intense mulberry, sweet-sour mebos flavours, firm tannins, long finish. **94** lower alc. at 12%. **91** with smoky, chocolate notes, prune scents/flavours, developing well. **90 VG** intense open nose, wild cherries, cinnamon hints. 13,1% alc.

★★★★ **Tinta Barocca** First-league **95** bright youthful purple colour, big fruity nose, cherry, ripe plums, brambleberry on earthy background. Full-bodied, plummy, sprinkling of pepper. Fresh finish. **94** altogether more lightweight, less intense colour; gentle cherry/plum tones. **93** carmine coloured, strawberry/pepper nose, cherry/plum flavours, dry tannins. 12,5% alc.

★★★★ **Port 93** similar to **92** in overt woodiness, sweet-vanilla ambience, harking back to house style of late 80s. **93** tawnier colour than pvs., fairly tannic, showing distinctive gutsy Malan touch. **91**, from super-warm year, fruity, pots of coffee, layer of chocolate. Usually about 50% tinta, 20% souzâo, 30% mix malvasia rey, pontac, tintas roriz, francesca. Always in 300 l barrels 4-5 years. Alcs. about 17,5%. Sugars, per Portuguese blueprint, reduced from pvs. ± 115 gms/l to ± 100.

ALPHEN CELLARS — By Gilbeys, Export Only

Pinotage Medium-bodied red, accessible fruit. **Dry Red** Light, easy drinking, **Sauvignon Blanc** Fruit/dry, crisp finish. Unwooded. **Chardonnay** Full-bodied, some toasty flavours. Partially barrel-femented.

ALTO ESTATE

Stellenbosch See Stellenbosch map

Tastings/sales Mon-Fri 9-5. Sat 9-12.30. Older vintages (some in magnum) available.
Owner: Distillers Corporation
Winemaker: Hempies du Toit (since 1976)
Vineyards: 100 ha.
P.O. Box 184, Stellenbosch 7599
Tel/Fax: 021-8813884

Hempies du Toit reckons the blaze that devastated a portion of the Helderberg on Feb 15th 1998 was a disguised windfall: "No need to use charred barrels," the human pantechnicon says with a broad grin, "the grapes were pre-toasted on the vine!" Du Toit, 5th generation vintner and only the third Alto cellarmaster since the first vintage in 1920, is looking to launch a cabernet from the historic neighbouring Annandale estate—this and Alto formed part of the original farm Groenrivier, granted in 1688. Annandale, by all accounts, was one of the biggest grape/wine producers of its day—in 1910, according to contemporary accounts, there were more than 500 000 vines on the property. Du Toit hopes to renovate the old cellar, dating from the 17th century and, possibly revive the long tradition of estate distilling—Du Toit's father Piet himself produced *eau de vie* in a still now on display in the visitor centre on Alto. Vintages **96-98**, all **Cabernet Sauvignon** from ± 8-year-old vines, are maturing in barrel and "looking good".

★★★★ **Alto Rouge** A Cape institution for over 50 years—launched 1947, same year as **Theuniskraal Riesling**—but far from ossified. Hempies du Toit has made bold, exploratory forays in a variety of directions with this wine, formerly shiraz-dominated. Up to **84** cabernet-shiraz-tinta barocca. In **85** tinta replaced by merlot, cab. f., the shiraz portion reduced, cab. s. increased. (**90** in this style **VG**.) **91 VG** these 4 varieties almost equal partners. **93** (lighter, with berry/mint nose) major switch to only 2 varieties, merlot, cab. s., former highly dominant for first time (90% of blend). **94** again merlot/cab. s., but proportions quite different: 51% cab. s. (with deepening cassis nose, chocs/herb/vanilla flavours, softish tannins but still lots of staying-power). Current release (**95**) signals return of shiraz—"which I really like" vintner says—23%, cab. s. (41%), merlot. Ageing well in bottle: resonant mulberry colour/aromas; full, firm palate with snatches creamy chocolate, some plummy fruit, 12,5% alc. What new pleasures will come next?

★★★★ **Cabernet Sauvignon** Current **91** (★★★) more modern style (though still in Burgundy bottle), dark ruby, blackberry, spice, liquorice, heather complexity. Mouthfilling concentration of fruit, mocha with fragrant oak backing. Long, firm finish. 12,7% alc. **90** still youthful, plummy fruit with herbal undertone, some tarry notes, good texture, long finish. **89 VG** big forceful bouquet, ripe plums/liquorice. Succulent but still chewy. Deep tannin, long finish. Great potential. These strapping but graceful unblended cabernets, from low-crop, unirrigated mountain vines. Released after 6 years' maturation (since **82** all in small French oak). Drinkable then, but generally best 10 years after vintage, can develop, hold for another 10 even 20 (as evidenced by 1997 **WINE** magazine tasting of 30 years of Alto Cab.—**67** outright stunner of the lot—majestically rich, intense; 2nd was **84**, followed by **95 WINE**★★★★ (first mainly from virus-free clones).

Port NEW **97** untasted. From shiraz, "a millennium wine", for release 2000.

ALTYDGEDACHT ESTATE

Durbanville See Durbanville map

Tastings/sales Mon-Fri 9-5.30. Sat 9-1. Also at De Oude Welgemoed Restaurant.
Owners: Parker family
Winemaker: Oliver Parker
Vineyards & Marketing: John Parker
Production: 5 000 cases. **Vineyards:** 120 ha.
P.O. Box 213, Durbanville 7550
Tel: 021-961295 **Fax:** 021-968521

This rustic, almost timeless estate encroached by brick-and-tile suburbia celebrated its tercentennial in 1998. Originally granted—score one for the women's movement—to one Elsje van Suurwaarde, the farm was producing wine on commercial scale as early as 1730. It passed into the hands of the current owners, the Parker family, in the mid-19th century. Nowadays laid-back winemaker Oliver Parker and partner-brother John, the marketer, grow an admirable, compact, somewhat off-beat—their **Barbera** is still only Cape wine from this Italian grape—always stimulating and well-priced range from marine-air-conditioned v'yds on the fringe of Durbanville. An anniversary **Bordeaux Blend** has been bottled to mark the occasion (see below).

**** **Tercentennial Bordeaux Blend 92** open, complex, delicious creamy fruity/oaky bouquet, hints of pencil-shavings, rich, blackberry flavours over vanilla spice, long clean finish. Still developing, tannins fairly firm. Lively acid should "bed down" in couple more years. **93** also tannic, should still ease into elegance. About equal parts cab. s., cab. f. and merlot. New Nevers oak, some American, 2 years.

**** **Cabernet Sauvignon** Neil Armstrong-type leap in **94**, **95** over compact, grippy **93**, "greenish" **92**. **94** is forward, open, sappy; ripe curranty black cherries on nose, echoing on slightly vanilla-toned, med.-bodied palate, firm but undaunting tannic squeeze. **95** very similar but features mulberries, lead pencils, vanilla-coated finale. These potential to age 5-10 yrs. 50/50 new/old clone, yr. large/small oak, some new. Pvs. tended to be more rustic, old-clone influenced.

*** **Pinotage 95** top in WINE (****) 1997 tasting of all major Cape pinotages of 95 vintage. Current **96** not as showy, elegant, needs time to develop; exceptionally smooth, drinkable, partly from 3,4 gms/l sugar ("unintentional"—says straight-arrow vintner), lowish alc. 11,5%, comfortable 5,2 gms/l acid. Yr used American oak. **94** big nose, ripe bananas; vanilla, chocolate on palate. **93** first in this modern mood.

*** **Shiraz** Toasty American oak is hallmark of **95**, nice plummy, ripe red cherry fruit reverberate on wild-herby palate to pleasantly tannic, spicy-tailed finish. Open-tank-fermented, yr in 40% American, French oak, none new.

**** **Chardonnay 98** one of the best yet from this cellar: complex, refined, well-oaked; drinks beautifully now with good ageing potential. Lemony tang offset by ripe-grape richness, vanilla/caramel butteriness. Needs yr to show hidden depths. 13% alc. 35% new Nevers-fermented, on lees 4 mths. Blend of 4 clones. **97** also very good, doing well in bottle. Rich butterscotch balanced by zesty lemon-lime.

*** **Sauvignon Blanc** Always a penetrating, thrusty (unwooded) white, **98** with "touch of moskonfyt (concentrated grape juice)" added to raise sugar to 3,4 gms/l for extra palate presence, silkiness. Gust of ripe gooseberries, frisky finish. Wide-bodied: 13,5% alc. Very nice. **97** has lost initial sharpish edge in bottle, gained honey patina.

*** **Gewürztraminer** ◀ Parker's signature dry style (unusual for Cape) particularly successful in **98**. Complex, fragrant almost sweet aromas of honeysuckle, litchi, rose-petal contrast most pleasantly—refreshingly, rousingly even—with decidedly dry, long palate. Lightly chilled, excellent aperitif. **95 VG**.

Barbera ◀ **95** has developed in bottle, brambly Karoo scrub aromas quite prominent in warm, organic, strong bouquet. Still unyielding on palate—ideally needs hearty dish backdrop. Unirrigated v'yds, 8-year-old vines. 12,9% alc., 6,7 gms/l acid. One year used American oak barrels. Pvs.: **92** dry, vermouth-like herbiness. **94** wafts ripe blackberries on background of fresh earth. **Chatelaine 98** untasted. Pvs. good value, semi-sweet for all occasions, 50% bukettraube, gewürz.

AMANI

Vlottenburg, Stellenbosch See Stellenbosch map

Tastings/sales Tues 9.30-5. Sat 9.30-1. Tasting fee R5 p/p. Group tastings for ± 12, cellar tours by arrangement.
Owners: Mark & Hillary Makepeace
Winemaker: Cathy Marshall (since 1998)
Viticulturist: Eben Archer
Production: 6 250 cases. **Vineyards**: 35 ha.
P.O. Box 12422, Die Boord 7613
Tel: 021-905-1126 **Fax:** 021-9054404
E-mail: makepeac@fast.co.za

Amani may mean peace in Swahili, but there's nothing sleepy about ad. executive Mark and Hillary Makepeace's fledgling winery. After an acclaimed maiden **97**—all five wines bagged Veritas medals — the operation went into hyper-drive in **98**: in the cellar, Oregon and St. Emilion-trained Cathy Marshall—whose impressive credentials include Blue White, Devoncrest and Ken Forrester Vineyards/Scholtzenhof—joined the team; Dr Eben Archer of Stellenbosch University came on broad as viticulturist; and small plantings of merlot and cabernet franc were established to raise the eventual proportion of red vines on the farm to about 30%. Aim of this distinctly un-peaceful activity is "to create world class Sauvignon Blanc, Chardonnay and Merlot", says Mark Makepeace.

*** **Sauvignon Blanc** unwooded **98** (newly bottled) not quite as demandingly fresh as maiden **97 VG**, but deserves time in bottle for herby, gooseberry-led attack to ease. Added complexity from fermentation with several yeast strains, variety of south, east slopes. 12,5% alc. 7 gms/l acidity. **97** has smoothed; bracing 9,1 gms/l TA better integrated. Food partners both; try with rich fish.

Blanc Fumé 98, like stablemates, features striking Afro-chic packaging. Nascent crushed nettle, flowery notes; seriously fresh, dry. ± 30% French oak matured, 4 months 1st/2nd-fill. **97 VG. Weisser Riesling** NEW **98** stylish, individual. Shot of sweet (80 gms/l sugar), botrytised, oak-matured sauvignon blanc gives delightful off-dry, muscat impressions. Very nice. Another "foodie"—try spicy/curry dishes.

AMBELOUI WINERY

Hout Bay

Here's something distinctly different for the millennium: sparkling Cap Classique grown and hand-crafted in leafy, upper-crust Hout Bay on the

panoramic seaward side of Constantiaberg. Available from late 1999, the limited-release pinot-chardonnay bubbly is made by the Christodoulous family in their tiny mountain-side winery with "a helluva lot of help" from Buitenverwachting's Hermann Kirschbaum, a close friend. Assurance industry executive Nick Christodoulous, wife Ann and children Lisa, Miranda, Christo, Alexis have chosen the name Ambeloui (Cypriot for "little v'yd") to represent both the winery and its range. Grapes are grown on the compact property at the relatively cool, sheltered Constantia end of the valley. Only ± 400 cases will be released.
Address:: 4075 Valley Road, Hout Bay 7800
Tel: 021-7907386 **Fax:** 021-7907873

ANDALUSIA WINES See Hartswater Wine Cellar

ASHANTI

Klein-Drakenstein, Paarl See Paarl map

Open for sales, tasting daily during season.
Il Casale Restaurant opening March/April 1999.
Owners: Ashanti Estates (Pty) Ltd
Winemaker: Jean-Vincent Ridon (since 1997)
Assistant Winemakers: Nelson Buthelezi, Johan Fortuin
Viticulturist: Louis Hitchcock
Production: 32 000 cases. **Vineyards:** 95 ha.
P.O. Box 934, Huguenot 7645
Tel: 021-8620789 **Fax:** 021-8622864
E-mail: cobramar@iafrica.com

"The grapes were coming through one door, the tanks were being delivered through the other!" reports effervescent winemaker Jean-Vincent Ridon of the 98 harvest at this brand-new cellar on a farm previously owned by Nederburg/SFW in the Klein Drakenstein area between Paarl and Franschhoek. The new proprietors are Manfred Schoeni, Michel Thuysbaert and investors from Europe and Hong Kong. Though Ridon has worked at Opus One in California, his soul-food remains French—he has cellar experience from the Loire, Alsace, the Rhône, and Burgundy—and he will return to Europe annually to make wine, keep updated. Foreign consultants will assist him with each harvest—in 98 these were Vincent Careme from Vouvray, and Cristian Bonot from Savigny-les-Beaune. Ridon sees the Ashanti hallmark as a blend of high technology (the cellar is an electronic enthusiast's dream) and "the traditional spirit of a French winemaker", which combination he feels captures an authentic Cape quality—"neither new nor old world, it has its own style based on 300 years of history and it is our goal to emphasize this natural character".

The farm, previously known as Languedoc, has its own nursery, and red wine varieties suitable to its deep red soils are being overgrafted—cab. franc, petit verdot, mourvedre, shiraz, malbec and zinfandel. 80% of the present vines are new-clone, average age 12 years. Another 82 ha. farm has been purchased: pinot noir, merlot and sauvignon blanc will be tried on its higher-altitude Simonsberg slopes (see **Signal Hill**). Assistants Nelson Buthelezi ("our Zulu wine warrior") and Johan Fortuin are being trained to become fully-fledged winemakers within the next couple of years, and will thereafter be sent abroad for a spot of French polish. Also travelling far and wide is the wine—50% is exported, to Belgium, Germany, the UK, France, USA, Mauritius, China, Hong Kong, Malaysia and Chile.

The excitement at Ashanti is palpable; here's a newcomer with big ideas, masses of energy and wines to watch.

All NEW

*** **Pinotage** Very modern, intriguing, purple-inky **98** with guts, character and a delicious French accent in the making here. Ripe banana aroma, dollop of American oak on nose/palate should tone down given a few years. Watch this one. 50% US, 50% French oak—40% new. 13,3% alc.

*** **Cabernet Sauvignon** Big, complex, interesting **98** cross-over cab. Not Bordeaux, not trad. Cape, something else: fusion of caramelised fruit, game, hints of grilled mushrooms on toast. Formidable 14,2% alc. From 7 different virus-free clones. Currently being Alliers-oaked.

*** **Chardonnay** Buxom but agile **98**: attractive lemon-lime nose, pineapple hints; smooth palate layered with butterscotch, barley-sugar; long fresh finish. High (14%) alc. well-masked. Year's oaking (80% new) before bottling/release. From low-yield v'yds.

Malbec Ripe mulberry, wild garrigue (or Karoo scrub) nose; raspberry, soft tannins on palate. Slips down easily, but watch it: hidden 14% alc. in this hot, **98** vintage. **Blush** Rather interesting French-style **98** rosé. Candied nose gives deceptive impression of sweetness to come; in fact satisfyingly dry on palate. Chill for chic summer salad partner. Blend pinotage, cab. s., merest touch of oak (one month for just 10% of cuvée). **Nouveau 98** for Paarl Nouveau Festival, fruity, straight-from-the-grape (80% cab. s., 20% pinotage) instant quaffing in virtually tannin-free zone. Not designed to last. **Sauvignon Blanc** Bold raw gooseberry dominates **98** aromas, with hints of tropical fruit, distant notes of green peppers. Very fleshy palate, warm finish (14,2% alc.). Very ripe purchased grapes from Simonsberg. 20% new oak-fermented. As was **97**—but grapes from Devon Valley—which more neutral, plainer, after year in bottle. Lower at 12,5% alc. Both very dry. **Peak 98** Blend 30% chardonnay, 70% chenin, latter comes through in ripe-peachy nose; by contrast, palate quite steely. Rather nice aperitif white. Alc. at 13% suggests sipping rather than swigging. Tiny, unobtrusive touch of sugar (3,7 gms/l) smooths, plumps, rather than sweetens. **Dragon** Big, high-kicking chenin, reflecting warm **98** vintage: ripe, yellow cling-peach nose, clean, smooth-textured palate, punchy finish (14% alc.), 4 gms/l sugar for richer dry effect. Aged on lees, 10% barrel-fermented. **Bouquet** Blend colombard, chenin, splash hanepoot, semi-sweet. Untasted. **French Kiss 98** dessert from chenin, 85 gms/l sugar, most elegant sweet wine in this range. Peach-apricot scents; smooth, non-cloying palate. Given a year or 2 could be rather delicious. **Vin de Careme** Named after, made under supervision of, Vincent Careme from Vouvray. **98** NLH from chenin, all new French oak-fermented. Freshly mown hay scents, rich honey flavour, doesn't taste oversweet despite more than 160 gms/l sugar. Grapes harvested in 9 batches ("more than Yquem," points out winemaker). **Vin de Paille** Unusual **98** dessert from colombard, grapes cool-dried for 2 months before new-barrel fermentation. Earthy, mixed dried fruit—almost "mebos"—nose. Like biting into a waxy honeycomb on palate. Endless aftertaste. Rather fascinating. 130 gms/l sugar. **Pearls** NV bubbly made for Ashanti by Villiera in the Grier estate's usual immaculate style: one of Cape's most reliable, all-purpose, friendly and classy MCCs. (Until Ashanti's own MCC comes on stream in future.) Export only.

ASHTON CO-OPERATIVE

Ashton, Robertson Valley See Robertson map

Tastings/sales Mon-Fri 8-12.30; 1.30-5. Sat 8.30-12.30.
Owners: 97 members

Sunday

LIFE

For only
the best
Platters
SIMONSBERG
The Cheesemasters

FFF

AAAAH

SIP

p Burble

M M

EUW!

NYUM

other exceptional South African wine.)

ed. Our Winelist of the Year inetasting dinners, our Wine e of sight, smell and taste. sense.

Opposite Left: A decisive endorsement of the Cape's potential comes from one of the wine world's most dynamic couples – stellar Californian winemaker **Zelma Long**, Executive VP of Simi in Sonoma, and her husband **Phil Freese**, international viticultural consultant (Thelema, De Wetshof among his local clients). In partnership with Michael and Jill Back, they've bought 40 ha. of vineyards near Backsberg; their combined credentials mark this as a most exciting new South African wine development.

Opposite below: Former sugar broker **Marc Wiehe** came to Stellenbosch from Mauritius, bringing a wine philosophy which reflects that romantic Indian Ocean Island's distinctively relaxed appetite for enjoyment. The spicy, tropical notes of some of his wines may be coincidental, but what's not is his passionate transformation of previously obscure L'Avenir Estate, in just 6 vintages, into a new Cape star.

Below: **Baron Benjamin de Rothschild** and Antonij Rupert represent the younger-generation forces behind an historic partnership between distinguished French and Cape wine dynasties. Their joint R and de R vineyards-and-cellar venture on Fredericksburg farm, between Franschhoek and Paarl, aims to produce wines – in keeping with the families' high profiles – that "the world will take note of," in the words of Dr. Anton Rupert.

Above: A new chapter in an illustrious French wine family's history opened in 1993 when **Anne Cointreau Huchon** and husband Alain succumbed to the charms and challenges of South Africa and bought the Stellenbosch estate Morgenhof. Bringing to the venture the glamour and *savoir faire* which has distinguished the Cointreau properties in Cognac and Champagne, the Huchons represented the first all-French foray into the Cape since the 17th century arrival of Huguenot refugees. Their lavish reconstruction, replanting and development programme has created a new image for the 300-year-old property: it's now a Cape "chateau" of considerable chic, with wines to match.

Opposite above: Russian-born **Mark Voloshin**, a former dentist, bought historic Hazendal Estate, in the Bottelary area of Stellenbosch, in 1994, and has since embarked on a major operation (the equivalent of root-canal treatment, perhaps?) to redevelop this property from the ground up. Replanted, rebuilt, comprehensively re-launched, Hazendal is now a Cape showpiece turning out appropriately stylish, contemporary wines.

Opposite below: Long Mountain is the Cape's answer to Jacob's Creek – both brands kick-started by Australian wine dynamo **Robin Day**, who jets between Asia, Eastern Europe, South America and Africa, on behalf of Groupe Pernod Ricard, in perpetual search of modern, ready-to-drink wines. His activities here have been deeply influential; he's not only created a successful new international label, but has also helped to recharge the batteries of his local sources – a string of co-op cellars now thoroughly alive to the challenges and rewards of the global market.

Winemakers: Marna Brink (since 1995), André van Dyk (since 1996)
Production: 22 000 tons. **Vineyards:** 1 000 ha.
P.O. Box 40, Ashton 6715
Tel: 0234-51135 **Fax:** 0234-51284

A new red-wine cellar has come on-stream at this industrious co-op to handle rising quantities of cabernets sauvignon/franc, merlot, shiraz, pinotage and popular cross ruby cabernet. "Traditional steen and colombard are waning," reports winemaker Marna Brink, "but chardonnay and other premium whites are booming, allowing member-farmers to get better prices." Most of production goes to the wholesale trade—Vinfruco is a high-profile customer—and private producers in the area. Looking further afield, the winery hopes to crack the export market in the future.

*** **Shiraz ◀ 97** bold step up from pvs. in attractive red berry, pepper, oak-spice trio, with gamey undercurrents adding complexity. Soft tannin/acid, for now or keeping yr or 2. Small oak 5 mths.

**** **Wit Muskadel Jerepiko ◀** NV Limpid amber-gold colour, luscious ripe-peach, raisin sweetness throughout, fine-grained texture with delicate acidity, crisp, clean finish. Before or after-dinner treat. 17% alc. **96** gold on young wine show.

*** **Rooi Muskadel Jerepiko ◀** NV Fortified dessert, current release (**97**) penetrating sweetness, silky texture, expansive, tangerine-peel twist provides a tangy counterpoint to grapey freshness.

Cabernet Sauvignon 96 10 mths oaked, fairly firm tannin structure, so could age interestingly or partner (rustic) food. Alc. 13%. **Satyn Rooi ◀** Agreeable, light, early-drinking, all-seasons blend of merlot, ruby cab., cab. franc. Current (**97**) dominated by ruby cab.'s signature green pepper-grassiness. Unwooded. **Chardonnay 98** fresh, lemon-scented, broadened by butterscotchy oak. Very nice. Pvs. barrel/tank-fermented, tropical, citrusy. **Sauvignon Blanc 97** untasted for this ed. Pvs. flinty, smoothly dry. **Colombard-Chardonnay** NEW **98** refreshing, pear-scented, gently dry, good fruit/acid balance. **Colombard 98** untasted, **96** quiet nose, nice fresh-fruity grip on palate, dry. **Gewürztraminer** Bottle age has emphasised spicy tones in amenable **97**, some rose-petal hints, light, off-dry, 11,5 gms/l sugar. **Laat Oes 98** powerfully scented, sugary side of semi-sweet, bukettraube, 224 gms/l sugar. **Spesiale Laatoes ◀** From **96** muscat de frontignan, delicate, gentle on palate, finely balanced, 11% alc. **97** in similar style. **Pétillant Blanc** Untasted. Pvs. fresh perlé, off-dry blend colombard, muscat. **Port ◀ 97** not "port" style but very nice; ruby cabernet fortified with 3-year-old brandy; perfumed, attractive spirity jive. **96** gold SA young wine show.

ASHWOOD WINES

Franschhoek See Franschhoek map

Not open to public.

Owners: Barry Cook, Neville Carew, Dave Kenny, Paul Meihuizen, Brett Paxton, Mike Wishart
Production: 200 000 cases
P.O. Box 68, Simondium 7670
Tel: 021-8741050 **Fax:** 021-8741867
E-mail: ashwood@new.co.za

This bustling wholesaler, with a subsidiary—Cape Contract Packaging—which bottles wines for several local producers, retailers (including Woolworths) and foreign buyers, has launched a new development phase. The first sod of its own winery on recently-acquired property in

Franschhoek was turned mid-1998. Building completion was due in time for the 99 harvest. Another new acquisition is a majority share in a nursery, which will supply material for the company's first own-vineyard plantings, also scheduled for 1999. The upshot is "control over the whole production cycle of wine from bud to bottle, thus ensuring quality and supply".

CAPE COLOURS range:
Pinotage NEW Friendly **97** spiced-plum aromas, generously fruity, soft ripe tannins, super-low acid, slight tannic twist in tail. **Grand Rouge** NEW to this guide, though top seller in range "for years" we're told. **98** blend 69% ruby cab., 17% merlot, 11% cinsaut, touch of cabernet. Spicy light fruitcake scents, softly/loosely-woven fruit. 4,6 gms/l sugar, so just out of official dry territory: taste confirms this. **Sauvignon Blanc** NEW **97** low alc. (11%), very crisp (8,4 gms/l acid) clean dry white; low-key nettle, green-pepper scents. **Chardonnay 97** quiet nose, modest flavours, crisp finish. **98** untasted, notes inform made "oxidatively to increase complexity, thereafter spent 3 months in wood". **Chenin Blanc 97** first release, rich tropical scents, soft, approachable. **98** untasted. Analysis points to dry, crisp, light style.
MICHAEL PAUL range: NEW
Chenin Blanc Faint green apple scents, livelier matching flavours in crisp **97**. Dry, light (11% alc.), brush of wood. The **Merlot** under this label is not local, it's from the Languedoc in France.
LE PARFAIT range: NEW
Rouge Individual casual quaffing: **98** cinsaut with warm raisiny nose, lightish body, redcurrant fruit flavours, lively acidity, tangy finish. **Blanc** From colombard, crisp, dry. Not perhaps "the perfect white" suggested by label, but nice enough peachy-floral attributes. **Stein** Light, no-frills, off-dry chenin.

ASTONVALE See Zandvliet

AUDACIA WINES

Stellenbosch See Stellenbosch map

Not open to public.
Owner: T.G. Strydom
Winemakers: Ernst Gouws (since 1998), Ansgar Flaatten (since 1999).
Production: 12 000 cases. **Vineyards:** 5 ha.
P.O. Box 12679, Die Boord 7613
Tel: 021-881 3052 **Fax:** 021-881 3137
E-mail: audacia@icon.co.za

An old property re-launches into a new era in this high-quality vineyard area of Stellenbosch, on the slopes of the Helderberg—a very good neighbourhood indeed, with establishments like Stellenzicht and Rust en Vrede nearby. Insurance industry *eminence* Trevor Strydom has refurbished a cellar which had been out of commission for nearly 20 years, and Hoopenburg's winemaker Ernst Gouws oversaw the first new-broom vintages; Ansgaar Flaatten joins the party for 99. New vineyards—the ratio is currrently 80-20 red to white—are being planted, and the 98 wines show lots of promise.

Cabernet Sauvignon 98 has makings of an interesting cab. Give 4-6 years. Youthful minerally, brambly scents, assertive tannins cloaking berry fruits on palate. **Merlot** Promising **98**, fresh plummy nose, some mulberry, touch chocolate, all re-emphasised on palate. Long, persistent flavour-flow. Very young, give it 5 years to grow. Both reds 13% alc. **Sauvignon Blanc 98** boiled-sweetish nose, very crisp, demanding palate. **97** far less bold. **Chardonnay** Latest **98** fresh tropical scents on vanilla backing, good butterscotch-toffee reverberates in aftertaste. Dry, 13% alc., part fermented/ matured in French oak. Perhaps best drunk quite young—**97** duller after year in bottle.

AUTUMN HARVEST WINES Boxed except Crackling (by SFW)

Crackling Pétillant colombard blend, lively, nice balance. Ready to challenge Virginia as country's top selling white. **Grand Crû** Dry colombard/chenin blend, bit bland. **Stein** Gentle semi-sweet, clean uncloying finish. From chenin. **Late Vintage** Extra sweetness, riper sunny flavours; also chenin. All NV.

AVONDVREDE

Stellenbosch

Not open to public.
Owners: Enthoven family
Winemaker: Jean-Vincent Ridon. **Viticulturist:** Gerda van Zyl
Vineyards: 9 ha.
Fax: 021-8755609

Another new string to the very active bow of French winemaker Jean-Vincent Ridon (see Ashanti, Signal Hill). On this Natte Valleij property, in the highly-regarded Simonsberg-Muldersvlei area, his goal is "to stay small and to make wine suiting the classic taste of the owner". To this end merlot joined cabernet in the vineyards in 1998: petit verdot and malbec plantings could be next. The model here is Ch. Bailly in Bordeaux ("a family friend"). Made so far are two vintages of **Cabernet Sauvignon 97**, and **98**, not available for tasting for this guide, but should be worth watching. Both were crushed by foot.

AVONTUUR ESTATE

Stellenbosch See Helderberg map

Visits: Open Mon-Fri 10.30-4.30, Sat 10.30-1. Tasting charge R10 refundable with case purchase.
Owner: Tony Taberer
Winemaker: Jean-Luc Sweerts (since 1989)
General Manager: Butch McEwan
Production: 30 000 cases. **Vineyards:** 60 ha.
P.O. Box 1128, Somerset West 7129
Tel: 021-8553450 **Fax:** 021-8554600
E-mail: avonwine@mweb.co.za

"Maverick" is a label that comes to mind, and rests easy with winemaker Jean-Luc Sweerts. Having been in each of his three "offices"—an "official" one, the cellar and his car—we can see why. Amidst seeming chaos, with documents awry, bottles stuffed into nooks here and crannies there, there **is** an order, a precision that he can access in an instant. The man's mind ("sorry, it goes in all directions") would appear to need bridling but that would stunt his creativity, of which there is no shortage. In a whirlwind—through the cellar he appears to be all over the place, even charmingly distractible. Yet out of the blue he will alight, like a butterfly on a flower, at a wine or an idea and all is revealed. Out of the maelstrom, order.

Like when he explains the roto-tanks with which he extracts the characteristic fruit concentration of his reds without harsh tannin, or when he proudly talks of wood treatments and his Swiss source of oak. The results are in the bottle, supplies of which are regularly depleted by loyal customers. Avontuur's signature and strength are its approachable, immensely drinkable reds, bursting with fruit and flavour, unrestrained by bracing acidity or green tannin. Blessed with a marvellous position on the slopes of the Helderberg, this cellar imparts a sense of still-to-be-tapped real potential. Then, much like the winemaker's thoughts, a stunner rockets in from nowhere to captivate and enchant. We'd all like the bridesmaid to have her day and her gems to be a little more regular perhaps, but that would detract from the element of surprise that adds to the allure of this individual property. *Vive la difference* is the cellar philosophy and Sweerts puts it into practice.

*** **Avon Rouge** NV ☺ ◀ Eminently quaffable, sumptuous juicy fruit shoe-horned into easy drinking package, broke the mould of austere dry reds a decade ago with still no competitors in sight. Recent bottlings may lack the broad, velvety texture and ripe plum of earlier releases, and indeed the firm structure sought by classicists, but there's still meaty depth and interesting spice from this blend of gently handled merlot and cabernet that make up the blend. Quick fermentation in roto-tanks that reduce tannin extraction is followed by brief exposure to oak. Wine to drink rather than store, more pleasure than challenge. (Latest R18 ex-cellar.)

*** **Pinotage Reserve 97** label deep violet, wild berry nose, cornucopia of gamey flavours, almond and hazelnut. Big in all respects, WINE****. Gear up on firm **96**, touch metallic, rescued by chocolate notes. Sample ripe **98** soft fruit, easy Avontuur tannins. Briefly oaked.

*** **Merlot Reserve 96** shows meaty, creamy depth, spicy oak, among best so far from this estate. **97** replete with ripe fruit of fine vintage, elegant rather than blowsy appeal that marks sample of opulent, gentian violet-coloured **98**. **92** WINE****. Standard bottling less oak, substance.

*** **Cabernet Franc 96** WINE**** example of Avontuur's ability to surprise. Variety tending to lean, sappy features, shows here with fleshy raspberry, tapered savoury *fynbos* notes. Welcome alternative to bigger, firmer reds, sound table-mate. 12% alc. from 10-year-old vines. Sample of **98** confirms purple, red berry fruit, oak vanilla.

**** **Chardonnay** Not for the faint-hearted; imposing, bold tropical island fruit flavours bolstered by significant oak. Unambiguous stuff, not classic but powerful mouthful. 3 labels. Flagship **Le Chardon Reserve** gets the full treatment, sweet oak vanillins buckle up ripe citric fruit. **97** more reductive, **98** massively rich, pineapple, mango and orange marmalade from intensely ripe grapes. **95 VVG**, WINE****, St'bosch wine show best oaked white, butterscotch-nutty tastes. Regular **Le Chardon** elegant, less wood. **Le Blush Chardonnay** deliberately coloured pink by fermentation in 2nd-fill red wine barrels after success of unplanned experiment. Unique in Cape, likely to remain so.

*** **Sauvignon Blanc 98** in tank, grassy grip, not quite up to piercing freshness of seminal **97 Reserve** (best by far on this estate); rich, round and fruity. Developed gooseberry, fig flavours, for drinking.

Baccarat Back with **96** after dormancy from **92**. Estate's serious B'deaux blend, 50/50 cabernet/merlot from best barrels of each and "only in exceptional years, when it makes itself," says Sweerts. **Cabernet Reserve 97** super concentration from Burgundian style pre-fermentation cold soak.

Dense cassis, tannic grip. Pvs. striking, wide, mouthfilling texture, but more rustic, nutty flavours. Regular label gutsy but lighter. **Pinot Noir 97** marks return of label. Tawny tints, delicately baked fruit flavours lifted by cherry freshness. Off main stream, individual drinking. **Frantage** NEW **97** intriguing blend of cabernet franc and pinotage. Latter fills out linear economy of former, fruity result. **Dolcetto** NV Unusual, from cabernet, merlot as for Avon Rouge, but sweet. No icon of craftsmanship, touch clumsy, but will appeal as rather distinct.

Blanc de Noir 98 off-dry, from cabernet, pinot noir. **Blanc de Blanc** NV Chardonnay dominates blend with sauvignon blanc, both oaked. Low-priced dry quaffer. **Insensata 98** semi-sweet, simple fruitiness. **Above Royalty** Pot-pourri of sauvignon blanc, weisser riesling, chenin, muscat make up attractive Natural Sweet dessert; soft ripe peach flavours, doesn't cloy. **95** developed honeyed nuttiness, **97** less complex. **Avon Brut** NV Cap Classique bubbly: chardonnay 60%, pinot noir 40%. Apple touches to yeasty/lemony nose, brisk mousse. Pvs. finished really dry—only 6 gms/l dosage, latest (**94**) now gentler 10 gms/l. Alluring pink version (also NV) drier.

AXE HILL

Calitzdorp See Calitzdorp map

Open to the public by appointment.
Owners: Tony & Lyn Mossop
Winemaker: Tony Mossop
Vineyard Manager: Sidney Cooper
Production: 8 000 bottles. **Vineyards:** 1 ha.
P.O. Box 12107, Parow Valley 7503
Tel: 021-6832200 **Fax:** 021-617271

Leather industry executive and Cape Winemaster Tony Mossop (and taster for this guide), together with corporate caterer Lyn, bought their small property in Calitzdorp in 1993 and proceeded to celebrate their wedding in this little Klein Karoo town. Egged on and assisted by fellow Cape Winemasters, locals Carel and Boets Nel, they planted a tiny 1 ha. vineyard with the help of the late Danie Nel of Boplaas: mostly touriga naçional, with about 20% tinta barocca, on rocky hillside territory, with just enough irrigation water to sustain the vines in this harsh environment. The small crop of low-yielding, highly concentrated grapes is vinified in one of the smallest and most rustic cellars in the country, using traditional Portuguese methods, including treading by foot in *lagares* (open tanks) for maximum colour extraction, followed by maturation in old 500 l barrels for 1-2 years. The wine is bottled in elegant 500 ml imported glass; this single-wine cellar is the only true Port specialist in the country. Axe Hill was named after the many ancient stone hand tools found in the vineyard, some of which are over a quarter of a million years old.

Vintage Port 1997 NEW, not rated, still in tank—for bottling end-98. A traditional blend of touriga and tinta barocca, first vintage shows dense chocolate, prune flavours of former, backed with elegant tinta fruit. Deep plum colour, a sturdy 19,5% alc., 90 gms/l sugar.

BABBLING BROOK

See Makro

BACKSBERG ESTATE

Paarl See Paarl map

Open weekdays 8-5. Sat, non-religious public holidays 8-1 Aug-Sept;

8-3 Oct-March.
Owner: Michael Back
Winemaker: Hardy Laubser
Vineyards: Clive Trent
General Manager: Charles Withington
P.O. Box 537, Suider-Paarl 7624
Tel: 021-8755141 **Fax:** 021-8755144
E-mail: info@backsberg.co.za

Some outstanding results, both vinous and social, from this well-established (1916) estate. The quiet launch—no flashy fanfare—in 1998 of the Freedom Road label, a partnership venture between Backsberg workers and management drawing grapes from hired vineyards nearby, has put nice wines on the market and real new money in workers' pockets. With this they're able to participate in a housing scheme in Klapmuts village. Probably for the first time in most cases, they're now able to build up their own real estate assets, freeing themselves and their families from the tied housing legacies of Cape wine farms—hence the label name.

The back label from the workers says: "Your enjoyment of this bottle brings us closer to the magic of owning our own homes and you are part of this dream."

Michael and Jill Back borrowed lines from *Jonathan Livingston Seagull* to express their feelings.

"When Livingston Seagull joined the flock on the beach it was full night. He was dizzy and terribly tired. Yet in delight he flew a loop to landing, with a snap roll just before touchdown. When they hear of it, he thought, of the Breakthrough, they'll be wild with joy. How much more of it there is now to living! Instead of our drab slogging forth and back to the fishing boats, there's a reason to life. We can lift ourselves out of ignorance, we can find ourselves as creatures of excellence and intelligence and skill. We can be free. We can learn to fly. The years ahead hummed and glowed with promise."

Said the Backs: "We hope you will enjoy this wine as much as we've enjoyed being part of this liberating process."

In other respects too, the estate continues to push ahead—specially viticulturally—to retain its model, all-round reputation established by Michael's father Sydney. Michael Back personally keeps the estate's projects computerised. Questions here are answered with specifics rather than conjecture, by a few taps on the PC at Back's left elbow (next to a soothing sound system) and then with a swift printout. "There's where we want to be in three years with the housing scheme," he announces, pushing across the figures.

There's also a big international picture here. "The world is filling up with good fruit now, from smartly managed vineyards and the consumer's choice has never been wider and better. We have to give him and her a good reason for choosing a bottle of Backsberg—and that means improving our wines all the time and getting them out at sensible prices."

**** **Klein Babylonstoren** Among the "safest" and most consistent of top-order barrel-aged Cape B'deaux blends, with two hallmarks: clean fruit and accommodating acidity. Among first of SA's "claret" style, oak-finished reds to include merlot, from mid-80s (roughly 50-60% cab. s. and 30%-40% merlot with balance of cab. f.). Latest **96** continues "thicker", ripe-and-sweet, richer quality noted since **94** and specially **95** which showed new levels of seriousness; winemaker Hardy Laubser still believes it "my best yet". Has not surrendered its long-time trademark of easy approachability—sometimes in past too easy, slightly insubstantial drinkability. Each to harmonise prior to bottling.

★★★ **Pinotage** An elegant rather than robust, extrovert pinotage, particularly noticeable in restrained bouquet, which has coarser edges of variety stripped out—a bonus or minus depending on personal preferences but here a more or less consistent trait for several vintages. **96** has same juicy, limpid feel on palate as recent pvs. but has some substance, grip in finish. Barrel-aged year in old French oak.

★★★★ **Cabernet Sauvignon** ◀ A lovely, middle-of-the-road drink, utterly free of post-prandial regrets—and denoting *balance* in wine. Cabernet is the focal point of Backsberg's stepped-up v'yd improvement programmes, revealing itself, specially since **95**, in more supple tannins, better-textured fruit—a progression seen too in Klein Babylonstoren above. Relatively difficult year **96** shows a firm, substantive and fruity grip on palate without intrusions of coarse tannin, neither on palate nor finish. It thus succeeds where so many Cape cabernets have tended to fail. **95**, from concentrated, hot year, also fine. Generally, with 10% merlot, unobtrusively oaked, perhaps even too unobtrusively. Always a considerable bargain. New clone spiciness has featured for several vintages. **94 SAA**. **91 VVG, SAA**.

★★★ **Merlot** The estate's characteristic minty edge in this varietal persists in latest **96**, with generous, sweetish impression—if not, overall, perhaps as impressive as some pvs. A cheerful, easy, balanced wine nonetheless—lightly oaked. **94** and **93** WINE★★★★, **92 SAA** Selection.

★★★★ **Shiraz** A triumph of chocolaty affability in **97**—the richness and ripe berry quality off-setting a mild varietal spiciness (which some might prefer to be more evident). But even shiraz-spoiled Australians would declare this "a beaut". And structurally seamless—as in no awkward acids, alcs. or tannins protruding disjointedly. **93** WINE★★★★ **VG**.

★★★ **Chardonnay** Hot vintage **97** perhaps shorter on freshness and lemony vitality of most pvs. years—from an estate which usually turns in dependable, sound, round, balanced examples. Mostly barrel-fermented (25% new, and used oak); plus proportion of tank-fermented. **95 SAA , 94** WINE★★★★, **93 SAA.**

★★★★ **John Martin** Very grown-up, ample, partly-oaked dry white from sauvignon blanc, with multi-layered flavours, tangy and fruity at same time. **97** seems quick to show some secondary, maturing flavours, with ripe, deepening gold colour.

★★★ **Chenin Blanc** ◀ Model, moderately-priced chenin, **98**, like most recent pvs. attractively scented, with tropical flavours. Just off-dry to round out palate, give very broad appeal (5,5 gms/l sugar).

★★★ **Sémillon** NEW in **98**. Barrel-fermented, broad-flavoured, already with unusual, advanced butterscotch undertones: dry. In small, maiden vintage quantity. Seems likely to mature quickly and made for the table and serious food—not casual, fruity-sipping, anytime wine.

Pinot Noir 96 dark-hued, rich-looking and -tasting, rather forward and pushy, with dry oaky-tannic finish. **95** obliging, extrovert with soft-carpet feel in mouth, spicy complexity. Critics might want more pinot typicity (leafy, gamey, mushrooms, etc) but this is a fine drink. (New clone.) Pvs. fewer flavours, less impressive colour. **Dry Red** Easy drinking, spicy, latest still follows Chianti/Chateauneuf practice of blending select white varietals with the reds. **Malbec** Last was **94** (v'yd seems to opt out alternative years): spicy, medium to light-bodied, with black cherry fragrance/flavour, hints of tobacco. **92 VVG**. One of few Cape examples of this French grape, red wine

"mainstay" of Argentina. **Rosé 98** merlot-pinotage mainly, off-dry, easy tasty drinking, slight nuttiness in latest. (**VG** for **95**.)
Sauvignon Blanc 98 some grassy scents with a certain bite—plus more substantial vinous body than pvs. **Rhine Riesling 98** delightful nose, light, ballerina-like body and weight, medium-dry (12 gms/l). **Special Late Harvest 98** sports forward muscat scents plus regular sweet 'n spicy palate: hanepoot about 25% with chenin, 34 gms/l sweetness. **Brut MCC** nearly 5 years on lees—very yeasty, light freshness on creamy/bready nose.
FREEDOM ROAD Sauvignon Blanc NEW **98** result of a Backsberg joint, worker-management project (see introductory notes above); balanced, dry white, straightforward sauvignon, with sufficient fruit and weight to render it very pleasant, all-purpose quaffing and food wine. 12,5% alc. From riverside Paarl vineyards managed by workers, vinified at Backsberg.
Export label: JENNSBERG
Cabernet-Merlot 97, grapes from neighbouring v'yds, nutty sweet-berried attractions, also some earthy grip finish.
SIMSBERG Pinot Noir NEW **97** with some potential and genuine pinot juiciness, flavours, very pleasant palate, plus solid rather than insipid finish.
★★★★ **SIMUNYE Sauvignon Blanc** NEW **98** maiden release from California's outstanding lady of wine, Zelma Long, and her viticultural consultant husband Phil Freese. Made in the Backsberg cellars. Grapes from Durbanville. Lovely, filled-out dry white; fresh, crisp sauvignon penetration, excellent balance overall with clean, elegant finish. This label eventually will adorn bottles with the Long and Freese grapes grown on their joint venture vineyards with Michael Back at Paarl. The vineyards, planted in 1998, will be devoted to the two cabernets and merlot and have been established with exceptional care.

BADSBERG CO-OP WINE CELLAR

Rawsonville See Worcester map

Tastings/sales Mon-Fri 8-12; 1-5.
Owners: 25 members
Winemaker: Carel van der Merwe (since 1993)
Production: 1 000 cases. **Vineyards:** 900 ha.
P.O. Box 72, Rawsonville 6845
Tel: 0231-91120 **Fax:** 0231-91122

For years dessert fans have been beating a path to the door of this cellar—conveniently near to the famous spa at Goudini—to buy its delectable silky-textured **Hanepoot**. Nowadays customers are as likely to ask for **Chardonnay** or **Sauvignon**, an indication of the steady march away from the stalwarts of yore to premium whites and reds.

★★★ **Hanepoot** ◀ Current **92** improving splendidly in bottle, acquiring warm honey glow. Delicious; delicate, tiers of spicy muscat, minty cold tealeaves, nuts. **90 VVG**, SA classwinner. Don't over-chill.
Pinotage NEW **98** lightly wooded, untasted. **Chardonnay** ◀ **98** the John Wayne of chard.: big, bold (alc. nudging 14%), oaky, toasty/limey; hints of marmalade, very crisp, shortish finish. Fermented on American oak chips. **Sauvignon Blanc** NEW ◀ **98** lively figgy scents, bit of grass, peppery seasoning, lowish alc. Very nice. ± 11%. **Late Harvest** Semi-sweet **95** chenin; tropical fruit, fresh honey overlay. **Vin Sekt** NEW **NV** Jovial fruity fizz from sauvignon.

BAKENSKOP WINES

See Jonkheer

BAREFOOT WINERY

Owners: Greg Mitchell, Peter Oxenham
Winemaker: Cathy Marshall
Production: 16 tons, 1 000 cases
Address: 18 Kiewiet Street, Stellenbosch 7600
Tel/Fax: 021-8879910 **Cell:** 083 454 3678
E-mail: wine@barefoot.co.za
Website: www.barefoot.co.za

Cathy Marshall, recently appointed winemaker at Amani Cellar, where the 99 Barefeet are to be made (other wines could join the pinot below), is guaranteed a calmer atmosphere for this private label next vintage. In 1998, with the picking of the pinot just two days away, she was still looking for cellar facilities—"major panic in the camp"—before Danie Steytler of Kaapzicht rode gallantly to the rescue. Marshall, with Oregon and French experience, has previously been a guest winemaker in a number of local cellars (Irina von Holdt's Blue White Chenin was one of her charges). Building an own-cellar is next on the agenda for her and Barefoot partners Greg Mitchell, an engineer, and education consultant Peter Oxenham, a step they began to contemplate in 1996 when the notion of this closed corporation was born, at a party in Muizenberg. There they and 17 friends gathered to stomp a ton of grapes the traditional way—*sans* shoes.

★★★ **Pinot Noir** NEW **98** with ripe strawberries on autumn forest-floor background, good clean oak, nice vanilla touch at end. St'bosch Kloof grapes, low-yield, 70% French 2nd/3rd-fill oak (Francois Frere), 30% in mix new/2nd-fill barrels. 13,3% alc. Made at Kaapzicht. Streets ahead of insubstantial **97**—12,5% alc., Devon Valley grapes, made at Devoncrest Winery.

BARRYDALE WINERY

Tradouw Valley, Klein Karoo See Klein Karoo map

Tastings/sales Mon-Fri 8.30-1; 2-5. Cellar tours by appointment. Tasting fee: R3.
Owners: 53 members
Winemaker: Bob de Villiers (since 1989)
Production: 25 000 cases. **Vineyards:** ± 300 ha.
Address: Van Riebeeck Street, Barrydale 6750
Tel: 028-5721012 **Fax:** 028-5721541
E-mail: barywine@dorea.co.za

This co-operative, established as a distillery in the 1940s, added fine-wine to its repertoire only relatively recently: the first bottling under the winery name was in 1985. Today Bob de Villiers' wines are in heavy demand, such that premium varieties are being established at the rate of some 80 000 vines a year. This breakneck pace will result in a doubling of wine-quality plantings soon after the millennium. "Then we'll be able to focus on the SA market, which is very important to us," De Villiers says. Welcome news for local fans who might feel short-rationed: over 95% of production is shipped overseas.

TRADOUW range:

★★★ **Tradouw Reserve** Continues established vintage-on-vintage blend variation within overall B'deaux theme. 20% cab. f. in **97** lends enticing savoury tang to cab. s. (75%) strawberries, merlot plums. Lightness, approachability are keywords, enhanced by very attractive sweet-oaky fruitcake finish. Mainly new 300 l Nevers oak, 12 months. Probably not best vintage to date: that honour, in Bob de Villiers' estimation, still goes to **95 VG**.

*** **Merlot** Key-change from Major of bright, luscious, easy-going **95** to Minor of sterner, more compact, less accessible (but no less fine) **97**. Latest release features merlot plumminess, touches of raspberry, dark chocolate, coffee leading to quite abrupt, not unpleasant finish. Overall mouth-impression is strict tannin, needing probably 2-5 years to relax. 8 months in French barrels, 70% new.

*** **Chardonnay** (pvs. called **Sur Lie) 98** unabashedly Australian-styled, with brash lemon-lime, zesty light-marmalade fruit, vanilla richness in tail. 5 months oak, full malo broadens mouth-feel, complexity. Mix of American/French clones. These best given time in bottle, usually ± yr. **97** has longer development horizon —perhaps 3-4 yrs. **96 VG.**

*** **Chenin Blanc/Chardonnay 98** 50/50 zigsaw that only time can assemble. Components—mouthfilling ripe guava, zippy citrus, "sweet" butterscotch-oak—all in place, more or less equal proportion. Allow 1-2 years for wood tannins to ease off, flavours to harmonise. Chard. 100% through malo, 5 months French oak, Alliers/Nevers. ± 13% alc.

*** **Sauvignon Blanc 98** powerful bone-dry white with ripe gooseberry, Granny Smith apple, pear-drop flavours; demandingly fresh. Best ± yr from vintage—time enough for youthful over-exuberance to abate. Alc. nudging 14%. Reductively made.

BARRYDALE range:

*** **Gewürztraminer** Hit all the right notes since maiden **96**. Latest **(98)** pure seduction: gentle rose-petal, litchi fragrances (definitely not the sort you'd associate with the Klein Karoo!). Freshened by light acidity; not a trace of bitterness that mars many a Cape gewürz. Gorgeous aperitif/dessert—29 gms/l sugar, with light alc. (11,3%). **96** (under Tradouw label) matured, ripened beautifully in bottle.

Tinta Barocca/Ruby Cabernet ☺ NEW **98** a distinctly different animal, but well worth catching. Fusion of high-toned rhubarb (from ruby cab.), damp-earthy (but not porty) tinta, exciting strawberry undertones. Succulent mouth-feel, super-quaffing. Moderate alc. (11,9%). Excellent example of a blend being stronger than the sum of its parts. **Chenin Blanc** NEW **98** fairly ordinary, dry, from 20-year-old vines.

BARTHO EKSTEEN WINES

Hermanus See Walker Bay map

Visits by appointment.
Owners: Bartho Eksteen and Ailsa Butler (UK)
Winemaker: Bartho Eksteen (since 1998)
Production: 1 000 cases, 14 tons (50% exported to UK)
Address: Suite 47, Private Bag X15, Hermanus 7200
Tel: 0283-24029 **Fax:** 0283-24029

Bartho Eksteen brought Wildekrans into production and was responsible for its rapid rise to fame. Now he's launched his own-name wine venture—based in the cool Walker Bay area that's become his spiritual/viticultural home. The back label on his first wine reads: "A deep desire to craft my own wine, a great passion for Sauvignon Blanc, years of dedication, and the appreciated support of fellow wine companions have resulted in a work of art which I am proud to put my name to." His signature appears over his own thumbprint! His first vintage is dedicated to his father, who passed away just as the 98 vintage began.

**** **Sauvignon Blanc** NEW from **98** grapes bought-in but grown under Bartho Eksteen's supervision. Pale straw green. A little tamer than one might have expected from him, but no doubt about the quality. Clean fig, gooseberry nose. Appears soft on entry but soon livens up with bright bouncy freshness, gooseberry, grass and herby notes. Elegant, dry, but complex with good mouth-feel. Long, zesty finish. 12,5% alc.

BAY VIEW **See Longridge**

BEACONSFIELD **See Bodega**

BEAUMONT WINES

Walker Bay See Walker Bay map

Tastings & sales 9-12.30; 1.30-4.30 weekdays. Sat am by appointment. Groups by appointment. Self-catering cottages for hire.
Owners: Raoul & Jayne Beaumont
Winemaker: Niels Verburg (since 1996)
Production: 8 000 cases. **Vineyards:** 48 ha.
P.O. Box 3, Bot River 7185
Tel: 02824-49733 (office); 49450 (cellar) **Fax:** 02824-49733

Raoul and Jayne Beaumont's historic Compagnes Drift farm at Bot River has come a long way since their début 93 vintage. The cellar—last in operation 40 years before the Beaumonts re-commissioned it—has not lost its rustic charm and remains one of the most characterful in the Cape winelands. The 93 renaissance began with a pinotage from old vines, and under the care of winemaker Niels Verburg, who joined in 1996, the range has expanded. After graduating from Elsenburg, he has worked in Sauternes, New Zealand, Western Australia and Chile. Jayne Beaumont continues to be deeply involved in shaping the wine styles and marketing strategies; and Raoul in nurturing the vineyards. Minimal handling is the philosophy here, except when Verburg takes the occasional tumble into the open *kuipe*. Export markets have opened up all around the world as their reputation has grown. Verburg rates the 98 vintage highly, as full ripeness produced voluptuous wines throughout the range. The vintage ended in an exuberant party to press the port by foot. 98 saw the first vintages of merlot, cabernet sauvignon and cabernet franc. Verburg believes the future is red here in Bot River; Beaumont's Shiraz is the first to be bottled in the Walker Bay area; a 98 Bordeaux blend named Ariane is waiting in the wings. The quantity of oak was more than doubled in 1998. Mourvèdre and sémillon have been planted.

★★★★ **Pinotage** A new-wave SA pinotage incorporating cool Walker Bay influence. **97** generous, big, lingering mouthful of rich, spicy plums with violet bouquet. Ripe, firm tannins and slight honeyed sweetness lend elegance. 9 months in 1st, 2nd and 3rd-fill French oak. 3 different yeasts add complexity. 12,5% alc. Traditional open fermentation. **Pinotage Reserve 97** barrel selection made for Diners Club, natural ferment only.

★★★ **Shiraz** Vibrant mulberry hue; spicy farmyard aroma merges into delicious dense cassis fruit in **97**. Elegant sweetness adds charm. 7 months French oak well integrated. 13% alc.

★★★ **Chenin Blanc** Prominent among new-style handcrafted SA chenins. **97** big, multi-faceted, dry, longer maturation potential than most. Penetrating lemony/apple aromas; honeyed caramel tones. Made more in Loire style. Long lees contact, oaking and fullness suggest longevity and food affinity. **Chenin Blanc Reserve** Still in barrel at time of going to press, **97** naturally fermented from low-yield 30 year vines. Only 1 500 bottles made.

★★★★ **Chardonnay** Full, buttered-toast style, with rich citrus flavours in **97**. Taut steeliness running through backbone to finely balanced finish. Oddbins buyer Steve Daniels says "I'll take it all if I can have it." 8 months French oak. 12,8% alc.

★★★ **Sauvignon Blanc 97** melange of tropical fruit flavours/aromas. Passion-fruit, grapefruit, touches of bell pepper. Zippy, fresh, crisp finish.

★★★ **Port 97** tinta barocca/pinotage blend, in drier style, wood-matured. Rich Christmas pudding flavours with coffee/chocolate tones. 900 bottles only.

★★★ **Goutte d'Or** Natural sweet from 20% botrytised **97** chenin. Fermented for 4 months. Sweet-sour raisin flavours, delicious piquancy. Elegance enhanced by dry, almost chalky finish.

BELLINGHAM

Franschhoek See Franschhoek map

Open Nov-Apr: Mon-Fri 9- 5; May-Oct: Mon-Fri 9-5, Sat 10-1. R5 per person tasting charge.

Light lunches during December/January.

Owner: Kangra Holdings (Graham Beck)
Winemaker: Charles Hopkins (since 1990)
Marketing Director: Jacques Roux
Production: 2 200 tons. 350 000 cases. **Vineyards**: 130 ha.
P.O. Box 134, Franschhoek 7690
Tel: 021-8741011 **Fax:** 021-8741712

"I'm 100% adrenalin-driven," says winemaker Charles Hopkins. He has to be, to match the pace set by owner Graham Beck ("I've never known a man with such vision") whose determination to turn this venerable Cape estate into a cutting-edge force by the 21st century is driving a massive building, renovating, replanting and expansion scheme here. The list of innovations is awesome: a new red wine fermentation and barrel cellar modelled on the Hospice de Beaune ("high-tech but old method," explains Hopkins, "I don't want to make wine by computer, I want to see, feel each tank"); a tasting tower (Italian-inspired); refurbishments and enlargements to the old white wine cellar (each cellar will eventually be able to crush 1 500 tons); landscaped gardens linking the two (Scotland the creative spur here); new plantings (the red/white mix is currently 36/65; by 2001 will be 50/50); and the addition to Hopkins' fruit sources of two new Graham Beck purchases, farms in the Firgrove-Helderberg area. "There's never a dull moment here," he says, and this was particularly true of the 98 vintage—"by far the most difficult harvest I've ever had"—which he handled in two cellars, one unfinished, separated by a long hike. In future each cellar will have its own manager, with Hopkins and a deputy commuting between them.

Bellingham's consumer profile stretches from those with super-twitchy, highly-calibrated noses—the Premium Rangers—to the more popular palate, catered for by both new-wave and long-established styles (the Johannisberger is still wowing the crowds after 45 years). "Our aim is to produce wines that are distinctive and exceptional across the ranges," says Hopkins. One of the Cape's most talented modern-generation winemakers, he's assisted by increasingly well-qualified staff, via Cape Wine Academy and practical equipment courses, visits to other cellars and a general "learning environment". A significant appointment is that of Howard Gqirana to manage the new red wine cellar, which also features a training office.

PREMIUM range:

★★★★ **Cabernet Franc** Hopkins' favourite variety; each vintage delightfully individual. Brilliantly hued **97** combines elegance, complexity. Outgoing nutmeg spice, leafy aromas lifted by discreet mintiness. Refinement continues with clean, light-textured but deep-flavoured palate, smooth tannin balance. Perhaps not as long-lived as dense **95 VVG**, just as good. **96 SAA** more open fruit, well-structured. All aged year in tight-grain French barriques, 3-monthly racking, re-barrelled.

★★★★ **Cabernet Sauvignon 95 VVG** only vintage to date. Benchmark traditional Cape cabernet; chewily ripe nuts, berries. Fruity concentration matched by dense but unobtrusive tannin. From 28-year-old dryland bush vines.

★★★★ **Pinotage 96** launched premium range to flying start: Perold Trophy for best Pinotage on 97 IWSC. **97** worthy follow-up, though tighter, less forthcoming fruit in youth, especially on nose. More sumptuous feel on palate, laced with fresh banana, dried fig sweetness; still with firm tannin wrapping. Will need year or two to open. From 23-year-old, low yield Bellingham v'yd. 13 months new wood, tiny portion American.

★★★ **Shiraz 96** gutsy but softish mouthful of sweet fruit flavours, black pepper spice. Should reach prime drinking by 2000. Alcoholic/malo fermentation finished in mainly new American oak, 10% used French, barrel-matured for further year. No **97.**

VINTAGE range:

★★★★ **Cabernet Sauvignon** Super **97**: traditional deep cassis, nuts aromas enriched with modern ripeness, classy well-absorbed oak. Very big, rich mouthful; densely packed fruit/tannins. Stand-out style but has length, breadth to reach grand maturity 7-8 years. St'bosch, Somerset West main grape sources. **96 (★★★)** similar fruit character; more medium-bodied, open. **96, 95 VG.**

★★★ **Pinotage** "Our bread and butter wine," says Hopkins. More style, personality than a mere staple, though: **97** with bright summer pudding red fruits, rounded out with oak. Soft, medium-bodied, has overall appeal. 8 months, used oak. **96 VVG.**

★★★ **Shiraz** Lively white pepper/spice fragrance highlights soft, chocolately palate of **97**; touch American oak sweetness enhances gamey hints. Satisfyingly substantial but without harshness; acids held at gentle 5,5 gms/l. **96** forward, open; **95 SAA** rich, compact.

★★★ **Merlot** Charming **97**: generous violet, mocha fragrance, freshening minerally overtones. Velvety palate, quite voluptuous but gentle tannin grip, medium body provide elegance. Already drinking well; should develop over next 4/5 years. **96** expressively fruity; could take slight chilling. All French oak-matured 13 months, portion new.

★★★ **Chardonnay** Change in approach with **98**. New style promises greatest sophistication; unblended sample reveals tight ginger biscuits, mango ripeness, sleek yet creamy feel; smoothly integrated fruit/oak. Up to 70% new wood, all French. Lees stirring, malo, other French touches. Hopkins' pvs. contention that "100% malo makes wines too dull" certainly not true here. Majority of grapes from Darling area. Possible higher rating once bottled. **95** barrel-fermented; pvs. 40% for more fruity accessibility but not sustained; good weight, suppleness.

★★★ **Sauvignon Blanc** ◀ One of Cape's best-value unwooded sauvignons. Despite hot, dry vintage, **98** brims with cool-climate intensity, introduced by green-flecked glassy translucence; powerful, incisively dry but not at all harsh. Steely, gooseberry attack promises to grow in bottle, unlike many more transient 98's. Selection 6 different v'yds inc. Devon Valley/Durbanville/Somerset

West grapes. Pvs. **95 VVG; 94 VG, SAA; 93 SAA** all noteworthy. **Classic** Gentle spice, mulberry sweetness in NV cab. s., shiraz, merlot blend; rounded, easy-drinking. **Rosé 98** cinsaut/pinotage blend; fruity, dry. **Premier Grand Crû** Medium-bodied, refreshingly dry with crisp, grassy tones. Sauvignon blanc/chenin blanc/Cape riesling NV blend. Still top seller in its class. **Sauvenay** ☺ ◀ Plentiful sauvignon fruit, rounded, softened by chardonnay in dry, flavoursome blend. Pleases show judges, consumers alike. **Johannisberger (Export label Cape Gold)** SA's top-selling semi-sweet white, NV, light-bodied, delicate grapey aromas, flavours; balanced, clean. **Natural Sweet** None since **96**, fruitily sweet, balanced 47 gms/l sugar; 11% alc. **Brut** ◀ Briskly dry sparkler; appealing chardonnay creaminess. NV charmat method.

BERG & BROOK VINEYARDS

Simondium See Paarl map

Visits: Open for tastings & sales, Mon-Fri 8.30-5 year-round. Sat 8.30-12.30 (Sept-May). R2 per person.
Owner: Berg & Brook Vineyards
Cellarmaster/Technical Director—Berg & Brook range: Nico Vermuelen (since 1995) with Woelie Wagener (since 1991)
Winemaker—Savanha range: Rudi Schultz (since 1998)
Vineyard Consultant: Dawie le Roux
Production: 4 000 tons
P.O. Box 15589, Vlaeberg 8018
Tel: 021-8742015 **Fax:** 021-8741402
E-mail: savanha@iafrica.com

Striding confidently towards the 21st century, a rank outsider which has suddenly burst out of nowhere, this booming wine operation is a new-age Cape phenomenon. Brainchild of pocket-sized, max-vision advertising man and wine author Graham Knox, it started off in 1996 as a fairly modest partnership between his Savanha bought-in wine business and 26 members of the former Simondium (Drakenstein) Co-op, with HQ in one of the least splendid wineries around. It's now listed on the Johannesburg Stock Exchange—all shares taken up, R20 million raised to build a new red wine maturation cellar—a huge vote of confidence for the company's expansionist vision. It now owns or leases 16 farms (700 ha.) in prime growing areas, runs the wine side of Dick Enthoven's Spier empire, and turns out some sensational examples of modern Cape wines.

Growers are practically beating down their doors to become suppliers, an enviable position in these times of acute wine shortages. And they're encouraged to do so via innovative incentives like, in 1998, a red-wine grape competition: neighbours Jackie Coetzee of Bloemendal (cab.) and Kosie de Villiers of Morgenster (merlot), both in Durbanville, won all-expenses-paid trips to Yalumba Winery in South Australia. While Berg & Brook, naturally, won grapes from their prize blocks, which have been incorporated into its Reserve range.

One of the judges was Alain Moueix, from the Pomerol Petrus family, B&B's red-wine consultant; he and Knox are partners in Klein Doolhof, a Wellington farm (see its first fruits below); through Moueix, B&B have to some extent cracked the most critical problem currently facing Cape wine—a shortage of planting material. He put them onto World Wide Vineyards, a French company which specialises in grafting; guarantees a 90% "take". By 2000 B&B will be harvesting from vines given this total personality-change. In addition, they're among only 4 producers which have official permission to import vine material. Advising on the white wines is Christopher Olivier, formerly a senior lecturer at Bordeaux

University, who said after his first visit to the Cape "I've not seen the same promise in Spain, Chile or Greece" (other countries in which he consults). However, he did insist on—and get—a significant revamp for B&B's white winemaking equipment. Music to the ears of Rudi Schultz (brother of Hartenberg winemaker Carl), who moves to this cellar from Eersterivier and a stint at Sonoma Cutrer, to beef up the team headed by Nico Vermeulen, ex-L'Ormarins, who has come into his own here.

RESERVE range: (name yet to be decided)

★★★★ **Merlot** Aim here to produce super-league, adrenalin-racing quality. First **97** on track (**98** even more promising). Striking Pomerol-like well-hung red meat, fresh minerally tones (no coincidence Pomerol's Alain Moueix consults here); lots of glycerol richness, sweet ripe fruit, melt-in-the-mouth tannins but opulence tempered with plenty of verve, elegance, for the classic feel, ageing potential more often associated with cabernet. Oak entirely supportive (broadens, enriches, rounds) rather than competitive. Extended skin contact, malo completed in new, Saury French barriques. Grapes from selected Durbanville, Bottelary Hills v'yds.

★★★★ **Cabernet Sauvignon** Delicate cassis, chocolate whiffs infused with cedar/cinnamon set tone of supreme elegance in **97**. Down-duvet texture, glycerol-rich sweet fruit, framed by ripe, friendly tannins; cabernets don't come much more tempting than this. But no overnight wonder; structured to last at least 7-8 years. Wellington, Sir Lowry's Pass v'yds.

Following Reserve range wines tasted as barrel samples; will be marketed under a separate, premium label, name as yet undecided: **Savanha Reserve Pinotage 98**: warm wood spice complexity, soft, dense, well-integrated oak, not intrusive sweetness from 40% American portion. No bitterness, vulgarity. **Shiraz Reserve 98** Similar gutsy, punchy style to **97** lots of spice, chewy flavours; grunty shiraz at its best. French/American oak-matured. Malo completed in barrel.

SAVANHA range:

★★★★ **Merlot** May be standard range, certainly above "standard" quality; classy **97** step up SA ladder. Combines opulence, refinement. Smells of intensely ripe, sweet red fruits plus tantalising spice. Palate swathed in mouthcoating plum/chocolate richness, velvety tannins, clean minerally frame. Fruit all there for current enjoyment, has good 4-5 years in store, if necessary. Malo completed in new/used French oak; 50% unwooded.

★★★★ **Shiraz** ◀ Rhône enthusiasts will associate with **97**. Striking pepper-spice fragrance woven with soft chocolate, gamey aromas; this decadent sweet/savoury impression lingers indefinitely on palate. Plentiful youthful oomph, flavour; tannins sufficiently comfortable for current irresistible drinking or 5 years down line. Beautifully judged oak: malo completed in shared French/American barrels, some new. Another step forward in Cape's shiraz revival.

★★★ **Cabernet Sauvignon** Full-bodied but elegant **97**. Forthcoming cassis ripeness, complementary dusty new oak bouquet. Gentle tannin frames approachable, long sweet fruit. Well-balanced, oaked.

★★★ **Chardonnay** ◀**97** evolving with ripe refinement. Complex oatmeal citrusy bouquet; full-bodied but supple, creamily soft; finishes just dry, generously long. **98** promises similar attributes, few notches up complexity scale. 100% oak-fermented with natural yeasts; malo completed.

★★★ **Sémillon** ◀ NEW Rich Australian-style with Cape elegance. **97** developing exotic lanolin, beeswax, lemony decadence; medium-bodied, dense taffeta feel, waves of flavour, ends on lingering lemon-biscuit note. **98** bigger, riper concentration, potential ★★★★.

Both excellent oak-fruit integration. French barrel-fermented, portion new.

**** **Chenin Blanc** ◀ One of few given classic chardonnay vinification which doesn't lose distinct chenin character. **97** top-rated dry chenin **** in WINE magazine Chenin Challenge; now with opulent dried peach, mango, nutty development; very rich, juicily dry; plenty to give still. **98** promises even greater ripe complexity. Barrel-fermented, through malo. aged on lees. Grapes from Durbanville, Paarl.

*** **Sauvignon Blanc** ◀ Restrained ripe sauvignon aromas of many **98**s give way to more substantial satisfaction on palate; refined fig/gooseberry cool climate intensity, broadened by rich texture.

Pinotage Forward warm spice, sweet plum fruits in **97** lifted by touch American oak; medium-bodied, juicy. Blend tank/oak-matured. **Pinotage-Cabernet Sauvignon** Uncomplicated 70/30 blend; **97** rounded, slightly earthy nose, more chocolate richness on palate; sound if unremarkable partnership. **Rosé** Far from traditional SA (and probably most other countries) rosé. **97** big, round, dry; captures lightness of a white with brambly nutty nuances, gentle tannin feel of a red; designed as food wine. Amber-tinged merlot/cab. s. (60/40); barrel-fermented. Pre-bottling **98** promises richer red fruit flavours, more supple dryness.

BERG & BROOK range:

*** **Merlot** ◀ Uncluttered ripe, spicy plum generosity in **97**; vibrant, crushed velvet feel; satisfying without being heavy; delicious chewy length. Has more substance than many early-drinking reds. Blend tank/barrel-matured.

*** **Cabernet Sauvignon-Shiraz** ◀ Savoury 70/30 blend from **97**. Generous pepper-spice bouquet; punchy fruit, cab. s. portion 3 months rounding in used French oak. Tasty everyday drinking with guts to last further year or two.

*** **Chenin-Chardonnay** ◀ Popular seller. **98** 70/30 blend, chardonnay lightly wooded for extra breadth, weight on palate. Chenin's extrovert tropical character with subtle vanilla enrichment, predominates. Big, clean mouthful, ideal with richer fish/white meat dishes.

Ruby Cabernet ☺ ◀ Berry-rich, unwooded **97**. Medium-bodied, chewily soft, sweet fruity persistence. **Pinotage** NEW Uncomplicated mouthful warm, spicy red fruits; **97** substantial but not heavy; fruitily dry. Unwooded. **Brookside Red** ◀ NEW 50/50 SA/French blend (French from Ch. Capion qv Saxenburg) **97** cinsaut, grenache, shiraz, merlot. Lots of spice, wild scrub, sweet plum tang; low tannins for immediate quaffability. **Chardonnay** ☺ ◀ **97** unwooded but with more assertive varietal character than most. Lively pale gold, green glints; smoky/oatmeal bouquet, sweet lemon flesh freshness, soft fruity finish enhanced by touch sugar. Best Buy in Wine Spectator. **Sauvignon Blanc** Unwooded **98**; quiet tropical fig tones, weighty dry mouthful. **Pinot Gris** NEW Smoky, lemon-grass aromas in fullish **97**, softened by 3,3 gms/l sugar. **Brookside Blanc** Honeyed-fragrance, juicy chenin; **98** balanced by 5 gms/l sugar. **Bouquet Blanc** Minty, spicy blend mainly Rhine riesling with 35% chenin, 25% muscat de frontignan; medium-bodied, clean fruity sweetness. From **97**. **Special Late Harvest** Botrytis-brushed **98**. 50% chenin with weisser riesling, bukettraube adding spice, flowery-muscat hints. Ripe mouthful; 48 gms/l sugar.

Klein Doolhof, Wellington farm owned by Graham Knox/Alain Moueix, has produced two "idiosyncratic" wines, a white and red, which Alain's father already has orders for in France. **Both tasted unbottled**: **White**, a 70/30 Sémillon-Chenin Blanc, Sémillon from 90-year-old vines, barrel-fermented on natural yeasts. Full, silky dryness with ripe beeswax aromas, savoury marmitey tail. **Red**, 80/20 pinotage/cinsaut blend (cinsaut old bush vines), ultra-ripe, cassia, allspice whiffs on nose, luscious concentration sweet raspberry fruit through to finish, but neither variety dominates, a different expression of both. Malo completed in small oak, portion new. Both 98s, tank samples; should rate at least ★★★ when bottled.

The following labels for export only:

BENGUELA CURRENT: grapes sourced from the West Coast between Vredendal and Piketberg. **Pinotage**, **Merlot**, **Chardonnay** ☺, **Sauvignon Blanc same as under Berg & Brook label.**

AGULHAS BANK: grapes sourced mainly from Breede River, which produces fuller-bodied wines. **Cabernet Sauvignon** Brambly ripe **98**; gentle tannin focus forward fruit; 3 months rounding used French oak. **Chardonnay** Up-front, spicy, tropical fruit style; extra flavour, bouncy texture from malo, small portion oak-matured. **98**, **97** spot on drinkability/satisfaction. **Chenin Blanc** NEW Full-bodied **97**; supple tropical nutty fruit, softness broken by slightly coarse tail. Portion lightly oaked. **Sémillon-Sauvignon Blanc** Unwooded, dry **97**. No **98**.

CHEETAH VALLEY: exclusive to US market. Chardonnay ☺, Pinotage, Merlot, same as under Berg & Brook label.

PIERRE SIMOND range: Unwooded and boxed wines—**Ruby Cabernet**, **Sauvignon Blanc**, **Riesling**, **Late Vintage**, **Stein**, **Rosé**. Also, fortifieds (**Hanepoot**, **Port**, **Sweet/Old Brown Sherry**.)

BERGENDAL — Budget range ex-Neethlingshof, Stellenzicht

★★★ **Sémillon 96** cut above rest of these quaffers. Light green/yellow colour; full lemon, herbal aromas. Good palate intensity. Altogether rather sophisticated.

Bergenrood Substantial aromas, flavours, mouth-feel. Well crafted **92** blend, no particular varietal showing (incl. cab. s., tinta). Good touch oak, satisfying. **Shiraz-Cabernet Sauvignon** ◀ Quality budget red, **91** blend. Galaxy of aromas: ripe plum, spice, chocolate, liquorice, almost sweetish tones. Soft tannins, long briary finish. **Cabernet Sauvignon-Shiraz** NEW though **96** (untasted). Vintner says: "Lively eucalyptus, mint, brush of oak; berry, peppery flavours, supple tannins. Good value." **Bergenblanc** NV easy drinking crisp dry white, mixed salad of varieties. **Johannisberger** ◀ NV White blend with delightful fruity bouquet. Good ripe flavours, smooth mouth-feel. Good balance, fresh, clean.

BERGKELDER

Stellenbosch

Tastings/sales Mon-Fri 8-5. Sat 9-1. Purchases railed country-wide. Cellar tours 10, 10.30 and 3 Mon-Sat.
Cellarmaster: Dr. Pierre Marais
Marketing Manager: Naas Erasmus
P.O. Box 184, Stellenbosch 7599
Tel: 021-8883400 **Fax:** 021-8875769
Internet address: www.bergkelder.co.za

The Bergkelder (mountain cellar), part of Distillers Corporation, handles its own prestige ranges, the Stellenryck Collection, Fleur du Cap, Grünberger, Kupferberger, Here XVII, each individually listed in this guide. Also Bergkelder Cellarmaster's Choice, a label marking one wine with which the Bergkelder's cellar chief decides to mark his career: so far only: **Cabernet Sauvignon 87**, barrel selection by retired cellarmaster Dr. Julius Laszlo. Present cellarmaster Dr. Pierre Marais is not yet ready to nominate his vintage of a lifetime.

Worcester North See Worcester map

Tasting/sales Mon-Fri 8-5, Sat 9-1. Cellar tours, group tastings, meals by arrangement.
Owners: The Lategan family
Winemaker: De Wet Lategan (since 1992)
Production: ± 30 000 cases. **Vineyards:** ± 300 ha.
P.O. Box 15, Breede River 6858
Tel: 02324-603/721 **Fax:** 02324-658
E-mail: wine@bergsig.co.za
Website: www.bergsig.co.za

Young De Wet Lategan, 6th generation wine grower on this panoramic mountain-fringed farm, makes an admirable, well-priced range that improves by the vintage. Most of the produce goes to the local trade—Woolworths, Spar are major customers—or is exported to far-flung markets such as Hong Kong, China, Belgium, the US. Only ± 10% is bottled under the estate label. "We run what amounts to a boutique winery within the larger cellar, bottling only what we consider the *crème de la crème*." 1998 saw the 155-year-old farm take root in cyberspace: a website featuring a profile of the estate, its personalities and wines went live at www.bergsig.co.za.

**** **Soet Hanepoot** ◀ NV Current release (**95 VG**) quite super; beautifully integrated, fiendishly moreish. Gentle floral, almost gewürz. rose-petal fragrance; honey-sweet fruit, lush texture, great length. From 25-year-old bush vines. Classwinner SA young wine show. ± 17% alc., 214 gms/l sugar.

Cabernet Sauvignon 97 sees return to streamlined, uncomplicated style after beefier **95**. Current has some ripe mulberry, raspberry tones, malleable texture. Pleasant, but not hugely complex. Mix of clones, yr used barrels. **94 VG**, classwinner at SA young wine show. **Pinotage** Has settled into medium-bodied, lightly fruity, easy-drinking mould, epitomised by **96**. Cherries, curlicues of smoke, unexpectedly grippy (not unpleasant) finish. 15 months large wood. Alc. 11,3%. **90 VVG**, well-rated by US Wine Spectator. **Pinotage Blanc de Noir** ◀ **98** bon-bon flavoured, light-bodied, delicate semi-sweet. Pleasant easy drinking. Sugar 18,7 gms/l, alc. ± 11,0%. **Chardonnay** ◀ De Wet Lategan is excited about **98**, reason isn't hard to see. Fresh lemon-lime aromatics, interesting smoky traces from sojourn in wood, crisp fresh-baked-bread flavours. Clean, nice! From decade-old vines; five different clones, mix of cooper/oak. Dry, alc. 12,6%. Tasted young. **Sauvignon Blanc 98** in same fresh-cut grassy vein as pvs. Light quaffer, from 16-year-old vines. 11,5% alc. **Chenin Blanc** ◀ **98** much more zingy version of rather tired pvs. (**95**). Fresh guava bouquet, crisp texture, gentle dry finish. ± 13% alc. **Gewürztraminer** Some gewürz. pelt you with rose petals, this one (**97**) gently strokes. Delicate floral palate, sweetish barley-sugar finale. 11,8% alc., sugar ± 17 gms/l. **91 VG. Chenin Blanc Special Late Harvest** Untasted. **Bouquet Light** Untasted. Pvs. perlé-styled semi-sweet. **Edel Laatoes 94** untasted for this edition (but pvs. track-record very good). Penetrating, rich, velvety-textured dessert from gewürz., chenin, bukettraube, dash of weisser riesling. **Painted Lady Demi Sec** Carbonated pink bubbly, sweet. **Port** ◀ **95** has grown a seriously complex bouquet—very ripe black cherries, Xmas pud, mulberries, slight oaky hints—palate shade less multifarious. Relaxed, not too sweet. Tinta barocca, 18 months large wood. ± 17% alc. Classwinner SA young wine show. **VG 94**. **92 VG**.

Paarl See Paarl map

Tastings/sales Mon-Fri 9-5. Sat by appointment.
Light lunches by arrangement.
Owners: Schwulst family
Winemaker: Gisela Schwulst
Production: 1 800 cases. **Vineyards:** 4 ha.
P.O. Box 7274, Noorder-Paarl 8730
Tel/Fax: 021-872-5618
E-mail: bernheim@iafrica.com
Internet: www.wine.co.za/bernheim

"Surprise, surprise, I can make wine!" Enthusiastic young Gisela Schwulst, fresh from Stellenbosch University, was elated—and apparently quite relieved—to discover that her family hadn't "wasted their money" on her education, after completing an "extremely challenging" first crush. Dad, an industrial chemist, and mother, a pharmacist, needn't have worried. Encouraged by no less a mentor than legendary former Nederburg cellarmaster Günther Brözel to make wine "passionately, fearlessly", the rookie winemaker took the fiery baptism in her stride.

All NEW
Chenin Blanc 98 in more vinous than up-front fruity mode, reflecting winemaker's aim of delicacy, understatement. Intimations of pineapple, melon, confirmed by marginally more overt tropical tones on palate. Overall effect, though, is stern, almost severe, so best with food. Unwooded, 13% alc. **Colombard 98** "limited edition" from small, low yielding (3 tons/ha.) v'yd, mix mature/young vines. Crisp, bracing, light at 11% alc. **Semi-Sweet 98**, from chenin, picked very ripe. Though technically semi-sweet, appears dry, very fresh. Agreeable guava, spiced apple wafts. 13% alc.

BERTRAMS WINES — Gilbeys

The Bertrams fans of old will be happily surprised by the new wines that are now W.O. Western Cape and no longer from Devon Valley. While the established style has been remarkably matched, there's a livelier lift to recent releases.

★★★ **Robert Fuller Reserve 96** from a year considered difficult shows some St Émilion likeness. Highly drinkable now but with good development potential over 5-8 years. Vigorous profusion of black berry, dry herbs, some spicy oak scents. Cab. s., merlot, 12% alc.

★★★★ **Shiraz** ◀ **96** purple/blue colour. White pepper, plum-scented nose with brambleberry, earthy tones which repeat on palate, fresh acidity, youthful tannin backbone. Warm, spicy, with elegant charm. ± 13% alc.

★★★ **Cabernet Sauvignon 96** a real Devon Valley look-alike. Deep garnet colour, with grassy, plummy, ripe strawberry aromas. These echo softly on palate, with vanilla and some toasty oak. 12,5% alc.

Bertrams still have a range of fine fortified wines at competitive prices, a **Ruby Port** and **Sherries** in all forms: medium dry, medium cream, full cream, santa petra and premier reserve.

Gilbeys Distillers & Vintners, P.O. Box 137, Stellenbosch 7599. **Tel:** 021-8086911. **Fax:** 021-8086000.

BEYERSKLOOF

Stellenbosch See Stellenbosch map

Visits: Open 9-5, weekdays, phone for Saturdays.
Owner: Beyers Truter and partners
Winemaker: Beyers Truter
Production: 42 000 cases
P.O. Box 107, Koelenhof 7605
Tel: 021-8822135 **Fax:** 021 8822683

Beyers Truter is fast beginning to resemble one of those venerable war veterans, decorated from beret to boots with so much shiny medal-ware you need dark glasses just to look at him. Latest, 1998 edition to his collection of finery was the Warren Winiarski Trophy (surely with ribbons and bar?) for the "Best Cabernet Worldwide" at the International Wine & Spirit Competition in London for the Beyerskloof **94**. Truter began to mark this contest as his personal territory in a major way in 1991 when he won the Robert Mondavi "Winemaker of the Year" trophy; followed in 1994 by its highest award for "Best Blended Red Worldwide" (these two for the wines he makes in his "day job" at Kanonkop). It's just as well, for fellow-competitors, that as a red-wine specialist he leaves the odd white category open for others to win. Truter's 1998 triumph garners him an all-expenses trip to Stag's Leap Cellars in California. The winning wine is specially significant in that it features the first grapes from this small property's own vineyards—used, in desperation, when Truter discovered to his horror that most of his earmarked bought-in grapes had been harvested under-ripe. Frenzied fancy footwork ensued to replace the offending fruit with the full-ripe Monty from Beyerskloof; this international award proves the vineyards' class.

★★★★ **Cabernet Sauvignon 96** better than ever, leading into five-star territory. Deep purple colour, ultra-ripe berry fruit nose with cassis, cherry. Exploding mouthful of fresh fruit is first impression, thereafter settling down to soft, but rich tannins and gentle, sweetish flow. Good vanilla/oak backing but nothing too pushy. Ready to drink now but full of potential to grow even better. Made in massive amounts which proves that big can be beautiful if handled correctly, sensitively. **95** deep, intense nose, ripe black fruits, cassis, cherry—minty tones—rich, full. Very drinkable now.

★★★★ **Pinotage 98** vibrant, deep, ripe mulberry colour. Better in every way than pvs. Ripe banana nose jumps out of the glass, flavours almost burst with ripe freshness. Raspberry, ripe plum, deftly handled oak giving bright spiciness, lovely sweet perfume. Excellent length of flavour, beautifully balanced. From unirrigated bush vines, 20-40 yrs old. 12,5% alc. **96** ABSA Pinotage Top Ten.

BLAAUWKLIPPEN

Stellenbosch See Stellenbosch map

Weekdays 9-5, Sat 9-1. Tasting charges.
Oct 1-Apr 30 horse-drawn carriage rides, 10-12/2-3; Coachman's lunch 12-2.30.
Owner: Graham Boonzaier
Winemaker: Hein Hesebeck (since December 97)
Viticulturist: Kolerine Kotze (since December 97)
Production: 600 tons, 40 000 cases. **Vineyards:** 100 ha.
P.O. Box 54, Stellenbosch 7599
Tel: 021-8800133 **Fax:** 021-8800136

A change of guard here, just before the 1998 harvest, saw Hein Hesebeck (Neethlingshof, Hazendal among his previous posts) taking over from Jacques Kruger (now fine-tuning chief for Long Mountain). Hesebeck immediately produced a couple of innovations: individually vinified Cabernet Franc and Merlot, scheduled to join the range in future. This property made its name with Cabernet Sauvignon back in the early 80s (Walter Finlayson then on duty), and Hesebeck plans to boost plantings of this variety and—a Blaauwklippen speciality—zinfandel. In WINE magazine's "track-record" ratings of wines reviewed between 1993-97, this cellar featured in the "Top 30 cellars" line-up, and its Cabernet and Shiraz among the "Top 100 wines".

★★★ **Zinfandel** This cellar's signature wine, aromatic, persistent **95** with raisin/berry spice, almond vanilla whiffs, smoky clove/coriander flavours, lightish lean finish. Less full than more richly textured and riper **93** which reveals herbal mulberry notes.

★★★ **Shiraz** Wafts of marzipan/oak dominate peppery, black cherry fragrance in **97**. Barrel character also evident in tannins, dry, slightly lean. **95** gamier, more obvious leathery tones. **93** softer, **SAA** selection. **90, 89** both **VVG**.

★★★ **Cabernet Sauvignon** Usually in smoky blackberry, leesy style. **96** ripe youngberry/plum fruit, refined mid-weight richness with Bordeaux-like elegance, jammy spice, long finish. **95** plumper aromas but also more austere palate with dry oak tannins, slightly leafy finish. **94** mélange of herbal, black cherry notes, nutty/dusty finish.

★★★ **Muscat Ottonel** ◀ **98** offers intensely spicy, litchi-like aromas lifted by crisp acidity, not obviously semi-sweet (13,1 gms/l sugar). Lingering finish.

Pinotage Limited release. **96** pungent raspberry/loganberry fruit, layerings of mineral, almond and earthy flavours, fine tannins, not jammy, complex, persistent finish. **Red Landau NV** featuring sweet blackberry fruit, medium to lightweight palate, spicy, accessible, blend of cab. s. and merlot. **Sociable Dry Red** Gamey, berry aromas, with strong farmyard whiffs, accessible. **Sauvignon Blanc 98** pronounced grassy aromas, limey, tangy lean finish. **97** similarly herbaceous, hints of fig, discreetly fragrant. **Chardonnay 98** tropical citrus aromas, with wafts of marzipan; tangy, pineapple flavours, crisp though not austere finish, fuller/riper than pvs. **Chardonnay/Sémillon** Mouthfilling dry white. **98** thatchier/limier than pvs. with herbal citrus flavours, tangy, almost lean finish. **97** fuller, with sweet spicy aromas, aromatically dry. **Sociable White NV**, delicately fragrant off-dry blend, fruit salad aromas, pale evanescent finish. **White Landau** Muscat-dominated off-dry blend, spicy flavours, easy drinking, chewy finish.

Special Late Harvest 98 apricot/pineapple aromas, sweet-sour flavours, rich but not cloying. **Vintage Port** Drier style, tobacco-like aromas, elegant rather than robust. **95★★★** "dusty" cedary notes, marzipan/prunelle flavours, dry palate, firm finish. **92** zinfandel/pontac blend tea-leaf aromas, delicately aromatic.

BLOEMENDAL ESTATE

Durbanville See Durbanville map

Open Mon-Fri 9-5; Sat 9.30-1.
Dinner Tues-Sat; Sunday lunch.
Owner/Winemaker: Jackie Coetzee (since 1987)
Production: 5 000 cases. **Vineyards:** 150 ha.
P.O. Box 466, Durbanville 7550
Tel/Fax: 021-962682

Jackie Coetzee's reputation for giving the most individual answers to the questions we ask all winemakers for each edition remains secure. For example: What are your cellar's plans for the future? "To be more relaxed!" he replies. Whether this is humanly possible for this already incorrigibly chilled-out, board-sailing, horse-riding, life's-a-breeze character is debatable, but his winemaking philosophy isn't. He says very firmly: "Do it because you enjoy it! Do your best. But never be satisfied." Asked where he's travelled in the past year and what he learned from his travels, he heads right off the wine map, to Mozambique and the deserts of Namibia, from where he brought back this wisdom: "No need to rush!" As good a winemaking mantra as any, come to think of it. His wines are as distinctive as he is, and specially admired by export customers in Germany, Belgium and Holland. They start off with the advantage of being grown in the excellent, cooler climes of Durbanville, conveniently close to the beaches near Table Bay. Greater worker participation in planning and realising Bloemendal's "vision for the future" is among Coetzee's current pre-occupations.

★★★★ **Cabernet Sauvignon** Good track-record, never run-of-the-mill. **96** latest release another real individual: mint, eucalyptus at beginning and end, liquorice all-sorts, black fruit pastilles in between, firm tannins. Bit of patience will be rewarding—these usually best 5-7 years after vintage. One year new oak, low-yield v'yd.

★★★ **Merlot 96** was richer, riper, much more forthcoming than lighter, **97**. But latest still gives satisfying if lower-key show of coffee, choc-cherries/berries, modulated by year in 2nd, 3rd-fill oak.

★★★ **Sauvignon Blanc** Perennially stunningly-scented, usual asparagus joined by fresh gooseberries in **98**, a thriving veg. garden of a nose, leading on to frisky, fruity, palate. Charmingly unserious. Fun young. But perhaps keep a bottle or two for later: pvs. have aged with interest. **97 WINE**★★★★.

Port From **94** shiraz, 3 years in barrel, exceptionally light, and in drier style. Reverse the usual order and try this before dinner, as an aperitif.

BLOUPUNT WINES

Montagu, Klein Karoo See Klein Karoo map

Tastings/sales Mon-Fri 9.00-5. Sat 9-4. Tasting fee for tour groups. Cellar visits by arrangement.
Owner: Phil Hoffman
Winemakers: Paul & Phil Hoffman (since 1997)
Consulting Winemaker: Sonnie Malan (Montagu Co-op)
Production: ± 4 000 cases
Vineyards: 1,5 ha. (11 000 closely planted vines)
Address: 12 Long Street, Montagu 6720
Tel/Fax: 0234-42385
E-mail: bloupunt@ilink.nis.za

After working 40 years for a major SA bank in various parts of the world, wine lover Phil Hoffman had retired to sleepy St James on False Bay when the (then) only chardonnay vineyard in Montagu came onto the market. The tiny plot, hugging the entrance to the historic hamlet, was duly bought and for 3 years the grapes were supplied to the local co-op — until son and economics graduate Paul Hoffman, encouraged by local and international accolades for winemaker Sonnie Malan's handling of the variety, decided to turn the operation into a stand-alone venture. The result is Montagu's first family-owned cellar, with self-taught father and son working the grapes under Malan's seasoned eye. The tone here is as amiable as the wines: "We're no experts. But what we lack in know-how we make up in enthusiasm!"

Chardonnay (wooded) NEW **98** (tank sample) delicious, handsomely packaged, too. Intense dried peach plumped out by broad, soft oak flavours. Gently dry finish. Emphatic step up from **97**, which perhaps too enthusiastically wooded for most palates. Fermented, aged with Nevers barrels, staves. 13,5% alc. Like sibling below, from ± 7-yr-old vines. **Chardonnay** (unwooded) ☺ NEW **98** (tank sample) marginally fresher version of seductive **97**. Luscious yellow-peach core, bouncy acid, lingering dry farewell. Mouthfilling flavours heightened by 13,5% alc.

BLUE CREEK VOORSPOED WINES

Blaauwklippen Valley, Stellenbosch See Stellenbosch map

Tastings/sales by appointment.
Owners: Rabie Smal, Piet Smal
Winemaker: Piet Smal (since 1998)
Production: 1 500-2 000 cases. **Vineyards**: 7 ha.
P.O. Box 3247, Matieland 7602
Tel: 021-8800522/887-6938 **Fax:** 021-8865462

Winemaker Jacques Kruger has moved to Long Mountain, leaving owners Rabie Smal and son Piet to make Blue Creek/Voorspoed wines on their rustic property in Blaauwklippen Valley. Since the last crush a new maturation cellar was built, pressing facilities upgraded for the single-varietal, single-product range, and workers' houses upgraded. Piet Smal, who took over winemaking duties from the 1998 harvest, says: "Current production is from bought-in grapes and the old cab. clone still growing on the farm. We're steadily replacing these seniors with new clones."

Cabernet Sauvignon 96 offering ripe bouquet of minty blackcurrant fruit, Virginia tobacco whiffs (a Blaauwklippen Valley trademark); soft coffee/chocolate on palate, firm but not astringent tannins, spicy, persistent finish. Oak evident, but well-layered. **97**, **98** untasted.

BLUE WHITE (Old Vines Wine Cellars)

Winemaker: To be appointed
Owners: Irina van Holdt and Francoise Botha
Production: 14 000 cases
Address: 50 Liesbeek Rd, Rosebank 7700
Tel: 021-6856428 **Fax:** 021-6856446
E-mail: oldvines@iafrica.com

A woman is permitted to change her mind, especially when the lady in question is energetic, enterprising, innovative Irina von Holdt, dynamo behind the classy, mould-breaking all-chenin **Blue White** label (we declare an interest, she's a taster for this guide). Von Holdt is credited—long before it became fashionable—with looking at the Cape's vast chenin v'yds and seeing ripe potential where others saw only barren leaf-cover. From the outset—here's the rub—the style was resolutely unwooded. "Blue White must never be a wannabe-chardonnay or just another wooded dry white," she maintained. But, as they say, customer is king and the brand's devotees demanded a wooded version. So she's launched a second wine, **Old Vines Barrel Reserve 98**—"*subtly* oaked", she stresses, to cosset rather than jostle with chenin's delicate fruit. On the commercial front, meanwhile, Von Holdt—with daughter Francoise Botha at her side—has had to "learn all the things they didn't teach you at Cape Wine Masters", like dealing with Sandton "business suits" and managing logistics of the first orders from Denmark, Japan (California, the UK are other export markets). But the mother-and-daughter team say they're loving every minute.

★★★ **Blue White** A wine with potential, "twinkles and shines" says Irina v. H. So it does. **98** not quite at full 4-star wattage when tasted in infancy, but track-record of this singular chenin shows it needs only a little time in bottle (few months, up to a year) to become fully illuminated. Very attractive fruity nose: honeysuckle, pineapple. Stack of plump, fleshy fruit on palate, with a keen lemon-like acidity. Super-fresh layers of apple and apricot add extra allure to the mouthfilling texture. **97** ★★★★ proves wine's staying/growing power: has the extra dimension of time, some grapefruit has emerged, there's still a fresh, zesty finish.

★★★ **Old Vines Barrel Reserve** NEW **98** a big-boned wine with green apple, pineapple and oaky, leesy notes on nose, generous, soft mouth-feel. Despite mellow palate has a firm, zippy finish. As attractive as this already is, will repay a year or two development in the bottle. Excellent potential. Barrel-fermented.

BODEGA

Paarl See Paarl map

Tastings/sales by appointment. Cellar tours, vineyard walks, guest cottage.
Owners: Jeremy Squier, Julianne Barlow
Winemakers: Julianne Barlow, Eugene van Zyl
Vineyards: Paul Wallace
Production: 2 000 cases. **Vineyards:** 12 ha.
P.O. Box 590, Kraaifontein 7569
Tel: 021-9882929 **Fax:** 021-9883527

After the very good **94** vintage Bodega—spunky little Joostenbergvlakte winery over the road from Villiera—seemed to say *hasta la vista*, grapes/wine grown on the property being sold in bulk to other wineries. But from the 1998 vintage, owner/winemaker Julianne Barlow, abetted by brother Jeremy Squier, advisers Eugene van Zyl and Paul Wallace, is again bottling the estate's distinctive upper-crust *vino tinto* under its own label. Identical wines are exported under the **Beaconsfield** label.

★★★★ **Cabernet Sauvignon 94** maturing invitingly, gaining rich vinous overtones. Velvety maroon, lovely waxy/cedar-oaky introduction with cinnamon, minty notes; clean, ripe fruit; smooth, good grip though tannins drying ever so slightly, so keep an eye. 13,5% alc. Large portion new-clone. Traditional methods, 12 mths French oak. **98** not ready for tasting.

Merlot 94 sweet red-black berry combo woven with spicy oak, decidedly dry finish, best with food. 13,6% alc. New clone.

BOEKENHOUTSKLOOF

Franschhoek See Franschhoek map

Open for tastings & sales by appointment only.
Owner: Newcom Investments (Pty) Ltd
Winemaker: Marc Kent (since 1996)
Assistant Winemaker: Enoch Hlaganyane (since 1996)

Vineyards: Pieter Siebrits (since 1997)
Production: 160 tons, 10 000 cases. **Vineyards**: 15 ha.
P.O. Box 433, Franschhoek 7690
Tel: 021-8763320 **Fax:** 021-8763793

Gnashing their teeth in envy: if that's not the reaction of many long-established producers to the sensational opening performance of this Franschhoek farm, we'd be surprised. In just a few vintages, relatively inexperienced (but worldly-wise on the palate) winemaker Marc Kent has turned out a string of pearls—wild and suavely cultured—which has introduced this new fine-wine contender in striking fashion. After a bit of a delayed start—it took the seven partners an age to agree on the design of the premium label—these wines are now off their marks and belatedly into the marketplace. The final design is as original as the wines themselves—it features seven classic Cape wooden chairs. (Presumably from beech—boekenhout—which is among the indigenous trees and bush which fringe the hillside vineyards.) The Porcupine Ridge second-label range (here's where the indigenous fauna shakes a quill) is designed for easy lunchtime drinking. (Boekenhoutskloof for more serious dinners, perhaps) and clearly hit that bull's-eye when the Merlot was chosen for the list of Chez Nico in London's Park Lane, one of only three UK restaurants awarded Michelin 3-stars. A selection table, so all fruit can be hand-sorted is but one example of the care taken at this cellar, which is soon to be expanded.

★★★★ **Shiraz** (may be labelled **Syrah**) Think along Rhône, even Hermitage lines (Marc Kent's benchmarks) with **97**, breakaway style for Cape. Luxurious opaque ruby brilliance contrasted by zingy white pepper, spice fragrance. Gutsy tannins, "garrigue" (scrub) wildness add to individuality, sophisticated dryness but not at expense of essentially sweet, soft brambly/violets fruit. Has fleshed out, got richer over past year; should become rounder, gain further complexity over at least 5-6 years. Matured in small French oak, significantly none new. 13,7% alc.

★★★★ **Cabernet Sauvignon** Cabernets don't come much riper, more velvety than mellifluous **96**. Built to show off waves of dense mulberry ripeness; creamy, melt-in the-mouth tannins, dense but not overly so. Halo of carefully-judged oak adds extra dimension. Brims with poise, freshness. Probably greater staying power than suggested in last ed., 7-9 years. An exception—and exceptional—in generally lighter vintage. F'hoek grapes; unfiltered. Small French oak-matured, 10 months.

★★★★ **Sémillon** One of best examples of area's signature grape. **97** released late 98 (delay mainly due to lack of decision on label design); extra year has allowed elegant, pure style to settle into itself. Initial silky-slip-of-a-thing impression, esp. lacy lemon, toast whiffs, is deceptive; intrinsic richness, weight glide smoothly, grow in mouth; elegance enhanced by balanced natural, not added 6,7 gms/l acid. Gently fragrant honey, lemon flower flavours, incipient waxy lanolin texture. Will develop over 2-3 years at least. F'hoek grapes, whole-bunch pressed, fermented/matured in new Burgundy barrels; through malo.

PORCUPINE RIDGE:

★★★ **Cabernet Sauvignon** NEW **96** full of open berry, nutty charm; supple ripe fruit, rounded tannin frame give elegant feel to solid 13% alc. Subtly satisfying. 100% small oak-matured for dimension rather than flavour.

★★★ **Merlot** NEW Chunky, uncomplicated style with soft, bouncy texture, creamy mocha tail. Aromatic plum-pudding, vanilla custard character may lack subtlety but adds to friendly nature of **97**. Malmesbury grapes. French oaked. On list of Chez Nico, London.

★★★ **Sauvignon Blanc 98** juicy floral, sweet gooseberry fruit, suggestion of leesy richness on palate, essentially crisp, delicate; drinkability enhanced by 3 gms/l sugar.

★★★ **Chenin Blanc** NEW Vibrant melon/fruit salad succulence in gluggable **98**. Long, clean ripe finish. One-third brushed with oak. Delicious aperitif.

BOLAND WINE CELLAR

Paarl See Paarl map

Open for tastings & sales, Mon-Fri 8-5; Sat 8.30-13. Cellar tours by appointment. Special gift packs, personalised labels to order.

Underground tasting venue serving light meals during festive season. Special winter get-togethers, featuring cellar's winter wines.

Owners: 116 shareholders

General Manager: Altus le Roux (since 1984)

Winemakers: Charl du Plessis (since 1991), Naude Bruwer (since 1996), Johan Joubert (since 1997)

Viticulturist: Jurie Germishuys (since 1998)

Production: 18 000 tons. **Vineyards:** 2 200 ha.

P.O. Box 7007, Noorder-Paarl 7623

Tel: 021-8626190 **Fax:** 021-8625379

E-mail: boland@wine.co.za

Internet: www.bolandwines.co.za

"Sometimes you need to focus on the obvious," says Boland's cellarmaster/manager, Altus le Roux. "It is vital that fine quality grapes are delivered to the pressing cellar. We must be prepared to pay for quality, and we must provide our growers with the means of achieving it. Good wine begins in the vineyard, so a specialist viticulturist is a key member of the team." Equally important is Boland's varietal guideline plan. It goes hand-in-hand with a quality-grading system that helps the winemakers identify small pockets of prime fruit. The new cellar capacity enables them to vinify these small parcels separately.

These innovations may be obvious, but the effect has been impressive. More premium varietals, better grapes all-round and more dedicated handling in the winery have all contributed to the leap in quality. To focus on but one example: Charl du Plessis gives **all** the cellar's whites extended lees contact—for a minimum of 6 months—to boost complexity.

★★★ **!Um Hap** Barrique-matured Bordeaux-style blend, **95** showing ★★★★ potential. (Cab. s. 43%, merlot 40%, cab. f. 17%.) Powerful blackberry/raspberry aromas, mint and almond layerings, fine tannins, soft juicy finish. Easy drinking but not uncomplex. Name derives from San legend.

★★★ **Cabernet Sauvignon** ◀ **94** new clone fruit driven, easy-drinking but not simple. Black cherry, cassis aromas, whiffs of mint, fine marzipan notes, showing good bottle age complexity.

★★★ **Merlot** ◀ Riper, richer, more densely fruited in **97** than pvs., plum/mulberry with lingering almond/vanilla fragrance, satisfyingly textured palate, sweet spice finish. **95** prunelle cherry aromas, lightish. **94** bigger but less ripe.

★★★ **Pinotage** ◀ **97** barrel-matured, with earthy, gamey aromas layering youngberry, smoky fruit. Ripe dense tannins, and spicy ribena-like finish. **95** simpler, with aromas of cherry. **94** leaner, more laid back.

★★★ **Chenin Blanc** ◀ Always good here, frequent competition winner, up-market quality at down-market price. Pear/apricot aromas, complex fruit-salad flavours, with crisp lime spice, mouthfilling, clean tangy finish in attractive **98**. Best drunk fresh, young.

★★★ **Chardonnay** ◀ Ripe tropical aromas in **98**, layered with marzipan, butterscotch spice; pineapple/grapefruit palate. Crisp, slightly limey finish. **97** smokier, with rich, leesy fragrance and flavours, cedarwood notes.

★★★ **Sauvignon Blanc** ◀ **98** herbal grassy fragrance, a little taut, green pepper flavours, slightly austere. **97** herbaceous with green fig notes.

★★★ **!Um Hap** Aromatic, full-bodied sauvignon/chenin blend, **97** with intense almond/melon aromas, pear/apple flavours, marzipan lime finish.

★★★ **Noble Late Harvest** ◀ **98** heady, botrytis/nutty aromas, mingling with peach-pear spice, sumptuously textured palate, citrus layerings, marzipan and lime, surprisingly crisp.

★★★ **Red Muscadel** ◀ **97** opulent, rose-petal fragrance, rich but not cloying, spicy stylish finish, persistent.

★★★ **White Muscadel** ◀ **97** litchi, cedary spice, stylish pear/pineapple flavours, prunelle accents, tea-leaf fragrance, ample length.

Nouveau 98 light, easy drinking red, blackcurrant spice, soft tannins. **Chenin Blanc-Chardonnay** Latest vintage not available for tasting at time of publication. But cellar's reputation for both varieties augurs well. **97** was first release, crisp, light, with a limey tang. **Riesling** ◀ **98** fine sweet thatch fragrance, fuller flavour than many, still easy-drinking. **Bukettraube** ◀ Delicate, muscat, cedary spice in **98**. Ample on palate, tangy off-dry finish. **Stein 97** apricot/pear fragrance, pineapple lime flavours, tangy sweet persistence. **White Muscadel Noble Late Harvest** NEW Not available for tasting for this edition, but cellar's track record with variety and style suggest this could be unusual and good.

BON VINO range (500 ml screw top dumpies):

Crisp Dry White Robust aromas of herb/citrus, full-flavoured. **Semi-sweet** Lime/melon flavours, tangy off-dry finish. **Dry Red** Smoky plum whiffs, soft tannins, easy drinking. **Brut** Carbonated sauvignon style bubbly, elegant fruit, crisp finish. **Vin Doux** Seductively light sparkler, with sweetish grapey aromas.

BON COURAGE

Robertson See Robertson map

Open 8-5; Sat 9-12.30, and public (non-religious) holidays.
Cellar tours by appointment.
Owner: André Bruwer
Winemakers: Jacques Bruwer (since 1990), André Bruwer (since 1965)
Production: 1 600 tons. **Vineyards:** 150 ha.
P.O. Box 589, Robertson 6705
Tel: 02351-4178 **Fax:** 02351-3581
E-mail: boncwine.rbtson@minds.co.za

This tightly-run family business is busy building its brand—particularly on the international front. "First study your markets before making any decisions," observes young Jacques Bruwer. Intent on bottling as much of their production themselves (hence the new stabilisation and bottling facilities being installed in 1998), they have carefully segmented their potential markets according to country, type of wine and point of purchase, whether restaurants, supermarkets or specialist wine outlets—always with the accent on the Bon Courage label, a user-friendly name inalmost any language—like the wines. In common with many of their neighbours the Bruwers are aiming to swing the grape balance in the vineyard to 50/50 red and white, with the emphasis on cabernet and shiraz.

*** **Cabernet-Shiraz 97** a 60/40 blend; bright cassis, walnut flavours with a dab of stewed fruit. 8 mths in used French oak. **98** a huge peppery, juicy mouthful with fennel whiffs—great potential.

*** **Colombard-Chardonnay ◀ 98** a top seller; juicy combination of guava and citrus from well-matched components, fermented separately and blended.

*** **Chardonnay Prestige Cuvée** Opens in **98** with gorgeous nutty, crème brûlée aromas, ripe melon and figs on palate; barrel sample shows potential. Watch this one.

*** **Chardonnay ◀ 98** pear, litchi on nose, supple, ripe peachy flavours. Unwooded. **97 SAA** selection.

*** **Sémillon ◀ 98** creamy citrus character, concentrated flavours; good expression of this often under-performing variety.

*** **Gewürztraminer ◀ ☺ 98** from 16-yr-old v'yd; huge flower arrangement of a bouquet—jasmine, honeysuckle. Really well balanced, off-dry lusciousness, no characteristic gewürz. harshness in finish.

*** **Gewürztraminer Special Late Harvest ◀ 98** made from 25% botrytised fruit: complex, oily, beeswax, almost muscat aromas. 11,5% alc. Previous Diners Club award winner.

*** **Jacques Bruére Cap Classique Brut Reserve 96** made in impressive subterranean brick-arched cave, shows rich developed apple and melon aromas, followed by sourdough bread flavours: a full-blown MCC, 50/50 pinot noir and chardonnay.

**** **Red Muscadel ◀ 94** a brilliant coppery-amber colour; huge raisiny, molasses whiffs, bursting with muscat opulence. Oily, voluptuously sweet flavours. Muscat de frontignan, 16,5% alc. **WINE****.**

**** **White Muscadel ◀ 94 VG** intense deep orange-gold hue, complex spicy, orange rind aromas, great richness and concentration on palate. A classic.

Cabernet Sauvignon 97 from new clones, red berry compôte flavours, delicate cedar whiffs from 9 mths in 2nd & 3rd-fill barrels. **Cabernet-Merlot 96,** russet rim shows age—easy drinking, but now. **Shiraz ◀ 97** bags of cherry-stone, prune aromas, smoky Rhône-like grip on palate. **Blanc de Noir 98** light, off-dry, strawberry, muscat—framed flavours: muscadel/shiraz blend. For easy quaffing.

Sauvignon Blanc 98 shy nettle, guava nose; austere, dry and flinty, with persistent finish. **Sauvignon Blanc Prestige Cuvée 98** similar profile, but mellowed by touch of wood, softer acids. **Chardonnay Reserve 97** had full-monty new oak treatment, now playing honeyed, floral notes; fat and rich, leesy flavours. **SAA** selection. **Blanc de Blanc ◀ 98** from chenin, has guavas jumping from glass—supple, off-dry for early quaffing. **Riesling ◀** Never disappoints here—**98** melon and hay aromas, light and semi-dry: 10% alc., 6 gms/l sugar. **Rhine Riesling 97** offers grapefruit aromas, bone-dry, with touch of terpene oiliness creeping through; zippy sweet 'n sour flavours. **Colombard ◀ 98** pungent guava character, farm-fresh, off-dry, for drinking soon. **Noble Late Harvest 97** from Rhine riesling: penetrating citrus-peach nose, delicious sweet/sour fruit. 112 gms/l sugar, 10,5% alc. Long finish. **Vin Doux Blush Sparkling Wine** Pale pink carbonated pinot noir, touch muscat. Spun-candy aromas; good acidity tones down 60 gms/l sugar. Alc.12,5%.

BONNIEVALE CO-OPERATIVE

See Robertson map

Specialising in colombard, fortified desserts, this rustic co-op bottles a small range for sale on the premises only. Wines available are **Colombard Dry**, **Colombard Effesoet** (off-dry), **Riesling**, **Kelkiewyn** (an off-dry colombard in 500 ml dumpies), **Late Harvest** (chenin/hanepoot), **Hanepoot Jerepigo**. Tastings/Sales Mon-Fri 8-12.30; 1.30-5. **Tel:** 02346-2795. **Fax:** 02346-2332.

BOPLAAS

Calitzdorp See Klein Karoo map

Open Mon-Fri 8-5; Sat 9-3. Tasting & sales. R5 tasting fee for buses. Cellar tours, video on request.
Owner/Winemaker: Carel Nel (since 1982)
Production: 25 000 cases. **Vineyards:** 70 ha.
P.O. Box 156, Calitzdorp 6660
Tel: 044-2133326 **Fax:** 044-2133750

Boplaas was de-registered as an estate in 1998—quite a radical step, but a decision not taken lightly by the forward-thinking Carel Nel. "The system had outlived its practicality as far as we were concerned," he maintains. "I recognise the principal factor holding us back from producing outstanding table wines of world-quality:—fruit. Sure, our standard range of Calitzdorp wines provides great value, and is in demand both here and abroad, but we need a couple of signature wines, and for these we like the freedom to buy in superior grapes from cooler areas." The leeway to do just this allows him to flex his muscles as a winemaker and will result in two levels of wine: the Boplaas range, known near and as far as Canada and Germany; and the Reserve range, vinified from selected fruit, aimed at the top of the market, such as the CIWG, of which Nel is a member. One effect of this change will be the disappearance of the Carel Nel range; grapes from his Ruiterbosch (Mossel Bay) vineyard will no longer be labelled separately, but blended into Boplaas *cuvées*. Of course, the championship Ports, all from Boplaas grapes, continue to grow in stature: further plantings of premium port varieties continue apace, particularly tourigas naçional and francesca. A win in the Klein Karoo vineyard competition, continued accolades for the Reserve Ports . . . the successes continue.

*** **Auction Reserve Cabernet Sauvignon 94** a blackish plum; complex chocolate, leather and tobacco nose; dry, elegant finish, approaching typical older claret profile. Drink/hold 3-4 yrs Muldersvlei grapes.

*** **Cabernet Sauvignon Reserve 97** showing classic whiffs of plum-cake and cigar box from 1 yr in med. toast Nevers barrels. Vibrant mulberry, cassis fruit, composite of New World plumpness and claret minerals. Made from Helderberg fruit, for release 1999.

**** **Vintage Reserve Touriga Naçional Port 95** This single varietal wine, from Portugal's premium port variety, planted in 1993 has developed more mature, gamey, meaty aromas, coffee-chocolate flavours, supported by spirited backbone: should last 7-10 yrs with ease. 18,8% alc., 95 gms/l sugar, 18 months Portuguese 500-litre oak. **SAA** Port trophy, 1997—served in 1st class 1998. **WINE******.

**** **Vintage Reserve Port 96** released at 1998 Calitzdorp Port Festival, blackish plum with bright crimson rim, potent chocolate, tar and bouillon aromas, more spirity grip than 18,5% alc. would indicate.

Massive structure, impressive length; best to date—10 yrs of vigourous life ahead. WINE★★★★(★). Reserves only made in exceptional vintages.

★★★ **Cape Vintage Port 96** now a traditional cocktail of tinta barocca, touriga naçional & souzão: still closed, holding its best for years to come: hints of cherry and cinnamon, plenty of smoky black fruits on palate. 18,5% alc. 2 years in old 500 l Portuguese pipes. As with all Boplaas Ports—sugars of 100 gms/l or less. **94** from cellar personally autographed by SA cricket skipper Hansie Cronjé.

★★★ **Ruby Port NV** ◀ From younger tinta barocca v'yds, most popular seller, shows dusty cherry and prune nose, lively firm grip. Gets closer to Portuguese style yearly.

★★★ **Port Late Bottled Vintage** NEW **93** has longer wood maturation, alluring prune, cocoa, liquorice aromas; a supple, plummy wine—sweet with dryish finish and solid grip. Alc. 19%.

★★★ **Cape Tawny Port** NV NEW Brilliant amber-russet hue; lively nutty aromas, touches of nutmeg, varnish, with crème caramel finish, plenty of spirited grip.

★★★ **Muscadel Reserve 97** musky, jasmine and honeysuckle aromas, backed with palate of exotic spices—altogether richer and more structured than standard bottling. Klein Karoo champ—17% alc. Special 375 ml pack.

Merlot 97 more solid than pvs., juicy cassis flavours to last 3-4 yrs. **Pinotage 97** "highly recommended" by *Wynboer*: cocoa, strawberries on nose—both this, merlot 8 mths in French oak. **Dry Red** NV Tangy, juicy blend of tinta barocca, merlot, cabernet franc (shows on nose). **Blanc de Noir 98** lively salmon pink, quaffable cocktail of pinotage, cabernet, shiraz: alc only 10%, sugar 18 gms/l. **Chardonnay 98** lightly wooded, shows vanilla, caramel aromas; firm limey palate. **Sauvignon Blanc 98** has nettles and lemons on nose, bone-dry, light, finely balanced. **Late Harvest 98** colombard/muscadel summer quaffer, semi-sweet with drier finish (22 gms/l sugar). **Golden Harvest 98** a grapey little number—similar blend, slips down sweetly (42 gms/l sugar). **White Muscadel 97** bouquet of honeysuckle and jasmine: light style—try with a block of ice in summer. **White Port NV** dusty beeswax nose, from chenin blanc; beats a cloying cream sherry as aperitif. Highly popular. **Red Dessert** Sweet spicy blend of muscadel/tinta barocca port; similar to young tawny. **Pinot Noir Sparkling 97** finely carbonated, pale blush-coloured, dry: hints of cherries, strawberries, tangy finish. **Vonkelwyn Soet 97** sweet hanepoot-based carbonated bubbly—78 gms/l sugar; lively, refreshing.

BOSCHENDAL

Groot-Drakenstein See Franschhoek map

Open Mon-Sat 8.30-4.30 (summer), 8.30-4.30 Mon-Fri and Sat 8.30-12.30 (winter). Vineyard and cellar tours by appointment.

Taphuis, Tel: 021-8741252. Le Pique Nique for picnic baskets. Open Nov 1-Apr 30. Le Café for light lunches. See restaurant section.

Owners: Anglo American Corporation (Amfarms)
General Manager: Gerrie Wagener
Winemakers: Mike Graham (since 1996), J. C. Bekker
Viticulturist: Spekkies von Breda
Production: 240 000 cases. **Vineyards:** 500 ha.
P.O. Box Groot-Drakenstein 7680
Tel: 021-8704000 **Tastings/Sales:** 021-870 4211 **Fax:** 021-8741864

A lavish, R22 million cellar revamp enters its last phase at this extensive estate, once owned by colonialist Cecil John Rhodes, now the property of the farming division of Anglo American conglomerate. The original barrel cellar is now devoted solely to Cap Classique bubbly production (and what a beauty—it's fashioned for year 2000 festivities). An array of unique "hanging" tanks—42 in all—has been installed in the new main cellar, sizes ranging up to 32 000 litres. GM Gerrie Wagener remarks, only half-jokingly: "We have taken all the excuses away from the winemakers. With the facilities they've got, now they have to produce the best!"

Winemaking chief Mike Graham, congenitally imperturbable, is equal to any challenge, particularly now that a symbiotic relationship has been developed here between viticulturists and winemakers: "Everyone has a good feel for the end-product, and we know that our efforts need to be tops from the ground up." The cellar team continues to do the wine globe-trot; Graham's self-taught French oiled the wheels in the Old wine world, while J. C. Bekker headed off to New pastures in 1998, working his second harvest of the year at Matanzas Creek in Sonoma, California.

Once almost solely a white-wine cellar, Boschendal can now handle 1 000 tons of red-wine grapes, and (see below) these relative upstarts are bringing a very rosy new glow to this excellent-quality (despite major quantity) line-up.

★★★★ **Red Blend** (to be named) NEW **97** merlot-cab. franc, 50-50 blend, opulent but elegant, packed with (★★★★★) potential. Booming, ripe dark berry nose—blackcurrant to the fore, oak off-stage—carries into palate plus layer of chocolate. Rich, sweet fruit flavours, ripe tannins.

★★★★ **Shiraz** Not long on this list, but already showing super form. **97** the full kitchen-garden bouquet—ripe berries, mint leaves, sprigs of wild Karoo scrub, chocolate, vanilla. Ditto on palate with fine-grained tannin, gentle spice. Might well pick up another star with age. **96** nose initially highlights wild scrub scents, expands into fresh, ripe berries. Cherry flavours, soft tannins, subtle oak on palate. Drinking well already, but deserves a little more patience.

★★★★ **Merlot** A winner since **95 (WINE ★★★★)** first entered the range. Latest **97** a velvety indulgence of plums, cherries, chocs, coffee—rich and ripe. For **96** read berries (sweet, small) rather than cherries, but otherwise similar notes, plus a scattering of leaves, hint of mint, dash of vanilla. Both most appealing already, but room to develop further.

★★★★ **Lanoy** This red blend—50% merlot, 30% shiraz, 20% cab. s. —becomes more serious by the vintage. In latest **97**, shiraz portion standing up to be counted: dark berry fruit pours out of potent bouquet, with dark chocolate, toasty oak. Ripe, juicy palate; clean spicy finish. Lighter **96** showed a plummier focus. Styled for drinking on release.

★★★ **Blanc de Noir** Far from the usual candy-floss quaffer made in this style. Easy-drinking, yes; drink-soon, absolutely; but now the thinker-drinker's B de N: a light pinot noir, with that classy variety keeping a minority of tinta barocca, ruby cab., cab. s. in check. Deeper colour than most, ripe strawberry scents/flavours, touch of sugar (4,5 gms/l) pushes it just out of the officially dry bracket, but little discernible sweetness—keen acid sees to that. Versatile food partner.

★★★★ **Premier Cuvée 97** from 85% pinot noir—15% chardonnay, intriguing pale purple colour. Full-bodied (13,5% alc.), but soft (seemingly no tannin), bounding with fresh strawberries, cherries. Pinot portion lightly oaked. Delightful food wine, pvs. have developed well in bottle.

**** **Grand Vin Blanc** Sub-titled Sauvignon Blanc on label—90% of blend, with splash chardonnay in **97**, no longer any Rhine riesling, as in pvs. Sort of style that needs year in bottle to get into full stride—now remarkably round, harmonious, lingering. Herby, grassy bouquet. 40% fermented small French oak, 7 months on lees.

**** **Chardonnay 97** a big, buxom beauty; voluminous nose, deep flavours—both featuring ripe peach, pear, apple and discreet oak—but in well-toned, not flabby style. Long finish. Could develop rather well. Noteworthy13,9% alc.

**** **Sauvignon Blanc** Distinctive *fynbos* bouquet, with grassy, boiled pear-drop notes contributing to complexity. Full but elegant palate. Made totally reductively in **98**. Good now, but a year in bottle has proved to do wonders for pvs.

*** **Chenin Blanc 98** seriously good, nudging****. J. C. Bekker has a passion for this variety; it shows. Aromas/flavours verge on the decadent—tropical top-notes sing out over riffs of spice, peach, lime, honeysuckle. Smooth, full on palate; long, zesty finish.

*** **Blanc de Blanc** Refreshing quaffing white—Cape riesling base in **98** (pvs. featured chardonnay as senior partner), with assortment of others. Freshly-baled hay with a dash of fruit-salad on nose; repeats on palate, plus hint of green olive.

*** **South African Riesling 97** shows how well this variety can develop in bottle: hay, dried peach scents; soft *mebos* flavour, pear-drop aftertaste with flick of lemon.

*** **Le Bouquet** From old hanepoot v'yd (planted 1948), specially guarded to prevent "illegal night harvesters". Intense muscat/honeysuckle/freesia bouquet in **98**, sweet tones but actually quite dry. Drink young. Also contains splash muscats morio/ottonel.

**** **Vin d'Or** Elegant dessert wine, 100% sémillon in **98** (first since **94**). Intense citrus blossom and honeysuckle bouquet, tied with a ribbon of orange peel. Palate features an array of fruits—citrus, tropical, melon, fig macerated with sweet spices. Delicious now, but if you can, wait 4-8 years. 13,5% alc. 120 gms/l sugar freshened by 8 gms/l acid.

**** **Brut 2000** NEW Nudging*****, as is only fitting for an MCC bubbly designed to accompany millennium fireworks. Will be expensive, scarce, book now: degorging began late 1998, is proceeding on demand. 60% chardonnay, 40% pinot noir, fruit selected bunch-by-bunch so as to avoid any less-than-perfect grapes. Worth the trouble—this is outstanding: really rich, creamiest mousse, deep flavour.

**** **Brut 92** big, with mouthfilling mousse, highlights both pinot noir richness, chardonnay citrus, in yeasty wrapping. **93** similar quality.

PAVILLON range:

*** **Rouge ◀ ☺ 98** the first vintage-dated release of this red blend. Mainly merlot, cab. s., 20% ruby cab. (No longer pinot noir.) Bright, bouncy, ripe plum/cherry quaffing.

*** **Blanc ◀ 98** chenin-based, with sémillon. Glinting lime-green colour, juicy texture, zesty finish. Tropical fruit nose, peachy flavours.

*** **Le Grand Pavillon Blanc de Blancs ◀** Bright, fresh NV MCC, creamy mousse, toasty citrus flavours, very easy-drinking.

BOSCHKLOOF WINES

Vlottenburg, Stellenbosch See Stellenbosch map

Tastings/sales by appointment.
Owner: Reenen Furter, Jacques Borman
Winemaker: Jacques Borman, Reenen Furter (since 1996)

Viticulturist: Reenen Furter
Production: 6 000 cases
Vineyards: 16 ha.
P.O. Box 1340, Stellenbosch 7599
Tel/Fax: 021-8813293

Culling of **Sauvignon Blanc** in **98** saw this boutique Vlottenburg winery edge closer to an all-red line-up. For now **Chardonnay** remains a popular fixture of the range, "but we're focusing on noble red varieties to ensure top quality," notes ex-radiologist Reenen Furter, who owns and runs the operation with son-in-law, La Motte's Jacques Borman. "Hand-made" is the watchword here, from the built-from-scratch winery and homestead to the small, individually crafted—and well-priced—range of wines. Admirers of the muscular house style will be delighted to learn that **98** was a blockbuster. "Deep colour, ample fruit and high extract foreshadow good bottle ageing potential," Furter reports, adding "not for the faint-hearted!"

**** **Cabernet Sauvignon** ◀ Delicious cassis-scented fruit, spice in **97** (tank sample), framed by bountiful ripe tannin, crisp acid; presages interesting development over 5-6 years. Embroiders, improves on commendable début **96 VG (***)**, which evolving in bottle en route to maturity around 2005. Two clones (166, 46); low yielding vines. French oak aged. Around 12,5% alc.

*** **Chardonnay Reserve** ◀ NEW **97** sashays across palate in copious stream of creamy toffee/vanilla; lingers beguilingly, finishes tenderly dry. From low-yielding vines, two clones. Fermented/aged French oak, 8 months.

Merlot 97 quieter version of **96 VG**, which has developed multi-layered brambleberry, tar, mineral bouquet. Like its house-mates, repays time in bottle. **Cabernet-Merlot Reserve 97** in same reined-in mode as **96**, with ripe prune, dusty oak nuances; but tannins even tauter, for longer keeping (6 years+). **Chardonnay** French/American barrel-fermented **96** now perhaps too oaky for most palates.

BOTHA WINERY

Worcester See Worcester map

Tastings/sales Mon-Fri 7.30-5.30. Sat 9-12.30. Cellar tours by appointment, guest-house/B&B 1 km from cellar.
Owners: 58 shareholders
Manager/Cellarmaster: Dassie Smith (since 1996)
Winemaker: Johan Linde
Assistant Winemaker: Johan Delport
Production: 20 000 tons. **Vineyards:** 1 360 ha.
P.O. Box 30, Botha 6857
Tel: 02324-740 **Fax:** 02324-615

New red wine cellar, new manager, new winemaker and—for good measure—new flagship for this deep-rooted co-op near Worcester, freshly made-over and looking decidedly younger than its 40-plus years. Super-experienced Dassie Smith—he snared two SA young wine show, 5 co-op grand champions during nearly 3 decades with Rooiberg—has taken over the revamped cellar from long-serving manager/cellarmaster André Stofberg. Genial Smith has lent his name (soubriquet, to be precise, his rather resounding names are Johannes Cornelius) to the new premium range, **Dassie's Reserve**, made by another recent arrival, Johan Linde, son of Nuy's acclaimed Wilhelm Linde.

*** **Dassie's Reserve Merlot** NEW **97** given intensity, dimension by just the right amount of (French) oak. Attractive floral, almost sweet top-notes—violet, honeysuckle—plummy fruit stage-centre, fresh mint, vanilla-oak primping in wings. Very nice. 13,5% alc. Value at ± R12 a bottle. "Standard" **Merlot** not in same league, tarry almost "sweet" nose, stemmy, difficult tannins.

*** **Dassie's Reserve Cabernet Sauvignon** NEW **97** rich, ripe raspberry fruit framed by lots of toasty oak, pepper seasoning, warm vanilla finish. French-oak-matured. Drinks well now, could hold 1-2 years. Gold on young wine show.

*** **Dassie's Reserve Pinotage** NEW **97** another fine young Dassie; this one is strapping, plummy, juicy, sweet-oaky, mouthfilling. 13,5% alc.

*** **Rooi Jerepigo** NEW ◀ **97** from pinotage, ruby cab., plus smattering of shiraz which lends pleasing peppery counterpoint to ripe plummy fruit; full, syrupy texture, sweetness freshened by limpid acidity.

**** **Hanepoot Jerepigo** ◀ This speciality of the house fires on 6 cylinders (and turbo) in out-of-the-textbook **97**. Clean, floral/fruity muscat nose, spirity freshness on palate, exceptional sugar/acid balance. Less than R10 a bottle.

*** **Ruby Port** ◀ **97** reprise of pinotage/ruby cab./shiraz varietal formula above, with nice peppery bite (that SA rubies often lack). Sweet plums, prunes, hazelnut/raisin undertones, nice chocolate coating. Value at R15 a bottle.

Cabernet Sauvignon 97 soft berry aromas/flavours, green pepper tones, fairly firm tannins so probably best with food or after 1-2 years. **Pinotage 97** attractive ripe banana, raspberry whiffs, but strict tannins make this something of a challenge right now. **Dassie's Rood** ☺ ◀ NEW **97** paragon of drinkability: ripe sappy fruit (plums, strawberries), easy tannins, velvety but not flabby mouth-feel. Cinsaut, ruby cab., cab. s., ready to party. **Chardonnay 97** dry, subdued. Drink young. **Blanc de Blanc** NEW **97** colombard, chenin, Cape riesling; slight honeyed tones, dry. Best in year of harvest. **Colombard Effesoet** NEW **98** alluring guava scents, chipper acid, not oversweet. **Colombard Late Harvest** NEW **98** fresh guavas, gentle semi-sweet. Drink soon. **Chardonnay Brut** NEW NV not a lot of chard. character but festively fizzy, clean, decidedly dry.

BOTTELARY WINERY

Koelenhof — See Stellenbosch map

Visits: Open weekdays 9-5.30; Sat 9-3.
Winemaker: Herman du Preez (since 1990)
P.O. Box 465, Stellenbosch 7599
Tel: 021-8822204 or 8813870 **Fax:** 021-8822205 or 8813102

Bottelary is currently emerging from its shell to stake its claim as a prime vineyard area: this cellar is part of the Stellenbosch Vineyards fusion (see that entry for more details).

Cabernet Sauvignon ◀ **94** developed tomato cocktail, roast coffee hints, merged into oak-maturation seasoning for sound, no-frills aftertastes. Old bush vines. Pvs. uncomplicated nutty-bramble flavours. **92** interesting funky, wild heather development. **Pinotage 97** pungent nose, austere finish. **96** bold, earthy flavours combine with grape's sweetness; unfussy, plain finish. Unwooded. **Blanc de Noir** semi-sweet, pleasant, simple. **Sauvignon Blanc 98** grassy nose, dry finish. **Premier Blanc 98** anytime, no-fuss off-dry wine, grassy, thatch notes.

BOUCHARD FINLAYSON

Hermanus See Walker Bay map

Tastings/sales: Mon-Fri 10-5. Sat: 9.30-12.30.
Owner: Klein Hemel-en-Aarde (Pty) Ltd
Winemaker: Peter Finlayson (since 1991). **Marketing:** Mike Clark
Production: 13 500 cases. **Own v'yds:** 14 ha.
P.O. Box 303, Hermanus 7200
Tel: 0283-23515 **Fax:** 0283-22317
European tel/fax: 33-380-214741
E-mail: finonrus@hermanus.co.za

"These wines are made for the table; their firmness quickly gives way in the company of de-boned, rare leg of lamb, barbecued," said Peter Finlayson last year. The rare lamb loin cutlet—hot off the fire—that accompanied the tasting for this year's guide was therefore not for sustenance, just to make the (very good) point, again. Finlayson's wines are much like him—quiet and considered until bursting forth with operatic power—and really do shine in the company of good food. It's no coincidence then that Norman Hardie, formerly sommelier at the Four Seasons Hotel, Toronto, is back full-time after a harvest in Volnay, Burgundy, bringing with him not only food & wine expertise but also French fluency. He's one of a new youthful duo keeping the "old men" on their toes. The other is Yolanda Mori whose lineage in Cape wine goes back a long way. Fresh enthusiasm apart, the style here remains firmly classic, viticulture (where the team believes 80% of the quality starts) taking its lead from Burgundy and wine styles bedded down in Old World classicism. Most apt for this, the Cape's first Franco—Cape wine venture.

With two flagship "Domaine" or home-vineyard wines, the Missionvale Chardonnay and Galpin Peak Pinot, now established—the latter to much acclaim—one may be forgiven for thinking that the label proliferation of bought-in grape wines would ease. No chance with this inquisitive winemaker, always willing to vinify separate batches in search of better tastes, better quality. Some labels work better than others, but the relentless pursuit of complexity continues. Not that matters of such grave concern as quality preclude a party. Bouchard Finlayson was the proud supplier of 30 cases to Bafana Bafana for the party after their opening match of the soccer World Cup against France. And a Pinot Noir Celebration is on the cards for the last week of 1999—to see out the millennium. "Is there any other way to celebrate, than with pinot?" they cheekily ask!

★★★★ **Pinot Noir** Accolades—and there've been plenty, including a British Airways First Class listing for **Galpin Peak 96**—don't ensure greatness, but where there's smoke there's fire. The path blazed by this, the first bottling to bear the label of the home v'yds overlooked by Galpin Peak behind the winery, is further forged by an exceptional **97** ★★★★★ from a super vintage. Dense crimson, combining raspberry with spice, solid yet restrained tannic weight, enduring length. The closest you'll get to the Côte d'Or south of Lyons. Quality at this level can never be cheap, at R90/bottle it isn't. **96** mocha, coffee, cherry interest, tannins still firm, **95** earthy notes, berry fruit emerging, lingering finesse. **94 (Overberg)** holding its colour, rustic nose, velvet texture, softening. Fruit of Burgundian clone 113, densely planted, pruned to French double guyot methods, now crushed differently to release less tannin, only 25% new oak. The wine, however, is huge; needs 4-5 years for oak, tannins, alc. acid components to settle, combine. Fruit dense enough to last. For some, will lack retiring elegance. But represents a salutary advance of Burgundian power in the New World. Pvs. from **91** variously labelled Walker Bay, Overberg, Elgin-Oak Valley.

★★★★ **Chardonnay Kaaimansgat** (Crocodile's lair, from Villiersdorp, Overberg). Heads the pack of several labels. Classically barrel-fermented, long lees contact, a Cape chardonnay which will last. **97** tapered citric fruit from gentle slow ripening, chalky finesse, protracted length. Chassagne-Montrachet-style. **96** pronounced lemon flavours in balance with wood/acid elements. **95** retains smoky overlay (perhaps still too oaky for some): rich, weighty, wine. WINE★★★★. **94** excellent notices abroad, including 92/100 in California's *Smart Wine* magazine. **93** WINE★★★★.

Missionvale Chardonnay 600 cases from Domaine grapes. **97** shows opulence from "concentrated" vintage. More open, obvious style; tropical melon, peach encased in butterscotch, palate fills out elegantly, not blowsy. Rich citric fruit, elegance suggest valley-specific individuality. Pvs.: **Overberg 96** from 3 scattered v'yd sources, including BF's own Walker Bay vines; limey, amply-padded on palate, for later substantial complexity. 50% oak-fermented. **Oak Valley-Elgin 96** noticeably oaked, richly constructed, bold fruit on palate. **Sans Barrique** Chardonnay NEW **97**, unoaked: clean lemon/lime fruit, mineral depth, tingling finish unfettered by wood. Primary lees contact adds complexity, no malo to retain bracing zip.

★★★ **Sauvignon Blanc** Three BF bottlings in **98**, all unoaked. **Walker Bay** Own v'yd fruit, potential alc. limited by close planting, pear rather than grass, tightly structured. **97** long-flavoured, uncompromisingly steely. Best with food. **Oak Valley** wild, opulent fruit, bold alc. from low yield, very ripe grapes. Definite food wine as was **97**, big style with "mega extract". Smaller quantities, 700 cases. **Old Lands** NEW Delicious, individual **98** sauvignon, lavender creaminess, fennel, leesy butterscotch flavours. Tiny yield 500 g grapes per vine, only 150 cases.

★★★ **Blanc de Mer** Highly underrated, delightful, just-dry white for summer patios. **98** more pinot blanc, some botrytis. **97** settled in bottle, round fruit-salad riesling notes, nutty almond husk character, varietally neutral in spite of mélange: chardonnay 36%, weisser riesling 27%, plus kerner, gewürztraminer, pinot blanc. Unwooded.

Oak Valley Merlot 94 available cellar door.

BOVLEI WINERY

Wellington See Wellington map

Tastings/sales Mon-Fri 8-12.30, 1.30-5. Sat 8.30-12.30. Cellar tours during harvest by appointment.
Winemakers' lunch during season.
Owners: 73 members
Winemaker: Marthinus Broodryk (since 1980)
Assistant Winemaker: Hendrik de Villiers (since 1996)
Production: 7 100 tons. **Vineyards:** 560 ha.
P.O. Box 82, Wellington 7655
Tel: 021-8731567/8641283 **Fax:** 021-8641483

Marthinus Broodryk, winemaker here for almost two decades, is seeing red. Not figuratively—what does he have to be incensed about with exports to the UK, Germany, China, Kenya, Zambia *et al* on the rise; a new 450-ton, everything-that-opens-and-shuts cellar in which to craft his easy-drinking, amiably-priced range? No, Broodryk is literally seeing red in the tide of premium red grapes rippling across the Wellington co-op's vignoble, as member-farmers cull workhorse varieties like chenin and establish merlot, cabernet, shiraz in their place. "We're working very closely with consultants to match varieties and soil types to ensure quality," the long-standing vintner says. "At the current rate of planting I'll be seeing red for the next 20 years!"

★★★ **Cabernet Sauvignon** ◀ Award-winning, good value/quality co-op cab., worth keeping a year or two. **97** good deep colour, blackberries, cassis, cedary spice turning into pepper on palate, untraumatic tannin grip, light-toned (11,5% alc.) without being thin. **92 VVG** and **VG**; **91 VG**.

★★★ **Rooi Hanepoot** NV Attractive tangerine-scented dessert, light-coloured almost rosé; citrusy flavours, fresh lifting acid cuts insistent sweetness.

Shiraz 96, like pvs., not in blockbuster style; made for easy swigging. Some spice, gamey hints, dried leaves, cherries/strawberries on palate. 12,5% alc. **Pinotage** ◀ **97** compôte of red berries, flavourful, some spice, amiable touch of tannin. Serve lightly chilled. Unoaked. 11,5% alc. **Merlot** NEW **97** very light, almost rosé colour; extracts of strawberries, cherries; light-toned/bodied. Our taster (recently returned from US) says: "Good cook-out wine." **Grand Rouge** ◀ **96** attractive quaffer, light, easy, nice touch of oak, cherry fruits. Cab. f., merlot. **Chardonnay** (unwooded) Unshowy, lowish alc. (11,5%), dry, melon overtones, fresh, relaxed. **Chenin Blanc** ◀ **98** youthful, clean just-dry white, guava-scented summer value-quaffing, lowish alc.: 11,5%. **Sauvignon Blanc 98** light gooseberry, dry. **Bayns Valley Cruchen Blanc** NEW **97** not much varietal character but easy, no frills gently dry swigging. **Riesling 97** untasted for this ed. Pvs. mildly nutty/grassy, no-frills white. **Blanc Imperial** NV semi-sweet chenin, easy, delicately fruity, light. **Bukettraube** Semi-sweet, light **96**. Drink young. **Gewürztraminer** ☺ ◀ **97** agreeably balanced, understated version of this sometimes overpowering variety, delicate semi-sweet aperitif. Low alc. (9,5%) for uncomplicated quaffing. 21 gms/l sugar. **Stein 97** off-dry white. **Special Late Harvest** Chenin blanc; 42,5 gms/l sugar, untasted. **Sec Vonkelwyn** ◀ NV Usually among nicest carbonated sparklers around, clean, fresh, much finer, more elegant than most. Light 11% alc. **Demi-sec Vonkelwyn** NV fiercely foamy, flowery, semi-sweet, light-bodied, 11% alc. **Brut** also on list. **Muscat d'Alexandrie** (previously labelled **Wit Hanepoot**) NV Bright yellow-gold dessert. Floral nose, spicy finish. After-dinner wine. 17,5% alc. **Port** untasted. Pvs. from ruby cab., cab. franc, rather pleasant in light, uncomplicated style.

Also, in "Wellington Dumpies", **Vin Blanc** (dry), **Stein** (semi-sweet white), Vin Rouge (dry red).

BOUWLAND

Stellenbosch

Wines available at Kanonkop Estate.

Owners: Johann & Paul Krige with Beyers Truter

Winemaker: Beyers Truter (since 1997)

P.O. Box 74, Koelenhof 7605

Tel/Fax: 021-8822447

Bouwland is an old Dutch word for cultivated land. This 130 ha. farm in the Bottelary area was purchased in 1997 and is currently being replanted; the enventual mix will be 80% pinotage and 10% each cabernet s. and merlot. Until its own grapes are available, fruit has been sourced from the foothills of the Stellenbosch mountains. The Truter-Krige brothers team-mates behind this development, with a specialist red-wine track record at Kanonkop—and Beyerskloof—are backing another winner.

**** **Cabernet Sauvignon-Merlot 97** brilliant cerise colour. Equally brilliant ripe fruit aromas, flavours. Juicy easy/early drinking with succulent blackcurrant, cherry, strawberry flavours, good depth and character. Supple, accessible, silky tannins.

BRAMPTON

See Rustenberg

BREDASDORP

See Sonop

BREDELL WINES

Helderberg See Helderberg map

Visits: Open Mon-Fri 8.30-5
Owner & Winemaker: Anton Bredell
Production: 1 800 tons, 3 000 cases own label
P.O. Box 5266, Helderberg 7135
Tel: 021-8422478 **Fax:** 021-8423124

Arid, inland Calitzdorp is the port capital of the Cape, some assert. Anton Bredell would disagree. Here, on one of the world's largest privately-owned port-growing properties, in the lap of the Helderberg—with the False Bay breakers mere minutes away—he's staking a most convincing claim to the Cape port-crown. Re-staking, we perhaps ought to say, because historically this was always prime port country. When Bredell scooped the General Smuts trophy for SA champion young wine at the 1998 national show—out of 2 304 entries—it marked the first triumph for a port in this competition since 1966, when his father, Koos Bredell, scooped the same laurels. But before that, just to drive home the point: a port from the Bredells' neighbouring property (recently acquired by Graham Beck) also won SA's top young wine prize! And eminent Portuguese producers (see notes on the flagship wine below) have recently confirmed that coastal Somerset West/Firgrove is no pretender to this throne. For those who wonder how long these ports last, a 1998 tasting note on the venerable **66** (Bredell has only two bottles left): "a bit sweet but absolutely gorgeous and still amazingly fruity".

Not that this is purely after-dinner and cigars territory. Some of the Cape's best red wines emanate from this farm. In 1993, Anton Bredell's **Cabernet Sauvignon** again brought the Jan Smuts champion young wine trophy back into the family. Much of Bredell's red wine production eventually surfaced under the KWV's prestige Cathedral Cellars label, winning a string of further awards. Cathedral Cellars' **95 Merlot**, winner of the best merlot trophy at the 1998 IWSC in London, came from this farm. A new chardonnay proves his prowess across the colour-spectrum.

All Bredell's "natural" wines are matured in 300 litre barrels, which are thereafter used for the ports.

**** **J P Bredell Cape Vintage Reserve Port** (Limited release) The Cape's best? Many believe so. Certainly not only a local benchmark, but much admired by some of Portugal's leading producers (Charles Symington for one) for its combination of power and refinement. It would be infanticide to drink **95 *******, bottled in October 1997, now. Even millennium year would be too soon. However it has remarkable depth of everything. Hints of plum, blackberry, green pepper are beginning to distinguish the nose. Texture is almost treacle-like, rolls across the palate in apparent slow motion. Deep, richly-layered fruit in drier (95 gms/l sugar), more classically Portuguese-pitched style (19,5% alc.). Bruce Guimaraens, guest of honour from the famous Taylor Fladgate and Yeatman port firm, sampled this at 1998 Calitzdorp port festival, and 40 minutes later claimed he still had the taste in his mouth. Parting words were: "That's a damn fine port, no matter where it was made!" 50/50 tinta barocca-souzão blend. **WINE****(*)**. There will not be a **96** as Bredell does not believe the wine has the legs to carry it to optimum maturity; it will go into the Helderzicht Reserve. **94** WINE**** awash in opulent chocolates, prunes but still great finesse; dry finish. **93** received rare, top ***** rating in WINE. First vintage was **91**.

**** **Bredell's Pinotage 96** retasted mid-1998, still needs another 2/3 years to start showing its best. Lots of ripe banana, cassis and well-rounded tannins. Has a not inelegant rustic charm. "No fining and only very basic filtration to make sure there are no *muggies* (little fruit-flies) in the bottle," says Bredell.

**** **Bredell's Shiraz 96 (WINE****)** big and beautiful with deep ripe plum and ground pepper nose/flavours. Still developing. "It has been taken by Air Namibia, and 96 Winery Road and a few other restaurants so I must keep stock for them. So won't have too much to sell to the public," informs Bredell. "I might not bottle the **97**. I'm not quite happy with it yet."

*** **Chardonnay** NEW Previously all went to the KWV. Good combination of limey/lemon and butterscotch, full on palate with long clean, lemony finish. Will need a year or two to show full potential. 10-year-old vines.

Bredell's Helderzicht Full Ruby. Helderzicht Vintage Character Port. Bredell's Cape Vintage Port 93. All these excellent of their kind, but now history. To be replaced by NEW **Bredell's Helderzicht Reserve**, NV, which not ready for tasting for this edition.

Helderzicht Jerepigo "A great favourite of the Vaalies," says Bredell, ("Vaalies": upcountry fans from pvs. Transvaal, now Gauteng) of this national award-winning dessert from weisser riesling, chenin. Follow-up to last release to be made if demand becomes overwhelming.

BRENTHURST WINERY

Paarl See Paarl map

Tastings/sales by appointment.
Owner: Adv. S.A. Jordaan S.C.
Winemakers: Adv. S.A. Jordaan with consultants (since 1994)
Vineyards: Johan Wiese
Production: ± 4 000 cases. **Vineyards:** ± 5 ha.
P.O. Box 6091, Main Road, Paarl 7622
Tel: 021-8631154 or 4246602 **Fax:** 021-4245666

Petit verdot in 1998 joined the line-up of traditional Bordeaux varieties—cabernet sauvignon, merlot and cabernet franc—flourishing on Cape Town Senior Council S.A. (José) Jordaan's small farm on the slopes of Paarl Mountain. "Compact is cool" seems to be the philosophy here: there's only one wine in the range, an elegantly packaged Médoc-style blend (though a limited release **Cabernet Reserve** is in the works) and production will not exceed a manageable 5 000 cases. Most is exported—Sweden, Russia, Mauritius, Ireland, Hong Kong are some of the far-flung offshore destinations.

*** **Cabernet Sauvignon-Merlot** First made in **94**, aim is "top-class quality that can compare in the international market". Engineered for elegance, undaunting firmness, ± yr in new/2nd-fill French oak, cab. s., merlot, dash of cab. f. Soon-to-be-released **96** rather good, ripe cassis fragrance with quite a fresh waft of mint, deep blackberry pile, med. body, trademark firmness. Drink (probably with food) or keep 2-3 years. String of accolades for **94-96**: "Recommended" by *Decanter* (UK) in 1997; wine mail-order club pick, medal Int. Wine Challenge; served on Sabena. **97** for release 1999.

BUITENVERWACHTING

Constantia See Constantia map

Visits: Open 9-5.
Restaurant: Lunch/dinner Tues-Fri. Sat dinner only. Closed Aug. Tel: 021-7943522. See restaurant section.
Owners: C. & R. Mueller, Trustees, Buitenverwachting Farm Trust
Winemaker: Hermann Kirschbaum (since 1993)
General Manager/Trustee: Lars Maack. **Vineyardist:** Pieter Reynold
Production: 50 000 cases. **Own vineyards:** 100 ha.
Address: Klein Constantia Road, Constantia 7800
Tel: 021-7945190/1 **Fax:** 021-7941351

GM Lars Maack's latest method of "industrial espionage" must be unique to any of the world's winelands—though it's a way that necessarily has a short shelf life—perhaps not helped much by blowing his cover in these pages. He, winemaker Hermann Kirschbaum and vineyardist Pieter Reynold are all quiet Harley-Davidson freaks. In search of new ideas, on how to run client hospitality tastings and to check on competitors' wine quality, the three of them last year pulled on the regulation black leather biker gear and helmets for disguise as much as for protection, and tore off—not to their customary haunts but to the Helderberg and Hermanus wine routes. Roaring into wineries unannounced in this way usually sees proprietors scrambling for cover in remote backroom offices, leaving the visiting "intruders" to sample wines and take a good look at everything in peace with unsuspecting staff. "We found much of interest," says Hermann Kirschbaum, with a huge Cheshire cat beam.

In fact, of course, they declare themselves if they find the winemaker at home and settle down to an incestuous gossip and exchange of ideas. As they did at Hamilton Russell Vineyards. There, Kirschbaum, as mischievous as he is inventive, reversed noisily a few times before parking, prompting Kevin Grant to stomp out calling for peace and quiet from the leathered invaders. "I've never seen such surprise on a face when we took off our helmets," laughs Maack.

The Buitenverwachting wines continue to show stylish finesse and awareness of contemporary trends precisely because this trio doesn't waste time gazing inwardly.

Completely re-planted in the 1980s—with smaller annual renewals since—and equipped with what is still one of the Cape's finest functioning wineries, Buitenverwachting has scored consistently highly for many years at major wine contests, including SAA and Diners Club. Its model worker relations—another pre-occupation of Maack's—and its first-class restaurant in one of Constantia's most beautifully rich architectural settings, make Buitenverwachting one of South Africa's outstanding wine showpieces.

**** **Christine** ◀ Estate's red flagship, excellent—and not only for its price. Altogether among first choice SA clarets: cabernet sauvignon (about 90%) with merlot. Latest **94** begins with very high class scents—spicy cinnamon swirls around a core of ripe plums, blackcurrants. Then follow the essentials of a classic—fine tannins, length in finish, a seamless production (slightly smoother, readier than original barrel samples suggested). Latest bottling follows fine, spicily oaked, clear-fruited **93**, similarly delicious **92**, with bouquet of ripe blackcurrants, cinnamon spices (a personal favourite). All from very low yielding cabernet v'yds; they steer a course between overt New World styles (with forward, simple fruit) and Old Cape (vinous austerity). Unstinted barrel maturation, a substantial proportion in new oak. Pvs. outstanding vintages: **89 VVG, 91** WINE****, **VG. 90 SAA, VG.** Also record for estate's discontinued **Cabernet Sauvignon**, last release **92**: succulent fruit, sweet, ripe prunes on palate after nutty, chocolate, cassis scents on nose. **91 VG, 90 VG.** Pvs. red labels also included **Buitenkeur** Merlot-dominated (about 90%) Bordeaux- style red blend, a **92**, approachable, well-oaked, some fresh-earthy qualities. **91 VG. Merlot 91** outstanding, huge wine, delivering minerally essences in dry but concentrated ripe fruit style. Chosen best Cape merlot by Diners Club Winemaker of Year judges.

**** **Sauvignon Blanc** Both latest **98**, **97** follow style established since **94**—deliberately, markedly different from many top Cape sauvignons, vinified to become slower starters, less fragrant than showy, fruity SA versions. ("There are many European drinkers who regard in-your-face fruitiness as offensive to classic ideas of dry vinosity in wine," says Kirschbaum.) But here pronounced development occurs in bottle after about 2 years—derived from initially long lees contact in tank. In bottle, they retain a clear freshness, with some flinty, Loire-like steeliness which acquires breadth. **97** with, initially, more restrained aromas in youth than pvs. "is to me best of the whole lot" says Kirschbaum, who appears confident it will develop same "back of mouth" penetration, flavours as others. Customarily released months after most SA sauvignons. **96** WINE****.

**** **Chardonnay** Another wine given the full oak treatment—which in **96** came out as very ample, forward, mellow (and slightly yellowing now, even somewhat blowsy) vintage. **97** might please classicists more—it's less forward, less soft. Regime here is classical barrel-fermentation for about two-thirds, plus broadening malolactic fermentation. They age for a few years—3-4—with attractive limey ripeness, though in some vintages the oaky overlay can be noticeable. **94 VVG, SAA**, gentle honeyed-oaky notes, creamy texture. **93 SAA. VG 91, 92.**

**** **Rhine Riesling** "This is a funny variety," says winemaker Kirschbaum, the voice laden with lament. "We'll never make a Mosel here in South Africa." Clearly, that's his wish, though he's sensitive to the patriotic—and realistic—notion the Cape could and should never produce an identikit German wine. **98** has rich scents, some honey (prematurely?), but nonetheless gets closer than most to a European style; fits pattern established here of consistently lively and light, very digestible, dryish version of Rhine riesling. A lime-tangy all-rounder, good with soups in winter, even a perky, red-wine-alternative backdrop to a braai in summer. Its lower than usual alc. (10,5%-11%) and lighter style generally are atypical of Cape Rhine rieslings though it strikes some oily terpene notes after a couple of years.

*** **Buiten Blanc** ◀ On many restaurant lists—with good reason at the price. Blend of sauvignon (60%) chenin—grapes mainly from fresh coastal Durbanville area. Has same youthful dry-fruity-spicy quality in latest **98**—as usual rounded off with 3,5 gms/l sugar: just dry and less austere than bone-dry.

*** **Brut Cap Classique NV** Softly fruity but balanced bubbly acquiring some biscuity qualities after 2-3 years. Classically bottle-fermented, about 50% pinot noir with pinot gris, chardonnay. (Between 8-9 gms/l sugar dosage.)

Noblesse None since **95** Rhine riesling dessert, with commendably low—for style—89 gms/l sugar; more complex ripeness of developing (initially lacked obvious botrytis blast); very smooth, soft finish. **WINE******. **91** ripe apricot bouquet, full, creamily sweet (about 140 gms/l sugar); partially oak-fermented.

CABRIÈRE ESTATE

Franschhoek See Franschhoek map

Open tastings & sales weekdays 9-1, 2-4.30, Sat 11-1. Cellar tours by appointment. Sat cellar tour (11) personally conducted by Achim von Arnim. Tasting fee R15 p/p.

Haute Cabrière Cellar Restaurant; lunches daily, dinner Fri & Sat May-Sept, Fri-Mon Oct-Apr. See restaurant section.

Owners: Clos Cabrière (Pty) Ltd (26 shareholders)
Winegrower: Achim von Arnim (since 1984)
Viticulturist: Renier Theron. **Cellarmaster:** Reinhard Schrimpf
Production: 400 tons, 25 000 cases. **Vineyards:** 22 ha.
P.O. Box 245, Franschhoek 7690
Tel: 021-8762630 **Fax:** 021-8763390
E-mail: carbriere@iafrica.com

"The true marriage of food and wine" is a Cabrière aphorism, coined to describe its Haute Cabrière Restaurant where the property's wines can be enjoyed with classy food—and possibly spurred by criticism of the austerity of some of the bubblies.

Sorica Nadel, officially Marketing Manager, is getting the office up to IT speed when not having to contain the ebullient Baron Achim von Arnim and Geisenheim colleague, cellarmaster Reinhard Schrimpf. Which can take some doing. Von Arnim's personal Saturday morning cellar tour—an essential item on any wine traveller's itinerary—is scheduled to start at 11 but Teutonic precision is not always observed. Nor is there a defined finishing time (don't commit to an early lunch). Neither of which can keep the fans away; many return regularly for new stories. While Von Arnim, a man of strong views, invariably colourfully expressed, is certainly the main act, others play essential supporting roles. None less than the deceptively quiet Schrimpf, reserved, meticulous, firm in the belief that his skill is best confined to the cellar. Give him a glass of the bracing Brut Sauvage, however . . .

Cabrière's other dictum—"Sun, Soil, Vine, Man"—is tangibly visible above the restaurant where ground is being prepared for further planting of chardonnay and pinot noir, the only two grapes from which the estate's extensive array of temptations is made. In the practical gravity-fed cellar a handful of Russian oak barrels have found a home (Schrimpf glows with pride), while the (chilly) Salmanazar Room at the lower MCC vault is Von Arnim's joy. Precipitated by the need for a seriously impressive sparkler to welcome the next millennium, 9-litre bottles of **Pierre Jourdan** gain further complexity. The first, outside of champagne house Pommery, to ferment in such a huge bottle: protective eyewear hanging at the entrance is not for show—several have exploded to date. All are pre-sold however, so start searching for your New Year host now.

Bubbles aside, the courtship with fickle pinot noir continues and a further ripe harvest in 1998 sees vintage-expressive patterns emerging. Criticised when a light **95** followed his powerful maiden **94**, again when the strawberry **97** came after the full flavoured **96**, Von Arnim proffers a sample of rich **98**. The power is back. Nothing can derail his other still wine, the immensely successful **Chardonnay-Pinot Noir**. On allocation to biggest clients—restaurants—its versatility at table is behind that success. And embodies the "true marriage" philosophy.

Haute Cabrière is the still wine label; **Pierre Jourdan** the label for MCC bubblies.

★★★★ **Haute Cabrière Pinot Noir** Blazed onto market with dense, firm, yet all too quaffable **94 SAA**, now softening, leafy vegetal character. Tarry wood features remain. **98** barrel selection retrieves style of understated depth, glowing ruby, savoury spice, soft cherry nose. Sheep wool waxiness, elegant throughout. **97** lighter, strawberry style. Cherry fruit, feminine. **96**—a bottling dedicated to Von Arnim's late mother Theodora—rich ruby developing russet tints, red berry and quince notes, grip without coarseness, super length. Delicious now. Bottle age shows in retiring **95**, earthy, vegetal, trifle slender. All partly new Tronçais barrel-oaked, careful handling in gravity flow cellar to maximise fruit, minimise coarseness. Grapes from now 7-year-old v'yds pioneering (in the Cape) narrow spacing, densely planted (new clones).

★★★ **Haute Cabrière Chardonnay-Pinot Noir** Cellar's most popular line, equal parts unwooded blend in "still champagne" mould; for early drinking. **98** pink tinge, ripe lemon, melon fruit, pinot weight on palate. **97** firm tannic mouth-feel, fair length. Usually just-dry. Unusual raspberry delicacy counters citric crispness. Pinot whole bunch-pressed. Suggested for "Mediterranean gatherings"!

★★★ **Pierre Jourdan Blanc de Blancs** Dark blue label. 100% chardonnay MCC bubbly. 4 months Argonne oak maturation adds vanilla richness to plush white grape texture. Slightly higher alc./sugar (12,2%, 4 gms/l) for broader mouth-feel. Dry finish, with lime focus to lift seafood.

★★★ **Cuvée Belle Rose** Salmon pink—like delicate blush of the wine—label in Pierre Jourdan MCC bubbly range. 100% Pinot noir, carbonic maceration for 5 days gives colour, avoids harsh tannin. Red berry flavours, full palate, trademark austere finish. For shellfish or pear tart. Cheese maybe. Generous feel from 5 gms/l dosage.

Pierre Jourdan Brut Savage Light blue label. Variant MCC style—unleavened by any sweet dosage—draws as many adherents as detractors. Arresting yeasty piquancy, bracing fresh finish. Bone-dry, "oyster dry" says Von Arnim. **Pierre Jourdan Cuvée Brut** Turquoise label; classic blend of chardonnay, pinot noir approaching equal proportions from **94** (bottled NV). Biscuit nose, elegant yeast flavours balanced by rich texture. Lip-smacking finish. 3 gms/l dosage. **Pierre Jourdan Cuvée Reserve** Cuvée Brut sold *en primeur* from estate only, aged min. 4 years on lees. For those who prefer more mature, less bracing bubbly. **Petit Pierre Ratafia** The complete chardonnay! Sweet chard. must fortified with chardonnay pot-still brandy (alc. 20%). Try chilled as aperitif, with ostrich liver, or to ratify treaties—its original use. **Fine de Jourdan** Uncompromisingly distilled from chardonnay, Limousin barrel-aged "marc"; fiery but also fine-flavoured digestif.

CALITZDORP WINERY

Calitzdorp See Klein Karoo map

🍷 Open weekdays 8-1, 2-5; Sat 8-12. Tastings & sales.
Cellar tours: By appointment.
Owners: 60 members. Founded 1928.
Winemaker: Alwyn Burger (since 1991)
Production: 3 000 tons. **Vineyards:** 85 ha.
P.O. Box 193, Calitzdorp 6660
Tel: 044-2133301 **Fax:** 044-2133328

Super-value port-style wines are the stars of this cellar in an area which has become known as the Cape's "little Douro". Alwyn Burger is now taking in increasing quantities of premium variety touriga naçional from his members' vineyards, bringing an extra dimension to these already fine consumer favourites. New equipment includes a Vello press and static drainers, while recent plantings are aimed at the increasing demand for reds; the export market is the next challenge. Tinta barocca, touriga, merlot, ruby cabernet and cabernet sauvignon have all been planted recently, and a new clone of sauvignon blanc. And staff are not being neglected in this rural area: several cellar hands have been sent on courses at Elsenburg college.

*** **Vintage Port** ◀ **96** in the now classic Calitzdorp mould, 18% alc., and lowish 80 gms/l sugar. Straight tinta barocca (expect addition of touriga again next year); offers soft mocha flavours, supple fruit and a surprisingly spirited grip at the finish. Easy drinking now; aged 2 years in 500-litre barrels. Drier than **95**, which contained a splash of touriga.

*** **Ruby Port** ◀ Biggest seller from the winery, particularly at the annual Port Festival when bootloads are carted away. Powerful prune, cocoa and marmite aromas, light, silky flavours. 18% alc., 85 gms/l sugar, tinta blended with 20% touriga: amazing value.

*** **Merlot** ◀ **97** barrel sample tasted for last edition has delivered the goods: sweet mulberry, vanilla-spice nose, flavours of chocolate, cloves, scented oak. A sound effort, from hillside v'yd, 10 tons/ha.

*** **White Muscadel** ◀ **97** brilliant orange-gold: fragrantly exotic muscat aromas, sleek, almost treacly palate, luscious finish.

Grand Vin Rouge NV ◀ 50/50 merlot, cabernet sauvignon; Swartberg vineyard, 1 yr French oak, offers cherry, forest floor aromas, dry savoury finish. **Blanc de Noir NV** bright salmon pink; cherry, barley-sugar flavours: semi-sweet (26 gms/l sugar). From tinta barocca. **Sauvignon Blanc 98** floral, passion-fruit nose, low acid, bone-dry. **Chardonnay** ◀ **98** pear/cinnamon notes, slight toastiness from 3 mths French oak, no malo: pleasant creaminess. **Vin Blanc NV** 50/50 off-dry sauvignon/chenin blanc blend, apple aromas. **Golden Jerepigo** Hanepoot/muscadel: unctuous, soft dessert wine. **Red Muscadel 97** lively pink hue, rich, sweet-grapey finish. **Soet Hanepoot** Pineapple, orange-rind flavours, sweet dessert wine, spirity finish. **Vin Doux** Hanepoot-based sparkler, carbonated semi-sweet (26 gms/l sugar).

CAMBERLEY

Banhoek, Stellenbosch See Stellenbosch map

Open Mon-Sat to 12.30, or by appointment. B & B guest cottages.
Owners: John & Gael Nel
Winemaker: John Nel
Production: 1 000 cases (500 ml). **Vineyards:** 2,1 ha.
P.O. Box 6120, Uniedal, Stellenbosch 7612
Tel/Fax: 021-8851176

This cabernet-merlot vineyard on the Helshoogte Pass linking Stellenbosch to Franschhoek is the consuming interest of John and Gael Nel, quantity surveyor and gourmet caterer respectively, whose tiny but very functional cellar leads almost directly and most conveniently off the kitchen of their home. What they lack in formal training (like so many newcomers bringing fresh perspectives to the winelands), they make up for in enthusiasm. "We are passionate about red wine!" they say, and it shows in their accomplished Cabernet, the **96** recently rated **** by WINE magazine. Also evident is the care taken in both vineyard and cellar—respected winemaker Kevin Arnold, a close friend, has been their sounding-board here. "With a farm on this small scale, we cannot afford to make any mistakes." Their single farm assistant, trained by Cordoba's Chris Keet, "has fantastic skills" and participates in profits, earning an incentive percentage of every case of Camberley sold.

*** **Cabernet Sauvignon** Serious style, but 500 ml bottles definitely appear to speed up maturation process, so drinkable earlier than most reds of similar gravitas. **96** first release WINE****. Lovely cassis fruit, tannins have smoothed (merlot touch in finish), exceptionally well-balanced, very dry, refined. All new French oak, 14 months. Drink now. **97** tasted before final blending: though alc. tad higher (12,5%) appears more delicate (was generally lighter vintage), tannins still to relax. New/2nd-fill barrels, 15 months. 600 cases only.

CAPE BAY WINES

Hermanus See Walker Bay map

Open for sales and tasting Mon-Fri 9-4.
Owners: David & Felicity Johnson
Production: 25 000 cases
P.O. Box 225, Hermanus 7200
Tel: 0283-23862 **Fax:** 0283-23867
E-mail: capebay@hermanus.co.za

Cape Wine Master, negociant, and winery owner Dave Johnson is crystal-clear about his goals with this range—which explains why it's been a huge hit locally and abroad. He seeks to provide the kind of wines "I like to drink and can afford to buy. Not wines for tastings but for drinking. Value for money. I get totally twitched by the high mark-ups put on my wines by retailers and restaurateurs. Those who have fair mark-ups sell lots!" In answer to the question "What's new in your cellar?" he replies: "Everything but me!" The wines are styled to his specs. at various cellars, in a variety of regions, with which he's had longtime associations.

*** **Cabernet Sauvignon/Merlot** NEW **98** replaces the pvs. Merlot. Unwooded, 50/50 blend. Ripe raspberry, blackcurrant leads into good, soft, juicy mouthful of fresh fruit. Easy charmer, for enjoying within a year or two of vintage.

**** **Pinotage** ◀ Bright mulberry colour in **98** with ripe mulberry, raspberry nose. Small berries repeat on palate, plus dark cherry, ripe plums. Attractive, if slight, gingerish note. Delightfully juicy yet decidedly dry finish. Versatile food wine. Unwooded. 13,6 alc.

*** **Mellow Red** ◀ ☺ 50/50 blend of **98** ruby cab./cinsaut. Light, bright, bluey-tinged red. Delightfully satisfying. Juicy, ripe, green pepper, fresh strawberry and raspberry fruitiness. Cheerful clean, no-frills instant gulpability.

*** **Chardonnay** Unwooded. **98** repeats more substantial style of packed with citrus, ripe peach nose. Full range of fresh citrus flavours, long clean finish. Ripe-flavoured, almost "sweet" (but it's bone-dry) mouthful, not specially complex but very agreeable. 12,9% alc.

Chenin Blanc NEW ◀ Fresh, tropical fruit nose, soft mouth-feel, clean finish. Easy quaffing, dry **98**. **Bouquet Blanc** ◀ Pleasant off-dry, fruity blend: colombard, clairette blanche, with subtle spicy-muscat interjection from fernão pires. Discreet 7,6 gms/l sugar in **98** (bit drier than pvs.) for smoothness rather than sweetness. Good with lightly spiced foods. 12% alc.

CAPE CHAMONIX WINE FARM

Franschhoek See Franschhoek map

Open daily 9.30-4. Tastings & sales. Also Hellinger schnapps and mountain-spring Eau de Chamonix. R5 for 5 wines charge.

La Maison de Chamonix: See restaurant guide for details. Playpark facilities.

Owner: IHDC Group—Chris and Sonja Hellinger
Winemaker: Peter Arnold (since 1992)
Production: 12 000 cases. **Vineyards:** 40 ha.
P.O. Box 28, Franschhoek 7690
Tel: 021-8762494/8 (Winetasting 021-8763241) **Fax:** 021-8763237
E-mail: chamfarm@icon.co.za **Website:** www.chamonix.co.za

Not remotely as elevated as its French ski-resort namesake, but this pretty farm does perch picturesquely above the Franschhoek Valley, and winemaker Peter Arnold's conviction that pinot noir and these high-altitude vineyards are made for each other is now being put to the test: in the Chamonix cellar are the first two barrels of this difficult (in SA), cold-climate-lover of a variety. Present plantings here—60% white, 40% red—are soon scheduled to go the other way about (5 ha. were replanted in 1998) to meet demand for red wines in the Chamonix export markets of the USA, Germany and Hong Kong. Arnold, trained at Germany's Geisenheim Institute, has both French and Californian experience; the former comes through strongly in wines like the compelling **Sauvignon Blanc** below, which should specially interest those who like their sauvignons to speak with a Loire accent.

**** **Sauvignon Blanc Wood Matured** A sock in the eye for the sauvignon-shouldn't-be-oaked brigade. We really liked the elegant **96**. We love latest **97**. A gust of assertive cat's pee aromas leads on to classically dry, refined, herby-tangy palate (hint of camomile), classy elongated finish. Individual, grown-up food wine. Invisible oak—fermenting/maturing 10 mths in "old" wood—which anchors rather than flavours—the secret here.

Cabernet Sauvignon Snatches tobacco pouch, green peppers; fruit concentration holding well in **95**, tannins softening. Needs sturdy food partner—pepper steak (rump not fillet)—for current drinking. Or wait 2-3 years. **Merlot 95** from St'bosch grapes, first crop, fruit has quietened down, tannins more exposed. Barrel-matured 18 mths, 20% new, 80% 2nd-fill. **Chardonnay Reserve 95** (top 100 place 1997 Chicago World Wine Champs.) beginning to slow; high-kicking (14% alc.), showy, all new-oaky, toasty character muted. Spotlight switches to (non-reserve, NEW) **Chardonnay 96**, also good performance at same wine champs (89 points) but significantly, in 1998. Buttered toast with grilled hazelnuts, marmalade fruit, very dry, longish finish. Neat French, rather than New World, air. 12,5% alc. 80% new oak. **Gemini** NEW **98** blend 80% sauvignon blanc, 20% chardonnay, no oak. Fresh-cut summer flowers bouquet, technically bone-dry but high 14% alc. lends sweeter note. **Blanc** ☺ Delightful, relaxed blend 20% chardonnay, equal parts chenin, weisser riesling, with personality quirks of each—citrus, ripe guavas, spice. Not quite bone-dry, easy low acid, undaunting 11,8% alc. for summer quaffing.

CAPE COLOURS

See Ashwood Wines

CAPE INDABA

See Natural Corporation

CAPELANDS

See Longridge

CAPE LEVANT, CAPE SOLEIL See Sonop

CAPENHEIMER Monis, Paarl

Delicate, sweetish, slightly sparkling chenin. Sells equivalent of 500 000 cases annually.

CAPE REFLECTIONS See Vinfruco

CAPE SAFARI See Cape Wine Cellars

CAPE VIEW See IWS and Kaapzicht

CAPE VINEYARDS Consortium Worcester co-ops, Bergsig Estate

CAPE VINTRY Kempens of the Cape

Dry Red Smooth, soft, piquant. Merlot, shiraz, cabernet. **Blanc de Blanc** 60% SA riesling, 30% Rhine riesling, gewürz. Not quite dry at 4 gms/l sugar. **Bouquet Blanc** Similar blend, with 5% muscat for extra-fruity fragrance, flavour; off-dry at 12 gms/l sugar.

CAPE WINE CELLARS

Wellington/Paarl

Sales S.A.D. Shop, Wellington. Mon-Fri 9-5. Sat 9-12.30.
Owners: S.A.D. Group, Wamakersvallei, Wellington, Bovlei, Boland Cellars
Winemaker/Team Leader: Jeff Wedgwood (since 1995)
Production: 175 000 cases
P.O. Box 508, Wellington 7655
Tel: 021-8731101 **Fax:** 021-8733112
E-mail: info@sadgroup.co.za **Website:** http://www.wine.co.za

Export markets firmly in its sights, Cape Wine Cellars—go-getting alliance of Wellington-based SA Dried Fruit Co-operative and four collective wine cellars nearby—is marshalling its forces to fire off 600 000 cases a year by 2005. A target that seems eminently reachable: the fledgling operation—1998 was only its 4th vintage—already ships some 175 000 cases annually to mainly Europe and Asia. The key, says cellarmaster Jeff Wedgwood, is intensive market research to ensure the wines are styled—and priced—to suit consumers' tastes. Through International Wine Services, the "flying winemaker" operation head-quartered in the UK, CWC taps Kym Milne MW—*Grapevine*'s 1998 Winemaker of the Year—to tweak the range for the quirky UK market.

KLEINBOSCH range:

Merlot 97 easy (despite 13,5% alc), ready-to-quaff version of variety; brush of strawberry fruit. **Cabernet Sauvignon** Modern-style **97** lightly oaked, undemonstrative; gentle almond, coffee wafts, hints of blackberry. Early drinking, slightly chilled, good with pasta. 13% alc. **Pinotage 97** rather pleasant example in lightish, juicy-fruit vein; made more interesting by attractive stalky traces. To quaff now. Alc. nudging 13%. **Chardonnay 97** ripe, sweet-citrus character when bottled, glazing over with honey. Low

11,7% alc. **96** (under a different label) **VG**. **Sauvignon Blanc** NEW **97** light, non-taxing, some gooseberry suggestions, very dry. Low alc. (11,5%). **Chenin Blanc (Early Release)** ◀ Winemaker says: "**98** bottled fresh, young; highlights apricot flavours typical of Paarl/Wellington". We get fresh apple, guava aromas/flavours; expansive tropical palate, lively, whistle-clean. Jolly nice. 13% alc. **Kleinbosch Bushvine Dry Muscat** ☺ ◀ NEW **98** hugely quaffable example of (in Cape) underrated style. 'Sweet' gently aromatic nose, full-blown muscat flavour, bone dry, delicious. Classic beach-party wine; sip solo or with fish/seafood, summer salads. CWC's top seller. Winemaker says: "(UK retail chain) Safeway will buy all we can make!" However small quantity obtainable locally through Makro. **Special Late Harvest** NEW **98** not ready for tasting. 100% weisser riesling, semi-sweet (47 gms/l sugar), low alc. (11%).

CAPE SAFARI range:

Cinsaut-Cabernet 97 soft, gently-fruited swigger, ready-to-go. Strawberry tones, snatches tobacco pouch. Cab. s. (25% of blend) oak-matured. Extra-low (4,6 gms/l) acid. **Late Sun Red** NV variation on cinsaut-cab. theme, ratio 85/15, unwooded. Featherweight palate despite 12,5% alc. **Blush** ◀ NEW NV delightful example of this style. Fragrant fruit-salad nose/palate (guavas, mulberries, *nogal*), crisp, quietly dry (17,5 gms/l sugar). Low alc. (11%). Ideal midsummer quaffing. Chenin, 20% merlot. Also in 2l box. **Chenin Blanc-Chardonnay 97** has acquired definite honey, candied pineapple overtones. Best young. **Stardust** NV off-dry (7,4 gms/l sugar) chenin/riesling/colombard. Light (11% alc.), no-pretensions quaffing. Also in 2l box. **Stein** NEW **97** replica of chenin/colombard/Cape riesling blend above, below. This one gently sweet at ± 18 gms/l sugar, unusual "chardonnay" citrus daubs on guava undercoat, non-cloying. **Late Harvest** NEW NV distinctly sweet (26 gms/l sugar), low alc. (11%). Also in 2l box.

CATHEDRAL CELLAR

Paarl See Paarl map

See KWV International entry for visit/tasting details.

Owner: KWV

P.O. Box 528, Suider-Paarl 7624

Tel: 021-8073911 **Fax:** 021-8073000

Gold at the Concours Mondiale Bruxelles, Belgium; best wine out of more than 1 800 at Selections Mondiales, Canada; Veritas double-gold; SAA trophy for Red Wine of the Year are some of the latest laurels for this top-of-the range export label, named after KWV's lofty, cathedral-sized cellar. Results, cellarmaster Kosie Moller explains, of (among others) a major upgrade/expansion of KWV's cellars at Paarl, investment of over R30-million in new oak, and a fresh winemaking approach: "We treat each wine as though it were created on an 'estate', giving the necessary individual attention." Stylistically, Moller aims for a New World vernacular "retaining an essence of its SA character". Three new labels—**Cabernet Franc**, **Shiraz** and **Port** —joined the line-up in 1998.

**** **Triptych 96** (knocking on ***** door) inky purple; fragrant, complex bouquet of spicy oak, earthy briar, rich, ripe berry fruit. Stylish, opulent palate, high-toned toasty oak, amalgam of red-fruit flavours: plum, blackcurrant, cherry. Finishes with gentle persistence. 60% cab. s., 28% merlot, 12% cab. f. Nearly 2 yrs new French oak. Allow to develop over 4-8 years. **95** pencils, blue ink on nose, brilliant, potent, bright qualities throughout. **94**, **93** both **VG**. **93** Gold IWSC, gold Ljubljana, best SA wine at Vinexpo 97. **92** top overall red at selections for 1995 **SAA**. Grapes mainly from Durbanville.

★★★★ **Cabernet 96** bright cherry red, dark berry fruit, restrained cedary oak. Wide-bodied, blackcurrants wrapped in dark chocolate. Elegant, fruit-driven, supple-tannined. Similar modern, richer **95** wears string of awards: **VVG**, best red at selections for **SAA**, gold at Concours Mondiale Bruxelles, best wine at Selections Mondiales. **94 VVG** bold, contemporary style. Ripe, curranty, black cherry fruit, good sweet oak. Firm tannins. Overall champion red Ljubljana, Slovenia, in 1997. **93 VVG**, **WINE★★★★**: from Helderberg farm of Anton Bredell, mix of clones. Same fruit tones but more chocolate, complexity. **92** heralded new-wave style, oak-matured new/2nd-fill barrels 18 months; ripe prune-nutty quality on palate. Developed extra complexity with time; **SAA**. All have acids at about 6,5 gms/l, alcs. close to 13% for good keeping.

★★★★ **Pinotage 96** serious, modern; inky, purple peeping through. Smoky/oaky nose: overtones of blackberry, apple-pie, ripe banana, palate raunchy, almost sweet; soft, supple tannins, long dry finish. Seductive, gorgeous, will reward 2-4 yrs in bottle. **95** in partly new wood 20 months, incl. dash of American oak, good modern style. **94** very good, aromas of bananas, pineapple carry through to palate. **94**, **93**, **92** all **VG**.

★★★★ **Merlot 96** bright mulberry colour, violets, soft chocolaty aromas, gentle mulberry flavours, plenty of development potential. 13,5% alc. **94** supple, ripe, fairly oaky. 18 months small French barrels 60% new/balance 2nd/3rd-fill. Ripe fruit, coffee, mint, green pepper on palate.

★★★★ **Shiraz** NEW **96** fine first release, richly constructed: dark red/purple, ripe red-berry bouquet, some green leaf, minty tingles, dark chocolate overlay. Fresh berry juice, gently spicy, medium-weight, fine-grained tannins. Hint of toasty oak, sweetish finish. Should develop well over 3-5 yrs. 13% alc.

★★★★ **Cabernet Franc** NEW **96** deep garnet, ripe black-cherry nose, blackberry, minty, stalky/stemmy (in positive sense); silky texture, pepper, mulberry, green pepper undertones; refreshing, bright almost sweet/dry finish. Plenty of potential.

★★★ **Sauvignon Blanc 98** (unwooded) "sweet" gooseberry nose, more texture than flavour, some nettly extracts. Big 13% alc. **97** showed quality of vintage. Crisp, nettly, bright, fresh. 12% alc.

★★★★ **Port** NEW **95** in traditional tall bottle with shapely neck (yet to be labelled). Brick-edged red. Deep plummy/minty nose, some smokiness. Succulent fruit, soft vanilla cadences, prunes, sprinkling of pepper. Lowish alc. (17%) makes for easy drinking. Quite dry finish.

Chardonnay 98 untasted. Oak-fermented, new 300 l barrels. **97** cellar samples show good fresh fruit, good oak. Grapes from Durbanville, Perdeberg.

CEDERBERG KELDERS

Cederberg See Olifants River map

Tastings/sales Mon-Sat 8.30-12.00; 1.30-5. Cellar tours by appointment. Fully equipped guest cottages, mountain walks, observatory nearby.

Owners: Nieuwoudt Family
Winemaker: David Nieuwoudt (since 1997)
Viticulturists: David and Ernst Nieuwoudt
Production: 3 000 cases. **Vineyards:** 15 ha.
Address: Dwarsrivier Farm, Cederberg 8136
Tel: 027-4822827 **Fax:** 027-4822825

Since David Nieuwoudt took over this high-altitude family cellar in the rugged Cederberg mountains in 1997, he has seized the challenge of mining the "incredible potential" of this stunning area with youthful enthusiasm. His first solo vintage, despite some of the wettest, coldest weather in decades, was a hit, nabbing two gold Veritas medals and a sought-after Business Class listing on SAA. Two new wines from the harvest—**Pinotage** and an early-drinker based on ruby cab.—made their début in **98**.

*** **Cabernet Sauvignon** Steady improvement culminates in classy **97** (tank sample), featuring high proportion (60%) new French oak. Intense blackcurrant, spicily oaked; vanilla, suspicion of mint. Dense fruit still in thrall of tannin—best cellared for yr while sipping charming **96**, which has acquired inviting baked-fruit aromas, dense chocolate flavours, soft seamless oak, savoury dry finish. Very nice.

*** **Cederberger** ◀ NEW **97** (tank sample) wide-bodied, ruby cab-driven quaffer. Bags of blackberry, cassis essences, ripe tannin; with cab. s., merlot. Ideal winter warmer.

Pinotage NEW **97** chunky style; beefy alc. (nudging 14%); gawky still, needs yr or 2 to acquire polish. One to watch. Young vines, 4 tons/ha., cold fermentation (20°), wood 14 months. **Sauvignon Blanc 98** cat's pee, grassy notes spill onto palate; compact, bone dry. Try with summer salads. 10-year-old vines, reductively made. **Chenin Blanc** Ripe melon, spring flower scents in **98**; most pleasant off-dry quaffing. **97 VG. Bukettraube 98** trumpets Thai curry, sweet-and-sour pork. Low-key muscat tones, semi-sweet but uncloying, fragrant. Just missed ***. **97 VG. Natural Sweet** NEW **97** botrytis-kissed chenin, dash of bukettraube. Glowing wafts of raisin, barely ripe apricot, stalky snatches, fresh. 100 cases. **Dwarsrivier Wit Jerepiko** Very sweet white from muscat d'Alexandrie. Barley sugar, quince essences.

CELLAR CASK WINES — Distillers, Stellenbosch

Premier Claret ◀ Recommended by WINE in its "Best Boxed Wines" tasting—further evidence of this range's improving quality at undaunting prices. Flavourful cab. s., shiraz, tinta barocca fusion, nice and smooth, med.-bodied 12% alc. **Select Johannisberger** Similar (red) blend to above but definitely for the sweeter-toothed: 48,5 gms/l sugar. This, Joh'berger below also in 340 ml screw cap bottles. **Premier Grand Crû** Floral/fruity, soft, easy-drinking, everyday jollity; chenin, Cape riesling, colombard, sauvignon blanc. Lowish alc.: 11,5%. **Premier Semi-Sweet** Basically PGC-blend adrenalised with 20 gms/l sugar. Caribbean tone, gentle palate. **Premier Late Harvest** For "sweeties": ripe, honeyed chenin prettiness; 28 gms/l sugar. **Select Johannisberger** Decidedly sweet white blend of chenin, riesling/colombard; rich, ripe fruit. 59 gms/l sugar.

CHAPEL CELLAR WINES — See Zanddrift Vineyards

CHÂTEAU LIBERTAS — SFW

In its seventh decade, this Cape stalwart shows no signs of fading either in popularity, nor in the bottle: 1940 still worth drinking. Cabernet-based; since late 80s merlot has added comfortable plumpness. Cinsaut's spice/strawberry jam sweetness remains finishing trait. Sells over 110 000 cases annually. ◀ Well-priced.

CILMOR — See Sonop

CINZANO — By Gilbeys, under licence to Cinzano, Italy

*** **Spumanté** Still a market force with usual attractive muscaty nose and bits of melon and tropical notes. Mouthfilling mousse with semi-sweet softness but pert carbon dioxide freshness. Delightful drinking for the sweet tooth.

Tiziano Rose-coloured, strawberry-nosed, bits of muscat, semi-sweet fizz. **Memoranti** Ripe apples, peach, passion-fruit on the nose and full semi-sweet mousse.

CLAIRVAUX CO-OPERATIVE

Robertson See Robertson map

Tasting/sales Mon-Fri 8.30-5.30, Sat 9-12.30.
Owners: 19 members
Winemaker: Kobus van der Merwe (since 1974)
Production: 30 000 cases
Vineyards: 125 ha.
P.O. Box 179, Robertson 6705
Tel: 02351-3842 **Fax:** 02351-61925
E-mail: clairv@mweb.co.za
Website: www.clairvaux.co.za

Not many cellars' price lists can be described as "eagerly awaited'; this one could. Invariably there's a gem somewhere in the line-up, as when **Hopp Johanna**—tongue-in-cheek reference to pop song: Gimme Hope, Joanna—made its (her?) début. Now it's the turn of Madonna—yes, the singing, dancing, pouting, grinding one—in another jewel: **Madonna's Kisses**. The sultry superstar lends her name to not one but two fittingly sweet, sensual styles—noble, special late harvest—a veritable bottled *smoochfest.*

*** **Goue Jerepiko** ◀ NV Very pleasant muscat aromas, quite spirity still, needs a little time, attractive brisk finish. From white muscadel. 17% alc.

Ruby Cabernet 98 "New World-style" says winemaker; but not over the top: juicy-fruity, strawberry/herby hints, light, undemanding, decidedly dry. **Blanc de Noir 98** peachy in most respects: very light colour, almost peach, gentle *pêche* wafts on nose, light palate. Semi-sweet. Also in 250 ml. **Sauvignon Blanc 98** delicate, light-bodied, grass/nettle-toned, dry. **Sauvignon Blanc-Chardonnay** NEW **98** 70/30 split. Clean, very dry. Light/medium-bodied. **Colombard-Chardonnay** NEW **98** works better than sauv. bl. blend above. Attractive peach, ripe pawpaw, soft mouth-feel, easy drinking. 70% colombard. **Chenin-Chardonnay** NEW **98 (70/30 blend)** 25% fermented on oak chips, lively green-apple scents, fresh, easy but rather oaky. **Rhine Riesling** ☺ ◀ **98** irresistible. Pretty peach/pear wafts, flashes of fragrant muscat, zesty finish; 12 gms/l sugar lends fullness, roundness rather than sweet impression. Medium alc. (11,8%). **Chenin Blanc 98** (export only) fermented on French oak chips—imparts terrific velvety texture, wood/fruit seamless. Clean guava flavours, kiss of vanilla in finish. **Blanc de Blanc** NEW **98** from colombard, tasty, mouthfilling ripe peach, green-apple flavours, light, fresh, off-dry but finishes whistle-clean. **Special Late Harvest Madonna's Kisses** ◀ NEW **98** full-blown SLH: very ripe tropical/peach/muscat flavours, decidedly sweet, deftly balanced by acid, finishes clean, crisp. Lowish alc.: ± 11%. **Special Late Harvest Soleil 98** cellar's accountant's favourite wine!—brisk seller "because it's so versatile". From chenin, muscadel; whiffs of tropical fruits/honey, light, easy. Sugar 45 gms/l. Also in 250 ml. **Noble Late Harvest Madonna's**

Kisses NEW **(89 vintage)** untasted. **Rooi Jerepiko NV** Pretty, deep rose colour, sweet, earthy. From red muscadel. **Red Muscadel** NV (**Hopp Johanna** in different dress) Friendly red muscadel dessert. **Golden Muscadel** NEW **NV** Untasted. Also in 250 ml.

CLARIDGE WINES

Groenberg, Wellington See Wellington map

Tastings/sales, cellar/distillery tours by appointment.
Private luncheons by appointment.
Owners: Roger Jorgensen, Michael Loubser
Winemaker/Viticulturist: Roger Jorgensen (since 1991)
Production: ± 3 000 cases. **Vineyards:** 12 ha.
P.O. Box 407, Wellington 7654
Tel: 021-8641241 **Fax:** 021-8643620
E-mail: claridge@dockside.co.za

Here's the scenario: Roger Jorgensen, ex-strawberry farmer in Kent, now prospecting diamonds from a 4x4 with custom-fitted brandy tank; spouse Maria, bird-watcher, computer ace; growing wine (and distilling brandy) at Wellington. Originating from so unusual a set-up, it's no surprise that Claridge is one of the most distinctive ranges around. Artisanal, barricade-storming, ABB (anything but bland)—Jorgensen's wines are all of these (in the best, quality-is-everything sense). In the past the range even might have been branded uncompromising, wines with a 'tude. But now—like Jorgensen's first (**94**) premium brandy, matured 4 yrs for release Nov/Dec 98—the winegrower is showing distinct signs of mellowing; he's "making more wine to customers' specs, as well as I can". Does this mean we're about to see a **Red Wellington** styled for braai popping? A spritzable **Chardonnay**? We think not. Then again, it's quite a leap from strawbs to sparklers. Anything's possible.

**** **Red Wellington** ◀ As personal as ever in gutsy, tri-athletic **95**, pumped up for the long haul. Complex—smells/tastes run gamut from ripe plums to "bitter" Dalmatian cherry, fruitcake, marzipan dusted with black pepper, trace of smoke in finish—huge weight (14,5% alc.!), mega tannin, almost tough. Will start drinking in 2000 earliest. From cabernet (mostly), merlot, touch cab. f. Aged 12-18 months in mixed cooperage, held yr in bottle before release. Like chard. below, 90% exported, snapped up by local restaurants (also on Blue Train), also in 500 ml. **96** (untasted) available Nov 99.

*** **Chardonnay** ◀ **96** a walk on the wild side: powerful smoky (almost animal) attack, rustic weight on palate, lashings vanilla/toasty oak, long lemon-zesty finish. Not your average tropical style. Food wine, also in 500 ml. Barrel-fermented, malo complete. 13% alc.

*** **Pinot Noir** Klein Opten Horst label. **95** developing authentic earthy, damp leaves over/undertones, hints of ripe cherry, aromatic fungi. Tannins still grippy—need 2-3 yrs. Light colour. Grapes from neighbour Naas Ferreira's farm, crop managed by Jorgensen. 250 cases.

CLOS MALVERNE

Devon Valley, Stellenbosch See Stellenbosch map

Tastings/sales by appointment Mon-Fri 9-5.
Owners: Seymour and Sophia Pritchard
Winemaker: I.P. Smit (since November 1997)
Production: 30 000 cases. **Vineyards:** 23 ha.
P.O. Box 187, Stellenbosch 7599
Tel: 021-8822022 **Fax:** 021-8822518

Seymour Pritchard—arch-perfectionist—should be pleased: while many estates scramble to jump on the pinotage bandwagon, he can bask in the knowledge that Clos Malverne hitched its star to the SA's signature grape long before it became *de rigeur*. The 1991 edition of this guide, reflecting on the Devon Valley winery's early vintages, noted: "Lavish oak maturation is a feature of the style [Seymour feels] . . . pinotage is every bit as worthy of such luxury treatment as more classic varieties." *A luta continua*. Pinotage represents half the current vineyards, features in 3 of the range including top-selling "standard" varietal **Pinotage**. Emphasis, new winemaker I.P. Smit—previously of Simonsig—reveals, is on producing more pinotage, pinotage-based blends. "We're experimenting with all sorts of combinations."

★★★★ **Auret** "Stunning and bold" is vintner's description of **96**, raised in 50/50 French, American oak. Stunning, yes—and for all its boldness, approachable, built for early enjoyment (but with legs for the longer haul). Pinotage, cab. s., merlot; blackcurrant dominant, some ripe cherries, lashings of toasty spicy-sweet oak, pleasantly fresh. **95** similar modern/approachable style, low-altitude acid/tannin. **94**, firmer structure. 4 stars from UK *Decanter*. **93 WINE**★★★★.

★★★★ **Cabernet-Shiraz** NEW ◀ **97** ready to do battle with some big-gun Aussie cab./shiraz blends. Orchestra of smells/tastes: ripe cherries, freshly turned soil, violets, toasted chestnuts, some gamey afterthoughts, velour of ripe tannin, fresh acidity lightening/brightening the performance, clean finish. Very drinkable now, solid development potential. Well priced at under R30 from farm. ± 13% alc. ★★★★ in **WINE's** "new releases".

★★★★ **Pinotage Reserve** These made in modern style, usually with French/American oak, toned-down acidities; however, patience is needed to bring out their full virtues. **95**, **96** (ABSA Pinotage Top Ten) and latest **97** probably best about 3 years from release. Alcs. generally over 13%, firm tannins allow (or, as in **97**, need) ageing. French-oaked **97** shows seductive, redcurrant/ripe plum hallmarks of house style, inflections of cloves, vanilla, toasty oak. Generous plummy fruit, resounding finish. Standard **Pinotage (★★★)** friendlier, lighter toned, for earlier drinking, gently brushed with oak. Both highly rated by British wine writer Jancis Robinson: "Devon Valley fruit in abundance and concentration."

★★★ **Devonet** ☺ **97** first-division super-quaffer, not quite bargain-priced at R25 ex-cellar but immensely drinkable, smooth, fresh. Sappy cherry-plum, comfortably upholstered, lovely vanilla warmth, mocha/sweet-oaky finish. For early drinking. 13,3% alc.

★★★ **Cabernet Sauvignon 97** a quieter sort of cab., unflashy, but good flavour concentration, ready to go. Combination ripe cassis/plum, almond top notes, sweet-sour palate tone, dark mocha in fresh finish. Pleasurable now or couple of years. 12 months French oak.

Sauvignon Blanc Wide-bodied **98** very drinkable solo or with food, gooseberry/grass resonances, zippy, dry. Reductively made, 13,7% alc. **SHEPHERD'S CREEK** is an alternative label.

COGMANS CO-OPERATIVE WINE CELLAR

Montagu See Robertson map

Tastings/sales Mon-Fri 8.30-5.30. Sat 8-12.
Owners: 41 members
Winemaker: Kootjie Laubscher (since 1993)
Production: 6 000 tons, 10 000 cases
P.O. Box 332, Montagu 6720
Tel: 0234-41340. **Fax:** 0234-42113

This combine, dating from the early 1940s, previously was known as Soetwynboere Co-operative—a title suggestive of its traditional sweet, usually fortified dessert range. Nowadays, under a different banner, the cellar offers a repertoire of amiable, well-priced table wines too.

COLD DUCK (Fifth Avenue)

Rosé sparkler; fresh muscat spice; sweet, gently fruity with lively bubble. Alc. at 8,5% makes it good starting point for many winelovers. NV.

CONSTANTIA-UITSIG

Constantia See Constantia map

Tastings/sales Mon-Fri 9.30-5, Sat 9-3. R1 per wine, refundable with purchases.

Constantia-Uitsig: lunch, dinner daily 12-3; 7-11: closed Mon lunch.

La Colombe: lunch, dinner daily 12-3; 7-11: closed Tues. 16-room country lodge. Conference facilities. See restaurant section.

Owners: Dave & Marlene McCay
Winemaker: Nicky Versfeld, at Steenberg
Consultant/Wine Director: André Badenhorst
Vineyards: André Rossouw
Production: 240 tons, 15 600 cases. **Vineyards**: 32 ha., eventually 40 ha. Made/bottled at Steenberg
P.O. Box 402, Constantia 7848
Tel: 021-7941810 **Fax:** 021-7941812
E-mail: wine@icon.co.za
Website: www.constantiauitsig.co.za

Here's a property in the heart of plush Constantia that offers a bouquet of attractions: you can stay—in a charming country lodge amidst the vineyards; possibly play—owner Dave McCay is a former first-class cricketer and the farm sports its own cricket oval; keep hunger at bay—at two of the Cape's most delectable restaurants; and of course, drink in style. The young vines here are now beginning to show their paces: a 95 cabernet-merlot blend was the only Constantia red to win a Veritas gold medal in 1997—and neighbourly competition is super-stiff in this cool, prime growing area, birthplace of the SA wine industry more than 3 centuries ago.

Born and bred in this historic valley of vines, Constantia-Uitsig's wine dynamo, André Badenhorst, is, however, no stay-at-home. During 1998 he visited Sancerre, Pouilly Fumé, investigated coopers and oak in Burgundy, and went twice to London, where, he believes, "wine styles are set . . . its vital to be aware of what's going on there . . . to find out what consumers are looking for." This is all part of the forward-planning for C-U's own cellar, to be built in the near future. Badenhorst's Elsenburg-trained son, Ardi, might well feature here—he assisted Steenberg's Nicky Versveld with the C-U wines in 1998, in between working two other harvests, in New Zealand and at Ch. L'Angelus. Experience in California and Australia is next on his itinerary before returning to home-ground.

*** **Merlot** Distinctly different from valley's other merlots, has similar potential. Fresh, spicy plum intensity of **96** has now developed warmer, rounded tones. Lightish-bodied, but with generous fleshy succulence, ripe lingering flavours. Well-judged oak (one-third new). Good drinking for next 2-3 years. Concentration from low 5-6 tons/ha. cropping. **97** for release under La Colombe label. Dense, mouthcoating flavours should lift **98** into higher league.

**** **Sémillon** Variety André Badenhorst is determined to crack; "Constantia is a natural home," he claims. Barrel-fermentation boosts quality, layers clean limey, honeyed freshness onto broad-shouldered base. Lovely fusion of vibrant new world flavours, old world elegance. **97** starting to show delicious complexity; still very fresh (fruit enhanced by 12,5% unwooded portion), worth watching development over another 2 years. **98** looks equally promising.

*** **Chardonnay Reserve** Harmonious **97**: expressive but not overwhelming creamy features, good flavours lead to long, softly dry finish. Big, 13,5% alc. Versatile food partner. Fermented, aged 11 months in barrel.

Cabernet Sauvignon Varying quality over first 3 vintages: **98** most promising. Ripe, full of soft sweet fruit, refined cassis, mint. **97** weak, thin. **96** gently charming: soft, juicy red-berry fruits; very gluggable. French oak-matured; one-third new. **La Colombe Vin Rouge** No set variety/blend; styled for easy drinking. Good fruit, low tannins. Next to be **97** merlot. **Chardonnay** NEW Unwooded **97**. Full-bodied; faint citrusy tang. **Sémillon** NEW Unwooded. **97** smooth, softly dry. Earthy, uncomplicated. **Sauvignon Blanc** Unwooded, **98** promises more figgy ripeness, richer texture than pvs. **La Colombe Vin Blanc** Restaurant's house wine. **98** unwooded chardonnay, sauvignon blanc, sémillon blend; rounded, gentle fruit, softly dry.

COPPOOLSE FINLAYSON

Stellenbosch
Owners: Rob Coppoolse, Walter Finlayson
Winemaker: Walter Finlayson
P.O. Box 4028, Old Oak 7537
Tel: 021-996334 **Fax:** 021-998004
E-mail: robc@igubu.saix.net

Originally part of a joint-venture with Slaley, the Coppoolse Finlayson partnership is now operating independently, armed with some of the wines and brands of the earlier alliance. The Sentinel range accommodates premium varietal wine, while the Mount Disa selection is produced for Seagram UK. A new brand, Cape Salute, to be released shortly.

SENTINEL range:

*** **Shiraz** ◀ **98** ripe, easy-drinking, raspberry/youngberry aromas, fine tannins, light spicy flavours, persistent. **97** accessible, with black cherry fragrance, smoothly textured.

*** **Cabernet 96** blackcurrant/brambly aromas, forward, not simple, firm elegant palate, lightish dry tannined finish.

Chardonnay 98 soft tropical aromas, oxidative butterscotch notes, very forward fruit, lime/grapefruit finish.

MOUNT DISA range:

Cabernet Sauvignon 96 mint/eucalyptus whiffs, light tannins, tangy blackcurrant flavours, very fresh. **Pinotage 96** youngberry/strawberry aromas, spicy palate, elegant, almost Burgundian finish. **Chardonnay 96** butterscotch, marzipan aromas, whiffs of tropical fruit, almost viscous textures, melon/lime layerings. **Sauvignon Blanc 97** green pepper herbal aromas, asparagus/grassy flavours, light not insubstantial, tangy, dry. **Cape Salute** Varnishy bouquet, with soft, light mulberry flavours in **97**, slight earthy textures, evanescent, quaffable.

CORDOBA (Also Mount Claire Range)

Stellenbosch See Helderberg map

Open by appointment only.

Owner: Jannie Jooste
Winemaker: Christopher Keet (since 1994)
Production: 7 000 cases. **Vineyards:** 30 ha.
P.O. Box 2282, Stellenbosch 7599
Tel: 021-8553744 **Fax:** 021-8551690

With postcard-perfect views of the Cape Peninsula and surrounding ocean from his mountain eyrie, vineyardist/winemaker/marketer Christopher Keet seems to have his head in the clouds. Far from it. His feet are firmly planted on the ground. Tireless, blending practical realities of farming this difficult terrain within a dedicated scientific paradigm, he relishes the latest addition to his burgeoning portfolio, that of marketing. Being connected with the product from soil to point of sale (ranging from Sandton to Tokyo) shows in the finesse of the wines, especially red (70% of production). Still alone in the cellar, Keet plans on employing a small complement of well-trained/motivated workers who take full responsibility for their tasks—and are well rewarded. The target production is 12 000 cases of quality, and a tasting facility allowing others to share the majestic view will eventually become a feature of this high-altitude Helderberg farm. Containing a massive mountain fire which burnt down the slopes to the thatch-roof cellar before the 98 harvest—destroying most of the fynbos—seems less of a problem than the marauding baboons which plunder his pinot noir at 600 m above sea-level. First duiker, then starlings ransack what they leave behind. The 1,3 ha. vineyard has yet to bear a ripe bunch. Most would weep. Not Keet, who calls this a "generous donation to the World Wildlife Fund". It's also something of a security barrier. If the pinot wasn't there, maybe the pirates would purloin his choice block of chardonnay, next in line.

With such a cool climate and eco-friendly practices (60% less spraying than prescribed), classically-structured wines come naturally. Cellar technique is designed to retain the "farmed-for" fruit flavours without harsh tannin. In an age of wines for imminent consumption, here's something of a maverick, a cellar offering reds of solid structure and layered, ripe tannin that will reward patient maturation.

★★★★★ **Cordoba Crescendo** Deep squid-ink colour, plush lavender, black pepper nose, dusty background. Dense cassis fruit cosseted in major—but soft—cloaking tannin. Echoing length. **95** first bottling of mainly cabernet franc (fickle elsewhere, very fine on these Helderberg slopes) blend with 20% cab. s., 10% merlot. Expensively oaked and tastes it, structure to last 10 years. A new benchmark, reflecting the individuality of Cordoba.

★★★★ **Merlot** Blood red, ripe cherry, mocha. Gutsy palate, soft tannic grip. Ripe fruit alive in **95**, bigger concentration than first **94**, lighter colour/texture although lively. For the new millennium.

★★★★ **Shiraz** Magnified red berry fruit, tobacco jostle with trademark soft concentrated tannins, powerful mouthful. **94** 18 months new oak. Only 400 bottles, release not decided.

★★★ **Cabernet 95** indian ink black, aromatic cedar, pencil shavings without grassiness, plump fruit amidst puckering tannin, step up on leaner, tight **94**.

★★★ **Chardonnay** Straw shot with green colour; subtle spiced oak second fiddle to tangy grapefruit core; understated baked bread warmth adds dimension. No flamboyant butterscotch in **98**. Whole bunch-pressed, barrel-fermented. Shy **97** slender, ends trifle tart. **96** heralded **98**, waxy frame for citric charm, finishes with finesse.

Sauvignon Blanc ◀ Fresh, bracing flinty fruit in reductive style (yeast selection, vit C application), river-stone briskness, penetrating, unwooded **98**. **97** bluegum herbaceousness, but steely dry.

MOUNT CLAIRE range:
Mountain Red ◀ Bright, blackcurrant, pepper and spice: firm; fruity, friendly, "braai wine" says Keet (modestly). Shiraz, cab. s., merlot, small portion oaked. **97** affordable R18 from farm. **Mountain White** ◀ **98** cool-climate chalk character from pinot blanc, sauvignon blanc; Rhine riesling adds aromatics. Just off-dry; with soft, natural acids. Anytime wine, will grace table extremely well at R15.

COUNT AGUSTA WINES — See Haute Provence

CRAIGHALL — Gilbeys, Stellenbosch

★★★ **Cabernet Sauvignon-Merlot** ◀ Huge seller, continues to improve. Attractive blackcurrant pastille-style nose in **96**, satisfying mouth-feel. Long, dry finish. Probably at its best within 3/4 years. Good outdoor food wine.

★★★ **Chardonnay-Sauvignon Blanc** ◀ ☺ Another consumer hit. **97** much fruitier than pvs., blend now 50/50. Budget price maintained by less barrel-age and intelligent use of chips. Lime-fresh, lemony nose, with fruit sweetness on palate but actually dry. Crisp, zesty finish. Remarkably classy when the large-scale production is considered.

P.O. Box 137, Stellenbosch 7599. **Tel:** 021-8086911 **Fax:** 021-8086000

CULEMBORG — Good value range by DGB

Pinotage-Cabernet Export-only blend, for relaxed everyday drinking. **97** pinotage on nose, well-rounded fruity palate. **Pinotage** ◀ **97** soft berry nose, fair complexity on palate, juicy cherry, plum, hint of banana. Tasty, easy drinking. No oak. 12,5% alc. **Blanc de Noir 98** attractive nose, fruity, off-dry from pinotage/cinsaut, delightful strawberry flavour/colour. **Chardonnay 98** with nutty, smoky aromas, fullish palate, fresh and lively. **Chenin Blanc-Chardonnay** Lime-vanilla aromas in **97**, lively, rounded, curvaceous dry white, most agreeable quaffing. Export only. **Colombard 98** shyly-scented, quite lean-green guava notes. Dry. **Chenin Blanc** NV Emphatically guava-toned off-dry, crisp refreshing, dry finish. **Stein** Identical to chenin above; for local market. NV. **Grand Crû** NV Bone-dry white. Same as export Colombard.

DIAMANTÉ (Perlé)
Blanc de Noir Bright pink, fruity off-dry, easy drinker with refreshing sparkle. **Crystal Blanc** Lively, fruity, muscat-flavoured semi-sweet, multi-varietal blend. Both NV.

CULLINAN VIEW — For Matthew Clark, UK

Cabernet Sauvignon 95 vinous rather than fruity, rustic, med./full-bodied, soft tannin. WO St'bosch, lightly wooded. **Pinotage 97** gentle redcurrant, juicy, very fresh. Unwooded, ex-Robertson. Early drinking. **Chardonnay 98** amiable peach-melba aromas, ripe, expansive fruit, long lemony finish. Lightly oaked, clean, easy drinking. Qualified ☺: only for export. **Sauvignon Blanc** Med./full-bodied **98**, water-white, unusual peach-blossom perfume on grassy background, soft acid, most agreeable. **Chenin Blanc 97** undemonstrative, gentle green-apple hints, fresh appley palate, bracing fresh. 13,5% alc., unwooded. **Colombard 98** fresh green-guava/grass, very brisk acid, bone-dry. Lowish alc. (11%).

CUVÉE CAP BY MUMM — See Twee Jonge Gezellen

DARLING CELLARS (pvs. Mamreweg)

Groenkloof See Swartland map

Open Mon-Thur 8-5, Fri 8-4, Sat 9-12. Tastings & sales. R5 tasting fee.
Owners: Private company-owned, 25 shareholders
Winemaker: Abé Beukes (since Dec 1997)
General Manager: Chris Rabie
Production: 300 000 cases. **Vineyards:** 1 860 ha.
P.O. Box 114, Darling 7345
Tel: 02241-2276/7/8 **Fax:** 02241-2647

New winemaker Abé Beukes, ex-Lievland, returns to his homeground of the West Coast and the place is certainly jumping: first, a name-change for the winery, previously known as Mamreweg. Darling, the hamlet which has woken up and started partying ever since it began to attract a new sort of resident—artists, writers, theatre-folk—is a far more fashionable label for a cellar which recently seems to have broken into a dance. There's been a creative re-organisation of the wines produced, into the premium Groenekloof range (after the highest point in this coastal wine and wheatland area), and the medium-priced DC range, with stylish new labels and bottles to match. Launching these at an hilarious lunch were Darling's most celebrated community leaders, the internationally acclaimed writer-satirist Pieter-Dirk Uys and his alter-ego Mrs Evita Bezuidenhout, South Africa's favourite drag-*tannie,* who is a personal advisor to every politician in the country, including President Mandela, for whom she likes to whip up Cape delicacies such as *koeksusters.* Uys, moving force behind the Darling Arts Festival, and a regular performer on his own stage here, has aimed the spotlight on this village; Beukes and his team are responding with a much more sophisticated but fun array of wines. These are helped on their way by new small French barrels in the cellar, a spanking bottling line, the appointment of a quality controller/ analyst, and vineyards newly-producing a much greater quantity of premium varieties. Beukes' aim is to capture the essence of this distinctive *terroir* in the bottle, and he regards patience as the greatest virtue towards this end. Europe, Canada and China are top export destinations.

GROENEKLOOF range:

★★★ **Cabernet Sauvignon** NEW Here's one you don't need to cellar. **96** bold cassis-cherry nose, fruity-nutty core, attractive mouthfilling quality, softish tannins. Clean, honest cab. **97 WINE★★★★** cassis/ mint scents, soft ripe fruit, very nice.

Sauvignon Blanc NEW Notch above usual everyday drinker in **98**: concentrated, very nice guava/gooseberry scents; arresting—almost quite stern—palate; long crisp finish. Above 13% alc.

D C Range:

Cabernet Sauvignon NEW Friendly casual quaffing. Ripe brambleberry, strong vanilla oak right through **97**. Low acid, 13% alc. **Pinotage** Unusual **97**: leafy forest-floor scents/flavours, quite stern tail. Low acid, 12% alc. **Shiraz** NEW Relaxed **97**, gentle spicy flavours. **Chardonnay** ◀ Pleasant everyday dry drinking, **97** oaked but shows no woodiness. **Sauvignon Blanc** Light (11,8% alc.). **97**, muffled guava notes, crisp finish. Dry. **Sauvignon Blanc-Chardonnay** NEW Versatile everyday dry white, floral nose, snatch of toffee, soft; fruitiest of this range in **97**.

DEETLEFS ESTATE

Rawsonville, Breede River Valley See Worcester map

Visits by appointment. Tastings, sales.

Owner: Kobus Deetlefs
Winemaker: Kobus Deetlefs (since 1989)
P.O. Box 36, Rawsonville 6845
Vineyards: 100 ha.
Tel: 0231-91260 **Fax:** 0231-91951
E-mail: deetlefs@wine.co.za
Website: www.wine.co.za/deetlefs

A change of name in 1998 for what used to be called Lebensraum Estate, but happily not a change of direction. The wines here are as seriously attractive as ever. Or might there be a bit more juice on the pedal now that Kobus Deetlefs is putting the family name up in lights with this sophisticated small range? The Deetlefses have farmed here at the foot of the Du Toit's Kloof mountains—throwing early shadows for long, cool nights— for 6 generations. "Growing up here has given me a great sense of pride in my heritage and a deep respect for the land that has nurtured us. This in turn gives me the confidence to expand our horizons using innovative ways of creating classic wines whose quality and style will reflect those deep-rooted values and traditions, but which will also point the way to a bright, bold future," elucidates Kobus Deetlefs.

*** **Sémillon** Those who thought our rave-review of **97** ("outstanding, properly understated") was over-the-top for a first release can stop quibbling and get into **98**. It's equally impressive. Sophisticated lanolin; lemongrass scents flow silkily into gentle, complex herbal flavours with faintest ripple of vanilla (30% was barrel-fermented, left on lees). The crisp, dry finish comes almost as a surprise—but an agreeable one. Excellent dining-partner, ageing prospects.

*** **Sémillon Reserve** NEW Another cracker. **98** with butterscotch, crème brûlée nose carries through to palate, velvety texture, fuller than above wine, smoky oak reverberates through aftertaste. Give 2-5 years in bottle and this should rate ****. To be made from the best barrels, only in exceptional sémillon vintages. Limited release, special packaging. "Statement wine," says Deetlefs.

*** **Chenin Blanc** Estate's trademark full, serious chenin style (unaided by any oak props) again evidenced: **98** super-beautiful ripe-peach nose; round, substantial on palate; impeccably dry. 13% alc.

*** **Chardonnay** Lemon, lime, lees aromas in **98**, lots of citrus flavours, whisper of oak (40% barrel-fermented), extend to fresh finish. Drink now, but this could also see in the millennium.

Pinotage NEW **98** first red release from estate, young, unusual, worth watching. Tasted in infancy: bold ripe blackberry nose plus lashings of oak, coulis of rhubarb, plums on palate.

DE FORELLEN

Stellenbosch

Tastings & sales at Lanzerac, 9-12.30; 2-4. R15 p/p. Cellar tours by appointment. All Lanzerac restaurant facilities.

Owner: Christo Wiese
Winemaker: Wynand Hamman **Viticulturist:** Truter Prins
P.O. Box 6233, Uniedal 7612
Tel: 021-8865641 **Fax:** 021-8876998

The De Forellen label alludes to Angus Buchanan who bought the Lanzerac farm in 1941 and bottled his first wines in 1947. Over the next decade he won 20 "first" prizes at the annual Paarl Wine Exhibition, champion red for 8 successive years. He was attracted to the Jonkershoek Valley to establish trout hatcheries and introduce these fish to the Eerste and other Cape rivers. He would spend hours patrolling the river banks, pruning trees to ensure they threw their shade in the correct spots of the river pools so that the trout had the conditions they preferred. The De Forellen (trout) wines also feature the names of Lanzerac owner Christo Wiese's daughters.

★★★★ **De Forellen Clare** ◀ **96** 80% cab. s., cab. f. Deep-coloured, medium-bodied with blackberry, cherry, green pepper aromas. Hints of vanilla from well-managed oak. Long, persistent finish. Good drinking now but will reward another 2/3 years in bottle. 12% alc. **97** brighter, deeper purple colour, richer all round. Sampled before bottling.

★★★ **De Forellen Christina** ◀ **97** a pinot blanc which Wynand Hamman believes has very similar attributes to chardonnay. First in **96** but not bottled. Small portion blended into **97** to give more depth. Unwooded, shows good clean citrus character. Hints of butterscotch, ripe quince. Good balance of acid and fruit. Lemony, clean finish. Malo in tank. Has benefited from time in the bottle; potential for further development over another year or two. Good food wine. 13% alc. **98** lighter, fruitier, fresher, crisper. Tasted before bottling.

DELAIRE WINERY

Stellenbosch See Stellenbosch map

Open Mon-Fri 9-5; Sat/Sun 10-4. Cellar tours by appointment. R10 includes glass. Tasting room with shop, deli, picnic area. Self-catering mountain chalets, cottages to hire.

Restaurant: The Green Door. Lunch Tues-Sun. Dinner in season only. See restaurant section.

Owner: Agrifarm International (Pty) Ltd, headed by Masoud Alikhani
Winemaker: Bruwer Raats (since 1997)
Viticulturist: Paul Wallace (consultant)
Vineyard Manager: Jaco v.d. Westhuizen
Production: 7 200 cases
P.O. Box 3058, Stellenbosch 7599
Tel: 021-8851756 **Fax:** 8851270
E-mail: delaire@iafrica.com **Website**: www.delaire.co.za

These "vineyards in the sky" on the crest of the Helshoogte Pass are re-establishing their credentials after a bit of a blip caused by re-shuffles in the cellar and vineyard management. Firmly ensconced since 1997 is young winemaker Bruwer Raats, whose enthusiasm has clearly lifted the range. One example of his dedication: on April 6, 1998, at 8 am he attended the birth of his son Daneël (3,6 kg). A mere three hours later he was back in the cellar delivering another baby, 3,2 tons of the 98 merlot. A new Bucher bag press and crusher-destemmer has provided practical aid; the barrel store has been refurbished and extended; and a helping human hand was lent during the 1998 vintage by a visiting winemaker from Pouilly Fumé. All cellar staff have been sent on cellar technology courses at Elsenburg College.

Raats worked the Californian 98 harvest at Cake Bread Cellars, and also travelled to the UK (London Wine Trade Fair) and France (Vinexpo and various coopers). Delaire's exports to the UK, Germany and the USA now take 30% of production, which is scheduled to rise to 10 000 cases by the year 2000. But Raats assures that Delaire will never become a slave to quantity: "We remain happily small enough to nursemaid individual blocks of vines, treating each separately from harvest through to vinification and maturation, thus ensuring maximum quality of well-balanced wines."

★★★ **Merlot** Delaire's new flagship red, **97** first release 1999: eucalyptus leaves on nose, ripe plums, tannins still tight when tasted mid-1998, but loads of promise. From low, 5 ton/ha. yield blocks, all new oak-matured 18 months. Only 200 cases made.

★★★ **Cabernet-Merlot** 55%-45% blend in **97**: plush berries, forest-floor/pine needle leafiness waft from glass, mocha flavours, excellent gently dry finish. New-clone, mostly bush vine cab. portion given 90% new oak for just under year, merlot 30% new oak 9 months.

★★★ **Chardonnay 97** has mellowed elegantly: citrus, spice notes, buttery flavours, still-fresh finish. Blend of 80% oak-fermented/matured (mostly French, touch American) with 20% unwooded wine.

★★★ **Sauvignon Blanc 98** step up on pvs. Wafts of gooseberries, freshly-cut grass lead onto palate. Good crisp finish. 13,3% alc. Merest touch of sugar (3 gms/l) achieves smooth drinkability along with technical dryness.

★★★ **Sauvignon Blanc** NEW **98** barrel-fermented/matured version, most successful: gooseberry, grassy scents brushed with vanilla, all elements nicely balanced on palate, vanilla twirl in tail for added drinking pleasure. 13,5% alc. Half blend oaked (briefly, 3 months), half unwooded.

Green Door Merlot NEW **98** to join second-label range. Oaked 8 mths, 2nd-fill—80% French, 20% American. 12,5% alc. Untasted. **Green Door Cabernet Sauvignon 97** nutty-fruity everyday cab. **Green Door Bubbly** Fresh, fruity, light, just off-dry (only 6 gms/l sugar) summer sparkler.

DE LEUWEN JAGT

Paarl See Paarl map

Tastings/sales Mon-Fri 8.30-5, Sat 9-1. Fee: R3 p/p for 6 "tastes".
Lunches weekdays 11.30-2.30. Specialities: chicken pot pie, bobotie.
Owner: African Farm Investments
Winemaker: Tania Neethling (since 1998)
Vineyards: André Hanekom (since 1985)
Production: ± 400 tons. **Vineyards:** 70 ha.
P.O. Box 505, Suider-Paarl 7624
Tel: 021-8633495 **Fax:** 021-8633797

Fresh European investment is re-energising and refocusing this historic farm on the southern slopes of Paarl mountain, whose name evokes the early days of the Dutch settlement when big-game rather than vines were the attraction. Imminent transformation into an estate will see an identity change to Seidelberg, a reference to the (unnamed) owner rather than a physical attribute of the farm. The range has been split: **Seidelberg** is the new flagship, selected from top-performing plots; **De Leuwen Jagt** is the value range. Up-and-coming Tania Neethling now is responsible for "dovetailing the range to the international taste profile, and producing accessible wines with structure and longevity".

SEIDELBERG range: All NEW.

★★★ **Cabernet Sauvignon-Merlot 97** (first under this new label) deep maroon colour, plummy, leafy, almondy flavours, minty background. Soft, creamy texture, unexpectedly dry finish. 13% alc. 12 mths French oak.

Upcoming **Chenin Blanc 98**, **Sauvignon Blanc 98**, **Chardonnay 98** all untasted.

DE LEUWEN JAGT range:

★★★ **Merlot** Invariably attractive here. **96** growing in complexity, attractive spicy fruitiness, marzipan accents. 13% alc. **95** ripe spicy plum nose, earthy-sweet flavours. **94 VG**.

Chardonnay 97 subdued citric flavours, soft, relaxed sipping. Unwooded. **95** gold SA young wine show. Wood-matured **93 VG**. **Chenin Blanc 97** earthy/waxy, hay/straw tones, dry, quite full, European-style vinosity rather than up-front fruit. **Late Harvest 96** Rhine/Cape riesling, not oversweet, 26 gms/l sugar. Drink young. **Muscadel 96** orange tinted, musk/almond scented sweet red dessert. Richly embroidered palate.

DELHEIM WINES

Simonsberg See Stellenbosch map

Open weekdays 8.30-5, Sat 9.30-3, Sun (Nov-Mar) 11.30-3. Cellar tours Mon-Fri 2.30. Sat 10.30. Vineyard tours (Oct 1-April 30) Mon-Fri 10.30.

Mon-Sat, 12.00-2.30, Sun 12.00-2.30 (Nov 1-Mar 31)

Owners: H.O. Hoheisen, M.H. (Spatz) Sperling
Winemaker: Philip Costandius (since 1987)
Vineyards: Victor Sperling. **Lab:** Karen Boshoff
Production: 80 000 cases. **Vineyards:** 150 ha.
P.O. Box 10, Koelenhof 7605
Tel: 021-8822033 **Fax:** 021-8822036
E-mail: delheim@iafrica.com
Website: www.delheim.com

Delheim's Philip Costandius reckons he'll be drinking a bottle of this cellar's 1988 **Grand Reserve** to see in the millennium. However, given how the profile of his winemaking has changed in the past 5 years, he may find himself opting for a younger red at the last moment. The turn-around in fruit quality has translated into wines that are denser, richer, fuller and infinitely more complex. The full benefits of the vineyard upgrade programme, with increased plantings of premium reds and grubbing out all of the marginal blending grapes are starting to make themselves felt in the latest releases. Flavours and tannins are even riper. More importantly, the sense of focus which has seen a decline in volumes produced and a substantial improvement in quality all round has become a feature of all of Delheim's investments: a new Bucher bag press, a massive upgrade in the cellar's cooling capacity, more—and better—barriques all reveal a willingness to respond to the challenge of international standards. With "job satisfaction the key words", as Costandius comments, good labour relations are also playing a part in Delheim's image.

**** **Cabernet Sauvignon** Convincingly new style, dense-fruited cab. s., **97** with cassis/raspberry aromas, rich textures, new clone spice layered with smoky barrrique (10 months in small barrels) fragrance. Weight and density belie its elegance. A further advance on **96** and **95**, both ripe, berry-rich, forward but not simple. Earlier vintages leafy, a little austere. Regular **VVG**.

**** **Shiraz 97** smoky, leathery, gamey aromas layered with plum/raspberry fruit, mouthfilling, lingering, rich, almost unctuous. Bigger and more complex than similar style **96, 95** and a generation away from much leaner **94** and pvs. Year in large/small oak.

*** **Grand Reserve** Delheim's flagship red since the 1980s, now strongly challenged by own stablemates. **95** riper, with blackcurrant/raspberry aromas, layered with herbal leafy whiffs, mushrooms, slight gaminess. Palate still a little taut, but softer than more minty **93. 92 VVG**.

**** **Pinotage 97** finely balanced youngberry/blackberry fragrance, ripe, soft-textured tannins, almost cassis-like spice. Great amplitude, finesse, length. More complex though no less drinkable than more forward **96**. Year in French oak vats.

★★★ **Pinotage Reserve** NEW Earthier, with more minerally varnishy overtones than above, also **97**: raspberry/loganberry spice, dusty, greenish mid-palate, minty dry finish.

★★★ **Chardonnay** Barrel-fermented tropical butterscotch fragrance, melon/marzipan flavours, fine lime grapefruit finish in **98**. Not quite as plump or forward in **97** with its smoky aromas, whiffs of vanilla, though this was riper, fuller than quite citrusy **96**.

★★★ **Gewürztraminer 98** rose petal/litchi spice, softer and fractionally sweeter than pvs., though with pure (100%) gewürz. character, delicate layered palate, soft melon texture. 15,5 gms/l sugar, 6 gms/l acid.

★★★ **Spatzendreck Late Harvest 98** powerfully aromatic, with distinct muscat spice layering pineapple, pear and rose-petal, sweetish finish, persistent. Blend of muscat de frontignan, gewürz., chenin, sauvignon and Rhine riesling.

★★★ **Edelspatz Noble Late Harvest 98** apricot/pear with whiffs of almost litchi-like fragrance, luscious but not cloying, caramel banana flavours, persistent finish. Blend of botrytised Rhine riesling, bukettraube 110 gms/l sugar.

★★★ **Rhine Riesling Noble Late Harvest** NEW **98** awaft with papaya/pineapple, richly textured palate layered with marzipan, long unctuous finish.

Merlot Plum mulberry fragrance, slight minty whiffs, cherry/raspberry midpalate, accessible **96**. **Dry Red** ◀ Minty, dusty, raspberry aromas in **98**, whiffs of varnish, earthy/minerally palate, a blend of pinotage, ruby cabernet, pinot noir, cab. s., shiraz and merlot, not simple, v. accessible.

Pinotage Rose Laid-back fruit with sweet, well-textured palate more dominant in **98** than pvs. (more aromatic) **97**. Cellar's top seller.

Sauvignon Blanc 98 nettly herby aromas, whiff of figs, slightly lean, taut, though with crisp long finish. Not as concentrated as pvs. **Sémillon 98** with delicate thatch/melon spice, herbal tones, fine but restrained. 67% fermented in large wood. **Heerenwijn 98** blend of colombard, pinot/chenin blanc: citrus/apricot aromas, crisp. **Grandesse 97** blend of sauvignon/pinot blanc, sémillon, fernão pires: spicy, aromatic, off-dry. **Goldspatz Stein** Honeyed grapey notes reveal clean fruit fragrance of equal blend. Colombard, chenin, rich melon palate, semi-sweet but not cloying **98**. **Special Late Harvest 98** lime/apricot aromas, sweet-tangy melon flavours, rich spicy finish. Blend of bukettraube, Rhine riesling. 48 gms/l sugar.

DE MEYE WINES

Stellenbosch See Paarl map

Sales only. By appointment, from Dec 1998.
Owner: Jan Myburgh Family Trust
Winemaker: Ernst Gouws (since 1998)
Production: 13 000 cases, 200 tons. **Vineyards:** 60 ha.
P.O. Box 20, Elsenburg 7607
Tel/Fax: 021-8844154

A new kid on the block, and what a block! The Muldersvlei-Elsenburg area of Stellenbosch has a long-standing reputation as a very superior neighbourhood indeed, featuring farms like Warwick, Simonsig, Kanonkop. The Myburgh family joined this select band of own-label producers in 1998, with their first vintage in a brand-new winery. A maturation cellar is the next building project: the aim is eventually to handle 500 tons. Winemaker is the very experienced Ernst Gouws, of Hoopenburg. Apart from the grapes noted in the wines below, these vineyards also include chenin, chardonnay and riesling. The reds in particular look promising.

Cabernet Sauvignon Infant **98** sample shows good fruit potential. Worth watching. Due for new French oak maturation. **Shiraz 98** with smoky leather scents, promising. Tank-fermented, 5 months new French barrels. **Pinotage** New-born **98** giving practically no hints about itself when tasted mid-year, this a wait-and-see wine. Scheduled for "slight" oaking. **Sauvignon Blanc** Unwooded **98**, bottled very early (May 1998). Unusual pear-drop, barley-sugar nose hints at sweetness to come, but bone-dry. Hint of grass, otherwise not strikingly sauvignon-like. One to fool your mates at a blind tasting. 12,7% alc.

DE TRAFFORD WINES (Mont Fleur Farm)

Stellenbosch See Stellenbosch map

Open any time by appointment.

Home-made (by Rita Trafford, a professional cook) lunch; tour and tasting groups 10-24, booking essential.

Owner: David Trafford
Winemaker: David Trafford (since 1992)
Vineyards: Mavis Trafford
Production: 34 tons, 2 100 cases. **Vineyards:** 3 ha.
P.O. Box 495, Stellenbosch 7599
Tel: 021-8801611 **Fax:** 021-8801611

No one can accuse David Trafford of trying to do things the easy way. His vineyards have been planted on land originally set aside because the slopes were inaccessible for grazing. Every aspect of the winemaking process is labour-intensive, from the decision to ferment only with natural yeasts ("no stuck ferments yet," he records gleefully) to the carefully timed rackings that spare the need to filter before bottling.

At the best of times the pressing season is the most stressful period: harvest decisions are not made by chemical analysis but by a constant regime of tasting the grapes to ensure that they are phenolically ripe. This is not a good time to have to break your routine to fight yet another mountain fire! Still, the vineyards were saved and he reckons the **98 Merlot** is the most promising wine of the vintage.

**** **Cabernet Sauvignon** Increasingly one of the Cape's more sophisticated reds. **97** dense blackcurrant/mulberry fruit from cleaned- up old clone vineyards. (Low-yielding (4 tons/ha.), even-ripening.) Has berry layerings, soft tannins; persistent, richly-textured. Malo in barrels. Fuller, more complex, greater length than equally ripe—though less weighty—**96** where spice and more ephemeral fruit outweigh palate.

**** **Merlot 97** ripe plum/mulberry aromas, sweet but not simple. Mainly French but also new American oak. Malo. Fuller and more sumptuous than **96***** whose finer, almost leafy character reveals slight gamey hints.

*** **Collage 96** a lighter, easier-drinking cab. s./merlot blend, slightly herby notes, quite taut on the finish. **95** mint/eucalyptus aromas, spicy tones.

*** **Pinot Noir 96** black cherry whiffs layered with hints of farmyard, firm-tannined rather than aromatic. Old BK5 clone. **95** less complex, simple berry fruit fragrance.

*** **Chenin Blanc 98 (Keerweder)** from grapes grown on neighbouring Keerweder farm. Smoky barrel-fermented aromas, nutty almond/apricot tones, less limey/pineappley than denser **97.**

*** **Chenin Blanc 97** (De Trafford vineyards) fine lime/apricot fragrance, whiffs of marzipan/prunelle. From old vines, ample development potential, less Chardonnay-like than pvs. elegant, almost austere.

★★★★ **Vin De Paille** De Trafford's signature white wine, a South African first with **97**. Full ripe fruit, rack-dried before fermentation, now showing plump, almost unctuous tropical tones, apricot/pineapple, hints of passion fruit. Alc. (16,6%), acidity (7,5 gms/l) and substantial wood-ageing concealed beneath spectacular fruit opulence. Long lived and lingering. **98** barrel sample tasted while still fermenting. Richer, sweeter, more voluptuous, at that early stage not as complex as benchmark **97**. But give it time . . .

DE VILLIERS WINES

Noorder-Paarl

Tastings/sales by appointment Mon-Fri.
Owners: Villiers de Villiers, Anthony Butler
Winemaker: Frank Meaker (since 1996)
Production: 25 000 cases. **Vineyards:** 180 ha.
P.O. Box 714, Noorder-Paarl 7623
Tel: 021-8638416 **Fax:** 021-8638480

"Keep prices low"—that's a business philosophy consumers everywhere can identify with, none more so than punch-drunk vinophiles who've been battered recently by some hefty rises. The De Villiers range, own-label wines from the historic Paarl mountain family estate, Nantes, certainly are fairly priced and, what's more, from 1998 offer something a little out of the ordinary: a **Cabernet Franc-Merlot** blend. "We're very excited about this wine," says Villiers de Villiers, co-owner of the winery which, in support of its labourers, particularly the children, maintains a trust fund replenished by, among others, proceeds from an annual auction of the estate's enviably compact range, made by Frank Meaker of nearby Ruitersvlei.

★★★ **Cabernet Sauvignon** ◀ Big, bold **97**, with soupçon of spicy cab. franc, improving well in bottle. Nice clean-oaky undercurrents throughout, long finish. Oak/chip-fermented. 13% alc. Winemaker says: "Delicate"; we say: beefy, muscular, in trademark Meaker idiom—but very nice! Snip at under R15 ex-cellar. Sold to Gall & Gall of the Netherlands as Heren van Oranje.

De Villiers Reserve Cabernet Franc-Merlot ◀ NEW **97** attractive ripe blue-plum nose, sweet-fruity tastes, fairly relaxed mouth-feel, nice fresh finish. Though drinkable now, winemaker's right: "Has long way to go." Components separately oaked, new/used barrels, Allier/Nevers, 8-15 mths. 13% alc. **Merlot** ◀ best-selling wine in range; **97** shows why. Big-framed, full of ripe plums, smooth, soft. Passa da pasta! 13% alc. **Chardonnay 98** kicks off splendidly with fresh pear-drop breezes, then falls away quickly to dry oaky finish. Needs time, winemaker reckons. So one to watch. Pvsly American-oaked, now French (Alliers), 6 mths. ± 13% alc. **Sauvignon Blanc 97** acquiring mantle of honey over tropical fruit-salad; fresh, crisp dry drinking. Sturdy 13% alc. **Chenin Blanc 98** lightly wooded, freshened by smidgen (Paarl) riesling. Ripe peachy tones, challenging dry. Quarter-century-old vines.

DEVONCREST

See Meinert Winery

DEVON HILL

See Sonop

DE WET CO-OP WINE CELLAR

Worcester, Breede River Valley See Worcester map

Tastings/sales Mon-Fri 8-5. Sat 9-12. Tasting fee (if no purchases made): 50c/wine. Cellar tours daily only in pressing season. Otherwise Wed, Fri by appointment.
Owners: 56 members
Manager/Winemaker: Zakkie Bester (since 1989)
Winemaker: Piet le Roux
Production: 15 500 tons. **Vineyards:** 950 ha.
P.O. Box 16, De Wet 6853
Tel: 0231-92710 **Fax:** 0231-92762

"Let's party!" is a conclusion that often springs to mind when tasting this friendly Worcester co-op's suggestively festive range, which is showing the benefits of modern cellar technology and a programme to match grape varieties to soil types. "In **98**, for the first time, we were able to cool the grape musts prior to fermentation, producing fresher, more concentrated flavours," say adroit cellar duo Zakkie Bester and Piet le Roux. Noteworthy additions are a premium range—oak-influenced **Cabernet Sauvignon** and **Chardonnay**—specially packaged in lipped bottles with labels by local young sight-impaired artists. Clearly these additions are meant to be taken a little more seriously, but they lack nothing of the break-dancing, *sakkie-sakkie* party-seeking exuberance of their stablemates.

*** **Droë Rooi** ☺ ◀ Yet another change to this super-quaffable keep-'em-guessing blend. Pvs. featured riffs on cab.-merlot-shiraz melody, dual/multi-vintage variations. **98** sees Bester/Le Roux jamming with 2 varieties, 2 vintages: merlot **98** (40%), cab. **98** (40%), cab. **97**. Result: delicious soft mouthful, ripe brambleberry fruit, oaky top-notes from French barrels/staves. 12,5% alc. Value at ± R12 ex-cellar.

*** **Hanepoot** ◀ **97** fresh, super-smooth honeysuckle/fuchsia-scented jerepigo from full-ripe muscat d'Alexandrie. Sweetness (185 gms/l sugar), lifted by fine acidity. Sip solo, or pour over ice-cream, fresh fruit salad. **93 VG.**

Blanc de Noir ☺ ◀ Habitually personable, al fresco quaffer all but yells "drink me" in **98**. Unusual blue-pink, delicate boiled-sweets aroma, clean, gently dry finish. From pinotage. Reasonably tame 12,5% alc.; drier-than-it-sounds 14 gms/l sugar. **Chardonnay** ☺ ◀ NEW Makes animated début with **98**. Breezy tropical fruit, vanilla suggestions; lovely silky texture, crisp, dry farewell. Super summertime sipping. Tank-matured on French oak staves. 13% alc. **Sauvignon Blanc** ◀ Herby, grassy, crisply dry **98** should liven up any surfin' safari. **Cape Riesling** ☺ ◀ **98** step up from pvs.; fresher, fruitier. New-mown hay, barley-sugar accents. Politely dry. "This is how we like our Cape Riesling!" **Clairette Blanche** ◀ Return to form in **98**. More character, nice grape, fresh hay nuances. Low alc. (10,5%) for easy drinking. **96 VG. Bouquet Blanc** ◀ NEW **98** amiable off-dry fernão pires/colombard/clairette blanche confit. Replaces Fernão Pires in range—"consumers couldn't get their tongues around name!" **Gewürztraminer Special Late Harvest** ◀ Ripe, almost voluptuous muscat essences in **98**. Nice crisp finish. Hugely appealing. Try with Cape Malay dishes. Frisky, grapey, slightly spritzy **Pétillant Fronté** ◀ usually flies out of cellar faster than any. **98** in fine fettle, light-hearted/bodied, off-dry. 100% muscat de frontignan, extra-low 8,1% alc., 29 gms/l sugar. Approved by the Heart Foundation. **Cuvée Brut** NV chirpy off-dry carbonated foamer from sauvignon blanc. 12 gms/l sugar. Morning-after friendly 11,5% alc. **Vin Doux** Gewürz./muscat de frontignan blend. Grapey zing, intriguing spicy hints. 65 gms/l sugar. Low 10,5% alc. For sweet-toothed party-animals. **Red Muscadel 97** easy after-dinner style. Ripe prunes, raisins; very sweet. Grapes from celebrated Nuy Valley. **Port** Latest **(97)** most agreeable, quite oaky, herbaceous. 90% shiraz, merlot, matured 3 months Nevers staves. In modern drier style (104 gms/l sugar).

DE WETSHOF ESTATE

Robertson See Robertson map

Visits: Open 8.30-4.30; Sat 9.30-1. Cellar tours by appointment.
Owner: Danie de Wet
Winemaker: Danie de Wet. **Assistant:** John Loubser
Production: 1 800 tons, 35 000 cases. **Vineyards:** 150 ha.
P.O. Box 31, Robertson 6705
Tel: 0234-51853/7 **Fax:** 0234-51915
E-mail: dewetshof@xpoint.co.za

His impressive stature matches the space he occupies in the SA wine industry. Danie de Wet is now a hyperactive KWV director, and has certainly made his mark abroad as one of the country's most proficient white wine makers. As he says, when surveying the beautifully proportioned replica of the old family home, the Koopmans De Wet House in Cape Town's Strand Street, now duplicated on his farm near Bonnievale: "A man must leave something for his children—I'll leave this. After all, they never knew the original . . . now they can have some idea of our past." But one of the most significant legacies this energetic man will leave is his approach to staff: for years the children of farm workers have enjoyed the facilities of a 5-star créche supervised by Lesca de Wet—kids delivered in the morning are handed back bathed, fed and educated each evening. The pair's involvement in community affairs is widely spread, from monthly management meetings with workers, to tractor drivers' courses; very much in tune with the expectations of overseas customers, who judge not only the quality of the wine these days. On that front, the cellar now boasts some of the most classy continuous cold stabilisation and bottling kit in the country, part of the plan to replace most equipment over the next few years. And watch out for the first reds from the estate—pinot noir in the offing, to match the range of award-winning chardonnays.

*** **Bateleur Chardonnay** This wine always a "barrel select" offering; complexity enhanced by sensitive wood treatment. **97** delicate lemon-cream nose, toasty, citrus flavours. 14,1% alc. promises great longevity—**95** still beautifully lively, with bright leesy finish.

*** **Chardonnay d'Honneur 95** intriguing buttery brioche nose, hint of toast, walnuts; still firm, developing lovely leesy, honeyed flavours from full oak treatment.

*** **Bon Vallon Chardonnay** ☺ ◀ **98** has gorgeous peach blossom aromas, hints of walnuts, thatch. A great, juicy mouthful—almost sweet, with balancing acid tweak. (3,2 gms/l sugar, 7,1 gms/l acid.) Surprisingly rich and complex for unwooded wine. **97** less voluptuous, more elegant, with melon flavours.

*** **Gewürztraminer 98** huge scented wafts of jasmine aromas, sweet pineapple/peach flavours; very light, supple style—only 7,8% alc., 89 gms/l sugar: Germanic touch.

*** **Rhine Riesling** ◀ **98** complex cinnamon, honey whiffs, bright lemony flavours, with hints of grapefruit, quince. Long, tart, firm, dry finish with plenty of scope for cellaring—try 5 years.

*** **Mine d'Or 98** like its name—yellow-gold of hue; shy, spicy Rhine riesling nose followed by well balanced limey flavours—another light, low alcohol, nicely balanced sweet wine.

★★★★ **Edeloes Rhine Riesling Noble Late Harvest 98** rich orange-gold hue, intense peach, apricot botrytis aromas which move on to silky tangerine flavours—perfect balance. 187 gms/l sugar, and a high 10 gms/l total acidity.

★★★★ **Muscat de Frontignan Blanc ◀ 98** an absolute delight: packed with orange rind and raisin fruits, a complex, elegantly fortified dessert wine with tangy acidity in finish. (6,1 gms/l, with light 15,3% alc.)

Chardonnay Finesse (**Lesca** in some export markets). Popular lightly wooded style, **97** with clean pear and melon aromas, bright refreshing lemony flavours—chardonnay to drink! **93** won Danie de Wet 1994 Diners Club Winemaker of the Year award. **Sauvignon Blanc 98** shows green grass/nettles on nose, some figgy whiffs; quite weighty, dry and supple. **Blanc Fumé 98** wooded sauvignon has herbaceous Karoo-bush aromas, slight hint of oak, crisper than above. **Blanc de Wet 98** with whopping peach and passion-fruit nose, chardonnay/sauvignon blend. Tangy, harmonious drinking.

Export labels: Tesco Reserve Chardonnay (★★★) with bracing pear, peach and vanilla character. **Tesco Robertson Chardonnay 98. Sainsbury's S.A. Chardonnay NV. De Wetshof Sainsbury's Chardonnay Reserve 98. Asda Cape Muscat de Frontignan** in marked Beaumes-de-Venise style (15% alc.).

DE ZOETE INVAL ESTATE

Paarl See Paarl map

Tastings/sales Mon-Sat 9-5, incl. public holidays (except religious holidays).

Owner: Adrian Frater
Winemakers: Adrian Frater (since 1952), Gerard Frater
Production: 300 tons. **Vineyards:** 65 ha.
P.O. Box 591, Suider-Paarl 7624
Tel: 021-8632375 **Fax:** 021-8632817

A warm welcome—and one of the Cape's most individual ranges—are what visitors to this enchanting winelands institution will find, promises Gerard Frater, easy-going son of proprietor Adrian. One or more family members—Gerard's siblings John Robert, Dan, sister Yogi, matriarch Suna or Adrian himself—are always on hand to offer opinions, advice about the range, which will delight connoisseurs of older vintages—a 1977 cab. is available—and fans of a more rustic, non-conformist style.

Chloë 75% cinsaut-cabernet blend, chocolate box flavours, dry, herby. **Yvette** Wooded sauvignon blanc; fresh herbal notes on nose; dry herby-savoury flavours, distinctly oaky finish. **Capri** NV 100% chard., doesn't broadcast varietal character but clean, dry, pleasant. **Late Harvest** NV from sauvignon, definitely sweet, vegetal sauvignon fruit peeping through. **Port** Star of the range: aficionados might disagree with "port" label; "fortified wine" perhaps more appropriate. Still, agreeable herby/fruity character, not oversweet. 17% alc.

DIAMANT

Paarl See Paarl map

Tastings/sales by appointment. Function hall for hire.

Owner: Niel Malan
Winemaker: Niel Malan (since 1992)
Production: ± 200 cases. **Vineyards:** 45 ha.

P.O. Box 509, Suider-Paarl 7624
Tel/Fax: 021-8631508

This diamond at Paarl is unpolished in the best, traditional winemaking sense. Grapes are crushed underfoot, bottled without filtration; results are unpretentious, elemental. Joining the micro-range in 1998 is an uncertified **Pinotage**, aged a year in barrel.

DIE KRANS

Calitzdorp See Klein Karoo map

Tastings, sales weekdays 8-5; Sat 9-1. Cellar tours Dec., April school holidays; self-guided vineyard tours year round (vineyard walk).
Vintners platters for groups of more than 10.
Winemakers: Boets & Stroebel Nel
Production: 650 tons, 15 000 cases. **Vineyards:** 60 ha.
P.O. Box 28, Calitzdorp 6660
Tel: 04421-33314/64 **Fax:** 04421-33562

Dedicated, high-aiming Boets Nel's vision for this cellar: "To be the top Port producer in South Africa." Keeping the sights as high as ever, he also believes in keeping the target moving. Contributing to this effort, he feels, will be the de-regulation of Die Krans as an estate: both he and assiduous brother Stroebel share the vineyard duties, certain that their concentration in this area will reap richer rewards than overkill technology in the cellar; they recognise the need to buy in some premium fruit from cooler vineyards, hence their quest for superior 98 sauvignon blanc grapes from Durbanville—permissible for non-estates. Planting more red varieties, including pinotage, merlot and cabernet, they acknowledge not only the region's suitability for these grapes in their environment, but the demands from foreign markets, particularly Benelux countries and Germany, where buyers have shown approval of reds from this cellar. "But we'll never buy in grapes for Port" assures Boets—coals to Newcastle! With new plantings of touriga naçional, tinta roriz and souzão building up steam, would they want to? Investment in a new crusher has improved quality of wines, he believes, particularly chardonnay: "softer, with much more fruit". A lightning trip through Tuscany, the Rhône and Alsace added to the thesaurus of viticultural knowledge of this Cape Winemaster, and convinced him that his sortie into the olive oil business would be a popular and worthwhile move. Look out, in 1999, for the 97 Klein Karoo Young wine show champion from Die Krans—its **Vintage Reserve Port**. It should be a clever investment if the **91** is anything to go by: it sold at the 1998 Nederburg Auction for R143 per bottle . . . compared to the R25 asking price on release.

★★★★ **Vintage Reserve Port** Less emphasis on wood maturation marks this **97**, latest in a line of established champs, only "declared" in exceptional years: 90% tinta barocca from low-yielding vineyards over 20 yrs old, with balance from newer plantings of souzão, tinta roriz and touriga naçional. Vibrantly plum-coloured, dense prune, tobacco, spice aromas. Fleshy, chunky mouthful of flavours, showing muscular tannic grip, sweetened with a concentrated mélange of all manner of red berries, backed by a healthy dollop of fine brandy spirit for posterity; potential ★★★★★, deservedly gold at SA young wine show. 19,2% alc., 89 gms/l sugar. 16 mths in mix of 500 l larger vats. **95** WINE★★★★(★) straight tinta barocca, now softening, but still with plenty of spicy chocolate, fennel, warm stewed fruits. **94** slowly coming round, showing intense prune flavours, still some years to go.

★★★★ **White Muscadel Jerepigo** In lighter, fruitier, less cloying style—altogether more modern; minimum raisins harvested, great care to ensure full ripeness. **98**, bright pale lemon gold, huge perfumed nose—jasmine, honeysuckle—followed by elegant silky texture with litchi and herb flavours. These age beautifully: become more nutty and caramelised, with glowing, mouthfilling finish. As in **97-95** all ★★★ , with addition of orange peel flavours. Around 17% alc. Watch for the upmarket, half bottle, silk-screened Reserve when released.

★★★ **Port (Cape Vintage)** Made every year, now lauded as one of SA's premium standard-vintage ports. **97** similar blend to Reserve. but tinta from younger v'yds: complex gamey, choc flavours—great grip and power, verging on ★★★★. 18,5% alc., 92 gms/l sugar, 18 mths in 500 l barrels. Striking black/white screen-printed bottle. As no Vintage Reserve declared in 97, portion blended into the **96** showing complex eucalyptus, cinnamon, plummy notes; more developed than **97**, similar structure, without touriga's choc aromas. **95** still has peppery, prune-like flavours, now drinking smoothly.

★★★ **Port (Cape Ruby** non vintage) ◀ Now with dash of touriga, souzão and roriz fleshing out the tinta barocca backbone, this fine Cape Ruby particularly admired by Fonseca's Bruce Guimaraens from Portugal, attending the annual Calitzdorp Port Festival tasting in July 98. Now also in handsome screen-printed bottle; plummy, nut and chocolate flavours, beautifully balanced—a marvel at the price: the most popular wine from this cellar.

Cabernet ◀ **97** bright green-olive, cassis character, softly-fleshed palate, supple tannins. **96** shows pleasing bottle development, warm stewed fruit flavours, less body. Part barrel maturation 2nd-fill Nevers oak. **Pinotage** ◀ **97** 8 tons/ha. from 23-yr v'yd: warm plummy nose, sensitive use of 2nd-fill French oak, juicy, savoury finish. **96** offers mulberry scents, warm peppery flavours. **Tinta Barocca** ◀ **97** with generous plum, smoky whiffs, light, unwooded, good value Chianti look-alike. **Vin Rouge NV** tinta-based blend, in 250 ml size for handy use.

Chardonnay ◀ **98** Afrikaans label: unwooded, mostly for Belgian mkt. 5 clones, elegant citrus, limey aromas, fat creamy palate. English label: wooded, mix of barrel/stave treatment: delicate melon and butterscotch aromas, subtle toasty finish. **Chenin Blanc** ◀ **98** continues pvs. trend towards more "serious" chenin. Ripe pear, melon notes, subtle oak treatment, bone-dry, elegant. **Sauvignon Blanc** NEW **98** from Durbanville fruit ("Calitzdorp too warm for this variety", notes Nel). Quiet fig, nettle aromas, steely and dry. **Golden Harvest** ◀ **98** fernão pires/gewürz. blend; basket of tropical fruit aromas, lovely tangy balance. Full-sweet at 39 gms/l sugar. **Late Harvest 97** similar blend to above, semi-sweet style (24 gms/l); a cellar door favourite.

Spumanté Finely carbonated hanepoot (60%), colombard (40%), sparkler; juicy, well balanced (11,5% alc., 48 gms/l sugar).

Heritage Collection White Jerepigo Profits to Gamka Mountain Nature Reserve; **97** (Pied Barbet label) pale polished gold; pungent hay, jasmine aromas, supple, elegant, full-sweet fruit. **96** (Gamkaberg Opal Butterfly label), nose more developed, now seems more oily and unctuous. Made from fully ripe chenin, fortified after 36 hours' skin contact to 17% alc.

DIEMERSDAL ESTATE

Durbanville See Durbanville map

Mon-Fri 9-5, Sat 9-3.

Functions (min 10, max 80) by special arrangement.

Cellar Tours: February and March

Owner: Tienie Louw
Winemaker: Tienie Louw (since 1976)
Vineyards: Div van Niekerk (since 1980)
Production: 8 000 cases. **Vineyards:** 170 ha.
P.O. Box 27, Durbanville 7551
Tel: 021-963361 **Fax:** 021-961810

1998 was the Louw family centenary at Diemersdal. It is also the tercentenary of the grant of the farm. Notwithstanding these centuries of tradition however, Tienie Louw believes that a combination of innovation and an ability to supply wines that cost less than their anticipated price point the direction he must follow. "Sell a £7-99 wine for £6-99 and you will survive the future," he maintains. The changes he plans include a new pressing cellar, stainless steel fermenters to help maximise fruit and colour extraction—particularly from his old clone vineyards—and a replanting programme to ensure a greater percentage of virus-free premium varietals. With his export wines vinified and distributed by SAVISA (see entry) he is responding not only to domestic market demand, but also to increasing international sales targets.

★★★★ **Shiraz** Standout, densely fruited, sumptuous **96**, raspberry/youngberry bouquet, gamey leathery whiffs, opulent texture, ripe plummy tannins, 65% French Nevers, 35% American oak. **95** sweeter, simpler style, with discernible farmyard aromas.

★★★★ **Pinotage** Plum/loganberry fragrance, whiffs of almond/prunelle, fruitcake notes, dense solid palate, clove layerings on finish of **96**. Plumper than more gamey **94**, in turn fuller than quite austere **93**.

★★★ **Private Collection** Cab. s. (75%), cab. f. (15%), merlot (10%) blend, ample fruit, firm tannins. **96** raspberry, cassis aromas, layered with fine prunelle fragrance, leafy, dusty notes, elegant not sparse. **94** blackcurrant, berry fruit, herbal whiffs. Riper than more eucalyptus-style **93**.

★★★ **Cabernet Sauvignon** First vintage **96** from entirely virus-free vineyards. Blackcurrant minty bouquet, jammy dry tannins, vanilla spice on finish. **94** ripe blackberry fragrance, intense palate, persistent. **93** fruit compôte, marzipan chocolate notes.

DIE POORT

Herbertsdale See Klein Karoo map

Tasting/sales Mon-Fri 8-5. Sat 8-1. Cellar tours by appointment. Wines also for sale at Wine Gallery, Mossel Bay. Tel: 0444-911811. Cellar tours by appointment.

Restaurant open only for group bookings, in advance; except during December holidays when open daily.

Owner/Winemaker: Jannie Jonker (since 1980)
Production: 10 000 cases. **Vineyards:** 80 ha.
P.O. Box 45, Albertinia 6795
Tel: 02934-52406 **Fax:** 02934-52347

A visit to Europe in 1998 proved an eye-opening experience for Jannie Jonker, whose estate at Herbertsdale, 40-minutes from Mossel Bay is one of the more colourful wine (and country cuisine) venues. After quizzing umpteen *vignerons*, traipsing through copious *vigneti*, he concluded that "SA's cellar technology and vineyard techniques are streets ahead of their Continental counterparts". Thus encouraged, Jonker is striding ahead with plans to quadruple red wine production, double output of his popular spirits which include an elegantly presented *eau de vie* from Langkloof apples, traditional *witblits*—"in grappa style"—and pot-still brandy.

Hemelrood 97 cabernet/pinotage in comfortable, light-toned partnership. **Cabernet Sauvignon 97** easy, personable, early drinking. **Pinotage** Vintner says **97** is "massive, fruity"; we think fruity yes, but light, easy; agreeable braai wine. **Premier Grand Crû 97** untasted, from colombard. Usually lean, clean. **Blanc de Blanc 97** off-dry, white muscadel, steen. **Frölich Stein** ◀ Semi-sweet, fruity summer picnic companion. **Lissa Jonker Hanepoot 97** buckets of fresh muscat flavour, unusual spiced-apple finish. Dessert made by teenager Lissa Jonker (uninhibited with father's alc.: 20,5%!). **Golden Jerepigo 96** bright gold, marmalade-scented, not oversweet, from muscadel. **Raisin Jerepigo 97** exotic variety: hárslevelü, unusual olive-grove scent; sweet, raisiny, long honeyed finish. **Rooi Port 97** congenial aperitif, from pinotage. **Camilla Perlé 97** White muscadel, semi-sweet, refreshing bubble. Other wines in range: **Cape St Blaize Dry, Late Harvest, Vin Brut, Demi Sec, Vin Doux, White Jerepigo, Red Jerepigo, Sweet Jerepigo, Selected White Jerepigo 83, Selected Red Jerepigo 81.**

DIEU DONNÉ VINEYARDS

Franschhoek See Franschhoek map

Tastings/sales Feb-Nov 9-4; Dec-Jan 9-4; throughout year Sat 9.30-12.30; Sun closed. Tasting fee R4 p/p for groups. Cellar tours by arrangement.

Owners: Maingard family
Winemaker: Stephan du Toit (since 1997)
Production: 10 000 cases. **Vineyards:** 26 ha.
P.O. Box 94, Franschhoek 7690
Tel: 021-8762493 **Fax:** 021-8762102

The Maingard family's traditionally white wine-denominated operation high above Franschhoek is charting a new course. Red plantings, including pinotage, shiraz, are joining award-winning cabernet sauvignon vines on the spectacular viewsite property. Allied to recent purchases of vineyards at nearby Normandie and La Cotte, this will result in a 70/30 premium red/white bias within 2 years. The transformation plays to the strength of young hands-on Stephan du Toit, who made red wine at Nederburg before taking over this high-potential cellar in 1997.

*** **Cabernet Sauvignon 96**, like pvs., hints at heights to which Franschhoek red can rise. Ripeness, concentration, balance, bags of fruity charm, approachability. Complexity, too, in profusion of cherry/berry extracts, toasty hazelnut/vanilla overlay. Lighter to medium-bodied (12% alc.) style; fine ripe tannin also distinguished **95, 94**. 50% Nevers barrels, none new. **93 VG**.

*** **Chardonnay** ◀ (Wooded) **97** follows trademark fusion of oaky-sweet butterscotch, lime zest. Fresh, tangy mouthfeel broadened—not overwhelmed—by higher alc. (13,5%). Oak-fermented, 10 months Nevers barrels, two-thirds new. Should mature well, develop greater complexity in bottle. Stand-out **92** gold in UK Wine magazine's International Wine Challenge.

Merlot Fine cherry/raspberry-toned, violet-tongued **96** perceptibly softer-edged than pvs, which needed 2-4 years for stern tannins to unwind. Plush texture, seamless oak. 50% aged 10 months French barriques, none new. **Rosé** Off-dry alfresco quaffer freshened by cherry, strawberry touches. 13% alc., 20 gms/l sugar. **Chardonnay** (Unwooded) ◀ **97** burnished by bottle-age, drinking nicely. Understated butterscotch, grapefruit suggestions; fine citrus tang. Easy, dry. Whole bunch-pressed. 13,5% alc. **Sauvignon Blanc 98** unwooded; extra-concentrated ripe tropical aromas/tastes, fresh, dry. Alc. kick in tail (13,6%). **Évêque 97** Noble Late Harvest from chenin. Subtle sherbet, lemon hints; inklings of botrytis, peaches, apricots; very fresh acid. 124 gms/l sugar.

DISTILLERS CORPORATION

Part of the Rembrandt Group, important producer of premium, medium and lower-priced wines, spirits. The Group is affiliated to Stellenbosch Farmers' Winery (SFW), Gilbeys, the KWV.

See also **SA Wine Cellars**, **Bergkelder**.

P.O. Box 184, Stellenbosch 7599
Tel: 021-8883200 **Fax:** 021-8870728

DOMEIN DOORNKRAAL

De Rust, Klein Karoo See Klein Karoo map

Tastings/sales Mon-Fri 9-5. Sat 8-1. Farm/cellar visits by appointment. School holidays: Mon-Fri 8-6. Sat 8-1. On De Rust-Oudtshoorn road.
Meals for groups of 10 or more by appointment.
Owners: Swepie & Piet le Roux
Winemaker: Piet le Roux (since 1996)
Production: 350 tons. **Vineyards:** 35 ha.
P.O. Box 14, De Rust 6650
Tel: 044-2516715 **Fax:** 044-2412548

Urbane proprietor Swepie le Roux—he's the KWV Director for Klein Karoo—and his son Piet make one of the most unusual—not to mention colourful—ranges in all the winelands. Charming silk-screened packaging, tongue-in-cheek labels ("Major", "Lieutenant"), shocking pink ostrich feathers—all create a delightful, highly original ambience. This, after all, is Kannaland (as the locals refer to the region)—a dreamy world-within-a-world where magic and reality converge. Domein Doornkraal is not only about frivolous bijou dusters and Chagall-like imagery, however. Piet le Roux, who took over the reins officially in 1997 (Le Roux Snr. had been winemaker since 1959!), has worked overseas (Mondavi Winery, California) and is keeping up to date with international trends.

*** **Merlot-Pinotage 97** in feisty form. Lovely plum, violet scents, ripe fruit, grippy but not unpleasant tannins. Lick of chocolate in almost sweet finish (3,5 gms/l sugar). Very drinkable now, has backbone to hold yr or 2. Nice!

Merlot NEW Variety makes agreeable choc-cassis flavoured impression in **97**, featuring curious sweet/dry mix of tannins, long clean finish. **Cabernet Sauvignon** NEW **97** first varietal cab. from this cellar—quite a serious wine. First impression (of barrel sample) is ripe strawberries, underpinned by very substantial tannins. Yr in barrel (still a way to go). In present state will need 3-4 yrs at least and/or ostrich casserole or other robust food. **Sauvignon Blanc** NEW **97** Light-flavoured (though not light-bodied at over 13% alc.), some gooseberry suggestions, off-dry at 6 gms/l sugar. **Steen-Sémillon** NEW **97** clean, dry, sémillon plays muted rôle. 13% alc. **Serenade** NEW **97** blend of steen, colombard, muscat; dry white. **Doornkraal Tinta Bianca Effe-droog** ◀ **97** vivid coral tint, light earthy aromas/flavours, challengingly dry-tasting despite 8,5 gms/l sugar. From muscat, merlot, pinotage. **Kuierwyn Sweet Natural 97** gentle fruity flavours. ("Kuier" is Afrikaans for dropping in on friends.) **Hanepoot** NV "Liquid raisins" is winemaker's apropos comment. His serving suggestion: "Pour over ice and spike with very dry gin, twist of lemon." **Kaptein** ◀ Blend red muscat/Pinta/chenin; wood-matured 3 yrs. Fruitcake/nuts/spirit on nose/palate. **Majoor** ◀ NV golden jerepigo steen. **Luitenant** ◀ From Zanté currants, muscat, wood-matured 3 yrs. Intensely fresh raisin-flavoured. Made by fortifying 50% at pressing, rest after partial fermentation: formula used by Swepie le Roux's father. **Pinta NV** ◀ Dessert jerepigo from pinotage, tinta barocca. Latest bottling (**96**) very individual with distinct porty overtones. **White Port** NV Not too sweet, matured 3 yrs in cask; firm, twist of citrus, gravelly finish. Try with ice as aperitif. **Port** NV Soft honeyed spices, chocolates. From tinta barocca, pinotage. **Tickled Pink** ☺ NV Blush-pink bubbly, salad of merlot, pinotage, muscat, steen, strictly non-serious, gently sweet. Swepie le Roux's comment: "Raises blood-sugar, loosens the tongue." Lowish alc. (± 11%), 60 gms/l sugar. Shocking pink ostrich bijou duster optional extra.

DOUGLAS GREEN

"The negociant rôle isn't fully undertaken or understood in SA," opines Douglas Green Bellingham's Marketing Director Jacques Roux, who keeps a hawk-eye on this admirable, fairly-priced, 100 000-cases-a-year range selected from various cellars by DGB's Gary Baumgarten, Johann Bruce, with Sterik de Wet, Johan Schreuder of KWV. The range, exported to Belgium, Sweden, the UK, Germany, is predominantly white (65%) though consumers' clamour for reds doubtless will have an impact here in the longer term.

Marketing Director: Jacques Roux
Tel: 021-8741690 **Fax:** 021-8741011

*** **Cabernet Sauvignon** ◀ Ever-dependable dry red has morphed into quite a serious wine. **96** minty, spicy, packed with ripe blackcurrants, pleasantly weighty, supple tannin. More approachable than **95**, which still needs yr or so to settle. **93 VVG, WINE****.**

*** **Cabernet-Shiraz** ◀ NEW **95** very drinkable, with all the positive attributes of this dry, hot vintage: inky colour, ripe fruit, fullness, plush flavour. Cherry/blackberry spectrum, gamey twists.

*** **Pinotage** ◀ **96** ripe red berries, appetising gamey notes, lots of flavour, foodily-dry finish.

St Augustine ◀ **95** quite a fat specimen, in line with vintage: deep colour, compôte red/black berries, some cassis, moderately grippy tannin. As always amiable tablemate. **93 VG**. Varietal rainbow: cabernet sauvignon, tinta barocca, shiraz, pinotage, merlot. **St Raphael** ☺ **NV** perennial easy-drinking, light-coloured/bodied red. Rosé colour telegraphs undemanding quaffing qualities; pinotage/cinsaut blend, loads of cherry-toned fruit. **Chardonnay 97** citrus/peach presence, oaky nuances, mouthfilling. **Sauvignon Blanc 98** gooseberry freshness. **St Morand** Range's top seller. Reason? "Value and style." Sappy juicy/fruity flavours, off-dry white, muscat finery. **St Anna** Semi-sweet white, ripe, grapey flavours, clean finish. "Non-intrusive conversation wine," our taster says.

DOUGLAS WINERY

Douglas, Northern Cape See Orange River map

Tastings/sales Mon-Fri 8-5. Cellar tours by appointment.
Owners: 56 members
Winemaker: Pou le Roux (since 1978)
Viticulturist: Danie Kershoff
Production: ± 7 000 cases. **Vineyards:** ± 500 ha.
P.O. Box 47, Douglas 8730
Tel: 053-2981910 **Fax:** 053-2981845

Winemaker Pou le Roux, part of the furniture at this far-flung, warm-climate winery near the confluence of the Orange and Vaal rivers—he joined 21 years ago—can't recall an earlier vintage than 1998: "Harvest started on Jan. 6th , finished on Feb 20th. Never seen the likes of it." If he and the growers had their way, climatic problems soon might be a thing of the past: they fantasise about a wind tunnel to bring breezes from the West Coast to cool the frazzled v'yds, though one imagines this grandiose scheme will remain something of a pipe-dream. Meanwhile, in the real world, the cellar plans to increase red wine production—now there's a workable idea!—and branch into the export arena "sometime in the future".

*** **Red Muskadel** ◀ **97** gorgeous, burnished amber tint, soft raisiny character, warm but fresh, not too weighty, lovely spirity tingle. **95** Class winner SA Show. 17% alc.

Pinotage ◀ **98** amiable braai partner, bouncy plummy flavours, fresh. Full bodied (13% alc), unwooded, early drinking. **Ruby Cabernet 96** with unusual green pepper-Karoo bush overtones, very dry, somewhat tannic. Unwooded. **Dry Red** 50/50 ruby cab/pinotage. Earthy/nutty grip, sweet-sour finish. Apparently custom-designed for BBQed mutton chops! **Mustique 97** bright coral-coloured blanc de noir from muscadel. Label says: "Seductively piquant." Yes, in muscat/honeysuckle mode, finishes dry though 10 gms/l sugar, lowish alc. (11%). **Colnay** NEW **97** chard./colombard blend, clean, discernibly dry, honey-tobacco-pouch finish. Very lightly wooded. **Colombard 97** light-bodied, muted litchi/guava, distinctly dry, undemanding. **Grand Cru** Dry white blend: chenin, cape riesling, colombard, sauvignon blanc. Untasted. **Gewürztraminer 97** lovely buttercup yellow, honey-sweet overtones. Sugar 26 gms/l; low alc. (10,7%). **94** SA gold. **Stein** NV Current (**97**) pleasant tropical spectrum, not overly sweet, nice. Light-bodied (10,9% alc.), chenin/colombard. **Late Vintage** NV, gentle muscat fragrance, light-bodied, semi-sweet, hanepoot/colombard, 26 gms/l sugar. **Soet Hanepoot** (Formerly Muscat d'Alexandrie). Untasted. Usually luscious nutty-sweet dessert, around 17% alc. **Rooi Jerepiko** ◀ NV An individual: smells/tastes (most pleasantly) of freshly ploughed furrows, light-textured, from ruby cabernet, not oversweet. **95** SA champion non-muscat fortified wine. Bargain at R10,50 ex-cellar. **Port** untasted. Also: in 5l boxes **Dry Red**, **Grand Cry**, **Stein**, **Late Harvest**.

DROSTDY WINES LIMITED (Drostdy-Hof Wines)

Tulbagh See Tulbagh map

Tastings/sales: Mon-Fri 8.30-12, 1.30-5; Sat 8.30-12. Tasting fee R5 p/p. Cellar tours 11 and 3 weekdays.
Owner: SA Wine Cellars
Winemaker/Cellarmaster: Frans du Toit (since 1968)
P.O. Box 9, Tulbagh 6820
Tel: 0236-301086 **Fax:** 0236-300510

Frans du Toit has practically patented the combination of magnetic value—quality—Schwarzeneggerish dependability which make for a consumer hit. Make that plural—not just one ace, but a fusillade of winning serves. It's this form which explains why both the **Chardonnay** and the **Light** are SA's top sellers; and why discerning WINE magazine readers have voted both the **Chardonnay** and the **Merlot** into their top-tranche of "SA reds/whites under R20".

*** **Merlot** ◀ **98** lots of ripe berries, good mouth-feel, very agreeable 5,4 gms/l acid, big 13% alc. Remarkable value/fruit/flavour, easy to drink. Very nice.

*** **Cape Red** ◀ **98** complex, ripe berry fruit nicely oaked, soft texture, long finish. Pinotage, shiraz, ruby cab.

*** **Adelpracht Special Late Harvest** ◀ **98** budget price but big mouthful, fruit-salad of aromas/flavours, fresh honey/lemon finish.

Mainly chenin with touch gewürz, hanepoot. Very good chilled aperitif or with fresh fruit (mango, peach in particular). 11,6% alc. 44 gms/l sugar.

Cabernet Sauvignon 95 animated strawberry/cassis flavours, big body, firm finish. Oak-aged, 13,7% alc., 5,8 gms/l acid. **Pinotage 96** plummy colour/flavours, lots of ripe banana, mulberry fruit, soft on palate, brush of oaky vanilla. 12,4% alc. **Ruby Cabernet 96** export only. Wild berry, mint, pepper bouquet/palate. Big mouth-feel. Showing surprisingly good bottle development (for price range). More than just a quaffer. 13,6% alc. **Claret Select** Soft, light, dry NV red; cab. s., pinotage, tinta barocca. Slight oak-ageing. **Chardonnay** ◀ SA's best-selling chard. **97** big, full, citric, light lemony grip, tropical touches in crisp, fresh finish. **Steen-Chenin Blanc** ◀ In-form **98**, delightful fruity-fresh, clean, crisp quaffing. **Sauvignon Blanc** ◀ **98** full, forward, fresh gooseberry, figs, hints meadowgrass. Crisp, exciting. **Extra Light** SA's best-selling light white. Low kilojoules/alc. (9%), soft but not wishy-washy. Chenin/colombard. **Premier Grand Crû** Dry white NV. Bright mélange of chenin/sauvignon, Cape riesling, colombard. Fresh, crisp, dry. **Stein Select** NV light, uncomplicated, easy white, ripe sweetness (18 gms/l sugar), elemental. **Late Harvest** Semi-sweet white (28 gms/l sugar), chiefly chenin. Untasted: **African Sky Crux** (ruby cab./tinta barocca), **African Sky Celeste** (sauvignon/sémillon).

Export wines available from cellar. **Two Oceans Cape Rosé** and **Sémillon-Chardonnay**; **Claret**, **Extra Light**, **PGC**, **Stein**, **Late Harvest** in 5 l, 2 l boxes, 750 ml, 340 ml bottles. Also from cellar only: **Ryk Tulbach Medium Cream** and **Pale Dry** sherries.

DU PREEZ WINES

Stellenbosch

Owner/Winemaker: Jan du Preez (since 1992)
P.O. Box 204, Stellenbosch 7599
Tel: 021-8879937 **Fax:** 021-8870566
E-mail: dupwine@intekom.co.za

Energetic Stellenbosch-based wine all-rounder Jan du Preez—maker, wholesaler, marketer, consultant, enthusiast—keeps several vinous balls in the air. His Du Preez Wine company, forged in 1994, deals in bulk wine locally, offshore, and exports bottled wines mainly to Europe. DPW has arrangements with SA private cellars, co-ops to market their produce overseas under their own label or a DPW-marque. Last but not least, the company markets its own select range under **Twin Oaks**, **Blouburcht**, **Migration** labels. Ruby cab. (under Twin Oaks) is a Du Preez speciality: he's exported it to Europe since 1993, most recently through a Bordeaux partner that imports 3 000 cases for sale into France "with very positive growth signs for the future". For more details, tasting/sales hours see Stellenbosch Wines Direct.

BLOUBURCHT range:

*** **Chenin Blanc 97** in upmarket blue bottle, concentrated fresh guava tang, easy, light, not too dry. A wine that suits its packaging. Lightish alc.: 11,5%.

MIGRATION range:

"Long I looked for a typical African name that would travel," says Jan du Preez. "Migration is perfect—a wine born in Africa that will migrate to all wine lovers, world-wide." **Cabernet Sauvignon 98** in stylish tall, slimline bottle, evocative front label. Too young to judge realistically, seems promising: good cassis, blackberry fruit, forward new-clone mint/eucalyptus scents, 13% alc. One to watch.

TWIN OAKS range: see Stellenbosch Wines Direct.

DU TOITSKLOOF WINE CELLAR

Worcester See Worcester map

Tastings/sales Mon-Fri 8.30-12.30; 1.30-5.30. Sat 8.30-12. Cellar tours by appointment.
Owners: 12 members
Winemaker: Philip Jordaan (since 1983)
Production: 11 000 tons. **Vineyards:** 680 ha.
P.O. Box 55, Rawsonville 6845
Tel: 0231-91601 **Fax:** 0231-91581

Staying ahead of the game in the global v'yd isn't simply a combination of climate, soil, grapes. People are important too—which is why Du Toitskloof, one of the pace-setting Cape co-ops, has promoted worker training to the head of its to-do list. "Everyone must become more involved in winemaking so we can keep improving quality," says assiduous winemaker Philip Jordaan. Early success is epitomised by Derrick Cupido, a veteran of 9 crushes with the cellar: the dab cellar hand passed his Elsenburg course with flying colours, earning the title of *dux*-student.

★★★ **Cabernet Sauvignon** ◀ Gets better and better. Preview of **98** almost replay of **97**, but more intense, flavourful, step up in every sphere. Spectrum of berry flavours, ripe tannins, fresh farewell. Needs bit of time. 13% alc. **97** ready; **96** best-value winner in mail-order club tasting. **92 VG.**

★★★ **Shiraz** ◀ **98** quantum improvement on pvs.; intense, mouthfilling, long, good complexity: smoke, leather, Karoo-bush over ripe, almost plump raspberry. Potential to develop impressively over 4-5 years. Tasted from barrel.

★★★ **Special Late Harvest** ◀ Consistently gorgeous from beginning to end. Delicate peach/pear-drop wafts, waves of ripe fruit flavour, zippy lemon-tinged finish invigorates 41 gms/l sugar. **96** champion Natural Sweet at SA young wine show.

★★★★ **Red Muscadel** ◀ **97** absolutely delicious, delicate; really not a winter warmer/after-dinner sweet. This comely pink, luscious, Turkish Delight-scented, non-cloying charmer, lightly chilled, is the perfect aperitif, daytime pick-me-up. Overall light touch enhanced by moderate alc. (17%).

★★★★ **Hanepoot Jerepigo** ◀ Always a star here, **92 VVG** no exception: deep gold, brilliant warm, creamy texture; ripe figs, smoky tobacco on distinctive palate; lusciously ripe, prolonged finish. "Stand-out year for hanepoot in Rawsonville," notes Philip Jordaan. **91 VG** bright marmalade colour/aromas. **90 VVG** gentler; more muscat, less citrus. Latest **95** untasted, but in house style, winemaker says.

★★★ **Cape Vintage** ◀ **95** ruby more than vintage style, very good nonetheless. Ripe plum compôte, raisins, dried apple rings, pleasing dark tarry notes; fresh, not overly weighty. Medium alc. (for style) at 18%. 2 yrs small French wood. Cinsaut, ruby cab. Well received at Calitzdorp's annual Port Festival. **91 VG** from cinsaut. 2nd rated co-op port in 1996 WINE tasting.

Pinotage ◀ Since firm but rich **92** one of most reputable co-op winery examples. **98** agricultural in literal, figurative, approbative senses: earthy, gutsy, dark/ripe prunes, plums, old-style acetone coating; but clean, packed with flavour. Begs for hearty stews, (steak)ranch fare. 13% alc. **96** Gold at SA show. **Merlot 98** similar to **96**: sauvignon-like cut-grass, capsicum with plum undertones, huge tannins. 13,5%. **Blanc de Noir 98** rosé-tinted, perfumed, good bite in finish, crisp. A summer food partner. Agreeably off-dry: ± 7 gms/l sugar, lowish alc. (11%), ruby cab. **Chardonnay 98**

characterful easy dry drinking, lemon-fresh palate plumped out by light vanilla oak. 13% alc. **96/95 VG**. **Riesling** ◀ **98** habitually delightful (and winery's fastest mover); if all rieslings were made this way, there'd be more reason to stay the Grim Grubber. Distinctive fresh hay/straw, tingly green-apple taste, bright finish, early/summer drinking deluxe. Finishes nice and dry (3,5 gms/l sugar). Lowish alc. (11% alc). **Blanc de Blanc** NV (500 ml) demandingly dry; could partner grilled sardines Lisbon-style. **Sauvignon Blanc** ◀ **98** gentle gooseberry flavours, soft acid. Enjoy while fresh, young. **Chenin Blanc** ☺ ◀ **98** model beach-party quaffer, lots of vibrant guava-scented flavour, agreeably dry, medium-bodied. Drink fresh off the vine. **Bukettraube 98** in ruminative mode: quiet, gentle, light, softly sweet. 11% alc., ± 17 gms/l sugar.
DUMPIE range (500 ml bottles with screw cap): **Dry Red, Blanc de Blanc, Late Vintage**.

EAGLEVLEI

Klapmuts, Stellenbosch See Paarl map

From Feb 99: tastings/sales Mon-Fri 10-4, Sat 10-2.
Owners: Steve and Jean Weir
Consulting Winemaker: Etienne le Riche (since 1998)
Production: 1 200 cases. **Vineyards**: 12 ha.
Address: Silver Leaves, Rhodes Drive, Constantia 7800
Tel/Fax: 021-7947179

Etienne le Riche, ex-Rustenberg, is the "flying winemaker" for this promising new cellar next door to Hoopenburg at Klapmuts. Le Riche's redoubtable skills are retained by New Zealand-born computer exec Steve and and wife Jean Weir, who landed on EagleVlei after ransacking the winelands for a nesting place for the "integrated winery" of their dreams. A 50-ha. property aside Elsenberg—advertised in Farmer's Weekly, *nogal*—caught their eye as much for wine-growing potential as breathtaking views and pristine natural wetland—a clutch of bird species, including an imposing male fish eagle, call this home. Said raptor provides the motif for one of the most eye-catching packaging concepts in ages, by design guru Anthony Lane.

★★★★ **Cabernet Sauvignon** ◀ NEW First-class début by this specialist red winery. Super-elegant **97**—with stylish heart/goblet-shaped ebony-on-old-gold label—showing all the markings of a high-flyer. No predatory aromas/flavours here: refined wafts of cassis, vanilla, cedary spice over layers of compact, ripe berry-fruit, refined oaky notes in background, distinctly non-clawing tannins. Delicious, approachable but with loads of ageing potential. All new-clone, fermented 5 days on skins; 8 months new/used French barriques. Grapes from Bottelary area. Dash of merlot from Jonkershoek. 12,8% alc. Value deluxe at R29.
Pinotage NEW **98** not ready for tasting.

EDWARD SNELL Wholesale wine/spirits merchants; Durban

"Value, value, value," is Snell chief David Hooper's on-target description of this ◀ relaxed, friendly range. **Dry Red** Light, fruity, cheerful quaffing. Mostly cinsaut, with shiraz, dashes of cabernet, merlot. **Dry White** Blend of chenin/sauvignon/pinot blancs. Tropical fruit flavours, dry finish. **Brut** Lively dry white sparkler, sauvignon/chenin blanc. **Vin Doux** Sweeter (35 gms/l sugar) charmat-method sparkler from chenin.
E. Snell and Co. (David Hooper). **Tel:** 031-9028877. **Fax:** 031-9028553.

EERSTERIVIER CELLAR

Stellenbosch See Stellenbosch map

Open weekdays 9-5.30; Sat 9-1.
Winemaker: Pieter Verwey (since 1997)
P.O. Box 465, Stellenbosch 7599
Tel: 021-8813886 or 8813870 **Fax:** 021-8813888 or 8813102

Individual, affordable wines from a prime vineyard area consistently produced here; this cellar now part of the Stellenbosch Vineyards merger—see that entry for more details.

★★★ **Grand Reserve** ◀ Quintessential Cape bargain. **96** colour softening, ripe cherry nose, stalky cabernet tightness softened with merlot in blend. 80% of merlot oaked, cab. s. unwooded. Distinctive plummy-nutty character. Pvs. **93 WINE**★★★★. Stacked with friendly ripe mulberries, fleshy palatability; new oak-aged 18 months. Includes Italian merlot clone. Alc. usually 12,5%. **94** 65% cab. s. no new oak.

★★★ **Cabernet Sauvignon** ◀ Solid quality-price ratio. **96** seductive, ripe-fruited plumpness. Barrel-aged, v'yd selected, from Helderberg area. Soupçon of merlot softens firmness. Dry, tannic finish.

★★★ **Muscat d'Alexandrie** ◀ ☺ Individual, aromatic dry version, introduced years ago by previous winemaker, Manie Rossouw. **98** billowing floral muscat perfume, firm, bone-dry mouthful. Good with Oriental fish dishes. **96**, **95** both **VG**.

Pinotage Unwooded; baked plums fill firm, rustic palate. Wild berry aromas and grape's sweetness abound in current **97**, dry tannins in tail. **94** was St'bosch red wine champion. Old bush vines. **95** hint of sweetness adds to accessibility. **Chenin Blanc** Fresh, clean, just off-dry. **98** tropical, thatch characteristics. **Sauvignon Blanc 98** fresh, grassy flavours, asparagus fullness, bone-dry finish. **Chardonnay-Sauvignon Blanc 97** interesting blend, wood chipped vanilla extraction adds creaminess. Crisp acidity.

HANSERET range:

Claret ◀ Easy quaffing, dusty berry fruit with touch of sweetness for smoothness. NV blend of multi-vintage merlot, cab. s., shiraz. **Edelblanc** NV blend, mainly sauvignon blanc, crouchen blanc; boosted with chardonnay, colombard, chenin. **Bouquet Blanc** NV semi-sweet, fresh grapey fragrance: Rhine riesling, hanepoot, chenin. **Late Vintage** NV pleasant semi-sweet, no rough edges.

EIKEHOF

Franschhoek See Franschhoek map

Open by appointment.
Owner: Tielman Malherbe
Winemaker: Francois Malherbe (since 1992)
Production: 3 500 cases. **Vineyards:** 35 ha.
P.O. Box 222, Franschhoek 7690
Tel/Fax: 021-8762469

In a quiet, unpushy way, talented young Francois Malherbe is making impressive wines on the family farm next to La Motte Estate in Franschhoek Valley. The former Dieu Donné winemaker's new **Bush Vine Sémillon**, from wizened oldsters planted in 1903—the year the Malherbe family acquired the estate—rates among the pick of the vintage. His **Chardonnay**, **Cabernet Sauvignon**—from considerably younger stock—are no slouches either. **Merlot**, from young vines, joined the line-up in 1998. Shiraz, a roaring success in the warmer valley-mouth where Eikehof is situated, was established during the year, adding a Rhône-tangent to the farm's established Bordeaux-Burgundy axis.

★★★★ **Cabernet Sauvignon** Demure, almost ascetic front label leaves you wholly unprepared for extrovert **97** inside, champing to get out. This really deserves peppier image to match vibrant deep ruby colour, forward (but nicely focused) ripe cassis/blackberry fruit, frisked with new-clone mint, chocolate coating, long minerally grip. Like all since first **93**, approachable but better after couple of yrs. 7 days maceration, 5 mths 300 l French oak, 12,8% alc., 9-year-old vines, 5,5 tons/ha. yield.

★★★★ **Bush Vine Sémillon** NEW **97** heady, complex: all sorts of ripe tropical, citrus fruit/flowers, oak-spice, vanilla; all reverberate on weighty, fresh-baked-bread palate. Low-crop vines nearly century old, whole-bunch pressed, 50% oak-fermented, matured French/American oak 6 months. Tank-fermented portion *sur lie* 6 months. Substantial 14% alc. Wine club selection. **98**, sampled from vat, similar but fuller, more gravitas. Don't hurry either. "Standard" **Sémillon 98 (★★★)**, from mix ancient/young, bush/trellised vines, in similar mould but shade less concentrated, melon-toned, very fresh. For earlier drinking. Whole bunch-pressed, oak-matured 2 mths, 13% alc.

★★★★ **Chardonnay 98** sample looks bright, fresh in buttercup yellow. Tastes good as it looks, tropical/butter flavours up-front, spicy oak in background. Full-bodied, crisply round. Now or for keeping. Whole-bunch pressed, 9-year-old vines, full-ripe grapes. 13% alc.

★★★ **Merlot** NEW **98** with attractive youthful cherry-red blush, reflected on medium-full palate; obvious toasty oak, chocolate-mint richness. Young vines show promise. 12,8% alc.

EIKENDAL VINEYARDS

Helderberg-Stellenbosch See Helderberg map

Visits: Open weekdays 9-5, Sat 9-3 (Oct-Apr), 9-12.30 (May-Sept), Sun 10-3. Charge for tasting. Cellar tours 11.30 & 14.30 (Dec-Feb).

Restaurant: Lunch: Swiss country Oct-Apr. Winter (soup, musselpot, bockwürst, fondue) May-Sept. Sun lunch mid-Nov to end-Apr. Fri evening Swiss cheese fondue June-Sept (book ahead). Facilities for functions, weddings. Eikendal Lodge B&B opening Oct 1998.

Owners: A.G. Für Planatagen (Switzerland)
General Manager/Winemaker: Josef Krammer (since 1987)
Cellarmaster/Winemaker: Anneke Burger (since 1991)
Production: 30 000 cases. **Vineyards:** 60 ha., 500 tons.
P.O. Box 2261, Stellenbosch 7599
Tel: 021-8551422 **Fax:** 021-8551027
E-mail: eikendal@netactive.co.za

It's a measure of the modesty of Josef Krammer and Anneke Burger that they politely intimate a request for restraint in any write-up. Trumpeting their wares is not their style. Considering the wines they let do the talking for them under cover of the elegant new Eikendal packaging, they stand little chance of remaining undiscovered. General manager Krammer's meticulous, measured planning is not obvious until one stands back and notices the depth and expanse of wines produced here: both white and red, varieties and blends, from entry-level up to reserve bottlings. With excellent value-for-money sewn in across the range. He's rejoined by

Burger who "travelled only as far as Vlottenburg" in the last year. After a short, sharp 1998 harvest at Hydro Holdings' Goedgeloof Cellar, she's back, relishing the challenge as cellarmaster. Advances being mapped out in the vineyard include grafting over of pinot blanc to in-demand sauvignon blanc, chardonnay and merlot, while shiraz has been added to the plantings. Successful experimentation with new red wine fermentation tanks sees their installation in time for the harvest in 1999.

★★★ **Classique** B'deaux blend, latest **96**, mostly cab. s. with merlot, cab. f. Brilliant ruby, cinnamon stamp, cassis berry fruit shines although surprisingly firmer than unblended cab. s. below. Muscular, tensely austere finish. **95** ripeness and layered chocolate/vanilla flavours added plushness, **94** also more accessible; sound fruit and oak. Pvs. good vintages include **89**, **90**, **92 VG**. Nearly 2 years in mostly new oak.

★★★★ **Cabernet Sauvignon Reserve** Generous, powerful red/black berry flavours enmeshed in spices, superb mineral flinty feel, firm tannins. Medium-weight, understated, not a brazen showstopper. 100% cab. s. (new/old clones in almost equal parts). Latest **96**, marvellous tapered depth of flavour, selected from 4 barrels where maturing for over 2 years. No **95**. Tiny quantity **94**, probably ready by 2000. Serious claret, released only when up to (formidable) scratch, and then sold only from cellar door.

★★★ **Cabernet Sauvignon** Unflamboyant, balanced example of cab., blackcurrant berry fruit lined up on elegantly weighted palate, gentle grip in **96**. **95** signalled significant step forward from pvs., deeper flavour, firmer texture, mix of old (nuttier, firmer) and new (fruitier, softer) clones. Fair proportion new oak adds spice. **93**, **90 VG**.

★★★★ **Merlot** ◀ Individual dry red, venison-tinted nose, violets, mineral flavours on stylish, Continental-appeal palate; flavour without stodgy weight. **97** reaffirms pace set by **96**. One of Cape's most charming, amazingly still R25 a bottle ex-cellar. **95** a yard back, reticent bouquet, slender texture. **94** WINE★★★★. Début **91** (all new barrel-matured) with intense spices, minerally, blackberry core, hoisted Eikendal among top merlot producers.

★★★ **Pinot Noir** Welcome return for label, last was **94**. Latest **97** tawny hue, earthy, baked cherry nose, super texture, grip on palate. Lingering richness. Reflects Burger's experience with pre-fermentation cold-soak extraction techniques in Sonoma and Oregon.

★★★★ **Chardonnay** ◀ **97** elevated label into Cape's premier league with citric fruit and oak flavour-play well judged for expressive, but elegant mouthful. **98** reflects ripe fruit of harvest, but with inimitable Eikendal elegance. Measured, creamy breadth enhanced by oak, refreshing lemon tang to finish. Balance in most years since **92** (champion SA white that year). Classically barrel-fermented, proportion new oak each year. Most through malo. **94**, **96** WINE★★★★.

★★★ **Sauvignon Blanc** ◀ **98** less wild than most, fresh, penetrating immediacy, more chalky, figgy, grassy flavours than blowsy ripe gooseberry. Crisp, lively. **97** set the trend.

★★★ **Special Late Harvest** ◀ Gleaming golden patina to voluptuous **98**, soft, ripe peach, guava, blast of rich sweet fruit backed by bracing 14,5% alcohol. Full, rich and delicious. **96** touch less intensity than pvs. Chenin blanc, latest drier at 36 gms/l sugar.

Rouge ◀ As good as always with latest, ripe, dusty, earthy **98**. Trusty, unfussy, clean Cape mélange: 60% cinsaut, with cabernet-merlot support. Briefly oaked. **Blanc de Blanc** Perennially fresh, supple chenin, sauvignon, pinot blanc dry white blend. **98** shows fruity persistence, fresh, crisp zip. Drink young. **Chenin Blanc** ◀ Ripe tropical fruit of **98** packed into, brisk, off-dry mouthful. **Stein** Same amiable chenin juiciness, backed by 22 gms/l sugar, fruit-salad finish. **Noble Late Harvest** Last was **92**, barrel-matured chenin blanc, alluring medley scents. **Mon Desir** Cap Classique Brut. Release of **96** awaited next.

DUC DE BERRY range:

C'est si Blanc NV (Brut) Crisp dry grassy charmat method sparkler. **C'est si Blanc NV** (Demi-sec) Gentle honeyed tropical fruit, 35 gms/l sugar. Both sauvignon/chenin.

EIKESTAD

See Vinfruco

ELEPHANT PASS WINES — Oude Kelder Farm

Franschhoek See Franschhoek map

Tastings/sales by appointment. Owl Cottage B&B. Tel: 021-8762946
Owners: Peter and Ann Wrighton
Consulting Winemaker: Jean Daneel (since 1998)
Vineyards: Krige Siebrits
Production: 4 000 cases. **Vineyards:** 8 ha.
P.O. Box 415, Franschhoek 7690
Tel: 021-8763666 **Fax:** 021-8762219
E-mail: wrighton@gem.co.za

Jean Daneel, Morgenhof's ebullient, super-competent cellarmaster—Diners Club Winemaker of the Year 1992 is but one of his outsize collection of laurels—is now crafting this boutique range for Peter Wrighton, former chairman of the Premier Group and high-wattage reviver/redeveloper of Oude Kelder farm on the old elephant-trail over the Franschhoek mountains.

★★★★ **Sauvignon Blanc 98** an exceptionally drinkable sauvignon. Guava-toned, grassy hints, unaggressive, plump, gentle acid "nibble". Food wine deluxe.

ETIENNE LE RICHE WINES

See Leef Op Hoop

EXCELSIOR ESTATE

Ashton See Robertson map

Tastings/sales Mon-Fri 8.30-5.
Owners: Stephen and Freddie de Wet.
Consulting Winemaker: Jaco Marais (since 1996)
Production: ± 80 000 cases. **Vineyards**: 300 ha.
P.O. Box 17, Ashton 6715
Tel: 0234-52050 **Fax:** 0234-52019

Grapes are by no means the only crops grown on Excelsior, Stephen and Freddie de Wet's vast, go-getting estate near Ashton—Zandvliet, Van Loveren and De Wetshof are neighbours—but one senses they are among the avuncular owners' pride and joy. The De Wets—they're third cousins to De Wetshof's Danie and second cousins to Zandvliet's Paul— supplied wine in bulk to the wholesale trade before switching to exports —UK chain Tesco is a major customer. Now they're also marketing the range locally under the estate label. "Consumers want fruit, fruit and more fruit—and that's what we give them." And, they add, "value for money"— indeed, decidedly pocket-friendly prices are a feature across the range.

All the following wines NEW.

*** **Cabernet Sauvignon** ◀ **97** (released 1998) absolute charmer, explicitly New World-styled. Bouncy, sappy strawberries, raspberries, unadorned by wood; succulent, mouthfilling, very long. Blueprint supermarket cab. (in the best, versatile, drink-today-or-keep-a-while sense), delicious now, should easily hold 2+ years. Bargain at ± R17. 13,8% alc. On UK shelves as **Tesco Robertson Cabernet Sauvignon**.

*** **Sauvignon Blanc** ☺ ◀ **98** rarity among Cape sauvignons at this price: flavour-packed, authentic sauvignon chalky/grassy cut, fresh non-aggressive acidity. 3,4 gms/l sugar fills rather than sweetens, lends delicious roundness. Unwooded. Steal at under R13.

Chardonnay 97 (unwooded) not quite as extrovert as housemates, but pleasant enough, undemanding. Clean, crisp finish. 13,2% alc.

FAIRSEAT CELLARS

Cape Wine Master Dick Davidson, sourcing wines mainly from around Worcester, reports that most of the 5 000-cases of **97** went to Germany, Taiwan. The Bundesrepublik will get most of **98**, too, after a successful listing on Lufthansa. Volume is slightly down, to 4 200 cases, owing to severe shortages of ruby cab. "But quality is as good, if not better than **97** thanks to lower yields, more mature vines." The striking label, featuring an original oil by well known Cape artist James Yates, has been widely praised.

Chardonnay 98 untasted, **97** creamy, accessible, layers of oak. 13,5% alc.
Ruby Cabernet 98 untasted, **97** inviting, ripe, substantial. 13,3% alc.
Enquiries: Fairseat Cellars, P.O. Box 53058 Kenilworth 7745. Tel 021-7971951. Fax 021-7629656. E-mail: fairseatilink.nis.za.

FAIRVIEW

Paarl See Paarl map

Open weekdays 8.30-5. Sat 8.30-1. Groups by appointment only.
Wine/cheese/tastings, sales. Nominal charge for tastings.
Owner: Charles Back
Winemakers: Anthony de Jager (since 1996) with Awie Adolf
Marketing: Jeremy Borg
Vineyards: 320 ha. (ultimately 75-80% red)
P.O. Box 583 Suider-Paarl 7624
Tel: 021-8632450 **Fax:** 021-8632591
E-mail: fairback@iafrica.com **Website:** www.fairview.co.za

The grass doesn't grow under Charles Back's feet. One wonders how he managed to expand his land portfolio to over 300 ha. and commence significant replanting programmes, build a cheese business that is now bigger than the wine side (from 200 litres of milk bought on day one to 20 000 now), initiate the Fair Valley empowerment project and be a founding member of the Spice Route Wine Company in such a short time. "I've a good team" is his response. And his staff clearly both learn from and inspire him all the while. Back thinks on his feet, and probably in his sleep.

Acquisition of a dryland Malmesbury farm with old bush vines almost doubles his vineyard area, and this is why Fairview has been de-registered as an estate: in order to allow freedom of vine planting and bottling. 25 ha. will be replanted per year as white varieties give over to reds. Back sees his terroir as similar to the Rhône and so shiraz, mourvèdre, carignan join pinotage, merlot and malbec in new cultivation. A smart new bottling line fits in next to over 2 000 barrels (doubled in 4 years) in the cellar, itself targeted for revolutionary revamp in two phases by 2000. "We're planning for the next cycle," says Back. The results of the last cycle show his team ahead of the pack. Viognier—all the rage in foreign markets—from vines planted 5 years ago (before it was even vaguely "sexy") is now in bottle while others look for stock or wait for plantings to mature.

Fairview's sights are firmly set on export markets where approaching 85% of production is destined. One can detect a hint of sadness in Back's voice when he reflects that Fairview is better known in London than Cape Town, despite its longtime reputation for remarkable value for out-of-the-ordinary wines—especially the top-flight examples. It's probably not what he would have wanted for this pioneering wine route name, but who are we to lament if other markets recognised the quality and grabbed it first? What was that about prophets in their own land?

**** **Shiraz** ◀ Estate's trademark wine—concentrated colour, packed pepper, liquorice wrapped in barrel, elegant cherry finish. Rhône-like milled pepperiness a glance at esteemed Hermitage producer Chapoutier whom Back recently visited. **97** severely cropped to maximise impact. **96** softer, grainy-textured, spiced nose. Sumptuous **93 Reserve** (**SAA**) won Dave Hughes Trophy at 1998 IWFS, remains decade's standout. Fine wooding adds sweet black cherry overtones. (Reserve labels discontinued.)

**** **Pinotage** ◀ **98** barrel sample from Malmesbury dryland bush vines, typical, modern Fairview red albeit from new source. Dense, deep, ripe berry fruit, smooth taste with French, American oak. Earmarked for **Tower** (special range) label. **97** more elegant, slighter, yet oozes charm. Cold-soak pre-fermentation enhances deep colour, frontal fruit. Low crop, cool vintage help. **95** under **Cyril Back** label (features "statement" wines), supercharged with personality and point of difference, named after the proprietor's late father. Huge, mulberry aromas, richly textured plum, neither sweet nor simple. Ripe tannins, opulent fruit, layers of almond/vanilla from American oak. **SAA**.

*** **Malbec** UK market experience prompted this commercial success, now backed by new plantings. Deep ruby intensity, cherry, sweet spice, savoury palate suggest gentle handling. **98** sample, dense ripe fruit. **97** long-flavoured, soft, silky, with tremendous appeal. Fairview stamp of fresh fruit flavour from destalking, no crushing, limited pump-over techniques. Still has to settle, but minerally-ripe plum/grape flavours have immediate impact.

*** **Carignan** NEW Startling purple, sherbet nose, earthy, dusty leather flavours with sweet fruity flair. **98** tank sample from Swartland bush vines, partner for new Pont L'Eveque-style cheese. 500 cases.

*** **Mourvèdre** NEW Approval for varietal bottling still awaited from cultivar committee of liquor authorities **98** deep ruby, dust edge to spice tempers fleshy cherry fruit. Vigour of vines requires restraint of marginal planting areas.

*** **Tower Red** First behind new label of reserve bottlings a blend of cab. s., merlot, malbec from **95**. Ripe fruit flavours woven through good tannins, integrated in tight-grain French oak to finish in a thoughtful, considered wine with less frontal, fruity simplicity than some in range.

*** **Merlot** Erratic vintage performance moderates star rating. Meaty, violets, soft raspberry fruit, firm tannin, acidic bite in **96**. **95** more serious, oak and fruit combine for finesse. **93 Reserve SAA**.

★★★ **Zinfandel 97** extraordinary, a (benign) monster. Thick, wham-bang, 16,4% alc.! Huge magenta colour, massively ripe "ribena" fruit, major alcohol, sweet American oak. Wow! And this achieved by natural fermentation. Needs oxtail and a taxi home. Small quantity bottled to record this amazing feat for local release, a little overwhelming for sensitive markets perhaps?

★★★★ **Chardonnay** ◀ Departure in style of **98** should convince local sceptics of right to feature in Cape's top shortlists. Show wine, flowing with citric fruit, milk-like texture from full malo, opulent new French oak. Swing-up style. **97** green-flecked gold, yeasty-rich flavoured, big buttery dry white, lively texture demands attention. Confirms *Decanter* top billing for gorgeous limey-lees depth, aided by crisper, more complex cool vintage. Blend of 4 v'yds, 4 different yeasts, 100% new oak barrel fermentation. Develops nutty, toasty layers after 2 years in bottle. **95 SAA**, WINE★★★★.

★★★★ **Sémillon** ◀ Oak fermentation enhances, doesn't mask varietal fruit, beeswax creaminess. Voluptuous dry white, its own character, neither sauvignon nor chardonnay look-alike. **97** smooth, mouthfilling complexity, vanilla sweetness, slightly honeyed, figgy. Low yields; seriously vinified as for chardonnay, complete with lees-stirring.

★★★ **Viognier** NEW Light, bright flint, fragrant, perfumed petally spice ensconced in creamy oak, wood shows on palate, but woven into whole, lingering tail, late alcohol (14%) lift. 1st harvest from 5-year-old vines, minuscule 1 ton/ha., fermented in 2nd-fill barrels, partial malo.

★★★ **Chenin Blanc** ◀ A barrel-fermented chenin with presence: honeyed lime, peach fruit, full, dry density; oak lifts, doesn't mask varietal charm of **98**. **97** striking volume on palate; a style pioneered by Charles Back now enjoying a revival as a serious dry white. No unwooded **98**.

Cabernet Sauvignon Classic minerally cedar nose, hints of eucalyptus, cassis fruit bit lean in **96**, **95** more generous fruit. Rather curious liquorice flavours add interesting sidebar to well-fleshed, dry red, finished (about 14 months) in barrel. Both outshine spicy/minerally **94**, **93 VG**. **Cabernet Franc** Perfumed, spicy nose, sappy "greenstick" palate. **97** attractive if austere. **Cabernet Franc-Merlot** Softer, meatier than above, merlot adding flesh to the ribs in **97**. Harvested extra ripe in **95**, expressive with minty aromas. Among most popular on this long list. **Zinfandel-Cinsaut** (Or sin-sin for short) **97** super-oomphy, only marginally less dramatic than potent straight "zin", nudged into composure and contained within limits of alcoholic power by 35% cinsaut; concentrated, surprisingly smooth. But heat and dust aplenty. Oaked too. Both varieties bush vines. **95**, rich, viscous; rated best SA red at the International Wine Challenge. Also whopping alc., over 14%. **Gamay Noir** ◀ Ripe cherry fruit bursts onto palate in **98**, brooding leathery tar features follow. No strawberry cordial here, full enough spice for pasta. Lower acidity of hot harvest means less brisk than enticing **97** which offered quick-drinking gamay fruitiness. **Dry Rosé** Light; dry lunchtime red of cinsaut, cab. f. and gamay. **Sauvignon Blanc** NEW **98** light grassy style, hints of hay, slight palate. **Colombard** ◀ NEW Only Back's team would part barrel-ferment (American/French) colombard! Result in **98** from bush vines is creamy, fruity, refreshing draught. **Weisser Riesling 98** very ripe floral spice from mountain grapes. Dry. **Pinot Gris** Not tasted. "Hanging on by its rootstocks"— may be discontinued. **Sweet Red** Ultra-ripe **98** shiraz fermented down to 20 Balling then fortified, back into barrel. An every-extremity winter warmer.

FIRST RIVER **See Stellenbosch Vineyards**

FLEERMUISKLIP See Lutzville

FLEUR DU CAP WINES

By Bergkelder

Consistent, quality, released-when-ready range from Bergkelder, safe bet on masses of restaurant lists, but increasingly offering more excitement than ubiquitous label might suggest.

★★★★ **Shiraz** ◀ Invariably reliable, deluxe red with considerable presence, complexity. Accessibility, with in-built pace-maker for keepability, are features as in current **96**, soft, mouthfilling, succulent, plush blackberry fruit, cigar box, pepper, spice, some eucalyptus notes; refined version of burly **94 VG**, still lots of development to come. Seductive softness, expansive, layered fruit, ripe tannins, (almost too) easy to drink now—cellaring should bring handsome rewards, as with pvs.

★★★★ **Merlot** ◀ **96** shows signs of rigorous selection: bigger even, bolder than **95** despite difficult, generally lighter year. Both top-league. Dark ruby, intense bouquet, rich cherry fruit mingles with exotic aromas of caramel, vanilla, mocha. Accessible but enough serious tannin for good development. 13% alc. Usually about 12,5% alc., 5,5 gms/l acid. **91**, **90 VG**.

★★★★ **Cabernet Sauvignon** Latest release **93** gentle, ripe berry aromas, sweet chocolate notes/texture. Supple, fruit woven through sweet oak. Regularly impresses international/local judges at the premier SAA wine list tastings. **92 VVG**. **92**, **89 SAA** selections. **90** has 3% souzão; similar to **89 VG**, **WINE★★★★**.

★★★ **Pinotage** Current **93** step up from pvs., raspberry, cherry on nose/palate. Should develop well. Grapes mainly from Alto, Middelvlei, Jacobsdal. **92 VG** lightish colour, gentle fruity nose, palate more forceful. **91 VVG**, **90 VG**.

★★★ **Chardonnay** ◀ **98** not available for tasting. **97** big, full-flavoured, citrus-packed, sweet-oaky, mouthfilling yet soft. 13% alc. **96** butterscotch, peach flavours. These often better after yr in bottle.

★★★ **Sauvignon Blanc 98** recaps broad-shouldered style of **97**, but bigger aromas/flavours, mouth-feel. Meadow-grass, gooseberries, piquant fresh-milled pepper accents, also sweetish tones but long dry, brisk finish. As usual, potential to develop in bottle.

★★★ **Riesling** (Cape) **98** once again in the blockhole with gentle palate, wafting floral fragrance. Satisfying just-off-dry white, 8 gms/l sugar lifted by freshness (6,6 gms/l).

★★★ **Natural Light** Jumps to higher quality-plane in **98**, fresh, full of flavour, among top Cape examples of the low-alc. style. Lunchtime white, mainly chenin with Cape riesling, sauvignon; off-dry, surprising full palate for low 9,5% alc.

★★★ **Noble Late Harvest 96** from chenin, developing well, honeysuckle, spicy, tongue-tingling palate, arresting tangy finish. 11,5% alc., 9,3 gms/l acid, 109 gms/l sugar.

Special Late Harvest Luscious **96** developed some lemonade, honeyed resonance. At 47 gms/l sugar a dessert for the less sweet-toothed. From chenin.

FORRESTER See Ken Forrester

FORT SIMON

Bottelary, Stellenbosch See Stellenbosch map

Open Mon-Fri 9-4. Sat & Sun 10-3 (Nov-Apr). Catering by appointment.
Owners: Renier and Petrus Uys
Winemaker: Marinus Bredell (since 1998)
Vineyards: 61 ha.
P.O. Box 43, Sanlamhof 7532
Tel/Fax: 021-9062549 **Tasting Room:** 021-9060304

Most unusual—for the Cape—architecture features in the cellar (Fort Simon) and the tasting quarters (Fort Anna) at this farm in the Bottelary Hills. Newly opened to the public, the buildings echo the lines of Namibia's famous German castles (complete with moats and ponds). This reference because the farm's late owner, Dr Simon Uys, was a medical practitioner in Namibia. He and his wife Anna purchased the property, known as Hou Moed, in 1961—when it was in a pretty derelict state—as a future retirement home. Vineyards were re-developed under the aristocratic eye of the late, legendary Dr Desiderius Pongracz of Distillers Corporation, with winemaking advice from Dr Piet Venter. The farm produce for years went to the Bergkelder. 1998 sees its first own-label wines, made by experienced former Louisvale cellar-chief Marinus Bredell, who has got this new-old Stellenbosch property off to a flying start.

All wines NEW

★★★ **Pinotage** Deep purple-coloured **98**. Raspberry, fresh tomato nose. Almost raspberry sweetness on palate with juicy plum fruitiness, sweet tannins. Still a bit chunky. Will need a while to settle. A good warmer for 1999 winter. Aged 6 months in ex-chardonnay oak. 13% alc.

★★★ **Merlot-Pinotage** Exuberant, ripe, strawberry and plum fruitiness with hint of grilled bacon in nose of **98**. Fruit repeats on palate with ginger spice, blackberry. Plump, apparently sweet but actually bone-dry. Well balanced, easy, satisfying drinking. 75% merlot, 35% pinotage. 13% alc.

★★★ **Merlot 98** concentrated blackcurrant nose with hint of violet. Same fruit on fleshy palate. Mocha after-taste. Reasonably muscular, will reward a year or two development.

★★★ **Shiraz** Super-ripe, chocolate, raisin, peppery Rhône-like nose in **98**. Big, full, with raspberry/cherry flavours. Oaky tannins and oomphy finish. Rather too youthful to rate realistically, but seems extremely promising.

★★★★ **Chardonnay** Grapefruit, barley sugar and vanilla scents introduce **98**, lead onto full palate with baked bread notes; toasty, well-handled oak in long refreshing finish. Fermentation in French Jupille and Allier barrels. On fine lees for 6 months and stirred regularly. 13% alc.

★★★ **Sauvignon Blanc** Aromatic **98** with green bean nose, good fruit complexity, alcoholic punch in zippy finish.

★★★ **Sauvignon Blanc-Chardonnay 98** combination of citrus, gooseberry with tropical notes and boiled pear drops whiffs. Full, scents re-echo in flavours; refreshing acidity and length.

★★★ **Wooded Chenin Blanc** ☺ Crowd-pleasing **98** easy drinker with lots of character. Elderflower, ripe pineapple scents on oaky background. Creamy, spicy, rich, mouthfilling, with subtle oak. Refreshing crispness in long finish. From 14-yr-old bushvines. 35%

fermented in new American oak, left 3 months on lees and blended back with fresh, fruity wine from stainless steel.

FRANSCHHOEK VINEYARDS

Franschhoek See Franschhoek map

Tastings/sales Mon-Fri 9.30-5. Sat 9.30-3. Sun 11-2. Tasting fee R5 p/p. Audio-visual of local wine industry. Large coach groups welcome. Function hall with braai.

Traditional Cape cuisine, coffee shop

Owners: 96 members

Winemakers: Deon Truter (since 1981), Driaan van der Merwe (since 1984)

Marketing: Marius Burger

Production: 100 000 cases

P.O. Box 52, Franschhoek 7690

Tel: 021-8762086 **Fax:** 021-8763440

This picturesque neoclassical winery, always swarming with visitors, became buzzier still in 1998 with the inauguration of a one-stop wine centre offering audio-visual displays, traditional Cape fare and facilities to taste a variety of wines from the famed Valley of the Huguenots. Inside the cellar, meanwhile, there was a bustle of an altogether different sort. "Everything ripened at once," says seasoned winemaker Deon Truter who, with Driaan van der Merwe juggles one of the winelands' more demanding work schedules. Apart from raising the co-op's own-label La Cotte range (named after the restored 200-year-old water mill on La Cotte farm, one of the first in Franschhoek to grow wine), Truter & Co. make wines for a medley of local and foreign customers including UK chain Tesco.

LA COTTE range:

Cabernet Sauvignon Special Reserve NEW **96** exceptionally light tinted/bodied. Tannic twist in tail. Wooded. **Cabernet Sauvignon** NEW **96** light-bodied, pleasant quaffer, braai-friendly; unwooded. **Pinotage Reserve** NEW **98** untasted, for release May 99. **Pinotage 96** limited first release drinking most agreeably. High-toned plums, raspberries; brush of wood. Pick of cellar's reds. **Shiraz** NEW **98** (untasted, still in barrel) first harvest from fledgling vines. **Cabernet-Merlot 96** equal proportions cabernet (oak-matured 10 months), merlot (tank-fermented); forward New World style. **Grand Rouge 98** gluggable, sweetish-toned dry red, from cinsaut. Feathery tannins. Under **Claret** in 500 ml screw cap. **Chardonnay 97** quaffing rather than sipping chardonnay. Crisp citrus flavours, broadened by buttery, toasty oak. Drink soon. 13,25% alc. **Chardonnay/Sémillon 97** extremely crisp, animated pineapple/tropical overtones. Dry, current drinking. **Sauvignon Blanc 97** casual dry drinking. **Sauvignon Blanc Special Reserve 98** gooseberry, grassy whiffs; fullish, dry, crisp finish. 13,67% alc. **Sémillon** Valley's signature grape in subdued mood in **97**. Fresh, dry, not overly complex. **Blanc de Blanc** NV mainly colombard with sémillon, chenin. No-frills dry swigger. Also in 500 ml. **Semi-Sweet** NEW Sugar-charged version of Blanc de Blanc above. Pleasant, lightweight. Also in 500 ml. **Port 97** challengingly dry at just 61,8 gms/l sugar, taut, tannic. Pvs. vintages markedly more relaxed, fruitier. **94 VG, WINE****, 92 VG. Sauvignon Blanc Brut** ◀ **97** fizzing merrily after yr in bottle. Very fresh, lemon-twist, gently dry. Carbonated. **Sparkling Demi-Sec 97** Scented hanepoot-chenin confection; pop-palate, lots of fizz. Semi-sweet charmer. Lowish alc. (11,8%).

FRANSCHHOEK VINEYARDS range: (previously for export, now available locally)

Sémillon Barrel Fermented NEW **97** step up from standard version above. Mouthwatering butter, vanilla on toasty oak. Very dry finish. 13,05% alc. **Chenin Blanc Barrel Fermented** NEW **97** appealing fresh apricot, peach accents. Demandingly dry. Barrique raised. **Chenin Blanc** ◀ NEW (Unoaked) Among stars of range. **97** soft, easy, ready-to-glug, enticing salad of peach, apricot. Deft fruit/acid balance. Off-dry. Fairly substantial alc. (13%) typical of year. **Chardonnay-Chenin Barrel Fermented** ☺ NEW **97** immensely quaffable dry white. Fresh desert-island fruit, sweet vanilla oak spiciness, mouthfilling, lovely length. ± 5 months new French barrels.

FREDERICKSBURG

See R & de R

FREEDOM ROAD

See Backsberg

FRIESLAND

See Kaapzicht

GILBEYS LIMITED

Stellenbosch

At present Gilbeys continues to produce its **Craighall**, **Bertrams**, **Alphen** (export), **Mondial** and **Robert Fuller** ranges (see entries for details). Gilbeys purchases grapes for these mainly from the Robertson area, which are then made up by KWV under the direction of Gilbeys' Wine and Brandy Operations Manager, Terence van Rooyen.

Major changes will be seen brand-wise at the wholesaler in future. In keeping with the policy of the past few years, Gilbeys will continue to have former employees, via their own companies, handle distribution and warehousing of certain products in certain areas. This policy could well be carried through to the wine brands and in 1999 these might be handled entirely by "outside" agencies.

P.O. Box 137, Stellenbosch 7599. **Tel:** 021-8086911 **Fax:** 021-8086000.

GLEN CARLOU

Paarl

See Paarl map

Visits: Open weekdays 8.30-4.45, Sat 9-12.30.
Owner: W. M. Finlayson/Hess Holding Switzerland
Winemaker: David Finlayson (since 1995)
Production: 20 000 cases. **Vineyards:** 45 ha. (108 ha. farm)
P.O. Box 23, Klapmuts 7625
Tel: 021-8755528 **Fax:** 021-8755314
E-mail: glencarlou@wine.co.za

David Finlayson is not a man to waste words—preferring to let his achievements speak for themselves. In the few years that he has been in charge of the cellar at Glen Carlou he has collected a noteworthy string of accolades, from 90+ scores in the prestigious US *Wine Spectator* magazine to multiple converts at the New York Wine Experience and Vinexpo Chardonnay tastings. Ask him what has changed his life in the past year and it's his marriage which tops the list. A young man who measures out his life in vintages, he observes, with some regret, that "experience is only gained one year at a time". Intent on not following whatever happens to be the fashion, he is driven by his vision of concentrated, unflamboyant wines, classically reflecting their time and place. It's a vision shared by Donald Hess, whose uncompromising quest for quality has boosted his Hess Collection wines into the top Californian league—Hess "head-hunted" Glen Carlou in 1995, when looking to further his aim of making world-class wines all over the wine-world, and bought in. A new maturation cellar, with a 2 000 barrel capacity, as well as a new planting programme, which has already seen 15 ha. of chardonnay as well as some shiraz and zinfandel increase the farm's vineyards by over 50% are proof of this Cape-Californian team's resolve to add further sheen to an already very polished operation.

★★★★ **Grande Classique** Bordeaux-style blend, cab. sauv., merlot, cab. franc, 80% new oak, 24 months barrel age, **96** smoky, almost gamey aromas, elegantly-textured rather than sweet-fruited palate, spicy, herbal finish. **Reserve 95** features 65% cab. s., 28% merlot, 7% cab. franc, 30 months in oak. Showing restrained Médoc-like density. Mulberry/loganberry aromas intense, concentrated cassis and tannin flavours, dry, spicy finish. **VG**.

★★★ **Merlot** Finely balanced fruit-wood character, **97** sweet cherry aromas layered with oak, accessible rather than dense, spicy, more weight than **96** where fragrance rather than palate was the keynote.

★★★ **Les Trois** Big-fruited, Médoc-style blend, softer tannins from second-fill oak. **97** very forward, blackcurrant, raspberry aromas, smoky almost sweet mid-palate, surprisingly long finish. **96** even fuller. **95** with higher percent petit verdot reveals denser, less fragrant character. Cab. s./f. are other partners here.

★★★ **Pinot Noir** Fast becoming a Cape classic. Mainly new clone **97** rich raspberry, black cherry aromas, some marzipan from 50% new oak, hint of farmyard, complex but not sweet, with fine, almost silky tannins and quite Burgundian finish. **96** less weight, finer fragrance, not as rich (WINE★★★★).

★★★★ **Chardonnay** ◀ Benchmark Cape Chardonnay showing increasing complexity as vineyards (and winemaker?) Finlayson mature. Pungent, tropical aromas, creamy, fine-fruited palate, great length, exceptional balance. **97** combines finesse and power: pineapple/apricot fragrance, almost frothy texture, sweetness deriving more from fruit than oak. 100% barrel-fermented, 6 months *sur lie*, spicy, fragrant, voluptuous. **Reserve 97** more extensive oaking, select cooperage, drier, slightly more tannic, smouldering richness, presently reined-in but showing marzipan, tropical notes. Won Paarl Vintners' 1998 Chardonnay competition, open to all chardonnays from this region. General verdict of 8 judges was: brilliant, world-class!

★★★ **Devereux** Strongly individualistic dryish-style chenin. **97** first vintage without noticeable sweetness, barrel-fermented, almost smoky mineral character, weighty not opulent, great length. Pvs. sweeter, more dependent for balance on touch of chardonnay in blend. **95** WINE★★★★.

★★★★ **Vintage Port** Blend of touriga naçional, tinta barocca/roriz, produced only in select vintages. **95** rich but not jammy, mulberry, prunelle scents, forest floor aromas, opulent, with lovely dry finish.

GOEDE HOOP ESTATE

Kuils River, Stellenbosch See Stellenbosch map

Tastings/sales, cellar tours by appointment.
Owner: P. J. Bestbier
Winemaker: Pieter Bestbier (since 1987)

Production: 9 000 cases, 600 tons. **Vineyards:** 80 ha.
P.O. Box 25, Kuils River 7579
Tel: 021-9036286 **Fax:** 021-9061533

Bucking the Cape trend to "go red', this low-profile family-owned, traditionally red-wine cellar at Kuils River (its name means "Good Hope") is heading in the opposite direction. A new fully-equipped section dedicated to white-wine production has been added to the cellar, and chardonnay will join the line-up in 1999. For the time being, the red blend, **Vintage Rouge**, remains Pieter Bestbier's top-selling label, both locally and in Holland, Germany—the biggest export markets—as well as Switzerland and Britain.

★★★★ **Vintage Rouge 97** sub-titled **Merlot/Cabernet Sauvignon**. Youthful red-purple colour; richness, complexity on nose: cassis over dried-leaf, pine, mint, raspberry. Attractive fruit-driven style, dollops soft chocolate. Clean, elegant, fine fruit/tannin balance, long, clean finish. Persuasive rather than powerful. First time Bordeaux-style blend (merlot 60%, cab. s.—pvs. few yrs. variations on cab. s., shiraz, pinotage). Three months 2nd/3rd-fill French barrels. 13,5% alc.

★★★★ **Cabernet Sauvignon** ◀ **91** amazing value. 50/50 virus-free/old-clone, well-developed ripe blackberry/brambleberry, some plummy, cedary wafts. Soft, charming palate, all above fruits with briary hints. Well-balanced, smooth, long finish. Very satisfying. 12% alc.

★★★★ **Shiraz** NEW **97** rich, extremely young blue-purple. Wafts of Karoo scrub, penetrating stalky/smoky aromas, waves of redcurrant, peppery spice. Full, similar array of deep-piled flavours, rich, velvety tannins. Soft even at this early stage. 12% alc.

★★★ **Sauvignon Blanc** ☺ **98** bright, green tinge; fresh tropical aromas, ripe pineapple tones. Slight earthy lift, crisp palate; gently accented by gooseberry. Very easy drinking.

GOEDVERTROUW

Bot River, Overberg See Walker Bay map

Tasting & sales: "every day by appointment". Conference facilities for 20 persons.
Winemaker: Arthur Pillman
Production: 1 000 cases. **Vineyards:** 8 ha.
Private Bag 37, Bot River 7185
Tel/Fax: 02824-49769

Retired engineer Arthur Pillman, who is of a similar vintage as Nelson Mandela, never fails to stagger the younger winemakers of the district with his energy and enthusiasm. His wife Elreda offers much support whilst running her own cattle herd. They started the 98 vintage with a substantially expanded cellar (no **97** wine was made while they were busy on that building project) and are now renovating and expanding the farmhouse. Pillman's love of Burgundy is shown in his choice of pinot noir and chardonnay as his leading varieties.

★★★★ **Chardonnay 98** rich, full, toasty flavours from 100% oak fermentation. Powerful structure, pert acidity with tangy citrus flavours, all in balance. 13% alc. Could top pvs. best vintage—**91**.

★★★ **Sauvignon Blanc 98** very individual. Quite steely, crisp acidity accompanied by tropical fruit/peardrop flavours. Good food wine.

The following reds were tasted as infant barrel samples. But all show the makings of extremely attractive wines. **Pinot Noir 98** for probable release

2000. In similar style to super **96** which performed well in many tastings. Violet bouquet, delicious cherry flavours, fine tannins. Great promise. **Cabernet Sauvignon 98** fine toasty wood, tannins. Great depth of colour, flavour, balance. **Pinotage 98** for release in mid-99. Preview shows deep ruby hue, open straw/thatch and raspberry aroma. Firm but unobtrusive tannins; sweetness with delicious brambleberry fruit. Gentle acidity.

GOEDVERWACHT ESTATE

Bonnievale, Robertson Valley See Robertson map

Tastings/sales by appointment.
Owners: Thys and Jan du Toit
Winemaker: Jan du Toit (since 1984)
Production: 15 000-20 000 cases. **Vineyards:** 110 ha.
P.O. Box 128, Bonnievale 6730
Tel: 02346-2845 **Fax**: 02346-3430

A taste of Tuscany travels to rural Bonnievale as brothers Thys and (vintner) Jan du Toit's plans to focus on red wine production gather momentum. They're establishing Tuscany's premier red, sangiovese, alongside cabernet, merlot, shiraz on the 110 ha. property, best known for its exceptional colombard. Cape riesling is being phased out, chenin steadily reduced to around 12% of the crop. Production marketed under the estate label will gradually increase to some 30% of the harvest; balance will continue to go to the trade in bulk.

*** **Chardonnay Sur Lie** ◀ **98** open lemon, mango aromas/flavours, relaxed, friendly, crisp. 90 days on lees, *battonage* every 10 days. 13,5% alc. R15 a bottle.

*** **Wooded Chardonnay 97** tasted in infancy for pvs. guide, in fact has developed: hidden fruits—specially limes—have emerged, merged with buttered toast wrapping. Very nice. Dry 12,9% alc.

Colombard ☺ ◀ Variety regularly in top form at this estate, since first **95 VG**. **98** perhaps not quite as much presence, zing as pvs. but bouncy, charming, fresh-picked guava-toned, crisp, bone-dry. Lowish alc. 11,4%. Classwinner on 98 young wine show. Drink young. **Sauvignon Blanc** Experimental **98** reductively made/*sur lie* 45 days, wide tonality: fresh-cut grass, passion-fruit, feline notes, good flavour, lively acid, alc. nudging 12%. **Crane Red** NEW **98** untasted. Cab. s. mainly, ruby cab. Wine sourced from local co-op for export.

GOUDINI WINERY

Goudini See Worcester map

Tastings/sales Mon-Fri 8-5. Sat 10-1. Cellar tours by appointment. Reception facilities.
Light meals for groups by appointment.
Owners: 42 members
Winemaker: Hennie Hugo (since 1985)
Production: 5 000 cases. **Vineyards:** 980 ha.
P.O. Box 132, Rawsonville 6845
Tel: 0231-91090 **Fax:** 0231-91095
E-mail: goudiniwine@lando.co.za

Is there anything (we asked Hennie Hugo, winemaker at this model co-op, forging a bright reputation on the international scene through the Pernod Ricard/Long Mountain connection) holding you back from making better wine? "Time!" was the succinct, somewhat out-of-breath reply. Looking at his 98 schedule, we understand why this hyperkinetic vintner didn't have a moment to elaborate: aside from keeping an eye on exports (Canada, the UK, Germany, Switzerland are primary destinations), he supervised the current cellar nip-and-tuck, turned the first sod for a brand-new red wine facility, networked with Cape Vineyards (export-driven consortium of Worcester producers) to further expand offshore operations. And he found time to make the cellar's first **Special Late Harvest**.

Ruby Cabernet ☺ ◀ **97** bright, cheerful in every way: brilliant mulberry colour, ripe berry/cut-grass bouquet, succulent plum flavours, easy-quaffing. Med.-bodied, dry, unwooded. **Pinotage 97** in lighter, drink-now quaffing style. 11,2% alc. **Umfiki** ("Newcomer") ◀ **98** early-release sémillon/chardonnay blend, bright, super-fruity, crisp; for early drinking. Mail-order club "best nouveau" selection. **Chardonnay** ◀ **98** maintains friendly, relaxed, early-drinking New World style of pvs. (**97**): crisp fruity acids, pear-drop/peach tones; smooth, wide-bodied palate (13,6% alc.); but **98** bone-dry where pvs. touched by sugar. Light brush of oak highlights fruit. **96 VG**. **Sauvignon Blanc** Doesn't shout "sauvignon" in **98**, but amiable, easy, crisply fruity nonetheless. Lowish alc. (11,8%). **Riesling 98** crisp dry white quaffing, for drinking in year of release; frequent regional champion. **Clairette Blanche 98** as always, laid-back light dry white. Screw-top bottle. Frequent local classwinner. **Chenin Blanc** ☺ **98** smooth, guava-fruity, fresh, gently dry (though off-dry on analysis). Really enjoyable anytime/anywhere quaffing. **Steen Late Harvest** ◀ **98** fruit-salady light semi-sweet, ± 23 gms/l sugar countered by fruity acids. Lowish 11,6% alc. **Special Late Harvest** NEW **98** first from this cellar, highly agreeable. Soft ripe tropical fruit, fresh, easy drinking for the sweeter palate. **Demi Sec Vonkelwyn** NV Fresh fruity fizzer, semi-sweet. Lowish 11,5% alc., 46 gms/l sugar. From sauvignon blanc. **Soet Hanepoot** ◀ **97** unusually subdued for this regular award-winning fortified dessert. In-form **96** had limey/honey notes, raisiny richness; luxurious silky sweetness doesn't cloy. 4 months in small oak barrels. Versatility to cope with summer heat (over crushed ice) or winter cold (by fireside).

GOUDVELD ESTATE

Orange Free State

Tasting/sales Mon-Sat 8-7. Cellar tours for groups. Tours of vineyards, cycad garden. Hall seating 100-120 for hire.
Braais for groups by arrangement.
Winemaker: Merkil Alers
Production: 4 000 cases. **Vineyards:** 18 ha.
P.O. Box 1091, Welkom 9460
Tel: 057-3528650

A bit of Free State wine history was made when this cellar, about 40 km from gold mining locus Welkom—bottled its first **Pinot Noir** in 1998. "Third time lucky," says proprietor Merkil Alers, recounting ill-starred previous attempts with the "heartache grape". "But well worth the trouble!" The winemaker is crusading for legislation to allow wineries easier participation in agricultural shows and similar events. "We want the public to taste and learn about wine," he says. Meanwhile Alers is looking for a buyer for his famous collection of cycads—SA's largest at about 600 plants, some apparently 2 000 years old. The following wines are on the list:

Pinot Noir NEW Lightly wooded, 11,5% alc., 5 000 bottles. **Semi Sweet Rosé** Herby/caramel flavours, pinotage. **Grand Crû** Dry chenin/

colombard/St Émilion blend. **Late Harvest** Rich, honey-sweet, **98** with hanepoot. **Colombard Jerepigo** Full-sweet, 18,5% alc., unusual. **Goue Nektar** Sweet white hanepoot dessert. **Port** Wooded pinotage; muscadel; sweet dusty flavours.

GOUE VALLEI WINES (Citrusdal Co-operative)

Olifants River See Olifants River map

Open for tastings & sales: Mon-Fri 8-5. Sat 9-12.30. Cellar tours by appointment.
Owners: 120 members
Winemaker: Bennie Wannenburg (since Dec 1996)
Production: 80 000 cases. **Vineyards:** 800 ha.
P.O. Box 41, Citrusdal 7340
Tel: 022-9212233 **Fax:** 022-9213937

Highlight of the year for winemaker Bennie Wannenburg was the luxury of handling the 98 reds in a brand-new cellar—vital to deal with the 30% increase in cabernet, merlot and pinotage over the past two vintages. Chardonnay is also coming into the winery in much greater quantity; and the total volume of grapes pressed will soon reach a projected ceiling of 14 000 tons which may be just enough to meet heavy export demand, especially from the UK, Belgium, Switzerland and Holland. For the past two seasons Master of Wine Jurgen von der Mark, from Germany, has come out to Citrusdal specifically to prepare the wines for Waverley Vintners in the UK. Wannenburg is encouraging his farmer-suppliers to plant more premium varieties—"we still get too much 'Frans'," he sighs, and if his Board of Directors read this, please will they note: new, and better oak is second on his wish-list!

Chianti ☺ ◀ NV **98** cinsaut brushed with wood (oak staves) for toasty fillip to herby, spicy notes. Cheerful little character of a dry red; in summer don't hesitate to chill. Pvs. also featured tinta. **Cabernet Sauvignon** Pleasant quaff—now 98, herby, vanilla-toned (8 months oak barrels). **Merlot** NEW **97**, gold medal SA National Wine Show, untasted. **Pinotage** Though **96** oldest red in range, still least easy-drinking. Ripe strawberries jostle with tannins. Drink with food. **Classique Rouge** Unwooded, light, everyday quaffing, NV **97**: sweet berries of ruby cab. boom through all-sorts blend. **Chardonnay** NEW Slightly honey-toned nose in soft, gentle **97**. Tiny portion was fermented on oak-chips. 12,5% alc. **Sauvignon Blanc** Light summer refreshment, dry **98** with cut grass character, sparky fruit acids. 11,2% alc. **Chenin Blanc** ◀ Waves of guava, tropical fruit, very soft, fresh, easy-drinking dry **98**, small helping of wooded chenin (5%) to raise interest level. Immediately topped a mail-order wine club tasting. **Blanc de Blanc** ◀ Pvs. off-dry, **98** dry. Rather pleasant easy quaffer, with guavas of chenin more noticeable than sauvignon blanc in blend. **Bukettraube** Smooth-quaffing **98**, pleasant sweetish muscat fruit flavours. 26 gms/l sugar. **Late Vintage** Tiny splash of white muscadel (5%) makes quite big wave in **98** semi-sweet. Majority partner chenin adds some guava to floral scents. Brisk finish. **Special Late Harvest** ◀ 90% chenin, 5% white muscadel, melon nuances, nice length, still-fresh finish to **97**, sweet, light white. 11% alc., 43 gms/l sugar. **Rosé Sparkling** As pvs. from grenache, NV but **98**. Pretty colour, strawberry flavour, semi-sweet, carbonated. **Brut** Attractive dry fizz from **97** chenin, clean, refreshing summer toast. (Pvs. sauvignon blanc.) Among most agreeable of its local kind. **Vin Doux** fruit-salad flavoured sparkler, **98** (65 gms/l sugar) not as sweet as pvs. 70% chenin, 30% white muscadel. **Hanepoot Jerepiko** ◀ Gold at SA National show for **97**. Still vibrant, fresh-tasting, not a heavy number. Try chilled, as aperitif. **Wit Muskadel** Amber-gold; raisiny-flavoured NV (**97**) dessert. smooth but thinnish. NV dessert. **Rooi Jerepiko** ◀ **98** change of variety, personality. Now from tinta barocca; pvsly pinotage. Fresh, fruity, unusually frisky for this dessert style—almost ruby portish. Also suitable as chilled aperitif. **Port 96** straightforward winter-warmer, on the drier side, earthy fig/currant fruit.

GRAÇA SFW

SA's top selling cork-closed wine; sauvignon-dominated with sémillon, Cape riesling. Best very fresh. Has bit of spritz, zingy lemony, green pepper aromas. Swings along with variety of foods, few grams "invisible" sugar add to all-round happy drinking.

GRACELAND VINEYARDS

Stellenbosch-Helderberg

Enthusiastic husband-and-wife team Paul and Susan McNaughton have chosen a poetic metaphor—the Three Graces of Greek myth: Joy, Charm, Beauty—to represent their new boutique range, Graceland Vineyards, crafted by celebrated winemaker Martin Meinert (ex-Vergelegen, now on home-turf at Meinert Winery in Devon Valley). Some 10 tons of cabernet and merlot from the McNaughton farm on the Helderberg were harvested in 1998 (February's fire fortunately didn't affect the "superb ripe berry grapes"), vinified at nearby Stonewall and are maturing in French oak for release in spring 1999. An *en primeur* scheme enables devotees to buy **Merlot** and **Cabernet Sauvignon** forward at advantageous prices.

Tastings/sales by appointment (or "take a chance").
P.O. Box 7066, Stellenbosch 7599
Tel: 021-8813121. **Fax:** 021-8813441
E-mail: pmcn@iafrica.com

GRAHAM BECK WINERY (also Madeba labels)

Robertson See Robertson map

Open for tastings & sales weekdays 9-5, Sat 10-3. Cellar tours by appointment.
Owner: Graham Beck
Cellarmaster: Pieter Ferreira (since 1990)
Winemaker: Manie Arendse (since 1992)
Vineyard Consultant: Johan Wiese
General Manager: Gary Baumgarten
Marketing Mgr: Jacques Roux
Production Mgr: Louis Jordaan
Public Relations: Ann Ferreira
Production: 2 500 tons, 150 000 cases. **Vineyards:** 175 ha.
P.O. Box 724, Robertson 6705
Tel: 02351-61214 **Fax:** 02351-5164, 61922 Mktg
E-mail: beckwine@madeba.co.za
Internet site: www.wine.co.za

"Quality is not a destination, it's a journey." Peter Ferreira's earnestness as he repeats this mantra is palpable: yet get behind those winking specs and into his head and discover the delightful combination of boyish humour and passionate perfectionism. As is obvious from the staff complement, Graham Beck Wines is Big Business—would you expect anything else from such a serious professional as the proprietor?—and it shows. Having a whole valley as a play-pen has its advantages, and this year another 22 ha. were planted, mostly Ferreira's favourite shiraz, and cabernet (expect a premium red in the range shortly), with case production rising another 25%. There's been architectural expansion too, to house a new bottling line, and provide more storage. Critical mass is something The Boss understands, and the result of all this investment has taken this cellar to world player status, in both price (read "volume") and quality. Having made their point as champion MCC producers, the team intends marking its territory with some equally good (read good value) table wines.

★★★ **Graham Beck Merlot** NEW **97** maiden vintage a solid 14% alc. Matured yr. in French/American barriques. Powerful, juicy mulberry and chocolate flavours; will develop over 3-4 yrs. cellaring.

★★★ **Graham Beck Shiraz** NEW **98** deep ruby; pepper, smoke and blackberries on nose—layers of prune and chocolate flavours, matured 14 mths. in American oak. Alc. 13,2%. **97** a lighter wine, elegant, supple, with fennel, prunes on finish.

★★★★ **Graham Beck Cuvée 2000** NEW Delicate amber-straw, 100% pinot noir MCC, bone-dry (1,2 gms/l sugar), with bright strawberry fruit on nose/palate. Austerity balanced by solid pinot weight and slight leesiness: will keep well past the millennium.

★★★★ **Graham Beck Brut Blanc de Blancs 92** yellow-straw colour, lovely citrusy, brioche nose. Premium cuvée whole bunch-pressed chardonnay, half being fermented in small Champagne barrels to enhance depth. 40 mths. on lees before degorging. Will last several years. **SAA** sparkling wine winner for 98. **WINE★★★★**. **93★★★** over 4 yrs on lees, more austere, serious than pvs., less wood apparent; could add another ★ with time.

★★★ **Graham Beck Brut NV** at 7 gms/l sugar drier than most bruts, a 50/50 blend of pinot noir and chardonnay; 2 yrs. on lees. Restrained elegance the hallmark—selected Sparkling Wine of the Year at 96 IWSC, UK.

★★★ **Graham Beck Lone Hill Chardonnay 97** offers crème brûlée and limes on nose, wonderfully succulent citrusy, custard flavours. 100% whole bunch-pressed grapes ferm. in wood, 40% new. **98** barrel sample full of tropical fruits, fatter but sleeker than pvs.; probably maturing sooner. A step up the chardonnay ladder for the cellar.

★★★★ **Rhona Muscadel 96** in tall, slim 500 ml flint bottle—pale burnished gold, essence of light, fresh grapiness in classic Beaumes-de-Venise mould: muscat de frontignan picked before over-ripeness, less sweet than some—182 gms/l sugar, with 17% alc. Delicious. WINE★★★★.

Graham Beck Cabernet Sauvignon NEW **97** shows sweet vanilla aromas, juicy, brambly flavours. Selected barrel bottled for 1998 **CIWG** auction. **Railroad Red** ◀ **97** a 60/40 cabernet/shiraz blend: 6 mths in older wood. Delightful, popular early drinker. **98** barrel sample is softer, with more shiraz, less cabernet.

Graham Beck Sauvignon Blanc 98 herby, gooseberry character, supple drinking. **Waterside White** ◀ **98** biggest volume seller, colombard/chardonnay 2:1. Supple, juicy, with chardonnay prominent. Smart new packaging, wax seal.

GRAND MOUSSEUX Sparkling Wines — SFW

Lively clairette blanche/colombard blend, sweetened according to style. **Vin Sec** Least sweet, well balanced, mouthfilling. **Vin Doux** Sweeter, very rich but offset by crisp, clean acid. With partner, Sec, the most ubiquitous toast in the land. **Grand Rouge** Light ruby; juicy cabernet-merlot fruit, sweetish, low 8,5% alc. **Spumanté** Billowing muscat de frontignan scents, sweet-spicy fruit. All NV.

GRAND PROVENCE — Carbonated sparkling from DGB

Cuvée Doux NV Sweetly grapey bubbly in popular style. From chenin, gewürz., bukettraube.

GRANGEHURST WINERY

Helderberg-Stellenbosch See Helderberg map

Visits: Open for sales Mon-Fri 9-5. Tastings as per sales hours on completion of new facilities—scheduled for Dec 1998. (Charge undecided.)
Owner/Winemaker: Jeremy Walker (since 1992)
Production: 75 tons, 4 800 cases; by 2001 should be 135 tons, 9 000 cases. Grapes sourced from 4 St'bosch areas.
P.O. Box 206, Stellenbosch 7599
Tel: 021-8553625 **Fax:** 021-8552143
E-mail: grangehurst@jaywalk.com

When Jeremy Walker grew out of his "starter" cellar, a converted squash court on his late parents' farm, he built another. Now that—a barrel storage building—is way too small and he plans to expand again in time for the 1999 crush. A 400 m^2 underground barrel maturation cellar will be topped by production and warehousing space at ground level. The "squash court" will still be roped into action, both literally and figuratively, and Walker's cellar-only operation (one of few to buy in all his grapes) remains firmly grounded in the individual, hands-on boutique genre. Not for him larger volumes or more labels, just "quality, quality, quality".

The latest plans are a move away from the "beg, borrow, steal" scenario. A new corking machine is earmarked to replace the one currently on loan from former classmate, Beyers Truter, and he's to continue his 1998 experiment with closed stainless steel fermentation tanks. Having previously fermented in traditional open "kuipe", Walker is impressed with the innovative tanks, complete with detachable floating lids which allow him to vinify small batches. It's all on the drawing board, all meticulously mapped out, all in the interests of boosting quality.

Micro-vinifying grapes from specific growers across the Helderberg, Firgrove, Devon Valley and Stellenbosch Kloof is clearly what allows for such individuality in the wines. Walker can draw countless samples to display the characteristics—of each site, modulated by differential cellar handling—that he wants in each of his complete wines. He was assisted in the "compact" ripe 1998 harvest by one of his customers, geologist Sam de Beer who swapped "gold mines for red wines" for 3 weeks. (He wryly hopes for $300 an ounce for the harvest results!)

★★★★ **Cabernet Sauvignon-Merlot** The profound impact of triumphant **95** with its densely opaque plum hue, plush, rich, classic claret flavours—blackcurrant, inky minerals, spice—and superb length, is reinforced by barrel samples of luscious **97**, in which mulberry and mint, mocha, tar and coffee, even taut tea-leaf flavours abound. Welcome after leaner **96** (★★★) with cassis fruit a tad short for tannic cloak although oak delicious; reflection of difficult vintage. Track record establishes Grangehurst as a leading Cape claret-style producer. **95** ★★★★★ 74% cab. s., with merlot, 20 months in 70% French, 30% American oak, about 35% new. **94** earned top 4-star *Decanter* rating, also **SAA**. French feel to it, echoing, dry finish. **93 Reserve** WINE★★★★. Ready. **92** début severe.

CIWG 1997 Auction Cabernet Sauvignon 95 swept boards as sole WINE★★★★★ from venerated vintage—rare indeed. Loads of extra oaking (30 months plus) mesh with rich mulberry fruit and mineral seam—much as in **95 Cab-Merlot** above. A serious treat—with ageing potential into 2005 but dangerously irresistible. **96** for 1998 auction from 6 barrels, purple, meaty richness, deliciously chewy, classic. 100% new oak. (Grapes from 2 Helderberg v'yds.)

★★★★ **Pinotage** Affirms position among top Cape examples with **97**: gutsy, meaty mouthful of plums, cherry, chocolate and cloves. Soupçon of wine from Hidden Valley grapes adds lanolin creaminess, mouth-clucking tannic finish. **96** followed lead of modern **95** but more herbaceous, farmyard character; savoury but lighter palate ends slightly bitter. Difficult to match considerable charms of super **95** WINE★★★★, elegant, riper tannins in contrast to bigger, coarser old-style pinotage. All barrel-aged (25% new), 65% French/35% American oak. (14 months for **96**, which longer than usual.) Contains portion cab. s. Pinotage grapes from 3 St'bosch v'yds, majority from Helderberg area. ABSA Pinotage Top Ten. **93 SAA.**

Auction Grangehurst/Hidden Valley Pinotage After stunning début with **95** at CIWG (around R100/bottle in 1996), **96** withdrawn from both 1997 and 1998 events as Walker not utterly satisfied. All-new oak, 50-50 American, French. Collaboration with Dave Hidden, owner of excellent Devon Valley pinotage v'yd which contributes to "standard" Pinotage, and supplies grapes for this, wine made at Grangehurst. Also, like regular above, has 15% cab. s. Sheep wool creaminess, loads of spicy cinnamon, trifle bitter.

Pvs. labels included: **Merlot 94**, one-off bottling. **Cabernet Sauvignon 93 SAA** Selection, sweet-fruity bouquet, succulent. **CIWG Cabernet-Merlot 94** chalky-dry charm—much less cabernet at 54%.

GRANITE CREEK

See Laborie Estate

GROENEKLOOF

See Darling Cellars

GROOT CONSTANTIA ESTATE

Constantia

See Constantia map

Open everyday except Christmas Day, Good Friday for tastings & sales 10-5 (6 in summer). Cost R9 for 5 wines plus glass.
Cellar tours: On the hour from 10-5, booking essential. R8 adults; R3 children, inc. tasting video.

Tavern: (021-7946255) Open daily 10-6; Fri-Sat 10-11. Country-style local and continental dishes. **Jonkershuis: (021-7946255)** Open daily 9 until late; Sun-Mon 9-5. Breakfasts, country lunches, teas. See restaurant section.

Run by: Groot Constantia Trust
Winemaker: Martin Moore (since 1993)
General Manager: Danie Appel
Vineyards: Kallie Bröcker
Production: 800 tons, 45 000 cases. **Vineyards:** 100 ha.
Private Bag, Constantia 7848
Tel: 021-7945128 **Fax:** 021-7941999
E-mail: gct@mweb.co.za

1998 was "the year of the cellar" at this historic estate, original nursery of the Cape wine industry since its founding as a farm in 1685, and now a national monument. Having spent recent years revamping the vineyards, winemaker Martin Moore and team-mates are now refurbishing the cellar—"it's time to give something to the goose" (which laid the proverbial egg), he says. All the large old wood has gone, replaced by small oak—from new to third-fill. (Not too much new—Moore is obsessive about wood playing a supporting rôle, never taking the lead.) He says, with discernible relief, that the barrel-cellar is now "a sight for sore eyes". A new port cellar (previously an art gallery) has been created—unusually, it's open to the outside; Moore maintains that some warmth and air circulation is necessary for the port. Mindful of the thousands of visitors who make Groot Constantia one of SA's biggest tourist attractions, cellar tours here are also being remodelled—the aim is to make them the most informative in the winelands, with explanations of all facets of winemaking, including bottling and corks. A private room in the cellar may now be booked for special tastings.

★★★★ **Gouverneurs Reserve** Flagship red, always finest selection and will vary each year, may yet be shiraz. Current **96** Bordeaux blend of 62% cab. s.,19% merlot and 19% cab. f. illustrates Moore's passion "to hide the wood". Gentle dusting of spice on refined berry fruits, intense cassis, touches of violet; compact, neatly built. Tannins soft and smooth, ready to drink, perfectly balanced. "I've never struggled with a blend like I have with this one," but like good art, Moore makes it seem all too easy.

★★★ **Cabernet Sauvignon 96** easy drinking, light savoury palate brimming with dusty dark-berried fruit. Unobtrusive oak (all third-fill and older) no distraction from full-frontal fruit. Slight brush of tannin on finish.

★★★ **Shiraz** Gamey **96**, with ripe blackberry fruit and good grinding of black pepper; soft tannins, smooth fruity finish. Preview of **97** more succulence, concentration from many "pump-overs" of fermenting juice.

★★★ **Constantia Rood** ☺ ◀ All-sorts red blend; ripe cab. berries demand attention, good oak, terrific sweet/sour tussle on palate, good long finish. Not serious, but seriously delicious.

★★★★ **Chardonnay Reserve** Fleshy yellow peach fruit in **97**, discreet toastiness, grows splendidly in glass. Developing beautifully, where others are bold this is graceful, refined.

★★★ **Chardonnay** Ready on release. **97** pristine, peaches and cream, uncluttered by oak to hide graceful curvaceous fruit. Mere 15% saw oak.

★★★★ **Sauvignon Blanc 98** astonishingly bold build, so fruit-crammed it has plumpness rarely seen in sauvignon. Cornucopia of ripe tropical fruits, even pineapple, with green peppers, nice touch of damp cellar, like Pouilly Fumé in good year.

★★★★ **Weisser Riesling** ◀ Always good, quite often dazzling, as in **96**. Newest **98** looks set to follow, "helluva promising," agrees Moore. Big, bold, ripe lemon with touches of coriander, rich glycerol feel. Harvested with 30-40% botrytis for added complexity. 18 gms/l sugar, seems drier, result of tingling acidity.

★★★★ **Gewürztraminer** Billowing rose-petal fragrance so intense one could dab behind each ear! Powerfully flavoured to match, picked full-ripe, almost meaty richness. Tastes dry despite 12 gms/l residual sugar.

★★★★ **Chardonnay Noble Late Harvest** Billowing apricots and honey, smooth, creamily textured, tangy fruit rather than barley sugar sweetness in **97**. Luscious apricots persist in long, long finish. No **98**.

★★★ **Tawny Port 94** estate's very creditable first tawny and certified, a first for SA. Delicious easy drinking, spiced fruitcake flavours, touches of demerara sugar. Good whack of oak.

Pinotage Always idiosyncratic version, **96** bears stamp of cool climate: more like tannic pinot noir. Cool, urbane, mulberry scented fruit, gruff tannins on finish. **Constantia Blanc** ◀ Unoaked blend of chard., sauvignon/ chenin blanc in **98**; ripe, rounded fruit, dry. **Kommandeurs Blanc** Everyday off-dry white, all chenin from bought-in grapes. Crispy. **Bouquet Blanc** ◀ **98** intensely aromatic, delightful semi-sweet from morio muscat, hanepoot. Sugar 14 gms/l.

GROOT EILAND WINERY

Goudini

See Worcester map

Tastings/sales Mon-Fri 8.30-12.30; 1.30-5. Cellar tours by appointment.

Owners: 17 members

Manager/Winemaker: Pieter Carstens (since 1996)

Assistant Manager/Winemaker: Marthinus Joubert

Production: 10 000 tons. **Vineyards:** 570 ha.

P.O. Box 93, Rawsonville 6845

Tel: 0231-91140 **Fax:** 0231-91801

This quintessential co-operative at Rawsonville is undergoing seismic changes as its game plan to evolve from a volume-producer into a quality-centred, consumer-driven winery shifts into higher gear. Cellar extensions, new equipment and training of workers all form part of the transformation, which clearly is bearing fruit in the much-improved line-up. "*Terroir* is key," says manager/cellarmaster Pieter Carstens, who spearheads the revolution, sounding more like a French *viticulteur* than a co-op winemaker in the Cape's famous "brandy belt". "We aim to please the consumer, but can only succeed if we use varieties we feel really suit the terrain."

Cabernet Sauvignon Amiable **97** developing swiftly in bottle. Pliant raspberry aromas/tastes; brief oaking adds agreeability. **Chardonnay** ◀ Cellar's top dog, budget buy. **98** pleasantly dry, easy drinker. Ripe melon nose/palate, wafts of citrus. Lingering farewell. 50% oak-fermented. 13,2% alc. **Meander** ◀ NEW **98** very drinkable amalgam of sauvignon/chenin/ colombard. Fresh, crisp, tropical fruit essences, off-dry (7 gms/l sugar). Named after rambling Breede River nearby. "Flying out of the cellar," reports Pieter Carstens. 11,5% alc. **Hönigtraube** Bukettraube (75%), hanepoot duet. Alluring rice pudding, muscat arpeggios. Semi-sweet (28 gms/l sugar), uncomplicated quaffing in screw top bottle. **Hanepoot 97** sweet (but not cloying) dessert, all fresh grapes, honeysuckle. 17,5% alc. Low acid. Very nice.

GRÜNBERGER WINES

By Bergkelder

Popular range in distinctive flattened round "bocksbeutel", traditional in Franken, Baden regions of Germany. Amazingly for price range, all carry vintage date (**97** tasted for this ed., **98** released end-1998). **Rosenlese** NEW something for sweet-toothed romantics: delightful blush-style, low alc. (7,5% alc.), luscious (74 gms/l sugar), rose-petal pink, strawberry-toned sipper. From pinotage. **Stein** bright, delicate fruity/floral aromas, off-dry, (15 gms/l sugar); mostly chenin, some sauvignon, gewürz. shows on nose. (Lowish 11,5% alc.) **Spritziger Wein** Gently carbonated white, sweetish (15 gms/l sugar), attractive sauvignon, sémillon, Rhine riesling, gewürz. fruit-salad (11,5% alc.) **Freudenlese** Low alc. (7,5%), decidedly sweet (75 gms/l) white **Natural Sweet**; mainly sauvignon, soupçon gewürz. Pretty floral-fruit scents.

GRUNDHEIM WINES

Klein Karoo See Klein Karoo map

Tastings/sales Mon-Fri 8-5. Sat 8-12. Stilling demonstrations March, April, mid-May. Cellar tours in harvest season.
Owner/Winemaker: Danie Grundling (since 1956)
Production: 12 000 cases. **Vineyards:** 20 ha.
P.O. Box 400, Oudtshoorn 6620
Tel/Fax: 0443-226927

Distilling know-how amassed over half-a-century on Susan and Danie Grundling's farm near Oudtshoorn is reflected in the delightful freshness of the fortifieds bottled under the Grundheim label, now in its third year and gaining something of a cult following. Prior to selling wine (and witblits, liqueurs) direct to the public, the Grundlings were noted purveyors to the wholesale trade. The rustic tasting room on the farm is worth a visit not only for the wines and spirits on sale, but also for Susan's witblits-preserved fruits (from prickly pears to watermelon) and a range of home-made folk remedies.

★★★★ **Red Muscadel** NV Bright, coppery dessert speciality of the house. Superb current release (**95**) shows marked vintage variation on pvs. (**94★★★**). Latest richer, fuller-flavoured, almost sumptuously muscat-toned, wonderfully fresh sprit/acid giving distinctly uncloying lift. Karoo bush, fresh dates in background add interest. Amiable after-dinner, fireside companion.

Wit Muscadel NV Not quite as compelling as red stable mate, most pleasant nonetheless. Honey, nutty; light muscat imprint on palate, quite hefty spirit grip. Regular medal winner. **Port** NV Freshly-ploughed earth, heathery *garrigue* follow through onto full, spirity palate. Clean dry finish. Attractive, though perhaps better labelled "dessert wine" than "port".

HAMILTON RUSSELL VINEYARDS

Hermanus See Walker Bay map

Visits: Open weekdays 9-5, Sat 9-1. Tastings, sales of wine and HRV olive oil.
Owner: Anthony Hamilton Russell
Winemaker: Kevin Grant (since 1995)
Vineyards: Stephen Roche
Production: 29 600 cases. **Vineyards:** 64 ha.
P.O. Box 158, Hermanus 7200
Tel: 0283-23595 **Fax:** 0283-21797

The shift is from "southerly" to "soil". When Tim Hamilton Russell established HRV in 1981, this site behind the seaside resort of Hermanus was selected as the most suitable, "most southerly vineyards in the Cape". It was about the closest one could get to the latitudes of Burgundy. Seventeen years on and new-generation proprietor Anthony Hamilton Russell—while tipping his cap to previous pursuits of cooler vineyard climes—is more interested in the soils.

Experience garnered with each passing harvest has allowed for demarcation of the best sites for the three varieties grown. Regal Burgundian grapes pinot noir and chardonnay prefer shale-derived clay-rich soils in this *terroir* so they have been replanted appropriately while sauvignon blanc roots in the free-draining gravel. Preferred clones, especially the Dijon selection of Pinot Noir, have replaced former stalwarts. It's all part and parcel of the desire—nay passion—to attain the oft-quoted HRV mantra of "Expression of Origin".

It's a passion that has led management recently to register the property as an Estate in spite of restrictions this places on a producer. The clarity and integrity of the concept of the smallest possible appellation, centred on *terroir*, resonates with the HRV philosophy. (But the act will also raise more than a few wry smiles of irony amongst those with longer memories—memories of founder-father Tim's frequent battles with the less-than-flexible authorities regarding quotas and use of the term "Vineyards" when Walker Bay was still a fledgling area in the 80s.)

Part of the philosophy is individuality and that's best reflected by the controversial launch of the Ashbourne label as the best single vineyard selection of the vintage, in 1996. Some bottles of the maiden pinot subsequently developed biological instability and the critics were quick to pounce. Had "Ashbourne" become "Crashbourne"? Hamilton Russell and studious winemaker Kevin Grant are disarmingly frank when asked to explain, which they do cogently, citing the absence of any filtration in pursuit of maximum flavour—a risky business—and ill-advised haste in its release. They will replace offending bottles with the sensational **97** when available, which one may expect. What shouldn't take one by surprise though, is how passionately they've seized the opportunity to learn from the mishap. The openness in debate, meticulousness with which their steps have been retraced and the zeal, not only to prevent a repeat but also to improve quality as a result, are breathtaking. These are hallmarks of a high-class estate which are reflected in the wines and deserving of the fabulous 97 vintage.

**** **Pinot Noir** The subtle but striking metamorphosis in style is complete with a stunning **97** (*****). Seldom do perfect weather conditions, physiological ripeness (when tannin and other grape component ripeness matches the degree of sugar ripeness), new clone vineyard maturity, a committed winemaker and passionate proprietor come together so timeously. Rich maroon colour, elegant cherry fruit and expansive velvet texture, gentle tannic structure, super grip, new clone pinot at its best. Vintage of the decade, a Cape masterpiece. **98** barrel sample from quicker ripened fruit, perfumed, plump baked cherries, fleshy mouthful. **96** is 80% new clone, showing smoky ripe elegance with liquorice hints, tighter tannin structure than in past; but also more pinot fruit and texture coating all round. **95** signalled transition with first significant infusion of Dijon clones alongside the slighter BK5 clone; developing tawny hue, retains substantive Burgundy style on palate. **94** plummy, slightly volatile. In spite of today's altogether different style, HRV regional consistency persists. And while many pvs. vintages had individual charm—**93**, **92**, **91**, **86**, **81** among them—the newest outclass them on all major yardsticks—balance, weight, pinot flavour and complexity, colour and tannin ripeness. Bridging these clone crossover years—was—and remains—HRV's general tracking of a European vinosity rather than a New World preoccupation with "fruit in your face", as Anthony HR likes to call it. The official line is that the *terroir* determines an HRV inimitability that is neither Old nor New World. In any event, the latest vintages confound—in a most impressive manner—those who might have thought HRV would be upstaged by local challengers bottling exclusively new clone pinot. **Ashbourne 97** second release of a v'yd selection, a gear or two (structure, concentration) up on HRV bottling—yes, it is possible—closed at present but full of promise of super elegance. Tiny quantities.

**** **Chardonnay** Vintage variations, which can be marked even in South Africa, are acutely delineated at small cellars such as

HRV—dedicated to reflecting the harvest. **98** barrel sample rich and toasty, very ripe pomegranate-like fruit, firm alc., while **97** shows pebbly, mineral tones, quiet citrus flavours. 8 months in Vosges/ Alliers wood from French coopers. **96** made in reductive style, fresh, open lemon-zest zip, less refined than usual HRVs which maintain a generally quiet classicism within these annual vagaries: balanced, with understated oaking, grape's natural limey tones displayed. **95** has developed remarkable richness, a glance at the Côte de Beaune? Wine Spectator 92/100 "this is something special". One of select few Cape chardonnays to keep for more than 4 or 5 years, retaining fresh, clean balance. **96, 92 WINE******.

Ashbourne 96 best single v'yd selection of vintage, no **97** as high standards not met. Highly priced.

*** **Sauvignon Blanc** Pvs. brilliantly edgy, steely, penetratingly bone-dry. **98** full, ripe, tropical and herb character, like **97**—which more minerally—from new v'yd, sandier soil, new Loire clone. Unwooded.

HANSERET

See Eersterivier

HARTENBERG ESTATE

Stellenbosch See Stellenbosch map

Open for tastings & sales weekdays 9-5; Sat. 9-3. Closed Sundays, religious holidays, New Year's Day. Tasting charges refundable with purchases. Cellar tours by appointment only.

Vintners lunches 12-2 daily except Sun. Picnic platters in summer. Soup, vetkoek in winter. Booking essential.

Owner: Mackenzie family
Winemaker: Carl Schultz (since 1994)
Vineyards: Frans Snyman (since 1996)
Marketing Director: James Browne
Production: 650 tons 46 000 cases. **Vineyards:** 98 ha.
P.O. Box 69, Koelenhof 7605
Tel: 021-8822541 **Fax:** 021-8822153

One of the Cape's new shining lights, a must-have label in an array of categories for any serious Cape wine enthusiast, and the jolly-quaffers exude style and class, too. Though intently focused on polishing the Hartenberg image, young director-duo James and Tanya Browne (she is the daughter of, in wine terms, deceptively rugged, altogether approachable co-owner Ken Mackenzie), and gifted cellar chief Carl Schultz are not one-track obsessives who talk trellising systems for fun. Fun they certainly have—it shows all over this eclectic, personality-packed range, which includes wonderful eccentrics like the Cape's only **Pontac**, a cracking **Zinfandel**, a dynamic flagship **Shiraz**, and—while others have hoisted the white flag over this variety—a **Weisser Riesling** as elegant as it is popular; along with most individual examples of all the other usual suspects. But these are people with a broader view and interests than wine alone.

Schultz manoeuvres his canoe through rapids from the Andes to the Drakensberg. James Browne, a football fanatic, did his best to cheer on Bafana Bafana in France during the World Cup, which quite coincidentally was scheduled to dovetail exactly with one of his frequent tasting and selling trips to Europe. Tanya Browne recharges at her childhood farm in Zimbabwe, where she exercises her formidable grasp of the intricacies of cattle-breeding and other agricultural matters. Both

Brownes rattled through Ethiopia in 1998, pronouncing its wines not as ravishing as its birds. (And yes, for followers of fashion, Mr Browne did don a different dashing neckerchief, his trademark accessory, each day of this bird-trip.) Such intervals of refreshment are vital to re-energise them for the task still ahead: having boosted the new-generation Hartenberg back into the Cape front-row, they're busy actively entrenching their position.

Carl Schultz recently worked at Domaine Monteillet in the Rhône to strengthen his grip on the farm's super-**Shiraz**. Vineyard manager Frans Snyman headed off to the 10th Australian Wine Industry Technical Conference to beef up on new trends, also visiting a number of cutting-edge Oz growers. Hartenberg's modern quality leap is very firmly rooted in its vineyards; recent innovations here include drip irrigation, to de-stress vines in times of drought, and the first use of a mechanical harvester, which worked from 2-9 am, ensuring quality cool fruit. 10 ha. of new-clone shiraz (the farm's best seller) were planted in 1998, along with more merlot, cabernet and chardonnay (the top-selling white). First harvest of the estate's first pinotage—grafted onto old auxerrois vines—is in 1999. Each vineyard's fruit is separately vinified; with blending and grading at a later stage. A single vineyard **Shiraz** is on the cards for exceptional years, as is a single-clone **Chardonnay**.

None of these advances would be possible without the commitment of all staff members. Hartenberg's enlightened empowerment policy includes assisting workers to acquire land on which to build their own homes.

**** **Shiraz** Local hero: (more Rhône than Australian but in final analysis, staunchly South African, a front-row Cape shiraz). **95** (nudging *****) SAA, VVG, impressive: elegantly bold, hints of exciting wildness. Warm, sensuous, dark roasted spice tones mingle with creamy chocolate, turn to savoury richness on finish; deliciously velvety but excellent structure will allow for hidden layers to develop. Possible peak around 2003-2005. Like following 3 wines, has assured, smoothly integrated feel. 22 months in oak, 10% new American, 30% new French, balance used French. Malo in barrel. **94** earlier maturing. Nice weight; satisfyingly dry. French oak-matured. **93 SAA** first in fresher vein. **90 VVG.**

**** **Merlot** Statuesque **95 SAA VVG**, most impenetrable red of its vintage when tasted mid-1998. Though very sumptuous, concentration of dense, spicy plum sweetness enveloped by solid tannin cloak. Will re-emerge, probably after year or two, to fulfil initial super potential. French oak-matured, 40% new, 22 months. Malo in barrel. **94** open plummy, chocolate fruit. **93** muscular, multi-layered, heralded estate's new-wave reds.

**** **Cabernet Sauvignon** A statement red, like rest of range. **95** a stunner; luxurious in all respects: deep blackcurrant brilliance; dusty roasted coffee bean bouquet; very rich, glycerol feel; serious, dry tannin backing. Like **94**, **93**, big, demanding but has intrinsic elegance of vintage. Small French oak-matured (40% new), unfined. **94** classically tailored; expansive ripe blackberry, chocolate. **93** dense chocolate, coffee richness. All built to last good 7-9 years.

**** **Cabernet Sauvignon-Merlot** Emphatically classy; **95** gains extra fruity layers—aromatic fresh blackberries, more lissome feel—from 40% merlot. Oaking regime—22 months, last 10 as blend in new Seguin Moreau, Taransaud barrels—gives extra flow, integration. Big mouthful, but compact, well-proportioned.

*** **Zinfandel** ◀ Tricky customer to get right but **96**, **95** (****) showing increasingly assured approach. **96** more forward, leafy raspberry freshness; plentiful sweet fruit disciplined by firm backbone. Well-balanced to absorb 13,8% alc., 6,8 gms/l TA. Spent 20 months in oak, mainly French (90%). Schultz believes too much American oak "sends wine over the top".

★★★ **Pontac** Cape's sole bottling under this varietal label gets better and better; Schultz admits lack of knowledge as to typicity encourages him to "get the wine to express itself". Comes of age with **95**: astringency of pvs. vintages replaced with enticing sweet morello cherry juiciness, liquorice richness, suggestion of American oak. Still distinctly firm, dry; candidate for interesting development over next 4-5 years. Would make good all-SA team with ostrich dishes.

★★★ **Cabernet Sauvignon/Shiraz** ◀ One of Cape's best-value reds; amenable at any occasion from braais (barbeques) to banquets. **96** (70/30 blend) has gained density in bottle; more depth to usual wild scrub, berry and sweet clove tang. Gentle tannins, rounded dry finish strike modern sophisticated note. Thoroughly friendly, attractive drinking. All oak-matured, used barrels, 15 months.

★★★ **Chardonnay Reserve** Ripe yet tightly-knit **97**; sleek, focused lines accentuate spicy, toasty tones. Undercurrents of subtle lees richness suggest greater breadth, complexity will develop after year or two. Fermented, matured 15 months new French oak. 20% through malo.

★★★ **Chardonnay** Moderation, balance keynotes in **97**: harmonious mix of citrusy freshness, roasted hazelnut richness; well-spread butterscotch-rich flavours, freshened, lengthened by lively citrusy thread. Friendly, satisfying, belies substantial 13,5% alc., 7 gms/l TA. Barrel/tank-fermented (80/20); no malo.

★★★ **Weisser Riesling** ◀ Warmer area, unfashionable grape; many Cape cellars have given up on it. Hartenberg couldn't/wouldn't, such is its version's success. **98** slightly higher sugar (20 gms/l cf 10 gms/l in **97**) to balance, lift distinctive spicy-limey keenness rather than sweeten. Good ripe mouthful contrasted by tantalising sweet/sour tail. 30% botrytis will encourage honeyed complexity over next year or two. Versatile with spicy or smoked foods (excellent Oriental cuisine partner); elegant, appetising aperitif.

★★★ **Chatillon** ◀ Unwooded dry white, varying blend. **98** insinuatingly attractive chenin blanc/sémillon (75/25); not a show-stopper but excellent table companion. Broad, interesting flavours, persistently fresh yet smooth.

Sauvignon Blanc 98 quietly convincing, steely, grassy notes; fattish but doesn't lack vigour. Less dramatic than pungent **97**. **L'Estreux** Showy Special Late Harvest, exotic mango/granadilla juiciness in **98**. 30 gms/l sugar neatly balanced by clean 6,4 gms/l acid.

BIN range:

Following 3 NV housewines: label features Bin numbers on Hartenberg illustration, all thoroughly good value, food friendly: **Bin 9** ☺ ◀ Invitingly bright zinfandel, shiraz, cab. s blend, perky berry-spice flavours, sound, substantial food partner. **Bin 3** ☺ ◀ Sauvignon/chenin blanc blend with waxy soft sémillon. Mouthfilling, unobtrusive fruit. **Bin 6** ☺ ◀ Ripe, juicily sweet morio muscat/chenin blend; delicious mouthful.

"OCCASIONAL" range (listed as **Montagne** in last ed).

Pinot Blanc, Sémillon, Auxerrois, Old Bush Vine Chenin Blanc only made when grapes of suitable quality; no **98**.

HARTSWATER WINE CELLAR

Vaalharts, Andalusia, Hartswater

- Tastings/sales Mon-Fri 8-4. Sat by appointment.
- Light meals daily in thatched winehouse, fully licensed. Conference facilities.

Owners: Senwes, 70 producers
Winemaker: Roelof Maree (since 1978)
Production: 5 000 tons. **Vineyards:** 350 ha.
P.O. Box 2335, Hartswater 8570
Tel: 053-4740700 **Fax:** 053-47409075

This former co-op, most northerly of Cape wineries—some producers' farms are over the Vaal River—converted into a company in 1998 after being absorbed into the Senwes group. With exports to the EU and other markets booming, the flagship **Andalusia** range was renamed to avoid confusion with Spain's fabled sherry region. Certified wines now appear under the new internationally trademarked **Hinterland** label; uncertifieds continue as **Overvaal**. Across both ranges, freshness, lightness are abiding features—welcome counterpoints to the scorching heat.

HINTERLAND range:
Ruby Cabernet Custom-built for summertime quaffing, as in **98**, fresh-fruited, light-bodied, relaxed. Takes well to chilling. Quite high (for cellar) alc. at 12,4%. **Chardonnay 97** clean, light, dry, unoaked (wood an unwelcome encumbrance in area's hot climate, winemaker explains). **Chenin Blanc** NEW **98** fresh guava tones, easy quaffing, at just 8,5% alc. Natural Sweet-style: ± 40 gms/l sugar. **Colombard** NEW **97** muted guava, appears decidedly dry (despite 16 gms/l sugar). Best well chilled. **Therona-Riesling** NEW **98** unusual blend makes pleasant undemanding quaffing. Amiable tropical fruit tastes, clean, light-bodied (10,6% alc.). **White Muscadel** NEW **98** very ripe guava on nose, full-sweet, raisiny palate. Try with ice as aperitif. 17%. **Erlihane** Only fortified SA dessert made exclusively from this grape. Light green-gold, very ripe almost decadent papaya, some other tropical hints (guava/pineapple), unctuous raisiny palate. 17%.
OVERVAAL range (NV, untasted): **Grand Crû**, **Nouveau Blanc, Late Harvest** (750 ml and 5 l box).

HAUTE PROVENCE VINEYARDS

Franschhoek See Franschhoek map

Tastings & sales daily 9-4. Closed Christmas & New Year's Days, Good Friday. Tasting charges R5 per person, refundable with purchases. Cellar tours by appointment only.

Luxury 5-bedroom guest-house; restaurant opening towards end 1998; open daily for lunch and dinner.

Owner: Count Riccardo Agusta
Winemaker: John Goschen (since 1994). **Vineyards:** Niel Maree
Production: 25 000 cases. **Vineyards:** 25 ha.
P.O. Box 393, Franschhoek 7690
Tel: 021-8763195 **Fax:** 021-8763118
E-mail: orders@agustawines.co.za
Website: www.agustawines.co.za

What's new at this Franschhoek farm? "Everything," says winemaker John Goschen. Re-amalgamation—after a split of 150 years—with La Provence next-door, owned by Count Riccardo Agusta, came about in 1998 when the Count bought Haute Provence from veteran foreign correspondent Peter Younghusband—who has "retired" higher up the valley to write his memoirs. The Count, who has other bases in Monte Carlo and St Moritz, claims to like Franschhoek best.

In the cellar, Goschen acquired a new press and pump "which changed my life". There's new packaging and labels too, a major factor here being objections from the French authorities to the use of the name Haute Provence, which is a designated vineyard area in the Apellation Controlee system. Hence the premium **Count Agusta** label (see below); and hence—end 1998—all Haute Provence-labelled wines had to be taken off shelves worldwide, to be renamed Agusta. New plantings will soon triple production to 600 tons—a third white, two-thirds red is the aim. More Californian-clone sémillon is being grafted onto weisser riesling vines, and Goschen worked the 98 harvest in California—after two trips to the UK to check out "the global competition". Workers' houses are being upgraded, a crèche and training programme established.

All these developments contribute to Goschen's ambition to make wines "that can truly be called world-class". Top foreign accolades have already followed local show awards for his **Chardonnay** and **Cabernet Sauvignon** in particular, alerting those in search of rising wine stars to follow. Goschen adds: "True happiness is to have an ambition and the passion to fulfil it."

COUNT AGUSTA range:

★★★ **Cabernet Sauvignon** Pvs. under Haute Provence label; from "imported" St'bosch grapes. **96**, **95**, both champions on Paarl show. Current **97** SA young wine show champ. Very showy chocolate mint/blackberry fruits; medium-bodied with satisfying elegance; has soft texture, tannin to drink now or keep but prominent minty fruit character suggests probably at most attractive up to 5 years. French oak-matured 14 months, none new. Unfiltered.

★★★ **Chardonnay** NEW For those who enjoy limey/buttered-toast power. **98** loads of rich fruit, sweet oak, alcohol emphasised by 85%. For buxom size, has balance which period of settling in bottle may reveal. Fermented in mainly French, some American oak, blended with 15% unwooded portion.

HAUTE PROVENCE (due to become AGUSTA) range:

★★★ **Chardonnay Reserve** NEW Big, fleshy **98**; forthcoming lemon marmalade aromas backed by toasty nuances. Mouthfilling juicy ripe fruit, gentle leesy bounce focused by crisp acid. Slight residual sweetness (approx 5 gms/l) should eventually add to pop-palate appeal. 20% fermented in Seguin Moreau barrels; remainder chip-fermented; malo completed.

★★★ **Blanc Fumé** Full-bodied, generously ripe sauvignon enriched with American oak chips, 5 months on lees. Silkily rich yet clean figgy concentration, length. Attractive though not over-subtle. Worth keeping for year or two.

★★★ **Chenin Blanc Reserve 98** extravagant in all respects; despite 14,8% alc. gives balanced impression. Chenin's ripe melon, honeyed fruit sings through softening influence of American oak chips, 15% sémillon. Good fruity density; technically dry but high alc./oak vanillins give sweetish impression.

Chardonnay NEW Unwooded **98**; quiet citrusy tones, pleasant leesy breadth; full-bodied but balanced. For early drinking. **Sémillon Reserve 98** boldly structured for somewhat retiring lemony, lanolin fruit; quite challenging acid, alc. kick in tail. **Sauvignon Blanc 98** powerful green fig, cheesy nose. Similar flavours cut by forceful acid. **Angels' Tears** Soft, gently sweet 50/50 hanepoot/chenin blanc blend. **98** with usual appealing floral/grapey aromas; 13,2% alc. quite demanding when tasted. **Muscat d'Alexandrie** Partially fermented, fortified to 18,5% alc. Sweetness tempered by clean orange peel tang. 75 gms/l sugar. From **98**.

LA PROVENCE range:

Sauvignon Blanc Unwooded **97**; refreshingly dry quaffer. **Fine White** Fresh, uncomplicated sauvignon blanc/sémillon blend for early drinking;

from **98**. **Brut** Same blend as pvs. wine, labelled NV; brisk carbonated bubble, dry. **Sparkling Chardonnay** NEW Carbonated, dry sparkler with lemony hints.

HAZENDAL ESTATE

Bottelary, Stellenbosch See Stellenbosch map

Tastings/Sales Mon-Fri 9-5, Sat/Sun 10-4. Tasting fee R10 p/p. Cellar tours by appointment.
Light meals Tues-Sun 10-2.30. See restaurant section.
Owner: Dr. Mark Voloshin
Winemaker: Ronell Wiid (since 1998)
Production: ± 36 000 cases. **Vineyards:** 66 ha.
P.O. Box 336, Stellenbosch 7600
Tel: 021-9035035/4 **Fax:** 021-9030057

Ronell Wiid, ex-Boschendal, took over the winemaking reins of this historic, lavishly restored estate at Bottelary mere days before the first grapes of 1998 arrived in the winery. Earlier she'd experienced a new arrival of quite a different sort—a bouncy son, born just three months before mom took up residency in Hazendal's imposing R7-million custom-built cellar. Unfazed, she completed the crush with baby Jasper more or less permanently attached to the hip! If this wasn't challenge enough, unusually hot, dry weather caused the farm's dryland bushvines to down tools—result: considerably lighter than usual crop. "We had to search for grapes!" A new range called **Kleine Hazen** joined the line-up in 1998—allusion is to surname of farm's German founder (1699), Christoffel Hazenwinkel; literally *hares' corner*. "From our nook of Stellenbosch we've conjured two sprightly cottontails!" the winemaker says. These, though value-priced, offer more than simple hare-today-gone-tomorrow quaffing—properly cellared, the **Shiraz-Cabernet** should repay at least 2-3 years in bottle. Meanwhile Wiid's assured touch has lifted the range a good few notches, vindicating Moscow-born proprietor Mark Voloshin's passionate belief in the property and auguring well for the future.

HAZENDAL range:

★★★★ **Chardonnay** Beautifully balanced, harmonious **98**, a mere fledgling, needs 1-2 years in bottle to start showing its potential. Brilliant buttercup yellow, spiked with green; open, zesty citrus, melon bouquet lashed with butter, honey; long crisp finish. Literally caresses the mouth. Definitely one to watch.

★★★ **Sauvignon Blanc** Brash, yellow-green **98** explodes with passionfruit, gooseberry, herbs. Full, almost sweet flavours (partly from lavish fruit) perked with pleasurable capsicum bomblets. Clean, crisp finish. Very good now, should develop well over 1-2 years.

★★★ **Chenin Blanc** (wooded) **98** a giant leap for chenin-kind over subdued, deciduous-toned **97**. Latest evincing complex (but not overbearing) nutty, guava/mango, minerally scents; sweet-oaky, yeasty overtones. Aromas repeat in full, fruit-packed palate to super-clean, persistent finish.

Special Late Harvest Light, honeyed **97** chenin blanc dessert losing first flush of youth. 39 gms/l sugar. No **98**.

KLEINE HAZEN range:

★★★★ **Shiraz/Cabernet** NEW **97** a fruit-driven charmer, delicious now but potential to improve 2-3 yrs. Vivid ruby/purple colour, minty/spicy top notes, attractive leafy undercurrents; soft tannins underpinning concentrated, ripe cassis. 13% alc.

★★★ **Chenin Blanc** (unwooded) ◀ NEW **98** completely different flavour spectrum to wooded version above, but delightful in own right. Bursts with fresh fruit—gooseberry, guava, lemon zest—modulating to crisp apples in deliciously dry finish. Enjoy in bloom of youth. 13,5% alc.

HEERENHOF — Vat range from DGB

Dry Red Cinsaut, soft, slightly earthy quaffing. **Premier Grand Crû** Straightforward dry chenin. **Stein** Chenin in riper off-dry mood. **Late Harvest** Fruity semi-sweet, fullish palate.

HELDERBERG WINERY

Firgrove — See Helderberg map

Open weekdays 9-5.30; Sat 9-3. Closed Sundays.
Country lunches daily except Sundays. Tel: 021-8422012. Book ahead.
Winemaker: Christo Roux
P.O. Box 465, Stellenbosch 7599
Tel: 021-8422371 or 8813870 **Fax:** 021-8422373 or 8813102

Excellent maritime/mountain-influenced vineyards provide the fruit for this winery, part of the new Stellenbosch Vineyards coalition (see that entry for more details).

★★★ **Cabernet Sauvignon Reserve** ◀ **95** full ruby colour/body (13% alc.), lanolin-creamy nose, oak accent on palate supports mix of ripe, sweet fruit, nutty solidity. The Reserve label is small bottling of richest cabernet, given extra oak maturation, partly in small barrels. **94** gorgeous oaken sweetness, hints of portiness add to interest. **94 VG**. **Regular** label shows firm vinosity, tighter unflamboyant claret style in **96**.

★★★ **Chenin Blanc Reserve** ◀ **98** consolidates more complex, substantial, oaked new-wave Cape chenin style—excellent colours, inviting limes/cloves bouquet, tropical melon taste on palate—food and talking wine. Fruit/oak combine well, broaden chenin beyond just simple fruit. 13% alc., 5 gms/l acid. Pvs. **97** rounded into honeyed harmony, colour richer gold.

Shiraz ◀ **97** attractive spice, slightly smoky-savoury aromas, dry finish. Tense restraint, R14 ex-cellar. **Merlot-Cabernet** ◀ **97** baked fresh plums, meaty, berry impact. No frills, unwooded dry red. **96** fleshy, **95** quite taut. **Pinotage 97** perfumed, bit volatile, hint of red berry. **96** lighter (11,5% alc.). **94 VG** usual sweet-berry character. **Cinsaut-Shiraz 96** Easy everyday stuff, some attractive vanilla notes. **Cinsaut-Cabernet 96** quiet nose, dusty dry red *vin ordinaire*. **Chardonnay 97** soft, oak-upholstered, balanced dry white. Partly wood-fermented. **Sauvignon Blanc 98** big, bold, ripe gooseberry fruit. Crisp mouthful. **97**, pleasant, no frills. **Chenin Blanc-Sauvignon Blanc** ◀ Well-priced dry white, unobtrusive table companion. **Sauvignon Blanc-Chardonnay** Food wine with substance, tangy dry finish. **Chenin Blanc** Off-dry. **98** floral, fruity palate, no dramatics, easy quaffing. **Cape Ruby Port 96** ◀ tinta barocca based, partly wood-aged, rich prune fullness, touch of chocolate. **92 VG**.

HERE XVII — By Bergkelder

Dependable, if not vastly complex carbonated bubblies from Bergkelder. **Here XVII Souverein** NV Clean, slightly sweetish finish; mostly sauvignon, some sémillon/Cape riesling. Officially dry but with ± 20 gms/l sugar. **Minuet** NV Brief rest "sur lie" gives this fruity, sweet chenin/sauvignon blanc sparkler its fuller character. Aromatic muscat snatches. 70 gms/l sugar. Lowish alc.: 10%.

HIDDEN VALLEY WINES

Stellenbosch

Visits: Open Mon-Fri 9-5. Sales from Grangehurst Winery.
Owner: Dave Hidden
Winemaker: Jeremy Walker (1996) with Guy Webber (from 1997)
Production: 800 cases. **Vineyards:** 6 ha.
P.O. Box 206, Stellenbosch 7599
Tel: 021-8553625 **Fax:** 021-8552143

Owner Dave Hidden's degree in viticulture/oenology and experience at SFW appear to bear less on his product than his inextricable links with Jeremy Walker of Grangehurst. After an MBA (UCT) and then BP corporate experience together, Hidden headed for business in "ozone-friendly propellants" while Walker circled back to wine. Hidden subsequently bought 23 ha. in Devon Valley and teamed up with Walker again, the latter making the wines for first a CIWG bottling (see Grangehurst) and now the Hidden Valley label from 6 ha. of old vines. A further 28 ha. on the Helderberg have been added to the portfolio and a cellar is planned. Guy Webber's association is likely to continue.

**** **Hidden Valley Pinotage** First **96** dark magenta colour, hints of lavender, lanolin charm, gentle fruit without bitterness, chewy tannic firmness needs food, time to soften. Individual. Sample of upcoming **97** proffers riper plum fruit spiced with cinnamon, clove, sweet acid balance. Perhaps even more appeal than its excellent stablemates in the Grangehurst listing; all new wood-aged, unblended pinotage from single Devon Valley, St'bosch v'yd, exceptionally juicy. American oak (60%) teams well with sweetness of grape.

HINTERLAND WINES

See Hartswater Wine Cellar

HIPPO CREEK WINES

Kempens of the Cape

Cabernet Sauvignon 96 gentle tannin, healthy berry-fruit. Fairly light-textured (though at 12,6% alc. not insubstantial). From St'bosch. **Chardonnay ◀ 98** once again marries drinkability and some complexity. Full-flavoured, supple-textured, tropical/limey fruit with leesy-oak vanilla. Barrel-fermented, through malo. **Sauvignon Blanc 96** firm, grassy vigour; medium-bodied, fruity-dry finish. **Chenin Blanc** Full-bodied **96** dry white; juicy melon in nose/palate/long aftertaste.

HOOPENBURG

Stellenbosch (But See Paarl map)

Tastings/sales Mon-Fri 9-4.30. Sat 10-1.
Owner: Ernst Gouws
Winemaker: Ernst Gouws (since 1992)
Production: 20 000 cases. **Vineyards:** 22 ha.
P.O. Box 1233, Stellenbosch 7599
Tel: 021-8844221/2 **Fax:** 021-8844904

Multi-award winner Ernst Gouws must be running out of wall space to hang his myriad commendations. Since his Hoopenburg range burst on the scene in 1992/93—"Hoopen-what???" was the reaction of many a (pleasantly) surprised consumer—self-effacing Gouws has become something of a fixture on the mail-order club (and several other) pop charts. 1998 was no exception: his **Pinot Noir 98** was preferred by *three* club panels. Lively fruitiness, approachability bordering on gulpability are the keys, plus a sturdy, carefully constructed undercarriage to raise the range above the crowd. **Pinotage** joined the line-up in 1998, made from Sir Lowry's Pass grapes.

★★★★ **Merlot** ◀ Consistently top-class, as in **98** brimming with succulent ripe strawberries/plums, toasty vanilla palate patina, gentle tannin squeeze, very long finish. Own grapes, rounded in French oak (some new).

★★★ **Pinot Noir 98** bouncy light/bright cherry colour, full basket of ripe strawberries, mineral threads. Delicious mouthful, in lightish/early drinking vein (but could have interesting—shorter-term—maturation possibilities). Lightly oaked. Mail-order club selection. Own-farm grapes, new-clone bushvines.

★★★★ **Sauvignon Blanc** ◀ **98** returns to form with a gooseberry-scented flourish after quiet, lightish **97**. Current release has all the tried-and-true Gouws mega-drinkability features: very ripe, almost lush fruit with piquant guava accents, amplitude enhanced by smooth whack of alc., soupçon of sugar to broaden farewell, brisk finish. As they say in Springs: What a boykie! 7,2 gms/l sugar, 13% alc. Grapes from Bottelary, Eersterivier. Bottled May 98.

★★★★ **Chardonnay 98** a real beauty, set apart by seriously smooth texture, toasty lime-marmalade bouquet, tropical flavours, bits of dried apricot, easy fruity tail. Surprisingly fresh for so rounded a wine. 50% wood-fermented/aged 6 mths. Swartland grapes. Nederburg Auction regular.

Cabernet Sauvignon 97 foursquare, soft brambly fruit balanced by gentle tannin; simple but pleasant drinking. Grapes from own farm, Herlderberg. **Pinotage** NEW **98**, tasted very young, seems something of an outsider in this otherwise accessible range. Uncompromisingly dry, tannic, needs lots of time or sturdy food. 3,4 gms/l sugar.

HUGUENOT WINE FARMERS

Wellington
Owner: Kosie Botha
Cellarmaster: Bill Matthee (since 1984)
Trade Enquiries: Gert Brynard, Manager
P.O. Box 7655, Wellington
Tel: 021-8641277 **Fax:** 021-8732075

This privately owned wholesaler at Wellington offers a range of dessert wines, port, muscadels, premium and medium-priced wines (many blended and matured in Huguenot's own cellars) plus liqueurs and spirits. Seasoned cellarmaster Bill Matthee believes the company offers good value for money across its range.

Cabernet Sauvignon In older SA style. Oak-matured 9 months. **Pinotage** Sweet plum fruit, oak-matured 6 months. **Cap Rouge** NV lightish blend 20% cabernet sauvignon, 80% pinotage, 7 months oaking. **Smooth Red** NV cinsaut with touch of pinotage, lightish pleasant quaffing. **Zellerhof Premier Grand Crû** NV Dry chenin/riesling blend. Fresh, fruity; softer than many of this style. **Stein** NV Semi-sweet chenin (24 gms/l sugar). Rounded, full, fruity. **Special Late Harvest** Ripe sweetness balanced by acidity. **Zellerhof Late Harvest** NV Chenin, ripe fruit style, clean, lingering finish. 24,5 gms/l sugar. **White Muscadel** NV Powerful grapey flavours, concentrated sweetness. **Red Jeripico** NV Tawny red muscadel, robust but rounded. **White Jeripico** From muscadel. Sweet-melon flavours, short finish. NV.

Hanepoot Deep gold NV dessert; rich full sweetness, fruity-honey finish. **Invalid Port** Sweet ruby-type style, medium-bodied. **Tawny Port** Bright tawny hues, richly sweet. **Nagmaalwyn** Full ripe-grapey flavours, finish; less sweet than usual for this style. **Valentine Cerise** Pinot noir pink sparkler. Also **Valentine Vin Doux**, white from chenin, clairette blanche. Soft and sweet. Both carbonated.

INGLEWOOD

See Neil Ellis

INKAWU

See Laibach Vineyards

INTERNATIONAL WINE SERVICES—PACIFIC WINES

Kym Milne MW, Alastair Maling and John Weeks are the formidable international talents behind this dynamic "flying winemaker" operation headquartered in the UK, tailor-making 600 000 cases for leading British retailers in conjunction with co-op and private cellars in Stellenbosch, Wellington, Robertson and Worcester. IWS's local partners are Vinfruco, Cape Wine Cellars and ArDéVi (see those entries for more details); its main customers include Thresher (Winelands label), Victoria Wine Cellars (Cape View), Tesco (Rylands Grove), Pinnacle (various), Safeway.

International Wine Services—Pacific Wines
Commercial Manager: David Cartwright
Address: 5 Baring Rd, Beaconsfield, Buckinghamshire, England HP9 2NB
Production: 600 000 cases
UK Tel: (1494) 680857; **Fax:** (1494) 680382
SA Tel/Fax: (021) 880-1282
E-mail: iwsinsa@new.co.za

CAPE VIEW range: For Victoria Wine Cellars
Chardonnay Barrel Fermented 98 foursquare, some interesting smoky nuances, clean, dry. 13% alc. Other labels in range (untasted): **Cabernet Sauvignon, Merlot, Cinsaut-Shiraz, Chenin-Sauvignon Blanc, Chenin-Muscat.**
KLEINBOSCH range:
Young Vatted Pinotage 98 gust of fresh raspberry leads on to soft, agreeably stalky palate. Very nice. Excellent food wine, versatile too. 13% alc. **Early Release Chenin Blanc** NEW **98** bottled within 3 weeks of fermentation. Quite robust, very different sweet-sour tropical palate. Dry finish. 13% alc. Other labels in range: **Cinsaut, Chenin-Sauvignon Blanc**. (See also under Cape Wine Cellars.)
PINNACLE range:

*** **Merlot** NEW **98** (tank sample) striking in all departments: mineral prickle; mouthfilling ripe plum, firm but yielding tannin, clean vanilla-scented finish; hugely drinkable. American oak influence during malo, maturation. Be seated, though: 14% alc.

Cabernet Sauvignon NEW **97** not particularly complex, some cassis snatches, unyielding tannin, but good spicy lift in finish. French oak 8 months. **Cabernet Sauvignon-Shiraz 96** holding, rather than improving. Soft ripe plum, smoky wafts, non-aggressive tannin, quite short. 65/35 blend, French/American oak 6 months. **Chardonnay** NEW **98** tasted in infancy, promises lovely tropical fruit, toasty oak, mouthfilling, long. Devon Valley fruit, 70% French oak-matured, 4 months. **Barrel-Fermented Chenin Blanc 97** acquiring honey-patina of age, primary fruit fading, 13,5%

alc. obvious. Better young. Fermented in new/2nd-fill French oak.

RYLANDS GROVE range: For Tesco

*** **Barrel-fermented Chenin Blanc 98** like pvs., excellent result from locally underrated variety. Expansive tropical fruit, butterscotch, vanilla; long, attractively woody. Fermented/partly aged in oak. Ideal chicken barbecue partner. Quite substantial 13% alc. adds presence (so can move from barbecue to dining table).

Other labels in range (untasted): **Cinsaut/Zinfandel Sauvignon Blanc, Chenin/Colombard**.

SAFEWAY range:

Merlot NEW **98** friendly, fruity, mellow.

Other labels in range (untasted): **Cabernet Sauvignon Cinsaut**, **Early Release Chenin Blanc**.

SIGNATURE range: For Thresher

Cinsaut ☺ Most attractive **97** benefiting from time in bottle. Gentle raspberry zephyrs, easy quaffing. Shows how much concentration of fruit/flavours can be wrung out of this grape, picked ripe (13,5% alc.), 3 months American oak.

WAMAKERSVALLEI range: For Tesco

*** **Cabernet Sauvignon 98** serious—seriously good—example. Resonant cassis, smoky/oaky-vanilla background, distinct, supple tannin. Good ageing potential, too. 13% alc. But all the above dependent on tank-sample we tasted making it into bottle! Same applies to **Merlot** below.

*** **Merlot** NEW **98** intense purple, almost opaque, lashings of oak, fruit to match, sternish tannins; give time to relax, knit. Very nice. 13,5% alc. **Pinotage 98** ripe, "sweet" raspberry, interesting stalky undertones, good intensity/texture. All-round oomph. 13% alc.

Other labels in range (untasted): **Cinsaut** NEW, **Chardonnay**, **Chenin Blanc**.

WINELANDS range: For Thresher

Shiraz-Cabernet Sauvignon 97 in easy, accessible style, above-average informal drinking, with spicy-berry tones, discernibly oaky. 13% alc. **Early Release Chenin Blanc** NEW **98** quite bold style, vinous rather than fruity; clean, crisp, dry. 13% alc. **Chenin Blanc** NEW **98** reveals appley side of variety's persona, affable, not overly complex.

Other labels in range (untasted): **Pinotage**, **Cinsaut-Tinta Barocca**, **Cabernet Sauvignon**, **Cabernet Franc** NEW, **Bushvine Chenin Blanc**, **Medium Dry** NEW (chenin blanc).

JACANA WINES

Partners: Norma Ratcliffe, Michael Kovensky, Michael Fridjohn
Winemaker: Peter Flewellyn (since 1995)
P.O. Box 2, Muldersvlei 7607
Tel: 021-8844410 **Fax:** 021-8844025

Reorganisation of the original partnership (Hugh Ryman is pursuing other interests) and loss of the lease on cellar space at Martin Meinert's Devoncrest see production dormant for the present. **Sauvignon Blanc** and **Cabernet Sauvignon-Merlot** still available from Norma Ratcliffe at Warwick. Pvs. releases included a top-quality **Pinotage Reserve (95** ****), easy-drinking **Cabernet Sauvignon**, approachable and quickly snapped-up **Cabernet-Shiraz-Merlot** blend, a spicy **Shiraz**, and "standard" **Pinotage**. Good whites too: ripe-buttery **Chardonnay**, serious, barrel-fermented **Old Bush Vine Chenin Blanc**, and **Wood-matured Crouchen** (Cape riesling).

Cabernet Sauvignon-Merlot 95 ageing colour, ripe berry fruit, spice, 20

months in oak, 14% alc., R29 ex-Warwick.
Sauvignon Blanc 96 full dry white aged 5 months on lees, big nose, sweet palate from residual sugar and bottle age, still alive, ginger beer notes, can confound as chardonnay. R17 from Warwick.

JACARANDA WINE ESTATE

Wellington See Wellington map

Tastings/sales Mon-Sat, but phone ahead. Cellar tours by appointment. Bed & breakfast.
Owner/Winemaker: Jan Tromp (since 1994)
Production: ± 300 cases. **Vineyards:** 2,8 ha.
P.O. Box 121, Wellington 7655
Tel/Fax: 021-864-1235
E-mail: 30330@beltel.co.za

"Our redoubtable pair—**Dry White 94** and **Wedel 95**—have regrettably come to an end," reports Jan Tromp, owner/winemaker at this pint-size, free-wheeling winery at Wellington. The retired accountant's words are chosen with bean-counter precision: consumers who tasted and enjoyed these formidable wines—earthy, super-individual chenins both—indeed will miss their idiosyncratic charm. But there are good tidings with the bad—new in the range are a cab/merlot blend (the first from Tromp-planted vines) and dessert from chenin. Also available ("on the basis of buy now, drink much later") are a couple of merlots and yet another *enfant terrible* (which does not mean it's terrible in English, merely a handful/mouthful!) This off-dry chenin, with alc. at over 14%, "has more legs than a canary", cracks Tromp.

Debutante NEW **97** cab. s./merlot blend, as mould-shattering as any Tromp creation: Bordeaux-lite! Distinctly slight coloured/bodied, envelope-pushing low alc. (10,2%). Vanilla spice, quiet fruit essences, savoury hints, subdued dry finish. Individual as a three-legged canary, quite pleasant too. **98** still in vat. **Merlot** NEW **98** (wooded and unwooded versions), not ready for tasting. **Schuss 95** dry chenin, untasted. **Chenin Blanc 98** (off-dry) not ready for tasting. **Jerepigo** NEW **96** friendly caramel aromas/flavours, balancing acid, lively fresh mouthful. Chenin, 18% alc., 170 gms/l sugar.

JAC CANARD Sparkling, for Hyperama by Robertson

Vin Sec Unpretentious quaffing bubbly, lightish, tropical hints, gentle sweetness. **Vin Doux** Fruit-salad character, relaxed, easy sparkle, sweetish finish. **Spumanté** full-blown sweetness, minty-muscat effervescence.

JACOBSDAL ESTATE

Kuils River See Stellenbosch map

Winemaker: Cornelis Dumas (since 1966)
Vineyards: 100 ha.
P.O. Box 11, Kuils River 7580
Tel: 021-9051360

1998 got off to a cracking start for quiet-spoken Cornelis Dumas on his pioneering pinotage-only estate at Kuils River: his **94** had been named one of SA's finest in the inaugural ABSA Bank Pinotage Top Ten competition. The handsome trophy joined the gold medal he'd won earlier at Vinexpo in Bordeaux—for the same wine—on the modest winemaker's mantelpiece. "I'm delighted. I've been working with pinotage exclusively since 1966, and always believed in it," said the man who's reputed never to have grubbed one of his vines.

★★★★ **Pinotage** Drift towards easier, fruitier style—begun with bemedalled **94**—continues in **95**. Pvs. vintages characterised by high alc. (over 14% in **89**), up-tight tannins needing time to relax. **94**, released June 1997, much more approachable, though with still robust fruit/tannin structure for development. **95** more refined, elegant than any to date, with usual berry-plum compôte, meaty hint. From 25-35-year-old unirrigated bush vines. Natural yeasts, fermented open *kuipe*, free-run juice, 18 mths 2nd-fill Nevers barrels, 13% alc. Pvs. vintages **88 VG**, **89**, **90** still somewhat restrained, with plum, vanilla prominent: **86** best vintage of decade. **VG 87**. **94** Gold Vinexpo, ABSA Top Ten.

J C LE ROUX — MCC, sparkling wines made by Bergkelder

This popular MCC sparkling brand returned to its roots in 1998 when its state-of-the-art cellar complex came on-stream in Devon Valley, Stellenbosch. The property, previously home of Bertrams, was acquired in 1996 and transformed into a specialised sparkling wine/Cap Classique production facility, complete with well-appointed tasting/sales centre, facilities for visitors to view the operations through self-conducted tours or with the help of a guide (the handicapped are fully catered for). On the drawing board are plans to restore the historic homestead, and open an oyster bar where "sparkling" cuisine will be offered. The link to the particular area of Stellenbosch—and origin of the brand—are illuminated by this inscription at the entrance: "In 1704, Jean le Roux, a French Huguenot from Normandy, settled in Stellenbosch. The House of J C le Roux pays homage to Jean le Roux de Normandie and descendants who practised viticulture here in Devon Valley."
Production Manager: Dr. Pierre Marais. **Winemaker:** Melanie van der Merwe. **Promotions Manager:** Dave Cobbold.

★★★★ **Pinot Noir** ◀ **90** lively, persistent mousse, soft, full, distinct pinot noir flavour/weight. Long, dry, biscuity finish. **89 WINE**★★★★ has developed deep straw colour, somewhat yeasty tones. Track record for some elegance since 86. These classically long-matured (4 years on lees), pinot noir-only MCC; properly austere Brut at 7,7 gms/l dosage.

★★★★ **Chardonnay** ◀ **91** delightful blanc de blancs, refreshing flavours, vibrant mousse. Fuller than pvs., attractive bright, fruity/floral nose, long stylish finish. **90** has developed gentle richness. **89 WINE**★★★★ showing mature yeasty ripeness (disgorged 1994). 85% chardonnay, 15% pinot noir, Brut at 8 gms/l sweet dosage. All malo complete, bottled without sulphur additions.

★★★ **Sauvignon Blanc 98** usual flinty character with manageable sauvignon fruit-acid grip. Fresh, bright, dry. Carbonated, 10 gms/l dosage, 11,5% alc.

★★★ **Le Domaine** Hugely popular sweet Asti Spumanté-styled NV, featuring extra-low alc. (7,5%); sauvignon headline, musky sidebars. Carbonated, 80 gms/l sugar.

★★★ **La Chanson** The red version; decidedly sweet, low alc. 7,5%, carbonated, two-thirds fruity pinotage with shiraz, 70+ gms/l sugar, NV.

JEAN LE RICHE — Carbonated sparkler by Simonsig

Vin Sec Gentle, off-dry blend, soft bubble, fruit-salad flavours. **Vin Doux** Chenin-based semi-sweet, with Rhine riesling, muscat influence.

JENNSBERG See Backsberg

JOHNSON & JÖRGENSEN Wellington

Range grown by Julian Johnson, made by his cousin Roger Jorgensen at neighbouring Claridge.

★★★ **Merlot 98** tasted in extreme youth, couple of steps up from pvs. **95**. Current glows deep-purple, youthful colour reflected on undeveloped nose/palate: ripe blackberries, wrapped in chocolate, spicy/toasty wood. Very nice. Needs year/2. **95** similar style, some savoury/caramel, coffee grinds.

Big Storm Shiraz-Merlot 96 named in memory of a late-1995 storm which reduced crop; dramatic, lightning-streaked front-label. Wine appropriately unquiet: pungent green pepper spiciness, earthy/stalky scents/flavours. For keeping.

P.O. Box 57, Wellington 7655. **Tel:** 021-8641237.

JONKHEER FARMER'S WINERY

Robertson Valley See Robertson map

Closed to the public.
Owner: Nicholas Jonker & Sons
Winemaker: Erhard Roothman (since 1970)
Viticulturists: Nicholas Jonker, Andries Jonker
Production: 100 000 cases. **Vineyards:** 139 ha.
P.O. Box 13, Bonnievale 6730
Tel: 02346-2137. **Fax:** 02346-3146
E-mail: jonkheer@mweb.co.za **Website:** www.wine.co.za

"Your guide will be the first to publish the news," reveals young Dirk Jonker, who helps run this sprawling family-owned farming, liquor wholesaling operation near Bonnievale. The Jonker clan, better known for their seriously delicious desserts, have been pushing hard to raise the quality of the unfortified range. To underscore their intent, they've elected to join the estate ranks (application was lodged in 1998, approval is awaited), introduce an own-brand premium range alongside the Bakenskop line-up. Packaging will be revamped and two red labels—**Pinotage** and **Tinta Barocca**—grafted onto the range. "All in all, an exciting time in Jonkheer's history!"

BAKENSKOP range:

★★★★ **Red Muscadel** ◀ **93** affirms cellar's standing as one of the top exponents of this quintessential Cape style. Shows breeding in brilliant coppery amber colour, ripe muscat fruit that jumps out of the glass. Fresh, spirity zest cuts through sweetness, leaves palate refreshed. Lightly chilled, makes excellent aperitif, anytime pick-me-up. Reserve champ, classwinner SA young wine show; Robertson medallist.

★★★ **White Muscadel** ◀ Effusively praised charmer, often with the stamina of a Giro del Capo cyclist. Current **(91)** beautifully integrated, creamily-textured, ripe-fruited, non-cloying, quite delicious. **(WINE★★★★) 93 VG. 92** SA young wine show champion; gold at 1994 London IWSC.

★★★ **Chardonnay** ◀ **98** unwooded, unlike pvs., but left on lees 14 days for extra complexity. Shows up in rich lees/yeast/butter tones, nicely balanced by crisp lemony tang. Clean, fresh finish. Very nice, good value too.

Cabernet Sauvignon 98 tasted young; angular still, tight, hinting at amiable development of pvs. (**95**). Yr in bottle should liberate closeted mulberry-driven fruit. **Merlot 98** smoky; suave-textured, easy drinking. With smidgen of cinsaut to enhance juicy/fruity accessibility. **Pinotage 98** untasted. **Tinta Barocca 98** untasted. **Sauvignon Blanc 98** oldish vines apparently catching their breath after burst of exuberance in **97**. Low-keyed, still nicely crisp, nettly. Reductively made. **Blanc de Blanc 98** untasted. **Weisser Riesling 98** sold out. Pvs. mail-order club best-value pick.

JORDAN VINEYARDS

Stellenbosch See Stellenbosch map

Open for tastings/sales weekdays 10-4.30; Sat. 9.30-2.30 (Nov-Apr); 9.30-12.30 (May-Oct). Tasting charges R7,50 per person, refundable with purchases. Cellar tours, groups by appointment only.

Owners: The Jordan family
Winemakers: Gary & Kathy Jordan (since 1993)
Vineyards: Ted & Gary Jordan (since 1982)
Production: 35 000 cases, 500 tons. White/red. **Vineyards**: 100 ha.
P.O. Box 12592, Die Boord 7613
Tel: 021-8813441 **Fax:** 021-8813426
E-mail: jordan@netactive.co.za
Website: www.wineroute.co.za

"A very strange year, 98," comments Gary Jordan. "Because it was in fact just 9 months." Indeed. A late-late 97 harvest followed by the early-bird 98 meant a very rushed pregnancy, and frenetic delivery theatre—all 500 tons were pressed in just one month at this cellar, with all-weekend picking unavoidable. On the upside, as Jordan adds, it was certainly "short and sweet", the warm weather delivering optimally ripe grapes. And this California-trained husband-and-wife team has proved equal to any winemaking challenge in the 6 vintages bottled at this superbly-situated family farm on a ridge overlooking both False and Table Bays. Recently expanded by the purchase of neighbouring, south-facing 7 ha. vineyards, the farm is boosting its plantings of cabernet and merlot, for reds which grow better by the vintage, and look set to challenge many longer-established stars. Just as the whites did immediately, scooping barrels of awards without pandering to any show-off, brazenly attention-getting tendencies. The Jordan style is an elegant but bold New-Old World fusion which perfectly suits their main marketplaces—"restaurants and top game lodges, so we aim for wines which complement food, but can also stand on their own". They also travel well—chosen for SAA 1st Class, Virgin Airlines, Air Namibia, Sun Air.

Success begins in the vineyards, with strict canopy management, and varieties matched to appropriate soils and slopes—on this farm they're fortunate to have the lot, north, south, east and west. And having begun their planting programme in 1982, more than a decade before wines were put in the bottle, they can call on mature vines with thoroughly grown-up fruit. High priority is placed on worker-satisfaction: a staff housing project has been completed, the existing crèche enlarged, and training courses are ongoing.

On a sobering note, for those who bemoan the rising price of wines: during their 1998 bottling, the Jordans found that corks alone cost more than they paid for this entire farm in 1981.

★★★ **Cabernet Sauvignon** Densely-fruited, modern but never overstated red. **96** particularly firm tannins, concentrated fruit for a generally lighter vintage. Palate should open to reflect bouquet's present cassis, minty charm. **95** serious, broadly-structured, mouthfilling nutty, tobacco layers, additional complexity from year in new Nevers barrels. Very classy. No **94; 93 VVG WINE****.**

*** **Merlot** Getting more stylish by the year. Bright raw-meat red, meaty-flavoured **96**; chunky, warming, tannins well-rounded, for current drinking, good for further 2-3 years. **97** (****) up quality notch: "more fruit from west-facing slopes," explains Gary Jordan. Luxurious ruby brilliance; complex violet, chocolate, roasted coffee fragrance; much firmer frame with dense, refined flavours. A friendly sophisticate. Second **97** (****) NEW, entirely from west-facing slopes, with Pomerol-style opulence, intense macerated plum/chocolate character, densely textured. New oak-matured; unfiltered, unfined. To be held back for further maturation. **95 VVG**.

**** **Chardonnay** One of Cape's most decorated, consistent chardonnays since maiden **93**. Combines distinctive personality with understated elegance, bridges gap between stand-out show winner and compatible food partner. Cooler **97** particularly intricate; dainty hazelnut, cream, citrus peel nuances with slow butterscotch crescendo in tail; elements seamlessly united. Well-contained, quite grippy; should confirm Jordans' belief that this is most ageable to date. **96 SAA, WINE****, VG; 95 SAA, WINE****, VVG; 94 SAA, WINE****, VG**. Mix clones (inc Davis, Burgundian), coopers, also new/used barrels, yeasts; 7 months on lees; through malo.

*** **Sauvignon Blanc**. Bold, characterful, but never over-aggressive even in broad, solidly built **98**. Structure in harmony with ripe gooseberry, figgy concentration; incisively clean. Everything in place to hold usual year or two.

**** **Blanc Fumé** Oak-enriched sauvignon, always expressively fruity but **98** particularly powerful. Clean, intensely ripe aromas; cascades of mountain-stream fresh flavours broadened by supportive sweet oak. Promises to uphold reputation as one of nicest of its kind. **97** fresh, cool figgy fruit lifted by sweet oak; smooth, creamy length. **97 WINE****, 96 WINE**** SAA, 95 SAA**.

*** **Chenin Blanc** Dry, partially (40%) barrel/chip-fermented **97**. Oak adds cassia spice/nutty infusion, extra dimension to tropical richness. Full body, concentration enlivened by ripe naartjie peel tang. 13% alc. **98** 60/40 tank/barrel-fermented.

*** **Chamelon Rouge** Soft, sweet-berried cab. s., merlot, cab. f. blend (62/25/13) in **96**, satisfyingly undemanding. **97** firmer, minerally nutmeg fragrance, lovely dark fruit variation on palate. All oak-matured.

Chamelon Chardonnay-Sauvignon Blanc ☺ Dry white blended for fruit, structure and compatibility at table. **98** uncommonly outspoken sauvignon character, rounded, creamy texture. 72/28 combination; small portion chardonnay barrel-fermented. **Rhine Riesling** Sprightly, just off-dry white; sugar well-absorbed by limey, spicy freshness in **97** (7,7 gms/l). Good partner to range of Thai dishes.

KAAPZICHT ESTATE

Bottelary, Stellenbosch Stellenbosch map

Tastings/sales Mon-Thur 8-6, Fri 8-4. Sat 9.30-12.
Winemaker: Danie Steytler (since 1979).
Viticulturist: George Steytler
Production: 15000 cases. **Vineyards:** 132 ha.
P.O. Box 5, Sanlamhof 7532
Tel: 021-9061620 **Fax:** 021-9061622

E-mail address: kaapzicht@new.co.za
Internet address: www.kaapzicht.co.za

"Bottelary is red wine country," reckons Danie Steytler, seasoned cellarmaster at this fast-rising family estate on Bottelary Road in Stellenbosch Valley. Steytler's reds" strong showing in competitions and consumer-panel tastings in recent years—cabernet in particular—bolsters his up-beat view of the area's viticultural potential. Merlot, he feels, does especially well on the estate, which first bottled wine in 1984 and now exports a wide, well-priced range to a number of countries, mainly the Netherlands, Germany, UK (and Channel Islands), Japan. As a result, much established chenin is being planted over with premium reds. "Five years ago just 10% of our grapes were red. Today the portion is closer to 40 and eventually it will be 65." In a noteworthy development, some v'yds will be established near farm labourers' homes so staff can manage these as their own. "We'll buy back grapes from them for our ranges," Steytler reveals.

KAAPZICHT range:

★★★★ **Cabernet Sauvignon Reserve NEW ◀ 96** further evidence of Danie Steytler's increasing confidence with this variety. Concentrated, powerful, abundantly wooded, needs time to show its potential. Gust of ripe red currants, lush-textured blackcurrant, generous sweet-oak backing. Elegant, very good potential. Value at just over R30 a bottle ex-cellar. "Standard" **Cabernet Sauvignon** no less fine, shade more accessible, tannins slightly riper. **95 VG. 93 VVG, WINE** ★★★★.

★★★★ **Pinotage Reserve** ◀ Among Cape's serious new-wave examples, **97** big in every department: opaque, bright mulberry peeping through; cherries, strawberries, banana woven with cedary wafts; attractive sweet-sour palate, decidedly dry so, like pvs., perhaps best not drunk instantly—give 4-5 years. Strapping 14,5% alc. 8 mths all-new French oak. Steal at under R30 a bottle. "Standard" **Pinotage 96** solid maroon colour, almost Burgundian hints on nose. Cherries, strawberries, array of red fruits throughout. Firm tannins, long finish. **VVG, WINE** ★★★★, ABSA Pinotage Top Ten.

★★★ **Shiraz** NEW Strong debut **97**, complex, plenty potential, fair rev of tannin—needs good few yrs. Attractive "wild" Karoo scrub, leather, brambles. 6 mths used, 3 mths all-new French oak. Gold 1997 young wine show. "Developing into one of my best wines," says vintner.

★★★ **Merlot** NEW Danie Steytler is excited about merlot in this terroir; classy, elegant **97** shows why. Ripe, plummy, lively sweet-sour tang, distinct tannin, needs 3 yrs+. 6 mths used, 5 mths all-new French oak. 13% alc.

★★★ **Sauvignon Blanc ◀ 97 VG** has developed Loire-like overtones in bottle. Tangy lemon, greengage, nervous acidity, fresh finish. Suggestion of sugar (3,2 gms/l) broadens palate. Very nice. Snip at ± R14 a bottle. 13% alc. **WINE**★★★★. **98** barley-sugar, hint of ripe fig. Might flesh out in bottle.

★★★ **Hanepoot Jerepigo ◀ 92 VG** in 1992/5, delicious, burnished gold-leaf colour, rich almost dense, still with fresh honeysuckle, freesia, musky bouquet/taste. 17,5% alc. Value.

Bin 3 Lightly wooded **97** features equal partners cab. s/merlot. Most pleasant, slightly earthy. For easy, early drinking. **Kaaproodt 96** flavourful, chocolate coating, chunky tannins need time or robust food. Cab. s., pinotage, merlot, lightly wooded. **Chenin Blanc** Among few Cape examples which have proved to grow in charm in bottle. **96** has developed smooth richness, semi-sweet, sugar 18 gms/l. **97** partly barrel-fermented, decidedly woody, needs time for fruit to come forward. 13% alc. **Weisser Riesling ◀**

97 shows flowery side of variety: geranium, light body (alc. 11,5%), soft, viscous, finishes dry despite 4,3 gms/l sugar. Good on its own or with food.

CAPE VIEW range: mostly for export

*** **Merlot 96 VG** lightly oaked, soft, ripe-plummy, easy-drinking, lightish-bodied (though 13% alc.).

Cabernet Sauvignon Latest **96** light coloured/bodied, "sweet" fresh-cut grassy tones, fair grip of wood-tannin. Allow few years to fill out, but may not quite match very nice, full-flavoured, already most accessible **95 VVG**. **Rouge de Kaap 98** ◀ Cinsaut, merlot, cab. s., tasty, ripe, pepper and spice, soft, drinking easily now. **Chenin Blanc 97** sturdy dry white quaffer. **Special Late Harvest Chenin Blanc** ◀ **97** 6,6 gms/l acid freshens and lifts sweetness, amiable guava tones; value.

FRIESLAND range:

*** **Merlot 96 VG** gentle, laid-back, medium-bodied, attractive plums, some minerally grip (though tannins ripe). Easy drinking now, but could wait 1-2 years.

Cabernet Sauvignon 96 still evolving. Green pepper, herbal nose/palate, dusty wood hints. After-millennium drinking. **Dry Red** NEW **98** relaxed cherries, strawberries, slight savoury notes, light-toned/bodied, most quaffable; mainly cinsaut, cab. s., merlot, dash chenin. ± R12 ex-farm. **Chenin Blanc** 2 versions, both **96**. Bottle age has been kinder to semi-sweet (18,4 gms/l sugar), very honeyed, undemanding quaffer. Citrusy off-dry incarnation just a tad sharp. Best young.

KANGO CO-OPERATIVE

Oudtshoorn, Klein Karoo See Klein Karoo map

Tastings/sales Mon-Thurs 8.30-1; 2-4.30. Closes at 4 Fri. Depot in Baron van Reede St., Oudtshoorn. Mon-Fri 9-5.30. Sat 9-1. Same tel. numbers.

Owners: 60 members
Manager/Winemaker: Pieter Conradie (since 1973)
Production: 4 500 tons. **Vineyards:** 260 ha.
P.O. Box 46, Oudtshoorn 6620
Tel: 044-2726065/6 **Fax:** 044-2791030

This Oudtshoorn co-op decided in 1998 not to bottle its own wines, rather to sell them in bulk. However, a range of **97** table wines and desserts—the house speciality—are available from the premises, and a sales outlet in SA's ostrich capital under the Rijckshof label.

KANONKOP ESTATE

Stellenbosch See Stellenbosch map

Visits: Open weekdays 8.30-5, Sat 8.30-12.30. Closed New Year's/Christmas Days, Good Friday.

Refreshments: Traditional snoek barbecue, sweet potatoes/home-made bread by appointment, for groups. Minimum 15.

Owners: Johann and Paul Krige
Winemaker: Beyers Truter (since 1980)
Production: 450 tons, 30 000 cases. **Vineyards:** 140 ha.
P.O. Box 19, Elsenburg 7607
Tel: 021-8844656 **Fax:** 021-8844719

This specialist, multiple award-winning red wine estate on the slopes of the Simonsberg dramatically enhanced its long-established reputation in 1998 by taking the brave decision not to release its **96 Pinotage**. This despite the wine having passed bottling stage, and despite the clamour from devotees who stand to suffer severe withdrawal symptoms once deprived of their favourite fix. But because of this, of course. As the Cape's pre-eminent pinotage-pioneering estate, the first to predict a bright future for this local hybrid—and show it worked—Kanonkop could not afford the slightest dip in its own high standards. The loss is significant—apart from the wasted expenses of bottling, proprietor Johann Krige laments: "There are also the expensive barrels it was matured in." (Kanonkop was the first to give pinotage royal oak treatment.) "We simply cannot run the risk of using them again just in case they were part of the problem."

Beyers Truter, widely-regarded as the king of pinotage, admits his bafflement. "No matter what awards we have won to date, we can't sit back any more and think we have the right formula for our winemaking. We must all become more technical and know how the chemistry is affected by our physical actions. And the more I work on this, the more I realise how little I know . . . It's not like politics. You can bluff the people but you can't bluff the wine."

He says, admirably frankly, that neither he nor many other winemakers know with complete certainty exactly how they achieve fine wines. It's all very well to improve vineyards and harvest better fruit, "but how do I really know that punching through 30 times in 24 hours is better than doing it 24 times? Not even the French are too sure about these things. Maybe I should have the must analysed each time it is punched through to see what difference it makes . . ." Here's a rare glimpse into the difficult, often make-or-break dilemmas which continually confront Truter and his peers. Wine does not make itself, and the old blood, sweat and tears cliché is a reality in every cellar.

However, undaunted, Truter continues his crusade for the very grape that dealt him an unplayable hand in 1996. He is busy developing a pinotage sauce which he wants the Wine & Spirit Board to certify! "It will be the best thing on ice-cream." He has somehow prevailed upon an innovative commercial manufacturer to create a new ice-cream with real pinotage fruit layered into it. And he is experimenting with a new savoury signature-dish, to be unveiled at the St'bosch Food & Wine Festival—*pinoguinea*. The local answer to Burgundian *coq au vin*.

★★★★ **Paul Sauer** One of Cape's most outspoken "statement" reds, since 70s. Big, bold, definitely packs in the front row; richly rewarding when given its due time—4 to 10 years or more. **95**★★★★★ gold at 1998 IWSC. 85% cab. s., 15% cab. f. No merlot. Deep purple. Spectacular wine with sweet, brilliant fruit and lots of new oak, now almost fully integrated. Palate an amazing concentration of ripe, juicy, essency berry fruits with cherry and blackberry prominent. The riot of berries mingles with vanilla, toasty oak. Beautifully balanced, packed with potential. **96** a powerful blend from 30-year-old vines that Truter believes were not as adversely affected by the vintage as young vines were. Yielding only 4,5 tons/ha. these have produced a big-bodied wine with abundant cherry fruit, rich and smooth palate, and a potency that really does belie the vintage. Tasted only a day or so after bottling but has all the components to be as good as the best. **Auction Reserve** Unavailable for tasting. **94 WINE**★★★★.

★★★★ **Cabernet Sauvignon 95** "still bloody nice, and getting better" says Truter. Blackcurrant accents, sweet, soft flavour-array, lovely vanilla notes creeping over some savoury flavour. Ripe, rounded tannin, deep-pile texture. From 30-year-old vines, 22 months in 225 litre barrels, third each new, 2nd-fill, 3rd-fill. 13,5% alc. **96** firmer, but similar character; will soften with time in bottle. **WINE**★★★★.

**** **Pinotage 97** nudging *****. Almost opaque purple with deep blue edge. Ripe bananas and full, soft red/yellow plum aromas. Almost sweetish palate impression, with massive fill-ability. Even in its youth soft, succulent, with hints of chocolate/vanilla. Long, sweet finish. As easy as it is to drink now, has tremendous potential for bottle development over 8-10 years. **95** ABSA Pinotage Top 10.

**** **Pinotage Auction Reserve** Everything the above is but more so. Deeper, sweeter, morello cherry as extra component along with ripe banana and blackberry. Big, full, yet as elegant as can be. Firm tannin reminds that the sweetness is from fruit/alcohol, not sugar. Given time is going to be fiercely fought-for by fans.

*** **Kadette Dry Red** ◀ Going on **** **97** supposed to be an everyday drinker but is too good for that: a superb rather than super-quaffer. Deep purple, fuller in all respects than **96** with ripe mulberry, leafy, cedary aromas, touch of mint. All repeat on palate with soft tannins, fresh bounce. Subtle oak throughout. Great food wine, remarkable value. **96** now in almost perfect balance, very classy quaffing.

KELLERPRINZ WINES — SFW

Sales equivalent to one million cases annually in returnable glass/box range. **Grand Crû** Bone-dry white, lightish; mainly chenin. **Stein** delicately scented, gentle semi-sweet. **Late Harvest** Honeyed scent, full-ripe fruit, clean bite of acid. **Rosanne** Rosé. Gentle fruitiness, sweetness moderated by some tannin. All NV.

KEN FORRESTER Vineyards—SCHOLTZENHOF FARM

Helderberg, Stellenbosch — See Helderberg map

Tastings/sales: 96 Winery Rd. Restaurant (Tel: 021-8422020), or by appointment Devoncrest Cellar, Devon Valley. (Tel: 021-8822363)

Lunch & dinner daily, except Sun night, at 96 Winery Road, opposite Helderberg Winery. (See Restaurant Section in this guide.) Self-catering cottage for hire.

Owners: Ken & Teresa Forrester
Winemaker: Martin Meinert (since 1998)
Vineyards: Johan Pienaar, Hannes Bredell
Production: 12 000 cases. 29 ha. (90% white, 10% red)
P.O. Box 1253, Stellenbosch 7601
Tel: 021-8552374 **Fax:** 021-8552373
E-mail: foodwine@satis.co.za
Website: www.forresters.co.za

Ken Forrester becomes positively boyish when telling of his latest coup, Forrester's Petit Chenin. The name is an oblique and characteristically irreverent reference to anatomical sites rather than merely matters of size. "A buxom, cheeky little chenin" he confides, in an adolescent change-room manner. Bottled in heavyweight glass with flanged lip (a bottle which larger merchants have been eyeing, without success) under Supreme corks, the first to carry a "100% guarantee of quality" and branded without the "Ken" to set it apart from more serious chenins under his personal label, it's been a roaring success. All 5 000 cases crossed UK till points within 3 months after advertisement in the London Sunday Times. The striking (alarming?) lime green and black label adds to the cheekiness. It wasn't initially intended that way, but when the printer inadvertently reversed the colours at the 11th hour, Ken, wife Teresa and young family decided they were onto something different. Local enthusiasts can look forward to it joining—from 1999—the barrel/bottle-aged food-friendly chenin blancs the Forresters are so passionate about.

Food remains firmly in their blood, of course. Unable to stay out of quality kitchens following their move to this Helderberg farm from Johannesburg, they established the relaxed 96 Winery Rd. Restaurant (just over the road from their vineyards), cosmopolitan in its mix of style and cuisine, in spite of an avowed intention to leave the foodie business to others. Partners in the immensely popular restaurant include gifted winemaker Martin Meinert who now takes full charge of this bevy of Forresters at his own Devoncrest cellar.

★★★★ **Chenin Blanc** Full but balanced, just-dry food wine, serious in intent, wood/bottle-aged for breadth to match cuisine. Super ripe guava fruit peeks out from early fermentation character of luscious **98**, freshly crisp when tasted mid-1998, will develop prior to release. Floral **97**, which firmly established the new-generation, weightier style, is taut and brisk, fruit evolving to richer plane. Bottling for Woolworths Reserve range touched with botrytis, slightly sweeter. **96** venerably full, honeyed, admirable lingering depth. From 25-year-old plus Helderberg bush vines, pruned for low yields, half barrel-fermented in used oak. Greater "mouth-feel" doesn't detract from grape's intrinsic delicacy. Interesting, lighter option for meals where unambiguous chardonnay could overpower. **95 WINE**★★★★.

★★★ **Petit Chenin** NEW **98** 100% full ripe chenin grapes, freshest fruit "lightly kissed with French oak". Limey, guava fruits burst through wood vanillins, fresh but full taste. "Clever" wine, economical oaking gives extra dimension without prohibitive cost, contact with spent yeast cells and full malo add luscious layers. Lots of flavour for early consumption.

★★★ **Sauvignon Blanc** Big, weighty style in ripe **98**, unwooded, briskly dry without hard acidity. Crisp, fresh, but definite bonus of ripe fruit, gooseberry rather than grassy flavours. **97** manages mix of fruity/gooseberry and flinty/stony qualities. Lasting impression in finish. 13% alc.

★★★ **Noble Late Harvest Chenin Blanc** Barrel fermentation in Sauternes style, peach, melon decadence cut with zinging citric lift. **98** drier style at 84 gms/l sugar, 12,5% alc., TA 7,7.

Blanc Fumé Green pepper crispness combines with buttery vanilla on creamy palate. Clean, dry finish. **97** second bottling after **94 WINE**★★★★, still alive. 50% tank and barrel-fermented, American oak. **Grenache-Syrah** Light, simple fruity-sweet quality, mulberry flesh, pepper, clove spice. **97** deeper colour, more substance than **96**. Unwooded Devon Valley grenache (two-thirds) teamed with Forrester-grown shiraz, oaked 9 months.

KERSFONTEIN

See Sonop

KEVIN ARNOLD FINE WINE

Stellenbosch

Visits: Open by appointment only.
Winemaker: Kevin Arnold
Production: 7 tons, 600 cases
P.O. Box 977, Stellenbosch 7599
Tel: 021-8800496 **Fax:** 021-8801007
E-mail: waterfordhil@icon.co.za

Those who wondered where accomplished winemaker Kevin Arnold had got to, after leaving Rust-en-Vrede, can now mark him down on a new spot on the Stellenbosch map—Waterford Farm (see also separate entry) up the Blaauwklippen road. Here, in a pumpkin-coloured, cleverly converted fruit packshed, he's in business with the farm's owner, IT industry dynamo Jeremy Ord: making the superb wine below and a striking sauvignon blanc under the farm label, and supervising the building of a cellar. Ord and Arnold intend dedicating their wines to their children; first to have his "own" label will be Kevin and Heather Arnold's eldest son, Robert Charles.

**** **Shiraz** NEW **98** grapes purchased from Overgaauw where a contract has been agreed to ensure future supplies. "I have never seen grapes like that in my whole life," says Arnold. "It must have been the almost perfect vintage and also a well-managed vineyard." The wine is stunning. Deep, bright purple; powerful bouquet: dense, ripe, dark plum fruit with touch of wild seaside herb, hints of liquorice and peppery spice. Youthful, concentrated palate is as rich and chewy as nose promises: stacks of dark fruit flavours, sweet vanillas. Rich, soft, with ripe tannins, almost gulpable now but a few years of age will reap magnificent dividends. 13,7% alc. Small French oak barrel-handled.

Cabernet Sauvignon and **Chardonnay** to follow. Both NEW.

KLAWER WINERY

Olifants River See Olifants River map

Tastings/sales Mon-Fri 8-5. Sat 9-12. Tasting fee R5 p/p for groups. Cellar tours by appointment.
Owners: 80 members
Winemakers: Len Knoetze, Sias du Toit
Consulting Viticulturist: Jeff Joubert.
Production: 25 000 cases. **Vineyards:** 1 100 ha.
P.O. Box 8, Klawer 8145
Tel: 02724-61530 **Fax:** 02724-61561

The 98 vintage was something of a revelation for winemakers Len Knoetze and Sias du Toit, newly installed at this revitalised West Coast cooperative. Moving to toasty Olifants River Valley from Tulbagh and Riebeek wineries respectively, they were bowled over by the quality fruit emerging from vineyards replanted on selected lime-rich sites. "We discovered the unbelievable potential of this warm-climate area. It's out there in the vineyards waiting to be picked!"

KLAWER range:

*** **Chardonnay** ◀ NEW Australian-styled **98** challenges conventional wisdom about quality of Olifants River whites. Quite delightful, lemon-lime tang; wide, succulent citrus fruit; inviting oak; long, zesty, dry finish. All too often Cape chardonnays are over- (or under!) whelmed by wood; this one is neither. Fermented on oak chips. Also defying accepted wisdom: highish 10 tons/ha. yield. Ideal picnic wine. A snip at R12 ex-cellar.

*** **Hanepoot** ◀ **98** bright, bouncy version of this commonly unctuous dessert. Arresting muscat nose; unusual tangy green-guava, mint inflections hint at freshening acidity which deftly lifts penetratingly sweet (close to 200 gms/l sugar) palate.

*** **Soet Wit Muskadel** ◀ **98** like Hanepoot above, distinctly uncloying dessert. Smooth, seamless melding of fruit, spirit. Complex muscat, peppermint, Turkish delight bouquet. Lusciously sweet, braced by lively acid, whistle-clean finish. Bargain at R11 from cellar door.

Vin Rouge Beefy in all departments; for robust constitutions. Not without some appeal, however, not least from handsome bottle in Mondavi mould. **Blanc de Noir** Unusual grenache-driven **98** redolent of Provence. Delicate coral-pink, gentle morello wafts. Semi-sweet, low alc. charmer. "Tourists rave about it!" **96**, only gold medal Bl. de Noir at Veritas. **Colombard** ◀ Oak-fermented **98** revealing merest hint of wood, zingy guava-toned flavour, dry. Shows what bit of TLC can do for variety. **Premier Grand Cru** ◀ Fresh, grassy chenin/colombard blend in **98**, crisp, invigorating, dry. Gives some meaning to the "premier" in PGC. **Sauvignon Blanc 98** attractively earth-toned, vegetal; for those who tire of tropical frippery. Emphatic gravel, nettle aromas/flavours, bone dry, lingers. Unwooded, low alc. (11,5%). **Chenin Blanc** Bigger dollop of sugar (6,7 gms/l) in **98** than pvs., still tastes dryish. Gentle guava eddies, pleasant, rounded, easy-drinking. **Late Vintage 98** untasted. **Special Late Harvest** Honey, pineapple in **98** follow through to finish. Good acid/sugar balance, charming sweetness. **95** won regional gold. **Red Muskadel** Very pale, almost Bl. de Noir-tinted **98** disguises very pleasant full-flavoured/sweet dessert; redcurrant aromatics. (208 gms/l sugar.) Regular show-winner. **Vonkelwyn Brut** NEW **NV** untasted. **Michelle Doux Vonkelwyn** Usually peachy pink carbonated sparkler from red muscadel, light cherry flavours, not too sweet. Low alc.

BIRDFIELD NEW Export range:

Includes **Chardonnay, (wooded) Chenin Blanc, Sauvignon Blanc, Colombard, Pinotage, Merlot, Shiraz.**

KLAWERVLEI ESTATE

Stellenbosch See Stellenbosch map

Open 9-5 weekdays; Sat 9-1. Tastings, sales, cellar tours.
Proprietor: Hermann & Inge Feichtenschlager
Winemaker: Markus Sieben (since Jan 1998)
Production: 4-5 000 cases. **Vineyards:** 44 ha.
P.O. Box 144, Koelenhof 7605
Tel: 021-8822746 **Fax:** 021-8822415

"Natural and pure" is how Hermann Feichtenschlager sums up his estate's philosophy, and fans of organic farming will be pleased to know that after a disastrous 1997 harvest, in which his gentle garlic-spraying regime was put to the sword by rampant mildew, 1998 has been "absolutely excellent. No sickness, no damage in the vineyards," he says. This will doubtless benefit from being handled in the cellar by new winemaker, Markus Sieben, from Geisenheim, Germany—which country, along with the UK and Canada, is an important export market for Klawervlei. While chenin is in the majority in these vineyards, 21 ha. of pinotage, merlot and cabernet are in place to meet increasing demand for red wines.

Cabernet Sauvignon 96 highly recommended by *Decanter* magazine: Lightweight, pleasant style, strawberry/earthy notes, attractive current drinking. **98** tasted in infancy while still tough on palate but could develop interestingly given 5-7 years, after ageing in new French oak. **Merlot** Stepping up by the vintage. Youthful **98** promising: ripe plummy nose, attractive morello cherries in chocolate on palate, firm tannins, agreeable vanilla flourish to finish. 13% alc. Should be even better than already agreeable **96**: ripe cherry scents carry to soft, succulent palate, delicious little hint of rhubarb. Very low acid for easy drinking, 12% alc., was highly rated by German wine magazine *Selection*. **Pinotage Limited Edition** NEW **98** light (11% alc.) barrel-sample tasted, character still embryonic, cloaked in oak. **Pinotage 96** equally light summer quaffer, seemingly unrelated to more substantial, weightier, more traditionally Cape **95**. **Chenin Blanc Reserve** NEW Dry **98** with ultra-ripe mango hints in nose, capsicum kick in tail, formidable 14% alc. result of super-hot vintage. **Chenin Blanc Dry** Wham-bang whopper of a white at 14% alc., not especially fruity/chenin-like, but very showy. **96** much gentler, softer, lemony character. **Chenin Blanc Bin 4** NEW Best chenin from Klawervlei in **98**: guava coulis nose, peach flavour, soft, smooth (altogether better foil for vintage-driven high alc.). **Chenin Blanc Off-Dry** Neutral **96**, just a hint of sweetness, 12% alc. **Chenin Blanc Late Harvest** Soft, sweet, lowish alc. (11%) white.

KLEIN BEGIN

See Nelson Wine Estate

KLEINBOSCH

See IWS, CWC

KLEIN CONSTANTIA ESTATE

Constantia See Constantia map

Tastings/sales: Mon-Fri 9-5, Sat 9-1. (Tours by appointment.)
Tasting costs: R10 per head for tour groups. Individuals, no charge.
Owners: Duggie & Lowell Jooste
Winemaker: Ross Gower (since 1985)
Vineyards: Kobus Jordaan (since 1980)
Production: 600 tons, 45 000 cases. **Vineyards:** 74,5 ha.
P.O. Box 375, Constantia 7848
Tel: 021-7945188 **Fax:** 021-7942464
E-mail: kleincon@global.co.za
Website: http://home.global.co.za/~kleincon

The English-language release of *Les Plus Grands Crus du Monde* as *The Great Wines and Vintages*, which lists Klein Constantia Vin de Constance amongst the top 44 labels in the world, will only increase pressure on tiny quantities. It's not as if it's unheralded. This modern recreation of the revered wine of Constantia that eased the exile of the defeated Emperor Napoleon on St Helena continues to impress abroad. It was featured at the 3rd Annual Raffles Wine & Food Experience (alongside Ch. d'Yquem) in late 1997 and again at the 1st Annual *Decanter* Great Winemakers Dinner at The Ritz, London in early 1998. Plantings of muscat de frontignan, from which the gem is made, have increased by 50%, but fruit from the new vineyards will find its way into the distinctive squat bottle only in 2005.

With refined understanding of the property's viticulture, certain blocks are being replaced. Sauvignon blanc gains more land with a clone offering open bunches that are less susceptible to botrytis; pinot noir takes root at the highest, coolest point of the vineyards. Owners Duggie and Lowell Jooste and winemaker Ross Gower bravely persist with elegant Rhine riesling in spite of its undeserved (especially from this cellar) lesser image.

Despite strings of accolades, more than a few critics believe Gower has still to produce his greatest reds. That reality may not be far off. To maximise the KC cellar capacity—designed for 1 000 tons but only crushing 600 tons due to low yields—the Joostes have purchased a run-down but high-potential red wine farm in the Helderberg. Warmer than KC, here the existing 8-year-old bush vine merlot will be joined by cabernet sauvignon and shiraz over the next 6 years. Able to exercise better control over the source than they could with bought-in grapes, the team will now be able to launch a second label. The commitment to quality, constant at this estate—once part of Van der Stel's and Hendrik Cloete's legendary Groot Constantia—since the Joostes bought in 1980, will guide this new direction in its history.

★★★ **Cabernet Sauvignon** Confirmation of medium rather than weighty style with latest **95**, yet delivers quite powerful flavours—touch of mint and spice off-setting dusty blackberry impact. Nicely oaked. With **94**, **93**, cleverly straddles "traditional" drier and "modern" fruitier styles. 100% cabernet but blend is 40% new, fresh, sometimes minty ("Schleip") clone—a Gower-initiated touch. Multiple accolades: **SAA** selections in **92**, **90**, **89**, **88**; **VVG 93**, **91**. Maiden, long corked **86** for Nederburg Auction.

Reserve 95 single vineyard, minty nose, classy cassis concentration, minerally, super tannic grip, like **94**, **93** 100% new clone.

★★★ **Shiraz 95** dense purple with sensuous, spiced pepper bouquet; full, generous, savoury fillip to cherry flesh. Matured in American oak barrels, adding sweet-spicy wafts. Most of these v'yds uprooted (only 1,2 ha., or 2% of the estate's total); what a pity. Pvs. vintages more leathery-earthy. **94 SAA. Reserve 97** for CIWG a corker. Very dense purple, milled black pepper and liquorice. Savoury twist to tannic tail. 50 cases.

★★★ **Pinot Noir 96 VG** mahogany tints, earthy cherry nose, ripe prune and date character. Like **95**, **94** from low yielding new clone 113 on high south-facing slopes. Handsomely oaked. **94** WINE★★★★. Unusually fermented by natural yeast. Barrelled, 50% new, in Burgundian-favoured Alliers, Vosges.

★★★ **Marlbrook** Enviable reputation of this label among Cape's more fashionable B'deaux-style blends. 55% cab. s., 40% merlot, 5% cab. franc in **95**, long stay in wood adds depth to still youthful, healthy colour. Tarry nose, restrained fruit, ripe tannin. **94** started switch from a merlot dominated (65%) **93**. **89** and first **88 VVG**.

★★★★ **Sauvignon Blanc** Big, impressive, unwooded, dry white Cape showpiece reclaims excellence with ultra-ripe **98**: overt capsicum, granadilla and fig, tapered fruit, imposing alcohol. 2 000 magnum bottling should see gentle buffing of edges over time. **97** *Decanter* Highly Recommended, developed grassy, gooseberry features, not as riveting as striking **96 WINE**★★★★(★), **VVG**, **SAA**. Initially shy nose evolves and palate broadens with fig, bell pepper richness. Solid show record began with maiden **86** which—hoisted on similar 14% plus alc. platform—suggests **98** will inherit longevity of Constantia *terroir*.

★★★★ **Sémillon 97** small CIWG auction bottling of dry sémillon, first from this estate. Fresh, grassy, almost sauvignon-like fruit. Dry, arresting. Stylish—a viable, welcome alternative to ubiquitous "mainliners" chardonnay, sauvignon.

★★★ **Chardonnay** Latest **97** step up on lighter, leaner **96**, in usual barrel-fermented style, deep, golden colours. Obvious vanilla oak aromas, ripe buttery fruit, finish lifted by characteristic lemon tang. Should develop butterscotch attractions, even Burgundian-like ripeness over a few years. Substantial. 7 tons/ha. yield, spontaneous malo, 50/50 new and 1 yr oak maturation for 6 months. **93** KLM, Singapore Airlines. **89 Reserve,** only **VVG** chardonnay at 1994 Veritas awards.

★★★★ **Rhine Riesling** Very ripe fruit, apricot, soft peach intensity, firm acid grip tightens 12 gms/l sugar in magical **98**, less botrytis than oily-textured **97** with sweet/sour tension, touch drier at 10 gms/l sugar. Unlike most non-dry whites, here the sweetness is not added back after fermentation, but results from shutting off fermentation when winemaker judges he has right balance. Result is an inviting fresh fruit basket. Good ageing potential (sp. in botrytis years: **97**, **96**, **95**), maturing into nutty, fruitcake and toffee-scented beauties.

★★★★★ **Vin de Constance** From Robben Island to Raffles? The world's most celebrated teetotaller, President Nelson Mandela, has been known to succumb to this tipple which holds its own with the best of Sauternes—even without botrytis, which Gower insists didn't infect the old Constantias. It's made from the same variety, muscat de frontignan, and is propagated from the very clones imported by Governor Jan van Riebeeck in 1656. Alongside full-blown "noble rot" stunners, Constance might not overpower, but it has its own riveting, complex minty, sweet lemon-honey impact, with an obvious but more restrained than usual muscat flair. Latest **94** propels the style, burnished gold, delicate lime nuances, enticing nut flavours, neat sweet tang. **93 WINE****** gold-tinted, clear-flavoured, ripe sunshine intensity of delicate muscat. Maiden **86** marvellously—and vividly—alive 12 years on. Intensely ripe grapes harvested at 40 balling, skin contact precedes slow pressing of very slippery berries before 18 months in old wood.

**** **Sauvignon Blanc Noble Late Harvest 96** opulently gorgeous, apricots, sweet/sour lime tang, lingering zesty finish (only 93 gms/l residual sugar). Fully botrytised sauvignon enriched by new barrel rounding. Nederburg Auction releases. In mould of equally intense **92**, brilliant, velvety eucalyptus dessert.

KLEINDAL — Vinimark 75 0ml range

Vinimark Trading Directors: Tim Rands, Cindy Engelke, Guys Naudé
Export Manager: Richard Kelley
Production: 10 000 cases
P.O. Box 441, Stellenbosch 7599
Tel: 021-8838043/4 **Fax:** 021-8864708
E-mail: info@vinimark.co.za
Internet address: www.vinimark.co.za

Stellenbosch *negociant* Vinimark Trading—one of SA's top independent wine wholesalers—represents a range of brands, producers including boutique wineries, co-ops, larger cellars (the company also imports a line of fine wines, ports, cognacs). Exports, managed by MW Richard Kelley, are booming and include the UK, Holland, Germany, the US, Japan. Kleindal is the house-brand; other ranges include Cullinan View, Table Peak (see those entries for more details).

Cabernet Sauvignon 95 vinous, quite rustic, med./full-bodied, soft tannin. WO St'bosch. **Pinotage 97** WO Stellenbosch; sweet acetone overlay, very light, dry. **Export version** untasted. Pvs. smooth, ready, unwooded, ex-Robertson. **Chardonnay** NEW **97** lighter style, gently citric, dry, very fresh; for Dutch, German markets. **Sauvignon Blanc 97** muted fruit in **97**, fullish, firm but not harsh, bone-dry. Best young. **Chenin Blanc** ◀ Enticing ripe quince, baked apple aromas in **97**, earthy tones too. Palate somewhat lower-keyed. Agreeable early drinking. Ex-St'bosch.

KLEIN GUSTROUW ESTATE

Jonkershoek, Stellenbosch — See Stellenbosch map

Tastings/sales by appointment.
Owners: Chris and Athalie McDonald
Winemaker: Chris McDonald (since 1993)
Production: 1 250 cases. **Vineyards:** 16 ha.
P.O. Box 6064, Stellenbosch 7599
Tel/Fax: 021-8874556

Proprietor/vintner Chris McDonald, with four vintages under his belt, is pleased with the consistency he's achieving in the flagship cab./merlot blend (the winery—newly inscribed in the register of Cape estates—also produces whites, but all go to SFW). A definite house style is emerging—masculine, meaty, fruity with good tannins—bearing the thumbprint, McDonald feels, of the "spectacular, beautiful and, in wine terms, increasingly important Jonkershoek valley". On a poignant note: Hamish, the Scottish Deerhound featured on the front label, has died. His spirit lives on in wine.

★★★ **Cabernet Sauvignon-Merlot** Preview of most promising **97** reveals distinctive muscular build, clean-oaky fruit foundation, warm vanilla seasoning. Current **96** released Oct 98 ahead of **95** ("not ready"), 65/35 blend, yr small French barrels (some new), low 7 tons/ha. yield, alc. 12,5%. **93**, cassis-toned, readying, needing 1-2 yrs; **94** gamey/earthy, some blackberries, grippy; **95** starting to bloom, concentrated, lots of tannin; **96** meaty—all initially tightly wrapped up, deserve time to unfold.

KLEIN SIMONSVLEI

Paarl See Paarl map

Tastings/sales, cellar tours by appointment.
Owners: Niel and Daan Joubert
Winemaker: Jan van Rooyen (since 1998)
Viticulturist: Daan Joubert
Production: 11 000 cases. **Vineyards:** 250 ha.
P.O. Box 17, Klapmuts 7625
Tel: 021-8755419 **Fax:** 021-8755462

Wine has been a feature of this "new" wine farm between Simondium and Klapmuts since its inception in the late 18th century. The property was granted by the Cape's viticulture-savvy governor, Simon van der Stel, around 1791 and the first grapes were crushed a few years later. Fast-forward to 1898, when the property passed into the hands of the current owners, the Joubert family, under whose auspices winemaking continues to this day. Production mostly has been sold in bulk to the wholesale trade or exported. Now, for the first time, a small range is available locally through selected wine shops, restaurants. Viticulturist Daan Joubert is the 3rd generation Joubert in charge of farming operations. Winemaker Jan van Rooyen twirled, sniffed, tasted his way through hundreds of samples during a 4-year stint in the QC section of the Department of Agriculture before moving to Louisenhof and now Klein Simonsvlei to make— rather than judge—wine.

NIEL JOUBERT range: All NEW

★★★ **Sauvignon Blanc** ◀ **98** very nice, unusual combination: ripe figs, fresh-cut grass—usually Cape sauvignons parade one or the other. Full, fresh, almost sweet impression (from 13% alc., 3 gms/l sugar), not aggressive. Mature vines, unwooded. Try with fuller flavoured summer salads.

Cabernet Sauvignon 96 a very laid-back cab. Lightly oaked, med./full-bodied, straightforward cassis, strawberries, traces of smoky oak, vanilla, gentle finish. 13% alc. Also: **Cabernet Sauvignon (Oak Aged) 96** matured 12 mths small oak. **Pinotage** not top 10 material in **96** but most agreeable, perceptible tannic tension, medium-bodied, low acid (4,8 gms/l), lightly oaked. From 22-year-old vines. **Chardonnay** ◀ **98** mouthfilling honey/lemon, smoky oak, crisp, dry. Could develop interestingly—one to watch. 13,5% alc. 30% barrel-fermented, 4 mths on lees, young vines. **Chenin Blanc** ◀ **98** broadside of attractive ripe guava, succulent, substantial, dry. For early drinking.

KLEINE ZALZE

Stellenbosch See Stellenbosch map

Tastings/sales Mon-Fri 9-5. Sat 9-1. Cellar tours by appointment.
Light lunches.
Owners: Jan Malan, Kobus Basson
Winemaker: Andries Eygelaar (since 1997)
Consulting Winemakers: Yves Barry (France), Gottfried Jost, Jan Coetzee
Viticulturist: Jan Malan (since 1984)
Production: 70 000 cases. **Vineyards:** 30 ha. (Stellenbosch), 200 ha. (Wellington), 20 ha. (Arniston Bay)
P.O. Box 12837, Die Boord, Stellenbosch 7613
Tel: 021-8800717 **Fax:** 021-8800716
E-mail: kzwines@mweb.co.za

"Supercharged" is almost too tame a word for the breathless state of this 17th century Stellenbosch farm, originally known as De Zalze. No sooner had new owners Jan Malan, grape farmer from Wellington, and brother-in-law Kobus Basson, Stellenbosch attorney, bought the property from Gilbeys in 1996 than they started refurbishing the ancient cellar from ceiling to floor (and below: a brand new red maturation cellar, capacity over 1 000 barrels, was cut into the granite subsoil). Around this buzz an upmarket residential development began taking shape, replete with guest-house and golf course designed by Peter Matkovitch. If that wasn't enough, the vintners bought a farm in up-and-coming Bredasdorp/Arniston Bay, planning to plant premium varieties on maritime-cooled hillside plots. Finally—*whew!*—the range, now in its second year, was completely overhauled and expanded.

KLEINE ZALZE range:

*** **Shiraz** NEW **97** in amiable soft-fruited style for current drinking or keeping up to 2 years. Some delightful "old-style" shiraz trademarks (brambles, smoke) backed by non-aggressive tannins. 13 months French/American barrels. Should partner gammon particularly well.

Cabernet Sauvignon NEW Gentle blackberry flavours in **97**, brushed with fresh wafts of mint. Light-bodied, undemanding. Kleine Zalze grapes, from ancient vines, matured in French barriques 13 months. **Chardonnay Barrel Fermented NEW 98** (vat sample) very nice, potentially ***. Aromas of light marmalade, freshly buttered toast follow through onto palate. Full, seemingly sweet mouthful (though bone-dry), brisk, tangy finish. Highish alc. 13,6%. Fermented/aged French/American oak, 7 months. Like sémillon below, needs ± yr from harvest to start showing its colours. **Sémillon Barrel Fermented** NEW Toasty-oaked, promising **98** sports ripe, vanilla-infused tropical tones, lithe texture, fresh, clean finish. Grapes from Cape "home" of sémillon: Franschhoek. Fermented in French oak, malo complete. Tasted very young, one to watch. 13,5% alc. **Sauvignon Blanc** NEW **98** very tame compared to "feral" version below. Subdued grassy notes, light flavour, very fresh. Durbanville, Franschhoek grapes, blended after fermentation, reductive treatment. **Chenin Blanc Barrel Fermented** NEW **98** (tasted young) strongly toasty (but very clean) wood still dominant. Unusual, attractive *mebos* tang, huge weight (15% alc.!), pleasant dry oaky finish. French barrel-fermented, briefly matured, malo complete. Durbanville v'yd. Potential *** (but not for delicate constitutions). **Chenin Blanc Bin 46** NEW Fresh guavas deluxe in tasty, wide-bodied **98**. Ripe, fresh-fruited, clean, ample—delicious all round. But watch that alc. 14,5%. Grapes from Franschhoek mountainside.

"Z" range:

Cabernet Sauvignon NEW **97** the sort of wine to chill out by. Easy, if fairly simple blackcurrant essences, gentle finish. Doesn't need food. Grapes ex-Wellington. **Gamay Noir** ☺ ◀ Nouveau-style quaffing doesn't get much fresher, bouncier than **98**. Vibrant cherry colour, forward sappy cherry aromas/flavours, dry, whistle-clean finish. Probably best young. Tank sample tasted. **Chardonnay** ◀ **98** unwooded, very clean (like rest of range). Beguiling peach/hazelnut wafts, attractive sweet-sour flavours, touched with walnuts, fresh citrus. Alcoholic oomph: 13,8%. Durbanville grapes. Partial malo. **Chenin Blanc Bush Vine** ◀ NEW **98** one of more interesting chenins of vintage, one to watch. Lovely ripe peach-apricot sorbet, sweet-oak, almond spicing; fresh, clean, extraordinary length. French/American oak. Potential ★★★, tasted very young. High-kicking: 13,8% alc. **Sauvignon Blanc** ◀ Here's a wild-child! **97** reeks of/perfumed with (take your pick) Karoo bush, nettles; explodes on palate, finishes dramatically with intriguing orange-zest tang. Very individual. Promises interesting development. Unwooded. "A very real Sauvignon Blanc" is winemaker's apt comment. 13,5% alc. **Sauvignon Blanc "Red Hill"** NEW **98** opposite of "sauvage" sibling above: gentle, soft, some grassy, gooseberry wafts, tame acid/alc. (12%). Wellington grapes, unwooded. Best young.

VINTNER'S CHOICE range:

Dry Red NEW **98** (blend being tweaked) cinsaut, cab. s., pinotage; earthy, robust, very fresh. No-frills dry quaffer. **Dry White** NEW **98** mainly sémillon, chard., some weisser riesling; grapes from Franschhoek, Wellington. Earthy, full-bodied everyday white. ± 13% alc.

KLOOFZICHT ESTATE

Tulbagh See Tulbagh map

Open Mon-Sat sunrise to sunset. Group tasting fee R5 p/p.
Guest cottage accommodation, breakfast on request.
Owner/Winemaker: Roger Fehlmann
Production: 1 500 cases. **Vineyards:** 5 ha.
P.O. Box 101, Tulbagh 6820
Tel/Fax: 0236-300658

One-of-a-kind Roger Fehlmann, "self-made, autodidactically groomed" winegrower and owner of this mini-estate, at Tulbagh, makes wine only when his spirit—and Nature, his "guide, mentor and all-powerful ally"—move him. Which, as it happens, isn't all that often. 1998 found him trekking through the US for the year, leaving fans of his Bordeaux-inspired **Alter Ego** nursing their steadily-maturing **93** release and, no doubt, wondering when a new incarnation of this "really idiosyncratic and unique" blend might appear.

★★★ **Alter Ego** Merlot/cabernet **93**, though getting on in years ("on a human scale in its early 30s," vintner says), still shows gentle "sweet" bouquet, good ripe blackberry fruit, sweet-sour flavours, fair grip of tannin. So drink now (with food) or wait to see what happens. Barrel-matured French, American, Hungarian oak. ± 12,7% alc.

KOELENHOF CO-OPERATIVE

Koelenhof, Stellenbosch See Stellenbosch map

Open Mon-Thurs 8.30-1; 2-5. Fri 8.30-1; 2-4.30. Sat 8.30-12.30.
Picnic tables, deli.
Owners: 75 members
Manager: Helmie de Vries (since 1969)

Winemaker: Louw Engelbrecht (since 1997)
Asst. Winemaker: Andrew de Vries
Production: 10 000 tons.
P.O. Box 1, Koelenhof 7605
Tel: 021-8822020/1 **Fax:** 021-8822796

Visits to Washington, Oregon and California in 1998 gave winemaker Louw Engelbrecht both inspiration and confirmation: "dedication makes good wine; and good wine can be made in large volumes". The key ingredients for what he calls the "not so simple" recipe for quality are healthy vineyards and correct clone-selection, his chief concerns in a determined drive to polish Koelenhof's image as a prime vineyard area. Showing many other wineries the way, Koelenhof has prioritised its workers' housing needs, assisting them with negotiations for state subsidies towards their own homes, and supplying building plans. Regrettably, Engelbrecht reveals, this worthy initiative is being slowed down by the quagmires of bureaucracy. No such brakes apply to winemaking activities, however: the red-wine fermentation cellar here is being extensively enlarged, and once completed will be able to handle more than double present volumes.

★★★ **Hanepoot** ◀ Classy **96** dessert: fresh minty-limey bouquet, creamy texture, lively personality, 187 gms/l sugar handled with a light touch. Delicious.

Cabernet Sauvignon ◀ **94** a big boy: dark, spiced plum fruit, touch of tar/liquorice, muscular finish. 13,8% alc. 2 yrs French oak. **Pinotage** Unwooded **97**: ripe plummy fruit, almost porty hints on nose, contrasting bite on palate. **Pinotage Rosé** ◀ Always agreeable here: **98** pomegranate colour, touch of caramel on nose, nice sweet-sour-spice, fruity combination on palate, all elements in right sort of harmony for this semi-sweet, fun, low alc. (10%) style. **Sauvignon Blanc** Assertive **98**: grassy, fresh herby aromas, palate to match. Smooth, dry, longish finish. **Koelenhoffer** ◀ ☺ Unsurprisingly cellar's top-seller, always spot on target—quaffer with touch of style, tiny sprinkle of 6,8 gms/l sugar, smooths rather than sweetens. Lively ripe apple nose, fruity-fresh palate, clean finish. Equal parts sauvignon/chenin blanc in **98**. Also in litre bottles with screw cap, good beach-party stuff. **Bukettraube** Semi-sweet **97**, delicate muscat notes fading. **Jerepigo 96** sweet dessert from chenin, quieter nose than pvs., more weight, similar tropical fruit/molasses tones. **Port 96** from merlot, ruby-type, year in barrel. Untasted. **Vonkelwyn Vin Sec** Low-alc., light, fruity, off-dry sparkler from **97** sauvignon blanc, colombard, chenin.

KRONENDAL See Natural Corporation

KUMALA See Sonop

KUPFERBERGER AUSLESE — By Bergkelder

NV Well-liked, lively blend of mainly chenin/colombard, dashes sémillon, Cape/Rhine riesling. Spicy semi-sweet (27 gms/l) white. Alc. 11,5%.

KWV INTERNATIONAL

Paarl See Paarl map
Paarl Cellar Tours: Mon-Fri 8-4.30, Sat and public holidays 8.30-4. Sundays 10-2.30. Booking essential. Tel: 021-8073008/7.
KWV Brandy Cellar: **Worcester**: tastings Mon-Fri 8-5, Sat and

public holidays 9-4 **Reservations:** Tel: 0231-20255
Executive Director: Willem Bestbier
Chief Cellarmaster: Kosie Moller
Production Manager: Sterik de Wet
P.O. Box 528, Suider-Paarl 7624
Tel: 021-8073911 **Fax:** 021-8073000

Mammoth investments in new cellar equipment and oak, updated techniques and what KWV International chief cellarmaster Kosie Moller calls "a greater degree of personal innovation" are steadily transforming not only the value-for-money **KWV** range below but the flagship **Cathedral Cellar** line-up (see that entry for details). Marketing and presentation are being spruced up to keep pace with quality and stylistic developments, as evidenced by the advent of trendy lip-topped bottles, easy-to-read labelling and sweeping rationalisation in the ranks—**Springbok**, a range for the US market, and **Paarl** (Canada) are being culled, and a number of items from the "standard range" have been nixed. The new easy/early-drinking range, **Robert's Rock**, is named after Col. Robert Gordon, a colourful figure in the early Cape who, apart from being a military commander, was a keen explorer and botanist (he gave his name to one of the dome-like rocks on Paarl Mountain). A Scot travelling to the Cape to command the Dutch forces, he didn't fare too well: under his watch the battles of Muizenberg and Wynberg were lost, resulting in the first British Occupation of the Cape in 1795.

★★★★ **KWV Cabernet Sauvignon 96** in same ripe-fruity mould as dramatically improved **94**, **95**; new red-wine cellar at Paarl paying dividends. Latest elegant, wide-bodied; blackcurrant pastilles, dark-roast coffee bean, almost sweet plumminess on palate, peppery/mulberry hints in the long finish. 12% alc. **95** rich, ripe berry fruit, mouthfilling, leafy, cedary, minty flavours. Plenty of potential, but already very accessible. Gold at Vinexpo. **94** developing in complexity. Generous fruit, mouthfilling, good clean oak.

★★★ **KWV Shiraz** From **96**, has improved out of all recognition. Latest **97** complex, very drinkable, plenty potential to develop over 3-5 yrs. Medium-deep colour, sweetly oaked, ripe blackberry fruit in soft, silky texture. 12,5% alc. **96** first of the new breed, complex, abundance of cherry/berry fruit, oak well-integrated, mouthfilling. **93 VVG**.

★★★★ **KWV Pinotage** Another quantum improvement, heralded by **94**. Fruit leaps out of glass in **97** (Burgundy-shaped bottle), oak, raspberry fruit lead from nose to tail, ripe bananas, plush plumminess. Clean, fresh finish. Bright mulberry red colour, tinge of blue. 12% alc. **94 VG** vast improvement on pvs. Big, fruity, (raspberries, bananas), bold, very satisfying. **VG**. **92 SAA** and **VG**.

★★★ **KWV Merlot 96** medium red, blue nuance. Bouncy green pepper aroma, blackberry, black cherry flavours coated with rich coffee/chocolate and well-judged oak. 12% alc. For now or next 2-4 years.

★★★ **Cinsaut**☺ ◀ **97** inviting light fresh strawberry aromas, mélange of strawberry/raspberry flavours. Soft, easy drinking, as suggested by fair, almost rosé colour. 11,6% alc.

★★★★ **Roodeberg** Steadily improving since **94**, this million-plus-litres-a-year smash is terrific in **96**. Bright ruby, quite deep; pleasantly ripe, green pepper scents; redcurrant, chocolate, spicy vanilla dance on palate, charming tannins, deft oaky flourish. Commercial style with some cachet. Handsome, tall, tapered claret bottle reflects quality within. 12,3% alc. 40/40 cab. s./shiraz, 15% merlot, also cab. f.

★★★ **Robert's Rock Shiraz-Malbec** NEW **97** youthful purple tint, fruit-driven style: juicy blackcurrant, sprinkling of cinnamon, easy drinker even at 13% alc.

*** **Sauvignon Blanc-Chardonnay** NEW ◀ Fresh peach, pear aromas/ flavours in **97**, brisk lemony finish, quite substantial. Lovely in bloom of youth.

*** **Chenin Blanc** ◀ **98** has all the right things in the right places, as did **96**, **97**. Floral, fruity, manageably off-dry (8 gms/l sugar), delicious. Unwooded.

*** **Cape Riesling** ◀ Bigger, fuller **98** than usual (13% alc.), as always honest, satisfying. Slightly grassy-herby, dry. For early enjoyment.

*** **Steen** ☺ ◀ guava-toned, lemon-zesty finish, dry. Delightful easy drinker.

**** **Noble Late Harvest 92** (half bottle) heady botrytis, honey, peachy succulence, flashes of kumquat. Gorgeous. 10% alc., 120 gms/l sugar. **90** raisiny, burnt caramel, from chenin, alc. 10,5%, sugar close to 130 gms/l. **89**, **88** both **VVG**, Riesling terpenes obvious on peachy palate. In unfashionably sweeter (150 gms/l sugar), lower alc. style (8,5%). Pvs. vintages aged with honeyed *élan*.

**** **Cavendish Cape White Jerepigo** Deep, golden brown hue, deliciously light-textured, though big-framed **79**, suffused with clean nutty grapiness. 12 yrs. 500 l casks. WO Boberg. 17,5% alc. **VVG**.

**** **Red Muscadel Jerepigo** ◀ **75** creamily smooth dessert, intense, persistent fruitcake, toffee-brittle flavours. **VVG**, a KWV 75th anniversary wine. Gold medal 1996 IWSC. **WINE******.

*** **Full Ruby Port** Earthy, dried-fruit character, dryish palate (± 100 gms/l sugar), 19,5% alc. Vat-matured 4-5 yrs. NV. KWV ports mainly from tinta barocca and souzão with small proportion of old-vine, high quality cinsaut.

*** **Full Tawny Port** "Vintage" style though no vintage actually stated. Amber-mahogany colour, coffee/toffee bouquet. Rich, full flavoured. **VVG**. Aged 8 yrs. 500 l casks.

*** **Limited Release Port 79** unlike Portuguese Vintage Port, this given extended ageing (in 500 l barrels), giving deep tawny appearance. Luscious nuttiness on palate. From cinsaut, pinotage, tinta barocca.

**** **Vintage Port 82**, like pvs. **69**, a show-stopper. Sweeter than current trend, fragrant fruit, hay, pleasant earthiness. Will reward keeping. Both **VVG**.

Rosé Sec Strawberries all the way in smooth, dry **98**. From pinotage. Drink within two years. **Cape Blush Blanc de Noir 98** pretty light coral, light-toned too, dry finish. **KWV Sauvignon Blanc** ◀ Quieter **98** than pvs., in line with vintage; crisp, touch grass, flinty edge. **Weisser Riesling** Light, easy-drinking **98** touched by muscat, arresting palate-tingle, just off-dry at 8 gms/l sugar. 13% alc. Drink young.

The following sparklers all NV: **Mousseux Blanc Brut** Light-bodied, bracingly dry, from chenin, pinot gris. Charmat method. **Musanté** Fruitily-sweet, low alc. (8,6%), perlé from muscat de frontignan; mintily refreshing, gentle prickle. **Pétillant Blanc** Unobtrusively fruity effervescent chenin, 19 gms/l sugar. Screw top. **Pétillant Rosé** Light, frothy pink from pinotage; pleasant sweet, ripe strawberry character. **Mousseux Blanc Demi-Sec** Similar chenin/pinot gris mix as Brut above. 37 gms/l sugar. Charmat method. Light-toned **Tawny 80** well balanced, complex, gentle, quite sweet, versatile: aperitif or digestif.

*A full range of "Sherries" also produced: **Mymering** pale-dry; **Renasans** pale medium-dry; **Onzerust** medium-dry; **Golden Acre** medium-cream; **1820 Cream** full-cream. Also medium-cream labelled **Very Old**, excellent lightly chilled. KWV fortified desserts, brandies are regular gold medallists on International Wine & Spirit Competition in London and local Veritas show.*

ROBERT'S ROCK range: All NEW

Merlot/Cinsaut Pretty violet, strawberry nose in **97**. Light, undemanding, agreeably fruity, for current drinking. Also with beefy 13% alc. Unwooded.

Chardonnay 97 untasted. **Chenin Blanc/Chardonnay 98** unpretentious early drinking. Some amiable lemon, apricot flavours. 66% chenin, chardonnay. 12,5% alc.

LABORIE ESTATE

Paarl See Paarl map

Tasting/sales Mon-Fri 9-5, Sat 9-1.
Laborie Restaurant & Wine House, picnics. See restaurant section.
Owner: KWV International
Winemaker: Gideon Theron
General Manager: Gawie Kriel
Production: 33 000 cases. **Vineyards:** 48 ha.
P.O. Box 528, Suider-Paarl 7624
Tel: 021-8073911 **Fax:** 021-8073000

Graceful Cape-Dutch buildings cluster under imposing Paarl Rock on this lavishly restored, richly historic estate in the suburbs of Paarl, offering panoramic mountain and valley vistas from the delightful tasting area and new tranquil lakeside picnic venue. Energetic cellarmaster Gideon Theron—he's a driving force behind Paarl Vintners, umbrella organisation for producers and communities in the area—conjures a handsome, characterful range with fine fresh touches such as **Pineau de Laborie**, fortified pinotage à la Cognac's classic aperitif, Pineau des Charentes.

★★★★ **Cabernet Sauvignon 97** a real attention grabber, best yet from this cellar. Deep mulberry colour; attractive green bell pepper, blackberry, mocha. Big mouthfilling flavours of ripe berries, vanilla, sweet spice, well-integrated oak. Varietal character shines through. 13% alc. Will develop with benefit over 4/6 years. **96** set quality rollercoaster in motion. Herby, berry/minty aromas, soft chocolate, eucalypt hint. Potential to develop over 3/5 years.

★★★ **Pinotage** Distinct bright purple in **96**, ripe banana, dry prune, attractive smoky/oaky char. Fruit resounds on palate, fairly firm grip, quiet finish.

★★★ **Merlot 95** year later, still youthful bounce; black cherry, baked fruitcake flavours. Potential to age further. 12% alc.

★★★ **Bin 88 Cabernet-Merlot 96** vibrant mulberry colour. Mulberry, violet nose, ripe plum flavour. Robust, flavourful, good with roasts and full-flavoured food. 60% cab. s., 40% merlot. 12% alc.

★★★★ **Sauvignon Blanc** Reductively-made **98** great step up in character, quality; full of nettle, green olive, ripe fig. Fresh citrus and herb tastes. Well-balanced, enjoyable unpartnered or with food. 13% alc. **96 ★★★** Green grass, nettles, fairly brisk, short. 12% alc.

★★★ **Chardonnay 97** great improvement on pvs., more fruit; citrus, melon, clean oak. Good mouth-feel, citrusy flavours, some butterscotch richness. Long clean, lemony finish. 60% barrel-fermented, malo. 40% tank-fermented, portion in barrel but no malo. 13,5% alc.

★★★ **Laborie MCC 92** all-chardonnay (Blanc de Blancs) bottle-fermented Brut; light delicacy, showing some age, some yeasty tang; dry, fine mousse. Next will include pinot noir. **VVG** and **WINE★★★★**. Drink now.

★★★★ **Pineau de Laborie** Gorgeous—gorgeously packaged—all-pinotage, all-South African dessert. In traditional Cognac mould—pinotage revved up by pot-stilled eau de vie to agreeably tingly 17% alc.—with individual flourish: super-fruity single v'yd selection, lightly brushed with oak. Luxurious, rich; sweet-prune, marzipan, chocolate confection, unchallenging sugar (90 gms/l). **96** in distinctive long-necked 375 ml cork-stoppered bottle with pinotage-coloured label. **Blanc de Noir** NV sparkler from pinotage, pinots gris/noir. Showing coppery colour, bottle age. Next is bottle-fermented. Current transfer method. **Alembic Brandy** See Brandy Section.

GRANITE CREEK range:
Export only Currently includes: **Merlot-Cabernet, Chardonnay, Sauvignon Blanc.**

LA BOURGOGNE

Franschhoek See Franschhoek map

Open by appointment.
Owner: MC Toop
Winemaker: Deon Truter, Franschhoek Vineyards
Production: 3 000 cases. **Vineyards:** 4 ha.
P.O. Box 78, Franschhoek 7690
Tel: 021-8762115 **Fax:** 021-8762689

"Joy of Life" is the name of this small ready-to-picnic range, custom-made by Deon Truter of Franschhoek V'yds from the distinguished 17th century farm's grapes. Ancient sémillon vines add their considerable character to the range.

Joie de Vivre Sémillon 98 shows some gravitas from riper, fuller vintage. Herby/grassy qualities, savoury finish. Partners wide range of (alfresco) food. Alc. 12,6%. **Joie de Vivre Sonny's Choice 98** off-dry, smooth texture, muscat whiffs, gentle aftertaste. Agreeable aperitif, sémillon/muscat d'Alexandrie, 11,2 gms/l sugar; 13,3% alc.

LA BRI

Franschhoek See Franschhoek map

Tastings/sales at Franschhoek Vineyards.
Owner: Robin Hamilton
Winemakers: Deon Truter, Driaan van der Merwe (Franschhoek Vineyards Co-op). **Estate Manager:** Johan Haasbroek
Production: 15 000 cases. **Vineyards:** 20 ha.
P.O. Box 180, Franschhoek 7690
Tel: 021-8762593 **Fax:** 021-8763197
E-mail: labri@wine.co.za

History and tradition have a rich resonance on this scenic property at the eastern end of Franschhoek Valley. Founded by Huguenot Jacques de Villiers in 1694, La Bri nurtures a living link with its winemaking heritage in a fraternity of ancient— still robust— sémillon vines. These venerable old-timers will be almost 100 years at the turn of the millennium, "which makes our **Chardonnay-Sémillon** the perfect wine to uncork on New Year's Eve 1999," reckons live-wire winemaker Driaan van der Merwe. "Ancient sémillon and youthful 9-year-old chardonnay represent a wonderful blend of past and future—the very essence of time captured in a glass!"

Cabernet-Merlot Reserve Latest **97** not available for tasting. **96** has developed most appealing ripe berry, plum overtones. Delicious, soft lunchtime drink. Cabernet 70%, merlot; small barrel-matured. **Rouge La Bri 97** cab.s.-merlot, for release early 99; untasted, should follow agreeable light-textured style. **Sauvage de La Bri** Cellar's top gun. **98** given extra heft by night, early morning harvesting. Fresh-cut grass, gooseberry aromas;

intriguing muscat, spicy threads. Can stand alone whereas very crisp, dry **97** better at table. **Chardonnay-Sémillon 98** (not ready for tasting) third each barrel-fermented chardonnay, unwooded chardonnay, old-vine sémillon. **97** unwooded; 73% chardonnay with sémillon from ancient vines. **Weisser La Bri 98** 100% Rhine riesling in lighter, off-dry mood. **Blanc de La Bri 97** sémillon (80%), sauvignon blanc. Peachy essences, dry.

LA COTTE WINES

See Franschhoek Vineyards

LADISMITH CO-OP

Klein Karoo See Klein Karoo map

Tastings/sales Mon-Fri 8-1; 2-5.
Owners: 110 members
Winemaker: André Simonis (since 1992)
Production: 9 000 tons
P.O. Box 56, Ladismith 6655
Tel: 028-5511042 **Fax:** 028-5511930

High alcs. were a feature of the 1998 vintage here as elsewhere, giving André Simonis' customarily lighter range—result of consumer demand in this sizzling semi-arid climate—comparatively rare mouth-widening oomph. This winery-cum-distilling operation bottles a small range under the Towerkop label (named after an unusual "cloven" mountain-peak nearby). The line-up (all **98**) includes:

Ruby Cabernet No-fuss, no-frills dry red swigging, unwooded. **Stein** Semi-sweet, though quite a bit drier (at 19 gms/l sugar) than pvs., from chenin. **Chardonnay** unwooded, dry, fully-ripe grapes from high-yielding v'yds (18-25 tons/ha). 13,5% alc. **Chenin Blanc** Fresh, med.-bodied extra-dry white: **Aristaat** After species of protea found only on slopes of Klein Swartberg at Ladismith. Fruit-salad of hanepoot, chard., chenin, Cape riesling. Clean, fresh, dry drinking. ± 12% alc. **Riesling** Clean, herby-dry white. 12,6% alc.

LA GRATITUDE

SFW

★★★ Major restyling in early 90s has repaid handsomely. Formula now set: mainly sauvignon with sémillon, barrel-fermented chardonnay; **97** has developed true complexity: very dry with warm rounded fruit, smoothness of chardonnay/sémillon offset by crispy sauvignon. Oak well integrated. Stylish dry white, a Cape standard-bearer in its field.

LAIBACH VINEYARDS

Muldersvlei, Stellenbosch See Stellenbosch map

Tastings/sales Mon-Fri 9-5. Sat 9-1. Tasting fee R5 p/p. Cellar tours, group tastings, picnic baskets by arrangement. Guest cottage. Venue for functions.
Owner: The Friedrich Laibach family
Winemaker: Elizabeth Augustyn (since 1997)
Consulting Winemakers: Stefan Dorst, Jean Daneel
Viticulturist: Michael Malherbe
Production: 12 000 cases. **Vineyards:** 36 ha.
P.O. Box 7109, Stellenbosch 7599
Tel: 021-8844511 **Fax:** 021-8844848
E-mail: laibach@iafrica.com

Fresh out of college and charged with running a brand new Swiss-German-owned winery next door to illustrious Warwick and Kanonkop, winemaker Elizabeth Augustyn kept her cool and made a most creditable (mainly white) début in 1997. Her expansively oaked **Chenin Blanc** finished in the top 10 in WINE's 1998 Chenin Challenge—out of more than 80 entries. Now, after a year in barrel, the Elsenburg alumna's impressive **97** reds get to strut their stuff, lending substance to Laibach's ambition to join the top echelon of Cape red producers.

LAIBACH range:

★★★★ **Pinotage** NEW Cape's proprietary grape gets full treatment in **97**—responds beautifully. Gorgeous ripe plums, banana; enticing smoky oak undulations. Intense berry/banana palate, ripe tannin, finely poised fruit-acid balance; has intensity to develop seriously well. 1 yr all-new French/American oak. Grapes from neighbouring farm. 13% alc.

★★★ **Cabernet Sauvignon** NEW **97** cornucopia of aromas: cassis, mulberry, blackberry, lead pencil; fine concentration. Berry compôte on palate, wisps of smoke, though not quite as complex as nose. Yr French oak. Very palatable now but potential to develop over 2-3 yrs. 13,5% alc.

★★★ **Chenin Blanc** (oaked) **98**, like maiden **97 WINE★★★★,** lavishly wooded in love-me-or-leave-me style. Fragrant green apples on base of spicy vanilla oak, ripe melon hints. Slightly austere wood tannins on clean dry finish when tasted in youth, but potential to soften, harmonise in bottle—as did **97**—given a little time in bottle. Picked very ripe; super-low yields. Barrel-fermented; though malo. 13% alc.

★★★ **Chenin Blanc** (non-oaked) ◀ Lovely tropical fruit essences in **98**, very ripe melon, guava dominating. Delicious full mouthful. 8,5 gms/l sugar heightens drinkability.

Merlot NEW Full-blown raspberries, plums, chocolate aromas in **97**; palate less intense, sharper. 1 yr 1st/2nd-fill French oak. **Cinsaut/Cabernet Sauvignon** NEW Soft berry aromas, flavours in **98**; a quaffer with a serious side, some backbone. Sample tasted in infancy, awaiting wooding/final blending. **Chardonnay 98** improves on more lemony **97**. Both partly barrel-fermented in all-new French oak. **98** with citrus, butterscotch, honeyed melon hints, promises interesting bottle development. **Sauvignon Blanc 98** (from bought-in grapes) grassy, light, not an attacking style. **Chardonnay-Sauvignon Blanc** ☺ NEW **98** oozes charm, quaffability, from delicious citrus nose to zippy Caribbean fruit palate. Unwooded. **Sweet Natural** NEW **97** Weisser riesling/chardonnay marriage. Scented peach-mango flavours. Very fresh acid more dominant on palate than 113 gms/l sugar. Vinified; matured 8 months 100% new oak. Will make way for Noble Late Harvest in botrytis years.

INKAWU export range:

Includes above (non-wooded) chenin, sauvignon blanc, chardonnay, cinsaut-cab. s. For specialised retailers, restaurants in Germany, the UK.

LA MOTTE ESTATE

Franschhoek See Franschhoek map

Open 9-4.30 weekdays, Sat 9-12.
Owner: Hanneli Rupert
Winemaker: Jacques Borman (since 1984)
Production: 15 000 cases. **Vineyards:** 104 ha.
P.O. Box 45, La Motte 7691
Tel: 021-8763119 **Fax:** 021-8763446

This prestige estate has now launched an inaugural—and long-awaited—chardonnay for local (and international) sale: and winemaker Jacques Borman has been intent to stake his claim to produce one with a difference, among the hundreds now available in South Africa. Like his good friend Giorgio Dalla Cia at Meerlust, he's eschewed a style with the immediate impact of fresh, fruity crispness, preferring a weightier, perhaps more long-lived one. "I'm looking for nuts—almonds—and limes in this chardonnay, plus keeping qualities." With the luxury of selecting just 40 barrels from 250 (the balance will not make the La Motte prestige range) he knows he has few excuses but to come up with the best.

Not that Borman, with 17 vintages under his belt, most of them with the Ruperts who own La Motte, is given to making excuses. With his impressive (and very French-influenced) track record, he hardly needs to. His responsibilities extend to more than just La Motte—to general Rupert wine empire advising (Fredericksberg, L'Ormarins), and now the widening search for new vineyards in Darling in the West and around Bredasdorp in the East. The discovery time is by no means over. Wine and winemaking is not a job. "It's a way of life, thank heavens," he says. "And now I'm off to the night shift," as we finish an afternoon tasting after 6 pm. He's going to the private family cellar, Boschkloof, over at Stellenbosch. Then home to Paarl. Much of his now relaxed worldly mien comes from trips abroad with Dr. Anton Rupert, an inexaustible fount of apt and wry aphorisms. But for his much wider sweep of business interests, Rupert would have been South Africa's Robert Mondavi. The self-effacing, down to earth Borman, one of South Africa's outstanding wine talents, knows how privileged he's been.

★★★★ **Millennium** Fine-grained, luscious B'deaux-style red, easy on eye (rich plummy hues in youth) and palate with clear but soft, fruity-and-mildly-oaky focus in current **95**. Usually about 50% cab. s., with some 30-40% merlot, balance cab. f. "I'm looking for elegance," says Jacques Borman, whose working visits to Lafite, Latour, Margaux have wrought the difference in these reds, chiefly by rigorous fruit selection in v'yd and a no-expense-spared oak regime. Still in circulation, the **94** among better years, complex bouquet with abundant, soft cherry/ripe berry fruit. Consistent laurels from overseas/local wine contests. About 16-18 months in Nevers barrels. These mature more quickly than cabernet below. The **91** Millennium, e.g., though with some dusty, earthy charm still, is fading compared with cabernet of same year.

★★★★ **Shiraz** Having made a name for what is a virtual single v'yd wine, Borman is obviously torn between this made "first love" and a favoured paramour in the Millenium above, a blend he constructs. Latest **95** shows a vigorous, grippy peppery side, going on vinous marmite, bold and somehow firmer, with less ripe cassis than some pvs. **94 VG** (one of best since **86**, which first showed modern Cape shiraz style) concentrated bouquet with black cherry, plum, pepper (20% new oak). 12,9% alc. **93** pepper, ripe cassis, preserved cherries on nose. Complex spectrum blackberry, nasturtium, hint of vanilla (10% new wood). 13% alc. **92 VVG** (no new oak). **91 VVG** Fine drinking now. **89 VVG**. Pvs. contained 5-10% cabernet. All matured in small oak.

★★★★ **Cabernet Sauvignon 94** latest release, racy claret style, firm and compact, without (flabby) frills of excess oak or sweetness, with grip, structure. Serious food wine. To keep for a while. **93** riper blackcurrant/cassis, clean vanilla, dryish tannins. Palate with herby/cedar touch. **92** currants/herbs, softening tannins. **91** tighter, lighter. **86 VVG**—and deserved, from a re-visiting in 1998—plenty of old-hay charm, still with some tannin scaffolding to lean on. But drink up. These all amply oaked.

**** **Chardonnay** NEW **97** limited release (available from estate only). Individually crafted—a doughy, yeasty offering, with almond-nutty flavours (in contrast to many conventionally crisp lemony stereotypes). Very amply barrel-aged, completely fermented by own wild yeast, in current Cape vogue (an older fashion in Burgundy) and through 100% malo softening routine. A selection of the best 40 of 250 barrels! (Balance for export, etc.) From 8-year-old vines.

*** **Blanc Fumé** Oaked; and, when young, big, bold and regularly each year, as with latest **97**, with some distinctive lusciousness—mainly from lees-and-barrel vinification. (About 8 months in partly new oak.) **96** big, with waning flavours, freshness replaced by honeyed vinosity and advancing, yellowing colours.

*** **Sauvignon Blanc 98** in respectable rather than flamboyant category (some pvs. have been much racier) but wholesome, clean, unwooded.

Merlot, export only. Second export label is **Roosenveldt.**

LANDAU DU VAL WINES (La Brie Farm)

Franschhoek See Franschhoek map

Tastings/sales at Haute Provence Vineyards
Owner: Basil Landau
Winemaker: John Goschen (since 1995)
Production: 500 cases. **Vineyards:** ± 14 ha.
P.O. Box 104, Franschhoek 7690
Tel: 021-8762317 **Fax:** 021-8763369

Everything keeps going right for former Toyota (and Gencor Industries) captain Basil Landau, ensconced on this meticulously restored property in Franschhoek. With talented consultant-winemaker John Goschen (of Haute Provence fame), he's producing some of the valley's most sought-after sémillon and sauvignon blanc. Henry Ford-style mass output is not, however, a hallmark of this micro-boutique operation—at just 500 cases, devotees have to look sharp to get a share.

**** **Sémillon 98** serious, sophisticated version of this at-home-in-Franschhoek variety. From 80-year-old vines. As in pvs. **97**, extraordinary concentration of waxy tropical fruit which, tasted in extreme youth, still jostles with lashings of clean toasty-vanilla oak. 1-2 years (at least) needed for harmony to develop. **95** WINE****.

*** **Sauvignon Blanc** John Goschen coaxes the whole gamut of tones from sauvignon in **98**: grass, gooseberry, feline purrings, river-pebble even; wide palate, fresh almost racy acid, bone-dry discernibly tannic finish makes this necessarily—propitiously—a food partner.

LANDSKROON ESTATE

Suider-Paarl See Paarl map

Tastings/sales Mon-Fri 8.30-5. Sat 8.30-12.30. Tasting fee R3 p/p. Guest-house, self-catering cottage on estate.
Lunch Nov-Apr 11.30-2.30.
Owners: Paul & Hugo de Villiers.
Winemaker: Paul de Villiers (since 1980).
Production: 1 300 tons. **Vineyards:** 275 ha.
P.O. Box 519, Suider-Paarl 7624
Tel: 021-8631039 **Fax:** 021-8632810

E-mail: landskrn@mweb.co.za
Website: www.wine.co.za/landskroon

Pocket-friendly pricing is just one of many attractions of this admirable range made by Paul de Villiers on the bustling family property at Paarl. Down the years the fifth-generation winegrower must have savoured the estate's magnificent views to Table Mountain innumerable times, but these days he's looking further afield—to the international market, where Landskroon is beginning to establish a presence. Steadily a customer base is evolving—Raisin Social, Tesco in the UK, Kinoshita in Japan—and, no doubt, more will follow. Styling his wines to please the international—and home—palate is the challenge, and to see how they do it in the Old World, De Villiers toured Bordeaux in 1998. "Fine red wine needs top-notch wood," he concluded. "Too much of a good thing is not good: wood should never be used in excess." Translating these lessons from Gaul into practice has already begun: the search is on for better quality oak for Landskroon's premium reds.

★★★ **Pinotage** ◀ **97** undoubtedly pick of the estate's reds. Ripe plums, mulberries, some varietal banana sweetness thrown in, gently firming tannins in finish. Moderate (alc. 12%). Pvs. holding steady in bottle, mail-order club "best value". **Reserve 96** clear, limpid plum colour, lots of juice, good tannin dryness on palate, very tasty finish. Medallist at IWSC in London. 9 mths new American oak. Good value all-round.

★★★★ **Port** ◀ absolute bargain at just over R20 ex-farm. Our comments on pvs. apply verbatim to stunning **95** (WINE★★★★): brilliant deep mulberry colours; voluptuous chocolate, berry aromas. Pronounced fruity sweetness highlighted by mature spirit fortification. Delicious, accessible. **94 (★★★)**, with earthier overtones, slowing a little, should be enjoyed now. One-third each mix of tinta barocca, tinta roriz, souzao. **95** Paarl show, mail-order club winner. **94, 93** (WINE★★★★). **94** SA champ (young wine show). **92 VG. 91** (more concentrated, reflecting vintage) and **90 VG**, both **SAA** selections/port trophy winners. 18 months wood.

Shiraz 97 (new clone) through American oak finishing school (50%) spicy, brambly, herbal scents—very reminiscent of glühwein (in attractive, aprés-ski sense)—quite acidic, tannic on palate, so needs time (4-5 years) or robust food. Paarl show gold. Pvs. more approachable, readier. **Cabernet Sauvignon 97** improves on pvs in all departments. Attractive bright colour, pleasant ripe strawberry/raspberry, moderate tannin, long. Pvs. challengingly tannic, needs 3-4 years. New clones now a regular feature. **Landskroon Tesco Cabernet Sauvignon** Good juicy bite, perhaps shade less substantial than standard cab. above. **Merlot 97** quite light coloured/bodied, some ripe strawberry wafts, palate subdued, less impressive than previous. Paarl show winner. **95 VG. Cabernet Franc** ◀ Individual, complex **97** has lots of smells/flavours to explore: peach-pip, cloves, some animal undercurrents plus estate's characteristic berry-tobacco aromas, medium-bodied, nice dry tannins in finish. Paarl show winner. **Cinsaut/Shiraz 97** ◀ deep coloured, attractive wild strawberry, fresh-milled pepper nose, sweetish palate, medium-bodied, easy—no angles. **Cinsaut 97** second vintage, sweet, not a lot of substance. **98** however, tasted from tank, a vast improvement, classic Cape cinsaut: plummy, sweetish sensations, pleasant tannic grip. Flavoursome. Best young. **Blanc de Noir 98** ◀ pretty pale coral, yummy candied strawberries, dryish (though ± 8 gms/l sugar). Versatile with food. Try Thai curries, summer salads. Blend of pinots gris, noir (50/50).
Sauvignon Blanc ◀ **98** very pleasant indeed, ample grassy tones, gentle palate, nice crisp finish. Dry. **Chenin Blanc (Dry) 98** ripe peach, flavours, pleasantly light, fresh. Has potential to develop in bottle, as in **97**. **Chenin**

Blanc Barrel Fermented 97 lovely rich, yeasty aromas, distinctly dry, somewhat tannic. 50% new oak. **Pinot Gris** ◀ **97** unusual variety, something "different" for the table: distinctive "grey" tinge, gentle floral wafts, balanced, dry white. Versatile with food. **Pinot Blanc** NEW **98** another rare (in Cape) variety, very affable peach-scented flavours, lightish mouth-feel (despite 13% alc.), dry oaky finish. Small wood-fermented/matured 2 mths. **Pinot Blanc-Chenin Blanc** ☺ ◀ **97** developing well in bottle: ripe, creamy mouth-feel, tropical/vanilla tones. Nice! (60/40 ratio). "Best value" wine club winner, wood-fermented. **Chenin Blanc (Semi-sweet) 98** lightweight, fresh, sweetish, doesn't shout. Moderate alc. (11%), 26 gms/l sugar. **Bouquet Blanc** ◀ **98** super-grapey, distinctive (but gentle) morio muscat aromas, smooth, tastes just off-dry (7,3 gms/l). 85% chenin. Another Thai-friendly "foodie". **Jerepico Morio Muscat 97** decidedly subdued, light, enjoyable nonetheless. Sip solo or pour over vanilla ice-cream. 17,5% alc. 178 gms/l sugar. In identical style to pvs., only lower-keyed. The only Cape fortified from this variety.

LANDZICHT WINERY

Jacobsdal, Free State

Tastings/sales Mon-Fri 8.30-1, 2-5, Sat 8.30-12. Cellar tours.
"Lapa" (traditional) braai area, guest cottage.
Owners: 45 shareholders
Winemaker: Ian Sieg (since 1984)
Production: 185 000 cases. **Vineyards:** ± 300 ha.
P.O. Box 94, Jacobsdal 8710
Tel: 053-5910164 **Fax:** 053-5910145

In a contest for cheeriest packaging, this admirable Free State winery with its breezy, party-waiting-to-happen image surely will romp into the finals. As for the range—light, often super-low alcohol numbers tailor-made for sociable quaffing—they're bound to get the nod for their bouncy, effortless style. Health-conscious imbibers are snapping up quantities of **Blümchen**, the top-selling label. "Yes, low alcohol is now in demand. And fruit yes!!" notes Sieg, in a delightful Joycean turn of phrase. This amiable Ulysses is engaged on a quest to craft wines that "excite consumers, make them euphoric".

★★★ **White Muscadel** ◀ **97** (current release, maiden vintage) undoubted star of the range. Low-key dessert, nice ripe grapey flavours. "You must have a few bottles of this for winter!!" **WINE★★★★**. Mail-order club winner.

Cabernet Sauvignon Style change in **98**: fuller, bit more oomph. Green pepper, nutty aromas/flavours. Quite tannic, needs 1-2 years. High-kicking (for cellar) 12,5% alc. **97** flew on SA Express wine list. **Rosenblümchen** NEW **98** colombard/pinotage quaffer; gentle bon-bon essences, quite sweet, low alc. (8,5%). **Chardonnay** ◀ **98** gaining more voomah by the harvest: pvs. 12% alc., this one 13,5%. Simple, but amiable citrus, butterscotch accents, zesty dry finish. **Grand Crû** Current (**97**) now tasting rather elderly. Best young. **Rein Blüm 98** light (10,5% alc.), semi-sweet, colombard/chenin. "Popular in-betweener at cellar functions," says winemaker. **Blümchen** Big seller, summery thirst-quencher, decidedly sweet **98**. 7,5% alc. **Gewürztraminer 98** (super-colourful label) discreet rose-petal, spice tones, semi-sweet. **97** exported to Holland. **Special Harvest** Earthy, muscaty sweet white. **Red Muskadel** Undemanding lighter-styled dessert, not over-concentrated. **Rooi Jerepiko 98** cabernet/pinotage blend. Exceptionally light for this style of fortified dessert, fairly neutral. 120 gms/l sugar, 17% alc. **Hanepoot** Pleasant enough, quiet style. **Vin Doux** Carbonated white sparkler, pleasant sweet-sour sherbet flavours.

LANGVERWACHT CO-OP WINERY

Bonnievale See Robertson map

Tastings/sales Mon-Fri 8-12.30; 1.30-5. Cellar tours by appointment.
Owners: 30 members
Winemaker: Johan Gerber (since 1987)
Production: ± 900 cases, 10 000 tons. **Vineyards:** ± 550 ha.
P.O. Box 87, Bonnievale 6730
Tel: 02346-2815 **Fax:** 02346-3059

Colombard, still this Bonnievale co-op's top-selling label in spite of strong emphasis on chardonnay and sauvignon blanc, was "exceptional" in 1998. Apparently the January heat-wave that toasted delicate aroma/flavour components in some areas had a lesser impact here in rustic Bonnievale on the Breede River.

Chenin Blanc NEW **98** first bottled chenin from this cellar. "Good fruit, long gentle finish" is winemaker's note. Off-dry. **Chardonnay 98** in delicately tropical style (though not insubstantial 13,6% alc.), now lightly wooded ("very subtly" says Johan Gerber, who feels a little time in bottle will be beneficial). **Colombard** ◀ **98** bargain-priced summer refresher, drink young. 12% alc.

LANZERAC This historic Stellenbosch name shared by farm/SFW

LANZERAC FARM AND CELLAR

Stellenbosch See Stellenbosch map

Open Mon-Fri, Sat.
Owner: Christo Wiese
Winemaker: Wynand Hamman
Production: 2 500 cases. **Vineyards:** 45 ha.
Consultant: Jan Boland Coetzee
Tel: 021-8865641 **Fax:** 021-8876998

A gentleman's agreement between Christo Wiese, who owns this historic farm, and SFW, long-registered owners of the trademark Lanzerac name required some fancy footwork, but the result is that both parties now share the name. (Though of course not the famously elegant country hotel, or the Wieses' own splendid homestead on the property!)

Excellent vineyards creeping up the mountain slopes cradling the cool Jonkershoek valley have been developed—consultant Jan "Boland" Coetzee of Vriesenhof had a big hand here; recent plantings include 2,5 ha. of sauvignon and malbec. The Wieses maintained their reputation as Stellenbosch hosts-with-the-most at a splendid alfresco party to celebrate spring, with tables arrayed down the length of Lanzerac's oak-fringed approach-avenue. Winemaker Wynand Hamman produced a special 250 ml red blend for the occasion—a take-away souvenir for the celebrity guests.

★★★ **Merlot 96** from 2nd crop, potential starting to show. Blackberry hints on nose/palate, undertone of vanilla, good dry tannin, long clean finish. **97** samples step up: deep mulberry colour, fruitier nose, sweet youngberry adding to palate—flavours. 12% alc. As vines mature this wine should become 4-star stuff.

★★★ **Cabernet Sauvignon 96** bouquet of sweet raspberry, strawberry re-appears amid ripe, soft tannins, layered over marzipan on palate.

Drinking well, has 4-6 years' growth potential. Year in French oak. 12,8% alc. **97** preview shows benefit of older vines, more experience with new winery ("a treat to work in," says Hamman).

★★★ **Chardonnay** Improving by the vintage. **97** third-crop has delivered broader nose, body than pvs. Bright straw colour, lively citrus (lemon marmalade) scents. Crispier, fruitier flavours, supportive oak, vivacious finish. 6 mths small Alliers oak (third each new, 2nd, 3rd-fill). Malo. Drink now, but could keep 2-3 years. 2,6% alc.

LANZERAC (STELLENBOSCH FARMERS WINERY)

As the Lanzerac farm cellar is relatively small, giant merchant-producer SFW continues to produce the historic **Lanzerac Pinotage** and **Rosé** at its Stellenbosch winery complex, in the massive quantities their long-established popularity demands. SFW markets all the Lanzerac-labelled wines, though these can also be purchased on the farm. Super-experienced SFW winemaker Jan de Waal is the power behind the wines below.

★★★★ **Pinotage** The first to be bottled in SA (and the world!) back in late 50s. Richly cloaked in vanilla-scented oak, sumptuous black velvet fruit, discreet tannins, **96** whispers luxury and opulence—the wine of boardrooms and high-powered dinners. Serious, could be drunk now, but try to wait 2-3 years, up to 6-8, for deeper impact. 100% new French oak—"shows what good oak and attention to fruit quality can do," says De Waal, who describes this as the best Lanzerac Pinotage to date. "**96** might have been a light year in some cellars, but not here." St'bosch vines, between 10-25 years old.

★★★ **Rosé** ◀ Recipe instructions for this perennial favourite: blend the fruitiest red of the vintage (so variety can vary from year to year) with freshest possible chenin. Positively **no** muscat! Result is a soft, semi-sweet, satiny-textured mouthful of strawberries, cherries, plums. Serve well chilled.

LA PETITE FERME

Franschhoek See Franschhoek map

No tastings, limited stocks for sale. Cellar tours by appointment. Individually decorated B&B cottages.

Farm-style light lunches/heartier meals. Open daily 10.30-4.30. Booking essential. See restaurant section. Wines below available with meals.

Owners: The Dendy Young family
Winemaker: Mark Dendy Young (since 1996)
Consulting Winemaker: Gerda van Zyl
Vineyards: John Dendy Young
Production: 2 000 cases. **Vineyards:** ± 8 ha.
P.O. Box 55, Franschhoek 7690
Tel: 021-8763016 **Fax:** 021-8763624

"Ours is probably the most unautomated cellar in SA—we use buckets to move the mash into the press!" The Dendy Young family's delightful mountaintop country restaurant-cum-winery at Franschhoek might look (and run) like a poster for the Arts & Crafts movement but, again, dedicated, enthusiastic vintners such as young scion Mark made top-drawer wines long before pneumatic pumps, stainless steel fermenters clanked onto the scene. So snicker not at the rustic methods:

taste what's in the glass—preferably on the veranda of the adjoining restaurant, with views—and cuisine, warm hospitality—so beguiling you'll not want to leave. All the wines are sold from and through the restaurant.

★★★ **Shiraz** NEW Experimental **98**, from v'yd in front of restaurant, appears somehow to have absorbed array of appealing *cuisine* aromas—crispy bacon, pepper, mixed spice, liquorice, smoky hearth—overlaying ripe plum. Food-friendliness enhanced by firmish tannin, sweet-oaky impression (though technically dry) in finish. 1 000 bottles. Lightly wooded, French/American oak.

★★★ **Merlot 98** "the most serious merlot made here to date"—shows in inky purple-black colour, concentrated plum/violet bouquet, ripe almost luscious mulberry/blackcurrant flavours, vanilla-oak coating. Firm tannins call for food/time. 13% alc. Bought-in grapes from St'bosch.

★★★★ **Chardonnay 98** mostly from family's v'yds high on Fr'hoek Pass, some valley bush vines. Expansive (but not heavy) layered mouthful: intense lemon-lime, lashings of butterscotch/crème brûlée, light marmalade topping, exceptionally long. Burgundian methods used: barrel fermentation (50% new), lees stirring. 13% alc.

★★★ **Sauvignon Blanc** "Best a year after vintage" reckons Mark D-Y. **98** seriously appealing even tasted in youth; powerful (as always), flinty core in aromatic wrapping of ripe gooseberries, fresh cut-grass, nettles, deliciously zesty dry finish. From father John D-Y's low-yielding, 3-ton/ha. v'yd, unoaked. **96 VG**. WINE★★★★.

★★★ **Fumé Blanc 98** 20% barrel-fermented, forward sauvignon attack modulated by "sweet" vanilla/oak capitulation; wide-bodied dry style, very attractive. Spot-on partner for smoked trout. Grapes from D-Y v'yds. **96 VVG**.

Pinotage 98 NEW an individual pinotage, bathed in Rhône-like scrub, ripe cherries, eucalyptus undertow. Tannins tight, allow 1-2 yrs to start unwinding. **Nectar du Val** NEW **Chenin Blanc** of pvs. years reappears with muscat in 98, easy-going, sweetish eucalyptus/pine-scented blend.

LA PROVENCE

See Haute Provence

L'AVENIR ESTATE

Stellenbosch

See Stellenbosch map

Open for tastings & sales weekdays 10-5; Sat 10-4. Tasting charges R5.
Luxury 9-bedroom guest lodge with pool. Own preserved and dried olives for sale.

Owner: Marc Wiehe
Winemaker: Francois Naudé (since 1992)
Production: 320 tons, 20 000 cases. **Vineyards**: 45 ha. 50/50 red/white
P.O. Box 1135, Stellenbosch 7599
Tel: 021-8895001 **Fax:** 021-8895258

No matter how lowly the grapes, how unserious the style, burly, invariably beaming Francois Naudé lavishes them with attention: even the clairette blanche in L'Avenir's new **Rosé** was painstakingly, reductively made, left on its lees for 6 weeks—treated like royalty. (Much to the bemusement of his cellar staff.) This is heart and soul winemaking, right through the range. From the dramatic, blaze-for-glory pinotage to an extraordinary chenin, a chardonnay which regularly shines in stiff French competitions, even the chic-and-cheerful white quaffer, these are wines of unusual charm and originality. L'Avenir's urbane, amusing, irrepressibly audacious Mauritian proprietor Marc Wiehe—formerly an international sugar-broker—sets the relaxed, adventurous tone here. Neither he nor Naudé, who came to winemaking after a long career as a pharmacist, have been remotely ruffled by the fact that they are relative wine rookies. L'Avenir means "the future", and here it has certainly worked. Since the first vintage in 92, this pretty estate with its elegant guest-house has made an impact. It is now a new Cape star—despite, traditionalists might think; because of, we aver—Naudé's fresh, often quirky cellar techniques, and Wiehe's congenital non-establishment approach. They are *amateurs* of wine in the true sense of the word.

Winning WINE magazine's Chenin Blanc Challenge in 1997 was yet further confirmation of L'Avenir's rapid rise, from an obscure farm delivering mainly to Nederburg, to the top estate wine ranks. Naudé's prize included a trip to the Loire and Sancerre: see our notes on the Chenin Blanc for stunning evidence of the inspiration he absorbed. But in the end, though these wines shine on shows, the Wiehe-Naudé conviction is that "wines are made to be drunk, not to be read". Naudé believes his secret weapon as a winemaker is that "I was a consumer for so long. I know what I like to drink and aim to make wines like that." Clearly, his tastes are widely shared.

**** **Pinotage** Naudé is passionate about pinotage and it shows. Festooned with awards: **96 VVG**, Pinotage Top Ten; **95 VG**; **94** Perold Trophy at IWSC for best Pinotage. Presently austere **97** will need more time than outgoing **96**; trademark fresh bananas, redcurrants reined in by firmish tannins. (30% from a first-crop v'yd, probably accounts for less concentration than pvs.) 13 months in new/used Vicard barrels. **Auction Pinotage** Exclusively from 30-year-plus vines. Opaque, brilliant **97** in soigné L'Avenir style. Lustrous, expressive fruit; dried figs, bananas brightening into summer-pudding, red berry freshness. Rich, creamy, with soft, very fine tannin. Generous oaking; "one mustn't be scared to use new oak on this variety," asserts Naudé. **96 WINE********, fetched very high R116,50/bottle average price at 1997 CIWG Auction. Equally multi-dimensional (with touches of coffee, wild game adding to fruity complexity); should last another 10 years.

**** **Cabernet Sauvignon 96 (***)** good reflection of lighter, more open vintage. Has traditional Cape nutty, grassy restraint but no green harshness (95% virus-free vines, 65% local clone). Supple, ripe red fruit flavours enhanced by 14% merlot, balanced tannins. 18 months in French oak, only 20% new to complement vintage. **95 VG**; **94 VVG**.

*** **L'Ami Simon (Merlot/Cabernet Sauvignon** export label) ◀ Quality early-drinking red, à la Bordeaux second-labels **97** (****) with instant drinking appeal, class; multi-layered minerally, sweet plum fragrance; creamy but fresh, with melt-in-the-mouth tannins. 58/42 blend, rounded out with year in used French oak. **96 VVG**, **SAA** blend with slightly less merlot; dense blackberry, cassis ripeness, full-bodied, smooth. **95 VG**.

**** **Chardonnay** Drinkability with complexity Naudé's goal here: admirably achieved in **97**, **96**; both medallists, top SA entries at 1997/98 French Chardonnay du Monde competitions. **97** slips down super-easily, has satisfying fatness, understated fresh hazelnut flavours. More Burgundian than New World. Long, softly dry; charming. (Usually about 60/40 barrel-/tank-fermented; oaked portion 9 months on lees, through malo; no malo in tank portion for fresh backbone.) 3-4 gms/l sugar.

*** **Sauvignon Blanc** Big, unwooded **98**; well fleshed-out ripe fig flavours, extending to easy but lively finish. Some Loire-like refinement on nose; good early drinking.

**** **Chenin Blanc** Naudé insists on botrytis-brushed, ultra-ripe grapes for this unwooded, off-dry chenin. The results have been stunning. **97 VG, WINE****** and Chenin Blanc Challenge award: boldly-structured; generously honeyed bouquet echoed in rich flavour concentration, long tangy-mango tail. 7 gms/l sugar balances rather than sweetens. Has good 2-3 year potential but looks set to be upstaged by absolutely delicious **98** (nudging *****). Higher botrytis/acid levels give more sophisticated sleekness. Firm, but voluminous, silky feel, great length. Outstanding promise.

*** **Vin d'Erstelle** ◀ A delightful non-ordinaire everyday drinking white, **98** as stylish as ever. Waves of juicy concentration spiced up with peppery zip. Blend approx. equal parts Cape riesling, colombard, Rhine riesling; last most prominent after year/2 in bottle. 7 gms/l sugar. Low yields, fully ripe grapes; extended lees contact. **96 VVG. 95 VG.**

**** **Vin de Meurveur Noble Late Harvest** Deliciously different dessert from colombard, a variety rarely seen in NLH style because not usually susceptible to botrytis, but in terms of its high natural acids (to balance sweetness) perfect for the job. **97 WINE****** scintillating sweet/sour tension; big but not unctuous; lots of tangy fresh apricot, orange marmalade peel flavours; long, whistle-clean finish. 13,3% alc. TA 9,5 gms/l. 144,5 gms/l sugar. (Naudé swaddled the tank in a duvet and electric blanket to get this wine fermenting; worth the pampering!)

Rosé Maison NEW **98** unconventional cinsaut/cab. s./clairette blanch blend; rare lambchop pink; spicy strawberry. cherry fruits; well-hidden 15 gms/l sugar.

LEBENSBRAUM

See Deetlefs

LE BONHEUR ESTATE

Stellenbosch See Stellenbosch map

Sales, tastings, 9-5 weekdays, 9-12.30 Sat. Special tastings, meals on request.
Owners: Distillers Corporation
Winemaker: Sakkie Kotzé (since 1994)
Production: 500 tons. **Vineyards:** 70 ha.
P.O. Box 56, Klapmuts, 7625
Tel: 021-8755478 **Cellar:** 021-8755478 **Fax:** 021-8755624

"Nothing's happened" over the past year insists winemaker Sakkie Kotzé. "Everything's the same." Oh yes? What about a visit by SA winemakers to a major Food & Wine Festival at Banff Springs in the Canadian mountains? Here, he says, the South Africans' sense of humour was enjoyed as much as the food (by Ina Paarman) and his and other wines. "You see," he explains, and gives a huge roar of laughter, "before, they'd had the French and the Italians, and, you know, they were a bit stiff compared to us!" Then there were the marketing and tasting presentations in California, Memphis, Atlanta, Washington. "They were amazed by our prices. My cab., selling at $16 is a bargain there—their equivalent goes for $30." Late in 1998 he flew off on a similar tasting/selling safari to Singapore. . . . Nothing's happened? There goes Kotzé's famous sense of humour again.

★★★★ **Cabernet Sauvignon 95** is next up and showing excellent form. Deep red/purple colour. Enticing berry fruit aromas, hint of mint. Ripe juicy texture with some (pleasantly) charry oak. Long clean finish. 12% alc. 18 months in 50/50 new/second-fill French oak. **WINE★★★★**. Small bottlings of **93** and **94** much in the style of the **91**: deep colour, deep fruity nose, concentrated flavours. Soft tannin, long, full finish. Was among SA's finest during 1980s. New-clone plantings showing in latest production.

★★★★ **Prima Merlot-Cabernet** Quality jump with super **95**, 71% merlot, 29% cabernet s. (40% in new 300 litre oak, balance in second-fill for 18 months). Elegant, well-ripened cassis and cedary oak aromas lead into blackcurrant, blackberry, chocolate, sweet vanilla and spicy oak flavours. Supple tannins. 12,2% alc. No **94**. **93** also merlot-dominated with 75%. Somewhat muted nose but good berry flavours, powerful finish. **92** ◀ developing well with ripe, black-berry succulence, showing elegance, lovely balance. 13% alc. 15 months in 35% new oak, balance 2nd-fill. **SAA** Selection. **91 VG** more herbaceous.

★★★ **Chardonnay 97** vintage conditions helped underline juicy, rich character, lovely balance of lees, oak and fresh citrusy fruit. Easy on the palate, satisfying now. Part (about 40%) barrel-fermented in new French oak, part tank-fermented; on lees 4 months, 7 tons/ha. yields. **98** similar style.

Sauvignon Blanc (Unwooded) A Cape sauvignon that needs a year in bottle to achieve its best. **97** ★★★★ developed good balance between herbaceous, grassy and gooseberry aromas and flavours. Well weighted but soft on the palate. Long, still crisp finish. **96** developed good, deep nettle character. **98** being similarly styled.

LEEF OP HOOP

Jonkershoek, Stellenbosch See Stellenbosch map

Tastings/sales preferably by appointment, guest cottage.
Owner/Winemaker: Etienne le Riche (since 1997)
Production: 60 tons/4 500 cases
P.O. Box 6295, Stellenbosch 7599
Tel/Fax: 021-8870789

Seasoned winemaker Etienne le Riche launched into a solo flight in 1996 after more than 20 years at blue-chip Rustenberg Estate. Operating out of a rustic refurbished cellar on tiny Leef op Hoop farm in Jonkershoek Valley, Le Riche tested the thermals with a **Leef op Hoop** (literally "Live on Hope', a wry allusion) **Cab. 96**, made from bought-in wine which he blended, matured, bottled, and—to his great delight—got a silver medal for on the International Wine Challenge. Then, in 1997, the amiable, soft-spoken winemaker spread his wings with a small range under his own name, made from bought-in grapes (rather than wines) from St'bosch. A **Cab.-Merlot** blend was specifically made for export to Belgium (which country, he notes frostily, is "not the place to be in winter"); others in the range were exported for the first time to the UK, Netherlands in 1998. In his second rôle as "flying" winemaker—around St'bosch, for the time being—Le Riche made the first **EagleVlei** wines for Steve and Jean Weir. As for the future, he sees himself specialising in "premium quality cab.-based wines" adding, in an entrepreneurial aside, "growers of top grapes who would like to see their produce treated in a classic, personal style are welcome to contact me".

★★★★ **Le Riche Cabernet Sauvignon Reserve 97** ★★★★★ concentrated, ripe, almost opulently fruity, seductive. Inky colour, cascading tiers of cassis, clean sweet-oak, mint; silky deep-piled richness on palate: mulberries, cherries, cedary oak, limber tannins persisting in long fruity finish. Superb, built for drinking now and well into next century. Winemaker says he'll ring in the new millennium with this—or (for auld lang syne) **Rustenberg Cab. 82**. Crème of Jonkershoek grapes, total 21 days open-tank fermentation/closed-tank maceration; 15 mths oak (80% new), light egg-white fining. 12,7% alc. "Standard" **Cabernet Sauvignon** marginally less fine, like a second-tier reserve. Lovely floral bouquet—perfumed violet top notes—mineral sensations, fresh ripe cherry sappiness. Perhaps lacking extraordinary complexity of Reserve, bit firmer, more compact, but undoubtedly in the very top league. Significantly shorter fermentation/maceration (6 days), 12 mths 2nd-fill French (Nevers) oak. 13% alc.

★★★ **Leef op Hoop Cabernet Sauvignon 97**, with drop of merlot, shade lighter than heroes above; chunkier tannins, shorter; still, a most satisfying, serious drink. Violet-scented, ripe cherry/berry flavours, very dry (so natural food partner). Alc. heading for 13%. Helderberg/Bottelary grapes, 3rd-fill barrique/4 500 l vat, 9 mths. **96** balanced, refined, probably best over next 2-3 years.

Cabernet-Merlot 96 (export only) fine, gently tannined blend; sweet cassis, nutty tones subtly embroidered with cedary oak. Accessible, lightish texture although not insubstantial (12,5% alc.)

LEIDERSBURG

See Stellenbosch Wines Direct

LEMBERG ESTATE

Tulbagh

See Tulbagh map

Tastings/sales Mon-Sat 10-5 and by appointment. Tasting fee R4 p/p. Cellar tours and light lunches on request. Guest cottage; breakfast/dinner on request.

Owner/Winemaker: Klaus Schindler (since 1994)
Production: 1 000 cases. **Vineyards:** 4 ha.
P.O. Box 317, Tulbagh 6820
Tel: 0236-300659 **Fax:** 0236-300661

"Excellent!" enthuses forestry scientist-turned-winemaker Klaus Schindler about the 1998 harvest on this tiny wine farm and guest-house on the Little Berg River near Tulbagh. **Sauvignon Blanc** and **Hárslevelü**, Lemberg's lynchpins, were especially successful and, according to Schindler, have the potential to rival the beefy 95s which he rates as his best to date. A highlight of the vintage was the first **Pinot Noir** from Lemberg's own vines, recently planted along with a small parcel of pinotage to give the property a red string to its formerly all-white bow.

Schindler's Sensual Red NEW **97** union of merlot (70%), cab. s. Perhaps not as fleshy as name would suggest. Quite angular still, green pepper notes. Needs 2+ years to soften. Alc. nudging 14%. **Pinot Noir** NEW **98** untasted. **Hárslevelü** Estate's signature grape. One of handful of Cape whites to improve in bottle; **96** now showing agreeable complexity, even some Loire-like touches to fynbos, spice on nose/palate. **97** with statuesque 14,8% alc. Generally lowish acids for smooth drinking. **Sauvignon Blanc 97** reprises kung-fu style unleashed with Schindler's maiden **95**: in-your-face tropical fruit aromas followed by sour/sweet (though technically dry) palate-attack; 13,6% alc. delivers extra kick. These perhaps best in youth (despite winemaker's assertion that Lemberg's wines, unlike most, are not released "much too early").

L'ÉMIGRÉ WINES

Vlottenburg, Stellenbosch See Stellenbosch map

Tastings/sales Sat 9.30-5, Easter holiday week and Dec 16-Jan 3. Self-catering guest cottages.
Owner: F.V. Gentis Trust
Winemaker: Frans Gentis (since 1992)
Viticulturist: Arnold Hugo
Production: ±3 000 cases. **Vineyards:** 67 ha.
P.O. Box 14, Vlottenburg 7604 (De Morgenzon Farm)
Tel: 021-8813702 **Fax:** 021-8813030
Website: www.icon.co.za/~mtison

Zooming demand prompted this hand-built, family-run winery on historic De Morgenzon farm in the Stellenboschkloof Hills to install additional cellar equipment and pump up production by another 1 000 cases in 1998. Vindication, indeed, of Frans Gentis' decision to retain a portion of his best co-op bound grapes to vinify and bottle under the L'Émigré and Azure labels. "We try to make the best wine possible from our low-potential soil," Gentis says. In line with modern trends the property's traditional varietal mix has diversified into noble grapes such as cabernet sauvignon and, most recently, shiraz. Sauvignon blanc comes into its own on the east and south-facing slopes—the current release is up there with the Cape's best. And the Port was highly rated at Calitzdorp's annual Port Festival.

*** **Azure Sauvignon Blanc 98** a cracker. Super-crisp sweet-melon, ripe fig flavours. Laser sharp acid (in the best, balanced, fruity-fresh sense), lengthy whistle-dry finish. Delicious. Limited quantity ("Fear we might have to ration," muses Frans Gentis).

Cimiterre Barrel-aged (14 months) cab. s. with smattering merlot, cab. f., malbec. **94** dried fruit, tobacco flavours. **95** shade mintier. **Shiraz 96** emitting spicy, sweet oaky signals, leaner style. **Pinotage 96/97**, like **95**, in unflashy, subdued smoky style. For current drinking. **Azure Chardonnay 98** untasted. Pvs. (**96**) labelled Reserve. (Used) barrel-aged dry white. **Azure Bouquet Blanc** NEW **98** rich, round, redolent of pawpaw. Supple mouth-feel (but alc. kick on finish). Soft, pleasant, just-not-dry quaffing. **Glorieux** Discontinued as Natural Sweet, reappears as Special Late Harvest in **98**. Soft golden syrup wafts, guava tastes. Not overly complex; best with dessert. From chenin. 42 gms/l sugar. 11% alc. **Muscat d'Alexandrie 96** very drinkable deep golden dessert, ripe tropical fruit with fresh muscat. Attractive. 170 gms/l sugar. **Port** Among this cellar's fast movers. **95** aligned with Cape trend towards drier, grippier style (100 gms/l sugar, 18,8% alc.). Pale, almost tawny. Radiates comforting hazelnut, Xmas pud, black cherry aromas/flavours. 2 yrs Spanish barrels. Should develop over 2-3 years. **96** lower-keyed. **94** more chocolate notes. From tinta barocca.

LE MOUTONNÉ

See Mouton-Excelsior Wines

LE PARFAIT

See Ashwood Wines

LIBERTAS (Export only, largely unoaked) SFW

*** **Cabernet** Impressive dark hue, good fruit concentration in **96**, still some abrasive tannin. 100% cab.

*** **Merlot** Grassy, dusty berry quality, softish tannins, attractive plump chewy fruit. Star of the range. 100% merlot.

Pinotage Warm stewed plum flavours in **96**, dry tannins, rustic. 100% p'tage. **Chardonnay** Modest, slender; some buttery notes, 15% oaked for added weight. **Chenin Blanc** Delicate floral aromas, light and lean, bone-dry. **Muscat d'Alexandrie** Grapey semi-sweet at 25 gms/l sugar.

LIEBERSTEIN SFW

The wine that started SA's unfortified drinking revolution, at one time was world's largest seller at 31 million litres a year. Now sales much lower, but still a few million. Everyday semi-sweet chenin blanc with some charm. NV.

LIEVLAND ESTATE

Muldersvlei, Stellenbosch See Stellenbosch map

Tastings/sales Mon-Fri 9-5, Sat 9-1. Cellar tours by appointment.
Owner: Paul Benadé
Winemaker: James Farquharson (since 1997)
Production: 15 000 cases. **Vineyards:** 60 ha.
P.O. Box 66, Klapmuts 7625
Tel: 021-8755226 **Fax:** 021-8755213

Scots-born James Farquharson, skirling in Lievland's cellar once more—he tuned up here while at varsity before performing at Cordoba, Rheebokskloof and Châteaux in St Émilion—had "a seat of my pants" return-crush in 1998. "Four days of hot—42 degrees plus—weather caused all our mid-season varieties to ripen at the same time. Then our crusher/destemmer broke down . . ." The young winemaker believes in minimal interference with natural processes in the v'yd and cellar. "My chief rôle is quality controller," says the Stellenbosch-trained vintner who, encouraged by (among others) *Decanter*'s five-star rating of the estate's **Lievlander** blend (the flagship cab./merlot **DBV** is no slouch either) will be striking fewer single-varietal notes and composing more ensembles.

★★★★ **DVB** Serious Bordeaux-style blend, cabernet franc-dominated (55%) in **96**, with merlot (29%), cab. s. Deep cherry colour, ripe curranty fruit, rich vanilla counterpoint to attractive charry oak. 15 mths oak, 50% new, mix of coopers. **94** gorgeous ripe plum, violet/almondy accents; med.-bodied, ripe fruit wrapped in abundant, unaggressive tannin. **93 WINE★★★★**; **92** stand-out year; **91 SAA, VVG**.

★★★★ **Shiraz** Fresh, sweet-spicy fruit trademark here. Evolutionary aspects include softer tannins, denser texture, drier profile. Switch to all-French oak (prior to **95** portion American oak) with some fermentation finished in barrel among methods used to achieve these goals. **97** (bottled 2 September 1998), punchy juicy fruit, engaging smoky/peppery threads, earthy Karoo scrub. 14 mths oak, ± 40% new. Preview of **98** shows v. good potential: dense cherry fruit, forward tobacco/coffee notes. **95** best of pvs. vintages; savoury touches add complexity to familiar spicy sweetness, richly embroidered, more oomph.

★★★ **Lievlander** ◀ Unpretentious mainly cinsaut blend with assorted varieties (including cab. s.). Never a fixed recipe. **97** easy-drinking, plenty of character. "Sweet" ripe fruit, strawberries, redcurrants, subtle oaky veneer. Upcoming **98** (from barrel) ripe mulberry, coffee tones, redcurrant peeps through. **96** more open, less intense and oak-influenced than **95**, which accorded *Decanter* 5-star peerage in 1997 tasting of more than 100 SA cab. blends. Quality quaffer.

★★★★ **Weisser Riesling 96** has developed thrillingly in bottle, long way still to go. Mouthfilling almost luscious lime-kerosene flavours, sprinkling fresh-milled pepper, 11,2 gms/l sugar and lowish 10,7% alc. add smooth, bright drinkability. **98** similar flavour spectrum, drier at 8,4 gms/l sugar, bit more fat at 11,6% alc. Very much a fledgling, needs time.

*** **Sauvignon Blanc 97** unwooded, crisp gooseberry, cut-grass, bracing acidic finish. Food wine.

**** **Noble Late Harvest Reserve 97** has acquired peachy, kumquat lusciousness, heady botrytis overtones, zesty lime dimension filled out by fresh acid, lends piquant vibrancy. Delicious. 127,8 gms/l sugar, 8,1 gms/l acid, 13,2% alc., fermented, aged 7 mths in oak, 55% new. Bronzy **96***** from bukettraube, chenin, Rhine riesling; decidedly sweet, non-barrel-fermented, caramel, raisin flavours.

Chardonnay 96 soft, enveloping lemon-lime flavours, leesy depth, very fresh. 13,2% alc. 9 mths oak, 75% new, malo in tank.

LINTON PARK WINES

Wellington See Wellington map

Tasting/sales by appointment.
Owner: Linton Park plc. **MD:** Malcolm Perkins
Winemaker: Ian Naude (since 1998). **Viticulturist:** T.C. Botha
Production: 14 000 cases. **Vineyards:** 120 ha.
P.O. Box 533, Wellington 7654
Tel/Fax: 021- 8731625
E-mail: iannaude@iafrica.com

Here's another example of foreign interests breathing new oxygen into the Cape winelands. Linton Park plc, a London Stock Exchange-listed company with international agricultural interests (tea, coffee, citrus, table-grapes in Australia, Chile, Malawi and Kenya), bought the old Slang Rivier property on the slopes of the Groenberg near Wellington in 1995. MD Malcolm Perkins immediately rang the changes. The 1809 homestead has been renovated, a brand-new 1 000-ton cellar built, and winemaker Ian Naude—who formerly handled grapes from this property at the Berg & Brook winery in Simondium—has moved to source, to oversee the first, 98 vintage of two own-label ranges for Linton Park. These show loads of promise and personality (see specially the Cab. below).

LINTON PARK range: (all NEW)

**** **Cabernet Sauvignon** Loads of promise; this **98** youngster heading for classy maturity. Blackberry/mint aromas, flavours, good vanilla backing; deep concentration throughout. Give 5-7 years. From farm's best cab. block, harvested/handled separately. New small French-oaked. 13,5% alc. Touch of residual sugar adds to richness.

*** **Chardonnay** Nice! **98** with lemon, some butterscotch notes expanding on palate, interwoven with good oak. More serious than Capell's Court below. 13,5% alc., as in above wine touch of imperceptible sweetness smooths, rounds. New French oak 10 months, malo. Grapes from farm's best chardonnay v'yd.

CAPELL'S COURT range: All NEW

*** **Chardonnay** Unwooded **98**: fresh, soft, tropical traits. Aperitif, table-mate—very pleasantly versatile. Dry but same residual sugar secret as most of these wines to enhance drinkability.

*** **Sauvignon Blanc** Gooseberry, grass scents, riveting freshness on palate, feels full, substantial (just under 4 gms/l sugar though tastes dry). Myrtle aftertaste. 13% alc. Unwooded.

Cabernet Sauvignon No-oak version, for early drinking. **98** with blackberry, grassy notes, soft, smooth-textured palate. Most agreeable. 4 gms/l sweetness enriches taste. **Shiraz** Huge, big-boom, talking-point **98** red: extrovert 14,5% alc., 6 gms/l sugar, deep dark violets in colour and nose, peppery palate, whack of finishing alc./tannins. Not for the faint-hearted; really rich food-partner required. But very young when tasted, and this is the sort of blockbuster that can knock out show judges. Wait and see.

LION CREEK WINES

See Napier Winery

LONG MOUNTAIN WINES

Owner: Groupe Pernod Ricard
Winemakers: Robin Day, Jacques Kruger (since 1998)
Production: 200 000 cases. White/red
P.O. Box 1324, Stellenbosch 7599
Tel: 021-8870836 **Fax:** 021-8870846
E-Mail: prsa@iafrica.com

Broad vision, lofty goals, deep resources, great initiative and a hugely confident approach characterise the winemaking activities of international group Pernod Ricard in the Cape. Australian dynamo Robin Day swept into the country in the early 90s, fresh from his phenomenal success with Orlando's Jacob's Creek—between similar wine-sourcing sorties to Eastern Europe, South America and Asia—and immediately bewitched, bothered and bewildered a string of rural co-ops and growers into collaborating on a range of wines styled to his market-rested specs: a revolutionary Cape-Oz breed notable for richness, softness, excellent finishes, readiness to drink. Bowen Botha, cellar chief at the bustling Robertson Co-op, helped Day pull all this fruit together, and now business and production have boomed to such an extent that former Blaauwklippen winemaker Jacques Kruger has been brought in as fulltime OC. He particularly relishes the blending scope he now has, with input from 13 different wineries.

David de Mardt, MD of Pernod Ricard in SA, and, like Robin Day not prone to thinking small, believes they have the potential to compete with a giant like Gallo. The intention, over the next 5 years, is "to develop the Long Mountain Wine Company into a world-class operation, by establishing Long Mountain as the number one exported South African brand, and a leading New World wine internationally". New sources of grapes are being secured, new brands planned, new labels designed. A measure of the wines' immediate success is their listing in the important UK outlets of Safeway, Waitrose, Tesco, Sainsbury's and Victoria.

★★★ **Merlot-Shiraz** ◀ Shiraz influential flavour component in **97** (80/20 blend); more savoury, gamey tones than spicy, minty **96**, has similar down-duvet, mouthcoating texture, attractive length. Successful if unconventional mix. Grapes from Vinkrivier, Robertson, Barrydale.

★★★ **Cabernet Sauvignon** ◀ **97** excellent example of cab. s. made for early drinking (and keeping year or two) without losing varietal intrinsics. Sufficient colour, fruit, structure for sound red wine feel; immediate accessibility achieved by fruit centre stage. Soft sweet plum, brambly appeal complemented by medium-bodied elegance, melt-in-the-mouth tannins.

★★★ **Merlot Reserve** NEW, more intense than standard range; achieved in **96** through deeper tannin, fruit layers, rather than higher alc. 9 months in cask, some new; oak still apart from, though balanced with rich spicy plum, bitter chocolate fruit. To be held back for further bottle maturation.

Ruby Cabernet 98 next available; previous **95 Reserve**. Unfinished sample tasted: distinctive wild berry, grassy fruit, perky but tannins trademark soft drinkability. **Sémillon-Chardonnay** ☺ Softly dry white blend, easy lemon-honey fruit, gentle persistence. **98** similar 75/25 mix to **97**. Worcester/ Rawsonville grapes. **Sauvignon Blanc** Clean understated asparagus, cut grass fruit in unwooded **98**; good weight, ripely dry finish **Chardonnay** Oak-influenced **97** with satisfying lemony butterscotch array; leesy soft palate freshened by crisp, fruity frame. Part malo, partly *sur lie*. From three widely scattered v'yds in Ceres, Barrydale and Vinkrivier. **Dry Riesling** (Rhine) **98** delicate lemony, spicy character; dry but bouncy, easy-drinking. **Chenin Blanc 98** with bouquet of spring flowers scent; gently yet well-spread flavours, softly dry.

LONGRIDGE WINERY

Helderberg-Stellenbosch See Helderberg map

Visits: Open weekdays tasting/sales 9-5. Sat 9-2. Imported wines available for tasting.
Refreshments: Picnic lunches (by arrangement, at 24-hour notice)
Owners: Exatrade Beverage Investments and Management
Winemaker: Ben Radford (since 1997)
Assistant Winemaker: Kirstin Katzenberg (since 1994)
Vineyards: Danie Zeeman. **Quality Control:** Zelda Petersen
Marketing Director: Johan Laubser
Production: 165 000 cases, 2 000 tons
P.O. Box 1435, Stellenbosch 7599
Tel: 021-8552004 **Fax:** 021-8554083
E-mail: longridg@iafrica.com

Hugely energetic, imaginative and professional—here's the sort of New South African wine company which is blasting away old Cape cobwebs and charging towards the new century, propelled by an altogether worldly-wise vision. For example: few other local wineries would think of listing "open-mindedness" as a philosophical cornerstone (along with integrity, reliability, innovation, and importantly—they really have fun with wine here—enjoyment). But at Longridge, a wide-angle, all-inclusive ethos is pervasive. It was typified by a symposium they organised in 1998 for foreign importers, primary focus not narrowly on Longridge but broadly on the Cape—its potential, its problems and solutions, the whole picture. Rival producers were among the speech-givers—unheard-of at a conference devised and financed by another producer! And the warts-and-all approach was refreshing—making the beauty spots much more convincing to international guests, who are as suspicious as anyone else of ridiculously rose-tinted puffery.

Staff policies are equally admirable. No patronisation nor paternalism notes our taster for this year's guide. "Staff here are obviously given every chance to prove themselves." Six workers in the cellar have completed the Cape Wine Academy's prelim. course; another staffer, now busy on a higher-level CWA course, has jumped from house-keeping to head the tasting room, visitors' facilities and promotions. The black oenology student Longridge is sponsoring through St'bosch University will find a slot at this cellar once she (yes, a double equal-opportunities strike here) gets her degree. Frequent international travel is part of the essential mind-opening process—quality controller Zelda Petersen, one of the first coloured women to hold such a position in Cape wine, is off to Australia to add to her skills.

Between MD Johan Laubser, right-hand-man (Burgundy-raised) Alex Dale, winemakers and viticulturist, Longridge staff in just a year clocked up 7 visits to Burgundy, 5 to Australia and the Rhône, 3 to Provence, plus sorties to source ideas from Champagne, Bordeaux, the Minervois, Cognac, Napa Valley, New Zealand, Spain and Italy.

Is anyone ever at home? Certainly, otherwise who would be handling a management buy-out proposal which was in negotiation as this guide went to press? Who would have organised the expansion of exports to North America, S.E. Asia and duty-free outlets? The cracking new labels/packaging for Bay View and Capelands (and the alternative **Meridian** label for a restaurant range)? And the biggest harvest yet, in 1998? Aussie-trained new winemaker Ben Radford, from the Barossa Valley, survived the deluge and is super-positive about the potential here "now that the industry has opened up". He and Burgundian *eminence* Martin Prieur, a longtime friend of Alex Dale, have introduced new micro-oxygenation techniques in the winery. A new Longridge maturation and vinification cellar is on the drawing board; in another expansionary move, Longridge has teamed up with the Joubert brothers of Veelverjaaght to complete a new barrel cellar (2 weeks before the 98 harvest) and to drive developments in their vineyards. More vineyard acquisitions are in the pipeline. The budget focus, notes Alex Dale, is on "people, quality, development".

LONGRIDGE label:

*** **Cabernet Sauvignon 96** in more yielding, charming mode than usual for variety; tannins here gently squeeze, elegantly frame layered array of sweet, crushed blackberries, fresh nuts. Genuine very ripe feel result of earlier-ripening, new-clone input. Despite apparent delicacy, doesn't lack presence, length, both enhanced by careful oaking, no filtration. Matured in small French oak, portion new, 15 months.

**** **Merlot** Stand-out red in range from **96**; classically styled, lots of velvety plushness, deep ruby lights, ripe plum, chocolaty fragrance, with soft cedary oak complement. Full, but gently structured, as was general tone for rain-affected **96** reds; pure ripe fruit density, broadened by subtle barrel influence, puts this one step ahead of crowd. Delicious now; should reflect what can be achieved even in difficult years until early part of new millennium.

*** **Pinotage** Outgoing fleshy succulence, plentiful sweet plum flavours make for immediately enjoyable **96**. Oak subtle background note, smoothing edges, adding to overall drinkability.

**** **Chardonnay** One of few Cape chardonnays to hold out promise of staying power, real maturation potential (not merely bottle age). Current **97** from cool, slow-ripening vintage, probably best in this genre. Despite strongly-hued appearance, both nose, palate very taut, minerally though not at all mean. Incipient pure lemon, oatmeal richness make appearance in gorgeous fantail finish; with further 12-18 months these should evolve in rest of wine. Oak also lends a note of firmness, dryness, though not intrusive flavours. Secret to invisible fruit/oak integration is delayed malo (in spring following vintage)—as prescribed by Burgundy's Martin Prieur—and use of tight-grained oak. Not a wine to hurry, nor to be hurried; nevertheless both **97**, **96** Virgin Atlantic 1st class selections. 85% barrel-fermented (about two-thirds new), spends year in oak before blending with 15% tank-fermented portion.

**** **Brut MCC** ◀ Generally medium to light-textured **94** gaining positive notes of oxidative fatness with extra year on cork. Yeasty, ginger biscuit features, sprightly bubble retain this MCC's essentially stimulating character. Styled the non-aggressive side of Brut. 50/50 chardonnay/pinot noir, by MCC specialist, TJ's Nicky Krone. **WINE******.

*** **Sauvignon Blanc 98** with not-to-be-ignored green pea, blackcurrant leaf piquancy; some flinty freshness too, should develop further as wine settles. Feisty, racy, as good sauvignon should be, but powerful fruit concentration overrides any potential abrasiveness. Spanking clean finish. Cool climate style with South African twist (i.e. natural, not contrived). Excellent partner to anything JUST out of the sea. Helderberg grapes. 12% alc.

*** **Chenin Blanc** NEW Insinuating honeyed ripeness in **98**; good breadth of flavour helped by soupçon oak vanillin; very clean, dry. Subtly satisfying rather than rich, demanding. This stable generally bucks trend for fat, fleshy dry whites; their trim, mineral character, is counteracted by weight of concentrated fruit extract.

LONGRIDGE/BAY VIEW range:

Most attractive quality-value range; from **98**, 95% own production.

*** **Cabernet Sauvignon** ◀ Supple, sweet-fruited **97**; oak carefully judged to round, add dimension. Well-integrated for current drinking, has backbone, depth to carry 2-3 years.

*** **Shiraz** ◀ NEW Modern, softly-structured **97**; rich chocolaty flavours, texture, slight spicy/violet overtones. Not vastly complex nonetheless satisfying mouthful.

*** **Cabernet Sauvignon-Pinotage** One of few in this unusual relationship where pinotage character doesn't predominate. **97** soundly structured, dry; intriguing tea leaf, tangy mulberry character, good fruity pliability on palate. 70/30 mix.

*** **Chenin-Chardonnay** ◀ Full-bodied, densely-textured 70/30 blend; sufficient flavour (butterscotch, roasted nuts) for interest, not too much to compete with richer pork and veal dishes, for which this ideal partner. Portion chardonnay component barrel-fermented.

*** **Chardonnay** ◀ Attractively-styled to reflect New World ripeness contrasting Old World elegance. Sweet lemon flesh freshened by minerally tautness gives aromatic intensity, lip-smacking, prolonged flavours. Clean, well-rounded dryness. Two-thirds barrel-fermented, some new.

*** **Sauvignon Blanc** ◀ **98** with unoaked sauvignon's invigorating dash , clean bite. Ripe gooseberry generosity, richly-textured middle too. Moreish.

*** **Chenin Blanc** ◀ Plenty of ripe flavour intensity, lushness in **98**; chenin's honeyed fruit augmented with touch attractive oak vanillin; extra breadth from comfortable leesy padding. Big but balanced, elegant. Stave-fermented; 4 months on lees.

La Revanche ◀ Popular French syrah/cabernet blend; introduced in retaliation against local wine prices, hence the name (Revenge). **97** currently available. **Ruby Cabernet-Pinotage** Unoaked **98** 60/40 blend. Solid ruby eye appeal; ripe friendly red berry fruits; well-rounded, chewy flavours for immediate drinkability. **Ridge Red NV** ◀ Versatile South African/French blend featuring tinta barocca, cinsaut with French cabernet, syrah. Plenty of juicy succulence, soft tannins, lifted by clean spicy tang in tail. Tasty, uncomplicated. **Merlot** Unoaked **98**; gutsy, full-bodied with rich sweet plum generosity. **Pinotage** Cheerful, gluggable **97**. Medium-bodied, abundant plummy flavours, gentle astringency. Partially oak-influenced. **Bay Blanc** Varying blend with goal of aromatic, crisp drinking. **98** from Cape riesling, chenin, sauvignon blanc, colombard; pleasant honey, fruit salad ripeness balanced by perky freshness. **Bouquet Blanc** Off-dry **98**; unobtrusive spice, muscat scents. Fruit, quaffability lifted by 11 gms/l sugar.

CAPELANDS Good budget range, all wines ☺

Merlot ◀ Full-bodied, gutsy **98**; plentiful rich sweet plum flavours, uncluttered by oak. **Ruby Cabernet** ◀ Unoaked **98** red; sweet, wild blackberry fruit, juicy lushness enhanced by gentle tannins; undemanding yet satisfying. **Classic Cape White** ◀ **98** exuberant but not pungent soft guava, dew-fresh herb fragrance; extra class from rich fruity density (short period skin contact, longer on lees), smoothly dry, long. 70% colombard, extra fruity touches from chenin, Rhine riesling. Everyday drinking, above-average quality. **Chardonnay** ◀NEW Fresh, bouncy **98**; easy toasty butterscotch tones. Well-balanced oak/fruit provides softly dry finish. **Sauvignon Blanc-Chenin Blanc 98** dry white, not ready for tasting at deadline. Mainly exported.

LOOPSPRUIT ESTATE

Bronkhorstspruit Mpumalanga

Tastings/sales Mon-Fri 8-4. Sat, Sun by appointment. Cellar tours, conference venue.

Traditional home-made fare Mon-Fri 8-4, a/h by appointment.

Owner: Mpumalanga Development Corporation

Winemaker: Jan Smit (since 1998)

Production: 10 000-12 000 cases. **Vineyards:** 20,5 ha.

P.O. Box 855, Bronkhorstspruit 1020

Tel: 013-9324303 **Fax:** 013-9333138.

This northerly winery has had more than its share of adversity down the years, but misfortune reached its nadir in 1998 with the sudden, untimely death of B.W. "Boet" Myburgh, winemaker and *primum mobile* for almost a decade. Infectious passion for wine, good-humoured stoicism—a survival skill he must have possessed before his tenure at Loopspruit: his previous tenancy was at Kango Co-op in the hot, dry Klein Karoo—kept his crusher running, so to speak, even when the crop failed utterly, as in 1997 (worms totalled the vineyard in four dispiriting days). As we noted in the pvs. guide, he succeeded in wringing amazing results out of the high-veld soil, including respectable chardonnay and cabernet. Jan Smit, incoming cellarmaster, says: "Boet's dream was to get all South Africans to drink and enjoy wine. We'll continue to pursue his vision."

Vin de Noir Off-dry blanc de noir from cinsaut; mellow berry/honey aromas, flavours. **Muxandré** Colombard, off-dry, with fresh palate prickle. **Goldenes Fest** Natural Sweet, tropical aromas/palate, long aftertaste. Colombard/muscat. **Rosé Demi Sec** Chenin, with muscat, cinsaut. Soft, not too sweet. Carbonated.
Witblits distilled from grapes, grappa-style; peach and apricot "mampoer" are also made.

L'ORMARINS

Franschhoek See Franschhoek map

Tastings/sales Mon-Fri 9-4.30, Sat 9-12.30.

Owner: Anthonij Rupert

Winemaker: Wrensch Roux (since 1997)

Vineyards: 200 ha.

P/Bag X6001, Suider-Paarl 7624

Tel: 021-8741026/8741024 **Fax:** 021-8741361

Seldom in the headlines, this grand Franschhoek estate owned by the youngest son of Dr. Anton Rupert, Antonij, quietly crafts a stylish, realistically-priced range that covers all the bases. Winemaker Wrensch Roux, a recent arrival from Bergkelder, handled a difficult 1998 crush with aplomb. A highlight was the first pressing of touriga naçional for the estate's **Late Bottled Vintage Port**.

★★★★ **Optima** Stylish cab./merlot blend, always generously oaked, now substantially more accessible in youth than pvsly. with v. good development potential. **95** showing supple merlot fruit, attractive mint and cassis vivacity; soft, full of warmth, richness. **94** fruity, fragrant, complex; creamy, almost milk-chocolate oak. 12,9% alc. **93** big, bold, violets/mint aroma, mouthfilling creamy vanilla, bold tannin. No **92**. **91 VVG**, ripe, sweet-perfumed, open juicy cherry, rich sweet oak. Developing great complexity. **90 WINE★★★★**, ready. 15-18 months oak, mostly new Nevers. Early 90s about two-thirds cab. s., 30-35% merlot, 10% cabernet f. From **94** merlot-dominated: ± 70% merlot, 30% cab. s.

★★★★ **Cabernet Sauvignon (La Maison du Roi)** Like companion above, far more accessible on release. Current **94** leafy, cedary with minty hints. Similar flavours, much softer tannins than pvs. Good balance, mouthfeel; classy long finish. Developing beautifully. 12,9% alc. No **93/92**. **91** was given more substance, wider dimension, touch of mint by new American clone, some 25% of blend. 13% alc. **90** forward, fruity.

★★★★ **Shiraz (La Maison du Roi)** Current **93** big open bouquet: brambleberry, briar, earthy aromas; all reverberate on palate with extra richness of liquorice, vanilla. Soft texture, very drinkable but enough alc. (13,9%) to ensure long development. **91** gentle, elegant, some plummy, baked-fruit aromas. **90** sweet mulberry fruit, deep concentration. All expensively, expansively oaked.

★★★ **Chardonnay 97** developing well, gaining deep toastiness, lemony richness, crisp finish. Mix French oak/tank fermentation.

★★★ **Grand Vin Blanc 97** more substantial than pvs., drinking well now. 60% chardonnay (half well-oaked), 20% Rhine riesling, 15% sauvignon, 5% gewürz. Fruity, fullish, smooth.

★★★ **Blanc Fumé 97** soft vanilla, grassy-fruity edges, usual substantial, big style. Barrel-aged sauvignon (3-4 months, more new wood than pvs.).

★★★ **Rhine Riesling** Has fine reputation, affirmed in light, lively, lovely **97**, showing bit of honeyed development. 9 gms/l sugar gives smoothness rather than sweetness. **96 WINE★★★★**.

★★★ **Guldenpfennig Guldenlese** NV white blend, very aromatic, rich, smells sweeter than the actual 20 gms/l. Gewürz., muscat ottonel, Rhine riesling.

★★★ **Noble Late Harvest 95** distinctive, smoky, earthy, botrytis dessert from bukettraube. Oak finish gave **93** and pvs. added, rounded dimension, but current **95** more in traditional Cape sticky-style. 140 gms/l sugar.

★★★★ **Port LBV 84** ripe sweet prunes, creamy chocolate, marzipan flavours. From souzão. 10 yr. wood-matured. Respectable near-20% alc., 110 gms/l sugar.

Sauvignon Blanc Unoaked **98** repeats **97**'s step up in quality (result of more stringent selection of fruit): peppery, hints of nettle; good grassy bite, fresh finish. 12% alc. **Pinot Gris 97** food-friendly, easy-drinking, soft dry white. **Méthode Champenoise Jean Roi** (after Huguenot founder of estate in 1694). Current **87** pinot noir-chardonnay. Oak-matured base wine.

LOUIESENHOF

Stellenbosch See Stellenbosch map

Tastings/sales Mon-Sat 9-5, also Sun 11-5 in season. Tasting fee R5 p/p.
Picnics in season, guest cottages, self-catering/B+B.
Owner/Winemaker: Stefan Smit
Production: 1 100 cases. **Vineyards:** 120 ha.
P.O. Box 2013, Stellenbosch 7599

Tel: 082 568 3006 **Fax:** 021-8897309
E-mail: lhofwine@iafrica.com

Seasoned cellarmaster/owner Stefan Smit—he earned his spurs on Koopmanskloof, the family farm nearby—is replanting this Koelenhof property at a gallop. Sauvignon is being established on cooler south-facing slopes and pinotage on relatively chilly eastern aspects ("I've noticed pinotage benefits from lower temperatures," Smit says). Customers and prospects in red wine-mad Far East, where Smit travelled in 1998, should find much to occupy their palates—and eyes—in this range: striking packaging featuring sleek, long-necked bottles and dramatic fine-art labels are features.

PREMIER COLLECTION:
Pinotage 98 step up from pvs. with sage and mint-like aromas, some plummy fruit flavours. Oaky touch, slightly rustic finish. Good, honest drinking. **Chardonnay 97** barrel-fermented, matured *sur lie*, herby/lemon character with honeyed tones. Full-bodied, throat-warming wine.

PERROQUET range:

*** **Louiesenhof Cabernet Sauvignon** Blend of new and old clones in **96**. Odd mix of tarry/green pepper scents. Juicy palate with blackberry fruit, snatches of vanilla. Refreshing twist of acidity in the finish.

*** **Louiesenhof Chardonnay 96** features cinnamon and burnt butter nose, grapefruit/lemon grass flavours. Tangy finish for early, easy drinking. Showy rather than subtle style.

**** **Louiesenhof Red Muscadel** NEW **92** example of lush, smooth-textured sweet dessert, tastes of fresh grapes in honey, doesn't cloy.

Red ◀ **97** early-drinking tinta barocca-based blend, gentle, ripe flavours, some toffees. **Rouge** NEW **98** from cabernet s. Light, bright, with raspberry, tobacco-pouch and spicy/peppery flavours. Easy drinker with pasta. **Pinot Gris 97** very light, dry, understated as this variety nearly always is, in the Cape. Unwooded. Best drunk young. **Chenin Blanc 97** not tasted. The aim was, however, "not a guava explosion, but a Stellenbosch character". **Chardonnay-Pinot Gris** NEW **98** addition to range. Not tasted. **Cape Tawny** NEW (Change from LBV) ◀ In stylish ceramic carafe. From low yielding tinta barocca, wood-aged 4 years. One of the driest at 80 gms/l sugar, 19% alc. (Smit a long-time port enthusiast and pioneer of more "Portuguese" Cape ports.)

LOUIS CAUVIN CAP CLASSIQUE — SFW

This sparkling wine range temporarily suspended. Featured two labels: **Chardonnay** Showing smoky, sweet biscuity aromas, now with significant bottle age. Two vintages released: **91**, **90**. Basically simple. **Pinot Noir 90** fading rosé; mature orangy rim. One-of-a-kind sweet Cap Classique, now tiring. A curiosity.

LOUISVALE

Stellenbosch See Stellenbosch map

Open weekdays 10-5; Sat 10-1. Self-catering guest cottage. Tasting charge: R5.
Owners: Hans Froehling and Leon Stemmet
Winemaker: Simon Smith (since July 1997)
Production: 320 tons, 22 000 cases. **Vineyards**: 14,5 ha.
P.O. Box 542, Stellenbosch 7599
Tel: 021-8822422 **Fax:** 021-8822633
E-mail: louisvale@iafrica.com

The winemaking team on this compact, critically acclaimed Devon Valley estate—Hans Froehling and Leon Stemmet, proprietors, art patrons and breeders of national champion Great Danes, and relative newcomer Simon Smith, ex-Weltevrede, the energetic young winemaker, must have logged up enough frequent flyer miles in 1998 to keep them travelling free of charge into ripe old age—the UK, Switzerland, Singapore and Thailand are just some of the countries visited to network with customers, prospects and contacts as part of the philosophy of "staying with production of 21 000 cases, concentrating on quality and service".

**** **Chardonnay** Biscuity-rich, buttery-citrus style, hordes of awards. **97** latest release best to date: high-toned, intense bouquet, scented with melon and grapefruit; spicy oak and complex malo character, usual trademark balance, integration. **96** has grown deeper, broader, with ripe citrus fruit on palate. **95** WINE**** has developed beautifully, with complex lemon and marmalade tones. 60% new oak (French/American). **94** creamy texture, mature toasted almonds. **VG 93**, among Top 100 at Sydney International Wine Competition.

**** **Cabernet Sauvignon-Merlot** Again in **96** riot of bright, juicy berries romps around with spicy oak on palate. Like **95**, offers dark berry, chocolate, toasty vanilla bouquet. **94** WINE**** mint, spice, fruit flavours. Ripe, soft. Improves with each vintage. 50% cabernet s., 35% merlot aged in part new American, 3rd/4th-fill French. Includes splash—15%—cabernet franc.

*** **Merlot 96** bright cerise-red; leafy, minty scents lead into intense cassis, sweet, ripe berry flavours. **95** still highly concentrated. Ripe fruit, abundant spice, dark chocolates, hint of mint. Soft tannins reveal mulberries, vanilla, fudge. American oak adds spice. **VG**. **94** developed beautiful berry fruits and soft chocolate nose.

*** **LV Cabernet Sauvignon 97** could be used to teach students just what pure cabernet fruit should be. **94** blackcurrants, black cherries, fairly chewy, with sweet berries/vanilla, some earthiness—first release from bought-in Devon Valley grapes. Drinking well; barrel-aged, incl. new American oak. Muldersvlei grapes. **Cabernet Sauvignon "Limited Release" 95** medium red/purple, deep cassis fruit nose, gentle dark berry fruits, touch of sweet oak, finishing with fine soft tannins.

LV Sauvignon Blanc-Chardonnay 97 continues on established, successful lines: about 60% sauvignon blanc, chardonnay, latter oak-fermented, oak-matured; good limey-leesy combination, broadening palate, **95 SAA**. **Chavant Chardonnay** ◀ Lightly oaked. Popular restaurant wine. **97** similar to pvs. Good citrus, buttery aromas, scents of vanilla, gentle palate, persistent finish. Develops well over year or two. **LV Chardonnay** (Unwooded) **97** tangy lemon/lime fruit, crisp, clean. Froehling says: "Belgians love this wine."

LOURENS RIVER VALLEY WINES See Morgenster Estate

LOUWSHOEK-VOORSORG CO-OPERATIVE

Rawsonville See Worcester map

Tastings/sales Mon-Fri 8-12.30; 1.30-5. Cellar tours by appointment, guest-houses nearby.
Owners: 36 members
Winemaker: Jaco Potgieter (since 1990), Anton Nel (since 1996)
Production: 14 000 tons. **Vineyards:** 820 ha.

P.O. Box 174, Rawsonville 6845
Tel: 0231-91110 **Fax:** 0231-91980

There's a fresh, new-broomy buzz about this winery, tucked into a quiet mountain-rimmed corner of Rawsonville. Overwhelmingly white v'yds of the old "heavy-bearing" sort are being ploughed up, replanted with trendy cab., merlot, pinotage, sémillon. The cellar, recently revamped, is getting specialised equipment for red production from the 1999 crush. Labelling, packaging have been spruced up, a new higher-echelon brand, Daschbosch, launched. "The next step is to pinpoint promising plots, coax the best fruit we can from them," says Jaco Potgieter, who makes ranges specially for export to Europe, the US, plus the local restaurant trade.

★★★★ **Louwshoek-Voorsorg Nectar de Provision** ◀ Acquired cult following from **87** inaugural; now in souped-up packaging, reflects stellar quality in bottle. First local version of Cognac's classic aperitif, Pineau des Charentes. Follows French methods: colombard, fortified with 5/3-year-old brandy, matured in brandy vats. Improves with age. Current **97** still young. Distinctive nose, flavours: ginger, aniseed; silky texture, spirity lilt. Chocolate coating becomes pronounced with age. 17,5% alc.

DASCHBOSCH range: All NEW

Cabernet Sauvignon 98 first cab. here, lots of leafy/stemmy undercurrents, easy impression heightened by pinch of sugar (5,9 gms/l). Drink soon. **Ruby Cabernet 98** Jonah Lomu version of this variety: beefy, bold, braai wine supreme (pass those fatty chops!). 13,4% alc. **Pinotage 97** first vintage; relaxed, friendly, quite light (though not in alc. dept.—13%), agreeable raspberry flavours, for quaffing now. **Chardonnay 97** pleasant, fairly simple, some vanilla diversion, 13,4% alc. **Sauvignon Blanc** 98 light cut-grass/ nettles, fresh, crisp farewell, dry. Lightish alc. 11,8%. **Cape Ruby Port** This bright, bouncy newcomer heralded by cerise colour, ripe mulberries top to toe, amiable spirit grip (moderate alc. for style—17,5%). Selected for Calitzdorp's annual Port Festival tasting.

LOUWSHOEK-VOORSORG range:

Premier Grand Crû NV Dry white, challengingly fresh. **Soet Hanepoot 98** straightforward muscat flavours. Takes well to chilling. Lowish alc. for style (16,7%).

LUTZVILLE VINEYARDS

Lutzville, Olifants River See Olifants River map

Tastings/sales Mon-Fri 8-5. Sat 9.30-12. Cellar tours by appointment.
Owners: 110 members
Production Manager: Jacques du Toit (since 1998).
Winemaker: Albie Rust (since 1990).
Production: 8000 cases. **Vineyards:** 1 830 ha.
P.O. Box 50, Lutzville 8165
Tel: 02725-71516 **Fax:** 02725-71435.

Soon after the millennium, this sparkling cellar on the cusp of the West Coast's alluvial diamond mining zone will begin bottling its first varietal reds—fruits of a sweeping programme to establish new premium v'yds on higher-lying sites away from the river; and upgrade cellar facilities, techniques to liberate latent quality in grape material supplied by the members. Appearance of **Sémillon** in the range in 1998 is a sign of the times, as is the first barrel-fermented white—a **Chardonnay** for release in early 1999. Availability of additional fermentation tanks allowed top-performing blocks to be vinified separately for the first time in 1998, with promising results (see **Sauvignon Blanc** below). "Workhorse varieties will remain a feature of the operation," says Jacques du Toit, "but we're moving towards a boutique cellar within the co-operative set-up." Developments in v'yd, cellar are matched in the human resources sphere where a worker's representative body has been established to liaise with management. The **Fleermuisklip** brandname is locally derived from a massive rock, shared as a shelter by bats and early explorers, now a national monument.

FLEERMUISKLIP range:

★★★ **Robyn** ◀ Usually jewel-bright (hence the name), uncomplicated red quaffer. **97** has tiger in tank: 13,5% alc. Delicious fruit (ripe brambleberries), gently tannic. Cab. s, ruby cab., merlot (50/30/20), unwooded.

★★★ **Chardonnay** ◀ **98** (wooded) attractive bright green-gold colour, persistent peach, mango, melon, buttery vanilla richness in tail. 13,5% alc.

★★★ **Sauvignon Blanc** ☺ ◀ **98** (tank sample) big step up from pvs in all departments. Arresting dusty green peppers, nettles, nice palate attack, smooth, fresh. West Coast seafood-friendly.

Blanc de Noir 98 rosé-tinted, high-kicking, decidedly sweet. From grenache. 25 gms/l, alc. nudging 14%. **Sémillon** NEW Noteworthy addition to range in **98**, marked by greener, tauter varietal traits rather than opulent waxy/oiliness. Fresh grassy hints, wide-body, smooth, spry finish. 13,3% alc. **Grand Crû** ◀ **98** among better examples of this catch-all style. Green-fruit flavours, fresh, upbeat finish. Summertime quaffer. **Bukettraube 98** a sweetie: delicate straw/rose wafts over pretty, muscat-scented palate. ± 19 gms/l sugar. **Chenin Blanc** "Remarkably pleasant, good acid/sugar balance" is winemaker's take on (tank sampled) **98**. We would add: pleasant, off-dry wine for sunset fish braais. **Late Harvest 98** sweet chenin, colombard. Honey overtones. 25,7 gms/l sugar. **Spesiale Laatoes** ◀ **97** has developed engagingly: lush pineapple, honey, vibrant sugar/acid tension. Labelled "Somer Soet" (Summer Sweet); we feel autumn afternoon might also be right occasion for this gem. From colombard, 48 gms/l sugar, Olifants River champion. **98** (tasted young) possibly not in same league. **Hanepoot Jerepigo** ◀ straight-from-the-vineyard grapiness, honeysuckle fragrance, assertively sweet. **Diamant Vonkel** Current release (**97**) tastes drier than ± 45 gms/l sugar. Attractive earthy hints, creamy palate, refreshing. Carbonated bubbly, colombard/sémillon. Nearby, diamond-rich West Coast is allusion in name.

MAKRO

If there was an award for the most improved purveyors of wine in the country it would have to go to Makro. Over recent years they have improved their range in quantity and quality and trained their staff to be able to handle wine-selling with greater confidence. Certain outlets have been specifically singled out, and upgraded with stocks to match the very best of the independent retailers; Woodmead, Gauteng; Milnerton, Western Cape; Springfield, KwaZulu-Natal and Centurion, Pretoria.

Not content to wait for whatever producers offer them, they've seized the initiative and commissioned innovative, exclusive-to-Makro styles straight from the cellars. One-off special releases, and custom-made wines are thus features of the range, which reaches excitement and quality levels many might not expect from this national discount chain.

Regular participation and purchasing at wine shows (for example the Calitzdorp Port Festival) add extra oomph to the line-up. **Babbling Brook**, easy on palate and pocket, has taken off. And here's where to find an array of those magnum-sized wines which make such generous-looking gifts.

Enquiries: Gary Barber. **Tel:** 011-8060500.

PRIVATE RESERVE ranges

★★★ **Overgaauw Touriga Naçional-Cabernet Sauvignon 97** pushing ★★★★. Spicy red is an apt sub-title on the label. Third cab. s. with touriga naçional. Plum, liquorice and spice with hint of oak. Soft palate with juicy feel. Easy but characterful drinking. Full of spice and chocolate. Drink now or over next 4/5 years. One year in used oak.

★★★ **Fairview Bin 422 Shiraz-Pinotage 97** purple hue, with mulberry, plum and ground pepper nose. Gentle on palate, which repeats fruit, more plum, hint of cherry. Elegant style with fairly firm finish. Good for drinking now and over next 2/3 years. 12,5% alc.

★★★ **La Bri Bin 411 Cabernet Sauvignon/Merlot 96** plum and ripe berry fruit scents, gentle charm. Fairly firm tannin and good texture. Ready for drinking, but can develop further.

★★★ **Morgenhof Bin 212 Blanc Fumé** Big gooseberry nose echoes on soft full palate, with myrtle and hints of vanilla. Gentle, toasty oak finish. Enjoy now or over another year or two. 12,5% alc.

★★★ **Stellenzicht Bin 223 Sauvignon Blanc/Chenin Blanc 97** gorgeous, full-flavoured, packed with tropical fruit and ripe apples. Very smooth with long, fresh, zesty finish.

★★★ **Backsberg Bin 215 Chenin Blanc** ☺ Intense waves of tropical fruit including guava and mango in **97**. Light, frisky on palate with just enough leesy/oaky character to offer extra dimension. From well-established 18-year-old vines. Four months *sur-lie*. 12,5% alc.

★★★ **Franschhoek Misty NV** ☺ Attractively packaged in frosted bottle. Delightful muscat whiffs, clean honeysuckle character. Bright, clean, fresh mouthful. 85% chenin, 15% muscat alex. Early, easy drinker. But be careful: high 13,5% alc.

★★★ **Backsberg Cuvée Brut Bin 606** Almost 5 years on lees give gorgeous yeasty/bready nose, soft creamy mouth-feel with herby dryness in the finish.

★★★★ **Boplaas Bin 608 Touriga Naçional Port 96** (In magnum) Deep ruby colour, attractive violets and mocha nose. Waves of similar flavours, excellent grip. Very tasty now but for max. pleasure give 5-10 yrs.

Franschhoek Vineyards Cabernet Sauvignon 97 (magnum) some charry oak notes with cherry pepper spice on the palate, slight tannic finish. Good with outdoor food. **Yellowwood Ridge Bin 450 Cabernet Sauvignon-Merlot 96** garnet-coloured with brick edge. Tarry, charry, dusty nose, some mulberry backing. Almost sweet flavours, certainly smooth. "Hot" finish with some raspy tannins. Good with fatty chops. 13% alc. **Franschhoek Vineyards Chardonnay-Chenin 97** ☺ grapefruit, guava aromas, flavours with vanilla leesy character. Good mouthful with clean, fresh finish. **Yellowwood Ridge Sémillon-Chenin Blanc** Lovely fresh lime, lemonade aromas and flavours. Soft on palate, clean, fresh finish in **97**. **La Bri Bin 216 Rhine Riesling 97** slightly honeyed nose with gentle citrus notes. Soft, spicy, peach/apricot flavours. Pleasant, easy, early drinking.

PREMIUM QUALITY SELECTION (exclusive to Makro)

★★★ **Zevenwacht Pinot Noir 97** made as a blanc de noir. Fermented in oak barrels and then further 6 mths. on the lees give distinct red wine character to bone-dry, strawberry-flavoured wine with touch of mushroom. Versatile food partner. 13% alc.

*** **Neil Ellis Sauvignon Blanc 97** deep, intense, nettly nose with gooseberry, herby flavours. Very accessible now, but will develop over next year or more. 13% alc.

BABBLING BROOK range:

*** **Cabernet Sauvignon 97** accessible red with enough potential to develop over another 4/5 years. Deep blackberry, raspberry fruit backed by sweetish vanilla and ripe tannins. 12,5% alc. W.O. Coastal Region.

*** **Pinotage 97** modern fruity style with fresh sappy texture. Cherry and ripe plummy flavours, soft tannins; easy but substantial drinking now and over next year or two. 13,5% alc. W.O. Coastal Region.

*** **Merlot 97** with raspberry, mulberry and hint of violet on nose; plummy, chocolate flavours. Touch of oak gives extra complexity. Soft mellow tannins for ready drinking. 12,5% alc. W.O. Western Cape.

*** **Ruby Cabernet** ☺ **97** wild berries/spice scents carry through to flavours. Light touch of oak. Good easy drinker, even chilled. 12,5% alc. W.O. Western Cape.

*** **Sauvignon Blanc** Full-bodied gooseberry delight with refreshing tropical tones and long, lemony finish.

Dry White 97 three-quarters chenin, with sémillon. Light guava and lime aromas/flavours with merest touch of oak. Delightful easy, early drinking. 11% alc. W.O. Swartland.

MALAN BROTHERS — Export range by Simonsig

Cabernet Sauvignon Herbaceous, berry-toned **96**. Uncomplicated, thinnish fruit. **Rouge du Cap** Light-bodied **98**; agreeable pinotage warm spice, plum character. Low tannins; good quaffing. **Chardonnay 98** forward citrusy, smoky aromas; bouncy palate, some leesy breadth. No-fuss drinking. Tank-/chip-fermented. **Sauvignon Blanc** NEW Pungent green-pea attack in unwooded **98**. Lively, fruitily dry white. **Blanc du Cap** Off-dry fruity blend weisser riesling, colombard, clairette blanche, hint morio muscat.

MAMREWEG — See Darling Cellars

McGREGOR WINERY

McGregor, Breede River Valley See Robertson map

Tastings/sales Mon-Fri 8-12; 1-5. Sat 9-12.30. Cellar tours by appointment.
Owners: 41 members
Winemaker: Danie Marais (since 1994)
Production: 10 000 tons. **Vineyards:** 500 ha.
Private Bag X619, McGregor 6708
Tel: 02353-741 **Fax:** 02353-829

1948, a momentous date in many respects, was the year this co-op was founded at McGregor, a lovely tranquil hamlet about 20 km from Robertson. The area's red soils, dry climate were conducive to wine grape cultivation and the fledgling venture flourished. Half-a-century on the operation still turns out some of the chirpiest, fruitiest, easy-quaffingest wines around, thanks in part to the skills of Danie Marais who joined from Bovlei in 1994. In his hands McGregor's **Colombard**, something of a legend in its own (and many, many consumers') lunchtime, has remained at the top of the winery's best-seller list.

*** **McGregor Village Red** ☺ ◀ **97** ruby cabernet in decidedly effervescent, playful mode. Gusts of raspberry, strawberry, sprinkling of green pepper, fresh, bit of tannin so needs food (pasta, light meats). Dry, lightly wooded.

Chardonnay NEW **98** quite a charmer: fresh, light, lemon-scented, with gentle traces of butter/vanilla (though unwooded), crisp dry finish. Drink young. 13,5% alc. **Colombard-Chardonnay** ☺ ◀ **98** mega-fruity, dry, very appealing everyday quaffer. Guava deluxe, medium-bodied, versatile at table. Chardonnay portion (20%) oak-fermented. **Sauvignon Blanc** ◀ **98** unwooded; grassy/nettly, crisp mouthful. Just not dry at 3,7 gms/l sugar, easy drinker. Early-morning harvested to enhance freshness. Drink now. **Chenin Blanc** ◀ **98** billows fresh guava on nose/palate, bone-dry despite impression of sweetness from very ripe fruit. A "foodie". **Colombard 98** a curiously subdued version of this habitually exuberant merry-maker. Off-dry (6,8 gms/l sugar). **Vrolijkheid Vin Blanc** NV Sauvignon-like grass/nettles (though from chenin), attractive bright fruit, quaffable. 500 ml screw top. **Vrolijkheid Stein** Semi-sweet chenin. 500 ml screw top. **Late Harvest 97** semi-sweet white blend. **Vonkelwyn Vin Sec** NV Lively off-dry carbonated sparkler. From sauv. bl. **Red Muscadel 95** pale onion-skin-coloured fortified dessert (17% alc.), very raisiny, sweet but not heavy. Aperitif (lightly chilled) rather than digestif. **White Muscadel 94** lovely golden tint, sultanas, raisins. In traditional SA sweet fortified dessert style, with some elegance. Serve lightly chilled. **Port** ◀ NEW NV Current release (**97**) Sweet-savoury dessert wine—not really "port", pleasant nonetheless. Label says: "savour glass as fireside companion", but better aperitif, lightly chilled. 17,5% alc. from ruby cab.

MEERENDAL ESTATE

Durbanville See Durbanville map

Open Mon-Fri 10-5. Sat 10-1. Closed religious holidays. Red wines marketed by Bergkelder.
Function, conference facilities.
Owner: J.C.F. Starke Trust
Winemaker: Soon Potgieter
Production: 1 000 tons
Vineyards: 132 ha.
P.O. Box 2, Durbanville 7550
Tel/Fax: 021-9751655
E-mail: hestarke@mweb.co.za

A new pressing cellar with the latest technology and new barrel maturation facilities were commissioned during the year, giving fresh momentum to this historic family-run estate's thrust into a modern, more fruity Cape style. A swing through Europe and participation in a number of local wine shows afforded Soon Potgieter and his team the opportunity to take the market's pulse and introduce customers to the new diner-friendly 500 ml packaging. Meerendal is one of the oldest Cape wine producers—vines were thriving here in the early 18th century—making the Durbanville farm a magnet for latter-day wine devotees who will find a friendly, relaxed ambience—and, of course, facilities to taste the range which now includes a **Merlot** and **Natural Sweet**.

★★★★ **Pinotage** Deep mulberry colour/scents in **95**. More mulberries and ripe, red plums on super palate. Fresh, fruity, almost juicy in modern style. Probably best enjoyed in its relative youth. 13,5% alc. **96** next up fared well at WINE's 1998 pinotage tasting—★★★(★). Blackcurrants more prominent in this, concentrated, elegant finish, needs another year or two for oak, tannins to amalgamate with fruit.

★★★ **Shiraz 95** more modern than pvs., but now losing initial fruitiness, showing more herby notes with firm finish.

*** **Merlot 97** first release. Clean, grassy, softly fruity with sweetish blackcurrant/vanilla notes, slightly rustic aftertaste. Easy-drinking. 12,3% alc.

*** **Cabernet Sauvignon 96** first release. Light green bean style with supple, fine tannins, hints of good blackberry. 13% alc.

*** **Sauvignon Blanc 98** full-bodied with clean, grassy gooseberry aromas/flavours. Nice softness on palate, fairly zippy finish. Unwooded, easy-drinker even with 13% alc.

*** **Chardonnay** Fresh tropical, citrus, peachy tones with faintest hint of toasty oak in **97**. Light fruit shows some alcoholic sweetness. Could have some development potential. 12,9% alc.

Gewürztraminer 98 gentle rose-petal aromas, with soft texture, low 11% alc. and unusually for this variety in the Cape, almost dry (3 gms/l sugar). **Natural Sweet** NEW **98** first dessert release from estate, untasted. 12,8% alc. 176 gms/l sugar.

MEERLUST

Faure, Stellenbosch See Helderberg map

Sales by appointment, weekdays from the estate; R30 per tasting charge.
Owner: Hannes Myburgh.
Winemaker: Giorgio Dalla Cia (since 1978)
Assistant: Chris Williams
Production: 40 000 cases. **Vineyards:** 150 ha.
P.O. Box 15, Faure 7131
Tel: 021-8433275 **Cellar:** 021-8433587 **Fax:** 021-8433513
E-mail: meerlust@iafrica.com

The young patrician and the older maestro—respectively in shy, urbane Francophile proprietor Hannes Myburgh and Italian winemaking chief Giorgio Dalla Cia—present the Cape's most formidable vini-cultured duo. And the Meerlust backdrop—like the wines—is all languid authenticity and continuity: this is the most stylishly lived-in Cape-Dutch architecture in the winelands and the view from the front door frames Table Mountain the way it has for the previous seven generations of Myburghs. The enormous kitchen at the back seats 30 (fits 80) and there's a roaring fireplace encircled by sprawled black and brown fox terriers. This is the strategic hub. Here, over unhurried lunches (pinot noir is the favoured tipple) and the hum of the ham slicer shaving the San Daniele and the urgent grinder of the espresso machine, and later a few snifters of the exquisite merlot Meerlust Grappa, they plot their next moves: where the best new wild mushrooms might be found next morning in the forests around Stellenbosch. And whether the 81 Pinot should be put up against the 91. (The stunning 95 and 96 are too young.) Or, wait, no, what about the Merlot 86?—"it has just enough organic decadence now"— says Dalla Cia. These are critical choices. Wines, like politicians, come and go—but usually more predictably. And they're generally pleasanter to have around the table. There may be this kind of wry, gentle cynicism here, but there's always an eagerness too to discuss absolutely anything—in the "spirit of the vine".

Not long ago, when the authors of this book were experiencing a "little local difficulty" in some quarters after some outspokenness on labour conditions in the winelands, the summons came to present ourselves at the Meerlust kitchen. There, as always, the discourse rambled wide and differing positions, fiercely held, were debated strenuously, unrancorously and with humour. Perhaps nowhere on a Cape wine estate do they live out, arrange their lives around, the true culture of the wine so naturally and with such unselfconscious pride. Wine is used as a mind-stretching, culture-defining, life-enhancing aid.

In 1998, Dalla Cia celebrated his 20th year at this most prestigious of posts. Taken on by Hannes Myburgh's late father, Nico, he brought a sensible world view of wine and winemaking: now, since the events of 1994, more generally fashionable in the winelands. (Hannes, who studied French at Stellenbosch and later worked in France, including at Ch. Lafite, is even more a "citizen of the world" than his father.) An unrepentant Eurocentrist, Dalla Cia quickly established the estate's wine persona and has held a steady compass since—with only occasional, and it's sometimes seemed not always with ungrudging alacrity, concessions to New World fruit faddism. "At table, with food, wines must be vinous and serious, not sweet and fruity and obvious," says Dalla Cia. Any rejoinder must take account of an unarguable fact: no Cape red wine label today has a bigger and stronger following, either at home or abroad. However, Dalla Cia did send his assistant, Chris Williams, to Ch. Bon Pasteur, last year to work under current international guru Michel Rolland. "The stress was on grape maturity, which means high sugars and low acids and silky, fine tannins," said Williams afterwards. "That's achieved with good soil drainage and canopy management."

Yes, among a thousand other things, Dalla Cia would add.

★★★★ **Rubicon** For many—including followers abroad—this remains an ultimate name and statement in Cape claret style. The upcoming, rich cherry, chocolaty **95** due out in 2000, will be a serious collector's piece, matching the four finest years of past decade or so—**86**, **87**, **89**, **91**. Rubicon remains the quintessence of refined understatement—serious, medium-textured vinosity, ripe but not overripe berry flavours, moderate grip from tannins, essentially dry rather than fruity-sweet. Winemaker Dalla Cia considers Rubicon a "better, richer, more complex wine than cabernet sauvignon on its own could ever be". Here, the blend is about 65-70% cabernet, 20-25% merlot, balance cab. f. New Nevers barrel-matured about 18 months to 2 years, through malo. Dalla Cia has never wavered stylistically: while others see-sawed between bold fruity "New World modernity" and "Cape tradition" this B'deaux-style standard-bearer has kept a constant course, for nearly 2 decades, openly aiming at European restraint and vinosity. Other vintages: **94** splendid array of layered fruit, tannin, oak; **93** presently still stands apart, slightly atypical bouquet—curious, intriguing mix of hay stacks, cigar boxes. **89 SAA**, *Decanter* 4-stars, among the UK magazine's "Top Wines of the Year" tasted in 1997. **87 VG**.

★★★★ **Merlot** Latest three: **94**, **95**, **96** (last not yet released) seem to become progressively more powerful, expressive. **95** a sturdy, minerally corker, squashed berry quality oozing everywhere. **94** more austere, with wild heathery aspects, though sweetish tinge, still needs (in 1998) 3-4 years more. **96** terrific, bold with enormous ripe fruity width on palate, lots of potential. These age well, but in past belonged in vinous, leaner category of Cape merlots. Dalla Cia looks for minerally, inky substance—"a typical merlot characteristic"—and believes more recent, bigger style will continue to show this quality. Among his favourites is still **86**—wafts of dried wild mushrooms, damp leaves—which this Friulian funghiphile maintains is the quintessence of well-matured St. Emilions. No local releases for 3 years, **90, 91, 92** (though bit exported). **89 SAA, VG**; **87 VG**. Barrel-aged, about 80% new oak. Always about 10% cab. s. seasoning.

★★★★ **Pinot Noir 96** second vintage of up-graded approach to this difficult variety. "Think through the wild strawberry notes on the nose and you'll get the truffles in the background," says assistant winemaker Chris Williams. "See, it's easy when you know how." This is the result of more serious, toasty oaking and general vinification including malo fermentation in (mostly new) barrels—echoing Burgundian-inspired approach to new chardonnay here, making for a Burgundian-styled duo. Much improved colour, richer bouquet, fuller palate contribute to more generous wine, as with **95**. Promising **97**, partly with fruitier new clone. Pvs.— pre-**94**—style leaner, more savoury (perhaps less berry) character, usually with lighter texture, leafy quality. Best years offer mushroom-gamey, leafy gilding; recent good years include sp. appealing **87**, **91**, **93**.

★★★★ **Chardonnay** Serious, weighty contender for top Cape chardonnay laurels with a difference—after début with **95**. Mellow, nutty, butterscotch and honeyed flavours. Achieves its gravitas by extra-long (18 months or so) extra-toasty barrel treatment—and 2-year plus wait before release. So comes ready-made with some bottle maturity, forsaking more common route of racy, lemony youthfulness. Some might say thus matches the sonority of its now very senior winemaker, Dalla Cia, an institution here since 1978 and for nearly two decades the only Italian winemaker in the Cape. **95** wide-bodied, dense, multi-flavoured, lush offering, layered with honey, toffee notes. **96**, **97** both promise trademark toastiness, density, plus lime-marmalade-honeyed quality. Classic barrel-fermented, in Alliers/Burgundy oak; then left there for ages, the dying yeast cells infusing their own (French-style) flavours, which eventually trigger the prized qualities of toasty decadence. May not plumb the depths of a better Grand Cru Burgundy, but in offering a weightier alternative to almost all Cape chardonnays, it provides a pleasing and serious drink.

Cabernet Sauvignon Bottled intermittently. Next one? Maybe 2002, says Dalla Cia. Last **93**, touch leaner than pvs. With coffee-smoky bouquet. **91** WINE★★★★, elegant, quiet rather than robust, but enough sweet ripeness in bouquet; lightish feel, balanced across palate. **86** also good. (These with about 10% merlot; 18 months oak, 80% new. Through malo.) **Meerlust Red 90, 92** upper-class quality, middle-class price, cab. s./merlot touch of cab. f. in **90**.

MEINERT WINERY (Devoncrest)

Devon Valley, Stellenbosch See Stellenbosch map

Visits: Sales by appointment, from end 1999
Owner, Winemaker: Martin Meinert (since 1998)
Production: 2 000 cases. **Vineyards:** 13 ha.
P.O. Box 7221, Stellenbosch 7599
Tel: 021-8822363 **Fax:** 021-8822363
E-mail: meinert@netactive.co.za

After nearly 10 years at prestigious Vergelegen, where he helped plan both vineyards and cellar, Martin Meinert has decided to devote himself full-time to the family vineyards here. A perfectionist—and something of a philosopher too—he'll produce specialist boutique reds in small but very collectible quantities, probably confined to just a trio of labels, when he's satisfied with his pinotage. Devon Valley is filling up now with more and generally smaller vineyards and Meinert's considerable skills—he's travelled the world of wine very extensively and has perhaps the best network of French wine connections of any South African winemaker, plus his very neighbourly attitude—will doubtless play a key role in the development of the valley's individuality. And his own vineyard and immaculate winery will be beacons here. His self-confessed weakest point—he finds "selling" (himself, his wines) difficult—is unlikely to be a hindrance: the wines are stylish and internationally-tailored.

★★★★ **Merlot 97** unblended varietal, deep and broad-flavoured. Grape and oak tannins mesh powerfully for very big impression overall. Needs couple more years. Plummy minerally merlot authenticity shows with a sappy, juicy and generous effect, the tannins (still to moderate, very adequate) notwithstanding. Only about 15% new French oak—but seems more!—and 14 months in barrel, with some American oak. **96** pretty much same profile, same unirrigated, low-yielding—6-7 tons/ha.—v'yds. Four-square, bold. Should last good 10 years. (Touch—5%—cab. s.) 13,5% alc.

★★★★ **Cabernet-Merlot** NEW **97**, a 70%-30% blend. From very low-yielding vines (5 tons/ha) intensely-fruity, ripe-tasting, with oak (14 months in barrel, 35% new French) and solid but unaggressive tannin in foreground, likely to remain for couple more years. Overall, dense wine, tasting very strongly of itself—with individuality, meriting collectors' attention. Should be stayer.

MERIDIAN — by Longridge exclusively for restaurants

Classic Red Light-textured, dry with spicy, meaty persistence. Versatile food partner. SA/French blend. **Classic White** Crisp, mouthfilling dry **98**. Refreshing guava, green herbs persistence. **Semi-Sweet** Fruity mix **98** colombard, riesling, bukettraube. **Brut** MCC Cava bubbly from Spain.

MERWESPONT CELLAR

Bonnievale See Bonnievale map

Tastings/sales Mon-Fri 8-12.30; 1.30-5. Cellar tours during harvest only by appointment.
Owners: 65 members
Winemaker: Dirk Cornelissen (since 1983)
Production: 10 000 cases. **Vineyards:** 650 ha.
P.O. Box 68, Bonnievale 6730
Tel: 02346-2800 **Fax:** 02346-2734

Better-looking, better-dressed Cape wines than these you'll search hard to find. The brand-new **Agulhas** label is a vision of modern chic, its elegant lipped bottles monogrammed with a dashing, expansive capital A. The old **Merwespont** range has been face-lifted in style, a vineyard photo-image washed with discreet, most attractive colour to match each wine. Altogether alluring. The Agulhas "Southernmost tip of Africa" front-label, and the back-label information that this is "a mere 86 km away" from the nearest vineyards (well, in vast Africa, that's no distance at all) do perhaps over-emphasise a maritime influence. But no matter. These are wines from a cellar clearly on a forward roll.

MERWESPONT range:
Cabernet Sauvignon ◀ ☺ Super **97** to match stylish new label. Gentle cassis scents/flavours, touches of tobacco pouch, soft tannins, manageable 12% alc. for right-now swiggability. At R12 ex-cellar a steal. **Chardonnay** ◀ **97** with delicate citrus hints, soft lemon-peachy fruit. Very low acid for easy sipping. Alc. 13%. Unwooded, dry.
AGULHAS range: All NEW
Cabernet Sauvignon 97 ultra-light, (11% alc.) low-acid instant gulping style, the sort of red which suits summer, and chilling. **Red** Soft, fruity, light, easy-drinking everyday blend pinotage, ruby cab., cab. s. **Chardonnay**

Low-key **97** with limey, spicy fruit. **White** Ultra-soft quaffer from third each chardonnay, chenin, colombard, on the dry side of off-dry. **Rosé** Charming coral-toned blend colombard, chenin, ruby cab. Latter's red wine flavours come through nicely. Gently fruity, just off-dry. Versatile aperitif, salad partner.

MICHAEL PAUL

See Ashwood Wines

MIDDELVLEI ESTATE

Stellenbosch See Stellenbosch map

Tastings/sales Mon-Fri 10-4.30, Sat 10-1.
Picnic baskets Dec-March.
Owner: Jan Momberg
Winemaker: Tinnie Momberg (since 1992)
Viticulturist: Ben Momberg (since 1992)
Production: 30 000 cases. **Vineyards:** 140 ha.
P.O. Box 66, Stellenbosch 7599
Tel: 021-8832565 **Fax:** 021-8839546

A highlight of 1998 for Momberg siblings Tinnie, winemaker, and Ben, viticulturist, and retired patriarch "Stil-Jan"— whose family established Middelvlei and first made wine here in the 1920s—was the **WINE** tasting of 19 pinotage vintages ranging from the earliest 1972 to 1994. Significantly the elder Momberg's **73**, made the traditional way in open fermenters, large oak vat ageing *et al* was the outright winner, followed by **80**; **86** tied with the **94** vintage, first of a new generation of Middelvlei pinotages vinified by Tinnie to accentuate fruit flavours (and accorded lush wood treatment). This style since has been adopted across the range, giving this well-liked label a fresh, contemporary feel. Developments in the cellar have been matched by progress on the labour front: the Mombergs, always pace-setters in this arena, have added a clinic to the community hall and crèche on the estate.

**** **Cabernet Sauvignon 95** bright mulberry colour; cherry-accented bouquet. Assertive palate, intense dark cherry/blackberry flavours wrapped around supple tannins. Smooth, harmonious with long, persistent finish. **92, 93, 94** sold out. **91 VG** growing in complexity, expressing bigger cassis, cherry fruit (result of riper picking than pvs.), ample oak. Nevers barrel-aged for healthy mix of oak-fruit tannins, penetrating, firm, classic finish. **WINE******. **90** less substantial. **89 VG**; **87, 86** both **VVG**.

**** **Shiraz 97** absolute stunner, ***** in the making, Rhône-like gravitas, 1997 SA champion young wine. **96** bottled but being held for further ageing, great potential. Since landmark new-style **95**, containing fruit from virus-cleaned vines (50/50 from old 1977 plantings, new 1990 plantings). **95** violets, vanilla, cherries on nose/palate, peppery, plummy depths, liquorice whiffs. No **92-94** (preferred to wait for cleaned-up clone production). **89-91** all **VG**.

**** **Pinotage** Latest **95** continues striking modern style, unleashed with **94**. Full-house of ripe plum, banana aromas, brimming with soft flavours, velvet texture, dollops vanilla, lithe tannins. **94** fuller, better than pvs. in all respects. Plums; ripe banana, vanilla, sweetish impression but bone-dry. **93** shows signs of new direction, more fruit, fresher oak. Both over 12% alc. No **92**. **91** barrel-aged, hearty but not coarse, medium-bodied (12,3% alc.); more than hint of pinotage "sweet" bounce, but enough fruit flesh to carry it, firmish tannins. **90** plummy nose, tannins quite unyielding. Bush vines.

*** **Pinotage-Merlot 97** 60/40 blend, fresh, modern, forward fruit. 13% alc.

**** **Chardonnay** From **96** lot more fruity presence, refinement. **98** probably best to date. Crisp, citrusy, buttery/oaky flavours, hints of peach poised over a spicy edge. Delicious. Available only on the farm.

MONDIAL — Gilbeys, Stellenbosch

*** **Chardonnay 97** innovative when first produced as a multi-origin blend from grapes throughout the Cape. Still widely sourced, features a goodly portion of healthy oak from barrel-fermentation. Lemon, lime nose, with fresh, toasty oak. Soft and juicy texture. Good fresh fruit and long, oaky finish.

MONIS — Fortified Wines, Paarl

Owner: Stellenbosch Farmers' Winery
Winemaker: Hans Losch (since 1959)
Production: 24 700 cases
P.O. Box 266, Paarl 7620
Tel: 021-8721811 **Fax:** 021-8722790

Hans Losch, one of SA's most seasoned vintners—40 years in the cellar—crafts this first-division, frequent Veritas award-winning range of fortified wines. The house of Monis was founded at Paarl by Roberto Moni, an early 20th-century immigrant to the Cape, scion of a prominent Tuscan winemaking family. The range, now under the SFW wing, includes a consistent range of sherries, **Pale Dry** (almost amontillado style), **Full Cream** (both **VVG** in 95), and **Medium Cream VG**. Limited lots of a **Monis Special Reserve** port are sometimes offered on the Nederburg Auction.

**** **VO Tawny Port** Mature mahogany; roasted coffee, caramel fruit, sweet, **VG** in 1995. **SAA** trophy winner. This, Reserve below star-rated as examples of traditional Cape liqueur wines, distinct from newer-style Portuguese-inspired "ports".

**** **Special Reserve VO Tawny** NEW to the guide but no spring chicken: **83**. Limpid tawny colour, dark caramel/honey tones; from mainly cinsaut, some tinta barocca, pinotage, bush vines in Paarl area, low 7 tons/ha. yield, 5½ years in wood.

Moscato NV ◀ Mellow Breede River red muscadel; succulent, uncloying sweetness, penetrating raisiny warmth. **VVG**.

MONS RUBER ESTATE

Klein Karoo — See Klein Karoo map

Tastings/sales Mon-Fri 9-5, Sat 9-1. Hiking trail in proclaimed conservation area.
Owners: Radé and Erhard Meyer
Winemaker: Radé Meyer (since 1990)
Production: 423 tons. **Vineyards:** 38 ha.
P.O. Box 1585, Oudtshoorn 6620
Tel/Fax: 044-2516550

"Do we have an e-mail address? Man, we barely have a telephone service!" laughs genial Radé Meyer, who runs this delightfully individual brandy distillery-cum-wine cellar at the foot of ochre-tinted Mons Ruber (Red Hill) near Oudtshoorn with brother Erhard. Change, Radé points out, happens languidly on Mons Ruber, rather like the gait of one of the farm's 800 ostriches on a cloudless February afternoon. But change *does* happen, as evidenced by increased plantings of red grapes and gradual introduction of chardonnay into the varietal mix. "A wild card but hopefully not a joker," is Meyer's take on the outlook for Burgundy's great white grape on far-flung, sun-baked Mons Ruber.

Cabernet Sauvignon NEW **98** (tank sample) gentle wafts of honey, straw; light, undemanding. Early drinker. **Conari** Current release **89**. Untasted; from cab. s. **Vino 98** (untasted) one of Radé Meyer's free-wheeling creations: a dry white from chenin blanc, sultana! Usually light (around 11% alc.); very different. **Cabernet Sauvignon Port 93** intriguing sherry/fruitcake aromas; chocolate liqueur tastes. Less sweet than most at 87,5 gms/l sugar. Oak-aged. **Cabernet Sauvignon Jerepigo 97** jewel-bright, light ruby colour; fresh sweet dates, chocolate pud essences. Lowish alc. Alternative name: **Elegantia**. **Muscadel Jerepigo 98** vivid orange-amber; barley sugar, sultana sensations. Full sweet, lifted by fresh acid. Alternative label: **Regalis**. **Muscadel Halfsoet** ◀ NEW Once-off **89** as personal as any of Meyer's tinkerings. Started (long) life as base for vermouth "but I changed my mind!" Emerges decade later as rather pleasant "medium-cream sherry", complete with Jerez-like nutty nuances. "Makes perfect sense—wine was stored in used sherry vats," reveals Meyer. **Hanepoot Jerepigo 98** (tank sample) full sweet, enveloping muscat aromas, stalky whiffs. Alternative label: **Bonitas**.

MONTAGU CO-OP

Montagu See Klein Karoo map

Tastings/sales: Mon-Fri 8-5, Sat 9-12.30. Cellar tours by appointment during harvest.
Owners: 70 members
Winemaker: Sonnie Malan (since 1972)
Production: 5 000 cases. **Vineyards:** 650 ha.
P.O. Box 29, Montagu 6720
Tel: 0234-41125. **Fax:** 0234-41793

Montagu, portal to the vast Klein Karoo region, is home to this co-op producing boutique-quantities under its own label (balance sold in bulk) at laudably low prices (ceiling price broke the psychological R10 barrier for the first time in 1998!). Member-farmers recently gave entrenched winemaker Sonnie Malan the green light to upgrade to the latest technology, enabling gentler pressing and mash cooling before fermentation.

MONTESTELL WINES Stellenbosch

Owner: Dr. Julius Laszlo
P.O. Box 1273, Stellenbosch 7599
Tel: 021-8870567 **Fax:** 021-8839555

Since he retired as cellarmaster of Bergkelder, Dr. Julius Laszlo has been more active than ever. Montestell, his wholesale wine operation headquartered in Stellenbosch, grows by leaps and bounds, with the main export customers for this well-priced range in Holland, Germany and the UK.

MONT ROCHELLE MOUNTAIN VINEYARDS

Franschhoek See Franschhoek map

Open Mon-Sat 11-4. Sun (Sept-April) 11-1. Cellar tours 11, 12.30, 3. Tasting individuals R5 p/p, groups over 10, R10 p/p. Tour & tasting individuals, R10, p/p, groups over 10 R15 p/p.
Owner: Graham de Villiers
Winemaker: Anne-Mareé Mostert (since 1996)
Production: 12 000 cases, plus 8 000 cases bought-in for Petit Rochelle. **Vineyards:** 26 ha.
P.O. Box 334, Franschhoek 7690
Tel: 021-8763000 **Fax:** 021-8762362
E-mail: montrochelle@wine.co.za

"The best fertiliser on a wine farm is the footprint of the owner in the vineyard," muses Graham de Villiers. But a businessman of his experience knows that efforts at improving wine quality go beyond such parochial notions. Chairman of the Franschhoek Vignerons and Vision 2020—an industry blueprint plan for the future—he was recently appointed Chairman of the SA Wine & Spirits Export Association (SAWSEA), irreverently referred to as "seesaw" following unseemly ructions. De Villiers' concern here is to re-establish a unified international presence for the wine industry. His footprints remain rooted in these mountain vineyards though, with Mont Rochelle an executive member of the Franschhoek Development Forum that is embarking on visionary plans to house disadvantaged members of the local community. An impressive Veritas double gold medal for her début 1996 **Cabernet** has not gone to winemaker Anne-Mareé Mostert's thoughtful head as she defines the property's style. Burgundian hand-sorting of grapes and new oak for her chardonnay are techniques she will introduce while experimenting with different vineyard blocks as the farm's own plantings begin to come on stream.

MONT ROCHELLE range:

*** **Cabernet Sauvignon 97** continues where **96 VVG** left off, deep vermilion colour, open minty nose, mulberry fruit on fresh palate. 10 months oaking keeps flavours reined in. Understated, but with depth of taste. Potential to develop further 5 years. **98** barrel sample bigger.

*** **Natural Chardonnay** Individual dry white. Sumptuous nose, plush buttery flavour achieved without oak, with clever use of lees contact, malolactic fermentation. **98** ripe lemon fruits filled out with lanolin waxiness, **97** developed honeyed nose, brisk steely palate.

*** **Oak-Matured Chardonnay 98** toasty nose from all new wood (from 3 different forests, 4 coopers). Hint of honey; ripe citric fruit under wraps in youth, waiting to emerge. 13% alc. contributes to sweetness in finish. **97** still youthful colour but richness developing on palate. **96 VG**, highly rated by **WINE** panel, smooth drinking at table.

Merlot 98 hand-pressed as in **97** but production doubled to 300 cases! Dense crimson, spicy pepper flavours, substantial tannins. **Sauvignon Blanc** grassy, herbaceous **98** flavours bolstered by invigorating alc., a food partner as in **97** which has retained its freshness after year in bottle.

PETIT ROCHELLE range:

Splendid Little Sauvignon Blanc 97 grassy aromas, dry and crisp. **Jolly Good Red** Light, pleasant everyday drink.

MOOIPLAAS ESTATE

Botterlary Hills See Stellenbosch map

Not open for sales to the public.

Owners: Roos family
Winemaker: Louis Roos (since 1983)
Production: 6 000 cases. **Vineyards:** 120 ha.
P.O. Box 104, Koelenhof 7605
Tel: 021-9036273 **Fax:** 021-9033474
E-mail: lroos@icon.co.za

New to local consumers—but with decades of winemaking experience—is the Roos family which has made wine on this estate in the distinctive Bottelary Hills area of Stellenbosch since 1963. Vinfruco is currently a leading buyer of its bulk wine for export to the UK and the rest of Europe, where winemaker Louis Roos visited in 1998—also attending the London Wine Trade Fair. Now an own-label has been launched for the first time with the attractive wines below. A **Pinotage** is soon to join the range, and a promising **Pinot Noir** is ageing in barrel. Red wine grapes are the main focus here and will shortly rise to 70% of total production.

★★★ **Cabernet Sauvignon** NEW First bottling was **95** with cherries, blackberries from nose to palate, clean finish, good honest current drinking. **96** quality leap in all respects: more of everything (except tannins), extra perk of mintiness on nose, very accessible. Moderate 12% alc., year in small oak.

Sauvignon Blanc NEW **98** respectable everyday drinking: grassy/gooseberry scents, fresh-fruity palate, crisp finish. Step up from first **97** bottling.

MOOIUITSIG

Bonnievale See Robertson map

Tastings/sales Mon-Fri 8-12.30; 1.30-5.30. Cellar tours by appointment.
MD: N.L. (Boet) Jonker
Winemaker: Chris Versveld (since 1970)
Assistant: Chris-Willem de Bot
Viticulturists: Adolph Jonker, Francois Claassen
Production: 4 500 tons **Vineyards:** 270 ha.
P.O. Box 15, Bonnievale 6730
Tel: 02346-2143 **Fax:** 02346-2675

The Jonkers, proprietors of SA's largest family-owned liquor wholesaler at Bonnievale, put a lot of effort into their table wine range in 1998. A new cellar, complete with impressive array of stainless steel tanks was completed in time to accommodate stepped-up production of premium varieties. These improvements coincided with the fairest weather in years, resulting in something of a red-letter harvest for the 50-plus year old business. "Quality was excellent," raves Chris Versfeld, resident winemaker for almost 30 years. To many consumers, though, Mooiuitsig remains synonymous with top-drawer, traditional Cape fortified desserts typified by the **Red Muscadel Liqueur Wine 78**—a majestic old-timer on the cellar's current list.

OUDERUST range:

★★★★ **Red Muscadel Liqueur Wine** ◀◀ *Two* value pointers for this ancient but deeply distinguished **78**, a real after-dinner conversation stop-starter, from its colour—like old, polished wood—to its densely treacly (but somehow not cloying), toffee-brûleé taste. Would be most luxurious over ice-cream, too. Rated Superior back in the old days. Sold at New World Wine Auction 1990.

Soet Hanepoot Amber-coloured, exotic spicy/honey scents, luscious fruit, long finish. **White Muscadel** Current release **(96)** sadly not up to standard of extraordinary **94** ****, with burnished gold colour, golden syrup on palate, lightened with lemon, freshened with ripe green grapes.

RUSTHOF range: All NEW

Dry Red 97 light coloured, bodied, pleasant enough. Lowish alc. (11.5%), pinotage, cab. s. **Premier Grand Cru 98** dry, crisp, clean, light-bodied, 11,5% alc. **Late Harvest 98** from sauvignon blanc, pinot blanc, colombard; semi-sweet, easy fruit-salad flavours.

MOOIUITZICHT range:

Cabernet Sauvignon 95 made for everyday, no-frills quaffing. 13,4% alc. **Pinotage 95** very deep, almost black colour, some muted berry flavours, sweetish overtones. High-kicking: 14% alc. **Blanc de Noir** NEW **98** fairground sweets on nose, palate, agreeable, quite sweet-tasting 15 gms/l sugar. **Chardonnay 97** citrus fruit becoming marmalade. Rather nice! Unwooded. **Sauvignon Blanc 97** starting to show bottle age, honey overtaking gooseberry fruit. **Riesling 98** dry white, very bracing. **Late Harvest** NV Semi-sweet white. **Premier Grand Cru** NV Crisp dry white. **Bonwin Ruby Dessert** NV ◀ Chestnut-coloured fortified winter warmer, with dark, wild honeycomb tastes. **Wit Muskana** Cognac-hued dessert, light rose-apple/petal scents, intense ripe grapey palate. Unusual. **Old Tawny Port** 5-7 year wood-aged, some Portuguese varieties. **Marsala** Red dessert, spice/dried peaches, apricots. Not just for preparing veal dishes!

Other traditional desserts from this cellar include: **Red and White Muscadel, Slabbers Golden/Sweet Hanepoot, Bonwin Golden Liqueur, and a range of Ports, Malmseys and Jerepigos.**

MÔRESON-MATIN SOLEIL

Franschhoek See Franschhoek map

Tastings/sales Dec-April: Wed-Sun 11-5; May-Nov: Tues-Sun 11-3. Large groups by appointment.

Môreson Bread & Wine Restaurant, lunch as above. Large groups book ahead, cater for special functions on request. See restaurant section.

Owner: Richard Friedman

Winemaker: Pierre Wahl (since 1998). **GM:** Anton Beukes

Production: 10 000 cases. **Vineyards**: 20 ha.

P.O. Box 114, Franschhoek 7690

Tel: 021-8763112/8763055 **Fax:** 021-8762348.

This is the spot to visit to get a distinctly different view of Franschhoek. The vistas from Richard and Evonne Friedman's delightful estate seem a bit fresher, more engaging, nearer the way it must have been when the Huguenots first took up residence in their "French Corner". Beyond ambience, visitors will find delicious—and, yes, different—cuisine served at the Bread & Wine restaurant, which opens out during summer to let diners admire the views. And, of course, there are the admirable wines of new winemaker Pierre Wahl, ex-Neil Joubert Wines, marketed under **Môreson** and, from 1998, **Pinehurst** labels.

*** **Môreson Premium Chardonnay** Light oaking characterises refreshing, highly palatable **97**, with zesty lemon, vanilla, buttery nose, broadening to butterscotch/toasty palate. Fairly weighty, perky lemon-acid tingle to neutralise heaviness. Oak-fermented, 60% new, 300 l vats, no malo.

*** **Môreson Weisser Riesling Noble Late Harvest 96** is developing rather splendidly in bottle. Original apricot snatches mutating into arresting marmalade, botrytis complexity, underpinned by zesty acidity. Very attractive dessert. 50% aged in wood 8 mnths. 10,5% alc., 17 gms/l sugar. First vintage. Available only at farm.

MÔ RESON SOLEIL DU MATIN range:
Cabernet Sauvignon 96 not the ripe-'n-ready pushover **95 (VG)** was. Current tauter, more tannic, needs 2-3 years to chill out. Lovely cassis, toasted hazelnut superstructure, founded on fresh-earthy platform. **Shiraz 97** once-off, one to watch. Smoky plums, concentrated mulberry flavours, supple but abundant tannin. Drinkable now but better in 3 yrs+. 13% alc., partial whole-bunch fermented. **Pinotage 97** (first vintage) has reached maturity; upfront banana, cinnamon bun, ripe, sweetish plummy flavours now showing well. Pleasurable tannic grip. 3 mnths American oak. **Merlot 97**, like pvs., one for the long haul. Has the right stuff: mulberry, chocolate, black cherries on palate, greenish (not unpleasant) overtones, long concentrated finish; all should coalesce into well-rounded merlot in 2-3 yrs. **Sauvignon Blanc 98** in unusual deciduous-fruit mood instead of usual gooseberry/vegetal; very pleasant, light, easy-does-it style; gently dry, unwooded. Good food companion, picnics too. **Sauvignon-Chardonnay** NEW **98** 50/50 combo (chard. on lees 3 mths), very pleasant quaffing, fullish, nicely round, tangy apricot/citrus tones. **Chardonnay** (Unwooded) **98** with fresh lemon nose, leading to rich bready palate, nice crisp finish. Comes across lighter-bodied than ± 13% alc. would suggest. Definitely a table companion. (Bread & Wine's Mediterranean fare?) **Chenin Blanc 98** returns to more familiar guava/pawpaw wavelength after detour into grassy/green spectrum in **97**. Ripe fruit (tropical, touch of peach), mouthfilling, crisp, dry. 13% alc. **95** *Decanter* (UK) ****. Off-dry. **Natural Sweet** NEW **98** most appealing, fresh-fruited botrytis dessert. Soft honey-melon is first impression, followed by subtle deciduous fruit, loads of tropics—ripe mango—sweet clean finish. Low 9% alc. enhances easy drinkability. **Soleil du Matin Cap Classique NV** Bottle-fermented, dry sparkler. Fresh, delicate aromas/flavours. 90% chardonnay, touch of chenin. Yr on lees.
PINEHURST range: Sold via SA/overseas wholesalers. All NEW
Shiraz 97 pick of this range. Dark smoky plums, sweet-oak finish, grippy tannin. Don't rush to open. 13% alc. **Cabernet Sauvignon 96** raspberries/mulberries, earthy hints, soft berry palate, quite tannic, needs ± yr. 13% alc. **Pinotage 97** subdued character, some banana/boiled sweets, drink young. **Chardonnay 98** delicate, yeasty/butter tones, citric on palate, best young. **Sauvignon Blanc 97** grassy, light-bodied/flavoured, challengingly crisp. 11,5% alc.

MORGENHOF

Stellenbosch See Stellenbosch map

Open Mon-Fri 9-4.30; Sat & Sun 10-3 (Nov-Apr).
Lunch 12-2 Mon-Sat, Sun Nov-Apr, picnics in summer, light lunches all year round.
Owners: Anne Cointreau-Huchon, Alain Huchon
Cellarmaster: Jean Daneel. **Winemaker:** Rianie Geldenhuys
Production: 25 000 cases. **Vineyards:** 80 ha.
P.O. Box 365, Stellenbosch 7599
Tel: 021-8895510 **Fax:** 021-8895266

Energetic Alain and Anne (Cointreau) Huchon—their French liquor connections/holdings include premier-league champagne, cognac and liqueurs—have transformed this historic (300+ years) Stellenbosch property into a chic Afro-French showcase. When they purchased the Stellenbosch property in 1993, the Huchons unleashed a whirlwind of construction (and reconstruction): the graceful Cape-Dutch buildings were restored; a Médoc-sized underground barrel maturation cellar—topped by formal French garden—built from scratch; to match, a new brick-vaulted barrel-ageing room for white wines plus Cap Classique production hall; offices were extended; the tasting room made over; forests cleared for new satellite image-mapped hillside v'yds of merlot, sauvignon, touriga naçional; stylish restaurant/catering facilities inaugurated for anything from weddings to business schmooze-sessions. Five years on hurricane-strength development is beginning to slow to mere gale force. Jean Daneel, Morgenhof's bemedalled cellarmaster (1992 Diners Club Winemaker of the Year, 1997 WINE Chenin Challenge laureate), smiles: "For the first time in years we're not building anything!" But, true to form, activity continues: new chardonnay, cabernet sauvignon, cabernet franc plots are in the pipeline; and to keep in touch with the international scene, talented winemaker Rianie Geldenhuys worked the crush in St Émilion. Meanwhile application to register as estate was made and plans finalised to consolidate the range around the new flagship **Première Sélection**.

**** **Merlot** A class act since dramatic début **93** (WINE****, SAA Selection, gold at 1997 Vinexpo). Latest **96** (**VVG** and nudging *****) inky purple/blue, aromatic nose with deep curranty, cherry and ripe plum notes. All carry through to palate. Mellow tannins hold dark chocolate, coffee; all adds up to bold complexity. 13% alc. **95** grand character, lots of violets, mulberries, blackcurrant, on nose. Mouthfilling, ripe tannin, vanilla background. 13,3% alc. **94 VVG** 40% new oak, 10% cabernet, liberal mellow tannins; dark chocolate, coffee aromatic intensity echoed on palate by thick, ripe flavours. Super-drinkable but still promises to grow. Early release not the policy at Morgenhof—Daneel and Huchons prefer wines to "shape up" on the property before being marketed.

**** **Première Sélection** NEW Five-star material. **95** mélange of 60% cab. s., 30% merlot, 10% cab. f. Dark ruby, intense aromas of cassis, dark cherries and vanilla, deep weighty feel on palate but not without some youthful bounce. Soft-textured, excellent balance. Some peppery spice leads into long exotic finish. Good now but will greatly reward some patient aging. Quite substantial 13,7% alc. **96** to follow, blended to taste and arrived at identical composition, however is bigger, meatier.

**** **Cabernet Sauvignon** "The best cab. goes into the blend," says Daneel. It must have been stupendous because **96** vibrates the backbone. Bursting with essency berry fruit aromas. Lashings of the same on palate. Multi-flavoured, hints of mint. Lots of promise. No **95**; all went into the blend. **94 VG** inky-dark red, minty nose. Gorgeous development. Big, soft, complex flavours: cherries, blackberries, fine tannins. From 4 different clones. **93** opulent, deep colour; ripe brambly, cassis flavours, also grassy tones (a plus of virus-free, local clone). Firm, dry finish. Barrel-matured 20 months, 30% new.

*** **Pinotage** A serious commitment to the future with this variety. New plantings include bush-vines and will result in increased volumes in 2002. **96** full of ripe black cherry, banana, soft, round and appealing but firm tannic frame. **95** from high-altitude vines. Distinctly Burgundian, ripe strawberries and plummy fruit, nice palate-weight, smooth but firm. Needs year or 3 to soften. None of the tropical flavours of **94**, which leanish but packed with bananas, spice, vanilla.

**** **Chardonnay** One Cape chardonnay well worth keeping. **97 VG** realising its original promise. A cracker. Everything the **96** had but more so. Fresh bouquet with discreet melon, fig and marvellously subtle oak. Lively repeat on the palate with touch of citrus; malo influence gives harmonious elegance. **96** elegant, classic, gently firm. 20% new oak not obvious, malo in barrel. Decidedly "Meursault". Just under 13% alc., rounding 3 gms/l sugar. **95** had 25% new oak (none in **94**), showed generous nutty warmth; buttery attributes cut by clean citrusy edge. **CIWG Auction Chardonnay** One-off **94**, toastier, fatter than standard, 50% new oak.

**** **Sauvignon Blanc** ◀ First grapes from new plantings of Loire clone boost quality, stylishness of **97**. Beautiful freshness and distinct grassy/gooseberry nose and flavours. 12,4% alc. **96** continues to develop in the bottle. Lots of gooseberry, myrtle, good grip. Still with full, fresh finish. **98** for later release promises hallmark cellar class.

**** **Blanc Fumé 97** a delicious "one off". Like the wooded Chenin, an experiment, mostly destined for Makro. Such a good wine it seems a shame it will not be repeated but Morgenhof feel they need to be focused on their core wines. Again 2nd and 3rd-fill casks from Meursault, 4 months on light lees. Full nose, soft, big palate, flavour-packed.

**** **Chenin** ◀ **98** even more appealing than pvs. Absolutely gorgeous. Almost sticks to the palate with mouthfilling creaminess. Stylish bouquet with complex barrel ferment and malo character underlying rich citrus, apple, cashew-nut notes, plus sweet vanilla. Classy **97** less oak, more delightful fruit. Limes, lemon, creamy, lovely. **96 VG** maiden won local WINE magazine Chenin Blanc Challenge. All taken by (see under) Makro. Fermented and malo in 2nd-fill Meursault barrels.

*** **Rhine Riesling 97** soft, well developed, super. Gingery/peppery tones and pear-like fruit. Just off-dry at 6,5 gms/l sugar and alc. of 12,9%. Ideal with eisbein, sauerkraut. Smooth, rich, and deep, soft, enticing character.

**** **Noble Late Harvest 98** from chenin. Hand-selected in vineyard, barrel-fermented, 6 months on lees. Complex bouquet: rich kumquat and mandarin fruit aromas, hint of guava. Well-structured, flavour-packed palate repeats all the fruit with added spice and vanilla touches but no evident oak. 15,1% alc.; 160 RS, 9,6 TA.

**** **Morgenhof Brut 94** same composition as maiden 65/35 chardonnay/pinotage **93** blend, but fresher, fruitier and more mouthfilling, with creamy, prolonged mousse. Elegantly dry Cap Classique. Barrel-fermented. **95** to be released before the **94** which needs longer to develop. **95** almost 3 years on lees before degorging. **94** will be 5 or more. Pvs. aged 20 months on lees. From **97** will be classic pinot noir/chardonnay. (No lack of family know-how here: Anne Huchon's sister Beatrice runs Gosset, in Champagne.)

Dry Red ◀ **97** wonderfully low priced. Certified Simonsberg and vintage-dated. Blend of young cab. s. 64%, merlot 20%, balance cabernet f., pinot noir. Contains some bought-in grapes. Almost a year in oak. Easy now but with development potential, 12,8% alc. **95 VG**. Pvs. cross-vintage blend, mainly cab. s. Eventually will carry the new label L'Atrium. **Blanc de M** ◀ ☺ **98** even more quaffable than pvs. Blend will vary with the vintage but will usually have sauvignon blanc as base with chenin, Rhine riesling. **Port 93** Jean Daneel's first attempt at a port; pinotage, tinta barocca. Lovely. 3,5 years in 300 litre barrels, to be labelled Late Bottled Vintage. Full-flavoured, can age profitably but very drinkable now. 75 gms/l sugar, 17,6% alc. **95** all tinta. No **96** due to downy mildew crop damage. **92 VG** tinta/pinotage/merlot blend, small/large oak-matured for over 2 years. About 100 gms/l sugar, roasted coffee bouquet, plummy palate. **91** developed sweet raisiny flavour. **90** tinta/merlot, powerful chocolate-plum character. Tannins to match. **88** rich nutty-raisin flavours, from pinotage, tinta barocca. Touriga naçional planted for future. Intention to move to Vintage style with higher alc.

MORGENSTER ESTATE

Helderberg-Stellenbosch See Helderberg map

Tastings/sales by appointment.
Owner: Giulio Bertrand
Winemaker: Wynand Hamman (Lanzerac)
Production: 1 000 cases. **Vineyards**: 33 ha.
P.O. Box 1616, Somerset West 7129
Tel: 021-8521738 **Fax:** 021-852-1141
E-mail: morgen@ilink.nis.za

Italian tycoon-turned-farmer Giulio Bertrand is delighted about the latest fruit of his "retirement" to the Cape: the first, 1998 vintage from Morgenster, his lavishly refurbished 18th century estate, next to Vergelegen. A year before, Bertrand celebrated another cherished goal: pressing of extra virgin oil from Morgenster's own fledgling olive groves —a project triggered, he says, by striking similarities between the landscape of his new country seat and that of his original home in Montemarcello. Virgin north-facing slopes fanned by summer breezes, were planted with merlot, cabernet sauvignon and cabernet franc: a St. Émilion-style blend the aim. Grapes for this flagship were vinified by Lanzerac's winemaker, Wynand Hamman. **Sauvignon Blanc**, from established vines, was also made by Hamman in the Lanzerac cellar, goes under the alternative label, **Lourens River Valley** (after the river running through the property) "not because quality is inferior but because we want to reserve the Morgenster name for the standard-bearer".

Morgenster NEW **98** untasted, blend of merlot, cab. s., cab. f., all new clones. Made in consultation with Pierre Lurton of Ch. Cheval Blanc, for release probably 1999. **Sauvignon Blanc** (Lourens River Valley label) NEW. Easy, non-assertive **98**. Grassy, nettly touches. Low yield vines. Unwooded. 13,5% alc.

MOUNTAIN SHADOWS See Vinfruco

MOUNT CLAIRE See Cordoba

MOUNT DISA See Coppoolse Finlayson

MOUNT ROZIER WINES

Sir Lowry's Pass, Helderberg See Helderberg map

Not open to the public.
Owners: Michael Rubin, Peter Loebenberg, Dave Lyddell
Consulting Winemaker: Ernst Gouws (Hoopenburg)
Consulting Viticulturist: Ernst Gouws
Production: 5 000 cases. **Vineyards:** 34 ha.
Address: Myrtle Grove Estate, Sir Lowry's Pass
Tel: 021-8581130 **Fax:** 021-8581131
E-mail: dlyddell@iafrica.com

"We have the soils, proximity to the sea—the *terroir*. We will make world-class wines." Dave Lyddell, brother-in-law Peter Loebenberg and partner Michael Rubin are infectiously enthusiastic about their budding maritime-climate winery near Somerset West, flying solo after taking off in 1997/8 under the wing of national discount chain Makro (a small range was custom-made for the group's operations). Boosted by initial success—**Merlot 97** was served on the Blue Train—the vintners are powering ahead with their own red wine cellar from the 1999 crush, and 18 ha. of premium reds to come on-stream over the next 5 years. "We'll remain a 5 000-case boutique outfit until 2004, then consider our position."

*** **Pinotage** NEW Lightly wooded **98** in relaxed, accessible style with plenty of ripe plummy fruit, agreeable earthy/leafy depths, seamless oaking, gentle tannic clasp. Medium body enhances overall early-drinking effect. Bottled July 98.

*** **Sauvignon Blanc 98** a sensual, made-for-drinking sauvignon, not cerebral twirling, mulling. Straightforward herby/gooseberry fruit, non-aggressive acid nibble, clean, uncluttered. Very nice. Unwooded.

Merlot 98 loads of ripe strawberries, plums burnished by brush of oak, easy tannins, fresh conclusion. Light-toned, most drinkable but only two-dimensional now, might gain third dimension (and ***) with time. 13,5% alc. **Chardonnay 98** a bit of a wolf in sheep's clothing: starts off gently enough, lemon-lime, pineapple sensations, soft vanilla, fairly light-toned; but 13,5% alc. overpowers delicate citrus fruit in the finish. So just missed *** when tasted in infancy, could smooth out agreeably given a little time. Lightly wooded, dry. 13,5% alc.

MOUTON-EXCELSIOR — Export Only

Tastings/sales by appointment.
Proprietors: Benjamin and Gerda Mouton/Universal Commodities and Communications.
Consultant Winemaker: Jan Coetzee (Vriesenhof) (since 1984)
P.O. Box 290, Franschhoek 7690
Tel: 021-4262684/5 **Fax:** 021-4262728

"Shortage of fine wine has placed renewed emphasis on the *negociant*. Our purpose is to ensure that demand from abroad—and from local wine lovers who have been loyal to their country's wines—can be met." That, in a nutshell, is the role of Universal Commodities and Communications, a specialist wine brokerage/export operation run by Ben and Gerda Mouton, representing the wines of Mouton-Excelsior, independent boutique wineries, co-ops across the winelands. UCC exports to the EU, Canada, China under three trademarks—**Mouton-Excelsior** (premium range), **Le Moutonné** (mainly whites), **Mouton-Excelsior Huguenot Reserve** (easy-drinkers/blends). The Moutons travelled to Scandinavia in 1998 to look at adding Nordic countries to their smorgasbord of markets.

**** **Le Moutonné Merlot** Flagship of this fleet, since **92 VG** all vintages a sell-out. Keeps well, too: **91** rated top of 60 merlots in 1997 WINE tasting, earned ****. Description applies, in general—and to current (**97**) in particular: "attractive eucalyptus and mint nose. Mint chocolate and cherry flavours. Powerful . . . firm tannins, dry, fresh and long aftertaste . . . should keep another 2 years." Usually with dash cab. franc; in barrel around 28 months.

*** **Mouton-Excelsior Pinotage 97** Bright ruby-purple colour, lots of ripe plum, toasted nuts, sprinklings of spice. Rugged tannins, high acid (7,7 gms/l) make this one to pour with robust food or cellar beyond 2000. Bush vines, Darling area.

MOUTON-EXCELSIOR range:
Cabernet Sauvignon NEW **97** lightweight, muted strawberry aromatics, fresh-milled pepper flashes, chocolate-plum flavour, distinct (fruit) tannin in tail. Unwooded. Breede River Valley grapes. 13% alc. **Chardonnay 97** Unwooded, quite substantial (± 13,5% alc.), dry. **Sauvignon Blanc 97** grass/nettle prickles, clean, dry.
LE MOUTONNÉ range:
Sauvignon Blanc NEW **98**. clean, gooseberries, zesty finish.
MOUTON-EXCELSIOR HUGUENOT RESERVE range:
Cabernet Sauvignon 94 small French oak, 24 mths, 5 rackings; fruit fading, gentle mocha essences taking over. Brush of sweetness from 3,5 gms/l sugar. **95** perceptibly fruitier, riper, some cassis, but fairly one-dimensional, early drinking. **Shiraz 97** given the full oak treatment (yr all-new French/American barrique). Charming "old style" smoke/leather aromas, sweet-sour palate tone, light in flavour department. Braai partner. 13% alc. **Pinotage 96** a light, gentle reminder of the way they used to make pinotage: ripe plum veneer, acetone undercoat, accommodating tannin. Nice. Just missed ★★★. Bush vines, St'bosch. 13,5% alc. **Chenin Blanc 97** no frills dry white. Helderberg grapes.

MULDERBOSCH VINEYARDS

Stellenbosch See Stellenbosch map

Tastings & sales by appointment only.
Owner: Hydro Holdings
Winemaker: Mike Dobrovic, (since 1991). **Assistant:** Desmond Hendricks
Production: 275 tons, 18 000 cases. **Vineyards:** 20 ha.
P.O. Box 548, Stellenbosch 7599
Tel: 021-8822488 **Fax:** 021-8822351

When big business takes over a small farm like this, one is inclined to fear the worst. Will its wines become safely commercial? Will—and here was the crucial question—winemaker Mike Dobrovic suddenly be transformed into a Suit? But on second thoughts—and after a second vintage under the clearly minimum-interference, maximum-support policy of Hydro Holdings boss Fred Wypkema, a real wine enthusiast—why the worries? Dobrovic, we should have known better, is congenitally a non-corporate animal, and he continues on his quirky, offbeat, absolutely individual course. The wines are better than ever. And they fly out of the cellar just as fast: sold out within 2 to 3 weeks of each release. (Due to this intense demand, they are now, mostly, pre-allocated. Casual buyers would be advised to be permanently on their marks, or to put in advance orders.) How does he keep doing it? Dobrovic has, as usual, a rich variety of theories. "Wine remains a massively complex substance," he says, "One needs an inordinate amount of luck and intuition. However, neither of those come without hard work." Like Gary Player, he believes "the harder I work the luckier I get".

He is also adamant that workers are critical to quality. Take his approach to harvesting: "By paying well per crate of grapes harvested—on top of a good salary—I encourage the pickers to work more methodically, and bring me just the grapes I've asked for—rather than picking anything and everything at a furious rate just to earn enough to live." When Dobrovic started at Mulderbosch, with previous owner Dr. Larry Jacobs, "we had very strong feelings that if we wanted to be happy with our product, the happiness would have to extend to everyone on the farm. I believe absolutely that we would never have achieved our quality without total commitment from all of us." Excellent 3-bedroomed housing, salary and promotion policies continue to anchor the Mulderbosch operation. Unlike on most farms—though here the smallness of the labour-force is clearly a factor—"each worker has his own vehicle; no waiting for the boss to drive them to town for shopping, and salary increases have been kept above inflation for 8 years." Dobrovic says this has resulted in unavoidable wine price increases—"but while quality continues we feel duty-bound to skim off the cream for our workers."

★★★★ **Sauvignon Blanc** 'The most unforgiving variety; if it's not picked at precise ripeness, you can forget it.' Mike Dobrovic's fine-tuned eye/palate ensures an exactness which delivers one of Cape's best wines, greatest sauvignons. Big (13% alc. is his minimum) but racy, agile, cool, extract-laden flavours unfold only gradually, before striking pinpoint balance between vigour, intensity, smoothness. **98** (nudging ★★★★★) as good as it gets. Incredibly rich, tangy greengage, fig concentration; unusually forward but has all back-up to hold for 2/3 years. At 13,5% alc. 7,8 gms/l acid, not to be taken lightly. Should outlast most other **98** sauvignons, pick up usual bags of awards. **97 WINE★★★★**; **96 WINE★★★★**, **SAA**; **95** only SA gold medal winner at USA Intervin, also only SA selection in German "Top 100 Wines of the World" list in 1996. (Since **92** vintage has made this list every year.) **94 SAA**; **93 SAA** White Wine trophy; **92 VG**.

★★★★ **Chardonnay** While experiments are ongoing (current focus on natural yeasts), style well-set: generosity (not exaggeration) suggests New World; elegant purity, drinkability reflects Old World. **97** similar to **96**, elegantly packed fresh lemon peel, roasted hazelnuts; understated complexity driven by fine fleshy texture, crisp, fruity-dry finish, but greater reserves for longer development. **97 CIWG** "Can we integrate 100% wood into our wines?" The result of Dobrovic's curiosity appears an emphatic "yes". Full-bodied, complex, with uncompromising dryness, some still youthful tannin. Sweet viscosity, subtle hazelnut richness nevertheless build to fabulous fan tail finish. Very grown-up, with trademark Mulderbosch refinement. Will reward 4-5 years' bottle maturation. Tank-fermented portion with 40%/50% barrel-fermented wine; always seamless integration, oak providing structure rather than flavour.

★★★★ **Steen-op-Hout** Oak-brushed chenin from old, low-crop vines. Awaft with acacia, honey fragrance, intense flavours, giving sweetish impression on palate, though ends bone-dry. Unblended sample of **98** promises similar to pvs., bigger build. **96 SAA** holding well; **98** should go further. **97 WINE★★★★**.

★★★ **Faithful Hound** Cape traditional in style, ultra-modern in drinkability. **96** merlot, cab. s./f., malbec, in gentle "user-friendly" mode of vintage; not deeply complex, but pervasive soft black fruit flavours, rounded by Taransaud Nevers barrels. **95** (★★★★) more serious, concentrated, with some claret-like dusty warmth. **94** for early drinking or ageing.

★★★ **Barrel-fermented Sauvignon Blanc** (previously **Blanc Fumé**) One of dwindling number in this style; always realises quality potential. Full-bodied, ripe-figgy, good food partner, matures well. Enriched by 60% barrel-fermented portion. Fruit initially quietened by malo, extended lees contact, though **97** showing more forward fig than usual. **95 WINE★★★★, SAA; 94 SAA.**

MURATIE WINE ESTATE

Stellenbosch See Stellenbosch map

Open Mon-Thurs 9-5; Fri 9-4; Sat 9-3. Sales & tastings. Fee R1,50 p/p

for tasting. Cellar tours by appointment.
Owners: Melck Family Trust
Manager: Simon Thompson
Winemaker: Bruno Lorenzon
Production: 200 tons. **Vineyards:** 32 ha.
P.O. Box 133, Koelenhof 7605
Tel: 021-8822330 **Fax:** 021-8822790

This farm in the excellent Muldersvlei bowl area of Stellenbosch, shadowed by the Simonsberg, is throwing its big party **before** the millennium—in 1999 Muratie celebrates 300 years of a most colourful history. Its first owner, Lourens Campher, challenged more traditional neighbours by marrying a freed slave. Much later on an early 20th century owner, Georg Canitz, was renowned for his avant-garde paintings and bohemian parties. The late Ronnie Melck, who began the modern winemaking renaissance here, and whose family are hoisting the flag even higher, was a legend in his lifetime, a man of great conviviality and character. This is no grey little place; its wines are appropriately personality-packed, and now made by Burgundian Bruno Lorenzon, whose Afrikaans cellar-speak is delightfully French-accented. He keeps in shape for the annual Argus Cycle Tour round the Cape Peninsula each vintage by personally handling the *pigeage* process in Muratie's traditional open-fermentation tanks. "Good exercise for the *vastus mediatus* and *lateralis*, and the *hip flexars*," he comments. The UK, Germany, Holland and Sweden are leading export customers.

**** **Ansela** Relatively young label, but already has fine pedigree. **96** deeply coloured, richly concentrated cassis, coffee bean, green pepper all carry to silky, sweetish palate. Counterpointed by dryish tannin and well-managed oak. Long, fine-grained finish with refreshing aftertaste. **95** luscious blend of SA champ cab. s./gold medal merlot. Most attractive aromas of cedar/spice. Ripe black and mulberry fruit emerging on palate. Long, clean finish. Very elegant. Not as rich or deeply-hued as **94** blend of 65% cab. s., 35% merlot, drinking beautifully now. Rich cassis/chocolaty tones, mouthfilling, sumptuous, berry-laden fruit, well-disciplined by oak. Eases into lingering dry finish. Well-rounded, full-bodied. Barrel-matured 9 months, none new. **VG 96**, **93** maiden vintage, powerful, juicy blend of 50% cabernet sauvignon, 30% merlot, 20% shiraz. Named after Ansela van de Caab, a slave freed in 1695, who married the first owner of this farm, helping establish its v'yds.

**** **Pinot Noir** Winemaker Bruno Lorenzon's home territory. **97** luscious, ripe bouquet of plummy fruit, almost essency, hints of spice, strawberries and violets. Complex palate needs 3/5 years to develop. Now showing wide range of flavours, from ripe plums through to slightly herbaceous. **96** lovely Burgundian whiffs of wild strawberries and compost follow through onto palate. Full-bodied (13,3% alc.), with sweetish strawberry flavours, dry tannins. Still too young for current consumption; keep for at least another 3/4 years. **94** dramatically deep ruby hue. Silky texture, expressive cherry fruit, very dry, tannic finish.

*** **Melck's Reserve** Made in memory of Cape red wine legend Ronnie Melck; **97** blend cinsaut/shiraz. Cherry/raspberry fruitiness on nose with addition of mulberries to palate. Fairly chunky but deep, succulent, fruity core makes for easy drinking.

*** **Cabernet Sauvignon 96** ripe blackcurrants and liquorice, backed by subtle oak; aromas follow through on the palate in compact French style. Fruit not overdone, tannins in check. Very drinkable now. **94** forthcoming, deep creamy chocolate, cassis bouquet extends to palate, fine tannin balance. Matured 10 months small, used oak. **93** penetrating spicy herby bouquet, palate packed with piquant mint, cassis. 8 months small oak.

★★★ **Merlot 96** restrained cassis/chocolate aromas; sweet-tempered ripe fruit, clean and succulent on palate. Tannins in finish softening. WINE★★★★.

★★★ **Amber** NV fortified muscat d'Alexandrie dessert. Delicate and not too sweet; clean, herby finish. 6 months in oak has tamed wilder edges of muscat. Label has painting by Georg Canitz (a previous owner) of soft, voluptuous model. Amber's sweet fruitiness lingers long after the last goodnight.

Shiraz 95 light coloured, brambly fruit nose, ripe youthful flavours, rounded tannins. **93** peppery/mulberry bouquet, rich texture held by fine dry tannin; some varietal savouriness. **Port** From Portuguese varieties tinta roriz/francisca/barocca, souzão, dash shiraz, aged in 110 gal. port pipes. **95** penetrating dry currants/earthly tones, taut, finely structured. At 97,5 gms/l sugar, driest to date. **94** earthy/coffee richness, robust fruity flavours, dryish finish. **92** concentrated cassis/walnut flavours, 8 months in wood.

NAKED TRUTH — Kempens of the Cape for Picardi

Red Uncomplicated, sweetish quaffing. Mainly pinotage. **White** ◀ Vin ordinaire that hits the spot. Mainly chenin blanc, crisp, dry. **Soetes** As name suggests, no-frills quaffing: older, rich, sweet wine (150 gms/l sugar). **Sparkling Brut** Gently dry carbonated white fizzer, ± 14 gms/l sugar. **Sparkling Doux** Muscatty sweet sparkler, fruity, clean. All NV.

NAMAQUA WINES — See Vredendal Winery

NAPIER WINERY

Wellington See Wellington map

Tastings/sales by appointment.
Owners: GRT Farming & Financial
Winemaker: Chris Kühn (since 1994)
Production: ± 160 tons. **Vineyards:** 21 ha.
P.O. Box 638, Wellington 7654
Tel: 021-8641231 **Fax:** 021-8642728 **E-mail**: dock@iafrica.com

Brandy is the latest development on Dr. Chris Kühn's white-grape-dominated farm at Wellington. A still is being erected for eaux de vie, set to flow from 1999. The farm's wine production is mostly exported, to America, the EU. **Lion Creek** is the second label.

THE NATURAL CORPORATION

Waving the flag internationally since 1990, brothers Gary and André Shearer have exported Cape wine to more than a dozen countries—chiefly the US, Germany, Canada, Switzerland, the UK, Holland—with enviable success. Seizing—rather shrewdly—on the Afro/ethnic/enviro theme, they've packaged the Natural Corporation's brands—Cape Indaba, Kronendal—as "the true spirit of SA wines" and dressed them in bold, bright, Madison Avenue robes. And the Madiba-generation has bought in, big-time—the Shearers have three State President's Export Award plaques, Chamber of Commerce certificates on their wall to underline their success.

Enquiries: The Natural Corporation, P.O. Box 5421 Cape Town 8000. **Tel:** 021-4195233. **E-mail:** info@natural.co.za **Website:** www.natural.co.za

KRONENDAL range:

Cabernet Sauvignon 97 epitomises relaxed, unceremonious quaffing: coffee-and-nuts character, some interesting tobacco nuances, soft. Swartland grapes. **Merlot 97** carefree, easygoing style, chocolate overtones, fascinating mushroom hints, partner for casual meals, barbecues. Low acid. **Pinotage 97** untasted. Paarl grapes. **Chardonnay 98** from Robertson, some lime wafts, congenial. **Sauvignon Blanc 98** from Swartland in unassertive style. **Steen 98** fresh, light dry white drinking, from Robertson.

CAPE INDABA range:

Merlot 97 agreeable, wafts of violets, tobacco, firmish tannins, light everyday drinking. Paarl grapes. **Pinotage 98** some fresh ripe fruit, easy, light. From Swartland. **Chardonnay 98** citrus-fruit driven, gentle touches of vanilla, lightly oaked. **Sauvignon Blanc 98** from Robertson, very pleasant, evincing classic Cape sauvignon features (ripe gooseberry, grass), fresh, off-dry. Drink soon. **Chenin Blanc 98** for quick-drinking, no-frills sweetish white.

NEDERBURG

Paarl See Paarl map

Open for tastings & sales Mon-Fri 8.30-5. Sat 9-1. Public holidays (except religious holidays) 9-5. Cellar tours Mon-Fri by appointment only, in English, Afrikaans, German, French R7,50 per person.

Light lunches, Nov to Feb, by appointment only. Conference facilities in conjunction with Cape Sun Intercontinental Hotel.

Winemaker: Newald Marais (since 1989). **Assistants:** Wilhelm Arnold (white wines); Ernie Leicht (red wines); Hennie Huskisson (auction wines). **MD:** Niel van Deventer. **Technical Director:** Ernst le Roux **Production Manager**: Louis van Wyk. **Farms/Viticulturists**: Hannes van Rensburg; Dirk Bosman, Dirkie Laubser (grape buyer). **Marketing:** Kim Green. **Public Relations:** Clive Torr

Production: 12 000 tons. **Vineyards:** 700 ha. 800 000 cases.

Private Bag X3006, Paarl 7620

Tel: 021-8623104 **Fax:** 021-8624887

E-mail: srust@sfw.co.za or jgradwell@sfw.co.za

Internet: www.sfw.co.za

Nederburg's first winemaker, Johann Graue, who put this respected, reliable, and sometimes unjustly underrated label on the map in the early 1940s might not recognise the place—or the wines—now, but his philosophy still guides cellar chief Newald Marais: "Good wine starts in the vineyard". Nederburg's own, and its many suppliers' farms are all focused on strengthening and broadening this foundation: massive plantings are underway, particularly of red wine varieties; the net is being thrown wider to pin down fresh sources of fruit from cooler areas such as Elgin, Darling and Durbanville. Marais believes that it's only the youth of these new vines which is holding Nederburg back from making even better wine. Meantime he is experimenting assiduously with less mainstream grapes such as petit verdot, malbec and sémillon; the aim is to beef up and further modernise the specialist Auction range. (Nederburg's annual auction, now in its 25th year, remains SA's wine equivalent of the Paris fashion collections.)

Ongoing cellar innovations include new crushers for the 98 harvest (soft, rubber-tipped, for gentler handling), and a small-scale cellar-within-the-cellar to pamper small parcels of special grapes will be in operation before the millennium. It's as a general practitioner, with a prescription for practically every palate, that Nederburg is most widely familiar (its **Rosé**, for example, soft and fruity, outsells all others). But what's often forgotten is that many such stalwarts started off their journey into general consumer consciousness as experiments here: the famous **Edelkeur** desserts, for example. And the inventiveness continues: a new **Sémillon NLH** (see below) will, we predict, become another Nederburg classic, and set new standards in this style category; Marais is also working on a barrel-fermented, dry sémillon.

Community development goes in tandem, as it should, with wine advances and booming exports. Nederburg's contribution here includes funding four day-care centres for the pre-school children of workers; four women's cultural and social centres, 10 different courses for skills development, and adult literacy classes. In less serious (or perhaps not?) vein, their rugby, netball and jukskei teams all participate in local leagues, their several choirs in festivals.

*** **Baronne** ◀ Cab. s., shiraz, merlot combination; honest country-wine style. **96** most successful red in standard range: strong ruby, aromatic smoky plummy warmth. Lots of open savoury flavours, slight gamey richness. Discreet unifying oak (50% wood-matured); fruity finish.

*** **Chardonnay** ◀ Consistently satisfying: drinkable, affordable. **97** more complex, sophisticated than usual, but as always, unintimidating. Clean nutty, leesy intensity, fruit broadened by subtle oaking. Elegantly long. **98** bigger. Half barrel-fermented/matured in mainly new, 2nd-fill, small portion 3rd-fill French oak.

*** **Chenin Blanc** Full-bodied dry white; 20% oak-fermented for extra richness. Aromatic ripe honey, mango bouquet; solidly built, slight fruit tart tang in tail. From old vines harvested fully ripe (no botrytis). **98, 97** both around 13,5% alc.

*** **Sauvignon Blanc** Generous unwooded dry white; matures graciously in Pouilly Fumé style; mellow figgy bouquet, steely but not harsh. **98** quieter in youth than exuberant **97** but promises similar reliable development. Mainly Durbanville, Elgin grapes.

*** **Rhine Riesling** Perenially appealing, versatile aperitif/spicier food partner. Delicate lemon, allspice fragrance, sprightly fruity acids drier than 10,5 gms/l sugar suggests, ends on refreshing note.

**** **Gewürztraminer** Regrettably to be discontinued. **97** cool spicy, litchi refinement; mouthfilling minerally flavours. Full-bodied but graceful. 16 gms/l sugar barely sweetens.

*** **Special Late Harvest** ◀ **98** classy chenin, gewürz., Rhine riesling blend. Elegantly aromatic, subtle botrytis influence. Big but balanced; honeyed succulence leads onto lingering, clean finish. 35 gms/l sugar well-absorbed.

**** **Paarl Noble Late Harvest** Undeservedly falls in Edelkeur's shadow. Super-classy, equally tempting botrytis-infused dessert: **97** mainly chenin, lifted by 30% weisser riesling. Intense white peach, tangy marmalade character; juicy richness offset by piquantly clean tail. Beautifully balanced, integrated.

Edelrood Cabernet s./merlot/shiraz blend (55/40/5% in **96**) in unfussy, all-purpose drinking mode. Sweet red fruit smoothness, discernible but not overdone oak. (70% wood-matured.) **Paarl Cabernet Sauvignon** Soft, unaggressive, characterised by leafy sweetness. **96** light-textured, straightforward, for early drinking. **95** (***) more striking, shows density, ripeness of virus-free vines in good vintage; firm but unintimidating tannins. Splash merlot in both; two-thirds oak-matured. **Pinotage 96** pleasantly light-textured lunchtime dry red. Half wood-matured; 10% pinot noir. **Duet** Unusual pinot noir/cab. s. blend (80/20 in **97**); easy raspberry/cherry ripeness, soft tannins. Half pinot wood-matured for firmer structure, fullness. **Rosé Sec 98** unshowy cinsaut/gewürz blend; versatile summer food partner. **Rosé** Best seller. Light, juicily gluggable, fresh wild strawberry tang in tail. **98** appealing dark rose colour. Cinsaut/gamay blend. 22 gms/l sugar. **Paarl Riesling** SA's top selling dry white. Reliable, unpretentious. **98** lightish body, pleasant meadow-grass freshness. 100% crouchen blanc (Cape riesling). **Premier Grand Crû** Lightish-bodied chenin, colombard, sauvignon blanc NV blend; quiet fruit, smoothly dry. **Prelude** Partially-oaked sauvignon blanc/chardonnay blend (74/26 in **97**); gentle nutty bouquet, smoothly dry. Versatile food partner. (Labelled **Sauvignon Blanc/Chardonnay** for export). **Lyric** Unwooded sauvignon b. Cape riesling, chardonnay blend; muted fruit, off-dry. **Elegance** ☺ ◀ Popular off-dry blend; flashy muscat aromas refined by about one third Rhine riesling in blend. Ample flavours highlighted by 11 gms/l sugar in **98**. **Stein** Dependable favourite; starting point for many winelovers, easy fruity sweetness, medium-bodied, balanced. From **98** splash gewürz adds extra style to Rhine riesling, chenin base. Outclasses many other semi-sweets. **Blanquette MCC** With delicate, lemon-cream fruitiness; refreshing, persistent bubble. From **94** chardonnay**; 95** riper lees character. **Kap Sekt** Fruitily dry **93** Rhine riesling, crouchen blanc, chardonnay blend. Clean peppery/peachy flavours; firm bubble. Charmat process, 9 months on lees. **Premiere Cuvée Brut** Reliable Charmat method bubbly; satisfying if straightforward chenin, crouchen/sauvignon blanc blend; softly dry. SA's biggest selling Brut. **Premiere Cuvée Doux** Same mix as Brut; lighter, sweeter; spicy-rich flavours. Mainly exported.

RESERVE range: currently 3 wines, mainly for export, limited quantities available locally. Unfinished samples tasted, all should rate at least ★★★ when bottled: **Cabernet Sauvignon** Modern **96**; aromatic fresh mulberry, spice nose, mouthcoating dense fruit, less open-textured than many from this vintage. Planned approx. 10% petit verdot addition should bring oak/fruit into balance. 14 months new/used Nevers casks. Cabernet from Elgin; petit verdot from Stellenbosch. **Sauvignon Blanc 98** broad-structured, ripe fig, gooseberry tones, concentrated viscosity to match 13,5% alc. Unwooded. **Chardonnay** Barrel-fermented **98**; elegant spicy, tropical complexity, fully ripe flavours balancing 14% alc. Promises classy mouthful. 6 months, new Tronçais oak. Durbanville grapes.

NEDERBURG AUCTION WINES

★★★★ **Private Bin R163 Cabernet** Oldest Auction red; mainly old clone (20% new in current **88**) giving traditional, laid-back, nutty tobacco tones. **88** (★★★) solid style, fruity softness just edging out drying tannin. Not for further keeping. Not in same league as seductive, charming **86 VVG**; long, sweet fruit intensity; beautifully balanced. Year in large new vats.

★★★ **Private Bin R161** Sweet-berried **90** cabernet (Schleip clone). Bright fruity length supported by dense, extracty texture, subtle oaking. 20% matured one year in small barrels; balance used large vats.

★★★ **Private Bin R109** Elegant 60/40 cab.s, merlot blend. **91** with mellowing cab. bouquet; lightish feel complemented by fresh, lingering blackberry fruits. Large oak-matured 13 months.

★★★ **Private Bin R103** Warmly smooth 75/25 cab. s/shiraz blend. Maturing, ruby patina reflected in spicy, ripe cassis mellowness of **90**; lingering savoury finish. Large, used oak-matured one year.

★★★ **Private Bin R115** Equal cab. s/shiraz blend. **92** fresh red berry, savoury bouquet; berries echoed on fleshy, chewy palate. Lively impression despite subtle rounding from year in large used vats.

★★★★ **Private Bin D234** Luscious oak-fermented/matured sauvignon. More Bordeaux than Loire, though firm flinty tones on **97** also nod towards Pouilly Fumé. Excellent oak/fruit balance; provides volume on nose, palate. Rich, dry with ripe figgy flavours. Very nice. Should develop further with year or two.

★★★ **Private Bin D250** Light-bodied, full-flavoured pinot blanc; subtle American oak (60% fermented/matured in equal mix new/used casks) enriches 11% alc. **96** dainty jersey cream, walnut maturity; supple rich feel on palate. Smooth, creamy tail.

★★★ **Private Bin D270 96** maturing with touches of Burgundian decadence, especially oily-rich, hazelnut bouquet. Broadly built chardonnay but not overwhelming; elegance enhanced by pickled lemon freshness in tail. Excellently judged oak: barrel-fermented/matured, 70% new.

★★★★ **Private Bin S354** Spicily sweet gewürz, Rhine riesling, SLH blend; typically exotic litchi scents, flavours contrasted by light, agile body; 70/30 proportions in **97**, less successful than usual: pleasant spice ends on slightly cloying but also touch bitter note. 10,5% alc. 39 gms/l sugar.

★★★★ **Private Bin S306** Exquisitely poised, expressive Rhine riesling. Delicate vitality pervades **96** from greeny gold tints to whispering limey finish. Gorgeous white peach, pepper spice hints—not merely sweet (43 gms/l sugar, SLH status). Delicious. **VG** for **93, 94.**

★★★★ **Private Bin S316 Weisser Riesling Noble Late Harvest** Local classic, full of charm, grace. For many, the jewel in Nederburg's dessert wine crown; better value than Edelkeur on auction. Characterised by aromatic pickled lime, tangy marmalade shot with botrytis; creamy palate threaded with racy, mouthcleansing acid. **96** unusually muted, slender pickled lime whiffs; lacks intensity, verve. **92 VG; 90 WINE★★★★.**

★★★ **Eminence** Another auction favourite; **96** forthcoming muscat de Frontignan fragrance; light, lively, minerally spice plays off against 80 gms/l sugar. **WINE★★★★** No **97. 95 94 VVG.**

★★★ **Edelkeur** Grandmother of Cape's modern dessert wines; regularly fetches amongst highest price for whites on auction. But perhaps being overtaken by younger, more vibrant, more complex Nederburg desserts, with lower sugar levels. **96** classic Edelkeur style; deep dried apricot, honeyed intensity, very full sweetness (at 11,9% alc. not heavy) cut by clean, bracing acid. Very correct, but short on excitement, intricacy. **95** less unctuous, some pointed volatility highlights vivacious sweet apricot fruits. More flightly, evanescent than most. **94** in fashionable trimmed-sugar mode: 84 gms/l cf 160 gms/l in **95,** being further matured before going on auction. **92 VVG. 91 WINE★★★★.**

★★★★ **Sémillon Noble Late Harvest** NEW **97** a new generation dessert. More French than German; big, rich (14% alc.), striking gold hue. Size balanced by seductively silky texture, sophisticated 70 gms/l sugar. Waves of flavour: fresh honey, subtle lanolin/beeswax nuances woven with equally discreet botrytis, all indicate delicious complexity to come. Unoaked. A future classic.

Private Bin 181 NEW Two vintages of merlot: **95** telling chocolatey richness, structure, length. **94** open, developed meaty character; smooth but bit meagre. **Private Bin R172** Plain **91** pinotage. New-vat matured, 13 months. **88, 87 VG. Private Bin R121** Fading **90** shiraz; vestiges of savoury smoothness in feeble framework. **87 VG. Private Bin D218** Barrel-fermented chardonnay/sauvignon blanc blend. **97** round, softly dry, neither variety dominates. Versatile at table. **Private Bin S333** Uncomplicated **97** muscadel/chenin (87/13) SLH. Lots of pear, granadilla, minty fruit; very sweet. **95, 94 VVG. Private Bin C92 MCC** One release of this chardonnay bubbly to date; **91** on **96** auction.

NEETHLINGSHOF ESTATE

Stellenbosch See Stellenbosch map

Visits/Sales: Open Mon-Fri 9-5, Sat-Sun 10-4. Cellar tours on request. **Stellenzicht** wines also for sale here. Farm tour with "braai" Nov 1-April 15. Closed Christmas Day, Easter.
Restaurant/Refreshments: Lord Neethling Restaurant, Palm Terrace 021-8838966
Owner: Hans-Joachim Schreiber
Winemaker: Schalk van der Westhuizen (since 1994)
Marketing and Sales Director: Ansias Londt
Production: 80 000 cases. **Vineyards:** 160 ha.
P.O. Box 104, Stellenbosch 7599
Tel: 021-8838988 **Fax:** 021-8838941

Home-grown, salt-of-the-earth Schalk van der Westhuizen is now charged with not only his winemaking responsibilities at Neethlingshof, but also with overseeing Stellenzicht, the development of two farms on Helshooghte, and Olives in the Vlottenburg area. These current "caretakerships" add up to a monster job which the genial giant seems to handle with ease. His earthy outward appearance is deceptive: he's as into electronic farming as anyone, and often found "tikking" at the computer keyboard with radio held to his ear as he keeps in touch with the team planting vines on Helshoogte. Directorial back-up includes proprietor Hans-Joachim Schreiber's son, Dr. Frank Schreiber, and Prof. Joel van Wyk (former head of the Oenology Department at Stellenbosch University) who both joined the board in 1997; but Van der Westhuizen remains the man directly at the coal face. Highlight of the year was the award of the IWSC's German Wine Institute Trophy for the best Botrytis Wine to the **1997 Neethlingshof NLH Weisser Riesling**. (Against some of the toughest competition the world can offer.) International financier Schreiber was the first major-league "foreigner" to invest in the Cape winelands, long before the boom began; his expanded portfolio of properties here make him a very big player indeed. And he's been ahead of the game in the integral matter of employees' benefits too—plans for workers here to be given access to own-home ownership on land Schreiber acquired nearby, are in motion.

Recent red vintages were not available for tasting at the time this guide went to press—they are maturing in the cellar pending decisions on specific release and bottling dates.

★★★ **Cabernet Franc** NEW **93** might not be a show/award-winning wine but very satisfying with curious mix of elegant sweet fruit and grassy, nutty, peppery flavours on smooth tannins. Could well be in the Loire Valley.

★★★★ **Lord Neethling Reserve** A "grown-up", drier-style **93** claret. Produced to celebrate the 10th anniversary of Hans Schreiber's purchase of the property, this is the most expensive Neethlingshof red: R80 a bottle, in 1998. (A **98** follow-up is being contemplated.) Serious, strong-tasting, developing well, gaining character, riper bouquet, with age. Fine nutty nuances in finish, even slightly heathery—perhaps from 15% shiraz. But cabernet 66%, and merlot, dominate blend, with solid, pliable ripe fruit tastes. Firm, compact, steers clear of easy-virtue "sweetness" on palate, which might explain why it took a couple of years to impress Veritas judges enough to award it **VG** in 1996. Not as silky or voluminous as some modern Cape reds, but just the ticket for those who prefer a less "in-your-face" style.

★★★★ **Cabernet Sauvignon** An altogether more elegant wine than pvs., **94** is developing beautifully in bottle. From 100% virus-free clone; lifts both colour/character. Bold, lively aromas of eucalypt, mint and leaf, subtle oak. Palate equally lively with leafy/mint, berry flavours, supple tannins. 12,3% alc. **93** solid, satisfying palateful, some mulberry notes, good fruit-tannin interplay. 90% from virus-tested vines. Less oak than pvs. vintages. **92** succulent, more forward, than **91** with pencil/cedar scents, restrained fruit. **VG 90**, **88.** The mostly "old clone" **87** excellent.

★★★★ **Merlot** One of the better offerings from **95** vintage: all berries, (straw./cherry), violets and sage-type herbs. Hint of sweet oak, rich and mouthfilling. 13,4% alc. **94**, for current drinking, combines both savoury, dried herbs, solid dry red compactness with enough ripe fruit to claim some classicism. Attractive bottle development. Close to being its best. Well oaked (8 months barrels, 1 year vats), minimally treated—filtration, fining, etc. Solid 13,5% alc. Through malo. **93 VG**.

★★★★ **Shiraz** ◀ Deep plums, smoky, Karoo scrub, silky mouth-feel, bit of milled pepper in **95**. Long full finish. **94** concentrated berry, liquorice, distinct earthiness, spicy/charry oak. Hints of smoky, peppery flavours. Good fruit-acid tension and grip in finish. Frequent classwinner, gold medal at local shows (**90**, **91**, **94**). 9 months small oak, 1 year large. Through malo.

★★★ **Pinotage** Usually solid, earthy, with firm tannins but **95**—which has developed well in bottle, shows fruitier style: bright plum colours, riper flavours, fairly sappy, good oak. **92 VG**.

★★★ **Neethlingsrood** (to be renamed **Cabernet Sauvignon-Shiraz** in future) Cabernet-shiraz mix (**93** 50/50) super drinking now. Herby Karoo scrub nose with some cherry flavours, quite easy tannin. Pvs.: e.g. **90**, cabernet, pinotage, merlot blend.

★★★ **Blanc de Noir** ◀ Always one of Cape's best pinks. **97** from cabernet s., cabernet f., pinot noir, gamay. Floral, fruity. Just dry (3,8 gms/l sugar).

★★★ **Sauvignon Blanc** ◀ Gets better by the vintage. **98** fine, bold, crisp grip, gooseberries, herbs and grassiness. **96**, **95** both **VG**, latter **SAA** Selection.

★★★★ **Chardonnay** Now an equal to sister cellar Stellenzicht's version. **98** good, classic citrus-lime qualities, 50% new oak-fermented. **95** showing attractive bottle development.

★★★★ **Sémillon Reserve** A rising star on the Cape scene. **98** powerful lemon/herbal aromas. Full intensity on palate; tangy, herbaceous fruit with beeswax overtones. Good length/balance.

★★★★ **Cape Riesling** ◀ Exceptionally poised—balanced mouth-feel—and attractive dry, green-apple and grassy, fruity fragrance; **97** particularly good. But still best drunk within the year. Unblended. (Pvs. with some Rhine riesling.)

★★★ **Gewürztraminer** ◀ Invariably beautifully rose-petal scented, lively off-dry (12 gms/l sugar) litchi aftertaste. **98** gentle, delicate and lovely, **97** stand-out vintage. **95 VG**.

★★★★ **Weisser Riesling** Poised, chic **97** blooming in bottle; glowing yellow/green; developing deeper, more intense lime, apricot aromas, riches and longer peach, apricot flavours. Combines delicacy with length on palate, clean, fresh finish. **96** also developing beautifully. Gentle alc. (10,7%) doesn't diminish impact—nor floral, aromatic intensity. Nor does off-dry 11 gms/l sugar reduce long, spicy vigour. (Pvs. sometimes drier.) **92** (dry) **VVG**; **96**, **95**, **93** (off-dry) all **VG**.

★★★ **Special Late Harvest 98** complex blend of furmint, weisser riesling, muscat de frontignan. Ripe, clean, fresh fruit salad aromas/flavours. Smooth, not as sweet as 39 gms/l would suggest.

***** **Noble Late Harvest, Weisser Riesling** Heady, sumptuous, botrytis dessert wine champion of Cape with consecutive wins **90** to **98** at SA shows. **98** most elegant yet from this cellar, with "low" 130 gms/l sugar. Delicious litchi, kiwi fruit on clean botrytis. Gorgeous. **96** sweeter—185 gms/l sugar—than most pvs. But **97** leapt to 240 gms/l. Not winemaker's intention; simply a fact of the vintage. Cool conditions prevented futher fermentation. Low alc. 9%. Rich, bright gold, usual intense apricots, peaches swirl about glass. Deeply impressive—**97** won IWSC Best Botrytis World Wide. German Wine Institute Trophy. **95** Top 100 Sydney International Wine Show classwinner. **93**, **91** both **WINE******. (**91** also a Sauvignon Blanc NLH, penetratingly delicious.)

Neethlingshoffer Soft, easily-downed off-dry (12,4 gms/l sugar) white blend: 50/50 Cape riesling, sauvignon blanc. **95 VG**.

NEIL ELLIS WINES

Jonkershoek, Stellenbosch See Stellenbosch map

Tastings/sales Mon-Fri 9-4.30.
Owner: Neil Ellis Family Trust, Oude Nektar, London Stone (Pty) Ltd
Winemaker: Neil Ellis (since 1986)
Production: ± 37 000 cases
P.O. Box 917, Stellenbosch 7599
Tel: 021-8870649 **Fax:** 021-8870647
E-mail: chrianto@iafrica.com

After more than a year of "constant battle", Neil Ellis Wines' new Stellenbosch home on Oude Nectar estate finally is complete—and with it Neil Ellis' and partner Hans-Peter Schroeder's ideal of consolidating their far-flung operation under one roof. Heretofore this pioneering, loudly acclaimed "virtual winery"— the first of its sort at the Cape and still one of the most consistent, successful—has led a migratory existence, with Ellis leasing cellar space (first Zevenwacht, then Louisvale, latterly Oude Nectar) and sourcing fruit from widely different areas like Elgin and Darling for the **Neil Ellis** label and other ranges. Now, 12 years on, the entire operation is ensconced at last in the splendid new Spanish-style cellar and visitor centre, boasting commanding Jonkershoek views. A cool feature, so to speak, is the underground red-wine barrel maturation cellar with its own waterfall—a diversion of the perennial mountain stream that feeds the farm dam—providing year-round natural humidity and temperature control. "Good for red-wine maturation," says Ellis, "very cost-efficient too." The old barrel cellar has been transformed into a temperature-controlled white-wine barrel maturation hall. Brand-new bottling and packaging facilities give Ellis total control of his wine into the bottle for the first time. Rising star Louis Nel, previously with Martin Meinert at Vergelegen, has come aboard to shoulder some of Ellis' winemaking duties. One of Cape wine's most thoughtful and innovative craftsmen, Ellis thinks shiraz is going to be SA's next great red variety. "I also still believe we can make great Rhine riesling in the Cape. Consumers will eventually come back to it."

NEIL ELLIS range:

**** **Cabernet Sauvignon** ◀ Purple-red **96** five-star in the making, in classic tall bottle. Great billowing nose, berry fruits to fore with hints of chocolate, subtle oak. Mouthfilling, succulent fruit (cherry, blackberry), beautifully balanced, with oak-aged suppleness. Fine, elegant. Very satisfying now but will reward ageing over 5-8 years. 12% alc. **94** WINE****.

**** **Cabernet-Merlot** ◀ **96** deep purple. Violets, ground pepper bouquet. Velvet-textured, silky smooth, sweet plummy flavours, ripe red berries, bits of choc/coffee. Some blackberry/black olive notes. Super drinking now, next few years.

★★★ **Pinotage** ◀ **97** vibrantly mulberry-coloured. Packed with juicy, ripe raspberry fruit, attractive fresh impressions from beginning to end. 12,5% alc. **98** (cellar sample) big and bold, almost inky purple. Fuller than pvs. From totally ripe fruit, made in open fermenters, regularly punched through, transferred to oak to complete fermentation. Packed with concentrated, spicy fruit. Promises much (a few more stars, perhaps?).

★★★★ **Pinot Noir 97** first vintage considered good enough to carry Neil Ellis label. From Elgin fruit. Nose a confusion of strawberries, raspberries, ripe cherry/plum. Ellis says: "Shows what a cool vintage can do." Silky concentrated fruit flavours, delicious length.

★★★★ **Chardonnay (Elgin) 97** glowing yellow-green, rich and complex bouquet with lemon, lime, touch of crisp acid under oak. Palate delivers what bouquet promised, with good concentration. Classy, elegant. (Blend of St'bosch/Whitehall.) **98** more lemon, lime scents, plus bits of butterscotch. Flavours are rich with tangy citrus, melon, some herbaceous tones. A big-big mouthful. Considerably intense, good balance, great style.

★★★★ **Sauvignon Blanc Groenekloof** ◀ **98** light yellow/green. Most attractive nose hovers between nettle, herby, citrus, gooseberry aromas; all carry through to well-weighted palate, soft, succulent, poised. Great length, super zesty finish. **95**, **96**, **97** WINE★★★★.

★★★ **Rhine Riesling 98** (tank sample) could rate 4 stars by time of bottling. Dry now but might get a gramme or two of sugar at bottling. Melon-scented with grapey fruitiness. Juicy, with grapefruity tang, good balance, zippy finish.

Note: No **98 Neil Ellis (Elgin-Whitehall) Sauvignon Blanc** was made. This invariably among finest, with track-record for racy, flinty penetration, mouthfilling length. Rain during the critical ripening period in 1998 spoiled these grapes; Ellis decided to skip a year, but assures this wine will be back. **97 WINE**★★★★.

INGLEWOOD: Value range by Neil Ellis. The red in this line-up varies with vintage: features fruit from young v'yds as well as overflow from the flagship Neil Ellis wines. Invariably very satisfying.

★★★★ **Cabernet Sauvignon-Merlot** ◀ Violets, strawberry, with some sweet chocolate in **97**. Mouthful of soft ripe berry fruits, well managed oak and ripe tannins. Drink now or in year or two.

★★★ **Sauvignon Blanc-Chenin Blanc** ◀ **98** blend with bright splash of Rhine riesling to lift the tone. Big, booming nose awash with tangy ripe lemon, fresh apple, hints of tropical guava and mango. The full fruit bowl on palate too, plus long lemon-zesty finish.

NELSON WINE ESTATE

Paarl See Paarl map

Tastings/sales Mon-Fri 8-5. Sat 9-4. Cellar tours by appointment. Guest cottage, conference, reception facilities.
Owner: Alan Nelson
Winemaker: Carl Allen (since 1995)
Production: 20 000 cases. **Vineyards:** 48 ha.
P.O. Box 2009, Windmeul 7630
Tel: 021-8638453 **Fax:** 021-8638424

Headline-grabbing news from this progressive Paarl estate in 1998 was of the first wines made by Klein Begin, a new worker-owned enterprise operating out of the current cellar on the farm. Earlier, with a nod to the labour corps's strong hand in bringing the Nelson range to award-winning status, proprietor Alan Nelson—he's a Cape Town senior advocate—had sold a portion of the v'yds to the workers. A community-owned winery, Klein Begin (Small Beginning), was duly formed and the first crush handled—with aplomb—by young Mathewis Thabo, cellar-assistant to Nelson winemaker Carl Allen. The trailblazing venture hit the ground running: its compact range (dry red/white, chardonnay) was promptly snapped up by retail chain Pick 'n Pay and appears on Western Cape, KwaZulu-Natal shelves under the **New Beginnings** label; it was also the first such range to be launched in the UK, by SA High Commissioner Cheryl Carolus. From these modest origins a dynamic operation is steadily emerging: first order of business is to replace traditional varieties with in-demand premium grapes. Thereafter the sky's the limit. Watch this space. Out of the limelight, meanwhile, development of Nelson winery continued unabated under the watchful eye of Carl Allen, Nietvoorbij's former winemaker. A new maturation hall was built, fermentation tanks installed, and a small sémillon v'yd established alongside new plantings of "Big Six" varieties.

★★★ **Cabernet Sauvignon** Delicious, serious **95** maturing handsomely in bottle, acquiring broader, nutty palate-tone. Deep plum colours, sweet-oaky bouquet, crushed-berry flavours, hints of cinnamon; savoury dry finish. Very good now, or in 1-2 yrs. 21 mths new/used oak. Both **95**, **94** gold on SA young wine shows.

★★★ **Chardonnay** ◀ **97** clean-lined, fine elegance all the way. Swirling peach scents, spicy oak, rounded palate, good fruit/oak balance, persistent dry finish. Follows **96**, champion SA young wine of its year. Barrel-fermented, then 5-6 months in new oak—which shows. Moderate alc. ± 11% enhances accessibility.

Shiraz 97 has absorbed something of the Rhône while in barrel: roasty, peppery Mediterranean scrub aromatics, brambly fruit, pleasant smoky eddies. Ripe tannins, discernibly dry. Medium-bodied. **95** lighter, gently rounded fruit, savoury finish, undemonstrative. **Merlot** Latest **96** individual, smoky, almost "sooty" notes (not unpleasant), fleshy plum flavours; ripe tannins still prominent. So best in 1-2 years. 12 mths partly new oak. **95 VG**. **Albenet 98** untasted. **97** friendly lightish-textured red, mainly cinsaut, frisson of shiraz. Unwooded **Chenin Blanc-Chardonnay** (formerly **Tinel**) **98** delicious ripe deciduous fruit, sunny. Good quaffer, mainly chenin blanc, dollop chardonnay. **Marguerite** Delicious semi-sweet white, muscat (± 60%), chenin blanc in **98**, with pretty powder-puff aromas, excellent lunchtime aperitif. Medium-bodied.

NEW BEGINNINGS

See Nelson Wine Estate

NEWTON-JOHNSON

Hermanus See Walker Bay map

Open for sales and tasting Mon-Fri 9-4.
Owners: David and Felicity Johnson
Winemakers: Johnson family with Bartho Eksteen.
Production: 5 000 cases. **Vineyards:** 4 ha.
P.O. Box 225, Hermanus 7200
Tel: 0283-23862 **Fax:** 0283-23867
E-mail: capebay@hermanus.co.za

Here's a family that's steeped in wine—David Johnson, Cape Wine Master, thriving negociant, winemaker, consultant, taster (for this guide, among others—so we declare an interest); wife Felicity (née Newton), multi-talented, able-bodied partner, confidant, catalyst; elder son Bevan, Stellenbosch-trained winemaker, working the 1998 crush at Chx. d'Angludet and Palmer in the Médoc; sibling Gordon, also Maties-tutored, stints at Cuvaison in Napa, Slaley (with Oz whiz-kid Ben Radford)—combining talents in the clan's new hilltop cellar at Walker Bay to craft a select range that's as easygoing, congenial as they. "We're all food-fanatics, so we make easy, light-toned (but never lightweight) wines that complement all sorts of cuisine," David Johnson says. Providing winemaking guidance and advice is award-winning former Wildekrans cellarmaster, Bartho Eksteen, who crafts his own-label range in the Johnson cellar. Grapes for Newton Johnson wines are bought in while ± 4 ha. of v'yds on the property come into production. Johnson also buys in wines (as distinct from grapes) from leading producers for blending and bottling on the property under the highly successful value-for-money export label, Cape Bay. A new tasting centre with panoramic views of the Hemel-en-Aarde (Heaven and Earth) Valley opens in November 1998.

**** **Cabernet Sauvignon-Merlot** ◀ 61% cab. s., 25% merlot, 14% cab. f. make up **97** blend. Blackberry and clean mintiness, together with ripe juiciness come through beautifully in this stylishly balanced, modern Cape red. Good depth and intensity, with some spicy, coffee bean oak notes. Pleasantly dry finish. Bought-in Firgrove grapes.

**** **Chardonnay 97** ◀ 40% barrel-fermented, balance in stainless steel with sprinkle of chips. No malo so as to retain fruit, deliberately not after full, buttery, showboat style, which may induce palate fatigue after a glass or two. Elegance is the objective. Mission accomplished. Lovely lemon, limey nose, rich, soft mouth-feel, nice clean lees character with overall complexity and finesse. Attractive hint of butterscotch and cinnamon. Great balance. Long, clean, fresh, citrusy finish.

**** **Sauvignon Blanc** NEW ◀ From **97** Walker Bay grapes with 6% wood-fermented sémillon. Warm reception at London Wine Trade Fair and not surprising. Packed with passion-fruit and gooseberry aromas/flavour. Appealing richness on palate; hints of elderflower tang, elegantly concentrated with excellent length.

NITIDA VINEYARDS

Durbanville See Durbanville map

Open weekdays 9-5; Sat 9-1. Tastings & sales. Cellar tours by appointment.
Owners: BV Veller, GV Veller, PB Veller
Winemaker: Riaan Oosthuizen (since 1996)
Production: ± 5 000 cases. **Vineyards:** 13 ha.
Address: Tygerberg Valley Rd, Durbanville
Tel/Fax: 021-961467

"We are a small cellar, and by staying small we feel we'll always have the flexibility and hands-on capability to produce wines of outstanding quality," is the message from the Veller family and winemaker Riaan Oosthuizen at this former cattle and sheep farm in the excellent viticultural area of Durbanville, brushed by the breezes of Table Bay. On top of its climatic advantages, Nitida (named after a protea growing wild on the property) also features 100% new-clone vineyards—equal spreads of cabernet sauvignon and sauvignon blanc in the majority, with smaller pockets of pinotage, merlot, cabernet franc and chardonnay, making up a 50-50 red-white wine profile. First to grab attention, from the début vintage in 95, was its dramatic Sauvignon Blanc; a début Chardonnay exudes chic, the new reds are full of promise.

★★★ **Shiraz** NEW **97** in lower-key but authoritative style: insistent meaty fruit. Long savoury finish. Drink from 1999.

★★★ **Cabernet Sauvignon** Modern **97** very drinkable already. Deep colour; wafting vanilla, warm blackcurrant pastilles; velvety texture, medium-bodied.

★★★ **Sauvignon Blanc** Always outspoken here "Yum-yum!" were our taster's first words on dipping into **98**. Brisk, nettly, green peppery excitement on nose; very dry, "sauvage" (wild), racy punch on palate. Tapers off a bit after all this feisty flurry, but even so, a real character, with something of a Loire accent. Good track record from **95 VVG**.

★★★ **Chardonnay** NEW Armani, not Versace, is attire worn by cellar's youngest offspring for her most promising **98** coming-out. Elegance, restraint are keynotes, gentle lemony fragrance, satiny butterscotch texture, long zesty finale. Very nice. Lightly wooded. 13% alc.

Merlot-Cabernet Franc NEW Interesting **97**: organic/fruity aromas, sinewy build (though soft tannins), herbaceous flavours. A good pizza, vegetarian red.

NIEL JOUBERT WINES

See Klein Simonsvlei

NORDALE CO-OPERATIVE WINERY

Bonnievale See Robertson map

Tastings/sales Mon-Thurs 8-12.30; 1.30-5; Fri 8-12.30; 1.30-4.30. Cellar tours by appointment.
Owners: 33 members
Winemaker: Tinus Els (since 1997)
Production: 3 000 cases. **Vineyards:** 660 ha.
P.O. Box 105, Bonnievale 6730
Tel: 02346-2050 **Fax:** 02346-2192.

"A warm Bonnievale welcome awaits all visitors"—so promises the Nordale brochure, and to judge from the compact range of budget-priced friendly, easygoing wines, that's exactly what callers will get. Responsibility for making the wines shifted to Tinus Els at the end of 1997, who took over from long-time cellarmaster Emile Schoch (he moved "upstairs" as general manager). Els (he's Els-enburg trained! and a *dux*-student to boot) brings experience gained as winemaker/viticulturist at Nelson Estate—bagging a brace of Veritas medals in 1995—and, more recently, Koelenhof.

★★★ **Chardonnay** ◀ Whoa! Here we have a quantum leap in **98** over rather listless pvs. This new, supercharged version is fresh, fruity, mouthfilling (it should be: 13,5% alc.!) with zesty lemon-lime tang in crisp, almost racy finish. Bargain at R12 ex-cellar.

★★★ **Red Muskadel Jerepigo** ◀ Delicious **96** has unusual green-fig preserve on nose, candied orange-peel plus usual raisins, chocolates on palate. Medium to light feel for this style of winter warmer. **94, 93** good too. Snip at ± R12 a bottle.

Vin Rouge ◀ Attractive, easy, strawberry/sage-toned **97**; blend of ruby cab./cab. s., lightly oaked in used barrels. 11,8% alc. Pvs. was ruby/pinotage blend. **Colombard** ◀ **98** the sort you'd choose to show what Robertson colombard is about: all fresh ripe guavas (plus other vaguely tropical notes), some muscat scents, persistent lime-toned finish. Clean, off-dry, easy-drinking. ± R8 from cellar door.

NUY WINE CELLAR

Worcester See Worcester map

Open Mon-Fri 8.30-4.30; Sat 8.30-12.30 for tasting. Sales ex-cellar (cases and 2-bottle packs only).
Owners: 21 members
Winemaker: Wilhelm Linde (since 1971)
Production: 9 500 tons. **Vineyards:** 500 ha.
P.O. Box 5225, Worcester 6851
Tel: 0231-70272 **Fax:** 0231-74994

First impressions are important—and any visitor to this immaculate co-operative cellar in the Nuy valley, tucked away off the R60 between Worcester and Robertson, cannot but be struck by the orderliness of it all. Founded 35 years ago, the winery has employed only two winemakers—Wilhelm Linde has been in residence since 1971, establishing not only the cellar, but also himself in the top echelon of producers of wines for sale in bulk to very selective customers like SFW, as well as an increasingly fine range of bottled wines, including two Diners Club award winners—for their signature **Muscadel**, and then for **Riesling** only three years later. It's not easy to extract hyperbole from the self-effacing, perfectionist Linde: "It's very difficult to talk about one's own achievements," he confides when pressed. Nevertheless, despite some frost damage which reduced the '98 crop by 10%, he feels confident that his wines continued to improve this past year, and is particularly happy with developments in his 21 members' vineyards, especially the red varieties.

*** **Cabernet Sauvignon** ◀ NEW **97** a serious bargain! Offers alluring mulberry and redcurrant aromas, a soft, modern wine, with finely-judged oak treatment. A worthy effort.

*** **Rouge de Nuy** ◀☺ **97** classic 60/40 cabernet/merlot blend, warm, sweet cassis-laden aromas follow on to brambly, just-wooded palate. Great to find such quaffing value in these days of ego-tripping over-priced reds.

*** **Colombard** ◀ **98 Dry**, shows subtle guava and pear notes, backed with usual zesty but elegant fruit and a promise of further bottle development potential, as shown by pvs. vintages.

**** **Red Muskadel** ◀ **97** brilliant ruby-topaz colour, earthy cinnamon spice bouquet, with a silkiness which spreads across the tongue in a burst of pure, sweet, fully ripe spirity-grape flavours. 225 gms/l sugar, 16,9% alc. . . . no compromises here. **96 WINE******

**** **White Muskadel** ◀ **98** consistently one of the finest in the land, this a brilliant burnished gold hue; the very essence of grapiness, with jasmine and exotic fruit aromas. Concentrated, succulent honey-sweetness fans into a spectacular peacock-tail of nectar and Karoo scrub flavours. Raft of **VVG**, **VG** medals; **85** Diner's Club Award winner. Regular at Nederburg auction. **96** WINE*****.

Sauvignon Blanc 98 has lively quince, pear wafts; austere, bone-dry flinty flavours and soft finish—improves annually. **Riesling** ◀ **98** hints of candyfloss; light, dry, lively undemanding style. **91** Diner's Club winner. **Chardonnay 98** ◀ elegant, restrained, unwooded; bone-dry with fine citrus character. **Chant de Nuit** NV Dry ◀ Sports spicy rhubarb aromas from bold dash of Ferdinand de Lesseps table grapes, together with chenin, colombard:

hugely popular. **Fernão Pires ◀ 98** off-dry at 10 gms/l sugar. Alluring spicy nose with a lemon twist—a zesty quaffer. **Colombard 98 Semi-sweet** at 19 gms/l sugar, bursts with pear, guava and melon aromas—lovely acid balance. **Sauvignon Blanc Sparkling 98** shows pinpoint bubbles from fine carbonation—whiffs of varietal fruit, sprightly off-dry finish (30 gms/l sugar).

OAK VILLAGE See Vinfruco

"OCCASIONAL" RANGE See Hartenberg

ODDBINS See Shoprite Checkers

O'HAGANS — For the Irish pub chain by Longridge

Ridge Red Soft juicy succulence in NV South African/French blend; clean spicy tang in tail. Tasty, uncomplicated. **Bouquet Blanc** From **98** bukettraube with gently toned spice, muscat freshness; 11 gms/l sugar gives appealing fruity lift.

ONDERKLOOF WINERY

Sir Lowry's Pass, Helderberg

Opening September 1999
Owners: Danie Truter, Beat Musfeld, John Harrison
Winemaker: Danie Truter
Vineyards: 32 ha.
P.O. Box 90, Sir Lowry's Pass 7133
Tel/Fax: 021-8581538 **Fax:** 021-8581536

Danie Truter, ex-Rhebokskloof, Hartenberg, is going solo—semi-solo, actually: 2 partners are helping him jump-start a new winery on Onderkloof farm near Somerset West. An existing building is being transformed into a cellar for the 1999 crush. Some 200 tons will be harvested. The first wines—**Chardonnay, Sauvignon Blanc, Chenin Blanc**—will be released in Sept 99; oak-matured Cabernet Sauvignon, Pinotage in 2000. New shiraz, merlot v'yds, cooled in summer by south-easterly breezes, will come into production around 2004.

OOM TAS — SFW

Reddish gold, spicy muscat character muted by other varieties. Smooth and dry, affectionately referred to as "No. 7", after inadvertent scratch mark on label. Sells equivalent of 2 million cases annually, all in returnable glass. NV.

ORANJERIVIER WYNKELDERS

Lower Orange River See Orange Rivier map for individual cellars

Tastings/sales at all the cellars (Upington, Kakamas, Keimoes, Grootdrink, Groblershoop) Mon-Fri 8-12.45; 2-5. Sat 8.30-12. Cellar tours Jan-March by appointment.
Owners: 750 members
General Manager: Noël Mouton
Winemakers: Jurie de Kock, Danie Volgraaff, Jannie Engelbrecht, Mathee van Schalkwyk, C. Venter
Production: 80 000 tons. **Vineyards:** 13 300 ha.

P.O. Box 544, Upington 8800
Tel: 054-3324651 (head office) **Fax:** 054-3324408

SA's largest co-op, so vast it has 5 cellars strung out along the lower Orange River around Upington, the region's nerve centre. High summer temperatures, and resultant high sugars here make fortified desserts the natural speciality. Sherries are also made from hanepoot and colombard.

Ruby Cabernet Unwooded dry red; in low tannin/acid mode. **Bon Souvenir** More mature blended version. **Dry Red** Pinotage/ruby cab. blend. **Pinotage** Sweet-plummy dry red. **Blanc de Noir** From ruby cabernet, off-dry. **95** SA show trophy winner. **Rosé** From ruby cabernet, semi-sweet. **Blanc de Blanc** Lightly wooded dry white blend. **Grand Crû** Dry colombard, 13% alc. **Chenin Blanc** Dry, 13% alc. **Colombard** Off-dry white. **Stein** Semi-sweet colombard. **Late Harvest** Colombard, semi-sweet. **Special Late Harvest** Similar, sweeter. **Nouveau Blanc** Sweet Natural from chenin. **Soet Hanepoot** Gold dessert. **Red Muscadel** From muscat de frontignan. **Jerepigo St Antonio** Dessert from chenin, fortified. **Dessert Wine** Fortified hanepoot, grapey bouquet, silky texture. **Red Jerepigo** From ruby cabernet. **Jerepigo White** Dessert from sultana; sweet fleshy taste. **White Muscadel** From muscat de frontignan.

OUDERUST

See Mooiuitsig

OUDE WELLINGTON WINE ESTATE

Wellington See Wellington map

Tastings/sales by appointment. Guest-house.
Owner: Dr. Rolf Schumacher
Winemaker: Vanessa Simkiss (since 1995)
Viticulturists: Vanessa Simkiss, Rolf Schumacher
Production: 2 000 cases. **Vineyards:** 18 ha.
P.O. Box: 622, Wellington 7654
Tel: 021-8732262 **Fax:** 021-8734639
E-mail: rrs@cis.co.za

If packaging is an indicator of the cellar style, then this bouncy purple-on-gold example bearing the image of "Wellington"—if you're thinking Duke of Wellington you're too highbrow; try footwear!—fairly shouts "individual and just a little impish". Which more or less describes the wine, called **Rubignon**, from fashionable American cross, ruby cabernet, with some cab. s. "We try to highlight the sometimes elusive characteristics of the variety," says winemaker Vanessa Simkiss, who uses traditional equipment where possible—additional old cement open *kuipe* were refurbished in 1998 to accommodate rising production.

*** **Rubignon** NV cross-vintage (**96/97**) ruby cab., cab. s.; developing impressive complexity—snatches damp earth, smoke, violets, ripe prunes; lush juiciness on palate, with almond/oaky undertones. Very appealing, distinctive. New (50%), used oak, 6-15 months. Next release (**98**) will be vintage-dated. Similar vineyard/cellar treatment.

Cabernet Sauvignon NEW **98** from late-picked grapes, open-tank-fermented, French oak-matured. 13,5% alc. Untasted.

OVERGAAUW ESTATE

Vlottenburg See Stellenbosch map

Open 9-12.30; 2-5 weekdays, Sat 10-12.30.

Owner: Braam van Velden
Winemaker: Chris Joubert
Production: 900 tons, 100 00 cases. **Vineyards:** 75 ha.
P.O. Box 3, Vlottenburg 7604
Tel: 021-8813815 **Fax:** 021-8813436

Time. That's one of the invisible, pervasive hallmarks of this admirable, innovative, determinedly low-profile range which, down the years, has included a number of notable Cape originals: first estate merlot; first touriga naçional vintage "port" (to name two). Braam van Velden, Overgaauw's quiet-spoken proprietor/winemaker, and protégé Chris Joubert (now officially in charge of the cellar after a 10-year apprenticeship) grow serious wines that need time, especially the reds, to reach their potential—up to 10-12 years in some cases. The vintners are convinced this long-held policy remains valid today, despite the (world-wide) canter towards earlier-drinking, buy-'em-and-swig-'em styles. That's not to say the range is unapproachable in youth—far from it—just that collectors exercising a little patience will be more amply rewarded. Not a philosophy with Gen X, instant gratification-appeal, perhaps, but one that's vindicated by experience. Van Velden points out that his **Cabernet Sauvignon 93**, not particularly well received by the critics when released, in the past year merited Veritas Gold, WINE★★★★, wine club selection and inclusion in several airline lists. "Proof that time is essential for the development of our reds," he says. Which is why Overgaauw's **Cape Vintage**, though made in higher quantities—just over 10 000 bottles a year compared to about 4 000 initially—to slake consumers' thirst, will become available only in 4-5 years. "That's the oak/bottle ageing we feel this style needs before it's ready for release." This same fashion-wary mindset guides the vineyard planting programme. "We won't be dictated to by short-term trends," Joubert remarks, "we plant what will do best on a specific site, within the parameters of the house style and our particular strengths as a winery, of course."

★★★★ **Cape Vintage** (The word Port does not appear on Overgaauw labels) **89** from tinta barocca, tinta francisca, souzão, cornifesto and malvasia rey is nearer 5 stars than 4. Bouquet has surprising fruit, raisiny richness, with nutty and prune tones. Full, smooth across the palate with wonderful warming sensation, good weight and spicy intensity. Elegant, dry, lots more development potential—10 years or more—but very good, satisfying already. 17% alc., 75 gms/l sugar. Fortified with 3-year-old rebate brandy. Matured 3 years in 1,300 litre oak vats and further maturation in bottle for 7 years at 14 °C cellar before release.

★★★★ **Touriga Naçional 94 Vintage** From Rolls Royce of port grapes, also near 5 stars, but for 1998 CIWG auction needs plenty of time to develop its full potential. 18,7% alc. Later vintages have higher alcs. This one has fragrant aromas, intense concentration, dry finish and spicy depth. Far too early yet for final assessment, let alone drinking.

★★★★ **DC Classic 96** (for 1998 CIWG auction) Immediate impact with full black cherry, raspberry nose, with heavy char backing. Hints of mint and spice. Mouthfilling silkiness. Super concentration of dark, berry fruit flavours, with masses of sweetish caramel/vanilla. Ripe tannins all the way through. Gorgeous now but will well reward some 8-10 years maturation.

★★★★ **Merlot** First in SA to bottle under varietal merlot label. **97** accessible earlier than most Overgaauw reds. Raspberry/cherry/strawberry bouquet with hints of violets. Soft, rich, warm palate re-emphasises fruit on nose. Gently oaked, wide spectrum of flavours waiting to develop. Give another 3/5 years to show full potential. From 16-year-old v'yds, about 11 tons/ha. Two years in French oak. **95 WINE★★★★**.

★★★★ **Tria Corda** This is definitely going on 5 stars. Produced only in exceptional years. **95** a stunner. 60% cabernet s., 25% merlot, 15% cabernet f. 2 years in small French oak. Nose dense with peppery, spicy, plummy, ripe cherry fruit. The palate is a marvel of a seamless marriage between sweetish fruit and oak flavours, surrounded all the way by soft tannins. A beautiful wine, already approachable but will reward another 8/10 years of ageing. No **96**.

★★★★ **Pinotage-Cabernet Franc** ◀ An Overgaauw red for now. Described on front-label as "fruity red". **97** lightish-bodied, plum-packed nose, sweet, ripe cherry flavours. Very drinkable but enough guts to develop another 2/3 years. 60/40 pinotage/cab. f. (pinotage from 30-year-old vines). Aged in third-use barrels for about a year. Good mouthful at ambient temp. or as summer quaffer chilled!

★★★★ **Cabernet Sauvignon 95** "will be a late developer like the **93**. That's our style", says Braam van Velden. Full of blackberry, mulberry, hints of herbs/spice, touch of mint/vanilla. Tasted mid-1998, still all pretty much apart. Palate is full and velvety, with soft tannins but also needs time to marry. But the potential is there. Matured in combination of new/old oak for up to 2 years.

★★★ **Sylvaner** ◀ Unique to Overgaauw since 1971. **98** very attractive spicy/peach nose with good, full body. "Sort of an airbus," explains Chris Joubert, "it's got a wide body and lots of length!" Very well balanced with rich grapey flavours, surprising natural tannins. Touch of sugar, 5 gms/l, makes for smoothness rather than sweetness. Unusual, appealing everyday drinker, but has long history of developing well in the bottle.

★★★★ **Chardonnay 98** one of the best. From 17-year-old vines. Fresh bouquet with melon, peach, lemon aromas. Marvellously subtle but distinct spicy aromas. Slight malo but far more fruit. (What malo there is, occurs naturally, is not inoculated.) Lively palate with lemon, lime, touch of fig, melon. Restrained, harmonious, elegant. Good now, potential to develop 6 months in combination of 40% new French, 30% 2nd and 30% 3rd-fill. 12,5% alc., 2 gms/l sugar.

★★★ **Sauvignon Blanc** ◀ **98** lighter than pvs.; bright peppery, nettly-grassy scents. Full and fresh palate with greenish gooseberry flavours, the greenage that seems peculiar to Overgaauw sauvignon. Delightful easy drinker.

Merlot/Touriga Naçional 96 (See Makro).

OVERHEX CO-OPERATIVE

Worcester See Worcester map

Tastings/sales Mon-Fri 8-5. Cellar tours by appointment.
Owners: 20 members
Winemaker: A. B. Krige (since 1996)
Production: 10 000 tons. **Vineyards:** ± 300 ha.
P.O. Box 139, Worcester 6849
Tel: 0231-75012 **Fax:** 0231-71057

Go-getting A. B. Krige, exposed to winemaking practices in Germany and France, is experimenting with oak barrel maturation at this overwhelmingly white-grape co-op near Worcester. Interestingly, some obvious characteristics imparted by wood are naturally present on the nose of the cellar's unwooded **Chardonnay**, a quirk of *terroir* that's driving up sales and encouraging member-farmers to establish the variety more widely, along with premium red grapes. A quality-focused "varietal blueprint" developed with KWV advisers guides the establishment of v'yds to ensure that vines take root in conducive soils.

★★★ **White Muscadel 94** gorgeous golden-amber colour belies lightish feel on palate. Delicious combination of raisin and fresh grape flavours, sweet but not cloying. Fine fortified dessert. 17% alc. **93**, **92** both **VG**.

Cabernet Sauvignon-Merlot 97 first red blend from this cellar (pvsly a cab. only). Very light, soft, some raspberries/cherries, chill for instant summer quaffing. Unwooded. 12% alc. **Pinotage 98** Cellar's first bottled pinotage, fermented on oak chips, untasted. Winemaker's note: "Fresh and dried fruit flavours, ripe tannins." **Chardonnay** ◀ **97** very nice unwooded dry style. Clean, fresh, citrusy; lots of fruit to balance crisp acids. 13% alc. **Clairette Blanche** ◀ **97** crunchy Golden Delicious apple flavours, lowish alc., just off-dry. Light, no-fuss, frisky drinking. **Chardonnay Spesiale Laat Oes 98** untasted for this ed., pvs. amiable citrus flavours, full, quite sweet. 38 gms/l sugar, 11,8% alc. **Colombard Semi-Sweet 97** drier than usual at 18 gms/l sugar; mouthful of fresh fruit-salad, nicely balanced by fairly crisp acidity. 11,5% alc. **Chenin Blanc 97** off-dry; first bottled chenin from this cellar, untasted. **Red Muscadel** Muscaty/raisiny fragrance/flavours in **94** very sweet dessert; piquant fruity finish. **Demi-Sec Sparkling** Carbonated **98** low alc. (10%) bubbly, sweet-sour palate (40 gms/l sugar), lots of foam.

OVERMEER CELLARS (5 lt vat range) SFW

Selected Red Cinsaut-based uncomplicated quaffer, cross-continental curiosity, as current is blend of SA, Argentinian wines! **Premier Grand Crû** Rather bland dry white, from chenin. **Stein** Friendly semi-sweet, some grapey fragrance. **Late Harvest** Sweeter chenin blend; uncloying.

OVERVAAL WINES See Hartswater Wine Cellar

PAARL PERLÉ DGB

Popular NV Semi-sweet pétillant white; chenin/colombard/hanepoot.

PADDAGANG RESTAURANT & WINERY

Tulbagh See Tulbagh map

Tastings/sales 7 days a week 10.30-4.
Traditional dishes; picnics
Owners: Paddagang Wines
Winemaker: Michael Krone
P.O. Box 303, Tulbagh 6820
Tel: 0236-300394 **Fax:** 0236-300433

Winemaking siblings Nicky and Michael Krone (Twee JongeGezellen, Tulbagh Co-op respectively), relatives and friends are the "froggy fraternity" behind this easy-drinking, unpretentious range with its witty labels designed to put a smile into the serious world of wine. Available from and named after the deservedly popular, authentically old-Cape Paddagang (frog passage) Restaurant, on the river in Tulbagh. All the wines NV.

★★★ **Brulpadda** Sweetish (but not cloying) port; tinta barocca, ruby cab. "Most serious of the paddas" is our taster's verdict—but not pretentious: easy, fruity, chocolate depths. Winter warmer, 120 gms/l sugar, 18% alc.

Paddarotti Dry red, 50% ruby cabernet, pinotage. Full-bodied, blackberry wafts, dark cherry flavours; quite grippy so best with (Paddagang?) food. **Paddamanel** Dry red, 50/50 cab. s., merlot. Bright fruit, cherries, definite tannic squeeze. **Paddajolyt** ☺ Sappy strawberry/cherry mouthful, round, quaffable. Cinsaut at its bouncy, jammy, fruity, froggy best. In summer, chill lightly. Lowish alc. 11,5%. Unwooded. **Paddadundee** Chardonnay, sauvignon (mainly), sémillon. Fresh, gently dry. Down-to-earth Tulbagh summer heat-beater. **Paddasang** Light-bodied, crisp dry white. Sauvignon blanc. **Paddaspring** NEW Jaunty, floral; "spring" in step from hanepoot injection, off-dry, lowish alc. (11,5%). Also chenin, sémillon. Just the thing to sip al fresco at Paddagang. **Platanna** Chenin; ripe, honeyed, semi-sweet (24 gms/l sugar). **Paddapoot** Delicate floral tone, caramel daubs, full-sweet; from hanepoot. 18% alc., 160 gms/l sugar.

PANAROTTI'S — For the pizza/pasta chain by Simonsig

Red Pinotage-based, quaffing red. **98** spicy, plummy fruit, soft, lightish build. **Dry White** Medium-bodied, soft dryness perked up with Rhine riesling, muscat fruit. **Stein** Elegant honeyed, semi-sweet; mainly chenin with spicy hints. **Vin Doux** Carbonated semi-sweet; chenin with muscat, Rhine riesling infusion.

PAUL BONNAY — Sparkling, for Pick 'n Pay, from Robertson

Rouge Vivid ruby bubbly; juicy, plummy fruit, invigorating bubble balance rich sweetness. **Brut** (Special Reserve Dry White Sparkling) Lively sparkler; citrus freshness contrasted by gently dry finish. **Vin Sec** Floral-muscat scents, flavours; bubble softened by 35 gms/l sugar. **Vin Doux** Rich, sweet (75 gms/l), but balanced; energetic bubble.

PAUL CLUVER ESTATE (De Rust Farm)

Elgin See Elgin/Walker Bay map

Open Mon-Thur 8-5.30; Fri 8-4.30; Sat 9-1. Cellar with viewing deck; art gallery. No charge for individual tasting, R10 p/p for groups of 8 or more. (Follow signs to De Rust.)
Owner: Paul Cluver
Winemaker: Andries Burger (since 1997)
Assistant Winemaker: Patrick Kraukamp
Marketing Manager: Liezl Cluver
Production: 9 000 cases. **Vineyards:** 54 ha. (60% white, 40% red)
P.O. Box 48, Grabouw 7160
Tel: 021-8590605 **Fax:** 021-8590150
E-mail: liesl@cluver.co.za
Website: www.cluver.co.za

The exuberance of youth—guided by the calm hand of experience—is driving this newly registered Elgin estate, in both the cellar and pace-setting Lebanon empowerment project. The latter, initiated by Paul and Songvei Cluver in 1994 when the future of the forestry workers' village was threatened by privatisation, embodies immense political and social significance—not only for the Elgin area but the whole Cape wine industry. Together with SAFCOL forests, they set aside 200 ha. of land—some forest, most arable—incorporating the 60-family community homes and other facilities. With the commitment of the community and a number of De Rust's own workers, as well as guidance from the Rev. Trevor Steyn of the Anglican Social Development Institute, the project started as a fruit farm with orchards of 46 000 pears and plums.

Vineyard development has now been accelerated and 16 ha. prepared for vine planting; a wine from sourced grapes is on the cards while the new stock matures. This is not a charity-donation scheme, but a self-help one. The land and establishment costs will have to be paid for eventually at a rate and pace mutually negotiated. But a community has been offered the bootstraps—and seized them—to haul itself onto a level of the farming economy hitherto denied it.

Winemaker Andries Burger (a Cluver son-in-law) positively gushes when talking of the virtues of Elgin as a cool, quality wine region. It's an identity worth isolating and behind moves to register as an estate and separate the cellar operation from Nederburg, to which grapes are still supplied. Although the move to their own cellar was eased by Burger's having worked at Nederburg, it clearly has had its difficulties. Burger candidly acknowledges hiccups in his first—1997—vintage back at home, which was followed by an extremely challenging 1998 harvest when the grapes ripened early—and simultaneously. But with experience in Bordeaux (Ch. Margaux) and Burgundy (Aloxe-Corton) and the vigour of youth, Burger can be anticipated to craft fine wines in future.

*** **Cabernet Sauvignon** NEW **97** a first for both cellar and Elgin. Proof of Burger's belief in cool climes for quality cabernet. Magenta colour, tobacco, cedar tones, minerally mouthful, restrained finish. Tight, restrained but a harbinger for the region, confirmed by samples of **98**.

*** **Sauvignon Blanc** Warm vintage packed into **98** with ripe gooseberry fruit, opulent constitution, high alc. 14,5%. **97** fresh, focused lime intensity, racy, flint finish. Remains best sauvignon yet off this farm: extraordinary 1997 season and lengthy pre-fermentation skin contact for first time. Tangy, dry, unwooded. 13,5% alc. Pvs. made at Nederburg. **96** more herbaceous than gooseberry; crisp, steely. **Barrel Fermented** version: subtler wood treatment for **98** but creamy oak buttresses ripe fruit and alc. **97** denser, fatter, rounder; partly barrel-fermented, spent yeast cells offering broader-spectrum flavours.

*** **Chardonnay** Latest samples of **98** signal change in direction: less of both new oak, 166 "muscat" clone. Nose quieter, palate more austere, creamy complexity with peach pip flavours. **97** assemblage from 80% new barrels showing unambivalent, marmalady-muscat clone; crisp citrus in finish. Should continue to mature into multiple-flavoured but subtle wine. Pvs. made at Nederburg. **96** delicate oak, mouthfilling ripe tropical flavours. Fuller, more complex than **95**.

Pinot Noir 98 (barrel sample) promises return to potential after disappointing **97**. Good colour extraction, baked cherry flavours. **99** will be exclusively Burgundian clones. Burger backing his belief in Elgin pinot with further plantings. **Weisser Riesling 98** massive, bursting with 30% botrytis and 14% alcohol. See-saw in style from taut, Mosel-like austerity of **97**, which off-dry. **Gewürztraminer 97** candyfloss character, mildly fruit-sweet at 10 gms/l sugar. No **98**.

PERDEBERG CO-OPERATIVE

Paarl See Paarl map

Tastings/sales Mon-Fri 8-12.30; 2-5.
Owners: 47 members
Winemaker: Kobus de Kock (since 1994)
Production: 15 000 tons. **Vineyards:** 2 300 ha.
P.O. Box 214, Paarl 7620
Tel: 021-8638244 **Fax:** 021-8638245

The 98 vintage was clearly a challenging one at this cellar, with hot weather boosting some alcohol levels rather higher than usual, notably in the dry **Chenin Blanc** which has always garnered loads of awards and hogged the spotlight. Now getting into the act, and demanding their share of attention are Perdeberg's charmingly different cinsaut dessert, and for the quaffing brigade in particular, a winner of a chardonnay-sauvignon blend. Winemaker Kobus de Kock's philosophy is succint: "Make wine in the vineyard."

*** **Cinsaut Liqueur Wine** Distinctive, complex, intriguing SA dessert. Antique red velvet colour; smells/tastes like plump, juicy raisins, with youngberries, nuts. Good—by contrast almost savoury—finish. Wine-writer Dave Hughes took an old example of this wine to Portugal not long ago; tasters there judged it "a super, light port"! 18,2% alc. 106 gms/l sugar.

Cabernet Sauvignon-Merlot ◀ Ripe plums, soft, easy-drinking **97**. Touch of sugar (6 gms/l) boosts smooth quaffability. **Pinotage 98** fruity, punchy style (14% alc.). Less tannic than **Pinotage Reserve 98**, which full, dense with quietish fruit. **Cinsaut 98** hot vintage upturned cellar's pvs. ultra-light, friendly style. 14% alc. looms over fruit. **Chenin Blanc Dry** Usually star of this show and others (frequent top-performer at SA Champs). Hot vintage of **98** didn't play ball: guava nose/palate muted, high 14% alc. repressing fruit crispness when tasted mid-1998. Pvs. more immediately forthcoming, penetrating. **Chardonnay-Sauvignon Blanc** ◀ ☺ Drink young to capture almost indecent cheekiness of **98**, bursting with pineapple, mango, sweet tropical scents, all vividly contrasted by bone-dry palate. Very nice! 13% alc. **Chenin Blanc Semi-Sweet** ◀ ☺ Much more immediately successful than dry version in **98**: lemons, limes, guavas, delicious carry-over to soft, easy-drinking palate. 12% alc., 23,6 gms/l sugar. **Late Vintage 96** honeyed, matronly semi-sweet from chenin.

PICK 'n PAY

Quality, friendly prices and a welcome air of fun are hallmarks of this increasingly vino-savvy super-hypermarket chain's range. All tastes and pockets are catered for here, if not in the wide selection of local wines from leading cellars (see below) then through value-for-money imports chosen (with advice from consultant Dave Hughes) from prime plots in the global vignoble. The offbeat—but not frivolous—**From Halves to Hogsheads** range offers mid-priced, easy-drinking wines with the extra frisson of discovery: new "Chapters" in the range follow the exploits—and vinous discoveries—of "Dick the Winebuyer". New in the range from 1998 is Fab with Food, a range selected specifically for its cuisine-enhancing properties. A variety of vats and "vinipaks" offers no-fuss budget quaffing.

Contact: Elsa Gray and Gigi Bisogno. **Tel:** 021-9345018. **Fax:** 021-9348975.

PICK 'n PAY PREMIUM range:

*** **Special Late Harvest** ◀ **98** 100% gewürz., concentrated, luscious, brushed with botrytis, quite sweet, light-toned/bodied (± 11% alc.), superior lightly chilled aperitif or dessert accompaniment.

Cabernet Sauvignon 97 from Helderberg Winery, in cellar's popular, quite firm but friendly, unbrash style. **Shiraz** NEW **97** Van Loveren is source of this peppery, smoky-scented, fruity-bold red, 13,5% alc. **Pinotage** NEW **97** Award-winning producer Rooiberg is supplier of this wooded pinotage, alc.: 13,7%. Modern, juicy, accessible style. **Ruby Cabernet-Cabernet**

Sauvignon NEW **98** untasted, from Ashwood. Ruby cab. 70%, grapes ex-Worcester. **Dry Red** ☺ Cheap, cheerful, charming easy soft quaffer, mouthful of fresh berries, brambly touches. Multiple blend includes ruby cab. Unwooded, from Van Loveren. Drink young. **Chardonnay 97** (wooded) from Backsberg, lemony tones, mostly barrel-fermented, proportion tank-fermented. **Chardonnay 98** (unwooded) from Ashwood, untasted. **Chardonnay-Sauvignon Blanc** ☺ NEW **98** unwooded, from Laibach Vineyards. Great charm, quaffability, citrusy/tropical tones. **Blanc Fumé** NEW **98**, 100% sauvignon blanc, two months on lees, from acclaimed sauvignon producer Welmoed, gooseberry, fig tones, dry, good food wine. **Sauvignon Blanc** NEW **98** from Berg & Brook. Restrained, ripe fig/gooseberry, good substance on palate, rich texture. **Blanc de Blanc 98** chenin/sauvignon blanc, from Van Loveren, tropical tones, fresh and friendly everyday dry drinking. Lowish alc. 11,5%. **Chenin Blanc** Crisp dry quaffer, ex-Darling Cellars, **98** unwooded. **Johannisberger NV** semi-sweet, spicy white from Robertson Winery.

FAB WITH FOOD range:

Shrewdly packaged, consumer-friendly range offering one-chop solution to perennial culinary conundrum: what wine with what food? Features recipes by top SA food writer/consultant/purveyor Ina Paarman.

Fantastic with Fish Fresh grass/sorrel notes in **97**, perky lemon-lime flavours, brisk finish, bone-dry. Fantastic? Well, let's say very nice. With fish? Absolutely, especially rich/oily cuts, seafood. Sauv. bl., unwooded, WO Robertson. **Chic with Chicken 97** light, fresh, lemon-lime zest. Chic? Oui, oui! With chicken? We say: fantastic with fish! WO Robertson, chard., lightly wooded. **Cool with Curry 96** vivid straw colour, assertive spicy/floral aromas/flavours, off-dry, light/med.-bodied. Cool? As Ice-T. With curry? You bet—ready to do battle with any spicy food, Thai/Indian curry included. WO Robertson, colombard/gewürz. **Divine with Dessert 98** delicate SLH, pretty muscat/rose-petal wafts, fragile sweetness, fresh, persistent. Divine? Perhaps a tad over the top, but rather good. With dessert? Try dew-fresh fruit instead. WO Robertson, colombard/gewürz. **Marvellous with Meat 95** chunky cab. s., heavily oaked, rustic. Marvellous? Well . . . With meat? We say: pizza, robust pasta, casseroles. WO St'bosch, lightly wooded.

Also: Perfect with Pasta (import).

FROM HALVES TO HOGSHEADS

Featuring amusing back labels with unlikely tales of how Dick the Winebuyer chanced upon each wine. Front label with witty warthog illustration by leading SA cartoonist Derek Bauer. These chapters are available:

Chapter 5 Fast-ageing **96** chardonnay. Bottle-age with toffee/caramel notes. Sweetish, simple. WO Robertson. **Chapter 7** ◀ Cap Classique ex-Robertson. Mature wheat hue, biscuity bouquet. Tangy baked apple flavours; clean, dry. From pinot noir, chardonnay. **Chapter 10** NEW **Liebfraumilch** NV (import from Germany).

5 litre "NO NAMES" vats:

Dry Red Attractively bright. Medium-bodied, plenty of fruit, softly dry. **Rosé Semi Sweet** Crushed strawberry scents; sugar balanced by fruity freshness. **Dry White Light** Unfussy vin ordinaire; low 9,5% alc., unobtrusive fruit. **Stein** Quaffable semi-sweet white; dainty muscat/floral fragrance; 10% alc. **Late Harvest** Fruitily ripe aromas, flavours; medium-bodied, semi-sweet white.

500 ml "vinipaks": Dry Red, Dry White, Stein, Late Harvest. See Robertson Winery.

RAVENSWOOD wines:

5 l, 2 l vats from Swartland. Dry Red Sturdy, reliable blend pinotage, tinta barocca, cinsaut, cab. s., ruby cab. Dark berries, non-abrasive tannins. **Vin de Noir** (2 l only) Easy-drinking, lightish from (10% alc.) pinotage. **Premier**

Grand Crû Lively dry white from chenin, colombard, clairette blanche; fruity, dry. **Stein** Semi-sweet chenin, tropical fruit flavours. **Late Harvest** Easy, sweet mouthful of chenin fruit.

2 l/500 ml packs from Robertson: Dry Red/Vin Rouge Sweet brambly nose, unpretentious, juicy flavours, tangy tail. Everyday quaffing. **Grand Vin Blanc/Premier Grand Crû** Crisp dry white; unfussy earthiness. **Cape Stein/Selected Stein** Uncomplicated white, lively tropical fruit juiciness, gentle sweetness. **Late Vintage/Harvest** Easy-drinking semi-sweet white; enduring tropical fruit ripeness.

PIERRE JOURDAN

See Cabrière

PIERRE SIMOND

See Berg & Brook Vineyards

PINEHURST

See Môreson-Matin Soleil

PINNACLE

See IWS

PLAISIR DE MERLE

Simonsberg See Franschhoek map

Visits: Wine tastings, sales Mon-Fri 9-5. Sat 10-1. Cellar tours by appointment.
Owner: Stellenbosch Farmers Winery
Winemaker: Niel Bester (since 1993). **Vineyards:** Freddie le Roux
Production: 35 000 cases, 800 tons
Vineyards: 400 ha. (80% of grapes go to Nederburg)
P.O. Box 121, Simondium 7670
Tel: 021-8741071 **Fax:** 021-8741689

Fans of the very distinctive wines from this showpiece SFW farm will be happy to know that supplies are beginning to catch up with demand—production has increased by nearly 50% since the inaugural **93** vintage: red wine lovers will be specially heartened—the expansion drive has targeted their tastes in particular. Red wine varieties now make up 25% of production and are rising; a new cabernet sauvignon vineyard comes on stream in 1999 to boost quantities of the property's best seller. Petit verdot and malbec plantings are scheduled for inclusion in a future blend. Extra tanks will increase cellar space for reds, which are already benefiting from the introduction of a new bag-press. Innovation is a cornerstone of winemaker Niel Bester's philosophy. Plaisir's low-acid, gentle, super-fine Cabernet was a modern Cape trend-setter from its first **93** release, proving to many sceptics (now frenetically following suit) that early-drinkers can also be classics. Short-term fashion fads are not, however, on his agenda—consistent top quality travels in tandem with trend-setting here. Bester's own travels in 1998 took in Canada, California and Washington State—off his usual beaten track to Ch. Margaux (whose Paul Pontallier was an early influence on the Plaisir style).

**** **Merlot** Individual, deep-flavoured, refined rather than buxom but doesn't lack authentic fleshy breadth. Latest **96 (***)** with similar chocolate mint-minerally freshness to first **95 SAA**, **VG**; more delicate, also less rich colour; oak nicely judged to highlight fruit, velvety softness. Aged one year, used 300 litre vats. Drinks well now, will peak sooner than concentrated **95**. **97** tasted ex-barrel could well top the lot; deep mocha opulence, more serious dryness with penetrating ripe blackcurrant flavours.

★★★★ **Cabernet Sauvignon** Other cabernets may now echo gentle, fine qualities of this groundbreaker, however, it remains a benchmark, not least for consistency of quality, performance. **95**, **94**, **93 VG**, all **SAA** selections. Such achievements made more creditable through wine's finesse; sometimes overshadowed in blind tastings by more robust cabs. Blood-red **96** in much same vein as pvs., touch less rich, dense but avoids thinness of many in this lighter vintage (harvested month later than usual). Charming mingling of soft sweet berries, delicate cedary oak hints; wood, as always, highlights, extends fruit. Will mature sooner than others, esp. bigger-tannined **95**, but just as pleasurable a table companion. **94** broad-structured, firm backbone with spicy, dark berry fruits; **93** ripe fruitcake flavours, velvety-soft. (All touched up with dashes of merlot, shiraz; very subdued but excellent oaking. Just over 13% alc. low acids, about 5,7 gms/l.) Prices have remained at an honest level considering wine's international class. Imported clone's ageing ability not an issue with Bester, who maintains "These are wines for drinking".

★★★ **Chardonnay** Elegantly rich **97**; balanced toasty, nutty, tropical complexity; satisfying, mouthfilling; size well-contained by clean fruity thread. 13,5% alc. 50% fermented/aged in new/used casks.

★★★ **Sauvignon Blanc** Until **98**, introverted, slow-to-develop style. **97** shows quiet gooseberry breadth, touches of Loire-like chalkiness. Boldly-structured but not flashy, nor aggressive; pleasant frictionless flow helped by 20% barrel-fermented portion. Good fruity resurgence on finish. First 3 vintages **SAA** selections: **96**, **95**, **94 VG** (100% oaked). Unbottled sample **98** promises fresher, steelier mode with vigorous ripe gooseberries, figs. Only 10% barrel-fermented. More forward than pvs.

PONGRÁCZ — By The House of J.C. le Roux

★★★★ Popular, showy Cap Classique NV, made at new J.C. le Roux cellar, Devon Valley, by talented Melanie van der Merwe. String of local, int. awards; latest: **WINE★★★★**, also **SAA** trophy, Schramsberg trophy best non-Champagne sparkler at IWSC, London 1994; served **SAA** 1st Class 1995. Two-thirds pinot noir, chardonnay; brut (11,5 gms/l sugar, 11,5% alc.), broadened by malo. Feathery, slightly yeasty delicacy; green-apple freshness.

PORCUPINE RIDGE — See Boekenhoutskloof

PORTERVILLE CO-OPERATIVE WINE CELLARS

Swartland — See Swartland map

Tastings/sales Mon-Fri 8-1; 2-5, Sat 8-11. Cellar tours by appointment, conference facilities.
Owners: 115 members
Winemaker: Klaas de Jongh (since 1980)
Production: 17 000 tons
P.O. Box 52, Porterville 6810
Tel: 022-9312170 **Fax:** 022-9312171

"To make wine as naturally as possible" is the philosophy of this co-op, where a new pressing cellar was inaugurated recently to keep pace with demand for quality wine.

POST HOUSE WINERY

Stellenbosch See Helderberg map

Visits: Open by appointment only.
Owner: Hermann Gebers
Winemaker: Nicholas Gebers (since 1997)
Production: 350 cases. **Vineyards:** 30 ha.
Address: Gebers Estate (Pty) Ltd., Languedoc, Firgrove 7110
Tel/Fax: 021-8422409

By all accounts Nicholas Gebers' first (1997) vintage on the Helderberg family farm was a hurly-burly, with cellar equipment begged, borrowed or press-ganged into service. But the grapes, despite being subjected to the indignity of crushing in an old tobacco press, turned into rather pleasant wines. The second Post House vintage shows greater assuredness, delicacy, auguring well for the future of this compact, delightful range.

Cabernet Sauvignon 97 has array of interesting tones—ripe prune, dried herbs, attractive savoury accents, wrapped in abundant ripe tannin. Mouth-feel lifted, focused by fresh acid; finishes clean. Drinks agreeably now but shouldn't come to harm over 1-2 yrs. **Chenin Blanc 98** attractive pale gold, reflecting ethereal appley wafts on nose. Palate more substantial, ripe-fruited, finishes on brisk, bone-dry note. Good with fish, seafood.

RAVENSWOOD

See Pick 'n Pay

R & de R—FREDERICKSBURG

Franschhoek See Paarl map

Visits: Due to open to public. Mon-Fri 9-4.30, Sat 9-1, cellar/vineyard tours by appointment. Tasting fee R5.
Owners: Anthonij Rupert & Benjamin de Rothschild
Winemakers: Schalk Joubert with Annemie van Royen
Production MD: Jacques Borman
Marketing: SFW
Vineyards: 200 ha.
P.O. Box 55, Simondium 7670
Tel: 021-8741648 **Fax:** 021-8741802
E-mail: info@fredericksburg.co.za
Website: www.fredericksburg.co.za

The flags are flying outside the tasting room at this illustrious cellar, but there's not a drop to drink. Yet. After a measured, high profile build up to the launch of the first labels, the inaugural wines—**97 Sauvignon Blanc** and **Chardonnay**—were withdrawn at the eleventh hour. They were deemed not up to the standard required of such a prestigious property. With a pedigree as long as this one, expectations run high.

R & de R is the premium label due to grace top-flight offerings from Fredericksburg farm on the slopes of the Simonsberg, neighbour to Plaisir de Merle. It's a formidable partnership between arguably the foremost families of French and Cape wine: Baron Benjamin de Rothschild (owner of Ch. Clarke, partner in Ch. Lafite-Rothschild, Bordeaux) with Dr. Anton Rupert and son Antonij (owners of L'Ormarins Estate among other considerable interests). Steadily developed since 1986, the spanking new 850 ton winery and underground maturation cellar were commissioned for the 1998 vintage, the **97**s having been vinified at "sister property" La Motte.

Youthful vigour is injected into the cellar in the form of unassuming winemaker Schalk-Willem Joubert who holds no formal training other than (perhaps more telling) apprenticeship to Jacques Borman, Production MD here and veteran proponent of the art at Hanneli Rupert's La Motte. He's joined by Montpellier-trained Annemie van Royen, of Flemish origin and fluent in the cellar vernacular. Both are endearingly humble, constantly broadening their horizons with travel (recently France and Italy) and by tasting wines of the world. They aim to enhance the quality grown in the vineyard with minimal handling; skin and lees contact and full malolactic fermentation adding extra dimensions.

One senses that Dr. Rupert's vision to see the Cape ranked with the best winelands of the world, and "not have it full of houses", is safe in these eager hands. His challenge, to make wines that the world will take note of, stands.

*** **Sauvignon Blanc** NEW Quiet bouquet, freshly cut grass, bell pepper herbaceous tones, tropical granadilla fullness on dry palate. **98** gentle alcohol in spite of warm harvest, this achieved from picking at staged degrees of ripeness. Left on spent yeasts for 4 months for richness. No wood.

Following wines tasted as barrel samples, before final form determined, and before labelling decisions made: i.e. under which labels—R & de R or Fredericksburg—they will appear. Release likely to be one year after bottling, timing not yet decided. **Cabernet Sauvignon/Merlot 97** delicious cornucopia of fleshy raspberry/forest fruits, smoky cedar, touch of mint. Palate packed with blackcurrant, leafy flavours. Coating ripe tannins. Grapes from Fredericksburg farm. After year in oak, varietal wines blended before further wood maturation—for better "marriage". Great potential. **Chardonnay 98** mélange of ripe lemon, melon, figs with toasty oak. Complexity likely from broad palette of flavours, different clones in various coopers' oak. Whole-cluster pressing, partial wild yeast fermentation in barrel, full malo.

REBEL — Range of vat wines

Dry Red Pleasantly spicy, fresh, full-bodied, dry. **Vin de Noir** Rosé-style off-dry wine, light, sound. **Premier Grand Crû** Medium-bodied dry white, easy sipping. **Stein** Gently sweet white, light, effortless. **Late Harvest** Grapey-muscat tones on nose/palate, clean finish, semi-sweet white.

REMHOOGTE FARM

Stellenbosch

Sales/tastings by appointment.
Owner: Murray Boustred Trust
Winemaker: Murray Boustred
Production: ± 500 cases
P.O. Box 2032, Dennesig 7601
Tel: 021-8895005 **Fax:** 021-8896907

Passion for the outdoors and game/trout farming experience awoke in Highveld construction and property development tycoon Murray Boustred a yen to go farming. A Hermanus *habitué*, unsurprisingly he gravitated towards the winelands and, shortly before the 1994 election, snapped up this run-down—but rich-in-potential—Stellenbosch property near L'Avenir and Morgenhof. About half of the 40 hectares have had to be grubbed and replanted; but established pinotage (some as much as 25 years old), cabernet sauvignon and merlot are in fine fettle, as demonstrated by the auspicious results of Murray Boustred's initial winemaking efforts, undertaken "with a lot of help from the neighbours!"

**** **Cabernet Sauvignon** Stylish, elegant début for this label in **95**, burnished deep plum colour with blackcurrant, forest scents, nuts and lead pencils. All reverberate on palate with splash of soft chocolate, plush tannins. Full, rich, decidedly drinkable now, but plenty development potential. 7 tons/ha., 2 yrs small French oak, 13,5% alc.

*** **Pinotage 97** generous full fruit nose, ripe banana, redcurrant, raspberries. Big juicy, mouthfilling, soft tannin, long full finish. Lots of potential over next 1-2 yrs. 8 tons/ ha. 18 mths combination new, 2nd/3rd-fill small French oak. 12,5% alc. **96** Soft fruity style with ripe plums, bit of wild scrub, soft mouthfilling substance. Ones to watch: both potential ****

REYNEKE WINES

See Uitzicht

RHEBOKSKLOOF WINE ESTATE

Agter-Paarl See Paarl map

Tastings/sales daily 9-5, including public holidays. Formal tastings by appointment, R7 p/p (includes cellar tour).

Continental cuisine, 11.30 until late. Tues 11.30-5.30. Closed Wed. See restaurant section. Own estate olive oil.

Owner: Keith Jenkins
Winemaker/Viticulturist: Daniel Langenhoven (since 1998)
Production: 20 000 cases. **Vineyards:** 90 ha.
P.O. Box 7141, Noorder-Paarl 7623
Tel: 021-8638386 **Fax:** 021-8638504
E-mail: rhebok@iafrica.com
Website: http://os2.iafrica.com:80/rhebok/index.htm

Young Daniel Langenhoven, Rhebokskloof's new winemaker/vineyardist, takes over the reins as new v'yd developments of mainly red grapes are poised to yield their first crops. Planting started soon after the historic 450 ha. estate was purchased by live-wire industrialist Keith Jenkins. "The terroir is excellent for reds," says Elsenburg-trained Langenhoven, who worked for a number of larger producers, including Mamreweg (now Darling Cellars), before moving to the family-run Agter-Paarl estate. From 1999 he'll be spreading his wings in the newly-extended cellar, featuring a custom-designed barrel maturation hall. "More and more of our wines, especially reds, will be oak-matured."

*** **Pinotage 97** unmistakably feistier than pvs., fuller flavoured, more intense. Gusts of ripe bananas, soft berries on nose, banana-black cherry on palate, supple tannin, fresh acid, persistent finish. Pick of the cellar's reds. Medium/full-bodied. Drinks easily now, shouldn't come to harm in 2-3 years.

*** **Chardonnay Sur Lie 98** features defty balanced fruit/oak, fine complexity. Bags of fresh limes brushed with honey, complementary spicy oak; clean, lovely butterscotch notes in finish. Six months in oak, 20% new. 13,5%.

*** **Merlot 97** classic merlot aromas/tastes: raspberries, cherries, soft chocolate—all brightened by dusting of sweet-vanilla oak. Approachable now, probably better from mid-99. **95 VG**, rated in top 10 of merlots tasted at Switzerland's "World Wine Festival", apparently outranking Petrus!

Cabernet Sauvignon 97 quite closed, hard to interpret, needs time to show colours. Some black cherry, mulberry dimensions, Xmas pud steaming in background, very taut tannins should relax in 1-2 years. **91 VG**. **Dry Red** ◀

NV Juicy mouthful of cherry fruit, lightly oaked, good quaffing. Gamay with 20% cab. s. **Gamay Noir** NEW **98** cut grass, red cherry essences, quite simple but pleasant, crisp acid. Relaxed quaffing now, but could age interestingly over 2-3 years. Lightly oaked, 13,5% alc. **Chardonnay Grande Reserve 98** big burly as ever—14% alc.—powerfully scented, dollop of oak. At this early stage wood masking fruit (in sample tasted), could integrate, age interestingly, so one to watch. Malo complete. **Grand Vin Blanc ◀ 98** smoothly fused chard. (80%), sauvignon, former briefly oaked for extra richness; softly dry. Pleasant citrus/honey toned quaffer. **Weisser Riesling ◀ 97** has not been idle in bottle: evinces rich honey, perfumed/floral notes, touch of botrytis; balanced, crisp, tastes dry despite 9 gms/l sugar. 13,3% alc. Drink now. **Harvest White** NV everyday dry white. From weisser riesling, chenin, sauvignon, fresh, light, understated. **Bouquet Blanc** NV perfumed weisser riesling/hanepoot/chenin blend, 14 gms/l sugar nicely lifted by acid. Summer sipping. **Tamay** Scented bubbly; off-dry, carbonated.

RICKETY BRIDGE VINEYARDS & WINERY

Franschhoek See Franschhoek map

Open 7 days a week. Nov-May 10.30-5; June-Oct 11-4.30. Cellar tours by arrangement. Accommodation: Paulinas Drift Retreat—executive suites.

Owners: Alan and Celia Tonkin
Winemaker: Boela Gerber (since 1998)
Consulting Viticulturist: Paul Wallace
Production: 20 000 cases. **Vineyards:** 22 ha.
P.O. Box 455, Franschhoek 7690
Tel: 021-8762129 **Fax:** 021-8763486

The hurricane of change that swept into this 18th century Franschhoek estate after international business consultants Alan and Celia Tonkin took up residency in 1997 refuses to abate. A fresh tempest from over the mountain has blown in Boela Gerber, former assistant winemaker at Stellenzicht (where he worked with one-man-whirlwind André van Rensburg, now at Vergelegen). Gerber flew solo at Stellenzicht during the 1998 crush following Van Rensburg's departure (see that entry for details), gusting into Rickety Bridge in June. The Tolkins' Texas-size blueprint for revitalising their stately riverside property, first known as Paulinas Drift, includes an all-new gravity-fed cellar which, Alan Tonkin notes with a nod to all contractors concerned, was completed literally as the 1998 harvest arrived. "Many suppliers who delivered and worked through the night to ensure that were were ready for the 1998 harvest have to be thanked. When the going gets tough, many in the wine industry pull together." The cellar design incorporates an attached visitor centre "to encourage an informative and personalised tasting experience". As a future "premier destination for wine lovers and international tourists", the estate will include upmarket guest suites (some will be completed during 1999), restaurant and terrace. Staff, the proprietors assure, will not be neglected—on the contrary, upliftment, development and training "have central focus".

PREMIUM range:

**** **Merlot** Rich, deeply upholstered **97** one for the longer haul. Almost opaque, glimpse of purple; red/blackberry compôte, dark-roast coffee, wide-framed. Tannins undaunting but at present too obvious, need few years to integrate. Very good.

**** **Malbec** NEW Unusual (in Cape) variety, expertly handled: smoky/toasty **97** plummy, blackberries in background, supple tannins, accessible yet good ageing potential.

★★★★ **Shiraz** Showy **96** dark-hued, attractive spice-rack nose, pepper-shaker on palate, punnets of red berries, some gamey suggestions, pliant tannins. Accessible now, will happily go few more years. 50% new American oak, 30% new French, 20% 2nd-fill. First ever **VG** for this cellar. "It felt good and certainly will be repeated," says proprietor. **97** spicier, more gamey, light chocolate coating; not as open, needs ± 3 years to unfurl.

★★★ **Cabernet Sauvignon 97** ripe plums, tobacco whiffs, toasty wood, cassis traces in finish, definite but not unpleasant grip. More linear, compact style, wood forward. 15 months new French barriques.

RESERVE range:

★★★ **Paulinas Reserve 96** red-berry aromas, sweet-oaky entry, spicy, dry-leafy touches. Still developing, needs ± 2 years. Blend cab. s./f., merlot, malbec, 18 months new American/French oak. Named after Paulina de Villiers, founder of farm 200 years ago. Special label, bottle, individual box.

PRESTIGE range:

★★★★ **Chardonnay** Blockbuster style continues in big, toasty, oaky **98**, brimming with ripe tropical fruit. This style needs time, as in **97** which developed well in bottle, ready now but should keep 1-2 yrs. Mango, pineapple wrapped in clean vanilla oak, persistent, long. Barrel-fermented/matured new French (Burgundian) oak, 4 coopers, various toastings, malo, "lees stirred once a week with a Jack White No 2". **98**, being fuller, riper, needs 2-4 years.

★★★ **Sauvignon Blanc-Sémillon** NEW **98** buttercup yellow, ripe gooseberry wafts, fresh-baked-bread on broad viscous palate, slight oaky tones, soft, easy, nice. 6 mths new American oak.

★★★ **Sauvignon Blanc 98** passion-fruit, slight grassy suggestions, big flavour but pleasantly crisp. **97** with serious fresh figs, grass, rather nice. Dry, unwooded, night-picked. Leap in quality over **96**.

★★★ **Chenin Blanc** Outdoorsy **98** delightful, crisp, fresh, guava-toned. Vintner says grapes picked lot riper than **97**, which blended with 15% sauvignon blanc.

Sémillon Wood quite forward in **97**, partially barrel-fermented/matured, new small American oak, 6 mths. Big mouthful, oaky-dry finish. Good food partner. **96** very restrained in youth, later developed peachy, floral notes. Best after yr in bottle.

CLASSIC range: Both NEW (untasted)

Chenin Blanc 98 unwooded. **Sémillon-Sauvignon Blanc 98** wood-fermented.

PAULINAS DRIFT range: (export label)

★★★★ **Cabernet Sauvignon 96** Though light in colour, deeply concentrated, basket of ripe red-berry fruit, long spicy-vanilla finish. ± 15 months new French oak. ± 12% alc.

RIEBEEK WINE CELLAR

Riebeek-Kasteel See Swartland map

Tastings/sales Mon-Fri 8-5. Cellar tours in season by appointment.
Owners: 63 members
Winemaker: Eric Saayman (since 1997)
Production: 18 000 tons. **Vineyards:** 2 200 ha.
P.O. Box 13, Riebeek-Kasteel 7307
Tel: 022-4481213 **Fax:** 022-4481281
E-mail: riebeek@mweb.co.za.com

Eric Saayman, who joined from Zevenwacht in mid-1997, wasted no time in implementing a programme to catapult this cooperative winery in the lee of Kasteelberg into the big league. A new red fermentation cellar, temperature controlled maturation hall, tank storage facilities were built; more premium varieties (mainly red) established; the range revamped; packaging/labelling updated—"We have a whole new image!"

★★★ **Dry Red** ☺ ◀ NV different, individual packaging (cf. reference on back label to "Eric Saayman . . . father of triplets, producing wine for a new generation"); light, fresh brambleberry/briar flavours, easy tannins, quaffable. Cinsaut, ruby, cabernet blend. Unwooded. Excellent value at ± R9 ex-farm.

Pinotage NEW **98** (tank sample) unflashy style: light-bodied, dry, unwooded. **Pinotage-Tinta Barocca** NEW **98** tasted very young. Interesting combo, has potential. Attractive smoky/savoury tones, perceptibly tannic. Oak-chip aged. One to watch. **Chardonnay 97** like pvs., friendly, fruity, fresh, merest hint of wood. Added interest from "sweet" toffee hints. Dry, 13% alc. 30% fermented/matured 6 months in new French oak. **Chardonnay-Sémillon** ◀ NEW **98** modestly priced chard. (70% oak chip-fermented), sémillon blend, with character. Zesty lemon-lime, butterscotch-toasty tail, briskly dry. Versatile with food. Value at ± R10 ex-cellar. **Chenin Blanc** (wooded) NEW **97** powerfully oaked (8 months 100% new French barrel-fermented/matured). Challengingly toasty, fruit barely peeking through when tasted young. **Chenin Blanc** (unwooded) **98** brisk, clean, from dryland bushvines. Agreeable quaffing. Swartland-picnic fare. **95 VG. Late Harvest** NV Clean, crisp semi-sweet white, from chenin. 22 gms/l sugar, 11% alc. **Anaïs** ◀ NEW **98** attractive, easy-quaffing semi-sweet hanepoot/chenin, fermented separately "to capture best qualities of each", then blended. Bowl of tropical fruit, fresh mango. Finishes drier than 20 gms/l sugar would suggest. Nice début. **Hanepoot Jerepigo** NV orange-gold dessert, very ripe fruit, penetrating sweetness. **Red Jerepigo** NV step up on white version above. Attractive dried-fruit, muscat scents, lively palate, clean finish. **Brut** NV carbonated dry sparkler from sauvignon blanc. **Vin Doux** NV sweet effervescent sauvignon blanc. **Port 97** (vat sample) relaxed raisin, Xmas pudding, gentle spririty glow. 6 months used barriques. One for the backpack.

RIETVALLEI ESTATE

Robertson See Robertson map

Winemaker: Johnny Burger
Vineyards: 172 ha.
P.O. Box 386, Robertson 6705
Tel: 02351-3596 **Fax:** 02351-4514

★★★ **Chardonnay 97** has lost the first flush of youth, developed gentle, most agreeable honey-citrus tones. Half barrel-fermented with malo, half in tank without malo. Best young.

★★★★ **Rooi Muscadel** ◀ **97** labelled simply "Estate Muscadel" but definitely "Rooi" in colour: light coppery orange; open, fragrant musky nose, delicious peppery flavour, spirity clean finish. Elegant, 200 gms/l sugar lifted by gentle acidity.

RIJCKSHOF WINES See Kango Co-operative

ROBERT'S ROCK See KWV International

ROBERTSON WINERY

Robertson See Robertson map

Tastings/sales Mon-Thur 8-5. Fri 8-4.30. Sat 9-1. Cellar tours by appointment, small wine museum.
Owners: 41 members
General Manager: Bowen Botha
Production Manager: Lolly Louwrens
Winemaker: Francois Weich (since 1997)
Assistant Winemaker: Eduard Malherbe (since 1996)
Production: 23 600 tons. **Vineyards:** 1 400 ha.
P.O. Box 37, Robertson 6705
Tel: 02351-3059 **Fax:** 02351-2926
E-mail: robkoop@iafrica.com

New in this energetic winery's wide, well-priced range is a duo of limited-edition Reserves, **Cabernet Sauvignon, Chardonnay** (a reserve **Sauvignon Blanc** is in the pipeline), displaying the familiar house style of relaxed, jeans-and-T-shirt quaffability, tweaked with a little spit-and-polish to further sharpen the image. Easy, earlier drinking and value for money remain the chief targets for this slick, market-savvy operation, with Bowen Botha, experienced GM and former winemaker, and a go-getting team testing new methods—night-harvesting of sauvignon, for example—to fine-tune the consumer-friendly formula. International input has left a huge imprint here, through the Pernod-Ricard Long Mountain connection and, as again recently, overseas sorties. Botha, visiting Italy, homed in on red wine-making (an own custom-built red-wine cellar is a goal); production supremo Lolly Louwrens, in New Zealand during the crush, gleaned tips on how better to handle sauvignon.

*** **Cabernet Sauvignon Reserve** ☺ ◀ NEW **97** velvety, delicious ripe berry-fruit basket, some attractive mushrooms, good balance; drinks well now but could stick around for a while: super-quaffer with ageing potential. 13% alc. **98** should drink from early 1999; fuller, bit more serious than **97**; toasted hazelnuts in background.

*** **Rheingold Special Late Harvest** ◀ Consistent semi-sweet, 100% gewürz. in very pleasing rose-scented **98**, with all-important botrytis enhancement. Concentrated, luscious, 47,5 gms/l sugar contained by honeyed persistence. Light-toned/bodied (11% alc.), versatility/complexity for lightly chilled aperitif, dessert accompaniment, sipping solo on a rainy day.

Cabernet Sauvignon ◀ **98** light raspberry wafts, some cassis; soft mulberries on palate, pleasant weight (13,5% alc. not intrusive), mere suggestion of tannin. Swiggability boosted by 3,8 gms/l sugar. **Merlot** Intense but presently closed **98** needs bit of time to show off soft plummy fruit, velvety texture. Earlier drinking style, enhanced by touch sugar (4 gms/l). Lightly oaked. Watch 14% alc. **Chardonnay Reserve** NEW **97** delicate citrus timbre, gooseberries playing in background, buttery texture, crisp, alc. 13%. Best young. "Standard" **Chardonnay** ◀ Hits the right notes in **98**: gently tangy citrus fruit, vanilla warmth, buttery richness, crisp finish, length. Oak-fermented, *sur lie* 2 mths, alc. 13%. **Colombard-Chardonnay** ◀ **98** most agreeable guava/citrus combination, broad palate, quite fat chard. presence, has complexity/structure to develop for yr or 2. Medium-bodied, easy-drinking. **Robertson White 98** honest, everyday white, lowish alc. (11,5%), off-dry. **Beaukett 98** delicate muscat scents, slightly spicy undertones. Very smooth, persistent, semi-sweet white. **Late Harvest** Untasted for this ed. Pvs. refreshing, light-bodied; colombard. **Santino Spumanté** Uncomplicated sweet frothy fizz. Carbonated. 1,5 l also available.

Following under WIDE RIVER label:
Merlot 97 slim-line version of variety: useful plummy fruit, mulberry-pie finish. Effect overall quite up-tight (contrast to rest of laid-back range) but not unattractive. 13% alc. **Pinotage** Unwooded, dark-hued **97** getting tad tired. **Ruby Cabernet** ☺ Chipper, cheery **98** all fleshy crushed dark berries; brush of tannin, youthful juicy glugging. Not insubstantial alc.: 13%. Drink young. **Sauvignon Blanc** Light-bodied **98** follows unshowy gooseberry/nettly style of pvs.; gentle tropical flavours, nice fruit/acid balance, grain sugar fills out palate. Easy quaffer. Partly night harvested, reductively made. Big seller. **Colombard** Classic Robertson fresh-guava colombard tang in **98**, fairly delicate flavour, fullish palate, dry.
Muscadel fairground-sweets character, lightish palate weight for style, 17% alc., 224 gms/l sugar. Mail-order club value-pick.
Following under SILVERSANDS label: (in conjunction with Vinimark): **Chardonnay 98** light citrus tones, delicate dry palate, crisp, alc. 13%. Undemanding quaffing.
ROBERTSON VINIPAK range: All ◀ Dry Red Berry, tangy herbs nose; juicily smooth palate. No-frills drinkability. **Dry White** Viscous texture, low acidity; fragrant floral/tropical hints. **Stein** Soft honeyed notes, manageable sweetness, clean. **Late Harvest** Ripe banana, fruit-salad flavours, mild sweetness. Unpretentious sipping.
See also **ROB ROY** range.

ROB ROY — 5 l range from Robertson Winery

Grand Crû Mouthfilling, smooth-textured, fruity dry white; tropical fruit salad character. **Selected Stein** Quaffable sweetish white; juicy palate, honeyed tail. **Late Harvest** Ripe tropical fruit persistence; easy, semi-sweet white.

ROCK RIDGE — See Vinfruco

ROMANSRIVIER WINERY

Wolseley — See Worcester map

Tastings/sales Mon-Fri 8-5. Sat 8.30-11.30. Cellar tours by appointment, conference/catering facilities.
Owners: 46 members
Winemaker: Albie Treurnicht (since 1998). **Viticulturist:** Hanno van Schalkwyk (KWV)
Production: 7 300 tons. **Vineyards:** 631 ha.
P.O. Box 108, Wolseley 6830
Tel: 0236-311070 **Fax:** 0236-311102

Radical recent changes in the approach of modern Cape co-ops are well illustrated at this energetic winery near mountain-ringed Wolseley. Locking sights on the fine-wine market, the members are spending some R3 million on a sweeping revamp, planting premium varieties, specifically merlot, shiraz; implementing plans "to raise the added-value portion, make us less dependent on wholesalers"; upgrading workers' skills, introducing principles of participative management—all at once! Little wonder that Albie Treurnicht, who handled his first harvest here in 1998, describes it as "the crush of a lifetime that I never want again!" Not that future vintages look any quieter: this painstaking winery—quality packaging; consumer-friendly labels; visitor facilities catering for the handicapped, excellent pricing are hallmarks—is one of the Cape's rising stars.

*** **Cabernet Sauvignon** ◀ **96** quality—and value!—red from its oaking to its minerally/berry/crushed black pepper character, long reach. Good drinking now (soft tannins), but shouldn't come to any harm in next 2-4 years. Snip at R16 a bottle.

*** **De Kijker Pinotage** ☺ ◀ **97** fresh breeze of plums, prunes, infused with Karoo scrub, disciplined tannins. Very nice! From 33-year-old v'yd. 15% barrel-fermented. De Kijker (look-out) a nearby landmark.

*** **Koelfontein Merlot 97** ◀ winery's first merlot and a real plum (mulberry, actually—ripe one at that), good concentration, chocolate, vanilla notes, firm tannin so wait 2-4 years or drink with rustic cuisine. Gold on young wine show. 13,5% alc.

*** **Ceres Chardonnay** ◀ **97** very nice indeed, pawpaw/passion-fruit over smoky oak, succulent mouth-feel, vanilla/light-marmalade to end. In similar mould is the "standard" **Chardonnay 97** (also called "Waverley'), featuring fresh (and dried) peach flavours, attractive sweet-sour finish, butterscotch notes. Both French barrel-fermented, matured (but Ceres version comes from mountain v'yd, ripening, picked" full month later—April 2, 1997). R13 each ex-cellar. Probably for early drinking.

**** **Koelfontein Chardonnay Noble Late Harvest** NEW **97** absolutely stunning late autumn-picked (April 4), botrytis-brushed dessert. Buttercup yellow, attractive lemon/lime sheen; huge complexity: peach, prune, mango, freshly picked dates, almond undertones, some vanilla-spice; silky texture braced by tingly acid, gentle tannic embrace; long zesty finish. Beautiful wine. Not filtered/stabilised (so may throw sediment). 117 gms/l sugar, 7,4 gms/l acid, 13% alc.

Vino Rood ☺ ◀ NV Current (**97**) charming quaffer, lots of ripe strawberries, plums, lightly wooded, fresh. Med.-bodied, perfect braai mate. Cinsaut/ruby cab. R12 a bottle. **Mosterthoek Sauvignon Blanc 98** single v'yd block, green-figgy/grassy, crisp, dry, attractive. Drink soon. 13% alc. **Grand Crû 98** amiable guava/green-apple flavoured easy/early quaffer, crisp, gently dry. Colombard/riesling. **Chenin Blanc 97** relaxing into middle age. **Ceres Colombard Off-dry** ☺ ◀ **98** distinctive guava flavour, lemon flashes, rounded by 10,5 gms/l sugar, delicious, gulpable, ± R8 a bottle. **Ceres Vin Blanc** ☺ ◀ **98** seductive early/easy drinker, guava-sweet, some mango scents, lemony brightness in finish. Winery's bread and butter, easy to see why. From colombard.

Grand Crû, Late Harvest also in 5 l boxes.

ROODENDAL SFW

*** **Cabernet Sauvignon** Current **95** gorgeous berry concentration, nice grassy touches. Tannins loosening, lovely rounded fruit, delicious mouthful. Small proportion oaked. Lighter, fruitier style, usually bottled in "odd" years; ready on release.

ROODEZANDT CO-OPERATIVE

Robertson See Robertson map

Tastings/sales Mon-Fri 8-5.30; 2-5.30, Sat 9-12.30. Cellar tours by appointment.

Owners: 63 members

Winemaker: Christie Steytler (since 1980), Hugo Lambrechts (since 1997)

General Manager: Abé Rossouw

Production: 25 000 cases. **Vineyards:** 1 400 ha.

P.O. Box 164, Robertson 6705

Tel: 02351-61160 **Fax:** 02321-5074

E-mail: roodez@mweb.co.za

What this scenically-challenged cellar at Robertson lacks in visual appeal—it's in the town's industrial precinct, next door to another factory-like operation, Robertson Winery—is more than offset by the engaging charm, consumer-friendliness of its range. And, one might add, its go-get-'em approach epitomised by GM Abé Rossouw and winemaker Christie Steytler. The seasoned cellarmaster, in line for the proverbial gold watch in 2000 after 20 years' service, is working hand-in-secateurs with technical advisers to spur members towards establishing premium varieties, specially reds. "We're determined to put Robertson on the map."

**** **Rooi Muscadel** ◀ NV Christie Steytler's red "sticky", usually a delight, scales new heights in current release (**97**). Pretty copper-toned colour introduces lush, smooth-textured dessert bursting with perfumed muscat fruit. Fresh acid lifts substantial ± 240 gms/l sugar, lends delicious crispness. A snip at ± R11 ex-cellar, as is white housemate below. **98** (tank sample tasted) bit paler than pvs., no less fine.

**** **Wit Muscadel** ◀ Traditional Cape dessert in practised hands here, regular show winner. **97** enchanting buttercup yellow, full, unctuous on palate, sweet but not cloying. Fresh grapey flavours livened by very attractive spirity oomph. "Best since 86" says winemaker. **98** (***) marginally lighter, not quite as much pizzazz. **96** lighter-textured, charming honeysuckle flavours/scents.

Cabernet Sauvignon 97 sports some really appealing ripe strawberry/raspberry flavours. Mineral-oak nose, abundant (but soft) tannins. Yr in 300-litre new/used French barrels. Food partner. 13% alc. **96 VG**. **Keizer's Creek** NV unwooded ruby cab./merlot/tinta barocca. Latest release (**98**) reverts to easy-going, early-drinking style. Ripe mulberries, pleasant tinta earthiness. **Chardonnay 98** a pleasant everyday chard. Not madly complex, but with fresh melon, intriguing smoky hints; unwooded. Drink in year of vintage. **Colombard-Chardonnay** For Tesco, UK, with cheerful zebra label. **98** guava-driven, vanilla-accented (though unwooded), fresh, dry. Amiable tablemate. **Colombard 98** uncharacteristically light-bodied at 11,7% alc., pvs. around 13%. Touch of guava, carnation; fresh, dry. Restrained style, grapes as always from Le Chasseur area. Drink soon. **Sauvignon Blanc** ◀ **98** (tank sample) rather nice: gooseberry/nettle, zesty, clean dry finish. Seems like amendable fish, salad partner. Unwooded, best young. **Vino Zante** NV (500 ml screw top) wears one of jolliest labels around. Crisp, just off-dry, 11,5% alc. 60% colombard, sauvignon blanc. **Late Harvest** NV current release (**98**) from muscat, chenin blanc; semi-sweet, lowish alc., foursquare. **Special Late Harvest** Winery's best seller. **98** fairly straightforward but with carefree sweet-muscat perfume. Low 10,5% alc. enhances quaffability. 45 gms/l sugar. **Sparkling Brut** NV Explosively fizzy, dry, carbonated, sauvignon blanc. **Sparkling Demi Sec** ☺ ◀ NV Different league to dry version above. Fresh, amicable muscatty sparkler, technically semi-sweet at 45 gms/l sugar but very clean, surprisingly crisp. Light 10% alc. Carbonated. **Port 98** though vintage dated, in ruby rather than vintage style. Light, very palatable, earthy toffee-butter essences. Wood-fermented/aged ruby cab., fortified with 3-year-old brandy spirit. First since **91**, which from tinta, merlot, ruby cabernet.

ROOIBERG WINERY

Robertson See Robertson map

Open weekdays 8-5.30, Sat 8-1. Cellar tours by appointment.

Guest cottages available. Farmstall and restaurant.

Chief Executive Officer: Johan du Preez

Owners: 34 members
Production Manager/Winemaker: Tommy Loftus (since 1990)
Production: 15 000 tons. **Vineyards:** 1 400 ha.
P.O. Box 358, Robertson 6705
Tel: 02351-61663 **Fax:** 02351-3295
E-mail: rooiberg@iafrica.com
Internet: www.interads,co.za/rooiberg/index.htm

With a palette of 35 cultivars, winemaker Tommy Loftus and his viticulturist Leon Dippenaar have their hands full. "It really gets right down to the vines, the grapes, the vineyards", enthuses the energetic Loftus. "But you've got to plant the right varieties in the right spots. We've been lucky having input from Phil Freese (Californian consultant viticulturist), who has taught some of our members plenty." A vicious frost lopped 3 000 tons off the 1998 vintage, but quality was excellent. A huge new Pera press with a capacity of 30 tons complements the cellar upgrade of the previous year; there have been significant plantings of reds, including cabernet sauvignon, merlot, and the shiraz which Loftus feels is particularly suited to the area, boosting the red-to-white ratio in line with requirements of major clients such as Woolworths.

*** **Cabernet Sauvignon ◀ 96** whiffs of green olives, cedar-wood; a zippy, modern-style cab. for easy, joyful drinking. **90 VG** still impressive, shows age well, with complex wafts of tea-leaves, dried fruits. Drink if you have.

*** **Shiraz ◀ 96** dense, smoky, peppery aromas; a Rhône look-alike. Tangy prune flavours, just a touch of sweet oak.

*** **Roodewyn ◀ 95** cabernet sauvignon, pinotage & merlot, ageing in style: brambly fruit, supple juicy flavours, backed by French oak.

*** **Colombard** ☺ **◀ 98** delicious, supple peach and guava-laden, semi-sweet (11,8 gms/l sugar). Regularly one of the best on the block in an area of stiff competition. **94** VVG. Amazing value.

**** **Rooi Jerepiko ◀ 96** one of the most decorated SA dessert wines around, this vintage set to elongate the swathe of **VVG** medals garnered since 91. Like drinking rich red velvet curtains, loaded with plums, chocolate and coffee flavours: a classic. Alc. 18,4%, made from pinotage.

*** **Ruby Port ◀ 95** not kow-towing to traditionalists, made from "non-Port" varieties pinotage and ruby cabernet. Consistent award winner, sweet earthy, gamey aromas, leading to classic fruitcake flavours, solid, spirited grip. **97** picked up SA young wine show classwinner laurels. **96** VG. **95** SA champion, VVG.

Pinotage 96 a modern style, supple, juicy. **95** lots of rich ripe plum, also fat, drinkable. ABSA Pinotage Top Ten. **Selected Red NV** youthful Chianti-style blend—usual cocktail inc. pinotage, ruby cabernet, shiraz, cinsaut. **Sauvignon Blanc 98** stylish, flinty, dry, with herby aromas. 94 **WINE******. **Cape Riesling** Time in bottle adds secondary flavours to **97**—but best young. **Premier Grand Crû** bone-dry cocktail of 5 varieties, most popular seller. **Chardonnay 97** with citrus, vanilla/barley sugar notes, now acquiring bottle-aged flavours; unwooded. **Rhine Riesling** Extra year in bottle fills out floral, off-dry flavours of **97**. **Bukettraube 98** grapey, mown-hay aromas, supple, semi-sweet: summer swimming pool quaffer. **Special Late Harvest 98** from chenin blanc: cream and custard aromas, light, sweet nectar character. (46 gms/l sugar.)

Rooi Muskadel 96 topaz-ruby, full-sweet, raisiny palate-coater: candied citrus, apricots, jasmine. **Brut Sparkling Wine NV** finely carbonated dry bubbly from chardonnay, sauvignon blanc. Pear, floral aromas—at the sweeter end of the brut scale. **Vin Doux Sparkling Wine NV** from 40% gewürz., 60% chenin blanc. Carbonated, 57 gms/l sugar, rose-garden nose.

Flamingo Vin NV ◀ coppery-pink sweet, "festive" muscadel-based bubbly.

ROOSENVELDT

See La Motte

ROSENBURG

See Uiterwyk

ROSEVALE

See Vinfruco

ROZENDAL FARM

Jonkershoek, Stellenbosch See Stellenbosch map

Tastings/sales, cellar tours by appointment.
Restaurant: Lunch & dinner (and accommodation) by arrangement.
Owner/Winemaker: Kurt Amman (since 1983)
Production: 3 000 cases. **Vineyards:** 7 ha.
Address: Omega Road, Stellenbosch 7600
Tel: 021-8838737 **Fax:** 021-8838738

Were it ever to be published, the book on Kurt Amman's approach to his craft might well be titled "Zen and the Art of Winegrowing". Ensconced in his boutique winery-cum-upper-crust auberge at Stellenbosch, the creator of Rozendal, one of the Cape's top rated Bordeaux-style blends has distinctly alternative, almost mystical—certainly intensely personal—views on winemaking. He's loath, for example, to reveal the varietal ratio of the blend—he doesn't want tasters/consumers to harbour preconceptions about his wine: "What does it matter if there is X-percent merlot or Y-percent cabernet? This is not important. What matters is that the wine must taste good." His wine-growing philosophy, zen-like in apparent simplicity, is: "We make wine as naturally as possible."

★★★★ **Rozendal 96** reveals itself in waves of seamless aromas—ripe black plums, cherries, vanilla-pod, hints of green stalk, dried leaves; on palate: silky-textured sweet-oaky fruit, well-worn leather, tobacco leaf, gentle mineral threads. Elegance, balance are hallmarks—nothing shouts (or whispers). Ripe fruit/tannins should carry to 2004 and beyond. 13% alc. **95 (WINE★★★★)** also very good, distinctive—among best of vintage. Pvs. often long-lived, **83** still a stunner; as are **86, 90, 94**.

Distillery: Open for tastings/sales by appointment. Tel: 021-8839307, Fax: 021-8872216. Helmut Wildever's products include marcs from chardonnay, gewürz, tinta barocca, muscat d'Alexandrie.

RUDMAN'S PORT

Rudman's Cape Tawny, chiefly from tinta barocca, blend of different vintages, average age 10-20 years; released late 1998 (untasted). "Livelier style than traditional SA tawnies," says supercharged, peripatetic port/cigar devotee and walking encyclopaedia, Theo Rudman, author of an internationally acclaimed cigar guide-book. Far-flung Rudman, habitually interfacing/networking via answering machine, in 1998 hit the OpryLand Hotel & Expo Centre, Nashville, Tennessee for the Retail Tobacco Association's *smoke-a-thon*-cum-trade faire; then hitched a lift in a zillion-dollar private jet to view Mexico's # 1 tobacco baron's eye-popping agricultural holdings in the lush San Andrés Valley near Veracruz. Somehow he found time to blend this Cape Tawny which, he says, still has "a fiery glow" despite its relatively advanced years.

Theo Rudman, Tel/Fax: 021-8553470

RUITERSVLEI ESTATE

Paarl See Paarl map

Tastings/sales Mon-Fri 8.30-5.30, Sat 9-2. Guest-house.
Lunch, tea, dinner 7 days a week. Belgian cuisine from Nov 98.
Owner: Faure Holdings (Pty) Ltd (John Faure)
Winemaker: Frank Meaker (since 1996)
Production: 50 000 tons. **Vineyards:** 280 ha.
P.O. Box 532, Suider-Paarl 7624
Tel: 021-8631517 **Fax:** 021-8631443

"Assertive, distinctive, some excellent reds in particular." Our taster really liked Ruitersvlei's unabashedly bold, often value-priced wines, made by high-octane cellarmaster Frank Meaker, who moved to this family-run estate behind Paarl mountain in 1996 after stints with Bergkelder, L'Ormarins, Trawal locally, and a sojourn in California. (He also makes the De Villiers marque and other ranges.) Meaker's leanings towards an upfront style doubtless were affirmed during a tour of Australia in 1998; but what made a more powerful impression was the Aussies' "mind-set of quality winemaking".

**** **Cabernet Sauvignon Reserve 97** big in all respects, deep purple colour, intense cassis/vanilla bouquet; ripe black fruits on palate; fairly suple tannin, approachable, contrast to **96** which sterner, less accessible. Both need time to soften, fill out. 13,2% alc. 15% American oak, used barrels, 1 yr, low-yield (3,5 tons/ha.) vineyard selection. **96** similar style, greater percentage new wood. Losing early gawkiness, harmony starting to emerge but needs more time. Taste again in 2 yrs.

**** **Merlot Reserve** NEW **97**, with soupçon merlot from **98** vintage, ripe with promise. Remarkable colour/fruit concentration, complexity; wide body, dollop ripe plums, sweet-cedary oak, coating of choc/mint, dark-roast coffee brewing in finish. Ripe tannins augur admirable future. Alc. 13,2%.

*** **Special Late Harvest** ◀ **98** tasted young, a peaches-and-cream delight from chenin. Interesting fresh *and* dried fruit inflections, ultra-smooth texture, non-unctuous lemon-zesty finish. Versatile; one possibility: elevenses with lemon-meringue tart.

*** **Paarl Riesling** ◀ Frank Meaker generally coaxes something special from this usually rather dull variety; **98** no exception. Earth-toned, thatchy, lots of refreshing off-dry sweet-sour fruit flavours. Natural light pasta, seafood companion. One of Cape's better examples.

Cabernet Sauvignon 97 (nudging ***) has markedly less presence, complexity than Reserve above, though most pleasant in own right; cassis, springling cinnamon, very dry tannin. Exported to UK, also available from farm. 13% alc. **96** gold/classwinner at Paarl young wine show.

Cinsaut/Cabernet Sauvignon ☺ ◀ **97** quaffable, but more complexity than average everyday swigger. Lightish blend (though this is relative: 13% alc.), 70% cinsaut gives sweetish, friendly dimension to cherry, strawberry fruitiness. Nice savoury flavours make it a "foodie". Snapped up by Gall & Gall, Netherlands. **John Faure Cabernet-Shiraz** NEW **97** another for current drinking, exclusive to Oddbins, UK. Brash, peppery, heaps of ripe raspberry. Rather nice. Sturdy tannin chassis, so food is recommended. **Mountainside Red** NEW **97** tinta, ruby cab., carignan, cinsaut. Winemaker covers all bases: "Pot-luck wine with easy-drinking complexities." We'd add: best lightly chilled. Alc. 13%. **Chardonnay Reserve 98** infant tank sample difficult to assess, as was pvs. Winemaker's note: "Still early days but tremendous potential". Some lime pointers, soft vanilla backdrop, dry, firm finish. 100% barrel-fermented, malo complete. Alc. 13,5%. **97** more subdued, dusty oak overtone, lightish marmalade flavours. **Sauvignon Blanc (Blanc Fumé)** ◀ Mount Nelson's housewine. **97** lightly wooded, striking nettly/fresh-baked-bread ambiance; categorically dry, assertive, so menu, please. Alc. 13%. **Sauvignon Blanc-Chenin Blanc** ☺ NEW **98** fresh fruit-salad featuring apple, pineapple, unusual scattering dried figs, lightly wooded. summer quaffing (with caveat: alc. 13%). **Bush Vine Chenin Blanc NEW 98** decidedly diferent sort of chenin: sweet-sour, citrus-toned (mainly lemon), probably good with Malaysian/Thai cuisine, dry; for Makro. "Our bush vines retained freshness despite heatwave," winemaker notes. Lowish 11,7% alc. **Chenin Blanc Reserve** ◀ In pvs edition we ventured **97** "could turn out rather well". Indeed it's still on the up, having developed warm hay-thatch aromas offset by tangy lemon grass. Oyster-dry finish. Partly barrel-fermented (10%, through malo), rest fermented on wood chips; on lees 3 mths. One to watch. Alc. 13% **Chenin-Chardonnay 98** went holus-bolus to UK. 70/30 dry blend, limes, smoky oak, velvety texture, crisply citric finish; agreeable but not air-headish: potential to develop. **Mountainside White** NEW NV sedate, easy off-dry Cape riesling/chenin blend, attractive hay, beeswax hints.

RUSTENBERG

Stellenbosch See Stellenbosch map

Visits: Open weekdays 9-4.30, Sat 9-12.30.
Bring your own picnics; tables and chairs provided under the oaks.
Owner: Simon Barlow
Winemaker: Rod Easthope (since 1996)
Vineyards: Kevin Watt
Marketing: Dave Hutton
Production: 65 ha. under vines at Rustenberg, 45 ha. at Nooitgedacht (Helderberg); 30 000 cases from 450 tons
P.O. Box 33, Stellenbosch 7599
Tel: 021-8873153 **Fax:** 021-8878466
E-mail: wine@rustenberg.co.za

"When it's dry it's dust and when it's wet, it's mud!" says Simon Barlow, happily tramping through the chaos created during rebuilding of the Rustenberg wine cellar. Not only bricks and mortar, but rebuilding the image, the sales plan and the workforce: reconstruction and development—redefinition all round—is on the go at this classic, deeply historic property. Barlow describes the process, in capital letters as a TOTAL concept: vineyards cellar and, marketing. "We are *totally* committed, the *whole* gambit. "The full Monty?" we ask. "If necessary we'll do that, too" he says, with a roar of laughter from the all-male team. "We will even deliver bottles late at night when our restaurant customers run out, *and* we're having fun doing it!"

The rustic feel of the place is to be carefully maintained; it is, after all, a working farm with a large dairy herd, plum and citrus orchards and now a trout farm, run entirely by staff under an empowerment scheme. Ongoing training embraces all areas of farming and estate management and has already reaped handsome rewards in terms of career development. Responsibility and answerability are important components of this process, the next stage will see managerial appointments from within the workforce. "Sustainability" is the keyword, Barlow believes.

Vineyard material is being imported from France and includes some exciting additions: shiraz, viognier, grenache, rousanne, marsanne, mourvèdre and newer clones of chardonnay. "Had to write a tome to get the vines in," says winemaker Rod Easthope, a transplanted New Zealander who's flourishing in these Simonsberg soils.

The three-tier plan has been tidied: Rustenberg has been de-classified as an estate, thus allowing white wines under last year's proposed Barlow Vineyards label to be integrated instead into the Rustenberg range. Grapes for these come from Barlow's farm Nooitgedacht, high on the Helderberg, a perfect climate for whites. The Brampton range emphasises up-front fruit (priced to sell below R30), Rustenberg is now the label for a premium range with Stellenbosch regional character (around R60-R70). Super premium Rustenberg single vineyard wines, one red, one white, made as purest expression of terroir (prices around R100) complete the trilogy.

**** **Rustenberg 96** sees return of this classic after two years' absence. Now bottled and final blend 70% cab. sauvignon, 15% merlot, 15% cab. franc. Less showy than Bramptons, restraint and breed of a true classic. Cassis-scented fruit, ripeness tempered by cedarwood overlay, the palate a revelation of how opulence can be disciplined by fine oak: 18 months in French, mainly Nevers, 50% new. Many-layered complexity, will need time: violets, berries persist in farewell. Released October 98, 5 000 cases.

***** **Peter Barlow**, present owner Simon Barlow's tribute to his late father who set unprecedented standards for the winery back in the 40s. First **96**, 100% cabernet sauvignon, from special portion of single vineyard. Already complex aromas of cassis and forest fruits, hints of cedar and violets recall the splendid **82** cab. Sweet-tempered dark-berried fruit gently supported by oak, fine-grained tannins make for deceptively easy drinking; epitome of fine Cape claret. Only 100 cases, release October 98, strictly on allocation.

**** **Rustenberg Stellenbosch Chardonnay 98** boldly scented and flavoured to match, ripe lemons and loads of toast. Opulent, dense fruit very showy in barrel sample; after polishing and finishing should recede to quieter brilliance. Assertive, confident style which reflects cool Helderberg terroir. Due for release Jan 99.

**** **Five Soldiers Chardonnay** NEW Named after five tall stone pines guarding the vineyard; **97** a study in understatement and subtlety, nudging *****. Repeating a Rustenberg tradition, fermented on natural yeasts, but all new oak (Dargaud Jaegle) for 12 months. Aromas of lemon peel and citrus blossom with touch of honeycomb translate easily onto palate. Tight, fine-grained citrusy fruit wrapped around steely, minerally core a reflection of Easthope's admiration for Puligny-Montrachet. Suggest leave in large red wine glass for 30 minutes for full flavour development.

**** **Q.F.1** NEW Fully botrytised **97** chardonnay ineligible for certification "due to Kiwi ignorance" confesses Easthope. A recent arrival, he was unaware of the Wine and Spirit Board's requirements but delivers the goods in terms of taste. Gorgeous ripe marmalade and fresh citrus play hide and seek on palate, rich and weighty but not oversweet at 130 gms/l. Named because of the Friday afternoon dash into the cellar for a "quick fix" after the week's work!

BRAMPTON wines: Good value label, flamboyant whites, fleshy reds; the focus firmly on varietal fruit.

*** **Old Vines Red** ◀ **97** NEW to range, 86% blend cab./merlot, balance red allsorts from farm, mainly from vines 25-30 years old. Full blast cab. grass/herbs palate shows inviting fleshiness, soft tannins, warm spicy undertone recalls Southern France. Good everyday red with style, substance. 10% new oak.

*** **Cabernet-Merlot** ◀ **97** immensely fragrant, wafting cinnamon and vanilla spice with dried herbs, touch of anise. Warm spicy fruit shows slight sweetness of ripe grapes, soft tannins. Gentle, seductive red, high score on hedonistic scale. Lighter, more subtlety than show-off **96**.

★★★★ **Cabernet Sauvignon 95** from top portion of production. Sleek and suave, tough cab. tannins banished forever, this one is plump and juicy showing attractive ripe mulberry fruit concentration. Has not been repeated as future Brampton reds will be blends "unless the wine dictates".

★★★ **Sauvignon Blanc** ☺ **98** full-bodied and ripe, reflects difficult hot vintage, less arresting than **97** (★★★★). Lovely whiffs/flavours of pineapple, tropical fruits, but also fig-leaf and nettles. Well-endowed, with lively acid core. Big wine at 13,8% alc.

★★★★ **Chardonnay** ◀ **97** showy, extrovert style replaces quieter **96**. Flamboyant peachy fruit with good dollop of butterscotch; palate shows more elegance though still generously built. Ripe, curvaceous fruit lifted by fresh acidity which saves it from total over the top exaggeration. On lees for 9 months, 30% barrel-fermented.

★★★ **Port** Brilliantly ruby-hued **94**, blend of 80% souzão, 20% cab. s. Attractive SA-style port, sweet and welcoming, showing some refinement. Smooth fruitcake flavours offset by freshness of cab.

Previous releases: **Rustenberg Cabernet Sauvignon** Over the years, a very individual signature on this prestigious, unblended cabernet. Almost uniquely in Cape, fermented with estate's natural wild yeasts. Many vintages showed tasty delicacy, almost Franco-European savouriness, smell of mushrooms and atmospheric underground cellars cut into the wines' grapiness. Best older vintages: **82**, **84**, both **VVG**—now on wane. Early tastings of **92** showed newer trend with fruitier emphasis, powerful fruit. These had less new oak than usually weightier **Rustenberg Gold**, B'deaux blend of about 50% cabernet s., 30% merlot, 20% cabernet f. **91 VG** elegant, sweet mulberry/plum flavours. **Pinot Noir**, usually quite lightly, old barrel-oaked, individual, varying from pleasantly organic (**92 WINE**★★★★) to some ripe vinosity (**93**). From old BK5 clone. **Rustenberg Dry Red** Famous name in Cape wine, often with nutty sweetness, more recently merlot ripeness. Formerly two-thirds cab., one-third cinsaut, harvested, crushed together. Now due for overhaul and newer cooperage from **96**. (Untasted.)

RUST EN VREDE ESTATE

Stellenbosch See Stellenbosch map

Open weekdays tasting & sales 8.30-4.30, Sat 9.30-1.
Owner: Jannie Engelbrecht
Winemaker: To be appointed
Production: 12 000 cases. **Vineyards:** 30 ha.
P.O. Box 473, Stellenbosch 7599
Tel: 021-8813881 **Fax:** 021-8813000

"When I first moved to Rust en Vrede I didn't want an office because I was farming," says Jannie Engelbrecht, rugby hero in his day, far-sighted entrepreneur, and proprietor of one of the Cape's blue-chip wine estates. "Now I need an office with all modern communication equipment, computer to farm, plus an understanding bank!" says the man who's overseen sweeping developments in the past year, including massive replanting of v'yds, construction of an underground cellar and offices. The extension was to have been for dry stores and packaging, but with the departure of long-time winemaker Kevin Arnold to embark on a solo venture, Engelbrecht did a "deep and serious" rethink, deciding to return to his former policy of using only new oak for maturation. "We did that for 10 years and got rave reviews. I'm confident this will again be the case." So—enter understanding bank manager—some 700 new barrels, mainly French, were purchased and duly delivered—at which point the new cellar underwent a dramatic function-change: now it's the maturation hall, stocked with more than 1 400 barrels (numbers will reduce as used barriques are sold off). A further Engelbrecht resolution has been to speed up replanting with virus-free vines to boost quality (and, not insignificantly, income). To date new clones have upped R&V's production from 12 000 to 18 000 cases; this will top at around 24 000.

★★★★ **Rust-en-Vrede Estate Wine** Authentic, arresting, appropriately Cape blend—dominated by cabernet sauvignon and estate's impressive shiraz. **95** smoky, oaky, red cherry bouquet. All repeated, in abundance, on fresh lively palate. Never a heavyweight but beautifully stylish and elegant. Long clean finish. 12,6% alc. **96** real knock-out stuff, especially in handsome bottle. (Tall and racy like Jannie E.) Deep purple-red. Massively rich aromas with an array of ripe cherry and blackberry fruit, spice, vanilla. Palate packed with these flavours too—deeply concentrated. Super vinosity. Almost explosively mouthfilling. After the fruit comes spice, green leaf, bitter chocolate, and a fine tannin surround. Great now but has plenty of potential to improve (to ★★★★★?) over 5/8 years. **93 VVG, 94 VG.**

★★★★ **Shiraz** Surprisingly powerful **95** bouquet with smoky, cherry, tea-leaf notes, bit of earth and hint of mint. Power carries to the palate with minty, berry fruit, ripe plum, clean persistent tannins. 12,5% alc. **96**★★★★ wow, what a wine! Embryonic ★★★★★. Deep mulberry colour. Fresh ground black pepper and green pepper on nose followed by lots of cherry, ripe plum. Palate packed with berry, plum, blackberry fruits, hint of Karoo bos and spicy, toasty oak. Soft persistent tannins, beautifully integrated oak. Good to drink now but with lots of development potential over next 5/8 years.

★★★★ **Cabernet Sauvignon 95** offers intense blackberry, redcurrant, mint aromas, with touch of eucalypt. All reverberate on the palate, where some dry herby character also shows. Elegant, a bit restrained now, should develop with benefit over next 2/4 years.

★★★★ **Merlot** Violets, mulberries and mint on **96** nose, light, refined and elegant. Long, fresh finish.

★★★ **Tinta Barocca** ☺ Soft, easy, juicy drinking in **97** but full of almost cheeky character. Succulent. Lots of small berry fruit. In limited supply, probably because it is Jannie Engelbrecht's own favourite everyday drink!

RUSTHOF WINES See Mooiuitsig

RYLANDS GROVE See IWS

SABLE VIEW SFW

★★★ **Cabernet Sauvignon 96**, generously fruity though still compact, dry; some sleekness from large oak.

★★★ **Chardonnay** Lightish style, lively lime and peach flavours in **97**, longish finish. 20% barrel-fermented.

Pinotage 96 unadorned pinotage; delicious ripe plum flavours, though not sweet, dry ripe tannins. Unoaked. **Sauvignon Blanc** Aromas of **97** now less forthcoming, still good honest sauvignon cut-grass/green pepper flavour. Smooth acid, gently dry. **Muscat d'Alexandrie**, made specifically for Asian markets. Grapey, fruity aromas, very showy. Semi-sweet at 30 gms/l. Good value export range.

SAFEWAY

See IWS and Cape Wine Cellars

SAINSBURY

See Vinfruco

SAVANHA

See Berg & Brook Vineyards

SAVISA

See Sonop

SA WINE CELLARS

Newly-formed (May 1998) sales and distribution company within Distillers Corporation. Handles the wines of the following producers (each individually listed in this guide): **Alto, Allesverloren, Bergkelder, Drostdy Cellar, Fort Simon, House of J.C. le Roux, Jacobsdal, La Motte, Le Bonheur, L'Ormarins, Meerendal, Meerlust, Middelvlei, Rietvallei, Theuniskraal, Uitkyk.** Most of the above may be visited, and their products tasted and bought on the premises.

Also runs the **Vinoteque** cellaring scheme for buyers purchasing young wine at an annual **Pre-Release** event. It sells a number of select old and rare wines at an annual **Special Release** occasion for the trade. For a moderate fee, these wines can be stored in perfect cellar conditions in Stellenbosch.

Vinoteque Manager: Stuart Buchan
Internet: www.bergkelder.co.za/vinoteq.htm
P.O. Box 184, Stellenbosch 7599
Tel: 021-8883200 **Fax:** 021-8870728
Toll free: 0800-225400

SAXENBURG

Stellenbosch See Stellenbosch map

Tastings/sales Mon-Fri 9-5; Sat 10-5; Nov-Feb Sun 10-4. Tasting fee R1,50 per wine. Cellar tours, special tastings by appointment only.

Guinea Fowl lunch Wed-Mon, dinner Wed-Sat. Closed Tues. See restaurant section.

Owners: Adrian & Birgit Bührer
Winemaker/Vineyards: Nico van der Merwe (since 1991)
Production: 25 000 cases; 20 000 red, 5 000 white. 300 tons.
Vineyards: 80 ha.; 120 ha. eventually
P.O. Box 171, Kuils River 7580
Tel: 021-9036113 **Fax:** 021-9033129
E-mail: Saxfarm@iafrica.com
Web site: users.iafrica.com/s/sa/saxfarm

Haute couture and *prêt-a-porter* are poles of star stylist Nico van der Merwe's range, spanning two hemispheres, widely differing *terroirs* and a colourful rack of varieties. Alternating between Saxenburg and Ch. Capion, the stylish sister estate in up-and-coming Languedoc (both properties are owned by Swiss real-estate tycoon Adrian Bührer and his wife Birgit), sturdy-framed V.d. Merwe says: "Saxenburg is the only SA wine farm operating on two continents with one team without losing out on quality, image or efficiency. I love what I do—it's a wonderful 7-days-a-week job!" All the more so when vintages like 1998 (at Cape) produce reds of "intense colour, substantial alcohol, body and excellent varietal character." These wines, he predicts, "will sit in new wood for ever if selected correctly" and mature beyond the 97s. Since staking claim to star status in sensational fashion by bagging 5 double-gold Veritas medals in 1993, this modest, hard-working winemaker has wowed critics and consumers with a meticulous, often innovative range like the bi-continental blends from the Stellenbosch property and its French twin. New in the range is **Gwendolyn**, a collage of shiraz and cab. sauvignon named after the Bührers' youngest daughter and already a huge hit with customers. "People want new styles, elegance and quality," explains V.d. Merwe. To follow are Franco-Cape combo's laced with trendy varieties such as grenache, marsanne and rousanne.

★★★★ **Private Collection Shiraz** Farm's flagship, SA benchmark distinguished by headily scented dark berries, violets, sun-drenched peppery wild scrub. Since V.d. Merwe's first vintage **91 VVG**, only under premium-quality PC label. **96** ★★★ currently overshadowed by magnificent **95**, but V.d. Merwe predicts it will follow maturity curve of now-ready **92**, which received R208 a bottle at 1998 Nederburg Auction. Ripe, truffly fragrance; American oak sweetness unusually noticeable. Supple, chewy, more open, lighter than most of these burly, warm individuals. **95 WINE**★★★★ (just missed 5★), **SAA. 93 SAA,** only SA wine in US *Wine Spectator* Top 100 list of 1996.

★★★★ **Private Collection Cabernet Sauvignon** Four vintages so far of this much-decorated, rich but defined 100% cabernet. Latest **95 SAA, WINE**★★★★, cassis intensity, expensive oak on finely concentrated nose. Similarly powerful but elegantly proportioned structure: ripe tannins still vibrant, yet to mesh with opulent fruit. Perfectly proportioned to stay course of maturation required. "Drink **96, 94** before this," recommends V.d. Merwe. Doubtless wait will be worthwhile. **94 VG** matured 14 months new Nevers barrels; unfined. No **93**; **92 SAA, WINE**★★★★**, VVG** good oak/fruit balance. **91 VVG** SA champion young red. **Cabernet Sauvignon** Usually more style than quality difference between standard and PC label. Lighter **96** ★★★ exception, Cape traditional nutty, cassis aromas, in quieter, less dense style. Oaking (20% new, all French) does not smother attractive fruit. More complex than other **96** standard reds but shows vintage accessibility. Ready before deliciously long, elegant **95.**

★★★ **Private Collection Merlot** Toasty oak, strength, sophistication than standard bottling. Matured in 100% new French oak. Well-absorbed by lighter-textured **96.** Charming silky feel, sweet red plum flavours. **95** ★★★★ (100% Saxenburg grapes from cooler slopes), **94** both opulent, dense tannin, but not short of finesse. Probable best drinking order: **96, 94, 95. Merlot** (standard) More immediate fruity charm, less complexity than PC; **96** already drinking well; satisfying plummy persistence, rounded dryness, Drink within 2/3 years. Like PC, includes 15% structural cab. s. **94 VVG.**

★★★★ **Private Collection Pinotage 96** possibly most successful in current PC range. Healthily ripe in all respects: ruby colour, mouthfilling tannins, luscious spicy fruit. Delicious but subtle style, well able to handle year in American oak (20% new). **95** richer, more tannic. **SAA, WINE**★★★★.

★★★★ **Gwendolyn** NEW (to this guide) Shiraz/cab. s. blend (55/45), named after Bührers' youngest daughter (blends named after other four Bührer children to follow). Sum greater than parts, esp. in **96;** shiraz offers soft, full texture plus ripe, truffly aromas; cab. s sound framework, complementary spice, cassis fruit. Digestible tannins, elegant drinking. **97** denser, with dark spicy, smoky character, drier finish, same refinement. All oak-matured, 15% new. Already best seller after PC Shiraz.

*** **Grand Vin Rouge (formerly Les Deux Mers Dry Red)** ◀ Very quaffable, interesting 70% French/30% South African partnership. NV **96, 97** blend, mélange of varieties—carignan, cinsaut, grenache dominate; cabs. s/f, syrah and tinta also in. Softer than pvs., maintains individuality, with bright cherry, black pepper, spice and wild scrub notes.

**** **Private Collection Sauvignon Blanc** Unwooded white, more than holds its own in predominantly red wine range. **98** richer, rounder than **97,** streamlined by 6,8 gms/l acid. Unflashy but concentrated tropical flavours, smooth fruity finish give wide scope for pairing with food. Good now; should have no problem holding another year/18 months in bottle. **96 WINE******, in top 3 of tasting. **95 VVG.**

**** **Chardonnay** Consistently elegant, but **97** should surpass all pvs. in sophistication. Inviting, complex Burgundian hints of ripe hazelnut, spice; good creamy mouth-feel lengthened by limey freshness. Components beautifully balanced, with sufficient reserves to develop over next 2 or 3 years. V.d. Merwe attributes superior quality to longer maturation for barrel-fermented portion (80%); 10 months cf 7 in **97**, all new French. 20% unwooded portion underlines elegance, intensity.

*** **Grand Vin Blanc (formerly Les Deux Mers Grand Vin Blanc)** Franco-Cape original blend: 70% chardonnay, 30% chenin blanc; NV (mix **98/97**). Local component 40%, mainly chenin, splash chardonnay, some wooded. More refined, complex than pvs. release: understated tropical, honey tones; quite rich, round, enlivened with subtle lime freshness, easy, dry conclusion.

*** **Private Collection Natural Sweet—Le Reve de Saxenbourg**. NV chenin blanc, weisser riesling, gewürz blend, no botrytis. Stimulatingly clean, forthcoming spicy tropical character, should develop more interesting layers with bottle age. 12% alc. 160 gms/l sugar.

Private Collection Le Phantom Brut Cap Classique NV pinot noir-chardonnay; 40 months on lees; tastes rather sweeter than 12 gms/l sugar. **Also** NV Cape riesling/s. blanc mix; earthy, briskly dry.

SEDGWICK'S OLD BROWN SHERRY

Jerepigo/sherry blend; pronounced raisiny character, rich, sweet.

SEIDELBERG

See De Leuwen Jagt

SENTINEL

See Coppoolse Finlayson

SHIP SHERRY

SFW

Old Cape label; jerepigo rather than sherry; somewhat neutral, sweet. Huge seller in Eastern Cape.

SHOPRITE CHECKERS

National Wine Buyer: Mark Norrish
Tel: 021-9804000 **Fax:** 021-9804075
E-mail: mnorrish@shoprite.co.za

A remarkable success-story here at this national supermarket chain mirrors international trends: wine as an essential item on the everyday grocery list, not some luxury purchase; bought—and consumed—with dinner, often on the same day; carefully priced so as not to throw that shopping budget out of whack. With almost 320 wine-licensed stores, Shoprite Checkers has a huge market for its own locally-sourced Oddbins brand and enticingly priced imports in particular; "critically important", says live-wire national wine buyer Mark Norrish, is tailoring the ranges for each store to its consumer profile. The core philosophy is value-for-money. Which does not preclude him from making the odd foray into the *haute couture* end of the market: in 1998 he was in Burgundy to assist with the making of a Premier Crû white. He has noticed a distinct shift, in popular consumer tastes, away from semi-sweet "stein" styles to off-dry; and a surge towards red wines. **Ruby cabernet** has been a special winner, moving into the vacuum left by increasingly higher priced "premium" red varieties. Except for the Grand Rouge, the bargains below all emanate from the Worcester area.

ODDBINS RESERVE range: All budget-priced
Ruby Cabernet-Cabernet Sauvignon Bin 127 Ultra-soft **98** with smooth fleshy fruit, chocolaty nuances, sweetish finish. **Ruby-Cabernet-Merlot Bin 179** NEW NV (**98**) smooth dry red, very soft tannins, blend from 2 farms. **Cinsaut-Ruby Cabernet Bin 41** NEW ◀ Very easy slip-down-the-throat stuff: light-coloured/bodied, gentle choc-box flavours, soft acidity. NV. **Ruby Cabernet-Pinotage Bin 151** NEW NV blend (**98** vintage), pinotage portion lightly wooded. Fairly bland dry red. **Grand Rouge Bin 151** ◀ NEW Franco-Cape, inter-continental blend, mix of unwooded grenache, syrah, carignan, cabernets s./f. from Ch. Capion, Languedoc and oaked cinsaut, tinta barocca, cab. franc from Saxenburg, St'bosch. **Rosé Bin 149** NEW Semi-sweet crowd-pleaser.

*** **Sauvignon Blanc-Chardonnay Bin 61** ☺ ◀ Charming **98** summer-refresher. Warm peachy nose, perky and fresh sauvignon dominates flavours, easy soft finish.

Wooded Chardonnay Bin 225 NEW Despite only 3 months oak, loads of vanilla, spicy cloves in **98**, tasted v. young. Reticent fruit could emerge given a little time. **Chardonnay Bin 141 98** NEW unwooded style: soft ripe-citrus bouquet, pleasantly peachy palate, rather brisk finish. 13,6% alc. **Chenin Blanc-Chardonnay Bin 217** ◀ NEW **98** blend, chardonnay portion oaked. Features Granny Smith apples throughout, nice vibrancy on palate. **Chenin Blanc Bin 76** NEW **98** slightly French-oaked, spiced baked apple scents, crisp green-apple palate, spice returns to finish. **Special Late Harvest Bin 125** NEW **98** from chenin. Lovely honeyed fruit nose, touches of apricot and sunny ripe fruit on palate, low acid, finish a bit staid. 40 gms/l sugar. Also **RITE** housebrand 5 l boxes from Robertson area.

SIGNAL HILL

Simonsberg, Stellenbosch See Stellenbosch map

Open by appointment only.
Owners: Ridon Family Vineyards (Pty) Ltd
Winemaker: Jean-Vincent Ridon (since 1997)
Viticulturist: Delphine Renier

Production: 400 cases. **Vineyards:** 5 ha.
P.O. Box 1050, Stellenbosch 7599
Tel: 021-8800908 **Fax:** 021-8800508
E-mail: ridon@iafrica.com

"The truth for me is the Burgundian way," says winemaker Jean-Vincent Ridon, who points out that in that corner of France "monks took 1 000 years to find the best soil". Perhaps a tad too long to wait even for a purist like Ridon, whose dream "to have 10 different vineyards, to be able to match cultivars/soil/climate as we do in Europe" kicks off with 5 ha. on the Kanonkop (Simonsberg) and Somerset West, a mix of own and rented ground. Future target is to build a boutique cellar on the Simonsberg, dedicated to experimental batches only. The approach will be traditional: no filtering, no cold stabilisation; with "classic" wines for ageing—"not to be drunk 3 months after harvest". He is close-planting in the vineyards, à la the grand crus in France, and conducting a test on ungrafted vitis-vinifera, à la Henri Marionnet, a friend from the Loire. "We still have a long way to go, but the potential is huge."

All NEW

Cabernet Sauvignon Concentration is first impression of **97**: blackberries on toast scents; more blackberries on palate, loads of vanilla; soft, ripe fruit tannins. Quite serious now, not for early drinking, but in 5-6 years could be gorgeous. From Muldersvlei grapes, some 20 yrs old, some new-clone 10 yrs old. Lavished with new, medium-toasted oak. **98** different régime (50% new oak), all old, very low-yield clone. **Muscat d'Alexandrie Natural Sweet 98** surprisingly unspicy, unmusky in infancy, but could grow up rather attractively. 13% alc., 65 gms/l sugar, old Simonsberg bush vines. **Vin de L'Empereur NLH 98** dessert, certainly not a conventional Cape muscat. Sunset-tinged gold colour, sweet but not cloying (160 gms/l sugar). New barrel-fermented. "A homage," says Ridon, to the old Constantia wines which were Napoleon's favourite.

SIGNATURE — See IWS

SILVERSANDS — See Robertson Winery

SIMUNYE — See Backsberg

SIMONSIG ESTATE

Stellenbosch See Stellenbosch map

Weekdays 8.30-5, Sat 8.30-16.30. Cellar tours 10, 3. Sat 10 am only. Tasting charges R3,50.
Owners: Malan Family
Winemaker: Johan Malan (since 1982) with Christopher van Dieren
Marketing: Pieter Malan. **Vineyards:** Francois Malan (since 1981)
Production: 160 000 cases, 2 400 tons
Vineyards: 270 ha.
P.O. Box 6, Koelenhof 7605
Tel: 021-8822044 **Fax:** 021-8822545
E-mail: wine@simonsig.co.za
Website: www.simonsig.co.za

A pioneering and distinguished Stellenbosch wine family, the Malans celebrated 30 years of bottling their estate wines in 1998 by sponsoring

South African performances of the "three young tenors from Milan"—former masterclass students at La Scala—an event which lends itself to an array of associations. Malan and Milan. The three (old? never!) brothers, Pieter, Francois and Johan Malan, now in full voice at the estate established by their father, feisty and farsighted Frans Malan . Simonsig's progression from a purely national to an international stage—exports now take 35% of production. The metaphorical linkages are endless. Just as are the Malans' ceaseless efforts to polish their performances in the marketplace (Pieter Malan on this podium), the cellar (take a bow, Johan) and the vineyards (encore for Francois).

Johan Malan sees specialisation as the way to go: "We've tried everything." (Latest experiment is the first verdelho crop, likely to be used in a blend.) "Now we want to cut down on the grocery list and concentrate on the quality of the wines we do best, without stagnating completely." Trouble is, he does them all so well. We wouldn't want to face the irate fans if and when their favourite tipple is culled—Simonsig's broad range epitomises consumer-friendliness, offering almost one-stop, every-palate, fine wine shopping! One certainty, however, is that the focus will be increasingly on reds—now up to 40% of production here—and "our wines will always reflect the vintage". No clever-tricks manipulation for this thoughtful winemaker. A new fermentation cellar went up during the 98 harvest ("a red wine vintage," he asserts, "like 84"); a new barrel cellar and more red wine tanks are imminent. Assisting with the first, traditional "submerged-cap" fermentation for shiraz—for gentler tannins, more flavour—was Stephanie Ogier from the Côte Rotie.

In the vineyards Francois Malan has been no less active. New 12 ha. planting plans target shiraz, cabernet sauvignon and pinotage, with pinot meunier for the bubbly and chardonnay. A new French harvester rolled out at 4am during the 98 vintage, ensuring grapes could be picked at optimum ripeness—and cooler.

Simonsig's broader interests include the Cellarmaster and Coastal Wines operations, distributing for 46 other wineries, "and there are always other ventures worth considering," says Pieter Malan. He believes they're currently at the new-generation crossroads. "The challenge is to create a platform for OUR children, all nine of them. All the girls already want to become winemakers! Our belief is that if we improve our service, the opportunities will open up." The vision which spurred Frans Malan to make the Cape's first MCC bubbly, and spearhead the launch of the first Cape wine route, remains in the family.

**** **Tiara** Cabernet sauvignon-led, vintage-dictated flagship. Impressive even in lighter-year **96** vintage: harmonious 81%/19% cab. s./merlot mix; oak flatters not obscures open-textured, fruity charm. Aged 19 months small wood, half new, 10% American. Ready sooner than rich, focused **95 SAA VVG**, best to date. **94** comfortably plump but doesn't lack backbone. Sweet plummy fruit extended by classy oaking.

*** **Frans Malan Reserve Pinotage-Cabernet** Goal here to create distinctive Cape blend: a New/Old World style fusion. **96** pinotage's plummy, red fruits to fore, accentuated by 6% merlot, 50% American oak (half new). Juicy mouthful, cab. s. adds lively tannins, solid core. Needs time to harmonise. **95** (****) more homogeneous mix red fruit refinement, subtle spiciness; very sleek, velvety. **94** first release, dominated by pinotage sweet ripeness. Small oak-matured, one year. (40-year-old bush vine pinotage.)

*** **Cabernet Sauvignon** Sophisticated, unostentatious. **96** particularly well-tailored; elegant interplay between cedary new oak, ripe fruit, fleshed out with 10% merlot; all in harmony with medium build.

★★★ **Shiraz** Less gutsy than some but never lacks honest shiraz flavours. Fresh blackberry, spicy expression in **96** evidence of new clone portion. Shows usual elegance, fine tannin; softened by gentle savoury, gamey nuances. 100% barrel-matured, all used. **94 SAA**. **95 Reserve** tasted for last ed. never released.

★★★ **Pinotage** ◀ Unwooded probably Cape's top pinotage in this category. **97** ★★★★ eloquent example of individuality, charm. Aromas reflect warm, spicy generosity of southern French reds. Dense, vibrant tannins well-meshed with plentiful, soft summer pudding red fruits; delicious spicy kick in tail. Should provide good drinking over coming 3-4 years. **94**, **92 SAA** Selections.

★★★★ **Chardonnay** ◀ **97** reaches plateau of elegance, complexity in excellent vintage. Gorgeous hazelnut, toast, spicy clove interweave; super-expressive, also refined. Full-bodied with supple, fleshy fruit framed, lengthened by firm structure; only 25% malo (cf 40% in **96**) for more fruity intensity. Oak complementary partner. Should perform on par with **96 SAA WINE**★★★★, **95 SAA**, mature longer, better than either. **Chardonnay Reserve CIWG** NEW **96** more obvious oak influence (100% new barrel-fermented/matured 16 months) doesn't swamp butterscotch, nutty concentration; broad-shouldered.

★★★ **Sauvignon Blanc** More richness, weight in **98** than pvs. from lees contact, vintage ripeness; gives greater volume, length to unwooded, cool gooseberry, figgy fruit aromas, flavours. Probably still best before mid-99. **97 WINE**★★★★.

★★★ **Weisser Riesling** ◀ From **98** has tipped over to off-dry, (5 gms/l sugar) "to give wider appeal in this diminishing category", explains Johan Malan. Retains usual peppery/grapefruit tang, beautifully pure, clean flavours with touch more juiciness than racily dry **97.** Closer in style to be-medalled **96 SAA, VVG, WINE**★★★★.

★★★★ **Kaapse Vonkel** White grape influence evident in current **95 (**★★★**)** as in Simonsig's/Cape's first commercial MCC in **71**; now chardonnay, then chenin. **95** (60/40 chardonnay/pinot noir) with fresh cream nose, gentle mousse; more fruity than yeasty but also some soft bready tones on palate. Needs more time to fill out, develop complexity of **92 SAA** trophy winner; **91 WINE**★★★★★ both 60%/40% pinot noir/chardonnay. No **94.**

★★★★ **Cuvée Royale** NEW Prestige cuvée to commemorate 30 years of bottling under Simonsig label; a **91** chardonnay (Blanc de Blancs). Has all warm biscuity, toasty lees ripeness expected from 4 years on lees; fine, persistent bubble emphasised by unforced Brut style (5 gms/l sugar), tasty sea-salty tang. Sophisticated, special-occasion MCC. 6 000 bottles.

★★★★ **Gewürztraminer** Regularly one of nicest SLH; good ageing potential. Bright, pale gold lights in **98**; intense spice, rose petal, litchi complexity; stimulating minerally feel lightens palate's obvious ripeness, gives tantalisingly long, refreshing finish.

★★★★ **Noble Late Harvest** From botrytised bukettraube. Infant **98** invigorating fresh honey, spicy aromas; full-bodied but lively, dainty feel. Antithesis of old SA syrupy style. 7 gms/l TA; 100 gms/l sugar. No **97**; **96 WINE**★★★★.

Adelberg ☺ ◀ Cabernet/merlot blend, **98** ripe chocolate, plum generosity on nose, palate with clean, spicy tail; dense but not harsh. Perfectly designed for everyday, uncomplicated drinking. **Chenin Blanc** ☺ ◀ **98** like dry Late Harvest: full-bodied but balanced, with uncluttered honey, melon juiciness. **Adelblanc** Unwooded dry blend, mainly colombard with chenin blanc, chardonnay: lightish, everyday quaffing. **Vin Fumé** Juicy, greengage sauvignon blanc expanded by oak-fermented portion. **98** good presence without overpowering fruit; successfully targeted as restaurant wine. Also

250 ml. **Mustique** Gently aromatic blend clairette blanche, weisser riesling, muscat ottonel, gewürz., schoenberger; **98** delicate muscat, spice, character enhanced by 9 gms/l sugar. **Franciskaner** Chenin-based semi-sweet, perked with some muscat fruit. **Late Bottled Vintage Port**. **94** from pinotage. Curranty, earthy bouquet, sweet berry palate, at 75 gms/l sugar, drier than most. Aged 3 years older French oak. Available from tasting room only.

SIMONSVLEI

Paarl See Paarl map

Open weekdays 8-5, Sat 8.30-4.30.
Lunch except Mondays.
Owners: 84 shareholders
Cellarmaster: Philip Louw (since 1988)
Viticulturist: Andrew Teubes (since 1996)
Production: 300 000 cases, 16 000 tons. **Vineyards:** 2 000 ha.
P.O. Box 584, Suider-Paarl 7624
Tel: 021-8633040 **Fax:** 021-8631240

The first vintage in Simonsvlei's brand new cellar was not without its problems. "The cooling equipment couldn't cope, though we dealt with that quickly enough," recalls cellarmaster Philip Louw, now into his second decade at this dynamic, top-echelon co-operative-turned-company near Paarl—a towering bottle-shaped storage tank on the premises, visible from the N1 motorway nearby, has been a trademark for years. "Then a couple of our new stainless steel tanks collapsed and we lost valuable—and desperately needed—premium varietal wine like cab. It was a nightmare time but now that it's over, I'm pretty satisfied with a lot of the wine we produced." Marketing changes scheduled for 1998 have also been a little slow in moving through the pipeline. Louw however remains ebulliently optimistic, and with good reason. His **Bushvine Chenin Blanc** won the hotly-contested inaugural Paarl Vintners Chenin Challenge—snaring an overseas study trip for the delighted winemaker—while the first vintage of the yet-to-be released super-premium range has been snapped up by wine clubs and the export market.

HERCULES PILLAR range: (may be renamed) All NEW

*** **Shiraz** Smoky raspberry/black cherry bouquet, toasty vanilla touches, sweet youngberry flavours mingling with spicy, leathery undertones, dry prunelle finish. **97** vintage.

**** **Chardonnay 97** plump butterscotch marzipan bouquet, layered with pineapple/pear fragrance, rich creamy-leesy flavours, sumptuous melon finish. Barrel-fermented, 30% malo. (Chosen by mail-order wine club.)

*** **Sémillon** Quince/melon aromas, whiffs of thatch, baked-bread palate, citrus notes in finish. Oak-fermented **98**.

SIMONSVLEI range: (Includes some labels from pvs. Reserve range.)

*** **Shiraz** ◀ Finely balanced berry-fruited **97** with leathery overtones, ripe but not fat. Spicy, gamey whiffs mingle with youngberry/loganberry fruit, fine tannins support dense though understated fruit flavours, persistent. Full malo, 8 months in wood. **96** smokier, with softer, more leathery whiffs, ripe tannins, spicy dry finish. **93 SAA selection**.

*** **Pinotage** Ripe raspberry/loganberry fragrance in **97**, tangy palate, almond whiffs. **96** varnishy youngberry fruit, earthy light-tannined palate, brambly finish.

*** **Pinotage Reserve 93** fuller, more jammy aromas, soft palate, easy drinking. **VG**.

*** **Cabernet Sauvignon 97** herby, raspberry fragrance, soft tannins, accessible, minty whiffs, dry not austere. **96** offers cassis, youngberry fruit, delicate marzipan mingling with cedary/tobacco flavours, tangy, persistent.

*** **Cabernet Sauvignon Reserve** Raspberry with dusty, gamey aromas in **95**, fine, slightly austere flavours, dry-tannined finish. **93** blackcurrant, tobacco whiffs, light almond accents, elegant tannins, spicy mid-palate, long finish.

*** **Cabernet Merlot** Youngberry/blackcurrant-scented **97** layered with minty, leafy aromas, spicy, soft mulberry palate. Long cedary finish.

*** **Sémillon-Chardonnay** Opulent grapefruit/thatchy aromas mingle in **97** with pineapple, lime apricot fruit, rich not flabby, light marizpan finish. 60% sémillon, 40% chardonnay, lovely balance of fruit and length.

*** **Chardonnay 98** toasty, butterscotch fragrance, lime/grapefruit flavours layered with almond, marmalade finish. **97** apple, citrus overtones, light whiffs of butterscotch, dry limey finish. Accessible, uncomplex.

*** **Sauvignon Blanc** ◀ **98** with grassy herbal aromas, intense nettly whiffs; gooseberry/asparagus flavours, dry not lean, richly-textured finish. **97** with more austere grassy fragrance/finish.

*** **Chenin Blanc** ◀ Benchmark Paarl Chenin. Loire-like apricot/tropical flavours, reined-in acidity. **98** fragrant, pear/pineapple fruit, fine citrus flavours, green apple tones, dried peach, tangy not lean. **97 Bushvine** more opulent, Paarl Vintners trophy winner.

*** **Chenin Blanc-Chardonnay** ◀ Melon/marzipan fragrance, aromas of apricot/tropical fruit, rich leesy palate, persistent **97**.

*** **Port** Sweeter, more voluptuous style, plum/cassis bouquet, prunelle notes, aromatic fruitcake finish. Blend of **94** pinotage/shiraz/tinta, oak-aged.

**** **Premier White Muscadel** Acclaimed **95** unctuous, intensely spicy, rose-petal muscat aromas, dense syrupy flavours. WINE****.

*** **Hanepoot Jerepigo** Pungent grapey, cedary fragrance, luscious, fresh uncloying finish though relatively mature **89**.

Bukettraube ◀ Muscat tobacco aromas, sweetish rose-petal palate, **98** finishing dry, surprisingly tangy. **Sauvignon Blanc Chardonnay** NEW **98** pungently herbaceous, with gooseberry/nettly overtones, crisp, but not austere. **Chardonnay Sauvignon Blanc** Fine grapefruit fragrance in **97** with whiffs of pear, elegant, appley/lime flavours, dry. **Hanepoot** NV Muscat bouquet, intense litchi flavours. **Humbro Red Jerepigo** NV Raisiny, with blackberry/fruitcake fragrance and flavours, densely-textured finish.

MOUNT MARBLE range (previously Lifestyle)

Simonsrood NV Easy-drinking mainly cinsaut (85%) blend, soft delicate tannins, spiced up with plummy ruby cabernet. **Blanc de Blanc** ◀ NV Tangy, chenin blanc/colombard combination. Pear, apricot aromas, gutsy, mouthfilling, persistent. **Riesling 97** smoky, thatchy aromas, delicately herbaceous flavours, crisp. **Stein** NV Compôte of chenin, riesling, colombard, delicately pear/melon-toned, easy drinking. **Late Vintage** NV Quaffably grapey, with pear/apricot overtones, uncloying. **Special Late Harvest** ◀ Opulent **98** with melon/apricot fragrance, mouthfilling; sweet lime/spice flavours, layer of pineapple, tangy fine finish. **Vin Doux Sparkling Wine** Aromatic, sweetish, easy drinking bubbly.

SINNYA VALLEY

Production: 44 000 cases.
P.O. Box 441, Stellenbosch 7599
Tel: 021-8838043/4 **Fax:** 021-8864708
E-mail: info@vinimark.co.za

A marketing success story with pan-cultural dimensions: conceived by UK-born MW Richard Kelley, Vinimark's Tim Rands; grapes from Robertson Valley, grown by members of the Robertson Valley Wine Trust; exported to far-flung Japan, Mexico, Sweden, the US; adorned with label-art featuring variation on a famous (Namibian) rock painting, White Lady of the Brandberg—debate rages about the enigmatic figure's origins: Egyptian? Phoenician?; and, to complete the rainbow brew, a San (Bushman) derived name: "Sinnya" is the Breede River (Wide River) that meanders through the valley.

*** **Cabernet-Merlot** ☺ ◀ Lightly oaked **97** with ripe brambles/plums, delectable vanilla overlay, spicy-oak finish. Accessible, velvet- textured, lingering sweet fruit. Satisfying, best young.

Chardonnay ◀ **98** lemon-zest, hint of spice, lovely fresh citric palate, persistent. Very nice. Lightly wooded; for US. **Colombard-Chardonnay 97** successful 70/30 blend. Quietish nose, crisp finish, dry. Designed for early drinking. **White 97** just off-dry (Rhine) riesling/gewürz; still going strong; fresh apricot, fragrant lemon nose. 6 gms/l sugar. Balanced, good intensity, lingering. Lowish 11% alc.

SLALEY CELLARS

Stellenbosch See Stellenbosch map

Owners: Hunting family
Visits: By appointment only.
Vineyards: Peter Tiffin (17 years)
Area under vines: 120 ha.
P.O. Box 119, Koelenhof 7605
Tel: 021-8822123 **Fax:** 021 8822109
E-mail: CVH@intekom.co.za

While the original partners to the Slaley joint venture have gone their separate ways, the vineyards and cellar have reverted to the Hunting family which has owned the farm for several generations. A division of stocks between the various parties has left the winery—one of the most modern in the area—temporarily devoid of much of its production. However, the deluxe wines remain, together with some of the most extensive premium varietal vineyards in Stellenbosch.

Both NEW

*** **Shiraz Hunting Family Reserve** Densely fruited and robust **97**, showing raspberry/loganberry aromas, toasty, minerally flavours, great amplitude on the palate, long spicy finish. **WINE******.

*** **Chardonnay Hunting Family Reserve** Pineapple/grapefruit bouquet, butterscotch, bready whiffs, concentrated tropical lime palate, rich tangy dry aftertaste in **97**.

SLANGHOEK WINERY

Slanghoek See Worcester map

Tastings/sales Mon-Thur 7.30-12.30; 1.30-5.30. Fri closes 4.30. Cellar tours for more than 5 persons by appointment, otherwise on request; guest-house.

Grietjiesdrift restaurant 500 m from cellar, open daily. Tel: 0231-91931.
Owners: 25 members
Manager/Senior Winemaker: Kobus Rossouw (since 1993)
Winemaker: Henri Swiegers (since 1998)
Production: 24 000 tons. **Vineyards:** 1 500 ha.
P.O. Box 75, Rawsonville 6845

Tel: 0231-91130. **Fax:** 0231-91891

Top seller of this progressive co-op near Worcester is the unusual (for Cape) **Riesling-Sémillon** launched in 1996. That the multi-award winning Slanghoek—the cellar won the 1998 Young Wine Show trophy for best points achieved for the second time in a row—should choose to bottle an exotic blend under its own label (bulk of production goes to wholesalers) suggests something of the push-the-envelope approach that prevails here. It's also reflected in a new, custom-built wine centre, which combines tasting, function facilities in friendly surroundings.

★★★ **Rooi Jerepiko** ◀ **97** cellar's first red dessert, still breaking/mending many a "stickie" lover's heart. Lashings of ripe plums, spirity top-notes; almost explosively fruity, mouthfilling. Plush-textured winter warmer. From pinotage. Classwinner SA young wine show, Worcester champion (as is Hanepoot below).

★★★ **Soet Hanepoot** ◀ **96** remarkably delicate for this style. Grapey/nutty bouquet, crammed with nutty flavours; expansive, long, gliding finish. **95 VVG**. **94** SA Champion. Good on its own, lightly chilled, or with fresh fruit.

★★★ **Special Late Harvest** ◀ Particularly successful in **98**; delicious fruity sweetness, finely balanced by tongue-tingling freshness. Delicate, clean muscat flavour. 43 gms/l sugar. From muscat d'Alexandrie. Terrific aperitif. **96 VG**.

Cabernet Sauvignon Private Reserve 97 revealing merest hint of wood despite 6 mths maturation large French oak. Uncomplicated, soft brambly fruit, gentle tannins. Early drinker. **Shiraz** Current release **(97)** first harvest from young vines. So lighter, early drinking (though fuller style in pipeline). Attractive, smooth, some herby/spicy accents, brush of sweet oak, 3 months in barrel. "BBQ" written all over it. **Pinotage 97** tasted very young, gawky still, tannins strict, some brambly fruit waiting to spring. Wooded. 13% alc. In winemaker's view, better than **Private Reserve 96**, Worcester show classwinner. **93** SA show classwinner. **Chardonnay-Sauvignon Blanc** ◀ **98** (labelled **Private Reserve**) fresh sauvignon grass/nettles dominant (though 50/50 blend), dry. Easy drinker. 13% alc. **Weisser Riesling** ◀ NEW **98** label states: "fruity"—so it is, in tropical mode, light, zippy flashes of muscat. Poolside sipping. 10,7% alc. **Riesling-Sémillon** ◀ Best-selling 50/50 partnership. Riesling dominant in fresh, very drinkable **98**, with honey-scented finish. Dry, 11,5% alc. **Noble Late Harvest** NEW **98** agreeable wafts of tropical fruit, dried peach; brisk, refreshing finish. Not very complex, perhaps, but friendly, balanced. Chenin (70%), muscat d'Alexandrie. 145 gms/l sugar, 7. gms/l acid. **Vonkelwyn** ◀ NV delightful sweet sparkler; light, fruity, attractive muscat fragrance. Low 10,5% alc., highly popular. **Port** Deadline prevented us from tasting **97** for pvs. edition; but we urged readers to follow Rossouw's advice and "Taste for yourself". Now, 12 months on, we get our turn; frankly, we like it! Modern, drier style (90 gms/l sugar), nice spirity nose/palate attack, plenty of fruit, probably for early drinking (though winemaker sees "lots of maturation potential"). Unwooded cinsaut. **96** different style, sweeter (113 gms/l sugar); gold medal SA show, classwinner Worcester.

SOMERBOSCH

Somerset West See Helderberg map

Tastings/sales Mon-Fri 9-5. Sat 9-1.
Owner: W.J. (Wally) Roux
Winemakers: Marius, Japie Roux (from 1995)
Production: ± 750 tons (± 200 own winery)

P.O. Box 12181, Die Boord 7613
Tel: 021-8553616 **Fax:** 021-8554457

There's a deepening Russian connection on this welcoming family farm exactly half-way between Somerset West and Stellenbosch. Brothers Marius and Japie Roux—they seem to have invented the phrase "laid-back"—showed their ever-improving range at the *Drinks Russia* expo in Moscow in 1997 and, to their great delight, since have been peppered with orders by the Russian wine broking fraternity. Germany (mainly), Holland and the US are further customers for Somerbosch's compact, well-priced range which was augmented in 1998 by the first **Pinotage** made on the property.

*** **Cabernet Sauvignon** ◀ Winery's top seller, usually medium bodied, showing particularly well in **97**. Rich, toasty oak underpins succulent fruit (v'yds next door to strawberry fields!), glides to extraordinarily long finish. **96** quite firm by comparison (though nicely ripe, not unpleasant by any means), fruity, spicy, cedary.

Merlot ◀ "Untamed teenager" of pvs. edition still quite animalistic (in nicest possible way), strapping (at 13% alc.). Some chocolate, coffee, berry flavours, non-stringent tannins. **Pinotage** NEW **98** untasted. **Chardonnay 98** has marginally higher oak-fermented component than pvs. (50%), shows in engaging vanilla/butterscotch platform for substantial tropical fruit. Tannins perceptible, so give yr in bottle to settle down. Alc. nudging 13%. **Chenin Blanc** ◀ Chenin in this terroir habitually wears unconventional citric garb, as in **98** with piquant lemongrass attractions, soft mouth-feel, bracing finish. **Sauvignon Blanc 98**, as in **97**, quite shy nose, firm palate, rather crisp finish.

SONOP WINERY

Paarl See Paarl map

Tastings by appointment.
Owner: Jacques Germanier. (SAVISA)
Winemaker: Thierry Fontannaz. **Manager:** Bernard Fontannaz
Production: 120 000 cases. **Vineyards:** 75 ha.
P.O. Box 1142, Stellenbosch 7599
Tel: 021-8872409 **Fax:** 021-8864838
E-mail: SONOP@iafrica.com
Website: www.sonop.co.za

Savisa's expansion plans were boosted with the takeover of Devon Hill in Stellenbosch and development of Cilmor in Worcester. It has been less than a decade since the Jacques Germanier Group made its first wine investment in the Cape. During that time it has developed an international trade covering most of the major European markets, and, more recently, Japan. The number of brands supplied through the various wineries increases annually, and while many of these names remain largely unknown to domestic consumers, they have acquired a real following in the export trade: African Legend is popular in the UK, while Grooteberg sells in Holland and Bredasdorp in Germany.

There are no secrets to the group's business plan: based on the simple view that good wine requires reliable grape sources, the South African operation has entered into long-term supply contracts with several established properties. Some, like Diemersdal, have handed over the vinification of export production to Jacques Germanier; others—like Kersfontein—deliver grapes to the Sonop winery to process in its ISO 9002 facility in Stellenbosch. The winemaking approach encourages early drinking fruit-driven wine styles, distinct varietal differentiation, and, where possible, organically approved and certified production methods.

CAPE LEVANT range:

★★★ **Cabernet Sauvignon** Spicy, soft-tannined, with rich dense texture. Raspberry/blackcurrant notes in **98**, riper than pvs., sweet berry flavours, elegant rather than robust. **96** lighter, more herbaceous, whiffs of youngberry/marzipan, nutty full finish.

★★★ **Pinotage 98** muscular, though not coarse, with pungent aromas, wild mulberry, almost gamey overtones, fine tannins, lovely amplitude in the mouth, rich-textured finish. **97** powerful ripe berry aromas, dense tannins, complex but accessible. **96** cherry fragrance, prunelle-like spice, earthy notes. **93 SAA** selection.

★★★ **Shiraz 98** fruit-loaded, powerful red, gamey/leathery aromas, layered with raspberry, hints of marzipan. Rich tannins, smoothly textured, surprisingly fine finish. **97** more peppery with robust, earthy flavours.

Merlot 98 accessibly fragrant, medium to light, mulberry and plum aromas, some minerally spice. Easy-drinking but with some length, finer texture than pvs.

DIEMERSDAL range:

★★★★ **Shiraz** Marriage of old and new styles in **98**: raspberry layered with earthy farmyard aromas, peppery dense tannins, vanilla whiffs from French/American oak. **97** more leathery but fuller and richer finish.

★★★ **Merlot** Fruit-dominated, easy-drinking red. **98** soft plum aromas, minerally, length rather than weight on palate. **97** more aromatic, also accessible rather than complex.

★★★ **Pinotage** ◀ **98** pungent youngberry fruit layered with mineral/acetone spice, dry-tannined, fine, more elegant than **97**.

Cabernet Sauvignon 98 elegant lighter-style red, herby, with green-leafy hints, lacking the dense blackcurrant aromas of fuller **97**. Early drinking.

CAPE SOLEIL range:

Wines produced for Cape Soleil are also marketed under the **Athlone, Bredasdorp,** and **Grooteberg** labels.

★★★ **Cabernet Sauvignon** ◀ Spicy aromas in accessible **98**, mint/eucalyptus with gamey whiffs, light dry tannins, more leafy than cherry-fruity **97**.

★★★ **Merlot** ◀ **98** plum/mulberry, with almost smoky, coffee overtones. Fuller, more chocolaty than **97**.

★★★ **Shiraz** ◀ NEW **98** raspberry/black cherry aromas, fine almost sweet tannins, accessibly fragrant, harmonious, spicy finish.

★★★★ **Sauvignon Blanc** Concentrated gooseberry/green fig fruit in **98**, voluptuous palate, tropical lime layers.

★★★ **Chenin Blanc 98** the full fruit-salad. Apricot/tropical/pear/pineapple notes, fleshy, with prunelle wafts in finish.

Pinotage 98 raspberry/loganberry aromas, earthy, spicy, with quite robust tannins, minty finish. **97** tobacco/berry scents, riper, richer than more varnishy **96**. **Chardonnay** Butterscotch, lime, grapefruit bouquet in **98**, layered in chunky, toasted vanilla oak, fruit hidden when tasted at early stage by barrel ferment character.

CILMOR range: All NEW

★★★★ **Cabernet Franc 98** features dense mint/eucalyptus fragrance, raspberry notes mingling with mulberry flavours, tangy mineral tannins, very elegant.

★★★ **Cabernet Sauvignon** Youngberry/herbal aromas, touch of mint, textured earthy palate, black-cherry spice, plump finish all add up to attractive **98**.

- ★★★ **Shiraz** Smoky, leathery aromas, mingle with raspberry, cherry/soft and plummy **98**.
- ★★★ **Merlot** Minty, with mulberry layers, some chocolate, in nettly, spicy, persistent **98**.
- ★★★ **Sauvignon Blanc 98** nettly, green pepper bouquet, grassy overtones, lime/quince notes in finish.

Pinotage Raspberry varnishy aromas, light palate, mineral/earthy character, delicately tangy **98**. **Chardonnay** Densely wooded **98**, with toasty butterscotch, vanilla layers over soft pear/grapefruit flavours, buttery. **Chenin Blanc** Medley of fruits in **98**. Apricot, melon aromas, tangy citrus mid-palate, crisp lemon/pear overtones, greengage notes in finish. **Colombard 98** with accessible guava/melon fragrance, forward though not simple, lime and pineapple palate, crisp, tangy.

AFRICAN LEGEND range: All NEW

- ★★★ **Cabernet Sauvignon ◀ 98** mint, blackcurrant notes, finely-textured tannins, whiffs of marzipan, fleshy but not flabby, long spicy finish.
- ★★★★ **Shiraz ◀ 98** smoky, leathery aromas, dense mineral spice, concentrated, whiffs of prunelle, long smouldering finish.
- ★★★ **Merlot ◀** Mulberry/coffee aromas, plummy dense tannins, ample spice and texture, rich and concentrated. Aged in second-fill French oak. From new clone vineyards.
- ★★★★ **Sauvignon Blanc 98** dense, pungent, gooseberry/pineapple fruit, asparagus aromas, soft-textured, lovely amplitude, fragrant, slightly nettly finish.
- ★★★ **Chenin Blanc ◀ 98** ripe apricot/pineapple notes, prunelle/marzipan spice, crisp but not tart, dense fleshy flavours.

Pinotage 98 raspberry, varnishy aromas, earthy, almost minerally texture, spicy long finish. **Chardonnay ◀ 98** fine, lime/grapefruit aromas, hints of butterscotch, spicy, tropical/pineapple palate. Delicate citrus-like finish, oak dominated in youth. **Colombard 98** crisp, light, with fruit salad/guava fragrance, tangy and dry.

KERSFONTEIN range: (NEW)

- ★★★★ **Pinotage** Super **98.** Concentrated raspberry/mulberry aromas, dense rich tannins; earthy, mineral textures and flavours. Intense blackberry spice, slight prunelle notes. Produced from 30-year-old dryland bushvines on Kersfontein farm, vinified by Sonop. Part barrel-fermented, malo.

DEVON HILL range: (All NEW)

- ★★★★ **Devon View Cabernet Sauvignon ◀ 97** dense blackberry notes, with smoky, almost gamey whiffs, fleshy though not jammy texture, sumptuous chocolaty finish.
- ★★★ **Pinotage ◀ 97** sweet raspberry aromas layered with marzipan, dense ribena-like spice, soft almost viscous tannins, rich creamy finish.
- ★★★ **Merlot 97** light plum aromas, leafy dry tannins, herbal scents, slightly lean flavours.
- ★★★ **Sauvignon Blanc 98** concentrated gooseberry notes, layered with lime, green figs, crisp not tart.

KUMALA range:

- ★★★ **Cabernet-Shiraz ◀ 98** gamey brambly aromas, blackcurrant fruit layered with oak, mid-weight, smoothly-textured (60% cab. s., 40% shiraz). **97** notwithstanding 70% cab. s. still dominated by farmyard smoky shiraz, fuller, more robust, than spicy, minty **96.**
- ★★★ **Cinsaut-Cabernet Franc** NEW **98** sweet fruit aromas infused with blackberry/mint spice, elegant, intense inky finish.
- ★★★ **Sémillon-Chardonnay◀** NEW **98** thatchy, almost herbal fragrance, lime/tropical palate, mouthfilling, crisp pineapple finish.

Cinsaut Pinotage ◀ NEW **98** sweet loganberry aromas, dense tannins,

earthy/tangy almost minty finish. **Cinsaut-Cabernet** ◀ NEW **98** smoky, slightly austere, blackberry fruit, well-textured, but not plump, lingering spicy finish. **Cinsaut-Ruby Cabernet** NEW **98** intensely fragrant, blackcurrant/mint bouquet, spicy palate, light but not instubstantial finish. **Merlot-Ruby Cabernet** NEW **98** big-fruited, elegant but uncomplex, mint/eucalpytus layers, plum notes. **Ruby Cabernet-Merlot** NEW **98** 60% ruby cab., 40% merlot. Concentrated, cassis-like fruit, minerally, fine-tannined texture, accessible.
Chenin-Blanc Chardonnay ◀ NEW **98** chenin (80%) dominates intensely fruity blend, dense texture, hints of vanilla, ripe grapefruit finish. **Sauvignon- Colombard 98** 50% sauvignon blanc, 50% colombard blend. Lime/citrus aromas, tangy flavours, short finish. **Colombard-Chardonnay 98** fruit- salad/guava fragrance backed with grapefruit tang, forward, aromatic, light, with crisp finish.
BREDASDORP range:
Ruby Cabernet ◀ **98** dense ribena fruit, thatchy/smoky flavours, accessible, mouthfilling, good quaffing wine.
Rosé 98 delicately spicy, marzipan/black cherry aromas, light tangy finish. **97** pinotage/cinsaut/pinot noir blend.

SOUTHERN RIGHT CELLARS

Hermanus See Walker Bay map
Owners: Anthony Hamilton Russell & Kevin Grant
Winemaker: Kevin Grant (since 1995)
P.O. Box 158, Hermanus 7200
Tel: 0283-23595 **Fax:** 0283-21797

Sauvignon blanc may well be this cellar's best seller, but its roots are in pinotage and that's where the development is headed. Joint-venture plantings of this early ripener on cool, clay-rich Walker Bay sites, identified and developed by HRV's Anthony Hamilton Russell and Kevin Grant, will contribute from the 1999 harvest; a 20 000 case production comprising 5 site-specific wines and a blend are planned. Of particular interest are the vineyards selected in each of the 3 river valleys leading into Walker Bay, replete with their own characteristics. Vintage fidelity and expression of *terroir* are to be expected from Hamilton Russell and Grant, who are researching a "value-added" chenin blanc to partner Pinotage as SA wines of note. Cognisant of the need for brands to have a "home" to which consumers can link an identity, they are expediting planning of a 30 000-case winery—and underground barrel cellar—on land next to Hamilton Russell Vineyards. An added ecological inducement is that the partners donate R1 for every bottle sold to research and develop Hermanus' worldwide attraction—the Southern Right whales which calve in the bay. Over R50 000 was raised in 1997 alone.

★★★ **Pinotage** Concentrated vermilion colour, full sweet-plum fruit substantial structure characterise this 100% pinotage. **98** (from barrel) shows ripe fruit; alc. 14% **97** spicy wood softens grape's trademark "sweetness". **96** faint hint of acetone, absent in later vintages; all side-step the gruff bitterness that can mar pinotage; astute Alliers oaking helps. Wild-yeast fermentation. **95 SAA** polished, rounded.

★★★ **Chenin Blanc 98** packed with peach, apricot, tangy complexity from barrel maturation; substantial alcohol 14% for full mouthful. Just-dry **97** (3,5 gms/l sugar) vanilla, canned guava flavours. Minute quantities (150 cases) at present but one to watch.

★★★ **Sauvignon Blanc** Gentle, unwooded sauvignon, treads middle path between overt fruit and river-stone flint. **98** grassy, alcohol "lift" 13,5%, **97** mature fig flavour, more filled out than pvs. **96**, **SAA**.

SPICE ROUTE WINE COMPANY

Swartland See Swartland map

Open by appointment.
Owners: Charles Back, Jabulani Ntshangase, John Platter, Gyles Webb
Winemaker: Eben Sadie (since 1998)
Viticulturists: Dawie Krynauw, Hans Neethling
Production: 450 tons, 34 000 cases. **Vineyards:** 182 ha.
P.O. Box 645, Malmesbury 7300
Tel: 0224-77139 **Fax:** 0224-77169

The gathering Cape wine renaissance may not have reached full bloom but it found at least some expression in 1998 in this new Malmesbury venture by four of South Africa's best known wine pioneers. Winemakers Charles Back of Fairview and Gyles Webb of Thelema, wine activist (and taster for this guide) Jabulani Ntshangase, and wine writer John Platter pooled their talents, headed up the Cape West Coast and produced their inaugural vintage in the first privately-owned winery at Malmesbury—a spankingly modern facility in a renovated tobacco shed. Back masterminded the winery, completed in a record three months. The group—an equal, four-way partnership—took its name, and some cues and concepts, from the spirit of adventure by early explorers plying the Cape sea routes—in search of spices to enrich the cuisines of Europe. The first views of Cape Town's Table Mountain by those explorers would have been the same as seen from the Spice Route Wine Company's cellars and vineyards today. The partners intend their modern adventure to be equally table-oriented—by focusing on warm climate grapes, shiraz, mouvèdre, viognier and others (including merlot!) whose flavours complement today's international mélange of cooking styles—so often animated by suggestions of cloves, limes, cinnamon, ginger, nutmeg, coriander, lemon-grass and others.

Sourcing grapes from their own, mostly old, bush vines as well as from surrounding vineyards in the wheatlands, the Spice Route partners were determined their wines, and specially the reds, would reflect—as completely and honestly as possible—the warmth and depth of the Swartland soils and climate. Previously, these grapes were delivered to co-operatives.

"We were convinced that by careful selection of grapes and specialist, small-batch handling in the winery, with the emphasis on deep flavours and fine tannins, we could produce some surprises," said Webb, who, with Back, oversaw wine operations. "And I think we've managed that; we surprised even ourselves," says Webb. The Spice Route partners chose Eben Sadie, a young and kindred free-spirit, trained at Elsenburg and with experience in Californian, Oregon and Rhineland wineries, to take charge of the cellar; and he's done a remarkable job. An avid surfer off the nearby West Coast beaches, Sadie rides the new-wave (big-wave?) of modern Cape wine with aplomb.

"This has been an altogether remarkable project," said Ntshangase, who became the first black commercial vineyard and winery owner in South Africa. "The combustible energy and ideas—and ideals—are matched by the wines themselves. After 12 years in the New York wine trade, I never dreamed we'd so quickly be able to fulfil such a 'New South African' dream; I just hope this gives courage and hope to others—and birth to more Cape wine projects with similar objectives where ideals can be underpinned by viability. It's really exhilarating for the Spice Route to be participating in a renaissance in this way. And with the energy we're devoting to training black winemakers [Ntshangase's campaigning and fund-raising have been the catalyst for several university bursaries] we'll complete the circle eventually and help secure a brighter, all-inclusive Cape wine future. "With world competition as it is now, we'll need all the efficiency and commitment we can muster. "And," he adds, "at the end of the day, the wines are what count: consumers don't drink ideals, they'll drink quality at a price they think is fair."

This is principally an export-targeted venture and the inaugural vintage has virtually been taken by London importers, Enotria Wine Cellars.

Declaring an interest: the co-founder, with his wife Erica, of this guide in 1980 and publisher until the last edition, John Platter, is a partner in the Spice Route. The Platters continue as consultants for this guide. The Spice Route wines were reviewed by Angela Lloyd.

All NEW

★★★★ **Andrew's Hope Merlot-Cabernet** ◀ Thrilling foretaste of other (considerable) **98** reds to come from this cellar. Custom-designed for accessibility as well as quality; winemaker Eben Sadie describes this 80/20 merlot/cabernet s. blend as "the softest thing we could find in the winery". It radiates warm plum/chocolate fragrance lifted by minerally spice; effortless waves of silkily-tannined dark fruit, plus intriguing "gout de Swartland"—a suggestion of the area's red-earth richness. Portion unwooded to emphasise fruit. Named after Jabulani Ntshangase's Malmesbury home.

★★★★ **Chenin Blanc** To wood or not to wood; Cape winemaking jury still out on this question but **98** eloquent advocate for barrel-fermented style; oak strictly backdrop-enricher to flaunting ripe mango, pineapple tang. Fruit intensity balanced by broadening fleshy weight, invisible 5 gms/l sugar. Ageing potential not in doubt; bigger question is how. From 36-year-old bush vines. Fermented in used French barrels, 8 months *sur lie*. Unfined; unfiltered. Smoked (West Coast) mussels; herbed chicken casserole sort of partners intended for this food wine.

★★★ **Long Walk Sauvignon Blanc** Vibrant outspoken **98**; alive with fig, passion-fruit and other tropical tastes. Generous build, tongue-tingling freshness, flinty clean tail, all are sauvignon thumbprints, but this scores with balanced leesy richness binding fruit to structure, controlling both—just—also adding texture. A juicy, uncomplicated but not simple, mouthful. 13,5% alc.

Preview of forthcoming attractions: following **98** reds not officially rated, to be bottled later 1999. All are big, 14%+ alc., very ripe but balanced, and so without evident excesses. When tasted mid-98, all bar (standard) Pinotage (★★★), rate ★★★★ (possibly higher). **Shiraz:** Spiced with 7% each grenache, carignan; densely textured, fine chocolate, allspice scents, also individual red earth warmth; elegantly rustic Cape style. **Bordeaux Blend:** Intensely ripe, but unintimidating cab. s./merlot/cab. f. blend, framed and fixed by merlot's sweet, juicy reach. Deep fleshy texture corsetted by balanced tannins, oak. **Pinotage:** Full-bodied, unfettered red fruits, extra spicy notes from well-absorbed oak, true varietal character (without vulgarity); exuberant astringency will need time to settle. From 35-year-old bush vines, low 3 tons/ha.

Then small bottling each of varietal Syrah, Merlot and (another) Pinotage selected as best wines in the cellar. **Syrah:** Full of sensual elegance, its class immediately apparent. Layers of chocolate, smoked bacon, sweet gamey aromas; big bear of a wine as good shiraz should be. **Merlot:** Fermented on own yeasts, shows sort of bitter chocolate/plum quality, fined-toned muscle mouth-coating flavours, associated with Pomerol. **Pinotage** (Premium label): Richer, more lavishly oaked than above version, portion finished fermentation in barrel; 45% new French oak encourages dried fig, banana aromas. In contrast, flavours have purer pinot noir quality. Oak sweetens, rounds tannins, but as with "standard" pinotage, will need time to soften.

SPIER CELLARS

Stellenbosch See Stellenbosch map

Visits: Open for tastings & sales Oct-Apr: Mon-Sun 9-5. May-Sept: Mon-Sat 9-5. Cellar tour and tasting by appointment only. Tasting costs R6; cellar tour & tasting R17.50 per person.

Restaurants: Jonkershuis for Dutch East Indian buffet; Taphuis, Café Spier for light meals. Tel. 021-8813096. See restaurant section.

Owner: Hollard Insurance
Winemaker/Viticulturist: Frans Smit (since 1995)
General Manager (Agriculture): Simon Springthorpe
Production: 650 tons. 45 000 cases. **Vineyards**: 57,4 ha.
P.O. Box 99, Lynedoch 7603
Tel: 021-8813351 **Fax:** 021-8813351 ext. 219
E-mail: info@spier.co.za

The winemaking side of this showpiece Stellenbosch tourist venue—with its own train and station, outdoor amphitheatre, restaurants and cafés, conference halls, picnic spots, the whole winelands trip—is being run by one of the new movers/shakers in the Cape, Savanha (Berg and Brook Wines). Spier bought shares in Savanha in 1998 and handed over vineyard and cellar operations. With an ultra-modern bottling line, the cellar can handle 900 tons of grapes, 30-50 tons per day. The aim now is to concentrate on a smallish range of premium wines; an historic lack of quality varieties on the farm is being addressed—chardonnay and merlot were planted in 1998, shiraz is coming up. Visitors may buy the IV Spears range on the property.

IV SPEARS label:

*** **Cabernet Sauvignon** Medium-bodied, harmonious **96**. Attractive brambly, cedary fragrance; oak highlights ripe fruit density, length; aged 14 months small French barrels. Has tannins, concentration to develop over 2-3 years. One of nicer cabs. in lighter vintage.

*** **Sauvignon Blanc** Easy sweet gooseberry fruit on unwooded **98**; vigorous, pleasant juicy length. 3,1 gms/l sugar. **96 SAA.**

**** **Noble Late Harvest 96 VVG** still young, vigorous; has developed gorgeous bitter orange peel tang; this plus lowish 10,45% alc. lend freshness/daintiness to essential creamy, fleshy luxuriance. 138 gms/l sugar. From botrytised, old vine bukettraube, given French Sauternes barrel-fermentation treatment.

Cabernet Sauvignon NEW ☺ ◀ Unwooded **97**; packed with inviting bramble/chocolate ripeness; very fresh, lively; built for early, pleasurable quaffing. **Cabernet Sauvignon-Merlot** Oak-matured; 60/40 blend in **95**, sold out. No **96**. **Chardonnay** Forward, butterscotch vanilla bouquet; similar flavours, ends on abrupt sweet-'n-sour note. From **97**. 13,5% alc. **Symphony** Dry sauvignon blanc-chenin blanc (65/35) blend. **96** now lacking melody. **Blanc Fumé** Understated figgy ripeness in partially barrel-fermented **97**; full-bodied, short finish. **Chenin Blanc** Full-bodied unwooded **98**; quiet ripe tropical, honeyed fruit should develop over year; smoothly dry. Pvs. portion barrel-fermented. **Bouquet Blanc** Pale gold glints in sweet floral/muscat-scented chenin/bukettraube blend. **97** undemanding, gentle 30 gms/l sugar.

SPIER WINE ESTATE

Stellenbosch See Stellenbosch map

Open for tastings and sales by appointment only.

Restaurant: Two planned: one formal with views over Stellenbosch-kloof, the other informal. Picnic facilities will also be available.

Owner: Hydro Holdings

Winemaker: Teddy Hall (since July 1998)
Vineyards: Johann Schloms
P.O. Box 548, Stellenbosch 7599
Tel: 021-8813808 **Fax:** 021-8813514
E-mail: info@spierwines.co.za
Website: www.spierwines.co.za

This is not to be confused with Spier Cellars. It is an entirely different establishment, in a different part of Stellenbosch, owned by a different company—Hydro Holdings, proprietors of Mulderbosch. Here was the home of the Goedgeloof cellar in which the original farmers of Spier, the Joubert family, made their wines. Now this estate is bursting into new life. The old cellar has been gutted and re-equipped. Ancient cement red-wine tanks have been incorporated into the design, but as points of interest rather than for use. Gardens have been landscaped with indigenous plants, and a bird-island created in a dam—putting in more than a few oars is passionate ecologist Mike Dobrovic, winemaker at Mulderbosch and OC here too. There's a wholescale replanting programme of premium varieties on the go. A think-first, act-thereafter approach—"let's get it right before we go on the market"—is evident throughout. For example, the restaurant planned to overlook the barrel cellar was not designed until the future restaurateur had been consulted.

SPRINGBOK

See KWV International

SPRINGFIELD ESTATE

Robertson

See Robertson map

Open Mon-Sat 8-5. Tastings & sales.
Owner/Winemaker: Abrie Bruwer (since 1983)
Production: 40 000 cases. **Vineyards:** 160 ha.
P.O. Box 770, Robertson 6705
Tel: 02351-3661/4728 **Fax:** 02351-3664

Talk to Abrie Bruwer for more than ten minutes and you will be totally confused: on the one hand, it's obvious he is a perfectionist. From his immaculate and functional cellar to his stylish and beautifully presented packaging and promotional material, much careful thought has been expended on every aspect of this up-and-coming business. Then hear the story of the pH meter (the piece of kit used to measure potential acidity in wines) "We use the lab. at Graham Beck now", he confides. "One year I forgot to order some buffer solution" (used to calibrate the gadget), "but I remembered being taught that saliva has the same pH as buffer, so I went through the vintage spitting on the electrodes: seemed to work, but my Dad thought it was a bit risky." The man is a mine of quirky quotes and homespun logic: on grape ripeness: "We don't pick on sugar—we look at seed maturity . . . we'd rather make a monumental stuff-up than a huge quantity of mediocre wine." He wishes he had a vintage every month to get more practice, rather than only one per year. And ask this passionate angler where he's travelled overseas this past year and what he picked up: "I learned that Mauritius is over-fished."

This farm on the banks of the Breede River, with its hard, lime-rich soils, bottles only its top wines, and will in future be more heavily planted to red varieties. Harmony with nature, some risky winemaking, such as use of natural yeasts on the grapes in some special ferments, instead of inoculation with cultured varieties, and ruthless restriction of yields in this prolific terroir have all propelled Springfield pretty close to the top of the heap. Future plans for the cellar include modifications to the red wine fermenters to allow working with whole berries: a new bottling line has created independence and total control from start to finish of these hand-crafted wines. Changes in the vineyards include re-aligning whole blocks to allow for more even ripening.

*** **Cabernet Sauvignon 97** (for rel. Feb 99) opens with green-olive, capsicum and cinnamon aromas, with bright cassis and vanilla flavours to follow. Bold, full-bodied, juicy; 50% matured in 2nd-fill French 300 litre casks: sparse 4 tons/ha, Schleip clone. **96** still youthful, similar profile. Who said Robertson wasn't budding cabernet country?

**** **Sauvignon Blanc Special Cuvée 98** from tiny yield of 4 tons/ha., fermented for over 3 months on lees, shows refined, elegant fig, pear and nettle aromas, followed by great concentration from 24 hr maceration on skins, and a pH of just over 3 from the limey soils. Minimal cellar handling ensures great length, not only on palate, but in the bottle: will age well over 4-5 years. **97 VG. 95** still a stunner which rocked many critics of the warm Robertson region.

**** **Chardonnay Méthode Ancienne 97** a real shot in the dark: bright limey yellow-green, with rich oily, citrus aromas, followed by pineapple, butterscotch. Huge, gutsy, muscular, no-quarter-given flavours, creamy finish. "Made in the ancient style of Burgundy," says Abrie Bruwer: natural yeast ferment for 55 days, 12 months on lees in French oak, unfined, unfiltered, unstabilised . . . can it be safe to drink? Certainly, if you can bring yourself to open the classy wax closure on the handsome bottle. Perhaps cellar for a year or three to bring out the best. A bold statement.

*** **Sauvignon Blanc ◀ 98** powerful, flinty pear, fig, gooseberry whiffs, latter flowing to grapefruity palate; highly reductive winemaking on night-harvested grapes picked at meagre 6 tons/ha. from 15-year-old vines, makes for well-structured ageworthy wine. "When we taste fig in the grapes, we pick," says the instinctive winemaker. When tasted, seemed more forward than Sp. Cuvée.

*** **Chardonnay ◀ 97** full-on butterscotch/toast aromas, followed by attractive limey flavours, hints of asparagus, hazelnuts. 24-day fermentation, 30% in new French barrels, full natural malo, 3 mths on lees and light filtration ensure interesting development. 13% alc., 3,2 pH.

Colombard-Chardonnay ◀ 98 rich, oily citrus-rind aromas, full-bodied (13% alc.) blend 77/23% colombard/chardonnay, some aged 2nd-fill Vosges barrels. Crisp tropical fruits of former follow to creamy, sweetish, easy-drinking finish: but a simple quaffer this is not. A sound, lightly-oaked dry white wine.

SPRUITDRIFT CO-OPERATIVE

Spruitdrift See Olifants River map

Tastings/sales Mon-Fri 8-5.30. Sat 8.30-12. Cellar tours as above.

Braai area for up to 60, conference facilities for up to 40. Book ahead.

Owners: 85 members

Winemaker: Erik Schlünz (since 1996)

Viticulturist: Jeff Joubert

Production: 28 500 tons. **Vineyards:** 1 400 ha.

P.O. Box 129, Vredendal 8160

Tel: 0271-33086 **Fax:** 0271-32937

Workers' conditions and incentives are priorities here: housing has been upgraded; a project to build nursery schools/crèches for farm-workers' children on strategic sites is on the go; winemaker Johan Rossouw and chairman of the board of directors Johan Voigt sit on the steering committee of the local school, and the cellar sponsors two of its rugby teams.

Cabernet Sauvignon ◀ Relaxed, no-fuss-drink-now **97** cab., very light (11,3% alc.) plus sweet blackberry flavours, low acid, for quaffability. Pleasant, clean, alfresco red, at home round a braai fire. **Merlot** Plummy nose, soft palate, easy-drinking **97**. **Cabernet-Sauvignon-Merlot** ☺ NEW Plummy aromas, fairly soft fruit (50/50 blend in **97**), just enough tannin to firm up palate. Rather nice pasta, superior braai red. 12% alc. **Pinotage** Quaff-now **97** for fans of traditional, high-tone-scented pinotage; fresh, lively flavours. **Chardonnay 98** "slightly wooded" says winemaker; pervasive oak when tasted mid-1998. Some butterscotch notes, quite a kick (13,7% alc.). Sip rather than quaff. **Chenin Blanc** NEW ◀ Bone-dry **98**, clean, fresh guava from beginning to end. Lightish (11,9% alc.) summer swigging. **Sauvignon Blanc** Drink-young **98** food partner: nettly, gooseberry scents, bright-fresh flavours. Dry. **Grand Crû** Light, dry, everyday drinking, pleasant guava nose, **98** chenin with 10% colombard. **Weisser Riesling** Light **98** semi-sweet (26 gms/l sugar) rather than pvs. off-dry. Untasted. **Late Harvest** Tropical-scented, honey-flavoured **97** semi-sweet chenin, light. **Rapsodie** NEW 70% chenin, 30% morio muscat **98** blend: semi-sweet, light, in popular "bouquet" style. Untasted. **Special Late Harvest** Pleasant, sweet, light with-pudding chenin, **97** has gained honeyed tones. **White Muscadel** Honeyed, clean, warm **97** dessert. **Red Muscadel** Pomegranate hued **98**, light, bunch of fresh, rich muscat grapes. **Hanepoot 97** golden yellow dessert, smooth, warm nutty tones. **Vin Doux Sparkling Wine** 80% chenin, 20% muscadel blend from **97**, light, sweet, festively fizzy.

SPUR WINES — For the steak ranch chain by Simonsig

Buffalo Red Light-bodied, fruity quaffing. Pinotage-based soft plummy, spicy flavours. **Desert Moon** Softly dry blend with spicy notes; medium-bodied, clean finish. **Autumn Rain** Mainly chenin blanc with muscat, spice suggestions; elegantly honeyed; smooth but not cloying. **Sparkling Rain** Chenin with Rhine riesling, muscat, soft, semi-sweet, carbonated bubbly.

STEENBERG VINEYARDS

Constantia — See Constantia map

Open wine tastings & sales weekdays 9-4; Sept-Feb. Sat 9-12. **Tasting charges:** Tour groups R5 per head. Cellar tours by appointment only.

19-room hotel. Restaurant open daily; breakfast 7-10, lunch 12-2.30, dinner 7-10.30; bar open 11 am-11 pm for oysters, wine, etc. Also golf club, meals, drinks. See restaurant section.

Owner: Johnnies Industrial Corporation (Johnnic)
Winemaker: Nicky Versfeld (since June 1996)
Vineyards: Herman Hanekom (since 1990)
Production: 25 000 cases. **Vineyards**: 70 ha.
P.O. Box 10801, Steenberg Estate 7945
Tel: 021-7132211 **Fax:** 021-7132201
E-mail: info@steenbrg.co.za; sales@steenbrg.co.za
Website: http//:users.iafrica.com/s/st/stf-wine/

Steenberg's wine philosophy matches every other facet of this historic estate, owned by Cyril Ramaphosa's mighty Johnnic group. Here's an elegant country hotel, fine restaurant, immaculate golf course fringed with luxury homes . . . unsurprisingly the aim in this estate's vineyards and cellar is to produce "a limited range of superb quality wines".

The vines are, mostly, still young—for example 1998 saw the first crops of shiraz and nebbiolo (the latter a first for South Africa, too). While the more-established sauvignon blanc has shown its class, with frequent awards, the red plantings are still to stretch their legs fully. But the potential here is exciting: vineyard guru Herman Hanekom believes that in Steenberg's more open sites, lighter soils, grapes ripen more easily than elsewhere in this premium wine valley, and he's confident that the estate's upcoming reds will challenge, if not beat, the neighbours. Certainly the quality leap from the **96** to **97 Merlot** indicates that these reds are on a roll. And a new wooded sémillon shows the versatility of talented winemaker Nicky Versfeld. He worked the vintage in Sancerre and Graves in 1997, and hopes to bring to his wines in Constantia, where the SA wine industry first took root more than 300 years ago, the sort of dedication and attention to detail—geared towards "wines which express the typicity of each area"—which he observed in France.

Steenberg's commitment to community development is noteworthy: the estate is financing one of the first black students of oenology and viticulture at Stellenbosch University and runs a crèche and literacy programme on the farm, while also contributing—with other nearby estates—to the running costs of the valley's primary school.

STEENBERG range:

**** **Merlot** Sophisticated **97** step up on impressive début **96**. Cooler vintage, older vines provide more substance, finesse, complexity. Deep minerally, chocolate peppermint cream fragrance; similar flavours in elegant silky wrapping. Relaxed tannins. Oak-matured (70% new). **96** luscious, intensely rich macerated plums, liquid dark chocolate; softly dry, gentle, probably best up to 4 years.

*** **Cabernet Sauvignon** Older vines, cooler **97** (****) vintage show: more body, complexity than pvs. Quiet fragrance: cigar box, tobacco leaf, whiffs of cassis. Correspondingly unshowy flavours set off by ripe, fine tannins. Barrel-maturation broadens dimensions, does not swamp elegance. French oak-matured one year, 50% new. **96** second bottling. Supple juicy fruit has developed warmer toasty, nutty tones. Retains ultra-soft texture with gentle tannin resonance. Drink now, or before 2000. Half matured one year in new Allier/Nevers barrels.

**** **Sauvignon Blanc** In top Cape league since **94**. **98** best yet. Two bottlings, different vineyards (distinguished on back label). First shows New/Old World cross-over character of **97 SAA**, **WINE** ****, **VVG** but broader sweep of figgy richness in **98**, a bit more swagger to its aristocratic profile. Elegantly prolonged flavours promise even more exciting development than **97**, which drinking very stylishly after year in bottle. Second **98** version more delicate, with flinty, sweet cut grass evanescence. Fine, crisp freshness; appetising poise.

*** **Sémillon** NEW **97** half-blend of barrel/tank-fermented wine with cool lemony, herbaceous delicacy, somewhat meagre, one-dimensional. **98** promises more 100% barrel-fermented, 30% new oak, complexity: highlights sémillon's rich texture, broadens ripe honey-and-lemon aromas. Expansive, ripely dry; good ageing potential.

**** **Sémillon** NEW Unwooded **98**; unusually distinctive for variety in youth without oak support. Richly-textured, weighty with creamy, lemony concentration, length. Polished grassy tang in tail. Generously built, 14% alc., but still shows farm's trademark balanced elegance. Already well integrated; should develop over next year or two.

Chardonnay 100% barrel-fermented, pleasantly juicy **98** promises more structure, concentration, drier lemony freshness than **97** with rich, tropical fruit, some mid-palate sweetness but quite elegant.

MOTIF range:

★★★ **Rouge Sec** Quality second-label red for early drinking. **97** cab. s./merlot blend (79%/21%) from young vineyards. Appealing violet, cassis fragrance; gentle chocolaty tones, minimum tannin interference. Oak-matured, all used, one year.

Rosé 98 unusual chardonnay, cab. s., pinot noir mix; unwooded; dry with soft raspberry flavours. **Blanc Sec 98** unwooded sauvignon blanc/sémillon blend. Fruitily smooth, early-drinking quaffer.

STELLENBOSCH FARMERS' WINERY (SFW)

Major South African merchant-producer, with leading brands in every sector and segment of the market; from its top-of-the-range Zonnebloem wines, to its popularly-priced, high volume sellers, SFW has had a significant influence on the tastes of most South African wine drinkers. Some of its brands (listed separately in this guide) still dominate their categories after more than half a century: La Gratitude, Château Libertas, Tassenberg, Lieberstein, Grand Mousseux, Lanzerac. There are also export-only ranges like Sable View and Libertas, and specialised products handled by separate teams, such as Nederburg, Monis and Plaisir de Merle.

SFW's activities extend to vineyard liaison work with the growers who supply grapes for its various brands, the management of an experimental nursery, Ernita, generating virus-free planting material, and the organisation of the annual Nederburg Auction, the industry's showcase wine event. The company is also involved in cultural, educational and sporting sponsorships. Its Oude Libertas open-air theatre presents an annual summer season of music, drama and dance.

SFW is controlled by the same shareholders (Rembrandt and KWV) as its major "competitor", Distillers Corporation, but operates independently.

Cellarmaster: Wouter Pienaar. **Winery Manager**: Koos Jordaan

P.O. Box 46, Stellenbosch 7599

Tel: 021-8087911 **Fax:** 021-8871355/8865414

STELLENBOSCH VINEYARDS Ltd

See Stellenbosch map

See also: Welmoed Wines, Eersterivier Cellar, Helderberg Winery, Bottelary Winery

Tasting/purchasing facilities at all above premises. Entire range can be ordered from Tel: 021-8822204, Fax: 021-8822205, or purchased at Twin Oaks, Main Road, Somerset West (Tel: 021-8527307).

Restaurants at Welmoed, Helderberg

Production: 30 000 tons, 400 000 cases, 3 500 hectares owned by 158 shareholders

Managing Director: Hermann Böhmer

Production Manager: Inus Muller

Head Winemaker-designate: Chris Kelly

Viticulturist: Francois de Villiers

Marketing Manager: Geoff Harvey

Commercial Manager: Marius Burger

Stellenbosch Bottling Manager: Frans Albertyn

Public Relations: Lucille Nel
P.O. Box 465, Stellenbosch 7599.
Tel: 021-8813870 **Fax:** 021-8813102

Hermann Böhmer and Inus Muller are men with a mission. Faced with the business, technical, legal and marketing intricacies of merging 4 former co-operative producers into a new commercial entity, Stellenbosch Vineyards Ltd. (SV), they've not lost sight of the human element, one that often accommodates change at a lesser pace. An opportunity to involve shareholders—the grape growing members of Welmoed, Eersterivier, Helderberg and Bottelary wineries—and staff in forging a new identity came with "Versus". More than just a vehicle for a large volume, entry-level brand, the conceptualisation, planning and launch of the product became a company affair. Different in every way—hence the name which signals going against convention—from its 1 000 ml format (not one litre—staff are "fined" for mentioning that, visitors come close) through a glossy ad campaign to innovative point of sale material (retail stands, restaurant ice buckets) and branded delivery vehicles, it has gelled "ownership" of SV for stakeholders from potentially disparate backgrounds. A new premium label is on the cards to maintain the momentum.

Discussion about merging goes back a long way but gained impetus in late 1995 and the 4 co-ops were consolidated into one in May 1996. This single co-op became a company in early 1997 and it immediately acquired Stellenbosch Bottling (Pty) Ltd as part of its long-term strategy to control all aspects of production. The motive was to offer diversity from a single entity to multiple clients, to shift from peddling commodities to adding value. The challenge has been to motivate grape growers to become wine farmers whose interest does not end with the cutting of bunches, and instil a profit rather than guaranteed minimum price motive. Part of the task is to persuade member landowners to invest in their vineyards ("where quality begins") as well as bring farm workers on board as benefiting parties. A community trust has been established to this end. The first candidate for a potential winemaking bursary scheme joined SV in 1998 and cash should flow into the trust once dividends come on stream.

The changes also affect a "stakeholder" cited by SV—the consumer. Branding alterations cannot be absorbed overnight and confusion is a risk. Three of the wineries—Eersterivier, Helderberg and Bottelary—were co-ops named prior to wine of origin legislation that then incorporated the area names they held. Negotiation has resulted in their retaining the well-known names if they remain wineries (and not individual companies) making wines of the region they initially served. The 3 will continue under the SV banner, with Bottelary being scaled down. "Welmoed" becomes a brand rather than winery (and draws material from all the others) while a "Stellenbosch" range joins "Versus" as company products.

There's solidity to the image projected by Böhmer and Muller. Youthful vigour blends with experience, international flair with salt-of-the-earth tradition. But what is common, is vision. No cloistered targets for this company. It intends to be both global, and in beverages rather than merely wine. One's sense is that it will take a great deal to derail the momentum.

*** **Versus** ◀ NEW Freshness is the focus, from bright straw colour to tropical peach aromas. Crisp grassy palate, hint of residual sugar cleaned by fresh zest. Unwooded blend chenin, sauvignon blanc. Innovative, clever product, good value retail under R20 per 1 000 ml. "Flying", says Böhmer.

SV FLAGSHIP range: (to be named)
Samples of premium reds intended for launch late 1999.
SV Shiraz 97 full ruby, aromatic vanilla spice, soft ripe tannins encase gentle fruit. **SV Cabernet Sauvignon 97** concentrated colour, tense blackberry fruit, zippy, good length.
STELLENBOSCH range: ALL NEW
Blanc de Noir Salmon blush, cherry fruit, tiring, off-dry finish. **Dry Steen** Nutty nose, honeyed peach, fruit fading. **Weisser Riesling** Floral rose-petal nose, neutral palate, off-dry. **Special Late Harvest** ◀ Golden, cling peach freshness, doesn't cloy. **Port** Plummy, nuts, spirit still raw.

STELLENBOSCH WINES DIRECT

Direct-to-your-door, duty-paid forwarding of Cape wine to other countries is the latest innovation of this high-voltage operation, spreading its tentacles from a Victorian office-cum-wine promotion centre at Vlottenburg. "Through our freshly-incorporated freight subsidiary, Cape Wines Direct, we take out the hassle, inconvenience and expense of going to air- and seaports," says Simon Lavarack, distribution specialist and owner of Stellenbosch Wines Direct. In anticipation of proposed liquor legislation, SWD's wholesaling and retailing operations have been split—local trade sales, exports now are spearheaded by former SWD shareholder/director Jan du Preez through his independent Du Preez Wines operation. Du Preez, an experienced winemaker, also selects wines for the SWD range, which aims to offer "easy, everyday enjoyment at affordable prices".

Open: Mon-Fri 9-5. Sat 9-1. Tasting fee R10 p/p.
P.O. Box 37, Vlottenburg 7604
Tel: 021-8813791 **Fax:** 021-8813740
E-mail: sales@winesdirect.co.za
Internet: www.winesdirect.co.za

SWD range: ◀ Unpretentious budget-priced quaffers.
Your Daily Red NV A cut above: forward spicy raspberry, appetising savoury hints, near-imperceptible tannin, easy. Very nice. **Your Daily White** NV clean, crisp, fruity/floral, ready to picnic or party.
TWIN OAKS range:
Cabernet Sauvignon 97 sweet-spicy cassis, full-bodied, a good pizza, vegetarian red. 13% alc. **Ruby Cabernet** ☺ **97** an unpretentious charmer, loads of blackberries, easygoing, slug-it-and-love-it. "This ruby bowled the French over," says Jan du Preez. **Dry Red** ☺ **97** red/blackberry *jus*, down-textured, easy, full-flavoured; lowish acids, med. body enhances gulpability. Pinotage, cab. s., ruby cab. **Sauvignon Blanc 97** gentle grassy sauvignon flavours, light honey coating, relaxed quaffing. **Chenin Blanc** Friendly outdoor/picnic companion **97**, light guavas, lively acid.
LEIDERSBURG range:
Features grapes from 18 ha. St'bosch v'yd owned by Jan du Preez, foreign investors. For local, export markets.
Cabernet Sauvignon Bunches of ripe cherry fruit in **97**, smooth, no angles, engineered to beguile. High 7 gms/l acid balanced by abundant fruit. "Will age well" is vintner's prognostication. 11,5% alc. **Grand Cuvée Rouge 97** light-bodied, dry red from gamay, cab. s., no-frills quaffing. Takes well to chilling. **Chardonnay** ☺ NEW Quaffable barrel-fermented **98**, ripe tropical fruit (mango in foreground), silky texture, good fruit/acid balance, vanilla-pod in finish. Easy, indoor/outdoor/anytime wine. Malo complete. **Grand Cuvée Blanc 97** riesling, colombard. Fruity, chewy, everyday dry white. Lowish alc.: 11,5%.

STELLENRYCK COLLECTION — Made by Bergkelder

★★★★ **Cabernet Sauvignon 94** confirms style-change heralded by big, resonant **93**. Current release certainly a sturdy lass but graceful—ballerina in diva's garb. Attractive sweet black-cherry bouquet, intense, persistent berry flavours, dark chocolate coating, expansive mouth-feel, good length, soft vanilla-toned finish. 13% alc. Gorgeous **93** booms green pepper, mulberry, fine oak. Loads of ripe, juicy fruit, spicy, charry oak. Has tannin architecture to develop further.

★★★ **Chardonnay** Forward, open **97** has developed peachy/oaky aromas, platter of fruits (peach, melon, fig), well managed oak. 13,5% alc. Pvs. more gentle flavours of peach, some citrus, vanilla, shy-scented but quite elegant. Barrel-fermented.

★★★★ **Sauvignon Blanc 97** at peak, should be consumed while showing good bottle age, harmonious light-toned citrus/tropical fruit. 11% alc. From St'bosch, Durbanville grapes. **95** string of awards: **VVG**, trophy at **IWSC** 1996, **WINE**★★★★. Before **96** wooded, labelled Blanc Fumé.

STELLENVALE — Gilbeys export range

Pinotage Medium-bodied, fruity, barrel-matured red. **Sauvignon Blanc** Unwooded, lively gooseberries, guavas. **95** SA champion white at 1995 young wine show. **Chardonnay-Sauvignon Blanc** Individual dry white, gentle oaking. Blend varies with vintage, consistently good food partner. **Chardonnay** New World white, vanilla/citrus personality. Barrel-fermented/matured.

STELLENZICHT VINEYARDS

Stellenbosch See Stellenbosch map

Visits by appointment only.
Owners: Hans-Joachim Schreiber
Marketing & Sales Director: Ansias Londt
Winemaker: To be appointed
Vineyards: Derrick Steyn
Production: 60 000 cases. **Vineyards:** 140 ha.
P.O. Box 104, Stellenbosch 7599
Tel: 021-8801103 **Fax:** 021-8801107
E-mail: nee@mweb.co.za

The rather large gap left in this cellar by the departure of big André van Rensburg to Vergelegen, on the other side of the Helderberg, had not yet been filled permanently when this guide went to press. But fans of Stellenzicht's dramatic wines need not fuss—all-important here (as Van Rensburg always stressed) are the excellent, cool-altitude vineyards which continue to be carefully tended by man-of-the-soil Derrick Steyn. And burly Schalk van der Westhuizen, OC of sister-cellar Neethlingshof, stepped ably into the breach for the 98 vintage—early tastings indicate the house "recipe"—chief ingredient quality fruit—has been successfully followed. Laurel of the year was the "Best SA White" award at London's 1998 International Wine & Spirits Competition for the (Van Rensburg-made) **97 Sémillon Reserve**. A follow-up **98** is looking rather good. Though this property's reputation continues to rest on its mainstream, premium dry wines, don't pass over its sweeter pearls: the NLH has a permanent spot in the Cape first team, and the White Muscadel is delightful. Some of the more recent red vintages (including Stellenzicht's famous Syrah) are being held back in the cellar, pending release-date decisions, and were unavailable for tasting this edition.

★★★★ **Merlot 95** absolute beaut. Deep, soft, velvet-textured, coffee bean, plum-flavoured delight. **94** forceful, with fruity-tension and grip; tight finish. 9 months in oak.

★★★ **Shiraz-Grenache** NEW Big, rich, finely textured **96** Southern Rhône-style blend. Warm, with sumptuous ripe, red berry fruits. Encouragingly modern. An excellent avenue for grenache.

★★★★ **Syrah** One of SA's most impressive and acclaimed new-wave reds, a convincing symbol of the modern Cape wine renaissance, specially in **95** and **94** (both nudging ★★★★★); those who bought at the time—you'll be super-fortunate to find either still around on retail shelves—were prescient (even at **95**'s R98 a bottle). Because there's no **96**—the vintage didn't deliver the prime quality fruit. Will always, in any case, be made in very small quantities, from low-yielding—2,25 tons an acre, 10-year-old—vineyard called Plum Pudding Hill. **95** deep plum hues, smells of rich spices, hints of wild, dried herbs, touch smoky; a twitch of heathery garrigue even, soft-textured, easy charm for a wine of such volume (alc. 14%) and substance, ripe tannins almost smothered by fruit; barrel-ageing barely discernible past the conentrated but limpid-textured taste of spicy grapes. Partly new, partly American oak barrel ageing. **94 VG**, in similar style, was judged better than Australia's fabled Grange Hermitage (**91**) by an international panel at Oz-SA Wine Test in 1995. **93 SAA** Selection All drinking splendidly. **95** should be superb as a millennium celebration, if you're able to resist it until then.

★★★★ **Cabernet Sauvignon** ◀ Top-class cab. **96** not available for tasting, but no reason to suspect won't be every bit as splendid, in modern Cape mood, as **95** (with tiny dashes merlot, cab. franc). **95** berry and mint nose, lush, ripe blackcurrants. Big and mouthfilling, developing with majesty. Cinnamon-scented **94 VVG** similarly mouth-broadening, substantial, featuring brilliant plum colour, ripe fruit. Both 17 months in oak—40% new—minimally handled; no stabilisation, no filtration. 13,2% alc., 6,2 gms/l acid. **94** has 13% merlot.

★★★★ **Stellenzicht (Red)** B'deaux-type blend of cabernet sauvignon/franc and merlot. **94 VG,** WINE★★★★, 69:9:22 ratios; fine quality ripe fruit—developing with age, soft, big mouth-feel, some coffee, chocolate aromas in fairly showy bouquet. Barrel-aged, 40% new. Alcs. between 12,5-13%. Next release may jump a few vintages to **98**.

★★★ **Merlot-Cabernet Franc** ◀ 77% merlot in **94 VG**; abundant soft cherries/berries on nose; mouthfilling dark choc/berry palate, well-integrated oak. Deep soft texture.

★★★★ **Sauvignon Blanc** Invariably one of Cape's finest. **98** with sweet/dry gooseberry character, full-flavoured, penetrating, sweet nettle/gooseberry softness on palate making for fascinating experience. **95**, Champion SA young wine, **VVG**, WINE★★★★. Due to lateness of vintage, **97 (WINE**★★★★) still to reach its potential but might be overtaken by **98** in overall quality. More moderate **VVG 96** (cooler vintage, lower alc. 12% and general profile) was still piercing, gravelly-stony, with long, very dry finish. 7,7 gms/l acid. **95** still full of gooseberry-flint flavours, drinking well.

★★★★ **Cuvée Hans Schreiber** This massive **97** Sauvignon Blanc was made in minute quantity, 500 cases, from highly selected fruit, late-picked, which shows in its 13,5% alc. Designed to develop over 4-6 years and revisited in 1998, still not for the faint-hearted. Combination of clean, crisp herbaceous tones and lively tangy, lemony palate with lots of gooseberry and nettle. Decidedly mouthfilling.

★★★★ **Sémillon Reserve 97** Cape Wine Academy trophy in 1998 for best SA white at IWSC, **WINE**★★★★. Full, well developed, powerful lemon/herbal aromas over leesy, vanilla tones. Broad on palate with intensity, length, beautiful balance—fulfilling intention "to make sémillon a main-line white". **96, 95 VG**. These food wines, with grassier, hay-like, savoury meadow flavours rather than full-frontal fruit. Preview of **98** very promising.

*** **Sauvignon Blanc-Sémillon** Delightful lime-fresh, ice-cream soda, honeysuckle and a touch of seaweed. Not surprised a **VG** in **97**. Pvs. more serious, dignified, but equally satisfying. Lots of presence at table. Excellent bottle development over year or two. **96 VVG, 95 VG**.

*** **Chardonnay 97**, and **96** more concentration than pvs., though all to date classically rich with lees, ripe melon and lemon scents; barrel-fermented. **95** gold at 1995 Mondiale Selections, *Decanter* top 100 in **95**, **VVG** in 1996. Low 3,5 tons/ha. yields.

*** **Sauvignon Blanc-Chenin Blanc (Formerly Heerenblanc) 98** big-boned, gorgeous wine packed with tropical fruit and ripe apples. Just dry (4 gms/l). **95** SAA selection, **VG**.

*** **Fragrance** Popular **97** as delightful as ever. Off-dry, muscat-scented white—muscats morio/alexandrie, erlihane. **96 VVG**. Well chilled makes charming aperitif.

**** **Noble Late Harvest** ◀ None since **96**; next might be **98**. Pvs. almost as decorated as sister property Neethlingshof's NLH. And in more guises here—weisser riesling (3 versions in **95**, two for export) plus sauvignon blanc, sémillon. Aims at drier style, but full character from less than 3 tons/ha. **96** weisser riesling WINE****, **VGG**. Full, gold and complex, rich with kumquat, naartjies, hint of oak. Spice and vanilla notes too. Not cloying. Local label **95** weisser: moderate sweetness, 129 gms/l; moderate alc. at 11,2%—tension between scintillating medley of ripe fruits, biting freshness. Acid 8,6 gms/l.

*** **White Muscadel** Gorgeous, well flavoured **97**, sweet muscat with good balancing acidity, making fine aperitif rather than digestif.

ST. ELMO'S

Restaurant range by Simonsig

Dry Red Light-bodied, pinotage-based blend. Uncomplicated plummy spicy flavours; soft tannins for easy quaffing. **Dry White** Soft, medium-bodied blend with gentle Rhine riesling, muscat influence. **Stein** Elegant, honeyed chenin, gentle spicy intrusions; smooth, easy-drinking.

STONEWALL

Helderberg See Helderberg map

Tasting/sales by appointment.
Owner: De Waal Koch
Winemaker: Martin Meinert (since 1998)
Viticulturist: De Waal Koch
Vineyards: 80 ha.
P.O. Box 5145, Helderberg 7135
Tel: 021-8553675 **Fax:** 021-8552206

This Helderberg hatchling operating from a gracious (stone) walled Cape-Dutch estate, boasting mature marine-cooled v'yds, has a knack of attracting top-of-the-vat winemaking talent. The inaugural (1997) crush was ably conducted by Mark Carmichael-Green, one of SFW's young stars; in 1998 thoughtful, highly experienced Martin Meinert—owner of Devoncrest and, with Ken Forrester, partner in nearby gourmet eatery 96 Winery Road brought his considerable verve to the operation. The ex-Vergelegen cellarmaster's know-how was inspanned by Stonewall proprietor De Waal Koch a mere week before harvest. "Luckily a talented New Zealender, James Graham, approached us at about that time and slotted in superbly," Meinert reports. "For both of us the challenge was to get to know the v'yds—*pronto!*"

★★★ **Merlot-Cabernet Sauvignon** (pvsly Stonewall Red) **97** impressive, complex, fleshy, most inviting. But should reward those patient enough to wait 4-6 more years for tightly-coiled tannins to relax, broaden. Merlot-cabernet s. (60/40), 20-25-year-old bush vines, French oak barrels ± year. Low-bearing cabernet—6-7 tons/ha.

★★★ **Chardonnay 97** showing all signs of matching winemaker's 6-8 year maturation horizon. Very young still, with a gymnast's muscularity, suppleness. Limey/toasty flavour profile, big mouthful (13% alc. plus). Barrel-fermented; from own, bough-in St'bosch grapes.

★★★ **Chenin Blanc 98** first of the Meinert-Graham progeny—and what a strapping young-un it is! Broad-shouldered (13,5% alc.), fresh (7,6 gms/l acid), clearly not your average chenin. But attractive, distinctive, too: intriguing herbal, litchi, lime (and more conventional guava) inflections, vanilla underlay. Partly barrel-fermented, extra oomph from some American oak. Tasted in extreme youth.

Sauvignon Blanc 98 another boisterous bambino. Fresh gust of gooseberry, nettle, bold pineapple/herby flavours, resounding finish. Unwooded, own bushvines, 7 tons/ha. yield, 13,4% alc.

STONY BROOK

Franschhoek See Franschhoek map

Tastings/sales Sat morning or by appointment.
Owners: Nigel and Joy McNaught
Winemaker: Nigel McNaught (since 1996)
Viticulturist: Paul Wallace
Production: 4 000 cases. **Vineyards:** 12 ha.
P.O. Box 22, Franschhoek 7690
Tel/Fax: 021-8762182
E-mail: mcnaught@iafrica.com

Nigel McNaught, a doctor whose hobby is growing and making wine, seems incapable of turning out any little grey specimens. Every wine in this range is a strong—verging on off-beat—character, and it's unsurprising that he pinpoints "individuality" as the cornerstone of his winemaking philosophy. He expands on his aims at this small Franschhoek farm: "To let the wines of the valley reflect their/its uniqueness without trying to mimic other varieties/areas." The white-red wine grape ratio is 55-45 here (relatively rare malbec is among the plantings), and it's the whites which have been the first to win serious local laurels. The McNaughts are currently pursuing plans for a wine to be made and marketed by their workers.

★★★ **Sémillon Reserve** NEW More flavour than many SA sémillons in **97**: lemons, limes, vanilla oak on nose/palate, chalky texture, good body, long-lasting zesty finish. WINE★★★★. From minute 3 ton/ha. yield, 70-yr-old bush vines; barrel-fermented 50% new, 50% 2nd-fill Nevers oak. Substantial 13,8% alc.

Shiraz Rustic food partner: **96** lightweight, pleasant smoky-gamey traditional traits, some spice with ripe plum-tomato flavours, tight tannic tail.
Chardonnay 97 WINE★★★★. Lime, lemon, candied citrus peel scents, crisp sweet-sour pear flavours, very dry finish. Barrel-fermented (half new; half

2nd-fill), oak-matured 10 months. **Sauvignon Blanc** Made for food: **98** in herby, very bright, brisk style.

STORMY CAPE

See Thelema

SWARTLAND WINE CELLAR

Swartland See Swartland map

Open for tastings & sales Mon-Fri 8-5; Sat 9-12.
Members: 102
Head of Production: Olla Olivier (since June 1996)
Winemakers: Andries Blake (since 1996), red wines; Kas Huisamen (since 1998), white wines
Marketing Manager: Charlto Opperman
Quality Control: Karien Lourens
Production: 25 000 ton capacity. **Vineyards:** 3 000 ha.
P.O. Box 95, Malmesbury 7300
Tel: 0224-21134/5/6 **Fax:** 0224-21750
E-mail: swynkelder@mbury.new.co.za

South African co-op wineries, currently on a renaissance roll, should tip their hats to this excellent cellar, which almost a decade ago blazed the quality-above-quantity, good-wine-not-distilling trail down which its peers are now stampeding. And pioneered a break-away movement from local merchant wholesalers which now sees almost every co-operative increasing the volume of wine made under own-labels—and for the export market. Long before that big boom reverberated generally round the winelands, Swartland's rich, ripe fruit (low yields, payments to growers on quality not volume have for years dictated the approach here) had been singled out by UK giants like Tesco and Sainsburys as an ideal provider of the modern, easy-drinking, ready-to-go wine style contemporary consumers clamour for. These big customers are still smiling—as is the Swartland team, which reports that South Africa is now "the country with the lowest number of complaints registered by consumers in these supermarkets".

New developments include the arrival of another two pneumatic presses—the cellar equipment is now spankingly modern from top to toe, including a state-of-the-art bottling line. No oak chips are used—it's either small barrels or staves. In the growers' vineyards, the emphasis is now on beefing up red wine production. The current 75-25 white/red ratio must, the team believes, become 50-50 to satisfy demand.

Consistency is the beacon here—not that easy when you're handling massive blends of 3 to 400 000 litres, as new white winemaker Kas Huisamen found in 1998. He's had stints in the Pfalz in Germany, and Ashton, Bergsig and Hartswater cellars, but his larger responsibilities at this admirable winery are "giving me grey hair *and* a grey beard", he says, happily. Overall cellar chief Olla Olivier, while scanning the big picture, nevertheless can't resist keeping his eye (and hands) in—see the Chardonnay Reserve below.

Most importantly for the consumer, this range remains quite remarkable value.

**** **Cabernet-Merlot Reserve** ◀ Now recognised as serious red in any company. Inviting chocolate and mint bouquet **97** leads to refined palate with subtle dark-berried fruit. Tannins very dry, still bit harsh, needing another year or two, but enough for the impatient. Dry nutty finish. No variety dominates, a true blend (cab. s., merlot, cab. f.)

**** **Pinotage Reserve** ◀ Regarded as one of the country's best.

Gorgeous waft of liquorice and redcurrant, with cloves and spice of good oak introduce **97**. Generous plummy fruit (prunes in liqueur), soft ripe tannins, long, long finish. Needs another 2 years, only 200 cases made. **96** ABSA Pinotage Top Ten.

★★★★ **Cabernet Sauvignon Reserve** ◀ Brilliant jewel-bright ruby **97**: touches of mint, redcurrant fruit. Dense, sweet fruit of ripe grapes, fine-grained and classy, oak still dominant but will come around because of excellent fruit concentration. Tannins deter early drinking. Barrel-aged.

★★★ **Dry Red** ☺ ◀ NV Terrific everyday red now a blend of ruby cab., cinsaut and pinotage. New styling features plump, juicy, ripe fruit as main attraction, supporting cast of smooth acidity with light brush of tannin, all winds up for resounding dry, grand finale. All applaud!

★★★★ **Chardonnay Reserve** New World style in **97** with forward citrus and smoky oak aromas. Full flavoured, rich; hot buttered toast, lime marmalade—the full breakfast special! Cellarmaster Olla Olivier says: "Step aside, I'm making this one," when grapes arrive.

RESERVE range: Made only when considered to be exceptional year, thus no sauvignon blanc or chenin in 1998.

★★★ **Sauvignon Blanc** ◀ **97** has developed beautifully. Now loads of green peppers and cut grass, even some Loire-ish damp cellar character. Fullish body, smooth acidity. A suave sauvignon.

Chenin Blanc Attractive floral/honey whiffs, in **97**; dry, fruit still fresh and lively but lacks concentration.

STANDARD range:

★★★ **Cabernet Sauvignon** ◀ Inviting cool fruit aromas of polished blackberry, dusty green peppers in **97**. Delicious sweet lip-smacking fruit; lightly oaked. Soft tannins, juicy, mouthwatering.

★★★ **Pinotage** ◀ In **98** cherry chocolate whiffs with touches of fragrant cinnamon, very attractive. Plump, pulpy fruit with mouthwatering tartness creates exciting zingy palate. "Swartland is pinotage country," says winemaker.

★★★ **Merlot** ◀ Subtle, feminine **97**, well rounded, graceful. Dark berry aromas with touches of mint; subtle medium weight fruit (no excesses here), creamy smooth feel but not rich. Fine-grained tannins, real elegance, dry finish. Ready to drink.

★★★ **Tinta Barocca** ◀ Waft of warm, ripe prunes, lovely touches of grass, ground coffee in **97**. Smooth, rich, chunky, with dry finish. Perfect with winter casseroles.

★★★ **Cinsaut** ◀ Delicious **98**, cherry liqueur aromas, soft fleshy fruit with good balancing acidity. Juicy, succulent version.

★★★ **Chardonnay** ◀ **98** lighter style with polished, well-rounded fruit; subtle oak (staves). Lovely peachy notes, cheeky stand-out wine.

★★★ **Riesling** ☺ ◀ Always a winner from this cellar. **98** fresh leafy wafts; bone-dry with bouncy fruit and soft, smooth acidity. Perfect for summer salads, drink immediately.

★★★ **Colombard** ◀ Fresh green guava aromas; very dry, lively fruitiness, soft, friendly **98**.

★★★ **Sauvignon Blanc-Sémillon** ◀ Unwooded blend. **97** has developed attractive dried hay/straw bouquet; still tasting fresh and vigorous, full flavoured, tart twist in tail. May be discontinued.

★★★ **Fernão Pires** ☺ ◀ Off-dry; fresh lemon/pineapple-scented fruit; soft, pretty, fairly low alc. at 10,5% makes **97** ideal lunchtime quaffer.

★★★ **Hanepoot Certified** ◀ NEW Pick of the crop, immensely fruity with honey and raisins, rich and weighty, unctuous. Spirit well integrated. A statement for hanepoot.

★★★ **Rooi Jerepiko** ◀ Warming, soothing wine; sweet, raisiny, with some liveliness. Attractive fresh-faced version.

Shiraz 97 vinous rather than varietal, but nice touches of black pepper, leather. Warm toasty fruit, matured with staves. Alc. 13%. **WINE** ★★★★. **Rosé** NV Chenin/pinotage blend. Smooth, fruity, semi-sweet at 17 gms/l sugar. **Blanc de Noir 98** heralds another change, now from cabernet sauvignon. Fruity, pretty aromas; sweetish, deceptively easy drinking. **97** from pinotage, candyfloss aroma/flavour.

Sauvignon Blanc ◀ **98** still quiet when tasted but nice touches of grass and gooseberry which translate onto palate. **Blanc de Blanc** NV Soft, dry white, light-bodied, from sauvignon blanc, colombard, chenin. **Premier Grand Crû** NV ◀ "Let's put some effort into it this year," said Olla Olivier, and it shows. Dry, crisp, with good fruity backbone and fresh-mown hay aroma. Chenin, colombard, SA riesling blend. **Steen 98** (same as Chenin Blanc) understated and newly bottled when tasted (chenin suffers severe bottling shock). Very dry with brisk acidity, fresh green apple flavours, steely and rapier slim. **Bouquet Blanc** NV Blend of colombard, bukettraube and touch of hanepoot, off-dry at 11 gms/l. Grapey, fresh with brisk acidity which makes for dry finish. **Bukettraube** Soft, easy **98** sweetie with some weight, pretty powder puff aromas/flavours. Mouthfilling. **Stein** NV charming semi-sweet from chenin; gentle fruitiness, good balance, all natural sugar, fermentation stopped at 17 gms/l sugar. **Late Vintage** NV Very fruity, from sun-ripe grapes, all natural sugar at 24 gms/l. **Special Late Harvest** Golden sunshiny fruit, gorgeous sweetness in **98** at 48 gms/l, touch of botrytis, soft acid.

Cuvée Brut NV Refreshing dry sparkler, whiff of green grass/nettles like a breath of fresh air, from sauvignon. **Demi Sec** NV crowd-pleasing bubbly, perfumed, very fizzy. Chenin/bukettraube blend. **Vin Doux** NV with generous dose of hanepoot, not sticky sweet. Carbonated, as are all these bubblies. **Rosette** NV low alc. at 8,5%, semi-sweet sparkler with some good red wine flavours. **Hanepoot** NV dessert; lighter crisp feel, looser weave than above, fresh grapey aromas, touch of coarseness. **Wit Jerepiko** NV fortified chenin, sweet but lively, not cloying. **Port** ◀ NV from tinta: vibrant, youthful fruity style, fruitcake flavours—with sweet red berries. Respectable ruby port style. Also: popular 5/2-litre boxed range.

SYLVANVALE VINEYARDS

Devon Valley, Stellenbosch

Tastings/sales Mon-Sun 8-6. Tasting fee R5 p/p refundable with purchase.

The Vineleaf at the Devon Valley Hotel. Mon-Sun, breakfast, lunch, supper; innovative Cape cuisine. See restaurant section.

Owner: David Nathan-Maister
Winemaker: I.P. Smit
Production: 1 800 cases, 25 tons.
P.O. Box 68, Stellenbosch 7599
Tel: 021-8822012 **Fax:** 021-8822610
E-mail: davidnm@solo.pipex.co.za

Looking to branch out of the computer business into something fresh, David Nathan-Maister drew inspiration from an unusual source: his former maths teacher. Not your common-or-classroom *trigmeister*, but Allan Mullins, tireless dynamo behind Woolworths' distinctly unbookish range, Cape Wine Master and esteemed wine judge, whose migration over the years from chalk to wine is a luminous example for anyone considering a career-move. Encouraged to start a vino-venture in the Cape, Nathan-Maister scoured the winelands before alighting on the famed Devon Valley Hotel which, sensibly enough, has its own well-established v'yds and (at present disused) cellar attached. Under the wing of Nathan-Maister and his wife Lee Ann, the hotel has been completely made-over—the top-drawer Vineleaf restaurant boasts an award-winning wine list showcasing wines of Devon Valley, CIWG and Nederburg auctions, Vinoteque and several private collections. In 1998 the first Sylvanvale wines were custom-made by I.P. Smit at nearby Clos Malverne from the current pinotage and chenin blanc v'yds.

Both NEW

★★★★ **Pinotage Reserve 98** inky purple, packed with concentrated plum, mulberry, ripe banana, spice; ripe, succulent fruit, juicy texture broadened by ± 14% alc., distinct but undaunting tannins. Tasted very young, but clearly packed with potential. From very ripe-picked grapes (pvsly part of Clos Malverne's production), fermented open *kuipe*, 3 days on skins. Malo in tank, transferred to new French oak 50/50 Allier/Nevers.

★★★ **Chenin Blanc "Laurie's Vineyard" 98** big, bold in all departments: heady narcissus whiffs, ripe peach, almost decadent mango, some cinnamon spiciness; all repeat on palate, passion-fruit, some citrusy flavours add uncommon complexity. High alc. (nudging 14%) gives sweetish impression though bone-dry; long lemon-zesty finish. Delightful on its own or with flavourful foods. From 20-year-old vines. Potential to become one of Cape's premier-league chenins.

TABLE MOUNTAIN — SFW

Chardonnay 97 Broad-shouldered version, attractive ripe peachy fruit, some coarseness on finish. **Cabernet Sauvignon 96** ripe plummy fruit with attractive berry touches; boldly flavoured, chunky wine though alc. at 12,5% not over-high. Sweetness in finish from ripe fruit. No oak. Export only, for Japanese market

TABLE PEAK — For Matthew Clark, UK

Ruby Cabernet 98 fleshy mouthful, crushed dark berry fruits, some grassy notes, slight tannin squeeze. Youthful, juicy glugging. **Riesling-Sauvignon Blanc 98** lean dry white, rather austere, briskly dry.

TALANA HILL — See Vriesenhof

TASHEIMER GOLDTRÖPFCHEN — SFW

Popular NV semi-sweet white, going strong for over 40 years. Spring blossom and honey bouquet, creamy ripe flavours, very soft acidity.

TASSENBERG — SFW

Part of SA wine lore ☺ . A legend, in fact, after being around for 60 years, and has devotees in a froth because it now contains 49% Argentinian wine, and percentage may rise, watch labels. "*Skande!*" (scandal) as the locals might shout. How could it happen to this most South African of wines? Easily. Demand for the local red outstrips supply especially when about 6 million bottles consumed annually. Current lighter than usual, wine-gum sweetness on nose; well rounded red cherry fruit, smooth but not jammy. An all-spice affair: cinsaut, carignan, tinta, sometimes a little cabernet.

TAVERNA ROUGE — Distillers, Stellenbosch

NV Slightly sweet-tongued (unusually for red) all-sort, usually pinotage, tinta barocca, shiraz, carignan, cabernet; budget-priced, easy, 8 gms/l sugar.

TENFIFTYSIX

Franschhoek See Franschhoek map

Open by appointment.
Owner/Winemaker: Michael Falkson (since 1996)
Production: 3 000 cases. **Vineyards:** ± 3 ha.
P.O. Box 244, Milnerton 7435
Tel: 021-5512284 **Fax:** 021-5512487

New Year's Eve 1999 will see Michael Falkson—hand-crafting, personally bottling a small range on 3 ha. in Franschhoek Valley— popping corks on a chardonnay MCC he created in 1998 specially for the occasion. "I look forward to share many bottles of **TenFiftySix 'Two Thousand'** with friends and family," says the leather, canvas goods specialist. Also new from this up-and-coming boutique winery is a **Blanc Fumé**—another of Falkson's experiments designed to produce "premium wines at realistic prices".

★★★ **Cabernet Sauvignon 97** (tank sample) improves on impressive maiden **96** (labelled **Reserve**) which struts attractive, individual choc-toffee resonances. Latest release clearer-fruited, minerally frisson, mulberry/vanilla notes in juicy-sweet finish. Tannins still firm, so don't rush to uncork. Potential for ageing 4-8 yrs. Selected by British Airways, as was **Chenin** below. **96** relaxed, most enjoyable now, could go 4-5 yrs.

Sauvignon Blanc 98 very quaffable. Billowing ripe gooseberry, almost sweet fruit (though officially dry), smooth, invitingly fresh. Alc. quite high at 13,7%. Pick of pvs. 3 vintages. **96 VG. Blanc Fumé** NEW Promising début with fruit-driven, unobtrusively wooded **98**. Ripe gooseberries, fresh cut-grass. Palate steely, almost tannic, needs time—or food—to soften impact. 50% French oak, 3 months, none new. Tasted very young. **Chenin Blanc 97 VG** perhaps more impressive in first flush of youth. **"Two Thousand"** NEW NV (untasted) chardonnay MCC sparkler specially for millennium.

TESCO See Vinfruco

THELEMA MOUNTAIN VINEYARDS

Stellenbosch See Stellenbosch map

Open weekdays 9-5; Sat 9-1. No charge for tastings.
Owners: McLean Family Trust & G. Webb
Winemaker: Gyles Webb (since 1988). **Vineyards:** Aidan Morton (since 1996)
Production: 28 000 cases, 360 tons. **Vineyards:** 40 ha. Leases 10 ha.
P.O. Box 2234, Stellenbosch 7599
Tel: 021-8851924 **Fax:** 021-8851800
E-mail: thelema@adept.co.za

Gyles Webb's musical tastes run to the classics and jazz—South African, Cuban, pianist Keith Jarrett—rather than Tina Turner, but if there's one modern Cape winery to which she might belt out praises, it's Thelema. "Simply the best." It's arguable, of course, as wine subjects always are, but ask anyone in the know, locally and abroad, to name South Africa's most consistent, international-quality winery and this former fruit farm on the distinctive Banhoek-Helshoogte side of the Simonsberg will almost certainly be the most frequently-cited. And that word "simply" is significant: Thelema's reputation does not swing on luxury chandeliers, marbled tasting halls, fancy labels, monumental cellars or lavish ad. budgets. This is a no-frills, unostentatious, hands-on family business, driven by a very hard work-ethic. Down-to-earth. Which is even more significant, because it's Webb's fundamentalist zeal in his vineyards which raises the Thelema game.

From the start, in 1983, Webb's conversion of orchards to vineyards won umpteen local viticultural awards. But each year he continues to introduce new angles and strategies in pursuit of the perfect grape. Resident vineyard manager Aidan Morton (well-informed by various Antipodean travels) and leading Californian consultant Phil Freese are on the case here. Latest innovation, a first in the Cape, is the planting of a permanent grass cover-crop between the rows. This will be lightly mowed rather than heavily ploughed (so as not to discomfort the vines), and help to curb excessive vigour. A newly-completed dam, replete with the trout the fish eagles haven't yet managed to cart off, feeds 5 km of main piping and 150 km of dripper lines, allowing for micro-irrigation answers to various weather vagaries. "There are plenty (and that means *plenty*) of new ideas to improve vineyard and grape quality," says Webb, and his latest 1998 planting—a new block of cabernet next to the cellar—will doubtless be the most pampered yet.

One of the busiest men in the winelands, he is a partner in, and hyperactive winemaking consultant to, the new Spice Route Wine Company on the West Coast. He's also heavily involved in neighbour GT Ferreira's plans to build a state-of-the-art 500-ton winery on his farm—featuring 40 ha. of vineyards—next-door. Ferreira, chairman of the Rand Merchant Bank is not one to settle for second-best. Already distinguished by Thelema, this little corner of Stellenbosch looks set to become even more sexy in future. Webb and Ferreira nipped off to Northern Italy and Bordeaux in 1998 to research designs for the upcoming cellar. In perpetual motion, Webb also visited Portugal (on the cork track), was a speaker at the Californian Merlot Conference—keynote address by Jancis Robinson, contributions from merlot eminences from all over the world, and was invited to showcase Thelema at the flashiest, most prestigious US wine event of the lot, **Wine Spectator's** New York Wine Experience.

Thelema's family character—physio/aromatherapist Barbara Webb must be the most over-qualified delivery-van driver in the winelands—was underlined in 1998 by the release of a Chardonnay named after, dedicated to—and picturing—Barbara's mother, Gyles's mother-in-law, Edna McLean, "chef-de-tasting room". Both wine ("a Dry White" the label says) and Ed (very fruity when necessary) are local treasures.

***** **Cabernet Sauvignon** Star-quality Cape cabernet, a New World gem bearing the Thelema signature: dense blue/black colours; supple, warm, rich mulberry and blackcurrant flavours; trademark ripe mintiness. Not for the faint-hearted or austerity-inclined, maybe, but the major stack-up of devotees queuing for its release day "clearance"—on July 1 each year—would stretch any air traffic controller. **95** is latest, with dry cedar sappiness, slightly less full than **94 Diners Club Winner** which remains, along with **93 SAA**, Webb's favourite. Former softening in bottle to unveil fleshy, earthy spice with chocolate mint. **92** WINE****, **SAA** proves that easy drinkability can be deceptive: keeping well (as these have from **91**, even **89**) despite friendlier tannins, being solid, substantial—around 13,5% alc.—to which 18 months oaking in 25% new wood adds longevity. **96** barrel samples reflect difficult, lighter vintage with flavours ranging from tealeaf, grassy notes to fuller Christmas cake plumpness without herbaceous undertones. Strict barrel selection likely to limit severely quantity of straight cabernet bottled for release in 1999.

CIWG Guild Auction Reserve Barrel selections of firmest, finest cabernet—amplified by spicy all-new oak maturation. Immense, dense—more tannic, even classier than above. For long keeping—even over 10 years. **95** extraordinary, rich choc-mint, blackberry fruit cloaked by stylish oak; soft, ripe tannins. Successor to **94**, **93**, both formidable, in taste and auction price. **90** has developed russet colour, Bordeaux like sweet tomato-cocktail nose. Earthy, dusty, dry finish of exemplary elegance. **Thelema Reserve Cabernet 91** only bottling so far.

**** **Chardonnay** Remarkable record for consistently hitting a top Cape note, showcases distinctive, rich, toasty ripe lemon/lime quality—sometimes verging on delicious pineapple and marmalade flavours. **97** packs zesty, citric punch of fully ripe fruit, barrel-fermented in 1/3 each new, 2nd, 3rd-fill oak from selected Burgundian coopers. Dominant wood will integrate during 1999, as will 14% alc. **96** tacked toward more classic, dry-lemon flavours, less ripe marmalade which scented pvs., but retains rich, creamy-textured mouth-feel. Weighty presence. Malo completed. First year the 166 "muscat chardonnay" clone omitted from blend and bottled separately. (See Ed's Reserve.) **95 SAA** mouthfilling. **94** WINE**** topped entire chardonnay entry for **SAA** 1995 selections for First Class (as did **93** in 1994—a record!).

Reserve Chardonnay 97 ***** a stunner. Classy, elegant (but full) French oak, rich buttery palate positively exploding with lemon/melon fruit, enduring length. Only 110 cases, release date pending. **93** only pvs. release, still astounding foreign palates of note with attractive, decadent profundity.

**** **Ed's Reserve 96** previously dubbed "Tall Poppy"—stood out in the blend—now mischievously labelled "a dry white" although back label admits it's chardonnay: enticing, perfumed, spicy aromas with flower petal tones, on rich, barrel-fermented cushion. Reminiscent of sweet-scented Viognier. Sure to be a hit.

**** **Merlot** In spite of Webb's pursuit of authentic varietal expression, the *terroir* of these v'yds has always seemed to blur distinctions between merlot and cabernet. Each offers the 3 hallmarks of Thelema: ripe berry bouquet; fleshy, luscious palate; warm, balanced finish. The famous Thelema mintiness often present in both too. Latest **95** serious colour from warm vintage, meaty aroma leavened with mineral, herb and wood-smoke characteristics. Cherry fruit, tannic grip. **94** a good year, though less demonstrative on palate than some pvs. Limited new oak (10%) in 18-20 month barrel maturation. Formidable record: **92 SAA**, best red of entire 1995 airline tasting. WINE****. Preview of **96** (barrel sample) mirrors light harvest, less meaty palate. Won't be released as varietal if doesn't develop to Webb's exacting standards. **97** promises to re-establish the lineage.

**** **Sauvignon Blanc** The cult continues. Adherents will not be disappointed by massive **98**, jam-packed with super-ripe gooseberry fruit, loads of flavour, seemingly indomitable alcohol (14,2%) mollified by touch of residual sugar. The benchmark **97**, racy, richer on palate than in past, noticeably flintier but still gorgeously fruity, has retained freshness, developed fig flavours. Whatever the harvest weather, this wine's sheer freshness and life places it, always, among very best of vintage. 100% sauvignon, no skin contact to limit harsh phenol extraction. Drinks best within 18 months of harvest.

Cabernet Sauvignon-Merlot Discontinued as separate label after **93** WINE**** in spite of success, including 1994 Diners Club Winemaker of

Year winner for **92**, only Cape red then to rate 90/100 in *The Wine Spectator*. **96** may see revival in this, or **Dry Red** form. **Rhine Riesling** Weather in **98** not conducive to normal delicate, dry style (**97**, **96**). **Muscat de Frontignan 98** in similar boat. Both came into cellar intensely ripe, were made as Late Harvests. Bottling depends on development.

Stormy Cape Chenin Blanc and **Dry Red** Purchased wine selected, blended, stabilised and bottled for UK agent, export only (local licensing restrictions).

THEUNISKRAAL ESTATE

Tulbagh See Tulbagh map

Tours/tastings by appointment.
Owners: Rennie & Kobus Jordaan
Winemakers: Kobus and Andries Jordaan
Viticulturist: Rennie Jordaan
Production: 130 ha.
P.O. Box 34, Theuniskraal, Tulbagh 6820
Tel: 0236-300688/9/0 **Fax:** 0236-301504
E-mail: wjordaan@iafrica.com

The 50th anniversary of Theuniskraal **Riesling** in 1997 seems to have injected fresh verve into this venerable, often innovative family-run estate at Tulbagh. The range is fresher, fruitier, more attractive than ever—something that would have pleased Andries Jordaan (grandfather of the namesake now jointly running the cellar with his uncle Kobus) who made the first Riesling in 1947.

★★★ **Sémillon-Chardonnay 98** more fruity than pvs., fresh juicy peaches, citrus zest reverberating on palate. Mouthfilling, clean, brisk finish. Blend now 50/50. Food-friendly, unwooded. Best young.

★★★ **Riesling 98** markedly better fruit, fuller flavour than pvs. Fresh-mown hay, pleasantly round mouth-feel, crisp, clean finish. Alc. 12%. Dash of sémillon adds presence.

Special Late Harvest 96 showing some honeyed notes, touches of rose-petal from gewürz., palate-pleasing fullness from chenin. Only from farm.

TOWERKOP WINES

See Ladismith Co-op

TRADOUW WINES

See Barrydale Winery

TRAVINO

See Trawal Wine Cellar

TRAWAL WINE CELLAR

Olifants River Valley See Olifants River map

Tastings/sales Mon-Fri 8-12.30; 2-5. Sat 9-12. Book ahead for cellar tours.
Owners: 47 members
Winemaker: Alkie van der Merwe (since 1995).
Production: 7 600 tons. **Vineyards:** ± 450 ha.
P.O. Box 2, Klawer 8145
Tel: 02724-61616 **Fax:** 02724-61425

Heard about the hunter who fortified himself with a breakfast of porridge spiked with dessert wine? "Makes you think, doesn't it?" inquires Trawal winemaker Alkie van der Merwe. "Point being that wine should be made to enjoy. That's what I aim for—quaffability." Evidently Van der Merwe's view is shared by international wine brokers who absorb the bulk of production, though a small portion is bottled for sale locally under the Travino label. **Blanc de Blanc** and **Classic Dry White** are firm favourites. A **Shiraz** was made for the first time in 1998.

TRAVINO range (local):
Pinotage 98 unpretentious traditional style, some uncomplicated banana, bit of coffee on finish, acetone overlay, with a kick. Alc. pushing 15%! **Merlot** Muted aromas in lightweight **98**, challenging tannins. **Shiraz 98** untasted. **Chardonnay 98** crisp, citric on palate, dry. Easy drinker despite high alc. (13,6%). Unwooded. **Sauvignon Blanc 98** untasted. **Classic Dry White 97** chardonnay/chenin/sauvignon fusion. **Blanc de Blanc 97** chenin/chardonnay combo. Best drunk young. **Muscat d'Or 98** untasted. **Late Harvest 98** carefree guava-scented quaffer. From chenin. 11,5% alc. **Special Late Harvest 98** heady wafts of ultra-ripe sultana. Semi-sweet, low alc. **Rooi Muscadel 98** untasted. Destined for oak treatment. **Wit Muscadel 98** untasted. Like red version above, earmarked for sojourn in barrel. **Spumanté Bellissimo NV** low alc., uncomplicated semi-sweet sparkler from sauvignon blanc, with grapey hanepoot accents. "All bubbly should taste this way!" raves Alkie van der Merwe.

TULBAGH CO-OPERATIVE WINE CELLAR

Tulbagh See Tulbagh map

Tastings/sales Mon-Fri 8.30-1; 2-5. Sat 8.30-12.
Owners: 90 members
Winemaker: Michael Krone (since 1998)
Production: 14 400 tons
P.O. Box 85, Tulbagh 6820
Tel: 0236-301001 **Fax:** 0236-301358

New winemaker, fresh ideas in this bustling co-operative cellar overlooked by the splendidly rugged Witzenberg mountain range. Michael Krone—brother of Twee Jonge Gezellen's Nicky—took leave from his nearby farming operation to handle the 1998 crush—enjoyed it so much, decided to stay. Elsenburg-trained, with extended stints at TJ, Excelsior to his credit, Krone's cellar experience was tapped to create the new premium collection—distinguished by upmarket packaging and labels depicting SA's largest collection of national monuments, on Tulbagh's Church Street. Parts of the range were culled in 1998 "so we can focus on jacking up the remainder".

*** **Merlot** ◀ NEW **98** flagship of new premium collection, big in every way. Inky colour, vivid purple edge. Burst of ripe plum, mocha, vanilla. Delicious succulent fruit, decidedly soft, round (partly from 14% alc.). Benefits from modified cellar regime (shorter maceration, gentler handling). Hints at potential for Tulbagh reds. Value at under R20 ex-cellar.

Camelot 98 very pleasant cab. s. (60%), merlot blend. Somewhat introspective nose, sweetish strawberry, mocha hints; full, fruity. Discernibly dry, so best with food. Try rich pasta. **Claret NV** Light-coloured/bodied, bon-bon scented dry quaffer. Braai-friendly, mainly from cinsaut. **Rosé 98** pretty rosewater-pink, wafts of almond, hay. Pleasant alfresco sipper for the non-dry fan. Chenin blanc/cinsaut. **Sauvignon Blanc** "Sauvage" side of grape's personality not much in evidence in subdued (bottle-shocked?) **98**. Some grassy tones, clean, dry. **Seminay Blanc ◀ 98** much livelier than solo Sauv. Bl. above. Fresh limey smells, round, clean, gently crisp finish. Appears slightly sweet (though technically dry). Blend of sauvignon, chardonnay, sémillon. Nice. **Blanc de Blanc** NEW **98** enlivened by frisky lime scents; soft citric palate, relaxed dry quaffer. From chenin, sémillon, hanepoot. **Late Harvest 98** one to cool a blistering day in Tulbagh Valley. Zingy, fresh. From chenin, 25 gms/l sugar. **Hanepoot NV** Current (**95**) sweet, spirity. **Vin Doux** Daintily pink sweet sparkler; volcanically fizzy. Chenin, colombard/pinotage, dab of cinsaut. Carbonated. Low alc. (11,5%), 61 gms/l sugar. **Port NV** Current (**97**) earthy, sweet-sour, quite robust. 18% alc., 100 gms/l sugar.

Grand Crû, Late Harvest, **Stein** and **Dry Red** available in 2/5-litre boxes.

TWEE JONGE GEZELLEN ESTATE

Tulbagh

Open weekdays 9-12.30, 2-5. Sat 9-12. Cellar tours Mon-Fri 11, 3; Sat 10.30. Large groups by arrangement.
Winemaker: Nicky Krone
Assistant: Henry Links
Marketing: Mary Krone
Vineyards: 274 ha.
P.O. Box 16, Tulbagh 6820
Tel: 0236-300680 **Fax:** 0236-300686

Nicky Krone is widely regarded as one of the Cape's most innovative Cap Classique exponents, and a maestro of quirky, fragrant and vastly popular white blends. But in the 60s, TJ used to turn out show-champion reds, so it's not so strange, therefore, to hear him talk with unabated enthusiasm about his red wine planting programme, and his latest baby, a project involving cornifesto, a little known port variety. "I've found some old planting material, and I've identified the perfect site. I'm only planning a hectare to start with, but I'm very excited by the prospect." Shiraz and merlot vineyards are joining his established pinot noir, and with the port, these will introduce a new era for this 300-year-old family estate.

★★★★ **Krone Borealis Brut MCC** One of the Cape's most distinguished bubblies, **94** with fine toasty aromas, whiffs of apple and lime, full on the palate, but entirely without clumsiness, dry baked-bread notes in finish. Finer, riper and more subtle than most, it consistently performs well in competition, winning the Diners Club award for the **93**. Blend of 50-50 chardonnay and pinot, leesy creaminess and fine persistent mousse are the hallmarks of all releases. Some bottlings are sold as **Longridge**, others as **Cuvée Cap by Mumm.**

★★★★ **Engeltjiepipi** Botrytis dessert wine: **96** opulent marmalade, pineapple fruit, lusciously textured, ample layerings of citrus and tropical flavours, uncloying finish. Pvs. **94** furmint, chenin and Rhine riesling, earlier releases included sémillon and gewürztraminer.

Pinot Noir NEW **97** first release of a TJ red for decades, was immediately snapped up by a foreign buyer, leaving only a minute quantity for sale from the cellar. Untasted. **TJ 39** Long-established, versatile, popular: delicately aromatic dryish white, **97** a blend of several varietals incl. Rhine riesling, chenin and muscat. **Sauvignon Blanc** Less perfumed than most, dry full flavours. **Chardonnay-Weisser Riesling 97** fragrant but crisply dry, terpene spice evolving with age. **TJ Light 97** sylvaner/muscat blend, delicately perfumed, bone-dry finish. **TJ Schanderl** Aromatic white, with apricot/pineapple notes, crisp acidity conceals sweetness. **TJ Night Nectar** Full-flavoured blend of chenin, furmint and sémillon.

TWIN OAKS WINES

See Stellenbosch Wines Direct

TWO OCEANS WINES

Made by Drostdy Wines, Tulbagh

Cabernet-Merlot ◀ Improves by the year. **98** fresh-fruited, medium to full-bodied, soft tannined. Low acid (4,9 gms/l) boosts drinkability. **Sauvignon Blanc 98** slides down as easily as ever. Just dry at 3,3 gms/l sugar, 12,4% alc.

UITERWYK ESTATE

Stellenbosch See Stellenbosch map

Open Oct-April Mon-Fri 10-4.30; May-Sept Mon-Fri 10.-12.30; 2-4.30. Sat year round 10-4.30. Cellar tours by appointment. Tasting charges: groups 10+, R5 per person.
Owners: De Waal family
Winemaker: Chris de Waal (whites, since 1976); Daniel de Waal (reds, since 1990)
Marketing: Pieter de Waal
Production: 1 000 tons, 20 000 cases. **Vineyards**: 115 ha.
P.O. Box 15, Vlottenburg 7604
Tel: 021-8813711 **Fax:** 021-8813776
E-mail: uiterwyk@iafrica.com

Triumph of the year for the talented, perennially modest De Waal brothers on this historic estate—in the family for more than 130 years—was the brilliant performance of red winemaker Daniel de Waal's first single-vineyard pinotage at WINE magazine's 1998 tasting of 47 examples from the **96** vintage of this local-hero variety. It swept the board, earning ****(*), cries of "Superb! Voluptuous!" and a unanimous first-place rating from the judging panel. Pinotage has long been a star here—going back, for example, the **91** was showered with praise by *Decanter* Magazine—but the De Waals' anti-fanfare nature has seen other labels snatch the limelight. No longer. Daniel de Waal's conviction that "South Africa needs great pinotages, not merely standard quality, to put the country and the variety on the map" was his motivation, and he poured a blend of local knowledge and French inspiration (from frequent working visits to St. Emilion in particular) into this wine. "You've got to go for broke," he says.

There have been advances on a variety of other fronts too: they've now settled on the trio of players for "distinctively Cape" blend, after 6 years of experimentation. And here the estate's excellent pinotage features again, in the anchor rôle. The first shiraz and viognier grapes are being harvested in 1999 (from grafted-over 15-20-year-old chenin vines), and Daniel de Waal's 1998 visit to the Rhône (with side-trips to Bordeaux and Sancerre) will inform his cellar approach.

Human resources are no less important: training and development of workers are actively pursued, workers have been part of management and planning for several years now. "We are progressing towards closer participation and management of the estate by our workers," says Pieter de Waal.

**** **Estate Cape Blend** Daniel de Waal's goal here: a unique, distinctive Cape red with creamy thickness of a Pomerol or St. Émilion. Pinotage captains the team, with cab. franc, merlot (cab. s. now dropped, "clashes with others"). Percentages vary with vintage. **96** equal parts pinotage, cab. f. plus 20% merlot: provides compatible, homogenous mix. Cab. f.'s leafy spiciness brings distinction, gentle elegance to creamy texture, red-fruit ripeness. Supple, accessible, even at early age, but has form, balance to carry through to interesting maturity. Pinotage from same vineyard as in Reserve wine below. First two vintages, **94, 93** (***) with cab. s., merlot. **94** (third each cab. s, merlot) sweet, fleshy, accessible; frisson of dry tannins. 18 months new French barriques. **93** début vintage (40% each pinotage, merlot, 20% cab. s.); dignified, understated fruitcake, plum and cherry flavours, gentle 5,4 gms/l acid. Small oak-matured one year. Estate-bottled.

**** **Pinotage** This Cape variety responds positively to Daniel de Waal's French-influenced winemaking approach: no bitterness or astringency, full of sweet bananas, figs, summer fruits, dense, succulent. **96** particularly lush, already enjoyable though maintains characteristic dry finish. Most need 4/5 years minimum. From **96** includes younger vineyards for fruitier, less tannic profile. 18 months in small oak, 40% new. **95 VVG** understated concentration, firm tannins. **94** deep colour, mouthfilling ripe berries, soft tannins. Voted best pinotage by Dutch Pers-Wijn magazine, October 96. **92 VVG** warm spicy aromas, **91, 90 VG** all Nederburg auction selections. No **93**.

Pinotage Reserve (may be renamed) NEW "I've waited a long time for this wine," beams Daniel de Waal. Stupendous **96** ***** from single, 45-year-old vineyard, always vinified separately, this first solo bottling. Bright, inky depths, hugely concentrated. Nose still to unfold completely mid-1998, but enticing hints of spice, black/redcurrants, chocolate cherries. Palate a burst of sun-dried figs, banana flavours; incredibly thick, glycerol-rich texture; soft, ripe tannins. Seamlessly absorbed Nevers oak adds final polish to this classy wine (aged New oak 22 months, half-yearly rackings). Built for long ageing, up to 8 years, but WINE panel which rated this champion pinotage tasted in 1998, remarked on its "soft accessibility" already. "Simply delicious!" they raved; we second that.

*** **Merlot** Change of direction in latest **96**; fuller-bodied, firmer tannins, more serious than pvs. Has spicy, chocolaty concentration; oak enhances overall complexity, class. (Matured 20 months Nevers barrels, 40% new. Yield 6 tons/ha. further concentrated by drawing off 20% juice prior to fermentation.)

Cabernet Sauvignon ◀ **94** traditional Cape nutty character; easy, open, soft undemanding fruit. Ready. Aged in older casks. **93** (***) broad, fleshy; keep a bit longer. **Chardonnay Reserve** NEW 100% barrel-fermented **97** for later release. Untasted. **Chardonnay** Essentially fruity style; **98** filled out with 15% oaked portion from **97**. **Sauvignon Blanc** Full-bodied, smoothly dry **98**; suggestion of ripe figs on nose, palate.

ROSENBURG wines: Grand Vin Rouge ◀ Straightforward **96** pinotage/cab. f./cab. s. blend with immediate red-fruit juicy appeal. Rounded in older oak barrels. **Sauvignon Blanc-Chardonnay** Crisp, dry **98** white. **Chenin Blanc** Quietly fruity, off-dry white. No **98**.

UITKYK ESTATE

Stellenbosch See Stellenbosch map

Tastings/sales Mon-Fri 8.30-5. Sat 8.30-12.30.
Owner: Distillers Corporation
Manager/Winemaker: Theo Brink (since 1994)
Production: 30 000 cases. **Vineyards:** 180 ha.
P.O. Box 3, Elsenburg 7607
Tel: 021-8844710 **Fax:** 021-8844717

Theo Brink, making the first **Chardonnay Reserve** on this historic (1712) Simonsberg estate in 1998, wondered how the 100% barrel-fermented and matured wine would be received. He needn't have worried: "Seriously good," was our taster's verdict on both this newcomer and the firmly-entrenched **Sauvignon Blanc**, about which Brink is "very excited". Indeed, the entire range is looking ship-shape, reflecting the energetic manager/winemaker's vast experience—he worked with, and later took over from legendary Bergkelder viticulturist-in-chief Desiderius Pongrácz—and intimate knowledge of the farm—Brink roamed the v'yds in youth and made his first wine here in 1974.

**** **Carlonet** Estate's flagship, venerable Cape label re-establishing its quality credentials with steadily improving releases. Latest **94** very fine indeed, demonstrative, rich, suavely-tannined for drink-now accessibility, longer-range cellaring. Crushed raspberry, cassis, clean cedary oak, fine length. Splendid **93** developing resonance, fullness. **92 VVG**. **91** slimmer but **VG**. No **90**. These all 100% cabernet sauvignon, mature vines (25 years+). Lavishly oaked, mostly Nevers, about 18 months.

*** **Cabernet-Shiraz** Style change, initiated with **94 VG** to emphasise fruity lushness, continues in deep-piled **95**, steeped in sappy red cherries, fragrant oaky overlay. Accessible now but with development potential, 50/50 blend, both matured partly new oak, mostly 2nd/3rd-fill 17 months. **94** garland of violet, cassis, spicy/earthy shiraz tones seamlessly integrated; full, ends with a flourish.

**** **Chardonnay Reserve** NEW **97** in bold, weighty Burgundy bottle, brilliant ripe-lemon colour, tangy pineapple fruitiness, toasty toffee-fudge coating. 100% new French oak-fermented, matured 13 months, malo complete. Should develop with benefit over 3/4 years. "Standard" **Chardonnay 97** (***) decidedly oaky, ageing well, fruity trio of lemon, melon, fig enriched by vanilla; fresh, brisk finish. 50/50 barrel/tank-fermented, barrel portion 5 mths matured, malo.

**** **Sauvignon Blanc** Often among most demonstrative Cape sauvignons, **98** almost baroque richness, power. Forward passion-fruit, gooseberry aromas, echo on big, racy palate filled out by 13% alc., elderflower tang. Crisp, refreshing ripe-nettle finish. **97** effusive gooseberry, figs, grass; full, peppery palate-presence, long, fresh finish. 12,7% alc.

*** **Cape Riesling** ◀ More of an individual than most from this usually demure variety, some fruity pizzazz, dependable. **98** particularly expansive, peachy/citrus burst on nose, considerable palate substance, boosted by 13,0% alc. **97** with bushels fresh hay, herby flavours, quite zippy.

UITZICHT FARM

Vlottenburg, Stellenbosch See Stellenbosch map

Not open to the public. B&B.
Owners: Reyneke family
Winemaker: James Farquharson (since 1997)
Viticulturist: Johan Reyneke (since 1988)
Production: ± 2 200 cases. **Vineyards**: 20 ha.
P.O. Box 61, Vlottenburg 7604
Tel/Fax: 021-8813261

Here's a brand-new range that's down-to-earth—literally and vinously. Crafted by talented young Scots-born, Stellenbosch-trained winemaker James Farquharson and Johan Reyneke, a varsity mate, on the Reyneke family farm, Uitzicht, the wines are designed to reflect, "without embellishment or artifice", the position of these vineyards on the maritime-influenced Polkadraai Hills. "We're passionate about this," says Reyneke, Environmental Philosophy post-grad and the operation's v'yd manager. His own occupation with typicity began, he reveals, in the 1980s after the family had moved to the estate and discovered Stone Age tools scattered throughout the v'yds—"timely reminder of the age-old relationship between Man and Nature".

REYNEKE range: All NEW

*** **Chenin Blanc 98** sampled in extreme youth, but breeding, potential evident. Ripe fruit, peachy/floral bouquet, wisps of guava. Fairly light effect despite hefty alc. (14,0%), fresh, dry. Partly barrel-fermented, new/used oak. 2,6 gms/l sugar. Striking packaging features etching of Stone Age tool—one of many found on the estate—on front label.

Cabernet Sauvignon 98 untasted. **Chenin Blanc-Sauvignon Blanc 98** some meadow-grass/granadilla tones, 13,6% alc. quite prominent when tasted in infancy, very fresh, dry. 20% sauvignon from young vines, rest mature chenin (30 years plus).

UVA MIRA VINEYARDS

Stellenbosch-Helderberg See Stellenbosch map

Tastings/sales by appointment.
Owner: Des Weedon
Consulting winemaker: Jan Coetzee (since 1996)
Production: 3 500 cases. **Vineyards:** ± 18 ha.
P.O. Box 1511, Stellenbosch 7599
Tel/Fax: 021-8801682

Here's another relative rookie on the Cape wine scene showing excellent form. The wines from these enviably-sited vineyards high on the Helderberg are made at Vriesenhof by Jan "Boland" Coetzee, but an own-cellar is soon to be built. 80% of current plantings are white wine grapes; 5 ha. of cabernet joined established merlot in 1998, along with a further 3 ha. of sauvignon blanc. Roobernet grapes will be harvested for the first time here in 1999.

**** **Chardonnay** Impressive, individual follow-up to lowish-key **96** in **98**: gorgeous ripe apricot scents lightly tinged with vanilla, cloves; emphasis equally on fruit on palate: fresh, intense, polished. Super all-round balance, long finish.

*** **Sauvignon Blanc** NEW Aromas of **98** a fusion of greenery—grass, mint, nettles—with whisper of gooseberry; more tropical tone to palate; all flavours, with flick of flint, come back in finish. Super. Immediately approachable. 13,5% alc. adds roundness.

VAN LOVEREN

Robertson See Robertson map

Open weekdays to 8.30-5, Saturdays 9.30-1.
Owners: Wynand & Nico Retief
Winemakers: Bussell Retief (since 1993), Phillip Retief (1998)
Viticulturists: Hennie & Neil Retief
Production: 140 000 cases. **Vineyards:** 200 ha.
P.O. Box 19, Klaasvoogds 6707
Tel: 0234-51505 **Fax:** 0234-51336

Expansion and new plantings continue apace—no doubt necessary to accommodate the full team of Retiefs now active in the business: partners Nico and Wynand have all four of their sons on the squad, active from the vineyards to the accounting department. Over the past 8 years 80% of new plantings have been red varieties, a trend set to continue in the foreseeable future, until a 50/50 mix is achieved. Not to say that the wide range will be reduced—"we produce a wine for every taste—we're a One Stop Shopping Centre" maintains winemaker Bussell Retief. "But the standards have to keep rising—the export honeymoon is over, and we need to stand together to stop our country's good name being sullied by poor bulk wine shipments." A winemaker crafting such fruit-driven wines has the right to make such a comment.

*** **River Red** ◀ ☺ **98** if available in sufficient volumes, could do for red wines what Lieberstein did for whites—a genuinely modern soft, juicy "super-quaffer". Blend of 60/20/20 ruby cabernet, merlot and pinotage, has fresh brambly aromas, a basket of red berries and plums on palate. Unwooded, for drinking within a year or two of vintage. Also sold in 500 ml screw cap bottle—now that's the way to go!

*** **Cabernet Sauvignon-Shiraz** ◀ **98** a classic New World blend, with European style. Vibrant crimson red, brilliantly defined currant and pepper aromas—both cultivars clearly visible; no pandering to "tutti-frutti" brigade; will mature seriously for 3-4 yrs.

*** **Chardonnay Reserve** ◀ **98** plump—13,5% alc., with intriguing toasty butterscotch aromas, right onto the palate. Just enough oak from 4 months' lees contact to show off well-integrated lime flavours. Like pvs. vintages, broad, but tightly structured.

*** **Special Late Harvest Gewürztraminer** ◀ **97** rose garden still billows mighty aromas after a year in bottle; a hint of oiliness with luscious, appealing tropical fruits and tangy, deftly balanced finish. 40 gms/l sugar.

Blanc de Noir 98 from red muscadel—pale straw-coral colour, a whole bouquet of jasmine blooms on nose/palate: a best seller in UK. 40 000 cases made. **Blanc de Noir Shiraz 98** uncomplicated, dry, firm French look-alike; will enhance spicy country cuisine. **Spes Bona Chardonnay 98** unwooded, from special v'yd block; pretty, creamy citrus flavours—for lovers of fruity chardonnay. **Colombard/Chardonnay 98** (70/30) deft touch of wood adds brülée flavours; supple, dry finish. **Sauvignon Blanc** ◀ **98** shows dusty green pepper, grapefruit nose, crystal clear fruit and acid harmony, lemony finish. Drier than pvs., 11,5% alc. **Pinot Gris 97** from variety grabbing more attention worldwide: reviewed last yr, supple and strongly built. Equally sound **98** in pipeline. **Hárslevelü 97** nose shows pears, nuts; brisk, juicy, assertive off-dry white—8 gms/l sugar. **Colombard/Sauvignon Blanc de blanc 98** an 80/20% blend; wafts hay and pear aromas—most gulpable. Sold in 500 ml screw cap bottle under **Vino Blanc** label. **Cape Riesling** ◀ **98** a definite notch up on good **97**, has grassy, mown hay aromas, persistent lime-and-spice flavours. Mail order wine club winner. Drink soon. **Fernão Pires 97** shows delicate muscat note, appley, off-dry character. **Rhine Riesling 97** now developing bottle-aged flavours. **Colombard 98** effusive fresh guava aroma, exceptionally supple, well-balanced semi-sweet (10 gms/l sugar). Another mail order club winner. **Red Muscadel 97** a bright, pale rose-hip pink, huge muscat-geranium nose, spirity, sweet, tangy flavours go on and on . . .

Papillon NV range of finely carbonated bubbly, chic packaging with "butterfly" labels. **Brut** ☺ ◀ Offers super value—70/30 colombard/sauvignon, whiffs of peach and grass, succulent just-dry finish. **Demi-Sec** equal parts Rhine riesling, colombard; semi-sweet, with honeyed aromas,

40 gms/l sugar. **Papillon Doux** a full-sweet pale pink party "spumanté"—or try with chocolate fondue. 80 gms/l sugar.

VAN ZYLSHOF ESTATE

Bonnievale See Robertson map

Tastings/sales by appointment.
Owner: Chris van Zyl
Winemaker: Andri van Zyl (since 1983)
Production: 11 000 cases. **Vineyards:** 30 ha.
P.O. Box 64, Bonnievale 6730
Tel: 02346-2940 **Fax:** 02346-3503

"I try to make fresh, easy-drinking wines," says Andri van Zyl, seasoned winemaker at this compact family-run estate near Bonnievale. Which he does with aplomb—his Chenin Blanc all but defines relaxed, informal lunchtime quaffing. For now the range is exclusively white—chardonnay (25% of current vineyards) being the focus—though 3 ha. of cabernet sauvignon should come on-stream soon after the millennium.

*** **Chenin Blanc** ☺ ◀ **98** Mouthwatering fresh peach melba, creamy, light but full-flavoured. Fine length, finishes dry with merest suggestion of ripe fruity sweetness, jaunty lemon tang in tail. Ideal lunchtime partner. Drink soonest. Low alc, 11,8.

Chardonnay 97 fresh pear-drop on nose; palate surprises with curious dusty oak (though lightly wooded—10% in new French oak), fruit rather muted. 13,5% alc. **Riverain Chardonnay 97**'s young vines tiring now after perky start; vineyard maturity should produce greater stamina. 13% alc. **Sauvignon Blanc 98** light, fresh, clean gooseberry flavours, gentle finish—suitable fish/salad partner. Best young.

VAUGHAN JOHNSON'S WINE AND CIGAR SHOP

Open for sales: Mon-Fri 9-6; Sat 9-5; Sun 10-5.
Owner: Vaughan Johnson
Address: Victoria and Alfred Waterfront, Pierhead, Cape Town 8001
Tel: 021-4192121 **Fax:** 021-4190040
E-mail: vjohnson@mweb.nis.za

If our ratings were based on budget considerations alone, Vaughan Johnson's selection of quality quaffing would be liberally sprinkled with 4, even 5 stars. Most of his own-label wines, bespoke-tailored to stretch the rands and flatter the senses of modern, busy, but demanding buy-today, drink-tonight customers, are priced under an astonishing and admirable R12 a bottle. Some slot in under R10. The elegant Mr Johnson has few rivals when it comes to nosing out stylish bargains, wherever they may be found (his own shirts, for example, from a tailor in Hong Kong), and his long-term arrangements with some top Cape producers ensure his range's consistency and continuity. Newest supplier in the loop is the Paarl winery Ruitersvlei, where Frank Meaker does the wine-design. Johnson's specs, remain constant: the wines must offer "great packaging". Both names and labels below are full of fun—as Johnson insists wine should be.

*** **Sunday Best** ◀ Full-blooded cab. s./cinsaut (90/10) mix; NV (**97**). Good mouthful, sweet brambly fruit, firm but not aggressive tannin. Has sort of structure, flavour to cope with Sunday roast. At R12,99 will allow for cost of roast too!

*** **As You Like It** ◀ Delicious modern-style red: bright ruby appeal, fresh spicy, brambly fragrance; soft, dense but not too heavy feel. Honest, country-style. Similar make-up to pvs. (50% cinsaut, equal parts shiraz/merlot, 10% cabernet) but reflects quality of **97** vintage. NV From St'bosch.

Waterfront Collection Captain's Claret ☺ ◀ Full-bodied cinsaut/cab. s. blend; light texture highlights spicy, strawberry tang. From Paarl. **Really Good Red** NEW Rejoins range towards end **98**. Untasted, blend not assembled at deadline, but mainly cab. s. make up ex-St'bosch shouldn't disappoint. **Good Everyday Cape Red** ☺ ◀ Warming cinnamon, clove tones in hearty no-nonsense cinsaut, ruby cab., tinta barocca, carignan blend. Spicily rustic, tasty wild tang but essentially low tannins, acid encourage immediate enjoyment. **Seriously Good Plonk** ◀ Flavour plus in current 60/40 pinotage/cinsaut blend from St'bosch; NV (**98**). Generous soft raspberry, fresh redcurrant fruit enhanced by comfortably soft feel. Quality of the most unpretentious sort.

Waterfront Collection Great White Sturdy but smooth Cape riesling/chenin blend from Paarl; undramatic floral, honeyed character. **Sunday Best** ☺ ◀ Nuttily mature chenin/chardonnay (75/25) blend; dry yet fruity mouthful, touch oak adds gravitas, roundness. Flavoursome without being too demanding. From Paarl. **Really Good White 98** mainly St'bosch sauvignon; unblended at deadline, but like others in range can be expected to live up to its name. **Good Everyday Cape White** ☺ ◀ Smoothly dry white, ex-Franschhoek. Mainly sauvignon with sémillon, chenin, colombard; combination of pleasantly understated fruit, good mouthfilling presence indicate versatility with food. NV from **98**. **As You Like It** Undramatic but flavoursome chenin; few grams sugar add to overall drinkability without dampening fresh fruity zing. NV (**98**) from Franschhoek. **Seriously Good Plonk** ☺ ◀ Fresh ripe figgy sauvignon, fleshed out with touch succulent chenin. NV **98**, big tasty quaffing. From St'bosch; 1 litre, screw cap; identified by Pik Botha lookalike, "cartoon" label.

VEENWOUDEN

Paarl See Paarl map

Open by appointment only. (R20 p/p tasting fee.)
Owner: Deon van der Walt
Winemaker: Marcel van der Walt (since 1995)
Vineyards: Charles van der Walt (since 1990), with Marcel (since 1993)
Production: 80 tons, 5 500 cases. Red only. **Vineyards**: 14,5 ha.
P.O. Box 7086, N. Paarl 7623
Tel: 021-8726806 **Fax:** 021-8721384

The most focused red wine vineyard and winery of its size—or any size—in the Cape? There might be a few who disagree, or believe it invidious to suggest it, but there's no gainsaying here are three—and just three—terrific, specific reds of real personality, grown from very personally supervised vineyards and a cellar so organised and functional that every operation is performed by the winemaker himself. And there's the owner: globe-trotting Swiss-based tenor Deon van der Walt, the inspiration behind this meticulous project. "He phones in about twice a week—always with ideas, suggestions, tasting notes," says Marcel, the brother and winemaker (and former golf pro). "He's constantly sending out great samples—he's very hung up on St. Émilion and Pomerol. Last week he sent us a Cheval Blanc 90—and the message was clear. Next week there'll be something else. Also, he wants everything just right. He knows so much about it all now he could easily make the wine himself." It's to St. Émilion and Pomerol—and their friend and international wine consultant Michel Rolland's place at Le Bon Pasteur—that Marcel has taken himself off to learn the finer points of dealing with merlot and cabernet. Rolland is an opera buff, so the Van der Walts hit it off on several levels—and Rolland in turn was a Veenwouden guest on his recent trip to South Africa. However, there is no formal consultancy arrangement.

"What I learn from Michel is a fanaticism about hygiene in the cellar. And ripeness in the grapes. Also, he really likes to work with—consult for—producers who are small enough to cope with the whole operation themselves, where there's personal control throughout," says Marcel. The 5 000-plus-case production a year from Veenwouden is just about right for this limit. The now well-known Rolland strictures about smooth tannins from ripe fruit and intense flavours and small yields, are also applied with an enthusiasm bordering on fanaticism here. The wines are very serious indeed, specially from the 96s.

★★★★ **Merlot** Is it too soon to declare this a collectible Cape classic after just 4 vintages—in which each has outstripped the previous? An irresistible, dense plushness achieved with latest **96**, confirms **95** (WINE★★★★ and magazine's top-rated SA merlot) was not random luck; it was in turn an improvement on **93**, **94**: a strengthening, enviable track record. From now buyers can look forward with confidence to a charming, serious reverberance in the bottle—5 years or so on. Latest (13% alc., 5,8 gms/l acid) and **95** (nudging ★★★★★) both show more confident ease in acidity, the longer hangtime in v'yds also means riper blackcurrant stuffing; abundant but sensitive oaking (24 months, 90% new barrels, five different coopers, one forest—Nevers) diffuses a spicy resonance that can only grow in complexity. **94** touch more accessible than maiden **93** but has backbone. All start with healthy deep purple brilliance, a good (longevity) sign. A 15% cab. s. stiffener widens the upholstery.

★★★★ **Veenwouden Classic** Many of the remarks above apply here too; there are two flagships! The vinification—and oak regime—virtually identical, as are results of (uncontrived) passion and care in v'yd and fruit selection. Low, intense yields (5 tons/ha.) and expensive cooperage (same as above merlot) are instantly reflected in a specialist, B'deaux-style blend. **96** reeks of confident, expensive ripe cedary/lead pencil and minerally spiciness; much like a strong, fine Medoc. 13,1% alc., 5,8 gms/l acid. The cabernet s. (50% plus) overrides merlot (30%) with firmer, more compact grip on palate. There's 13% cab. f., 4% malbec for seasoning. **95** ★★★★★ fine black fruits, cedary fragrance; less overtly sumptuous but no less concentrated than varietal merlot above (50% cab. s., 42% merlot, 6% cab. f., 2% malbec): perfectly proportioned, fine tannins infused with sweet, silky fruit. Deliciously long. These need at least 2-3 years before they start opening; should mature with interest for 9-12 years. **94 VVG** (64% cab. s., 37% merlot) dense-textured, chocolaty-rich fruit, dry finish.

★★★★ **Vivat Bacchus** This may be the quickest-maturing and third on the price list, but here's a splendidly limpid, slightly spicy but high-toned, beautifully (that is modestly) oaked red blend, principally merlot. **97** (66% merlot with cab. f., malbec and cab. s.—15%, 12%, 7% respectively); 12,8% alc. 5,7 gms/l acid. **96** with many similar scents, ripe fruit, cinnamon, but grippier, firmer tannins—perhaps readier in another couple of years. **96 (VG)** 58% merlot, 18% each cab. f., malbec, 6% cab. s. Though a year older, is probably still two or three years less ready than latest **97**. Small oak-matured for 10 months, 5 months each used/new barrels. (Nearly half wine drawn off skins prior to completion of fermentation to produce a softer, readier effect in bottle.) First **94** a more rustic specimen.

VERDUN ESTATE

Vlottenburg, Stellenbosch See Stellenbosch map

Tastings/sales Mon-Fri 9-5. Sat 9-1. Tasting fee R10 p/p.
Owner: Francois Tolken. **General Manager:** Mike Harrison
Winemaker: Marius Lategan (since 1997)
Viticulturist: Pieter Rossouw
Production: 15 000 cases. **Vineyards:** 83 ha.
P.O. Box 79, Vlottenburg 7604
Tel: 021-8865884 **Fax:** 021-8877392
E-mail: verdun@icon.co.za
Internet: www.wineroute.com

Diet Coke-toting stock market maven Francois Tolken—no stranger to the ups and downs of the investment game—must be thrilled with the way his Stellenbosch wine venture is turning out. A new-look Verdun—tee-totalling Tolken bought the famous Vlottenburg estate in 1995 from a direct descendant of the 18th century founder—has emerged in a sweeping make-over. An architect-designed cellar renovation has been completed; new equipment installed; barrels procured; new wine-tasting area with panoramic v'yd, mountain views completed; 14 ha. replanted to cab., pinotage, sauvignon, shiraz. Establishment of new v'yds, under the eye of Johan Pienaar of KWV, continues apace—18 ha. in 1998/99 for a total of 83 ha. by the millennium. Meanwhile former Gilbeys/Eersterivier winemaker Marius Lategan plays the estate's repertoire of established vines like a virtuoso (2 of the maiden **97** range were picked by mail-order clubs), while v'yd-whiz Pieter Rossouw keeps the grapes—and 4 ha. of plums—on the straight-and-narrow.

**** **Chardonnay** ◀ Unusual kumquat-perfumed **97** ripening in bottle, showing remarkable depth, refinement. Ripe melon, lemon, spicy aromas, attractive crisp lees/citrus-toned texture. Delicious now, but deserves 1-2 yrs to reach peak. 60% barrel-fermented; partial malo. 13,2% alc. Youngish vines, low 3,5 tons/ha. yield.

*** **Chenin Blanc** ◀ **97**, from 11-22-yr-old vines in some of farm's best soils, evolving into something special. Rich Caribbean-fruit, limey/bready dimension on wide, zesty palate. Classy, potential to further improve over 2-4 years. Partially oaked, just off-dry at 5,5 gms/l sugar. Best wooded chenin in mail-order club tasting.

*** **Sauvignon Blanc** Striking **97** reflects something of sauvignon's "wildness"—peppery, distinct freshness (8 gms/l acid), green fig tang—moderated by suggestion sweet oak, which also broadens mouth-feel. Partially barrel-fermented. Mail-order club selection. 13% alc.

INTERLUDE range:

Gamay Noir Grape synonymous with this estate; **83** was last vintage. American-oaked **97** clearly a modern incarnation: forward sweet-sappy mulberry fruit, touched up with spicy wood. Lightish body but satisfyingly chewy, fruitily persistent. 11,7% alc. Drink within 2 yrs. **Blanc 97** mainly chenin with Rhine riesling, gewürz., chardonnay. Spicy/litchi juiciness; well-balanced mouthful, distinctly dry. Drink soon.

VERGELEGEN

Helderberg, Stellenbosch See Helderberg map

Tastings/Sales: Open daily 9.30-4, incl. Sun, except Christmas/ Workers' Days, Good Friday. Guided winery tours daily 10.30; 11.30; 3. Also "Interpretive Centre", gift shop, historic homestead, library and gardens. Entrance fee: R7,50 (snr. citizens, scholars: R5) includes winetasting at homestead, guided tour, access to gardens.

Restaurant/Refreshments: Light lunches, teas, Lady Phillips Tea Garden/Rose Terrace (April to Nov 9.30-4, daily). See restaurant section.

Owner: Anglo American Farms Ltd

Winemaker: André van Rensburg (since 1998). **Assistant:** Louis Nel

Vineyardist: Niel Roussouw (since 1995)

Production: 65 000 cases. **Vineyards:** 103 ha.

P.O. Box 17, Somerset West 7129

Tel: 021-8471334 **Fax:** 021-8471608

The arrival in early 1998 of burly winemaker André—"I don't beat about the bush"—Van Rensburg, the passionate iconoclast who put Stellenzicht on the map, has added excitement to a Vergelegen wine renaissance brilliantly launched by the departed Martin Meinert. With GM (and viticulturist) Gerrie Wagener, Meinert laid the foundations here 10 years ago for a spectacular revival but he's now decided to devote his future to the family vineyard in Devon Valley, Stellenbosch.

Van Rensburg will go down in South African wine lore for one remark, worthy of Marie Antoinette, aimed at fellow winemakers who whinged about unlevel playing fields after South Africa's salutary 79-21 points defeat in the celebrated wine taste-off against Australia in 1995: "Let them plant vegetables," he said. People in polite white apartheid society were not supposed to talk to each other like that—not in public anyway. But Van Rensburg was laughing all the way into his rising bag of laurels: his 1994 Stellenzicht Syrah had just trounced the canonical Aussie Grange (91) in the same contest.

How was such a free spirit about to settle into the often cramped bureaucratic Anglo-De Beers environment of Vergelegen? He now rationalises his move—to those puzzled after he loudly swore undying fealty to the hills and soils of Stellenzicht—by insisting that his ultimate loyalty is to the Helderberg Mountain range common to both properties. "Don't you dare call me an Anglo man!" he explodes. Then, gesturing at the craggy backdrops behind, "I belong to Vergelegen and this Helderberg mountain of mine." A pause. "But maybe I'm a De Beers guy—they're diamonds aren't they? Well, I like diamonds."

So much for the jesting—and the puffery, even bombast, in this case is quite unnecessary. Van Rensburg is among the finest winemakers of his generation and he's quickly set his own powerful imprimatur on the Vergelegen wines of 1998. They're spectacular. Vineyard and fruit selection, and the crazed attention to minute detail, have shown in an even more focused line-up, achieved chiefly by isolating the finest fruit sources *within* each vineyard—and culling with an objective ruthlessness that comes more easily to someone who hasn't planted the vineyards himself! "There's only one way to approach a vineyard and that is to treat each one as the most special one in the world—and then search out the best grapes and individual vines," he says. "My constant fear is that we might not do justice to the grapes." The dispassionate winnowing out—which extends to some inherited wines in barrel—means there'll be no **97** Vergelegen Cabernet or Merlot labels (except perhaps a small bottling of Reserve Cabernet). He'd like to plant more cabernet franc; the Helderberg is probably a "discovery'" region for the grape. But his fixations about syrah means he wants to plant more of that too. Wines from already established, and critically (good) low yielding pinot noir vineyards have produced something much, much better than he's ready to admit (but which will probably be sold or blended off, at least this year). A tip of the hat must be due to GM Wagener for hiring the redoubtable Van Rensburg. Managing such huge passion and talent is not for the faint-hearted.

★★★★ **Mill Race Red** ◀ Great-value, top quality B'deaux blend. **97** is 60% cab. s., 40% merlot, 14 months in both French, American oak, with frequent rackings to achieve softer texture and mouth-feel. Altogether a quality B'deaux style blend at a super price—about R20 off the property. Due to merciless culling (e.g. no **97 Cabernet Sauvignon,** nor **Merlot** labels from Vergelegen) there's top quality fruit in this supposedly second-label red. Largely virus-free v'yds impart some exceptionally nice (a minty-cassis combination) fruitiness. 13,5% alc. 6 gms/l acid. From **95**, **96 VG**: former richer, fuller than coltish, lively, more slender-textured younger wine.

★★★★ **Merlot** No **97** nor **96** bottling for an exceptionally promising—in **95**—Verglegen label, was set to become, perhaps still will, this prestigious cellar's flagship red. From own v'yds. **95 VG** finely but densely structured, showing distinctive, plummy charm, with luscious opulence—ultimately easier to drink than initial **94** which acclaimed by visiting British MWs. Between 12-14 months in barrel—including from French Taransaud coopers. Barrel selection for **CIWG** auction bottled separately.

★★★★ **Chardonnay Reserve** This a contender for the finest handful of Cape chardonnays: from **96 VG** single v'yd (Schaapenberg) productions—with very classy, integrated, super-fresh but elegant, limey penetration. **97 SAA** achieves similar grace, balance, perhaps even more concentration (and possible future ★★★★★ rating). As in some of the greatest Burgundies intent on individuality and a reflection of *terroir*, this is also the result of painstaking vinification: all-new barrel fermentation, at extra-slow (six months) pace, by natural yeast, 100% malo. Dense, intense fruit copes with thrust of new oak with ease, and, as with **96**, there's no trace of over-oaked heaviness or bitterness in finish. ("This is seriously good winemaking," says current winemaker Van Rensburg, apparently immodestly, until he adds: "unfortunately it was made by my predecessor.")

★★★★ **Chardonnay 98** fresh, readier bottling than above. Contrasts with Reserve in various respects: less oaking (70% oaked, partly new barrels), only partly through malo. "We don't want too much oak here—that would not be doing justice to the grapes. Actually in some cases, oak is simply a wine adulteration!" says Van Rensberg. First was **95**, when clean, appetising—not too fat—style was set by pvs. winemaker Martin Meinert.

★★★★★ **Sauvignon Blanc (Schaapenberg)** NEW premium label. Very few sauvignons are made for the thinking drinker. Here's one. **98** all grapes from single Schaapenberg v'yd on Vergelegen's higher slopes. Unwooded. Convincingly different; with full, penetrating flinty-dry steeliness, shorn of the braggadocio fruitiness that briefly—for a year or so—hoists many flashy Cape sauvignons to fleeting stardom. This a serious, racy, gravelly individual, which should bear comparison with fine world-class line-up—and should last 3-4 years. Priced to match. 13,5% alc. 7 gms/l acid. Supersedes pvs. **Reserve Sauvignon Blanc (★★★★) 97, 96 (VVG)** very small quantities, also exclusively Vergelegen v'yds. More in New Zealand style, completely unwooded, very fresh, almost raw fruit, green pepper quality, dry, mouth-parching finish.

★★★★ **Sauvignon Blanc 98** different from pricier above: deliciously, substantially fruity and long, long flavours. Some bought-in grapes, but from latest bottling, about 80% own Vergelegen grapes. All pvs. have qualified for top status, with racy, fruity palatablity. **96 SAA, 97 SAA.**

★★★ **Vin de Florence NV** Most attractive, spicy off-dry four-way white blend (including 28-year-old, ungrafted chenin blanc from

Durbanville, plus Rhine riesling, sauvignon blanc, muscat. Latest **98** (though labelled NV) less sweet at 8,5 gms/l than pvs. at 9,7 gms/l for broader appeal and to double as aperitif/food wine. The 97 bottling, **SAA**.

★★★★ **Noble Late Harvest Sémillon** NEW **98** beautifully green-hued stunner, barrel-fermented (on skins), showing plenty of nervous fruity acidity—some apricots, over-ripe limes etc.—for stylish length; a twang of nutty tannin in finish steers it clear of any syrupy cloying conclusion. All from Vergelegen grapes, 100% botrytis.

VERGENOEGD ESTATE

Stellenbosch See Helderberg map

Open Wed 2-5, Sat 9.30-12.30 or by appointment.
Owners: Haydn Wright and John Faure
Winemaker: John Faure (since 1983)
Viticulturist: Haydn Wright (since 1994)
Vineyards: 120 hectares
P.O. Box 1, Faure 7131
Tel: 021-8433248 **Fax:** 021-8433118
E-mail: verest.@mweb.co.za

In the few years since John Faure and Haydn Wright have jointly assumed control of Vergenoegd, this estate—closest to the ocean of all its Stellenbosch peers—has experienced something of a tide change. Gone are the old style robust reds and in their place a serious line-up of classy, but unflamboyant, premium wines. The bulk of the farm's wines are still sold through the KWV, but limited volumes are bottled on the property for local market sales. Vergenoegd aficionados have come to discover that the cellar is dedicated to making intense, concentrated wines with good maturation potential. "Young and fruity does not really fit into the Vergenoegd image," says John Faure bluntly. Instead wood ageing capacity has been increased to accommodate an average of 18 months in oak, with one third of the barrels renewed each year.

★★★★ **Reserve** Intense, opulent Medoc-style blend. **95** concentrated mulberry, blackcurrant notes, succulent dense flavours, super-ripe tannins, marzipan/plum finish. 60% cab. s., 35% merlot , 5% cab. f. **94** cassis, prunelle aromas, firm tannic palate. **93** full, rich blackberry fragrance, taut dry finish. **92** dustier, less evident fruit. **90 VVG.**

★★★ **Cinsaut/Merlot** ◀ Cinsaut (80%) based, mainly large oak-aged. **95** fragrant currant/raspberry aromas, mulberry mint overtones, easy drinking, but with violet minerally complexity. **95** pungent sweet strawberry fragrance, accessible, not insubstantial. **94** light, easy-drinking.

★★★ **Cabernet Sauvignon** Blackcurrant youngberry aromas in **95**, with leafy notes, leaner tannins, herbal whiffs, still closed. **WINE**★★★★. **94** spicier, more forward berry fragrances mingling with earthy, mineral flavours.

★★★ **Merlot 96** spicy mint aromas, whiffs of cloves, slight eucalyptus hints, firm not lean tannins, persistent finish. 80% new French oak. **95** mulberry/lemon grass aromas, supple but not evanescent palate. 10% new wood, remainder 3rd/4th fill. **94** 90% merlot, 10% cab. f., blackcurrant/cocoa aromas.

★★★ **Shiraz** Plump mulberry/plum fragrance and textures in **95**, with almond notes, peppery whiffs, supple ripe tannins. Fuller, more accessible than **94** with dusty, leathery overtones, dry tannins. **92 VG.**

**** **Cape Vintage** Coffee, chocolate aromas, marzipan/plum pudding flavours infuse **95**, with cranberry notes, dense sumptuous finish. 100% tinta barocca, 2 years barrel-aged. **WINE****.** **94** dryish, mineral leafy fragrance, long earthy finish. Slightly fuller than **93**.

VERSUS

See Stellenbosch Vineyards

VILLIERA ESTATE

Paarl

See Paarl map

Open weekdays 8.30-5.00, Sat 8.30-1.00.
By special arrangement: Champagne breakfasts; St Vincent's Day Celebration dinner.
Cellar Tours: Self-guided or by appointment
Owners: Grier Family
Winemaker/Manager: Jeff Grier (since 1984)
Vineyards: Simon Grier (since 1983)
Production: 1 800-2 500 tons. 100 000 cases. **Vineyards:** 300 ha.
P.O. Box 66, Koelenhof 7605
Tel: 021-8822003 **Fax:** 021-8822314

Jeff Grier's triumph in the 1997 Diners Club Winemaker of the Year award—for his **Traditional Bush Vine Sauvignon Blanc 97** (****and stellar ◀)—surprised no-one, pleased everyone: Villiera's cellarmaster ("coopmaster", but for smiling Fortune—he planned to study poultry farming at Stellenbosch but switched to wine growing at the last minute) has long enjoyed the respect of his peers, as much for his easygoing open-mindedness as for his contribution to Cape wine. His successes in the past few years—Champion Paarl wine, an array of Veritas Double Golds, now Winemaker of the Year (the first for Paarl in more than a decade)—are the result of more than mere dedication, meticulous attention to detail. Working in concert with his cousin Simon, who manages the estate's viticulture, he has upgraded v'yds, internalised the "terroir" of the farm's individual sites. Ever-increasing availability of premium varietals (recently joined for the first time by shiraz and pinot noir); riper, more concentrated flavours at harvest-time; gentler cellar handling; a real sense of the nuances of the best vineyards have all contributed to a spectacular improvement in Villiera's wines, and an undisputed place among the top echelons of Cape estates. But, equally admirably, success has not been translated into high-echelon prices. Good value is a strand woven right through this range (see our ◀ strewn like confetti), from top-flight bubblies and luxurious-tasting still wine classics to jolly quaffers. The award-winning **Sauvignon Blanc** is amazingly affordable.

The Griers have also dedicated themselves to a community upliftment programme and in 1998 established a tertiary education fund.

**** **Crû Munro** ◀ Densely-fruited, accessible, richly textured **96** Bordeaux-style blend. Cab. s. (56%), merlot: raspberry, cassis aromas, layered with prunelle, ripe grape tannins, oak (25% new French) still evident on palate, great persistence. **95** plummier, with more obvious vanilla, from 50% new French barrels. **94 SAA** Selection less primary fruit, denser palate. **88 VVG**.

**** **Merlot** ◀ Powerful though not coarse, ripe-fruited, stand-out example in **97**. Dense mulberry aromas, viscous texture, plum layerings, marzipan. Great amplitude on palate. 60% new French oak, malo in tanks. Increasingly riper, fuller from **95** onwards, spicy youngberry aromas, 25% new French oak. **94** leaner, more prominent tannins (cab. s. in blend) **VVG 89**, **91**, frequent **SAA** Selections.

★★★★ **Shiraz** NEW Intense raspberry aromas in **97**, with spicy blackcurrant whiffs, delicately gamey, with tangy mint flavours, fine tannins, long finish. From low yielding bush vines, part barrel-fermented, full malo. Unfiltered.

★★★ **Pinotage 97** with smoky, varnishy aromas, wild strawberry tones, firm tannins, sweet oak finish. From bush vines, part barrel-fermented (60% US, 40% French).

★★★ **Cabernet Sauvignon** Easy-drinking, lighter style, forward fruit, blackcurrant/raspberry aromas, soft texture, layered with vanilla, delicate spice on finish. Malo in tank, 12 months in oak (70% French). **95** with cassis, marzipan, spice tones, friendly drinking. **94** leaner, with mint/eucalyptus notes. **88**, **89 VVG**.

★★★ **Pinot Noir** NEW Wild mulberry aromas, spicy sweet strawberry/brambly flavours, whiffs of oak in this **97**. From newer (PN52, PN9) clones, Accad-style long cold pre-fermentation maceration. Dense rather than fragrant with wood tannins evident; needs more time to relax.

★★★★ **Bush Vine Sauvignon Blanc** ◀ One of Villiera's stars in herbaceous, gooseberry-toned **98** from untrellised vineyards. Loire-like aromas, tropical, asparagus top-notes, accessible not simple, persistent. **97 WINE★★★★**, Diners Club award-winner. Intense, complex melon grassiness, still ageing well. **96** leaner, more herbaceous.

★★★★ **Sauvignon Blanc** ◀ Lighter, easier-drinking **98** from trellised vineyards, gooseberry, tropical aromas, fragrant green fig palate, dry not lean finish. **97 (WINE★★★★)** more concentrated, aromatic, **96** lighter, leaner.

★★★ **Blanc Fumé** Smoky, gooseberry-scented **98**, layered with marzipan, dense herbal/vanilla flavours, soft dry finish. Mainly from old, low-yielding vineyards, 75% French oak-fermented. No malo. **97** similar gunpowdery fragrances. **WINE★★★★**. **96** more perfumed from American oak.

★★★★ **Chenin Blanc** ◀ **98** features beautifully layered pineapple, apricot fruit, dry not tart, with sweet cantaloupe flavours, vanilla aromas from light oaking, 45% bush vineyards. **97** denser, with more intense fruit spice. **96 (WINE★★★★)** crisper, apricot/pear flavours.

★★★ **Chardonnay** Fine tropical grapefruit aromas in light (but not lightweight) **98**, delicate marzipan/butterscotch spice, persistent flavours. 60% new French oak, malo in barrels, **97** leesy, with prominent pineapple fragrance.

★★★★ **Rhine Riesling** ◀ Intense apricot/melon bouquet, whiffs of terpene, botrytis nuttiness, high acid (8 gms/l) belie late harvest sweetness of **98** (28 gms/l). **97** drier, more obvious terpene aromas now dominating pear/apricot fruit.

★★★ **Gewürztraminer** ◀ Litchi/rose petals waft off **98**, with terpene notes (13% R. riesling blend) dryish, slightly bitter finish.

★★★ **Sonnet** ◀ Accessibly off-dry **98**, apricot/litchi aromas (64% chenin blanc, 30% muscat, gewürz.) rich, plump, fragrant palate. Intense persistent finish.

★★★★ **Tradition Premiere Cuvée Brut** ◀ Single **92** vintage of one of the Cape's benchmark bubblies. Fine toasty/buttery aromas, slight smokiness, sumptuous but elegant vinosity. 65% pinot noir, chardonnay, 5 years on lees, 18 months on cork before release.

★★★★ **Tradition Carte d'Or Brut** Barrel-fermented chardonnay (50%) blended with unwooded pinot noir, fuller biscuity, leesy character, buttery textures, fine mousse. Up to 5 years on lees.

★★★★ **Tradition Rosé Brut** ◀ Bready/toasty aromas, light raspberry notes, fine leesy palate, melon/lime finish. Pinot noir/chardonnay with 10% pinotage adding weight and colour. 18 months on lees.

*** **Tradition Carte Rouge Brut** Villiera's signature MCC fragrant rather than toasty, elegant melon/pear bouquet, less tart than earlier vintages, due perhaps to partial malo, year on lees. 45% pinot noir, 15% pinotage, remainder equal parts chardonnay/chenin blanc.

*** **Vintage Port 95** ◀ LBV style, plummier, more developed bouquet, tobacco, tea leaf aromas, fruitcake flavours, drier, spirity finish. 55% shiraz, 25% gamay, pinotage. 3 years in used wood.

BLUE RIDGE range:

Rouge Early-drinking, lighter-style red. **97** smoky/gamey aromas (60% shiraz, 25% carignan, 15% gamay), softish tannins, light tangy finish. **96** similar style, with some cab. s. for structure. **Blanc** ◀ Accessible, lightly fragrant, dry white. **98** apricot/pineapple fragrance, crisp grassy undertones, some spice, good length, quaffable but not simple.

VILLIERSDORP CO-OP WINE CELLAR

Overberg See Worcester map

Tastings/sales Mon-Fri 8-5. Sat 8.30-1. Cellar tours by appointment.
Coffee shop, light meals.
Owners: 90 members
Winemaker/Manager: J.P. Steenekamp (since 1989)
Viticulturist: Danie Conradie
Production: 8 000 tons. **Vineyards:** ± 500 ha.
P.O. Box 14, Villiersdorp 7170
Tel: 0225-31120/31151 **Fax:** 0225-31833

1999 will be J.P. Steenekamp's 10th year at the helm of this large co-op at Villiersdorp founded in the 1920s to produce *moskonfyt* (unctuous jam made from concentrated grape juice). As pilot of a fair-sized ship—members' farms are scattered from land-locked Worcester to Hermanus on the seaboard—Steenekamp has had his share of challenges down the years. As in 1998, when the January heatwave nuked some of the more delicate grape flavours. Still, top-selling **Chenin Blanc** emerged in fine fettle and **Rosé**, newcomer to the always well-priced range, is quite delightful—a super-quaffer supreme.

*** **Western Cape Cabernet Sauvignon-Merlot** ◀ **96** sappy fresh raspberries, punnet of cherries; on palate ripe plums, appetising vanilla/oaky overtones. 13,4% alc.

*** **Western Cape Merlot 97** not a panting-puppy sort of merlot, more reined-in, with charry oak dominating plummy fruit. **96**, by contrast, is all gambolling friskiness, raspberry-fresh, plummy, nice toasty oak-vanilla in (wagging) tail. Around 13% alc.

*** **Overberg Rosé** ☺ NEW Undersubscribed style in SA—why?—because there aren't enough fruity, dry-tasting (though technically semi-sweet) examples such as this **98** in circulation. Consummate outdoor wine. 13,3% alc.

Overberg Pinotage Untasted. **Overberg Chardonnay 98** weighty on palate yet light-flavoured, flashes of peach, demandingly dry. **Overberg Sémillon 98** more texture than fruit—feel the flavour!—interesting enough on own terms—some melon, herbs. Food wine. **Western Cape Sauvignon Blanc** NEW **98** light straw wafts, lemonade flavours, formidably fresh. **Overberg Chenin Blanc** ◀ Gentle, clean bouquet, quieter than usual in **98**, but most attractive. Ripe guava flavours balanced by crisp, citric finish; off-dry. Drink young. **Overberg Colombard 98** ◀ Untasted. When on-song (drink immediately) with guava/fermentation aromas, off-dry. **95 VVG**. **Overberg Colombard-Chardonnay 98** built on woody/citric foundation, guava superstructure, lemony masonry; arrestingly dry, so needs rich/oily fish (coal-seared barracuda steaks). **Overberg Riesling** ◀ Some entrepreneur should can **98** nose—smells romantically of Elgin farm: steamy haystack, apple orchard on a summer's day—super-dry, long. **Late Vintage** ◀ **98** semi-sweet guava essences, honey licks, 27 gms/l sugar **Hanepoot Jerepiko** Unheralded wafts of cloves in **98**, pale gold dessert resonating with sweet, spicy muscat, honey flavours, 17,7% alc. **Villiersdorp Vonkel Demi-Sec Sparkling Wine** Lowish-alc. (11,5%), explosively foamy, fresh, clean, some sweet Granny Smith flavours in background. 45 gms/l sugar. **Wes Kaap Port** ◀ **NV** evinces earthy tinta barocca tones, contrasting nicely with fresh strawberry accents. Not too sweet, alcohol quite high (nudging 20%) in Portuguese style.

VINFRUCO

Stellenbosch, London

Having established itself as a colossus in Cape wine exports—800 000 cases in 1997/98—this Stellenbosch-based powerhouse began tweaking its approach in 1998. Two new ranges were launched: **Cape Reflections**, the flagship, and **Rock Ridge**, the medium-high priced line-up. These newly sprouted wings are designed to manoeuvre Vinfruco, heretofore exclusively a midfield player, to within striking distance of the premier-price goal post. The game-plan is to sell roughly one-third of production in upper-echelon price categories, while pulling out the stops to develop a portfolio of strong consumer-friendly brands, especially in the prized, super-competitive UK market. Savvy, universally respected Lynne Sherriff, Vinfruco's head of European marketing—she's one of only two Masters of Wine from SA—has established a beachhead with direct hits such as Arniston Bay, the wildly popular chenin-chard. blend that (way cool, dude!) has its own website. And though there might be obstacles—lack of a wider selection of typical South African varieties is a perennial one—there's enormous potential too. International Wine Services' Kym Milne and his "flying winemakers" continue to have a huge impact on the styling and techniques of many of Vinfruco's partners.

Enquiries: Lynne Sherriff, Vinfruco, Farnham House, Farnham Royal, Buckinghamshire SL2 3RQ, England. **Tel:** 01753-647093. **Fax:** 01753-818821. Or Vinfruco, Pinotage House, Brandwacht Office Park, Stellenbosch, South Africa. **Tel:** 021-8866458 **Fax:** 021-886-6589. **E-mail:** Dalena-Koen@unifruco.co.za

**** **Cape Reflections** NEW **95** the flagship, auspicious "creative collaboration" between winemakers Anton du Toit (Vinfruco), Jan "Boland" Coetzee (Vriesenhof), Braam van Velden (Overgaauw), Neil Ellis (Neil Ellis Wines). Lush, complex carpet of blackcurrant, ripe plum, green walnuts, leafy/spicy flashes. Serious but not stuffy, approachable. Abundant supple tannin will see wine into next century. Cab. s. (70%), merlot, small barrels, 18 mths. Handsome packaging showcases hand-written tasting notes by winemakers.

*** **Oak Village Cabernet Sauvignon 96** jolly nice. Laser-etched clarity of fruit/oak/tannin throughout, lovely ripe cab. fruit (cassis, brambles), spicy sweet-oak. 30% small barrels, medium-bodied. WO St'bosch.

*** **Rock Ridge Cabernet Sauvignon** Imperceptibly wooded **97** an intelligent compromise between supermarket, home-cellar: ripe fruit—cherry, cassis—bolsters immediate drinkability; firm tannin imparts some longevity (3-5 years). Clean sweet-oak wraps it all up. WO Coastal, 60% French/American oak. Funky crypto-Celtic labels a feature of range.

*** **Rosevale Cabernet-Merlot 97** a star; fresh, fruity all the way. Almond-scented mulberries, cherry notes lurk, lots of silky tannins, mouthfilling. Early drinker.

*** **Eikestad Cabernet-Merlot** NEW **97** very nice, fresh, almost jaunty blackcurrants, ripe cherry mainstream, sweet-oaky sidelines. Mouthfilling, exceptional length. WO Stellenbosch. Medium-bodied.

*** **Oak Village Vintage Reserve** Some splendid Rhône-like scrub in medium-bodied **97**, also ripe raspberry, cassis, briar. Tannin quite firm, so best with hearty/rich food (springbok pie?) or solo in 2-3 years. Cab.s., merlot, cinsaut, shiraz; unoaked. **95** SAA selection.

*** **Oak Village Chardonnay 97** has improved with bottle-age, very pleasant, harmonious. Zesty grapefruit, fair whack of wood up-front, non-angular palate, broadening butterscotch/vanilla in tail. Stellenbosch grapes, lightly oaked.

EIKESTAD range:

Pinotage Select Reserve NEW **97** plummy, ripe-fruited, smooth, racy finish. Lightish alc. 11,7%. 6 mths oak.

OAK VILLAGE range:

Pinotage-Merlot Blend changes to 50/50 in **97** (pvs. 60/40), brings ripe plums to fore; also rich toasted hazelnut, minty allusions. Very drinkable. WO Coastal, alc. nudging 13%. **Pinotage 97** "fruit-driven" is winemaker's tasting note—yes, and dimension-adding smoke carrying through to palate. Really nice drinking wine, also good with light meats. Medium-bodied. WO Coastal. **Chenin Blanc-Chardonnay 97** 60/40 blend, unwooded. Very ripe (almost decadent) pawpaw, Granny Smith apple hints. Boland grapes. **Chenin Blanc 96** Ordinary, everyday dry white quaffing; 12,5% alc. **Chenin Blanc/Colombard** NEW 70/30 blend. Crisp, fresh, fruity, dry. **Sauvignon Blanc 98** grass/nettle nose; fresh, mouthfilling, easy drinking, dry. 13,2% alc.

MOUNTAIN SHADOWS range:

Cabernet-Merlot 97 cab. s. (60%), merlot blend, very acceptable. Blackcurrant, ripe cherry complexion, nicely rouged with oak. Label features *Mimetes*, one of Cape's rarest protea species, flourishes on high slopes.

ROCK RIDGE range: NEW, exclusive to Marks & Spencer.

Chardonnay 98 low-keyed but thoroughly enjoyable. Piquant grapefruit gives pleasant palate-tingle, round, gentle finish. Lightly oaked. Nice on its own, versatile with food. WO Robertson, 13,3% alc.

ROSEVALE range: WO Robertson.

Ruby Cabernet 98 untasted. **Chardonnay 98** wide range of aromas, flavours, comfortable mouth-feel, very clean. Most acceptable. Potential *** (tank sample tasted). Watch that 13,8% alc. **Colombard-Chenin 97** Robertson's calling card in strangely "sauvage" mood—pungent almond/narcissus, challenging acid. Not the ideal advertisement for region. Could partner game fish. Lowish alc. (11%).

SAINSBURY range: NEW unoaked

Cabernet 97 lovely "old Cape" cab.—ripe mulberries, pleasant stalky seasoning, green leaves. Versatile at table. Try succulent lamb chops. Unoaked. **Cinsaut-Pinotage 97** a qualified super-quaffer (☺)—if you can afford the airfare. Delicious, medium-bodied, with almost Rhône-like pepperiness tempered by sweetest of strawberry fruit. Easy/early drinking. Cinsaut (70%)/pinotage, unoaked.

TESCO range: NEW

Cabernet Sauvignon Reserve NV Tarry, some savoury notes. Lightly oaked, 12,7% alc. **Merlot 98** with magnificent strelitzia on label (grapes from KwaZulu-Natal perchance?). Soft, plummy, mouthfilling, dryish tannin but nice all-round. Versatile food mate, but watch 13,7% alc. **Cape Cinsaut 96** just what you'd expect from this variety in Cape: juicy strawberries, sweet impression (though officially dry), super-soft, easy. Takes well to chilling. **Cape Chenin Blanc 97** ordinary but amiable in guava-ish sort of way. Off-dry.

Other wines marketed by Vinfruco:

Arniston Bay Chenin Blanc-Chardonnay 98 another unobtainable (for SA consumers) superquaffer (☺). Styled, packaged for Sloane Rangers (and wannabes): good wine (easy, succulent guava/lemon-lime scented fruit, soft acid, merest touch of sugar); great packaging (features see-through "amphora" style bottle; visual by legendary local ceramicist Esias Bosch). High kicking: 13,7% alc. Roaring success in UK.

Bin 1-21 NEW **98** starts very invitingly (loads of ripe plums) but falls a little short in flavour department (stayed behind in Bin 1-21?). Merlot, ruby cab. Exclusive to Marks & Spencer. WO Western Cape.

Vinfruco collaborates with International Wine Services (see separate entry) on certain wines for Marks & Spencer, Sainsbury's, Safeway, Tesco. Including the following labels: **Winelands**, **Cape View**, **Rylands Grove**, **Pinnacle**.

VIRGINIA — SFW

SA's top selling white wine; equivalent of 1 million cases annually. Off-dry/semi-sweet NV, easy drinking, mainly chenin. Slogan: "the man's wine"!

VLOTTENBURG WINERY

Stellenbosch — See Stellenbosch map

Tastings/sales Mon-Fri 8.30-5. Sat 9-12.30.
Winemaker: Kowie du Toit (since 1973)
Viticulturist: P.G. Slabbert
Owners: 21 members
Production: 9 000 tons. **Vineyards:** 900 ha.
P.O. Box 40, Vlottenburg 7604
Tel: 021-8813828 **Fax:** 021-8813357

This is the only co-op on local WINE magazine's list of Top 30 SA cellars, based on stars awarded by the publication's panel from 1993-1997—a noteworthy but not entirely unexpected achievement: Kowie du Toit's wines have an established, very consistent reputation—reds in particular—not to mention a cult following among consumers. Laying hands on the budget-priced range is something of a challenge, however: bulk of production goes to SFW; only a fraction is bottled under the house label and sold from the winery. "We try to offer value for money," is Kowie du Toit's accurate observation. "Quality is the future. We want the market to realise that co-op wineries are willing and able to trade salvos with the big guns!"

★★★ **Merlot ◀ 97** new star of cellar's reds. Fat juicy mulberry fruit, violet wafts, some chocolate essences; wide, mouthfilling, soft; roasted hazelnut in finish. Delicious solo or with pasta, lamb/pork roast. 13% alc. **96** developing excitingly in bottle, getting broader, more seductive. Drink or wait to see what happens. **93 VG**.

★★★ **Cabernet Sauvignon ◀ 97** up to usual high standard. Generous dollop of ripe cassis, raspberry, black cherry/berry on palate, subtle vanilla flavouring, gentle tannin grip, length. Delicious now, should improve over 2-4 yrs as did **96**, ready now. **92 VG**. **94**, **93** both **WINE★★★★**.

★★★ **Chardonnay ◀ 98** vast improvement on pvs., packed with ripe citrus flavours, broadened by buttered toast, yeast, vanilla. Fine

balance between power, refinement. Good potential—one to watch. 100% oak-fermented/aged 5 mths. 13,5% alc.
Pinotage 97 follows recent style but shade leaner, more astringent. Smoky scents, laid-back fruit. Pvs. regular show winners, WINE picks. **Reserve Blend** Changes to shiraz (60%), cabernet in latest **97**. Deft oaking showcases interesting earthy, smoky nuances. Should drink well from early 1999. **96 VG** probably *à point*. **Rouge** ☺ ◀ NV engineered for quaffing. Cinsaut, pinotage (with all their friendly attributes leaping out of the glass), "sweet" raspberries, soft, round, mouthfilling, quite simple but most enjoyable. "Best value for money in Stellenbosch!" gushes winemaker. **Blanc de Blanc** NV Engaging guava tones, off-dry chenin, sauvignon blend. **Sauvignon Blanc** ◀**98** somewhat restrained but easy drinking, gently fruity, crisp, refreshing. Best drunk young. **Chenin Blanc** ☺ ◀ **98** most appealing baked apple, guava smells, ripe papaya, melon; 13,5 gms/l sugar freshened by acid, gentle mouthful, clean finish. 13,4% alc. **Gewürztraminer** Nederburg Auction favourite. Good dose of sugar in **98** (25,7 gms/l) lifted by tingly acid, delicate rose petal, muscat hints, full-bodied (though med. alc. at just under 12%). Versatile food partner, alfresco sipper. **Special Late Harvest 98** quietish nose, mild summer fruits (melon/papaya), sweet-sour palate. **Muscat de Hambourg 98** pretty light garnet colour, attractive bon-bon flavours, round, smooth, decidedly sweet. Unusual variety: one of only 2 bottled in Cape. **Hanepoot** ◀ NV light-textured, fresh, grapey throughout, smoothly sweet. Nice. Lowish alc. (for style) 16,5%.

VON ORTLOFF

Franschhoek See Franschhoek map

Tastings/sales, v'yd, cellar tours by appointment.
Owners: Georg & Evi Schlichtmann
Winemakers: Georg & Evi Schlichtmann (since 1993)
Production: 3 600 cases. **Vineyards:** 15 ha.
P.O. Box 341, Franschhoek 7690
Tel: 021-8763432 **Fax:** 021-8764313

Form follows function—Georg and Evi Schlichtmann, super-industrious growers of the select Von Ortloff range at Franschhoek, are in Le Corbusier-ish frame of mind these days. The couple— he's an ex-BMW bigwig and she an internationally acclaimed architect—have planned and built a smart new steel-framed, all-bells-and-whistles cellar on their model hillside property, Dassenberg. "Evi's lucid design created a landmark that harmonises with the landscape," says the admiring spouse, "a perfect expression of the architectural dictum: form follows function. Unfortunately the same cannot be said of our unruly sauvignon vineyard, which sprouts green shoots faster than you can say secateurs!" Troublesome though it may be, the Schlichtmanns are obliged to discipline the vines' wayward vigour: their winemaking philosophy—"Vineyards! Vineyards! Vineyards!"—includes strict control of yields to boost fruit quality.

★★★★ **Chardonnay** ◀ 97 Refined, delicious, stylishly packaged; perfumed with ultra-ripe (almost decadent) marula fruit, sweet-oaky spice; full, polished mouth-feel, crisp, lip-smacking butterscotch-fruity finish. Assured oak/fruit/acid balance, like dancing with a partner who's substantial but light on the feet. Barrique-fermented/matured (9 months, Nevers, 50% new). Winemakers say ageing potential of 5-7 yrs. We say fat chance: all will be drunk long before.

★★★ **No 7 Merlot 97** super-drinkable; as chard. above: lovely cherry/berry aromas, some green pepper notes, ripe satsuma plum adds 3rd dimension to palate, abundant ripe tannin. Ready, won't come to harm over 2-3 yrs. 12 months small Nevers oak (30% new). Alc. 13%.

Cabernet-Merlot 96 cab. s.-dominated (after merlot-driven **95**), made for the long haul. Complex nose—ripe plums, damson, sweet violet wafts. Tight tannins need couple of years to unwind. Tank-fermented; separately matured 16-18 months new/used small French oak. ± 75% cab. s. 13% alc. **No 5 Sauvignon Blanc 98** attractive gooseberry, grassy nose, interesting ripe guava nuances. Very fresh, trips lightly round palate. Super summertime drinking. Unwooded.

VREDENDAL CO-OPERATIVE WINERY

Olifants River See Olifants River map

Tastings/sales Mon-Fri 8-5.30, Sat 8.30-12.30. Closed public holidays. Cellar tours by appointment (includes audio-visual).
Owners: 160 farmers
Cellarmaster: Willem Loots (since 1996)
Winemakers: Dominique Waso, Alwyn Maass
Viticulturists: Jeff Joubert, Paul Wallace
Public Relations: Elrine Bester
Production: 60 000 tons. **Vineyards:** 2 200 ha.
P.O. Box 75, Vredendal 8160
Tel: 0271-31080 **Fax:** 0271-33476
E-mail: vredwine@kingsley.co.za

The numbers, to say the least, are impressive: 20 000 tons of chenin, 20 000 tons colombard, 12 000 tons "other varietals" (riesling, bukettraube etc.); not forgetting premium varieties like chardonnay, sauvignon and a burgeoning red grape harvest—over 60 000 tons in all—turned into wine under one roof. Despite vast volumes, SA's biggest single winery on the remote, rural Cape West Coast is obsessed with "quality, quality, quality". Cellarmaster Willem Loots says: "Veritas gold in 1997 for our **Caberet 96** blend (the first **VG** for an Olifants valley red) stiffened our resolve to burnish the range, especially reds." As a result the cellar spent a cool R25 million on a sweeping cellar revamp, built a state-of-the-art laboratory, introduced exacting quality control, made a promising start with strict v'yd selection (fruits of which see below) in a bid to tease that extra bit of freshness, flavour from the grapes. Also v'yd modernisation, canopy management, early-morning harvesting, picking at peak ripeness; incentivised schemes to upgrade labourers' housing; measures to involve member-farmers in day-to-day operations. Small wonder that exports—to the UK, Switzerland, Benelux—are roaring. The challenge will be to maintain momentum in the face of sledgehammer competition. "We must correctly read world markets and learn how to keep customers happy," muses Loots.

*** **Maskam Cabaret** ◀ First-time inclusion of cabernet sauvignon (55%, with ruby cab., cab. franc) plus grown-up oaking (12 mths French barrique, over half new) in **97** underlines cellar's drive to become lion-killer in red arena. Good deep colour, full green pepper/fruity palate, ripe tannins, cedar-oaky wind-down. Not overly complex but nicely balanced, flavoursome, well priced. Alc. 13,5%. **96 VG. 94** Jan Smuts Trophy for best SA wine of year, top 5 of **WINE** "co-op selection" tasting.

*** **Maskam Special Late Harvest** Botrytis-brushed **97** quite delightful; packed with ripe guavas, ample width, juicy lemon zest, brisk 8,1 gms/l acid adds decidedly zippy tone to palate; from 75% botrytised chenin—which shows—white muscadel.

Maskam Classic Red 97 mainly merlot, shiraz, some ruby cab., matured

90% 3rd-fill French, 10% new American oak. Ruby cab.'s green pepper lead nose, also ripe cherry, peppery hints, vanilla coating; soft plums add furthe dimension to palate. Finish quite tannic so needs food/time. 13,2% alc **Gôiya G!ãan** ◀ (Name directly translated from Kung—the San language—means Wine Red), hits the spot in **98**, plummy fruit, animated by gree pepper, freshly milled spice, early/easy drinking; mainly ruby cab., wit pinotage, shiraz. Undemanding quaffing with some panache. **Goiya Kgeisj** ☺ ◀ Pronounced Hoya-heyshe, joined by firm click; meaning "first wine" in Kung. Marketing tour-de-force, cellar's biggest brand, backed by soli winemaking. **98** 50/50 chard./sauvignon, dressed in wildly colourful Afr hues specially for Euro-sippers; bold, funky stylised lion on front labe reflecting big, quaffable pussycat inside. Dry, 13% alc. 3 l box exclusivel for UK (also available from cellar).

Following two single-farm, single-block wines, recognising co-op's fines quality, premium-variety grapes:

Dessie Chardonnay 98 2nd consecutive star-turn for Ryan Engelbrecht's Dessie farm; oaked (unlike pvs.), malo complete, though effect quite subtle hints of pawpaw, butterscotch, vanilla, nicely balanced, fresh finish **Maskam Sauvignon Blanc** NEW **98** from farm of Pammies van Zyl front-of-the-scrum style, forward grassy character, gooseberry/guava wav ing from the bleachers, bracing finish. Crowd-pleasing stuff. 12% alc.

Maskam Delicate 98 untasted. Pvs. chardonnay, sauvignon blanc colombard. For early drinking. **Maskam Piquant 98** untasted. Pvs semi-sweet, early drinking. **Maskam Soet Hanepoot** NEW **98** white musca dessert, latest addition to Maskam range, from block selected by v'yd hotshot Andrew Teubes, free-run juice, fortified to 17% alc. Knock-out nose (honeysuckle/narcissus), palate very sweet. **Maskam Rooi Muscadel** NEW **98** repeat of white version above: beguiling nose, decidedly sweet.

NAMAQUA range: International export label

Includes **Colombard-Chardonnay 98** guava/lime, vanilla hints, fresh friendly. Under **Elephant River** label in UK. Also **Colombard**, **Cheni Blanc**, **Chardonnay**, **Classic Dry White** (box).

A **South African Dry White** (box) is also sold to Tesco.

NAMAQUA range: Local label

In screw top and 5-litre casks: **Laat Oes**, **Stein**, **Grand Crû**. Also Namaqua fortified desserts: **Soet Hanepoot**, **Rooi Jerepigo**.

ASDA range:

Selected, made for ASDA supermarket UK: **Colombard-Chardonnay 9** 70/30 blend, colombard fermented on oak staves, chardonnay unwooded Amiable guava, lime spectrum, subtle wood, fresh. Early/easy drinking.

VREDENHEIM ESTATE

Vlottenburg, Stellenbosch See Stellenbosch ma

Tastings/sales Mon-Fri 8.30-5. Sat 9-2. December 9-3.30. Tasting fee R1 p/p. Cellar tours, lectures, group tastings by appointment.

Light lunches, traditional meals in summer season. Catering, functio area.

Owners: The Bezuidenhout family
Winemaker: Elzabé Bezuidenhout (since 1987)
Production: 8 000 cases. **Vineyards:** 86 ha.
P.O. Box 369, Stellenbosch 7599
Tel: 021-8813878 **Fax:** 021-8813296

The rustic Vlottenburg farm with 360-degree v'yd and mountain views, owned by the Bezuidenhout family, is a delightful destination in summer when light meals are offered in the breeze-cooled courtyard outside the cellar. Low-profile winemaker Elzabé Bezuidenhout lets her wines—and her expressive naïve-art labels, a riot of colour—do the talking.

VRIESENHOF—TALANA HILL—PARADYSKLOOF

Stellenbosch See Stellenbosch map

Visits: Sales Mon-Thur 8.30-1, 2-5; Fri 8.30-1, 2-4. Tours by appointment.
Owner: Jan Boland Coetzee
Winemaker: Jan Boland Coetzee (since 1981)
Production: 25-30 000 cases
P.O. Box 155, Stellenbosch 7599
Tel: 021-8800284 **Fax:** 021-8801503

Jan Coetzee is, uncharacteristically, a little bewildered. Having celebrated the cool, extended 1997 harvest with its composite, gently ripened fruit, along comes the gutsy 1998 season showing full, ripe alcoholic wines in the mould of the formidable, long lived 1974s. A recent glut of good vintages—**95**, **97**, **98**—leaves him uncertain as to which is his favourite. After years of toil, he's not complaining and will take them all. A string of land swaps results in Coetzee consolidating his vineyard portfolio but means he has to plant anew, 53 ha. in total, 20 ha. on Talana Hill and 33 ha. at Vriesenhof. For somebody who left Kanonkop after a decade for Vriesenhof in 1981 and who has consulted in the establishment of, amongst others, Buitenverwachting, Graham Beck, Cordoba, Yonder Hill, and Lanzerac, this may seem like a chore. Not to Coetzee who is blessed with unstinting vigour and, his daughters tell, sleeps little.

Energy is required to keep pace with this zealot in the cellar. Coetzee has developed a fine understanding of his vineyard sites, how and where the planted cultivars perform best, but he's constantly tuning the oak treatment—forest of origin, cooper, degree of char, match with variety, etc.—and is fascinated by sulphur and longevity. Graphs are plotted to determine the influence of everything he can possibly alter, even the glass in which wine is bottled. Coetzee has also deftly altered the signature style of his red wines, perhaps a little more slowly than some would have thought. The unyielding, sinuous muscularity of his earlier reds has given way to more accessible, early-drinking fruit, but never in an up-front New World manner. One couldn't help but notice, on departing, a line up of decades-old, mature classed growth Bordeaux awaiting serious tasting. The benchmarks must be touched from time to time.

★★★★ **Vriesenhof Kallista** ◀ Trademark of the property, nutty integrity and classic tightness, measured wood—no opulent oak sweetness—but with inky, high-toned, violet-perfumed echoes. Latest **96** leaner vintage, sappy grassiness but some meat on the bone. Fuller, rich **95** and **94** are in regular groove, with standard 18 month maturation in small used and large oak. 50% cabernet s. shows, balance merlot (30%) and cab. f. Samples of **97**, **98**, suggest wines of power will follow. **92** WINE★★★★. **91 CIWG** magnum bottling continues to impress. Older vintages show herbaceous austerity—prized by traditionalists.

★★★★ **Vriesenhof Pinotage** ◀ Mélange of flavours from differentially cellar-handled fruit. Coetzee's preference is for sweet banana, but includes less obvious spicy touches for elegance. **97** more classy than frank **96**. Good supple palate, restrained finish steering clear of bitterness. Oaking barely noticeable. **98** samples bursting with ripe fruit.

★★★ **Paradyskloof Pinotage** ◀ **97** fragrant tropical papaya, banana, cloves. Ripe yet tapered mouthful. With albeit lighter **96**, slots into style of upgraded **95**, forward and grapey. Can show slightly stemmy edge to black chocolate finish.

★★★ **Vriesenhof Cabernet Sauvignon** Blend of old, cleaned-up and even some new clones give veritable palette of flavours; herbaceous grassy, earthy linear tones, shoe polish, mineral glints and fleshy blackcurrant fruit. Densely structured palate, guiding tannic edge to **96**. Samples of **97** show fullness to match **95**, **94** nutty and firm in classic style lifted by caramel, toffee succulence sp. in **94**. Alcohols (12,5%), tannins within moderated limits. **93** muscular firmness although riper tannins than some pvs. (which harder, more austere). **91 WINE★★★★** and **92** are "fusion" wines, crossing over from 1980s style to easier, less lean character. (From **93** mostly virus free cab. v'yds; Coetzee still doesn't trust the keeping qualities of the imported new clones.)

★★★ **Talana Hill Royale** Similar *terroir* and under same guiding hand but mostly (80%) merlot with cab. franc blend makes for noticeably more delicate, fine-grained claret. **96** tea-leaf, grassy leanness, **97** will realign succulence shown with **95**, **94**. A St Émilion-style wine. **93** a "feminine vintage".

★★★ **Chardonnay (Vriesenhof and Talana Hill)** Both made in atmospheric Talana Hill winery. Medium-weight, barrel-fermented, full **98** showing peachy/apple pie features with limited lemon tang. Ripe fruit not overwhelmed by tightly managed oak. Moderately-toned **97**. Talana Hill a step up on Vriesenhof stablemate. Neither has completed promise in bottle—yet.

Paradyskloof Cabernet Sauvignon/Merlot ◀ Lighter style, but fleshy **98** meaty fruit tempers terse claret substance. **Paradyskloof Sauvignon Blanc/Chardonnay** ◀ **98** opulently ripe gooseberry, green fig wildness of sauvignon matched with oak-fermented chardonnay, touch of chenin blanc. Above its station.

WABOOMSRIVIER CO-OP

Worcester See Worcester map

Tastings/sales Mon-Fri 8-12.30; 1.30-5.
Owners: 47 members
Winemaker: Chris van der Merwe (since 1987)
Production: ± 10 000 tons. **Vineyards:** ± 800 ha.
P.O. Box 24, Breede River 6858
Tel: 02324-730 **Fax:** 02324-731

This animated mountain-fringed co-op celebrates its 50th anniversary in 1999 with the planned inauguration of a new high-tech red wine cellar. A commemorative **Ruby Cabernet** is scheduled to be bottled, as much to celebrate the winery's founding as recognise the pole position this versatile grape occupies within the varietal mix.

Ruby Cabernet ◀ **96** in smoothly fruity, easy dry style, lifted by hints of oak. **Cinsaut 97** juicily fruity, relaxed quaffing. **Grand Crû 97** with touch sugar for quaffability; some colombard guava juiciness. **Sweet Hanepoot** ◀ NV golden dessert, fruity, nutty bouquet; dainty, smooth texture; non-cloying finish. Matured in large vats. **Chenin Blanc Late Harvest 98** gently sweet fruit-salad character. **Perlé 98** from chenin late harvest, with spritz. **Rubellite Demi-Sec NV** Chenin/pinotage blend (85%/15%). Cherry pink carbonated bubbly; fruity-sweet, crisp. **Port 95** wood-aged, pinotage/tinta barocca blend. Curranty flavours, light-textured. **94** Worcester Young Wine Show gold.

WAGENBOOM WINES See Waboomsrivier Co-op

WAMAKERSVALLEI WINERY

Wellington See Wellington map

Tasting/sales Mon-Fri 8-1, 2-5, Sat 8.30-noon. Cellar tours during harvest by appointment.
Owners: 54 members
Winemakers: Chris Roux (since 1970), Pieter Rossouw (since 1975)
Production: 11 500 tons. **Vineyards:** 1 450 ha.
P.O. Box 509, Wellington 7654
Tel: 021-8731582. **Fax:** 021-8733194
E-mail: wamakers@mweb.co.za
Internet: www.wamakers.co.za

Here's a co-op that's got it together: a varied range, easy quaffers all with character aplenty, smart packaging, loyal local following, thriving exports to the Netherlands, Germany, the UK. And—a generous dollop of techno-savvy: in 1998 the cellar was wired with a state-of-the-art computer-management system while, in the burgeoning realm of cyberspace, a custom-made Wamakersvallei website went live, allowing potential customers, curious vinophiles around the globe to pop in for virtual tastings.

*** **Merlot** ◀ NEW **96** hero of this cellar. Delicious, soft, succulent; ripe black cherries, agreeable touch of tar, medium-bodied.

Cinsaut ◀ **95** light-bodied red, sound everyday drinking. **94 VG.** Soft berries, spicy ripeness; low tannin. **Cabernet Sauvignon 96** light-flavoured/bodied, savoury, herby notes. Early/easy-drinking. Without being dismissive, this is great with hamburgers! **Pinotage** Change of style in **97**: more delicate, gentle; red currants, puff of acetone, lively fruit, engaging sweet-sour tussle on palate. **93 VG.** Unwooded. **Chardonnay 98** attractive fruit-driven style, not overdone, peaches-and-cream palate, harmonious. **Sauvignon Blanc 97** dry, just a tad world-weary now. Best young. **Riesling 97** gentle dry white. Lowish alc. (10,5%). **Chenin Blanc** ◀ NEW Pretty, easy-drinking off-dry **97** is developing well in bottle. "Sweet" ripe apricot whiffs, almost perfumed, also on palate, low acid, gentle finish. Very nice! **Stein 97** untasted. From chenin. Low 10,5% alc. **Late Harvest 97** subdued nose, weightier on palate, quite sweet, 21 gms/l sugar. Low alc.: 10,5%. From chenin. **Muscat d'Alexandrie** NEW Full-sweet **98** dessert, amiable muscat/thatch aromas, unctuous, low alc. for this style (16,5%). **Port 95** hints of dried figs, fruitcake; dense, rich spicy texture, sweet finish. From cab. s. Low alc.: 16,5%.

WAMAKERSVALLEI Tesco Range See IWS

WARWICK ESTATE

Simonsberg See Stellenbosch map

Visits: Open weekdays 8.30-4.30, Sat by appointment. Tasting R5.
Owner: Stan Ratcliffe
Winemakers: Norma Ratcliffe and Marcus Milner
Production: 200 tons, 20 000 cases, **Vineyards:** 60 ha.
P.O. Box 2, Muldersvlei 7607
Tel: 021-8844410 **Fax:** 021-8844025
E-mail: ratcliffe@warwickwine.co.za
Website: www.warwickwine.co.za

One meets the most interesting people in the convivial Warwick cellar. The tasting for this guide coincided—unexpectedly—with a visit of the advance party of an American sommelier association planning a Cape sortie. No problem to the Ratcliffes, especially winemaker Norma with her inimitable way of managing people, who inspanned all for an extended, almost jocular sampling of the range. Behind the bonhomie, of course, is serious wine. Best selling flagship **Trilogy** flies British Airway/Comair, Richard Branson loves it and the label was recently listed with 3 star Michelin restaurant Georges Blanc in Burgundy. That's when it's not fetching the highest price paid for red wine at the Nederburg Auction (R600 per magnum for **88** in 1998).

But cabernet franc is clearly the favoured child here. 10 years after having brushed aside the incredulity of her peers (not out of character for Norma Ratcliffe) that she was bottling it as a varietal, the **94** won an unprecedented WINE★★★★★ in April 1998 to add to the Dave Hughes trophy for the best Cape red (**95**) at London's International Wines and Spirits Competition (IWSC) in 1997. The launch of the 96 was orchestrated by daughter Jenny, "food presenter extraordinaire", with kitchen marvels all based on Warwick wine. This in keeping with "the ultimate"—wine with food—which accords with their cellar philosophy that wine is to be enjoyed from start to finish.

Not only wine. The new, vast wood maturation cellar was initiated in June 1998 by winemaker Marcus Milner and local (young) winemakers with "Action Cricket" and lots of fresh **98 Cabernet Rosé**. (We are not aware of the standard of umpiring.) Milner, who started at Warwick as a casual 8 years ago, is credited by Ratcliffe for contributing to their success as well as being a genius at cellar management. These talents were tested to the full in the chaotic "we have to pick now" 1998 harvest when tank space had to be found, and re-found, on the turn. His second crush of the year was at California's Flora Springs, home of Ratcliffe soul-mates, the Garveys and their namesake blend **Trilogy**, before returning to get married in December 1998. He proposed to Cathy Lane atop the last murderous hill of the Argus Cycle Tour (participation in which would appear to be a condition of service here) but Norma Ratcliffe's question remains: Do married winemakers make different wine compared to when they were single? No doubt samples will be laid down to test the hypothesis at a later date. With gusto, of course. Warwick is that sort of place.

★★★★ **Trilogy** Violet-scented intensity adds to the allure of concentrated colour, tarry tones introducing tense cassis softened by meaty merlot contribution. Full black berry fruit tightly contained within considerable structure of acids and tannin. Latest **96** bucks the trend of most as lighter, leaner red vintage, full of well-fleshed fruit currently behind veil of tannin. A "thinking vintage", no recipe could be applied, only experimentation, checking and further fine-tuning. **95** a rung higher, demonstratively riper, deeper fruit concentration and, particularly, more malleable finish. Usually about 60% cab. s., 30% merlot; 10% cab. f. 12-16 months in 225 l, new and used French oak (Nevers, Alliers, Vosges), each variety aged separately before final blending; careful egg-white fining to minimise flavour stripping before bottling. Earlier bottlings had reputation as classically slow developers, touch harder. Prestigious listing at Georges Blanc—"pity, with the state of the rand, that we won't be able to afford to eat there" rues Ratcliffe.

Femme Bleue Special new barrel-aged selection for **CIWG** Auction. **96** a cracker, new-oak vanilla, aromatic savoury cherry fruit, dominant cabernet intensity on palate. **95** dramatic, sweet-scented, cinnamon aromas; loaded oak-tannins impose a clench-fisted finish.

★★★★ **Cabernet Franc** ◀ Norma Ratcliffe, who elevated this variety to separate "noble" status in SA (first in 1988) but still defers to Bellingham's Charles Hopkins as the arch-exponent, believes it to be an unlikely cross between cabernet sauvignon and sauvignon blanc—hence the compendium of flavour. Grassy, sappy refinement to chewy fruit, mocha interest, barrels add spice. Samples of **97** display investment of strenuous cropping ("70% left on the ground" laments vineyard curator Stan Ratcliffe), current **96** earthy, more rustic tenor. **95 WINE★★★★, SAA** fine, focused bouquet of violets, minerals, carried off 1997 IWSC Dave Hughes Trophy ahead of big name cabernets and blends. This is 100% varietal (except for shot of merlot, cab. s. **93**) with moderate alcs.—**96**, **95** at 12,5%—and easy acids—5,5 gms/l range. **94** WINE★★★★★ but Ratcliffe, while deferring to experts, still prefers **95**. Earlier characteristics were heather, brambleberry, desiccated herbs. Lean rather than ample-muscled, showing—specially since **94**—firm claret-style intensity through to finish. Oak regime now more or less settled at 14 months in new/2nd.

★★★★ **Old Bush Vine Pinotage** ◀ Tawny tints to ruby colour, stewed fruit and ripe plums flow on fleshy palate, **97** product of extended harvest, slight biting finish. Some bottles labelled without "Old Bush Vines" qualification, still same wine but may become collectors' items! **95 VVG** sweeter, juicier fruit, won all the prizes: excellent example of how modern treatment of this uniquely Cape grape can produce antithesis of old stereotype—the coarse, blunt paintstripper. **96** followed suit: WINE★★★★. Balanced alcs. in 12,5% range, acids around 5,5 gms/l. 9 months in small (10% new, rest 2nd, 3rd-fill) 90% Nevers oak reins in pinotage's wilder flashes, provides classy, quite firm finish. All 100% pinotage, from 26-year-old bush vines, low 8 tons/ha. yields. **96**, **95 CIWG** auction bottlings bigger.

★★★ **Merlot** Style confirmed with **96**, minty, violets, mulberry, broader, more yielding fruit, retains elegance suggested in **95 SAA**, **94 SAA**, **VG**. Latter reflects warm, full-bodied vintage, mouthfilling ripe plum fruit flavours. Fine balance, soft wood tannins. Touch of cab. s. in **96** 5%, 10% in **93**.

★★★ **Cabernet Sauvignon** Latest **96** retreats into shell of austerity and tight, mineral tones after riper, new clone fruity qualities of warm, dry vintage **95**. Cedar wafts, pencil lead tingle and though closed, bristling fruit attractive. Similar to **93**, **90**, more reserved. Average 6 tons/ ha., 16 months 30% new, rest 2nd-fill Nevers. **94 VVG**.

★★★ **Chardonnay** Showy mélange of citric fruits, broad leesy texture and oak—though much less than before—in flashy, ripe **98**. **97** initiated new style, less noticeably oaked (only 4 months, new), citrus/melon fruit to the fore. Much more modern and drinkable than honeyed, oaky-spicy forerunners such as **96**. Low yields, 4 month lees contact, full malo, not cold-stabilised.

Rosé ◀ **98** coppery-tinted, 100% cab. s., dry, and dried herbs nose. Very popular. **Tentklip** 2nd-label cab. s., with touch cab. f., merlot.

WATERFORD WINES

Helderberg-Stellenbosch

Tastings/sales by appointment.
Owner: Jeremy Ord
Winemaker: Kevin Arnold
Vineyards: 14 ha.
Address: Waterford Farm, Blaauwklippen Road, Stellenbosch 7600
Tel: 021-8800496 **Fax:** 021-8801007
E-mail: waterfordhil@icon.co.za

A striking example of the new energy and financial muscle currently re-shaping the Cape wine scene is the launch of the first wines from this 120 ha. property up the Blaauwklippen road, in a fold between the Helderberg and Stellenbosch mountains. Potentially prime vineyard area—only 14 ha. currently features vines—its 50 ha. of arable land, fringed by mountainside, streams and indigenous forest, is due for major development. Owner Jeremy Ord, Johannesburg IT industry heavy-weight, has joined forces here with seasoned winemaker Kevin Arnold (ex-Delheim, Rust-en-Vrede), who is overseeing the construction of a Mediterranean-style winery due to swing into action for the 1999 vintage. (See also the entry under Kevin Arnold Fine Wine.)

★★★ **Sauvignon Blanc** NEW **98** grapes off the farm (from 8-year-old vines) that were previously delivered to Vriesenhof. It is a long time since red wine specialist Kevin Arnold has made white wine, so he enlisted the advice of Villiera's Jeff Grier. The result is a noteworthy success—potentially ★★★★. Picked very ripe. Billowing ripe gooseberry and fresh sweetcorn nose. Very full and rich on palate, with touch of sweetness rounding off youthful edges. Substantial mouthful but already very drinkable. Enough within to carry it into full development over 2-3 years. 13,4% alc.

WELGEGUND — Wellington

Johannesburg power brokers Alex and Sheila Camerer—he in business, she politics (as a top office-bearer in the National Party); he's also a director of Devon Hill Winery—took over a tiny plot of ancient, shy-bearing carignan vines when they bought their 50-ha. Wellington property 10 years ago. The crop all went to Bovlei co-op, but in 1997 the Camerers bottled a varietal **Carignan** under the Welgegund label. A **98**, again by Guy Webber, since has become available. Available from Devon Hill; The Oaks Wine Merchants, Cape Town; 500 cases. ± R20 a bottle. **Welgegund** (Alex Camerer) **Tel:** 011-4476748 **Fax:** 011-4424386.

Carignan NEW Spanish variety widely grown in Languedoc-Roussillon, some in Italy, Calif., S. America etc.; half-dozen SA estates, v. small quantities. **98** distinctive, but doesn't trumpet; light-tinted/bodied, exotic Karoo scrub, basket of berries, distinctly dry, low alc. 11,6% alc. 20-yr-old dryland bushvines yielding 5 tons/ha.

WELGEMEEND ESTATE

Paarl — See Paarl map

Open 2-4 Wed; 9-12.30 Sat or by appointment.
Owner: W.A. Hofmeyr
Winemaker: Louise Hofmeyr (since 1992)
Manager/Viticulturist: Ursula Hofmeyr
Production: 3 500 cases. **Vineyards:** 12,6 ha.
P.O. Box 69, Klapmuts 7625
Tel: 021-8755210 **Fax:** 021-8755239
E-mail: safred@iafrica.com

The 1999 crush at this much-admired Paarl estate marks the 20th anniversary of the Bordeaux-style blend at the Cape, the first commercial example crafted by land-surveyor-turned-vintner Billy Hofmeyr in 1979—with unstinting help and encouragement from Ursula, loyal spouse and partner-in-wine—and released the following year. In realising his tenaciously-held ambition to transplant the style of the Médoc to the Cape, Hofmeyr blazed a since well-trodden trail and secured his place in local wine lore. His illness saw Hofmeyr's talented daughter Louise take over the reins in 1992—under her thoughtful aegis most of the wines remain in the Bordeaux mould, made largely from the varietals—and in the manner—of the reds of the Médoc. Unsurprisingly they are not "new world" in character, and the differences between them arise from marginal adjustments in the winemaking process as well as in the percentages of each varietal comprising the blend. In this they reflect Billy Hofmeyr's philosophy, as well as daughter Louise's creative, yet assiduously hardworking approach to perfecting her craft.

★★★★ **Welgemeend Estate Reserve** ◀ South Africa's original Bordeaux varietal blend: **96** Fine, "dusty" Médoc-style bouquet, whiffs of violets, raspberries, elegant mineral textures, blackcurrants layering the earthiness, persistent, spicy finish. 54% cabernet s., 27% merlot, 19% cabernet f., from selected v'yds, older vines, later harvested due to virus. 12-18 mths in barriques, some new wood. **95** wild mulberry/mineral aromas, palate discreetly spicy. **94** uncharacteristically plump, cassis/coffee notes. Path-breaking **79** (distinguished service award), tasted for this ed., still vigorous, deep maroon tint reflecting good concentration, intensity. Open, refined bouquet, soft-toned, layered: honeycomb, leafy hints over generous ripe cassis, clean cedary wood, whiffs of acacia, tobacco. Aromas develop in glass: slight savoury and toasty notes, all above echoing on palate. Medium-bodied (picked to yield alc. ± 12%), ample flavour—cassis, light honey-chocolate overlay—clean dry finish, very fresh. Elegant, linear style; sets tone for succeeding vintages. Harvested from 14 Feb 1979, 70% cab. s., 10% each merlot, cab. f., malbec, vines ± 5 yrs old, small French oak 12-18 mths.

★★★ **Douelle** Malbec-based blend, generally more rustic than Estate Reserve. **96** brambly aromas, whiffs of quince, lighter, more austere palate, hints of black cherry, fine, not lightweight. 28% malbec, 26% merlot, 25% cab. s, 15% petit verdot, 6% cab. franc.

★★★ **Amadé 96** youngberry/loganberry fragrance, smoky, leathery, with light truffle/earthy notes, mineral spice on finish. 39% pinotage, 31% shiraz, 30% grenache (not all estate grapes), 12-18 mths in small wood.

Soopjeshoogte Lighter, easier drinking, more accessibly priced second label of Estate Reserve: **96** strawberry notes, black cherry/herby layerings, firm tannins, plum-like textures on finish. 67% cab. f., 25% merlot, 8% cab. s.

Tipple Hill NEW Pinotage-shiraz blend from **96**, raspberry/prunelle aromas, fine dense tannins, delicate mineral flavours, plum/mulberry finish.

WELLINGTON WYNKELDER

Wellington See Wellington map

Tastings/sales Mon-Fri 8-5.
Owners: 51 members.
Winemaker: Gert Boerssen (since 1980)
Production: 20 000 cases. **Vineyards:** 1 547 ha.
P.O. Box 520, Wellington 7654
Tel: 021-8731163 **Fax:** 021-8732423

"An outstanding red wine year," comments winemaker Gert Boerssen on the small but beautiful 98 vintage at this cellar, which while currently taking in 80% white varieties, continues to steal show awards and consumer hearts with its reds in particular (though never underestimate its chenin blanc). New vineyards of pinotage, cabernet, shiraz and merlot are beginning to push up the red ratio—the eventual aim is 40% of production—but Boerssen faces the same problem here as colleagues all over the Cape—an acute shortage of plant material. (No-one, least of all industry authorities, it appears, anticipated today's red wine boom.)

*** **Pinotage** ◀ ☺ Perennial winner here, regular Veritas, SA young wine show golds. **97** less exuberant than terrifically bouncy **96** but same cinnamon bun scents, plus cherries this time. Juicy, sweetish-seeming palate. 12,8% alc.

*** **Cabernet Sauvignon** ☺ Super **96**. Honest, approachable, soft tannins, ripe but not over-the-top fruit. A most swiggable style. 3rd-fill oak one year. Bush vines, low-yield.

*** **Shiraz** NEW Further confirmation of Wellington's red-wine potential. **97** though from first-crop vines full of confidence. Friendly leather, smoke aromas, fullish, quite meaty flavours, lovely spicy, lengthy finish. Drinking well.

Chenin Blanc ◀ Waves of ripe guavas, tangy-fresh palate, dry **98**. Good summer lunch companion. **Chardonnay** NEW **98** first oak-fermented version from this cellar; lean, crisp style, very dry. **Sauvignon Blanc 98** unshowy dry white.

WELMOED WINES

Lynedoch See Stellenbosch map

Visits: Open Mon-Fri 9-5.30, Sat 9-5, Sun 10-4.
Restaurant: Brad's Original Kitchen serves lunch 10-4.30 daily, except Tuesdays. Tel: 021-8813310
Head Winemaker-elect: Chris Kelly
P.O. Box 456, Stellenbosch 7599
Tel: 021-8813800 or 8813870 **Fax:** 021-8813434 or 8813102

Supplied by well-situated vineyards, many brushed by Atlantic Ocean-breezes, this winery is now part of the new-wave Stellenbosch Vineyards venture (see that entry for more details).

*** **Shiraz** ◀ Russet-flecked ruby, cinnamon, clove and nutmeg-spiced varietal tones raise tenor. **96, 95** above average. Matured used oak for 1 year. 12,5% alc., easy 5,4 gms/l acid, unaggressive, glycerol-textured finish. Some pvs. notched up good show results; **92, 91 VG**.

*** **Pinotage** ◀ Both **96, 95** big, broad array of flavours, prominent bon-bon, boiled sweets attraction. Beware light to medium colours/ texture—weighty with 13,5% alc. Frontal, fruity finish, mocha interest. French oak-matured, 1 year. **94** boasts vanilla notes of American oak, powerful vinous finish. **93 VVG**.

**** **Sauvignon Blanc Reserve** ◀ Consistently excellent. **98** arresting, fresh, crisp ripe gooseberry, green fig, very dry. Full; food rather than stand-alone wine (14% alc.). Enjoy before next harvest. **97 WINE****, 96 VVG** (one of only five to achieve it that year).

*** **Sauvignon Blanc** ◀ More approachable and less opulent—but as attractive in own right—than **Reserve** above. **98** elegant grassy flavours, uncompromising flintiness in finish would "cut" the richest fish dish.

Cabernet Sauvignon Reserve 94 among better medium-weight cabs.; bricking with age, quiet bouquet, fairly ripe fruit, firm in older, dustier style. **93** individual waxy-mint aromas. Both **91, 90 VG**. **Rouge Royal** NV Mainly cinsaut, aged in large oak; pleasant, gamey bouquet, easy on palate, medium-weight. **Blanc de Blanc 98** light-bodied, fresh, easy flavours, drink within year. **Chardonnay Reserve 97** barrel-fermented in older, tempered oak; pleasant creamy texture, tad short of citrus complexity, 13% alc. **Chenin Blanc Reserve 98** part barrel, part tank-fermented, soft oak lifts quiet nose, wood fills out pleasant palate, refreshing dry. **97** also touched with oak. **96** unwooded, off-dry. **Chenin Blanc 98** off-dry "all-purpose" easy white.

WELTEVREDE ESTATE

Bonnievale See Robertson map

Open for tasting & sales: Mon-Fri 8.30-5; Sat 9-3; cellar tours by appointment.

Light lunches served Mon-Sat 12.-2. Self-catering cottage—"Ons Huisie".

Owner: Lourens Jonker
Winemaker: Nicolas Rust. **Assistant/Vineyards:** Philip Jonker
Production: 30 000 cases. **Vineyards:** 100 ha.
P.O. Box 6, Bonnievale 6730
Tel: 02346-2141 **Fax:** 02346-2460
Website: www.weltevrede.com

KWV chaiman Lourens Jonker sets a good example when it comes to the development of the community on his estate, as one should expect from a man in his position. This model property boasts a day-care centre for workers' children, run by daughter-in-law Lindelize, offers adult basic education courses, and a home ownership scheme. Despite a severe frost scare in October 97, the 98 vintage was rewarding, with much excitement in the cellar as the first cabernet and merlot came in. The cellar's philosophy is to balance New World techniques with traditional European flavours, creating wines unique to this "Valley of Wine and Roses"—anyone who has driven the lovely road from Robertson to Bonnievale will identify with this title. Young winemaker Nicolaas Rust can be congratulated on some great work in the cellar in his baptism year; this young team, including Jonker's son Philip, is well-set for the future.

*** **Chardonnay 97** shows restrained, well-mannered aromas of peach, pear, with hazelnut overtones—most elegant for totally barrel-fermented wine; wood and lees character in complex harmony. **96** still shows piquant leesy favours. **95** with Burgundian character starting to form—toffee, butterscotch notes; only available on the farm. KLM 1st class selection.

*** **Privé du Bois** ◀ **97** popular wooded chardonnay/sauvignon blanc—one of the earliest oaked whites made in SA. Blended after fermentation, aged on barrel-fermented chardonnay lees in French oak for 5 mths. Shows restrained limey nose, a hint of vanilla on palate. Should reward a couple of years cellaring. **95 VG, 91 VVG**.

*** **Sauvignon Blanc** ◀ **98** fresh, grassy, green pepper aromas, hint of grapefruit: dry, elegant nettle-flavoured Loire style. Work in v'yd paid off—canopy management, frequent pre-harvest tasting for optimum ripeness—to produce the best yet from this cellar.

*** **Rhine Riesling** ◀ ☺ **98** honeysuckle aroma followed by quite delicious fruit/acid; after a disappointing (unreleased) **96** and a somewhat better **97**, latest crop proved to be outstanding. 8 gms/l sugar neatly frame the fruit acids on an off-dry palate; make for super drinking—and for a year or two in the cellar.

*** **White Muscadel** ◀ **96** now **Ouma se Wyn** after grandma Lisbeth Jonker. Creamy golden syrup aromas, essence of fresh muscat grapes, melded with spirit into succulent mouthful of beautifully balanced flavour. Consistently among Cape's most delicious desserts.

★★★ **Philip Jonker Brut 95 (MCC)** a first from chardonnay only—a blanc de blancs. Whole-bunch pressed, selected *cuvée*, 3 years on 2nd lees in bottle. Rich, deep straw-green, complex appley flavours, full- bodied mature sparkler.

Merlot-Cabernet Sauvignon 98 NEW for release late 99: traditionally made (feet, basket press, the works). Lourens Jonker asked for "no comment" from taster at this stage; sorry, can't pass up the opportunity to note: your first red baby shows lovely vanilla, mulberry character—lots of potential. **Blanc de Noir 98** salmon-tinged, plump and jolly semi-sweet from muscadel grapes. 15 gms/l sugar. **Blanc de Blanc 98** fruit salad of sauvignon, colombard, chenin, dash of crowd-pleasing muscat de frontignan: nicely strung, taut and juicy flavours, sweetish finish. **Cape Riesling 98** (also bottled for Woolworths), pear and lucerne aromas, surprisingly full for only 10,5% alc.; dry, a splash of Rhine riesling for seasoning. **Colombard 97** last appearance; is making place for reds. **Gewürztraminer 98** billowing rose-garden aroma, soft friendly palate—11 gms/l sugar. Small crop depletes supply still further of this very popular. off-dry. **Therona Special Late Harvest 98** shy baked apple nose, soft, sweet succulence to follow; fragrant, light-bodied, sweet (26 gms/l sugar). **Woolworths Muscat de Frontignan—Colombard 98** a real island fruit salad, the two varieties complement, with musky aromas and bright acidity. **Red Muscadel (Oupa Se Wyn) 98** from red muscadel v'yd planted 1926! Deep plum-red, almost port-like aromas, lively and youthful sweet dessert tipple, plummy flavours. **Muscat de Hambourg 97** refined red fortified dessert; spicy, elegant—17% alc., 177 gms/l sugar.

WELVANPAS WINES Retief Family Cellar

Wellington See Wellington map

Tastings by appointment.
Owners: The Retief family
Winemaker: Dan Retief Jnr. (since 1993)
Production: 1 600 cases
Vineyards: 45 ha.
P.O. Box 75, Wellington 7654
Tel: 021-8641238 **Fax:** 021-8641239

The spectacular Groenkloof/Du Toitskloof mountains form the backdrop for this family-run winery near Wellington, where winemaker Dan Retief Jnr. crafts a compact, thoughtful range reflecting the benefits of higher-lying plots.

WESKUS WINES See Winkelshoek Wynkelder

WHALEHAVEN

Hermanus See Walker Bay map

Tasting & sales Mon-Fri 9.30-5. Sat 10.30-1. Animal farm for children. Self-catering cottage available.
Winemaker: Storm Kreusch (since 1995 inception)
Production: 4 000 cases
Private Bag X10, Hermanus 7200
Tel: 0283-21585 **Fax:** 0283-21917
E-mail: whwines@hermanus.co.za

Here is a small cellar with a cool-climate wine focus and a reputation that grows with every vintage. WhaleHaven sources grapes from a vineyard in the Hemel-en-Aarde valley, one in Elgin, and a third in the Stanford area. Stellenbosch University trained owner/winemaker Storm Kreusch made wines at Delheim, SFW and HRV before starting her own cellar. Her background also includes years of overseas training and experience in Italy, France, Germany. WhaleHaven is a family affair, with each member playing a rôle, from a 5-year-old gumbooted daughter who works the pump, to the year-old toddler who ingeniously mops the cellar floor with whatever she's wearing at the time! Meantime, mother aims at making hand-crafted top quality wines with distinct elegance. "Let the wines develop naturally, don't force them" and "Don't push pinot" are two typical Storm Kreusch injunctions—and they're clearly valid. Her **96** was rated top in a WINE magazine SA Pinot tasting, and was selected for the prestigious Blue Train wine list.

★★★★ **Pinot Noir** Sleek and stylish SA pinot. **97** echoes pvs. with pronounced stone fruit flavours, bouquet of violets, absolutely delicious. A sleeper now but will develop beautifully. **96** second vintage, from Elgin grapes: 86% new clone, 14% BK 5. **WINE★★★★**, topped local pinot ratings. Lovely, strawberry nose. Delicious sweet-sour piquancy on palate with supple tannins but firm grip. Elegant dusty finish, highlights spicy cherry fruit. Year in small French oak. Unfiltered. 12,8% alc.

★★★ **Merlot 96** dense fruit, deep mulberry colour. Rich chocolate/coffee bouquet leads into full-flavoured brambleberry fruit. Kreusch describes it as having Barolo character. Alc. 13%. 8 months French oak. Elgin grapes. **97** barrel sample most promising.

★★★ **Cabernet Sauvignon 96** deep cassis upfront fruit, coffee aroma with delicious berry/cherry flavours, minty touch. Slight sweetness in finish. Dash of cab. franc. Developing beautifully. 14 months French oak.

★★★ **Baleine Noir** Shiraz/merlot blend with immediate drinkability. **97** spicy/raspberry fruit, gentle finish and tannins, a summertime, lunchtime wine.

★★★★ **Chardonnay** Equal blend of **97** Elgin/Walker Bay grapes show cool climate influence. Nutty apricot and marmalade aromas precede layered creamy/citrus flavours; crisp refreshing acidity creates elegant food-friendly mouthful. 10 months oak (mainly Taransaud) integrates well, lending structure. 13% alc.

★★★ **Sauvignon Blanc 97** Given time in bottle before release. From single Walker Bay vineyard. Lively grassy, asparagus bouquet. Developing in chic style, with racy Sancerre-like acidity/steely fruit. Superb food wine, calls for wild Agulhas shellfish.

WIDE RIVER WINES

See Robertson Winery

WILDEKRANS CELLARS

Overberg See Walker Bay map

Tastings & sales Mon-Fri 9-5; Sat 10-1. Guest-house in Houwhoek. Cellar tours by appointment.
Winemaker: Jacques Fourie
Viticulturist: Barry Anderson
Production: 10 000 cases. **Vineyards:** 42 ha., 135 tons.
P.O. Box 200, Elgin 7180
Tel: 02824-49829 **Fax:** 02824-49902

A new era begins at Wildekrans with the appointment of winemaker Jacques Fourie, who started his career with ex-KWV chairman Pietman

Hugo at Rawsonville. Fourie studied at Elsenburg from '88-'90. The class of '90 obviously had a strong attraction for cool climate wines; as classmates Niels Verburg (Beaumont) and Kevin Grant (HRV) are now neighbours. A spell at Bellingham followed in '91, then 3 years at Delaire. Fourie worked at Chalkhill in California during '96, his first overseas experience. He was particularly impressed by the degree of experimental work, particularly with natural fermentation. On his return Fourie was consultant for Klawervlei for the '97 vintage after which he moved to Wildekrans. "Everything I need is here —cool climates accentuate the varietal taste and I must also give full credit to Barry Anderson (viticulturist). I like to work to real physiological ripeness, I don't care if I have 14%+ alcohols as long as the ripeness is in balance."

Fine vineyards and the distinctive Walker Bay micro-climate have helped Wildekrans win loads of laurels, including SA Champion young red (1996); "Wine of the Show" for the Chenin Blanc Reserve at the 1997 London Wine Trade Fair; and a rating, in *Decanter* magazine, as one of the two Cape cellars on a list of "the 21 hottest wineries in the world to watch".

★★★★ **Pinotage** Dashing examples of succulent, new-wave, cool-climate pinotage since **93** début. Latest **97** vibrant mulberry hue, dripping with sweet, spicy, plummy/berry fruit, tangy acidity solidly backed by dry tannins. Shows harmony, elegance with good weight and grip. Caramel touches on finish. From bush vines, 13,2% alc. 8 months in new and 2nd-fill French and American oak. Early **98** barrel sample shows immense promise.

★★★ **Cabernet Sauvignon 97** lighter style reflects vintage, ruby colour, cloves on nose. Elegant, spicy fruit gives way to steely, minerally finish. 12 months French oak still showing. Deserves time, drink after millennium. 12,7% alc. **96** Grand SA champ, Jan Smuts trophy at 1996 young wine show. Deep, full, with minerally fruit (includes cherries) and soft ripe tannins, toasty oak notes. Only 600 cases made from 3-year-old vines.

★★★ **Merlot** NEW Fine garnet tones in **97**, with smoky, toasty wood showing. Palate has rackful of spices; chicory, pepper. Good accessibility with balanced, youthful, elegance and tannins.

★★★ **Sauvignon Blanc** Definitive Walker Bay cool-climate style. **98** pungent green pepper nose. Racy palate reflects mix of degrees of ripeness; tropical, almost floral tones mingle with weightier figginess. Pert acidity creates delicious food wine with fine steely finish.

★★★ **Chenin Blanc Reserve 98** has depth and weight to help balance hefty 15% alc. Peachy, vanilla bouquet, palate crammed with nutty, lemony fruit. Complex blend of 50/50 Seguin Moreau American oak/steel ferment with 5% each of sémillon, sauvignon blanc.

★★★ **Chardonnay** Toasty, marmalade aromas in **98** follow into creamy, lanolin tones on palate from 70% wood fermentation. Supple tannins balance with lively citrus fruit. Will develop, broaden within 12 months.

★★★ **Sémillon** NEW Not a lightweight, **98** with full, toasty, spicy aromas. 50% fermented in all new, equal blend of French/American oak. Fine food wine with richness balanced by grip and tangy finish.

WINDMEUL WINERY

Agter-Paarl See Paarl map

Sales weekdays 8-5. Tastings by appointment.
Owners: 53 members

Winemaker: Hein Koegelenberg (since 1990)
Assistant Winemaker: Riaan van der Spuy
Production: 12 000 tons. **Vineyards:** 1 500 ha.
P.O. Box 2013, Windmeul 7630
Tel: 021-8638043 **Fax:** 021-8638614

The quality-tsunami engulfing the winelands has spread to rustic Agter-Paarl, causing members of this forward-looking winery to plant premium red varieties at a high rate of knots. "We're also widely establishing premium white grapes," reports the winemaker. Highlights of 1998 include a new high-tech pressing facility, revamp of packaging and labels, and conversion from a co-op into a company. "The challenge is to remain on the crest of the wave. Time will tell," Hein Koegelenberg adds on a sobering note, "if the vision we are following is the right one."

*** **Pinotage** ◀ Nostalgic **98** runs gamut of old-style pinotage aromas/flavours: ripe, juicy redcurrants, spicy stewed plums, estery top notes leading on to wide-bodied, fruity-textured, sweet-sour finish. *Lekker!* Snip at ± R12 ex-cellar. From ancient shy-bearing v'yd. 13,5% alc.

Cabernet Sauvignon/Merlot Light ruby-pink appearance disguises front-of-the-scrum style in **97**. Very ripe, weighty, distinctly dry, vanilla-spice in tail. 11 mths new French oak. 13,0% alc. **Merry Mill Red** ☺ ◀ NEW Pvs. rather quaffable **Cinsaut** reappears in exuberant "let's party!" 500 ml screw top packaging. Ripe plum compôte, vanilla spice, "sweet" plump fruit add to super-smooth drinkability. But watch it! Alc. way over 14%. Lightly wooded. **Chenin Blanc** Floral display, usually a sideshow, is main act in **98**. Very nice weight, roundness, "sweetish" (though technically dry) finish. 13,3% alc. Thelema buys in from Windmeul for its second-label **Stormy Cape** chenin, another pointer to its quality. **Sauvignon Blanc** ◀ Very showy **98** redolent of overgrown veggie patch: grass, nettles, green pepper gusts; vibrant fruit on palate, pleasant just-not-dry finish (soupçon of sugar 3,1 gms/l). Very nice. Low ± 11% alc. **Merry Mill White** NEW **98** sauvignon-dominated, dry, no-frills quaffing blend.

WINELANDS Range

See IWS

WINE WAREHOUSE

Tastings/sales Mon-Fri 8.30-5.30, Sat 9-1.
Owner: Oscar Foulkes
Address: 8 Ravenscraig Road, Woodstock 7925
Tel: 021-4482371 **Fax:** 021-4478589
E-mail: oscarf@iafrica.com

A chain of compact, specialist retail wine shops offering personalised service and informed advice is the latest outlet for husband-and-wife team Oscar and Andrea Foulkes's boundless energy and enthusiasm. Three Enoteca ("place of wine") stores are up and running in/around Cape Town—one in the original Wine Warehouse, Woodstock, also trendy Heritage Square (soothing summer shade provided by Cape Town's oldest vine) and upper-crust Newlands. Features include a budget-priced own-label, comprehensive range of top SA wines and selected imports.

*** **Oscar's Reserve Sauvignon Blanc** ☺ ◀ Striking front label featuring titillating oil by New Zealand-based artist Jacqui Colley, aptly reflects qualities of frisky-fruity **98**, chalky/grassy, fresh, suggestion of sugar fills rather than sweetens. Unwooded. Alc. 12%.

★★★ **Oscar's Reserve Chenin Blanc** ☺ ◀ Super-quaffable, barrel-fermented **98** packed with tropical fruit, sweet-oaky flavours, gently dry. Solo sipping or at table. Value at R15 a bottle. Both from (undivulged) leading wineries.

WINKELSHOEK WYNKELDER

Swartland See Swartland map

Tastings/sales Mon-Fri 8-6, Sat 8-13. Tasting fee R1 p/p. Conference facilities for ± 50.

Daily 8 am-9 pm.

Owners: Hennie Hanekom, J. J. Brand

Winemaker: Hennie Hanekom (since 1984)

Address: Off national road (N7), Piketberg 7320

Tel: 0261-31092 **Fax:** 0261-31095

They say you haven't lived unless you've tasted fresh West Coast crayfish with a frosty glass of Hennie Hanekom's **Grand Crû**. "They" might have a point, for these everyday quaffers are tailor-made for braaiing, picnicking, partying or simply chilling-out with friends. Distinctive brandies and fortified wines are features of the range, sold from new premises on the N7 highway.

Vin Rouge Dry red blend of pinotage, cinsaut. Moderate alc. **Grand Crû** Dry white colombard/chenin blend. **Blanc de Blanc** Colombard/chenin, off-dry. **Late Harvest** semi-sweet chenin sipper.

WOOLWORTHS

Enquiries: Woolworths Wine Department

Selection Manager: Allan Mullins (CWM)

Senior Buyer: Ivan Oertle

P.O. Box 680, Cape Town 8000

Tel: 021-4072777/4072762 **Fax:** 021-4614935

E-mail: wwioe@woolworths.co.za

This super-successful and versatile quality chain-store range is, at source, a credit to many of the finest winemakers in the Cape, whose creative talents flourish throughout the line-up. But equal billing must be given to the duo marshalling the crowds, here keeping them in line (with consumer tastes), there allowing them to break ranks and surge in new directions (to set new trends), deciding when a wine may kick up its heels and toyi-toyi, or when it should restrain itself to a quieter sort of demonstration.

Cape Wine Master Allan Mullins is the front-man, ceaselessly criss-crossing wine country to confer with longtime suppliers and winkle out new ones, endlessly tasting, blending, and fine-tuning in their cellars to arrive at what he knows from experience, or feels intuitively, Woolies' customers will enjoy drinking with their meals. Mullins is the man who must take the front-line flak—from, for example, a couple at the (KwaZulu-Natal) Mercury Wine Week, who accused him of taking the fun out of the wine. "Woolies' wines are so reliable that we just know what we're going to get with each bottle," they complained! Surely the most complimentary sort of gripe. In fact, it's not an altogether fair comment. Woolies is very often a ground-breaker—as in a new (still in development so untasted for this edition) sulphur-free, lightly oaked Chardonnay-Chenin commissioned from Villiera—in response to consumers with headache-inducing sensitivity to even the modest sulphuring (lower than some countries) of SA wines. This will go on trial in the W. Cape, and will carry a sell-by date. Trendy new packaging for many of the wines appeals to an increasingly younger set of consumers.

And here's where Mullins' right-hand man, the practical power behind the sweeping vision, takes a bow. Ivan Oertle makes it all happen, with his meticulous grasp of detail, consumer and store profiles; what will fly, where, in what quantity and at which price. While Mullins may do the big tango moves, so to speak, it's Oertle whose steady partnering skills make them possible. The duo travelled to Europe in 1998 to source new labels for Woolies' popular imported array—an affordable Spanish range which premierèred late in the year was among their finds. Reliability, reasonable prices, food-friendliness remain the bottom lines here. But there's more than enough drama and excitement too in a line-up which long ago rose above the negative associations of "supermarket plonk" to position Woolworths very firmly in the Cape's prime wine territory.

RESERVES

*** **Cabernet Sauvignon Reserve** Sensitive hand required, such as (Villiera winemaker) Jeff Grier's, to make success of light **96** vintage. Rather than try to force greatness out of the wine, natural assets, however transitory, are allowed to speak for themselves. Bouquet of modern (new clone) ripeness: sweet red cherries, berries, fused with complementary spicy oak warmth. Ripe plum, chocolate flavours balanced by soft springy tannins, medium-weight. For current drinking or over next 18 months.

*** **Pinotage Reserve** A new producer for forthcoming vintage wine was under negotiation when this guide went to press. Pvs. **95** ◀ from Jan Coetzee of Vriesenhof, developed some Rhône-like spice, good savoury concentration, ended with solid tannins. Blended with 10% merlot, 15% from **96**. Oak-matured 2nd-fill for 1 year. From 25-year-old bush vines.

*** **Shiraz Reserve 94** ex-Hartenberg showed gamey decadence with peppery spice concentration, from both fruit/oak. Smoothly accessible; savoury length. Sold out by mid-1998, new producer for next release.

*** **Cabernet Sauvignon-Merlot 96**, though 57/43 blend, is merlot-driven. Healthy, ruby; lightish but not simple chocolate-mint, berry fruit with carefully-judged oak overlay. Gentle tannins allow sweet plum fleshiness full play. From Neil Ellis, St'bosch. **95** more unyielding than 50/50 blend might suggest; good minty/minerally thrust, firm, fine tannins. Grapes from Helderberg, Devon Valley, Jonkershoek v'yds, old/new clones, oak-matured 18 months partly new barrels.

*** **Cabernet-Shiraz Reserve** ◀ New World-style; **95** lighter than punchy **94**; apart from some residual savoury gaminess, more of a pleasant-drinking dry red than distinctive blend. French oak barrel-ageing. From La Motte.

**** **Constantia Reserve Sauvignon Blanc** ◀ A gem in the Woolworths range. From Buitenverwachting whose sauvignon is amongst best if slowest to develop. **97** hitting top gear only 18 months after vintage; gorgeous figgy, cheesy, rich bouquet; deep, sumptuous feel yet ends with flinty clarity. Demands nothing else but simply prepared goat's cheese. No need to hurry this, will stay the course for another year or two.

**** **Chardonnay Reserve** ◀ **97** St'bosch star from masterly Neil Ellis. Gorgeous; chardonnay at its most harmonious, complex. Strong wheaten translucence. Ripe but delicate hazelnut, oatmeal character; gives drier feel than more usual tropical flavours; broad, fat but never clumsy; winds up with lingering, whipped lemon-butter freshness. Quintessential elegance; a bargain R29,99. Barrel-fermented, all French, 20% new; 70% completed malo.

*** **Barrel Reserve Chenin Blanc** Woolworths Wine of the Year. Bold, friendly sums up both man behind the label and his wine. Restaurateur Ken Forrester (his 96 Winery Road is a magnet for tourists/winemakers alike) is a chenin enthusiast; his wine, naturally, styled as food partner. **97** with botrytis overtones suggests Thai or Provençal dishes. Still quite tight; technically dry but gives sweetish impression; should develop mellow honeyed quality as wine ages to complement pale gold brilliance. Well-judged oak provides sound frame. Made by Martin Meinert at his Devon Valley cellar.

REDS regular labels:

*** **Merlot** ◀ Drinkability with class achieved even in difficult **96** with Jacques Borman's input. Picks on best features of slender vintage; soft fruit, uncomplicated charm; subtly oaked to emphasise gentle chocolaty length. Agreeable early drinking. Matured mainly in once-used casks, smattering of new wood. From La Motte Estate, Franschhoek.

*** **Grand Rouge** ◀ Classy, ready to drink Bordeaux-style mix. Slightly higher merlot content than usual lends tempting sweet fruit balance to lighter **96**. Sensitively put together by La Motte's super-blender, Jacques Borman with Mullins' assistance. "I doubt there's better value on the counter," asserts Mullins. Current vintage, 51% cab. s., 36% merlot, 13% cab. f., best over next year; some earlier vintages, pre-**94** had more ageworthy depths.

*** **Cabernet Franc-Merlot** ◀ NEW Little-used combination (50/50 in **97**) giving true "claret" lightness. Graceful leafy, spicy fragrance; cassia spice also dominant theme on palate; packed with flavour which feathery tannins allow full show. Barrel-matured, none new. Another individual from De Leuwen Jagt, Paarl.

*** **Three Springs Red** NEW French/South African blend from Saxenburg/Ch. Capion's Nico v d Merwe. Individual bright cherry, ground black pepper spice and wild scrub flavours, beefed up with touch more cab. s. than Saxenburg version. NV **96, 97** combination; many varieties, mainly carignan, cinsaut, grenache with cabs. s./f., syrah and tinta.

Cabernet Sauvignon (Vin de Cuvée) NEW Lightly-oaked **97** from Bergsig. Interesting but undemanding berry/cedary nuances, soft chocolaty texture rounded off with gentle tannin grip. **Shiraz** Sound, gutsy red from Rooiberg. **96** shows pleasant white pepper, spicy character; firm but rounded tannins. Partially oaked. **Jug o' Red** Sound vin ordinaire. Gluggable raspberry, cherry sweetness; softly chewy. Mainly ruby cabernet with cinsaut, cab. s., merlot. Ex-Worcester. **Selected Cape Red** ☺ ◀ NV Fresh, fruity quaffer. Appealing bright colour, uncomplicated spicy, juicy Santa Rosa plum fruits. Unwooded cinsaut, cab. s., ruby cab. mix from Simonsvlei. **Maison Rouge (Vin de Cuvée)** ☺ ◀ Friendly, soft-textured NV red, "perfect drinking any time of day or night" says Mullins, who designed it that way. Mainly ruby cabernet with cinsaut, cab. s., merlot. Plentiful soft cherry, raspberry sweetness, pleasantly chewy with no fighting tannins. From Worcester, blended at Du Toitskloof co-op. **Pinotage (Vin de Cuvée)** Soft raspberry tang in lightish, unwooded **96**. Fresh, down-to-earth style from Rooiberg. Customer favourite.

Rosé Fruitily-sweet, fun pink; plentiful dainty muscat appeal, lightish, easy-quaffing. Villiera grenache, muscat, chenin blend. From **98**. **Blanc de Noir** Full-flavoured pinotage from Swartland. Wild strawberry/savoury ripeness reflects warmer **98**; 9 gms/l sugar ensures smooth drinkability, compatibility with Provençal-type dishes. **Nouveau Rosé** Fruity, off-dry (11 gms/l sugar) blend of whites, reds by Villiera. Spicy muscat overtones to mainly chenin blanc; light 10,5% alc. **Nouveau Rouge** A drink-quick, don't-think wine of quality: gamay (with 5% pinotage) from Villiera; dry but very soft.

SPRING COLLECTION

*** **Spring Red** French/South African blend from Saxenburg/Ch. Capion's Nico v d Merwe. Soft, quaffable with individual bright cherry, ground black pepper spice and wild scrub flavours. NV **96**, **97** combination; many varieties, mainly carignan, cinsaut, grenache with cabs. s./f., syrah and tinta.

Fernão Pires ☺ ◀. Ideal low alc. lunch companion: soft, pretty, with fresh lemon/pineapple-scented fruit; off-dry. **Chenin Blanc-Colombard** Refreshing, light **98**; unflamboyant fruit enhanced by 5 gms/l sugar. Drink young. By Graham Beck, Robertson.

FIRESIDE REDS

Pinotage Light-textured **97**; easy raspberry sweetness, some firmish tannins in tail. Could be lightly chilled. From Bergsig. **Merlot** NEW **96** from Languedoc. **Traditional Glühwein** NEW Blend of red wine, herbs and spices; ideal served heated on cold winter's night. Screw cap. 9,5% alc. Sales took off immediately.

SUMMER DAYS COLLECTION

Chardonnay Lightly wooded; from Deetlefs Estate, Worcester. **Semi-Sweet** Undecided at deadline; possible chenin blanc, Rhine riesling, gewürz. blend, 18 gms/l sugar. Also NEW **Sangria.**

WHITES regular labels:

*** **Chardonnay-Pinot Noir** Pale-hued, "still-champagne" blend but picked riper, therefore fruitier than champagne without bubbles. Style encourages subtlety with satisfaction, compatibility with many dishes; delicate raspberry nuances lifted by unobtrusive 4 gms/l sugar. **98** little sturdier than usual, ripe berry concentration reflection of vintage. Remains well balanced, individual. From Achim von Arnim's Cabrière Estate. 12% alc. (Pinot from Cabrière's outstanding, densely-planted new clone v'yd.)

*** **Chardonnay (Vin de Cuvée)** ◀ Moderate creamy, lemony complexity; subtle oak enrichment; grows on to lingering finish. Whole greater than parts in quietly satisfying **97**. **98** of same family, slightly bigger, more concentrated. From Robertson Winery.

*** **Sauvignon Blanc Premier** NEW Well-positioned intermediate style between Robertson/Buitenverwachting sauvignons. Mouthfilling but not too heavy; authentic fig, flinty character, even touch ripe cheesiness on palate but delivered with gentle push rather than varietal punch. 12% alc. From Wildekrans, Walker Bay area.

*** **Rhine Riesling** ◀ "Our customers love riesling with a bit of age," Mullins confides. Jeff Grier's **97** should prove very popular; has maturing terpene hints but oiliness subdued by limey-peppery tang; full-bodied, fruit kept at high-pitch by 8 gms/l sugar. Should acquire even more attractions with more age.

*** **Three Springs White** ◀ NEW Epitomises new genre of Cape whites which focus on texture, food compatibility rather than over-in-a-flash fruit, or sickly cream-'n-vanilla richness. In **98**, sémillon's soft, bouncy texture, oaked-chardonnay's subtle breadth and chenin's fruity lift bind in harmonious, food-friendly style. Delheim is source.

*** **Chenin Blanc-Chardonnay** ◀ Partnership with distinctive ginger-spice attraction, from 60% barrel-fermented chenin portion. **97** showed good zest, also fruity pliability to soften well-focused dryness. Combination which favours Thai food. **98** follows usual established pattern. From De Leuwen Jagt, Paarl.

Sauvignon Blanc (Vin de Cuvée) Best-selling white in range. **98** invigoratingly fresh, light, nicely poised gooseberry ripeness, flavours in no hurry to fade. Consistent performer from Robertson Winery. **Blanc de Blanc (Vin de Cuvée)** ☺ ◀ Comfortably-matched 60/40 chenin/sauvignon blanc blend. **98** with grassy freshness, complemented, softened by tropical juicy flavours. Easy, dry finish. From Villiera. **Jug o' White** Buxom 1½ litre screw cap jug with handle; filled with ripe, fruitily long chenin, balanced with clean acids. **Selected Cape White** ◀ NV Uncomplicated, fresh colombard from Rooiberg. Quaffability, dainty guava fruit encouraged by few grams sugar. **Chenin Blanc (Vin de Cuvée)** Wispy floral understatement in **98**; best as young, fresh as possible. 6 gms/l sugar. From Rooiberg. **Cape Riesling** Lightish, fresh-tasting **97**; Cape riesling neutrality perked up with 10% splash peppery Rhine riesling. From Weltevrede, Robertson. **Bianca Light** "Feather light," says Mullins of **98**; long time low alc. favourite, (under 10%). Gains good winey taste from fresh muscat flavours, approx. 12 gms/l sugar. Muscat frontignan, furmint, riesling, sémillon partnership from Delheim. Health considerations have seen sales soar since early 98. **Nouveau Blanc** Off-dry, blend of muscat ottonel, chenin, light alc. From Villiera. **Selected Late Harvest** No nonsense chenin/colombard mix; shy fruity aromas, very sweet. From Simonsvlei. **Muscat de Frontignan-Colombard** NEW Appealing muscat daintiness in **98** 65/35 blend; fruit emphasised by 14 gms/l sugar. From Weltevrede, Robertson.

FESTIVE range offered in gift pack with non-wine products in other departments of this store: range varies according to product, price and demand.

SPARKLINGS

**** **Méthode Cap Classique** ◀ Blue Label, **Vintage Reserve 92** "Quite decadent" is Mullins' summary of this Champagne method bubbly. Its classic varietal make-up—pinot noir, chardonnay (65/35)—and ripe year encourage such description, as does suggestion of oxidative fatness on creamily rich palate. Languorous fine bubble important rôle-player too. Sophisticated individual, requiring only plate of caviar to seal the scene. 5 years on lees, 18 months on cork; 10 gms/l dosage. Also from Villiera.

*** **Méthode Cap Classique** (Red label) ◀ Woolworths Wine of the Year. Hallmarks of value, reliability matched by sound authentic traditional-method character in this NV Brut. Latest introduced by appealing wheaten brilliance; red grape influence apparent in full bouquet; round, ripe biscuity flavours, creamy bubble; softly persistent. By experienced bubbly producer, Villiera's Jeff Grier. Styled closely on estate's own Tradition; 50% pinot noir, 20% chardonnay, with equal parts pinotage/chenin for local individuality. Moderate 11 gms/l dosage. Much-prized by Woolworths' customers.

*** **Brut Rosé** Quite frivolous, strawberry-fruited when first released, around 3 years. With further year acquires more sophisticated but not unfriendly dryness sparked by brisk, fine bubble. Spicy ginger biscuit tang broadened on palate by red wine fullness, 9 gms/l sugar. Sales strongest around Valentine's Day but good with food anytime. NV MCC; blend pinot noir 40%, pinotage 25%, with chardonnay 35%. From Villiera.

Following three carbonated bubblies from Rooiberg: Spumanté Rosé NV, romantic, frivolous fizz from red muscadel. Ginger spice nose, wicked wild strawberry tang, 43 gms/l sugar all attractive. Label (on following two bubblies too) less appealing. **Spumanté** NV sparkler with dainty exotic fragrance, juicy sweetness, languid bubble. Unusually-styled gewürz. About 60 gms/l sugar. **Brut** Effervescent, refreshing NV bubbly. From perky sauvignon; its hugely popular, dry but soft feel effected by 14 gms/l sugar.

1 LITRE TETRAPAK: *from Simonsvlei, NV.*

Dry Red Fresh, fruity cinsaut, cab. s., ruby cab. blend. **Blanc de Blanc** Chenin blanc, colombard mix; soft, dry. **Late Harvest** Semi-sweet, from chenin blanc.

WOOLWORTHS BOX WINES: *5 litre box range, produced monthly to ensure freshness; all NV, medium-bodied, 11-11,5% alc. from Simonsvlei.* **Dry Red** NEW Uncomplicated spicy, plummy cinsaut, cab. s., ruby cab. mix. Fresh, easy drinking. **Grand Crû** NEW Sprightly chenin-colombard blend; dry. **Stein** NEW Semi-sweet chenin; 18 gms/l sugar. **Bouquet Blanc** NEW Fruity chenin, muscat, Rhine riesling blend; 11 gms/l sugar.
250 ml TETRAPAKS: *Handy snacking, picnic wines from Simonsvlei.* **Dry Red** Juicy, soft cinsaut, cab. s., ruby cab. blend. **Dry White** Gently fresh chenin/colombard blend. **Late Harvest** Semi-sweet white with tropical chenin fruit.

YONDER HILL

Helderberg-Stellenbosch See Helderberg map

Visits by appointment.
Owners: Frikkie & Danila Naudé
Winemaker: David Lockley. **Consultant:** Jan Coetzee
Production: 2 330 cases. **Vineyards:** 10 ha.
P.O. Box 914, Stellenbosch 7599
Tel: 021-8551008 **Fax:** 021-8551008
E-mail: yonder@lantic.co.za

"A road runs through it," say David Lockley wryly as he surveys his new winemaking domain. After stints at Blaauwklippen and Rickety Bridge, he's explaining plans to upgrade this Helderberg cellar, currently housed in two buildings separated by the farm road. An expanded production facility will be followed by an 800 barrel maturation cellar, tasting room and vinoteque—all before the 1999 harvest! Lockley, known meticulously to measure the ratio of fruit to foliage from selected sample vines in the vineyards he tends—all in the pursuit of balanced vigour—will be working with omnipresent Jan Coetzee to maximise the black grape (especially merlot) potential of this small property. All the wine produced will find its way into Yonder Hill bottles from 1999 with 14 000 cases being the target for 2001.

★★★★ **Merlot** ◀ Signature rich, mocha, mineral scents, meaty mouthful, ripe tannin caress. **96** super length, more elegant than tannic **95**, which beginning to open up after long wood maturation; plummy, smooth-textured. **94** lean after acclaimed **93** WINE★★★★. 1,2 ha. plantings may be expanded due to success of the variety in the Clovelly soils.

★★★ **iNanda** Meaning "beautiful place", returns to form. Oriental spice, mulberry, mint flavours napped in deep-pile tannins. **96** still in oak, **95** needs time for components to integrate. Blend of 65% cab. s., 20% franc, 15% merlot. Lean, volatile **94** disappointed after **93** WINE★★★★.

Deux-Cabernets Cabernet duo: 70% sauvignon, 30% franc. Sappy, tea-leaf, old style, austere. **Chardonnay 97** herbaceous, organic, lacks varietal stamp, less oak than pvs. (sp. **95**). **96** light gold, ripe marmalade, nuts, but tiring.

ZANDDRIFT VINEYARDS

Suider-Paarl See Paarl map

Open Mon-Fri 10-5. Weekends by appointment. Tasting fee R10 p/p.
Stone Chapel Cellar, lunch, dinner for groups by appointment. Mon-Fri 10-5, weekends by appointment. Function facilities.
Owner: Zanddrift Vineyards
Winemaker: Riaan Marais (since 1996)
Production: 18 000-20 000 cases. **Vineyards:** 31 ha.

P.O. Box 541, Suider-Paarl 7624
Tel: 021-8632076 **Fax:** 021-8632081
Website: www.zanddrift.co.za

A corner of Tuscany in the winelands, courtesy of Italian prisoners-of-war who constructed the farm's charming stone buildings—and rustic bell-towered chapel after which the range is named—in the early 1940s. Riaan Marais, assisted by an all-woman cellar team—newly qualified or taking courses in winery management—made a variety of new styles in 1998, including a yet-to-be-named limited-release **MCC**, and experimental wood-matured **Chenin Blanc**.

CHAPEL CELLAR range:

*** **Capella Reserve** ◀ NEW **98** among tastier new-wave wooded chenins, result of trial run. Engaging yeasty/buttery nose, bags of flavour, wood seamlessly woven into crisp texture. Very attractive fruit/acid balance, clean, long. "Seems to have been really successful!" is winemaker's comment.

Cabernet Sauvignon NEW **98** untasted. **Pinotage** NEW **98** (tasted very young) exception to winery's easy drinking style—(fruit) tannins very demanding, so a food wine. Some nice ripe plum/mulberry on nose, almost "sweet" fruit on palate. Unwooded. **Sémillon Chapel Reserve** (P'vsly **Sémillon**) Lightly wooded, dry **97** has acquired green-grassy notes, touch of oiliness; acid still very fresh. 350 cases. **Tuscany Spring** Cellar's numero uno (along with **Route 303** below), mail-order club tasting winner. **97** very agreeable quaffer, no angular challenges. Dry, chenin (85%), sémillon. **Route 303** Current release (**97**) showing bottle age in marked honeyed overtones. Best young. Dry, Cape riesling/colombard. **Le Soleil 98** untasted. Off-dry white from farm's award-winning chenin blanc. **Chenin Blanc Natural Sweet** NEW **98** untasted, botrytis grapes. **MCC** NEW **98** untasted, from chenin, 260 cases.

ZANDVLIET ESTATE

Ashton See Robertson map

Open weekdays 9-5, Sat 9-1.
Group lunches for 12-24 by appoint. Tel: 0234-51823.
Owners: Paul and Dan de Wet
Winemaker: Paul de Wet (since 1971). **Vineyards:** Dan de Wet
Production: 75 000 cases. **Vineyards:** 147 ha.
P.O. Box 36, Ashton 6715
Tel: 0234-51146 **Fax:** 0234-51327

"You want to hear about my dream?" Paul de Wet is standing in the veld surveying a huge, gently sloping grass-covered vista at the upper reaches of the estate, populated at present by a few hundred unconcerned springbok. "I'd love to build a new winery and a visitors' centre here one day, when we've completed all our new vineyard plantings on these hills—but it must be world-class." Since breaking his ties with wine giant Distillers a few years ago, and weathering the rough financial consequences, he is now on a roll. "Anything holding us back? Nothing—we're going!" This seasoned farmer is like a youngster with a new toy. The enthusiasm is palpable, behind the languid, somewhat perplexed exterior. Long famous for his signature **Shiraz**, produced from old vineyards on the valley floor, Paul de Wet recognises Zandvliet's need to move with the times—better vineyards in better locations, more modern wine styles, and, of course, to make it all viable, larger volumes. From its present 147 ha., expect to see 250 by 2003, and 300 eight years into the millennium: the target is 60% reds (cabernet, shiraz, pinot noir, merlot), 20% chardonnay, and the rest planted to other white varieties. Few winemakers are blessed with terroir which allows them virtually to re-shape their entire vineyard on virgin, once ostrich-covered land. Local viticulturist Francois Viljoen, together with Sonoma-based consultant Phil Freese are helping to develop these limestone-rich slopes, aptly named Kalkveld—"Chalky Field"—check out their first fruits below. And community development is proceeding apace: "We've earmarked a vineyard from which a percentage of profits will flow to a Zandvliet Community Trust Fund—to underwrite a pension fund and sponsor tertiary education."

ZANDVLIET range:

★★★★ **Kalkveld Shiraz 96 (French oak-matured)** NEW A fine start, the first Zandvliet labelled "grown, made and *bottled*" on the estate. Bright cherry aromas, backed with cinnamon, pepper, in elegant but plush Rhône mould. Dry, supple finish. 18 mths. 2nd-fill oak.

★★★ **Kalkveld Shiraz 96 (American oak-matured)** NEW A lighter hue than above, scented vanilla notes persist on the palate; more New World style, but dry elegant finish.

★★★ **Estate Wine Special Reserve** NEW Classic **97** blend of selected barrels of separately vinified merlot and cab. s., an intense, deep plum hue; mélange of cloves, fennel and chocolate aromas. Tannins still in foreground. Needs a year or three for 4-star potential to emerge.

★★★ **Merlot 96** 1st bottling—fleshy redcurrant aromas, sweet Christmas pud. character, tannins still quite aggressive, juicy finish. First vintage off vineyard; 7 mths. new French, American oak. **VG**.

★★★ **Cabernet Sauvignon Special Reserve 96** similar cellar handling to above—fennel/cigarbox aromas, clarety mineral flavours. Elegant, not showy.

★★★ **Chardonnay 97** offers wonderful toffee, brioche aromas, tightly-wound New World flavours and Burgundian grip. In American/French barrels for 10 weeks on lees for malo and twice-weekly *batonage*. **98** barrel sample shows butterscotch, pineapple flavours, solid structure—14% alc.

Shiraz 95 has shy cherry-mulberry nose, thinner and more austere than more recent vintages (above). No concession to in-yer-face jammy style here, but much-liked by more traditional Cape shiraz fanciers since **75** vintage.

ASTONVALE range: marketed by Bar Valley Wines, PO Box 55, Ashton 6715. Tel, fax as for Zandvliet.

Shiraz ◀ **97** smoky, clove, pepper and currant aromas, bags of juicy flavours and just a sniff of oak. Côte du Rhône-style. **Chardonnay 98** unwooded, with clean pear, melon aromas, bracing lemon flavours—refreshing balance. **Sauvignon Blanc 98** shy crushed guava aromas, easy drinking, with hint of sweetness in finish (4,5 gms/l sugar). **Colombard 98** intense fresh pear, passion-fruit nose, bright fruit-salad flavours. **Colombard-Sauvignon Blanc 98** a 80/20 blend, with former dominating; a supple tangy drink.

ZANDWIJK WINE FARM

Paarl See Paarl map

Tastings/sales Mon-Fri 8-12.30; 1.30-5. Closed Sat.
Owner: Mendel Kaplan
Winemaker: Leon Mostert (since 1983)
Production: 7 000-8 000 cases. **Vineyards:** 12 ha.
P.O. Box 2674, Paarl 7620
Tel: 021-8632368 **Fax:** 021-8631884

"What can I tell you? There's nothing new in our cellar, no headline grabbing highlights—just the usual range of quality kosher wine," says vintner Leon Mostert, re-trained in Israel to perfect the techniques needed to meet super-strict "kosher le pessach" requirements. Actually there *is* a highlight: 1 October 1998 marked Mostert's 15th year at this unique Paarl winery. "I've become part of the stock," he quips. The range includes **Klein Draken Dry Red**, a cabernet/merlot blend; **Chardonnay** fermented/aged in wood; **Sauvignon Blanc**, off-dry; **Rhine Riesling; Klein Draken Dry White** from chenin; **Zandwijk** for Kiddush, Havdalah—a sacramental wine.

ZEVENRIVIEREN See Zevenwacht

ZEVENWACHT ESTATE

Kuils River-Stellenbosch See Stellenbosch map

Open daily 8-5 for sales & wine- and cheese-tastings, cellar tours. Guest accommodation, banqueting, conference facilities.

Open daily, specialising in South African country cuisine. Picnic baskets. See restaurant section.

Owners: Harold & Denise Johnson
Winemaker: Hilko Hegewisch (since 1996)
Viticulturist: Francois Baard (since 1997)
Production: 55 000 cases. **Vineyards:** ± 200 ha.
P.O. Box 387, Kuils River 7580
Tel: 021-9035123 **Fax:** 021-9033373
E-mail: sales@zevenwacht.co.za
Internet: www.zevenwacht.co.za

Here's a hot contender for the list of must-see destinations in the winelands. Harold and Denise Johnson's visitor-friendly estate at Kuils River offers a galaxy of pleasures, ranging from sweeping views of Table Mountain and *two* oceans, *nogal*, to upper-crust South African cuisine served in the 18th century manor house, a national monument; picnics; wine and cheese tastings in the convivial visitor's centre (resident *fromagers* Paul Rogers and Thandile Nikelo make an own-label range of matured English cheddar in a spotless factory on the farm); guest cottages; conference centre; children's play park; helicopter pad—all these and, of course, Hilko Hegewisch's first-division wines, reflecting the former Boschendal cellarmaster's deepening knowledge of Zevenwacht's v'yds and soils. A range from grapes from Harold Johnson's Banhoek v'yds is also made here by Hegewisch under the Zevenrivieren label.

ZEVENWACHT range:

★★★★ **Shiraz NEW** ◀ Dramatic début **97** shows fine concentration despite lightish colour/tone. Brilliant ruby, attractive fresh-milled pepper attack offset by ripe red plums, touches of violet; all resonate on palate, light almost crisp tone (though muscular 14% alc.), peppery long finish. 10 mths large French oak, 5,7 gms/l acid, 2,3 gms/l sugar. Preview of ravishing **98** (★★★★★ in the making): toasted/roasted aromas à la Côte Rotie, sumptuous fruit, dense, ripe tannin. Still in barrel yet already approachable; 5-7 year maturation horizon.

★★★ **Cabernet Sauvignon-Merlot 98** (first since **96**) tasted very young, definitely one to watch, potential ★★★★. Complex, ripe blackcurrant, chocolate, fresh-ground coffee, lead pencil, liquorice; concentrated flavours, intriguing camphor hints, firmed with classy oak cab. 65%, merlot; partly wooded. **96 SAA** trophy runner-up; roasty, toasty, matured separately in new barrels; softish profile, for drinking before 2000.

★★★ **Cabernet Sauvignon** NEW **98** tasted in extreme youth, very ripe, fleshy, meaty, rich vanilla, supple tannins, agreeably dry.

★★★ **Pinotage** ◀ Preview of **98** attractive deep purple colour, good concentration, sappy almost like fruit-cordial, soft ripe tannin. Very showy style, 50% wooded, whereas **97** substantially lighter, quieter; redcurrants, savoury finish, greenish tannin. 40% in large French oak.

★★★ **Chardonnay** ☺ **98** crowd-pleasing, fruit-focused style, lightly oaked, dried-peach flavours, lemon twist in tail. Broad-beamed (13,5%).

★★★ **Chenin Blanc** ◀ Hegewisch's Vouvray exposure (he won a trip to the Loire in **WINE**'s first Chenin Blanc Challenge with one of his Boschendal creations) evident in **98**: complex, long. Dew-fresh apple blossom bouquet, fleshy sunripe melon, smooth. "Fat but elegant" is vintner's apropos comment. 13,5% alc.

★★★ **Zevenrood** ☺ ◀ Fresh black berries, ripe plum notes on NV fruit-led blend. Bright, juicy flavours, low tannin; nice touch rounding/firming oak. Cabernet, merlot, shiraz, 10% oak-matured. "Sells like hot cakes," says vintner.

Sauvignon Blanc 98 green pepper hints, touches tropical fruit, pleasing plumpness. A mellow fellow. **Reserve 97** (untasted for this ed.) also available. **Pinot Noir-Chardonnay** Slightly nutty nuances in **97** have deepened into attractive toasted hazelnuts; pleasing fullness, weight from pinot (and: alc. 13,5%; 3,6 gms/l sugar). Interesting, serious food wine. **Gewürztraminer** NEW to this ed.; actually pvs. regular returning to range after short hiatus. **98** made by assistant winemaker Lizelle Gerber, in familiar dry style; delicate rosebuds, lemony fruit, whistle-clean finish. Very nice. **Rhine Riesling 98** untasted; pvs. amiable off-dry fruity style, good at table. **Blanc de Blanc** ◀ Current (**98**) gentle fruit-salad of chenin, Rhine riesling, sauvignon blanc, chardonnay. Smooth, everyday dry sipping. **Bouquet Blanc** ◀ **98** dainty (despite 13,7% alc.), rose-scented off-dry. 15 gms/l sugar.

ZEVENRIVIEREN range:

★★★★ **Shiraz** NEW Preview of **98** robed in deep purple, good whiff of expensive leather, smoke, ripe plummy flavours, fleshy texture. Very nice, good potential.

★★★ **Cabernet Sauvignon** NEW **98** tasted from barrel, quiet nose that should perk up nicely in time, judging from dark velvety palate which tastes of blackberry jam on toast; undaunting tannic comeback in tail. Our taster's recommendation: keep 3 yrs. and serve with rare roast beef. Partly wooded.

★★★ **Chardonnay** Assertive, concentrated **98**, ripe peachy fruit, liberal dusting of spicy oak, big mouthful, touches of butterscotch, long. Tasted very young, should evolve into ★★★★. **96** relaxed, easy drinking.

Sauvignon Blanc NEW **98** ideal summer picnic wine: salad bowl of green aromas, quite streamlined, fresh, lots of zing.

ZOMERLUST — Sourced by Vinimark

5 litre vats: Dry Red Juicy quaffing; ripe blackberry fruit, bit of finishing tang. **Blanc de Blanc** Fullish dry white, no-frills earthy flavours. **Stein** Lively fruit-salad flavours, friendly sweet white. **Late Harvest** Easy-drinking semi-sweet; papaya/melon ripeness enhanced by extra sweetness. **2 litre packs: Dry Red** Tasty mouthful, juicy brambly fruits; gluggable, finishes with clean fruity bite. **Blanc de Blanc** Brisk dry white; inoffensively steely, flinty. **Stein** Semi-sweet, easy tropical fruit, lightish. **Late Harvest** Similar to Stein; more richness, 28 gms/l sugar.

ZONNEBLOEM WINES (SFW)

Winemakers: Wouter Pienaar (Manager) since 1983 (joined SFW 1963). Jan de Waal (reds) since 1969. Razvan Macici from Romania (whites) since 1998.
Winery Manager: Jan Cilliers
P.O. Box 46, Stellenbosch 7599
Tel: 021-8087911 **Fax:** 021-8871355/8865414
E-mail: Kgreen@sfw.co.za

"South Africa first" is the firm guarantee given by the powers that beat the drum for this premium-quality SFW label. Music to the ears of local wine fans who complain increasingly that (as with Cape fruit and even crayfish) too much of SA's finest local produce disappears over the export horizon. Volumes here happily allow for a maximum spread of satisfaction. Biggest annual seller of the bunch is Cabernet Sauvignon (40 000 cases), followed by Pinotage at 35 000 cases. The most-wanted white wine sells a mere (by comparison) 18 000 cases annually. But such considerable quantities do not preclude what Wouter Pienaar describes as the "serious quality" focus here: Zonnebloem's annual Fine Art Label competition for local artists is designed to emphasise that very point—that these wines are individually created rather than mass-generated. Underlining this approach is Zonnebloem's **Reserve Cellar Collection,** a regular pre-Christmas release of special older vintages. In 1998 this offers reds from the vintage of **90** (750 ml) and **88** magnums.

★★★★ **Lauréat** Cab. sauvignon/franc, merlot blend; signature style is creamy smooth, with blackcurrant aromas, fleshy, generously-endowed palate. Rich, dark fruit, ripe tannins, well-integrated oak. **95** ★★★ lighter wine; sweet merlot, tannins still a bit tough, needs another year. **96** sample back to form, shows more ripeness, concentration.

★★★★ **Cabernet Sauvignon** Stepped into New World from **94** with deep intense colour, fragrant blackcurrant aromas and touches of grass/dusty green pepper; juicy bramble/cassis freshness, ripe tannins. Current **95** shows consistency of style, but better than pvs. All St'bosch grapes, 100% barrique-matured, small proportion new. **96** dense, dark, brooding.

★★★★ **Shiraz** Riveting (for shiraz fans) complex aromas combine with intensely ripe, dark-berried fruit dusted with black pepper, touches of tar and smoke in **96**. Sweet, succulent fruit with immense concentration but no lack of elegance. 85% matured in small oak of which 40% new/second-fill, rest old *stukvats*. Already drinkable. "The only pity is there's so little," says winemaker Jan de Waal. **95** very elegant, loads of ripe, purple-tinged fruit. **Shiraz Fine Art Label 95**, developing well, has come together beautifully, all rough edges gone. Sweet touch on nose, palate. More new oak than regular.

★★★ **Pinotage** Honest, friendly version **96** with sweet red-currant/red cherry aromas, touch of pinotage ester; tangy sweet/sour fruit, tannic comeback on finish. Lighter than many at 12,5% alc. Best after 5 years says De Waal. **95** sweet cinnamon bun and raspberry fruit, subtle oak finishing. **94** intensely ripe plums.

★★★ **Merlot** Smooth, elegant, with dark-berried fruit, lovely easy flavours, soft tannins for early drinkability, almost feminine charm. Ideal for restaurants. **96** riper, more richness in warmer year.

★★★ **Cabernet Sauvignon Blanc de Noir** Refreshing change from norm

98—made dry unlike almost every other in this category. Attractive onion skin hue, good meaty red wine flavours, fresh tang in tail.

*** **Chardonnay 97** developing attractive buttered toast bouquet, touches of marmite. Elegant, restrained flavours, smooth peachy fruit, good whack of oak on finish. "Growing well," says winemaker Macici.

*** **Sauvignon Blanc Fine Art Label** More of everything: grass, green peppers and loads of tropical fruit contribute to plump **98** profile. Grapes from two special vineyards in Helderberg and Devon Valley. Alc. 13%

*** **Premier Grand Crû** ◀ Colombard-chenin blend, exuberant fresh guava aromas/flavours in **98**. Crisp and lively show-off version. "Fantastic with fish" says winemaker Macici.

*** **Rhine Riesling** ◀ Especially delicious **97**, has smoothed to spicy richness. Sugar at 8 gms/l not noticeable, merely adds weight, fullness.

**** **Special Late Harvest** ◀ Sunny but serious. Arresting aromas in newest **98**—wafts of apple blossom, pineapple, ripe quince touched with good dose of botrytis. Generous ripeness at 44 gms/l sugar but crisp acidity adds lift and excitement. Has everything for ageing, botrytis will intensify.

*** **Blanc de Blanc** ☺ 85% chenin blanc, juicy fruit and all-round pleaser, firmed/freshened with 15% sauvignon blanc. More fullness, ripeness in juicy **98**.

Sauvignon Blanc Tropical fruit and Cape gooseberry ripeness in **98**. Easy drinking, smooth acidity, nice grassy/green peppers on finish. **Noble Late Harvest 96** chenin blanc-Rhine riesling mix; intense fruity richness, not unctuously sweet.

LIMITED EDITIONS

**** **Cabernet Sauvignon** Dark ripe blackberry whiffs in **95**; tightly packed cassis fruit held in check by fragrant, vanilla-scented oak, all new. Opens slowly in glass; sleek, very concentrated, a fine wine. In dark green Bordeaux bottle with lip.

*** **Pinotage** Less showy than regular p'tage, **95** has had a year in all new oak. Excellent concentration, dense berries, touches of tar, liquorice. Still quite tough and tannic, but has more than enough fruit.

(New labels, since previous edition of this guide, in **bold** *type.)*

AUXERROIS Hartenberg (Montagne)

BARBERA Altydgedacht

BLANC DE NOIR
Avontuur, Bergsig, Bon Courage, Boplaas, Boschendal, Bottelary, Calitzdorp, Cape Country Blush, Cellar Reserve, **Clairvaux,** Culemborg, De Wet, De Zoete Inval Blush, Domein Doornkraal Tinta Bianca/Sweet Natural, Douglas, Du Toitskloof, Hazendal, Jonkerskloof, Kango, Klawer, Kronendal, KWV, Landskroon, Lutzville, **Mooiuitsig,** Neethlingshof, Oranjerivier, Ravenswood, Rebel, Simonsvlei, **Stellenbosch Vineyards,** Swartland/2 *l*, Van Loveren (2), Weltevrede, Woolworths, Zonnebloem

CAPE "BORDEAUX" BLENDS (cabernet s. blend with one/all/some of following: merlot, cabernet f., petit verdot, malbec), Altus, Altydgedacht, Avontuur Avon Rouge/Baccarat, Backsberg Klein Babylonstoren, Bertrams Robert Fuller Reserve, Blaauwklippen Red Landau, Boland !Um Hap, Bon Courage, **Boschendal,** Boschkloof Reserve, Brenthurst, Buitenverwachting Christine/Buitenkeur, Camberley Cabernet Sauvignon-Merlot, **Cape Bay, Cape Reflections,** Cape River Isle, Cape Vintners Grand Reserve, Claridge Red Wellington, Constantia Uitsig La Colombe Vin Rouge, Cordoba, Craighall Cabernet/Merlot, **De Forellen,** Delaire Cabernet-Merlot, De Leuwen Jagt Cabernet-Merlot, De Trafford Collage, Delheim Grand Reserve, **De Villiers Cabernet Franc-Merlot,** Diamant Dry Red, Diemersdal Estate Private Collection, Eersterivier Grand Reserve, Eikendal Classique, **Eikestad Cabernet-Merlot,** Fairview Cabernet-Franc Merlot/ Tower, Franschhoek La Cotte Cabernet-Merlot, Glen Carlou Grande Classique/Les Trois, Goede Hoop, Grangehurst Reserve, Groot Constantia Gouverneur's Reserve, Hartenberg Cabernet Sauvignon-Merlot, Helderberg Merlot-Cabernet, Hermanusrivier Cabernet Sauvignon-Merlot, Jacana, **Jacaranda Debutante, Jennsberg Cabernet Sauvignon-Merlot,** Kaapzicht, Kanonkop Kadette/Paul Sauer/Auction Reserve, Klein Constantia Marlbrook, Klein Gustrouw, Kloofzicht Alter Ego, Kumala Reserve, KWV/Cathedral Cellars Triptych/Roodeberg/Paarl, L'Avenir L'Ami Simon, **Lemberg Sensual Red,** L'Émigré Cimiterre, L'Ormarins Optima/Reserve, La Bri Rouge La Bri, La Motte Millennium/Cabernet-Merlot, Laborie/Granite Creek, Lanzerac Farm Cabernet Sauvignon/Merlot, Le Bonheur Prima Merlot Cabernet, Leef op Hoop, Lievland DVB, Lost Horizons, Louisvale Cabernet-Merlot, **Makro La Bri Bin 411 Cabernet Sauvignon/Merlot/Yellowwood Ridge Bin 450,** Meerlust Rubicon, Morgenhof Prémiere Sélection/Dry Red, **Morgenster,** Mountain Shadows Cabernet-Merlot, Mukuyu, Mulderbosch Faithful Hound, Muratie Ansela, Napier Lion Creek Dry Red/**Medallion**, Nederburg PBin R109, Neil Ellis Cabernet-Merlot, Nelson, Newton Johnson Cabernet Sauvignon-Merlot, Overgaauw Tria Corda/DC Classic, Overhex, Paradyskloof Cabernet-Merlot, Perdeberg, Rozendal, Rustenberg/Brampton, **Seidelberg Cabernet Sauvignon-Merlot,** Simonsig Tiara, Simonsvlei Premium, Sinnya Valley Red, **Spice Route/Andrew's Hope,** Spier Cellars IV Spears, **Spruitdrift,** Stapleford Private Cellar Cabernet-Merlot, Steenberg Motif Rouge, Stellenzicht, Stone Wall, Swartland Reserve, Talana Hill Royale, Tesco Cabernet-Merlot, Thelema Cabernet Sauvignon-Merlot/Cuvée Rouge, Tradouw Tradeaux Reserve, Tulbagh Camelot, Two Oceans Cabernet-Merlot, Veenwouden Classic/Vivat Bacchus, Vergenoegd Reserve, Villiera

Cru Monro, Von Ortloff Cabernet-Merlot, Vriesenhof Kallista, Warwick Tentklip/Trilogy/Femme Bleue, Welgemeend Estate Reserve/Soopjeshoogte, **Weltevrede Merlot-Cabernet Sauvignon,** Windmeul, **Winelands Cabernet Sauvignon-Cabernet Franc,** Woolworths/Grand Rouge/ **Cabernet Franc-Merlot**, Yonder Hill Deux Cabernets/iNanda, Zandvliet **(2)**, Zevenwacht, Zonnebloem Lauréat

BUKETTRAUBE
Boland, Bovlei, Du Toitskloof, Goue Vallei, Koelenhof, Lutzville, Nuy, Rooiberg, Simonsvlei Premium, Swartland, Welvanpas

CABERNET SAUVIGNON
Africa Collection, **African Legend, Agulhas (Merwespont),** Allesverloren, Alphen, Alto, Altus, Altydgedacht, **Ashanti,** Ashton, Athlone, **Audacia, Avontuur**/Reserve, **Babbling Brook,** Backsberg/Hillside, Bay View, Bellingham (2), Berg & Brook Savanha/Savanha Reserve/Agulhas Bank, Bergkelder Cellarmaster's Choice, Bergsig, Bertrams, Beyerskloof/Reserve, Blaauwklippen/Reserve, Bloemendal, Blue Creek, Bodega/Beaconsfield, Boekenhoutskloof, Boland, Bon Courage, Boplaas/Carel Nel, Boschkloof, **Botha,** Bottelary, Bovlei, Buitenverwachting, Cape Colours, Cape Country, Capelands, Cape Levant, **Capell's Court,** Cape River Isle, Cape Selection, Cape Soleil, Cape View (Kaapzicht), Cape Vintners, Cederberg, Chamonix PB 3/4, **Cilmor,** Clos Malverne, Constantia-Uitsig, Cordoba, Cullinan View, **Darling Cellars/Groenekloof,** Delaire, Delheim, **De Meye,** Destinaire, De Trafford, De Villiers, **Devon Hill, De Wet,** De Zoete Inval, Die Krans, Die Poort, Dieu Donné, Diemersdal Estate/Export, **Domein Doornkraal,** Doc Craven, Douglas Green, Drostdyhof, Du Toitskloof, **EagleVlei,** Eersterivier, Eikehof, Eikendal/Reserve, **Excelsior,** Fairseat, Fairview, Fleur Du Cap, **Franschhoek Vineyards** (**2**), Friesland, Goede Hoop, Goedvertrouw, Goue Vallei, **Graham Beck,** Grangehurst, Groot Constantia, Grooteberg, Groot Eiland, Hartenberg, Haute Provence, Hazendal, Helderberg, Hermanusrivier, Hippo Creek, Hoopenburg, Huguenot, Inglewood, **Intaba,** IWS Wamakersvallei, Jacana, Jonkheer, Jordan, Kaapzicht (**2**), Kanonkop, **Kevin Arnold,** Klawervlei, Kleinbosch, Klein Constantia, Kleindal, **Kleine Zalze (2), Klein Simonsvlei (2),** Koelenhof, Kronendal, Kumala Reserve, KWV/ Cathedral Cellars, Laborie, **Laibach,** L'Avenir, **Le Moutonne, Linton Park,** L'Ormarins, La Motte, La Provence, Laibach, Landskroon, Landzicht, Lanzerac Farm, Le Bonheur, Leef op Hoop, Leidersburg, Libertas, Long Mountain, Longridge, Louiesenhof/**Rouge**, Louisvale, **Makro Franschhoek Vineyards**, **Louwshoek-Voorsorg Daschbosch,** Malan Bros, McGregor, Meerendal, Meerlust, Merwespont, Middelvlei, Mons Ruber/ Conari, Mont Rochelle, **Mooiplaas,** Mooiuitzicht, Môreson/**Pinehurst,** Morgenhof, Mouton Excelsior, Mukuyu, Muratie, Nederburg Paarl/P/Bin R163/P/Bin 161, Neethlingshof, Neil Ellis, Nelson, Nitida, **Nuy,** Oak Village, **Oude Wellington,** Overgaauw, **Paul Cluver**, Pick 'n Pay, **Pinnacle,** Plaisir De Merle, **Porcupine Ridge, Post House**, Rainbow Ridge, R de R-Fredericksburg/Reserve, **Remhoogte,** Rhebokskloof, Rickety Bridge, Robertson (**2**), **Rock Ridge,** Romansrivier, Roodendal, Roodezandt, Rooiberg, Ruitersvlei/Reserve, Rust en Vrede, Rustenberg (2)/Brampton, Sable View, **Safeway,** Saxenburg/Private Collection, Sentinel, Simonsig, Simonsvlei Reserve/Lifestyle, Slanghoek PR, Somerbosch, Spier Cellars IV Spears (**2**), Springfield, Spruitdrift, Steenberg, Stellenryck, Stellenzicht, Swartland, Ten Fifty Six, **Tesco,** Thelema Reserve/Cabernet Sauvignon/ CIWG Auction, Tulbagh, Uiterwyk, Uitkyk Carlonet, **Uitzicht Reyneke,** Vergenoegd, Villiera, Villiersdorp, Vins Du Cap, Vlottenburg, Vredenheim, Vriesenhof, Wamakersvallei (2), Warwick, Wellington Wynboere, Welmoed, Welvanpas, WhaleHaven, Wildekrans, Woolworths/Reserve, **Zanddrift,** Zandvliet, **Zevenrivieren,** Zevenwacht, Zonnebloem

CABERNET FRANC
Avontuur, Bellingham, **Cilmor, KWV Cathedral Cellar,** Landskroon, **Mukuyu Select, Neethlingshof,** Warwick, **Wildekrans**

RIESLING (CAPE or SA)
Berg & Brook Pierre Simond, Boland, Bon Courage, Bonnievale, Boschendal, Bovlei **(2)**, De Wet, Du Toitskloof, Fleur du Cap, Goudini, Jacana Wood Matured Crouchen Blanc, KWV, Ladismith, Louwshoek-Voorsorg Daschbosch, Mooiuitsig, Nederburg Paarl, Neethlingshof, Nuy, Ouderust, Rooiberg, Ruitersvlei, Simonsvlei Lifestyle, Swartland, Theuniskraal, Uitkyk, Van Loveren, Waboomsrivier, Wamakersvallei, Wellington Wynboere, Weltevrede, Woolworths

CARIGNAN
Fairview, Welgegund

CHARDONNAY
African Legend, Alphen, Altydgedacht, **Ashanti,** Ashton, Astonvale, Avontuur Le Chardon/**Le Chardon Reserve/**Le Blush (Pink), **Audacia,** Backsberg, Badsberg, Barlow Vineyard, Bay View/Reserve, Beaumont, Bellingham, Berg & Brook Savanha/Agulhas Bank, Berghof, Blaauwklippen, **Bloupunt,** Boland, Bon Courage/Reserve, Boplaas, Boschendal **(3)**, Boschkloof **(2)**, **Bredell,** Bouchard Finlayson Kaaimansgat/Walker Bay/Oak Valley, Buitenverwachting, Calitzdorp, Cape Bay, Cape Colours, Cape Indaba, **Capelands,** Cape River Isle, Cape Soleil, **Cape View,** Chamonix **(2)**, **Cheetah Valley, Cilmor,** Claridge, Constantia Uitsig, Cordoba, Culemborg, Cullinan View, Deetlefs, Delaire, De Leuwen Jagt, Delheim, Destinare, De Villiers, **De Wet,** De Wetshof Finesse (Lesca)/ Bateleur/d'Honneur/Grey Label/Blue Label Sur Lie/Green Label, Die Krans, Diemersdal Estate, Dieu Donné, Douglas Green, Drostdyhof, Du Toitskloof, Eikehof, Eikendal, Fairseat, Fairview, Fleur Du Cap, **Fort Simon,** Franschhoek La Cotte, Glen Carlou/Reserve, Goedvertrouw, Goedverwacht, **Goue Vallei,** Graham Beck, Groot Constantia/Reserve, Groot Eiland, Hamilton Russell (2), Hartenberg (2), **Haute Provence (2),** Hazendal, Helderberg, Hippo Creek, Hoopenburg, **Intaba,** Jacana, Jonkheer, Jordan, **Kevin Arnold, Klawer,** Kleinbosch, Klein Constantia/Reserve, **Kleine Zalze, Klein Simonsvlei,** Koelenhof, Kronendal, Kumala Reserve, KWV Cathedral Cellar/**Robert's Rock**, L'Emigré Reserve, Laibach, L'Avenir, L'Ormarins, La Motte, La Petite Ferme, Laborie/Granite Creek, Lanzerac Farm, Le Bonheur, Leidersburg, Libertas, Lievland, **Linton Park,** Long Mountain, Longridge/Capelands/Bay View, Loopspruit, Lost Horizons, Louiesenhof, Louisvale/Chavant, **Louwshoek-Voorsorg Daschbosch,** Malan Bros, Mamreweg, Meerendal, Meerlust, Merwespont, Middelvlei, Mondial, Mont Rochelle, Montestell Reserve, Môreson Premium/ **Pinehurst**, Morgenhof/CIWG Auction, Mouton Excelsior, Mukuyu, Mulderbosch **(2)**, Napier, Nederburg/PBin D270, Neethlingshof, Neil Ellis (2), Nelson, Newton Johnson, **Nitida,** Oak Village, Overgaauw, Paul Cluver (2), Pick 'n Pay/Halves to Hogsheads Chapter 5, **Pinnacle,** Plaisir De Merle, R de R-Fredericksburg, Rhebokskloof/Sur Lie Reserve/Grande Reserve, Rickety Bridge, Rietvallei, Robertson **(2)**, **Rock Ridge,** Romansrivier Ceres, Ruitersvlei Reserve, Rustenberg **(2)**/Brampton, Sable View, Saxenburg, Sentinel, **Shoprite Oddbins Bin 225,** Simonsig **(2)**, Simonsvlei (2), Spier Cellars IV Spears, Springfield **(2),** Steenberg, Stellenryck Collection, Stellenvale, Stellenzicht, Stone Wall, Stony Brook, Swartland (2), Talana Hill, Thelema (2), Tradouw Sur Lie, Trawal, Tulbagh, Uiterwyk **(2)**, Uitkyk **(2)**, Uva Mira, Van Loveren, Van Zylshof, Verdun, Vergelegen, Villiera, Villiersdorp, Vlottenburg, Von Ortloff, Vredendal, Vriesenhof, Wamakersvallei (2), Warwick, **Wellington,** Welmoed, Weltevrede, WhaleHaven,

Wildekrans, Woolworths Robertson/Stellenbosch Reserve/Summer Days, Yonder Hill, Zandvliet, Zevenwacht, Zonnebloem (2)

CHARDONNAY-SAUVIGNON BLANC BLENDS
Bellingham, Boplaas, Bottelary, **Chamonix,** Citrusdal, **Clairvaux,** Craighall, **Darling Cellars,** De Wetshof, Eersterivier, **Fort Simon,** Helderberg, Jordan, **KWV, Laibach,** Lost Horizons, Louisvale, Lutzville Fleermuisklip, Merwespont, **Môreson,** Nederburg (2), Nordale, Paradyskloof, Perdeberg, **Pick 'n Pay,** Rheboksklooff, Shoprite Oddbins Bin 61, Simonsig, Simonsvlei, Slanghoek, Spar Country Cellars, Stellenvale, Uiterwyk, Van Zylshof, Vredendal, Weltevrede

CHENIN BLANC or STEEN: Dry
African Legend, Barrydale, Bergsig, **Bernheim,** Boland, Bovlei, **Cape Bay, Cape Colours,** Cape Chenin, Cape Indaba, Cape Soleil, Cape View (Kaapzicht), **Cilmor,** Clairvaux, Cullinan View, Deetlefs, De Villiers, De Zoete Inval Capri, Drostdyhof, Elephant Pass, **Fair Valley,** Fairview, Fraser's Bay, Friesland, Goue Vallei, Groot Constantia, Grooteberg, Haute Provence, **Hazendal**, Helderberg/Reserve, Hippo Creek, Inkawu, Jacaranda (2), Kaapzicht, Klawer, Klawervlei **(3)**, Kleinbosch **(2)**, **Kleine Zalze, Klein Simonsvlei,** Kronendal, Laibach, L'Avenir, Ladismith, Landskroon, Libertas, Longridge Bay Blanc, McGregor, Montagu, Montestell, **Mouton Excelsior,** Naked Truth, Napier, Nederburg, Oak Village, Oranjerivier, Perdeberg, Pick 'n Pay, Rickety Bridge, Romansrivier, **Ruitersvlei,** Safeway Early Release, Shoprite Oddbins Bin 75, Simonsig, Simonsvlei (2) Somerbosch, **Spruitdrift, Stapleford Private Cellar, Stellenbosch Vineyards,** Stormy Cape, Swartland/Reserve, **Sylvanvale,** TenFiftySix, Van Zylshof, Wellington, Welvanpas, Windmeul, Winelands **(2)**, Woolworths (2), Zevenwacht

CHENIN BLANC (OAKED)
Agulhas Bank, Ashanti, Beaumont/Reserve, Berg & Brook Savanha, **Blue White,** De Trafford, Die Krans, **Fort Simon, Franschhoek Vineyards,** Hartenberg, Haute Provence, Hazendal, Helderberg, Jacana, Jordan, Kaapzicht, Ken Forrester **(2)**, Kleine Zalze, Laibach, Landskroon, **Longridge/**Bay View, Louiesenhof, **Makro Backsberg Bin 215, Michael Paul,** Pinnacle, **Porcupine Ridge**, Post House, **Riebeek**, Ruitersvlei Reserve, Ryland's Grove, **Shoprite Oddbins Bin 76,** Southern Right Cellars, **Spice Route,** Spier Cellars IV Spears, Stone Wall, **Uitzicht Reyneke,** Verdun, Villiera, Vinfruco, Wamakersvallei, Welmoed, Wildekrans Reserve, Woolworths, **Zanddrift,** Zevenwacht

CHENIN BLANC or STEEN: Off-dry/Semi-sweet/Stein
Autumn Harvest, Backsberg, Bellingham Johannisberger, Berg & Brook Brookside Blanc/Pierre Simond, Blue White, Bonne Esperance, Boschendal, Bovlei (2), Cape Colours, Cape Country, Cederberg, Cellar Cask, Chamonix Blanc, Cogmans, Culemborg, Die Poort Frölich, Du Toitskloof, Eclipse/Mystery Reserve, Eersterivier, Eikendal (2), Franschhoek, Friesland, Goudini, Grünberger, **Hartswater,** Helderberg, Huguenot, Jacaranda, Kango Herfsgoud, Kellerprinz, Klawervlei, Koelenhof, Kronendal, Ladismith, Landskroon, Landzicht, Langeberg Wonderfontein, **Langverwacht**, **L'Émigré Azure Bouquet Blanc**, **Le Parfait,** Lutzville, McGregor Vrolikheid 500ml, Mike's Kitchen, Môreson, **Mukuyu Meadows/Vat 10,** Nederburg, Overhex, Overmeer, Paddagang Platanna, Party Pack, Perdeberg, Pick 'n Pay No Name, Porterville, Ravenswood, Rebel, Riebeek, Rite, Rob Roy, Rooiberg, Simonsvlei, Spar Carnival/Country Cellars, St. Elmo's, Stapleford Private Cellar Emerald Steen, Swartland Stein/5 *l*, **Tesco,** Tradouw, Trawal, Tulbagh, Vaughan Johnson As You Like It, Villiersdorp,

Vinipak Robertson Selected, Vlottenburg, Vredendal Namaqua/Namaqua Stein/5 *l*, Waboomsrivier, Wamakersvallei, Wellington, Welmoed, **Winelands Medium Dry,** Witzenberg Select, **Woolworths Box Wines Stein,** Zellerhof, Zomerlust

CHARDONNAY (UNWOODED)

Agulhas (Merwespont), Athlone, Berg & Brook/Benguela Current, Bergsig, **Bloupunt,** Boschendal Bin Reserve 104, Bouchard-Finlayson Snowline/**Sans Barrique**, Bovlei, Cape Country, **Capell's Court,** Cape Soleil, Cape View, **Constantia-Uitsig**, Coolstream, De Wetshof Bon Vallon, Diemersdal Export, Dieu Donné, **Excelsior,** Goedverwacht, Grooteberg, **Hartswater, Haute Provence,** Kango, **Kleindal,** La Provence, Ladismith, Landzicht, Langverwacht, Lanzerac, Louisvale Chavant, **McGregor,** Mooiuitsig, Mont Rochelle, Montagu, Mount Simon, Nordale, Nuy, Overhex, **Robertson,** Roodezandt, Rooiberg, Rosevale, **Shoprite Oddbins Bin 141, Sinnya,** Somerbosch, Spruitdrift, Vredendal/Namaqua, Wamakersvallei, Wellington, Winelands

CINSAUT

Goue Vallei Chianti, KWV, Landskroon, **Le Parfait Rouge,** Perdeberg, **Safeway,** Signature, Swartland, **Tesco,** Wamakersvallei **(2)**, Wellington, Woolworths Spring Collection

CLAIRETTE BLANCHE

De Wet, Goudini, Overhex

COLOMBARD: Off-dry/semi-sweet

Bon Courage, Bonnievale, Botha, Cape River Isle Stein, **Clairvaux Blanc de Blanc, Hartswater,** Klawer, Landzicht, Louwshoek-Voorsorg Daschbosch, McGregor, Montagu, **Mukuyu Meadows/Vat 10,** Nuy, Oranjerivier, Overhex, Romansrivier Off-dry/Vin Blanc Special Reserve, Rooiberg, Stapleford Private Cellar, Swartland, Van Loveren, Villiersdorp, Weltevrede, Woolworths Selected Cape White

COLOMBARD: Dry

African Legend, Ashton, **Bernheim,** Bonnievale, Cape Country, Cape River Isle, **Cilmor,** Cogmans, **Cullinan View,** Douglas, Goedverwacht, Langverwacht, **Le Parfait,** Nordale, Nuy, Oaklands, Robertson, Roodezandt, Swartland, Vredendal Namaqua, Vredenheim

DESSERT WINES (fortified) HANEPOOT

Badsberg, Bergsig, Bonnievale, Boplaas, Bovlei, Calitzdorp, De Wet, Die Poort (3), Domein Doornkraal, Du Toitskloof, Goudini, Goue Vallei, Groot Eiland, Huguenot, Kaapzicht, Kango, Klawer, Koelenhof, Landzicht, Langeberg Wonderfontein, Loopspruit Guinea Fowl, **Louwshoek-Voorsorg,** Lutzville, Mooiuitsig, Opstal, Oranjerivier/Dessert Wine, Riebeek, Rooiberg, Simonsvlei, Slabbers Golden, Slanghoek, Spruitdrift, Swartland **(2)**, Tulbagh, Villiersdorp, Vlottenburg, Vredendal **(2)**, Waboomsrivier, Wellington

FERNÃO PIRES

Nuy, Swartland, Van Loveren, Woolworths Spring Collection.

GAMAY (see also under Nouveau)

Fairview, Kleine Zalze, **Rhebokskloof,** Verdun Interlude

GEWÜRZTRAMINER

Altydgedacht, Ashton, Barrydale, Bergsig, Bon Courage, Bovlei, Delheim,

De Wetshof, Douglas, Groot Constantia, Landzicht, Nederburg, Neethlingshof, Villiera, Vlottenburg, Weltevrede

HÀRSLEVELÜ
Lemberg, Van Loveren

KOSHER WINES
Zandwijk Chardonnay, Sauvignon Blanc, ZWR2, Klein Draken/Dry Red/ White, Zandwijk, Rhine Riesling

LATE HARVEST (often from Chenin Blanc)
Ashton, Autumn Harvest, Badsberg, Berg & Brook Pierre Simond, Bergsig, Bonnievale, Boplaas/Golden Harvest, **Botha,** Calitzdorp, Cape River Isle, **Cape Safari,** Cape Selection, Cellar Cask, Cellar Reserve, Cogmans, Culemborg, De Leuwen Jagt, De Zoete Inval, Delheim Spatzendreck, Die Krans, Die Poort, Douglas, Drostdyhof, Du Toitskloof, Goederust, Goudini, Goudveld, Goue Vallei, **Hartswater,** Heerenhof, Huguenot, Kellerprinz, Klawervlei, Kupferberger Auslese, Landzicht, Langeberg Wonderfontein, Loopspruit, Louwshoek-Voorsorg Daschbosch, Lutzville, McGregor, Montagu, Mooiuitsig, Nuy, Oranjerivier, Overhex, Overmeer, Panarotti's, Perdeberg, Pick 'n Pay No Name, Ravenswood, Rebel, Riebeek, Rite, Rob Roy, Robertson, Roodezandt, Rooiberg Late Vintage, Simonsvlei, Spar Carnival/Country Cellars, Spruitdrift, Spur, Swartland/5 *l,* Trawal, Tulbagh, Villiersdorp, Vinipak Robertson, Vredendal Namaqua/5*l*, Waboomsrivier, Wamakersvallei, Wellington, Weskus, Witzenberg Edelgoud, Woolworths (2), Zellerhof, Zomerlust

"LIGHTS"
Bersig Bouquet Light, Cape River Isle Dry White Light, Drostdyhof, Fleur du Cap, Mukuyu Meadows, Pick 'n Pay No Name, Sprizzo, TJ, Tulbagh Extra Light, Woolworths Bianca/Nouveau Blanc/Nouveau Stein

MALBEC
Ashanti, Backsberg, **Rickety Bridge**

MERLOT
Africa Collection, **African Legend, Audacia,** Avontuur Reserve, **Babbling Brook,** Backsberg, Bay View, Beaconsfield, Bellingham, Berg & Brook/ Savanha/Savanha Reserve/Benguela Current, Bloemendal, Bodega/ Beaconsfield, Boekenhoutskloof, Boland, Boplaas, Boschendal, Boschkloof, **Botha,** Bouchard Finlayson Oak Valley, **Bovlei,** Buitenverwachting, Calitzdorp, Capelands, Cape Levant, Cape River Isle, Cape Soleil, Cape Vintners, Cape View, Carel Nel, Chamonix, **Cheetah Valley, Cilmor,** Constantia-Uitsig, Cordoba, Delaire (**2**), Delheim, De Leuwen Jagt, Destinaire, De Trafford, De Villiers, **Devon Hill,** Diemersdal Export, Dieu Donné, Domein Doornkraal, Drostdyhof, Du Toitskloof, **Eikehof,** Eikendal, Fairview, Fleur Du Cap, **Fort Simon,** Friesland, Glen Carlou, **Goue Vallei, Graham Beck,** Grangehurst, Groot Constantia, Hoopenburg, **Intaba,** Jacana, **Jacaranda,** Johnsen-Jörgensen, Jonkheer, Jordan (**2**) **Kaapzicht,** Klawervlei, Kleinbosch, Kronendal, KWV/Cathedral Cellars, La Motte, Laborie, Laibach, Landskroon, Lanzerac, La Petite Ferme, Libertas, Longridge, **Long Mountain**, Lost Horizons, Louiesenhof, Louisvale, Meerendal, Meerlust, **Michael Paul,** Mont Rochelle, Morgenhof, Mouton Excelsior, **Mukuyu Select,** Muratie, Neethlingshof, Nelson, Overgaauw, **Pinnacle,** Plaisir de Merle, **Porcupine Ridge,** Rhebokskloof, Rickety Bridge, Robertson, Romansrivier, Ruitersvlei, Rust en Vrede, **Safeway,** Saxenburg/Private Collection, Somerbosch, **Spice Route,** Spruitdrift, Steenberg, Stellenzicht, Swartland, **Tesco,** Thelema, Tradouw Tradeaux, Trawal, **Tulbagh**, Uiterwyk, Veenwouden, Vergelegen, Vergenoegd,

Villiera, Vlottenburg, Von Ortloff No 7, **Wamakersvallei,** Warwick, Wellington, WhaleHaven, Wildekrans, Woolworths/**Fireside Red**, Yonder Hill, Zandvliet, Zevenwacht, Zonnebloem

MOURVÈDRE
Fairview

MUSCAT D'ALEXANDRIE
Cogmans, Die Krans, Eersterivier, Haute Provence, **Kleinbosch,** L'Émigré, Libertas, Louwshoek, Mons Ruber Vino, Sable View

MUSCAT DE FRONTIGNAN
Montagu Mont Blanc, **Stapleford**

MUSCAT OTTONEL
Blaauwklippen

NATURAL SWEET
Ashanti/Vin de Paille, Avontuur Above Royalty, Beaumont, Bellingham, **Boschendal, Cederberg,** De Trafford Vin de Paille, De Wetshof Mine d'Or, Klein Constantia Vin de Constance, **Laibach, Meerendal, Môreson,** Nederburg Auction, Vredenheim Angel's, **Zanddrift**

NEBBIOLO
Steenberg

NOBLE LATE HARVEST: From botrytis-affected grapes
Ashanti, Backsberg, Barlow Vineyard, Boland **(2)**, Bon Courage, Buitenverwachting, **Clairvaux,** De Wetshof, Delheim, Dieu Donné, Eikendal, Fleur Du Cap, Groot Constantia, Ken Forrester, Klein Constantia, **Koelfontein,** KWV, L'Avenir, L'Ormarins, Laibach, Lievland, Louwshoek-Voorsorg Daschbosch, Môreson, Morgenhof, Nederburg (**5**), Neethlingshof (2), **Rustenberg,** Saxenburg Private Collection, Simonsig, **Slanghoek,** Spier Cellars IV Spears, Stellenzicht (2), TJ, **Woolworths,** Zonnebloem

NOUVEAU
Ashanti, Boland, Fairview Gamay Noir, KWV Early Autumn White, Oranjerivier Nouveau Blanc, Simonsvlei Lifestyle Nouveau Pinot Noir, Woolworths Nouveau Rouge
Note: Several cellars produce small, one-off, immediately consumed bottlings for local Nouveau festivals.

OTHER OAK-FERMENTED/MATURED WHITES
Babbling Brook, Berg & Brook Agulhas Bank Sémillon-Sauvignon Blanc, Boland !Um Hap, Boschendal Grand Vin Blanc, Groot Constantia Blanc , Kumala Colombard-Sauvignon Blanc, L'Ormarins Grand Vin Blanc, La Gratitude, Oranjerivier Blanc de Blanc, Overgaauw Sylvaner-Sémillon, Stellenzicht Sauvignon Blanc-Sémillon, Stony Brook Sémillon-Sauvignon Blanc, **Woolworths Three Springs White**

WHITE BLENDS: Off-dry/Semi-sweet
Agulhas (Merwespont), Altydgedacht Chatelaine, **Ashanti Bouquet,** Astonvale Chenin-Sauvignon Blanc, **Avontuur Insensata,** Bay View Bouquet Blanc, Berg & Brook Bouquet Blanc, Bergendal Johannisberger, **Bernheim,** Blaauwklippen White Landau, Boland/Bon Vino, Boschendal Le Bouquet, Cape Bay Bouquet Blanc, **Cape Safari Stein,** Cape Selection Bouquet Blanc, Cape Vintry Blanc de Blanc/Bouquet Blanc, Cape Safari Stardust White, Cellar Cask Johannisberger, Delheim Goldspatz, **De Wet**

Bouquet Blanc, Die Poort Cape St. Blaize, Douglas Green St. Anna/St. Morand, Douglas Stein, Eersterivier Hanseret Bouquet Blanc, Goede Hoop Vin Blanc, Graça, Groot Constantia Bouquet Blanc, Groot Eiland Honigtraube/**Meander**, Hartenberg Bin 6, **Hartswater Therona-Riesling,** Haute Provence Angels' Tears, Koelenhof Koelenhoffer/Koelenheimer, Kupferberger Auslese, La Bourgogne Sonny's Choice, **La Petite Ferme Nectar du Val,** L'Avenir Vin d'Erstelle, L'Ormarins Guldenpfennig Guldenlese, Landskroon Bouquet Blanc, Landzicht Rhein Blum/Nouveau Blanc, Lieberstein, Madeba Bouquet Blanc, **Makro Franschhoek Misty**, Malan Bros Blanc du Cap, McGregor Vrolikheid, Nederburg Elegance/ Lyric, Neethlingshof Neethlingshoffer, Nelson Marguerite/Tinel, Oranje-rivier, **Paddagang Paddaspring,** Panarotti Stein, Pick 'n Pay Johannis-berger, Rhebokskloof Bouquet Blanc, **Riebeek Anais,** Rite, Robertson Beaukett, Rob Roy Selected Stein, **Ruitersvlei Mountainside White,** Simonsig Mustique/Franciskaner, Sinnya Valley, Spier Cellars IV Spears, **Spruitdrift Rapsodie,** Spur Autumn Rain, St. Elmo's Stein, Stellenbosch Wines Direct, Stellenzicht Fragrance, Swartland Bouquet Blanc, Tasheimer Goldtröpfchen, TJ Schanderl, Trawal, Tulbagh Stein, Uiterwyk Rosenburg, Verdun Interlude Blanc, Vergelegen Vin de Florence, Villa Rossini Bianco, Villiera Sonnet, Virginia, Vredendal Namaqua/Piquant, Vredenheim Honey Harvest/Debuut, Wamakersvallei Bon Ami, **Woolworths Muscat de Frontignan-Colombard/Box Wines Bouquet Blanc,** Zevenwacht Bouquet Blanc

OTHER CHARDONNAY BLENDS

Arniston Bay Chenin Blanc-Chardonnay, **Ashanti Chardonnay-Chenin, Ashton Colombard-Chardonnay,** Bayview Chenin Blanc-Chardonnay, Berg & Brook Chenin Blanc-Chardonnay, Boland Chenin Blanc-Chardonnay, Bon Courage Colombard-Chardonnay/Crouchen-Chardonnay, Boschendal Pinot Noir-Chardonnay/Premier Cuvée, Cabrière Pinot Noir-Chardonnay, Cape River Isle Colombard-Chardonnay, Cape Safari Chenin Blanc-Chardonnay, **Chamonix Blanc, Clairvaux Colombard-Chardonnay/Chenin Blanc-Chardonnay,** Constantia-Uitsig La Colombe Vin Blanc, Culemborg Chenin Blanc-Chardonnay, Fairview Crouchen-Chardonnay, **Franschhoek Vineyards Chardonnay-Chenin Blanc,** Glen Carlou Devereux Chenin-Chardonnay, Kumala Chenin Blanc-Chardonnay/ Sémillon-Chardonnay/Colombard-Chardonnay, **KWV Robert's Rock Chenin Blanc-Chardonnay,** La Bri Chardonnay-Sémillon, La Cotte Chardonnay-Sémillon, Louisenhof Chenin-Chardonnay/**Chardonnay-Pinot Gris,** Madeba Waterside White, **Makro Franschhoek Vineyards Chardonnay-Chenin Blanc**, McGregor Colombard-Chardonnay, **Riebeek Chardonnay-Sémillon,** Ruitersvlei Chenin Blanc-Chardonnay, **Shoprite Oddbins Bin 217 Chenin-Chardonnay,** Simonsvlei Chenin Blanc-Chardonnay, Sinnya Valley Colombard-Chardonnay, Springfield Colombard-Chardonnay, **Stapleford Private Cellar Colombard-Chardonnay,** Stellenzicht White, Theuniskraal Sémillon-Chardonnay, Tradouw Chenin Blanc-Chardonnay, TJ Chardonnay-Weisser Riesling, Tulbagh Seminay, Vaalharts Overvaal Nouveau Blanc, Van Loveren Colombard-Chardonnay, Villiersdorp Colombard-Chardonnay, Vredendal Namaqua Colombard-Chardonnay, Wildekrans Caresse Marine, Woolworths Grand Vin Blanc/Pinot Noir-Chardonnay/Chenin Blanc-Chardonnay/**Chardonnay-Chenin Blanc,** Zevenwacht Pinot Noir-Chardonnay

OTHER DRY RED BLENDS WITH CABERNET

Agulhas (Merwespont), Alto Rouge, Astonvale Shiraz-Cabernet, Backsberg Dry Red, Bay View Ruby Cabernet-Pinotage, Bellingham Classic, Berg & Brook Cabernet-Shiraz/Savanha Pinotage-Cabernet,

Bergendal Shiraz-Cabernet Sauvignon/**Cabernet-Shiraz**, Boland Bon Vino Dry Red, Bon Courage Cabernet Sauvignon-Shiraz, **Botha Dassie's Rood,** Bouwland, Bovlei Grand Rouge, **Brampton Old Vines, Cape Colours Grand Rouge,** Cape Safari Late Sun Red/Cinsaut-Cabernet, **Cederberg Cederberger,** Cellar Cask Select Johannisberger, Chateau Libertas, Clos Malverne Auret/**Cabernet-Shiraz**, Culemborg Pinotage-Cabernet, De Zoete Inval Grand Rouge, Die Poort Hemelrood, Douglas Green St. Augustine/ **Cabernet-Shiraz**, Edward Snell Dry Red, Eersterivier Hanseret Claret, Eikendal Rouge, Goede Hoop Vintage Rouge, **Goedverwacht Crane Red**, Goue Vallei Classique Rouge, Groot Constantia Constantia Rood, Hartenberg/Bin 9, **Hazendal Shiraz-Cabernet Sauvignon**, Huguenot Cap Rouge, Inkawu, Jacana, Jordan Chameleon Rouge, Kanonkop Kadette Dry Red/Kadette Export, Kleinbosch Cinsaut-Cabernet Sauvignon, **Kleine Zalze Dry Red,** Koelenhof Koelenberg, Kumala Cabernet-Shiraz/**Cinsaut-Cabernet**, KWV/Roodeberg, **Laibach Cinsaut-Cabernet Sauvignon,** Ladismith Dry Red, Leidersburg Grand Cuvée Rouge, Lievland Lievlander, Longhorn Dry Red, Loopspruit Guinea Fowl Rouge Reserve, Madeba Railroad Red, **Makro Overgaauw Touriga Naçional-Cabernet Sauvignon,** Meerlust Red, Morgenhof Dry Red, Mukuyu Meadows Coteaux, Muratie Melck's Reserve, Nederburg Baronne/Edelrood/P/Bin R115 P/Bin R103/Duet, Neethlingshof Lord Neethling Reserve/ Neethlingsrood, Nelson Albenet, Nuy Rouge de Nuy, Oak Village Vintage Reserve, Overgaauw Pinotage-Cabernet Franc, Paddagang Paddamanel/ Paddajolyt, Pick 'n Pay Dry Red/Halves to Hogsheads Chapter 4/**Ruby Cabernet-Cabernet Sauvignon**, Pinnacle Cabernet Sauvignon-Shiraz, Ravenswood Dry Red, Rickety Bridge Paulina's Reserve, Rooiberg Roodewyn, Ruitersvlei Cinsaut-Cabernet/**John Faure Cabernet-Shiraz**, Rust en Vrede/CIWG Auction, **Saxenburg Gwendolyn**/Grand Vin Rouge, Shoprite Oddbins Bin 127/**Bin 51**, Simonsig Frans Malan Reserve Pinotage-Cabernet/Adelberg, Somerbosch Cabernet Sauvignon-Cinsaut, Spar Country Cellars Ruby Cabernet-Cabernet Sauvignon, Stapleford Private Cellar Cordon Rouge, Stellenbosch Wines Direct, Swartland Dry Red, Uiterwyk Estate Cape Blend, Uitkyk Cabernet-Shiraz, Vaughan Johnson's Sunday Best/As You Like It/Waterfront Collection Captain's Claret/**Really Good Red**, Vergelegen Mill Race Red, Vlottenburg Rouge, Welgemeend Douelle, Weskus Vin Rouge, West Peak Red, Winelands Shiraz-Cabernet Sauvignon, Woolworths Cabernet-Shiraz Reserve/Selected Cape Red/**Box Wines Dry Red**/Dry Red/**Three Springs Red/Spring Red**, Zevenwacht Zevenrood

OTHER DRY RED BLENDS

Alphen, Ashton Satyn Rooi, Avontuur Baccarat/**Frantage**, **Barrydale Tinta Barocca-Ruby Cabernet**, Bayview Ridge Red/Ruby Cabernet-Pinotage, Bergendal Bergenrood, **Vinfruco Bin 1-21,** Blaauwklippen Sociable Dry Red, Blue Ridge Rouge (Villiera), Bonne Esperance Red, Boplaas Dry Red, Boschendal Pavillon Rouge, Bredell's Red Blend, Calitzdorp Grand Vin Rouge, Cape Bay Mellow Red, Cape Colours Cinsault-Ruby Cabernet, Cape River Isle Dry Red, Cape Vintry Dry Red, Cape View Cinsaut-Shiraz, Cellar Cask Premier Claret, Cogmans Claret, Delheim Dry Red, Destinaire Grand Rouge, Die Krans Vin Rouge, Domein Doornkraal Merlot-Pinotage, Douglas Dry Red, Douglas Green St. Raphael, Drostdyhof Claret Select/ Cape Red, Du Toitskloof Dry Red, Fairview/Zinfandel-Cinsaut, **Fort Simon Merlot-Pinotage,** Franschhoek Valley Jolly Good Red, Harewood Hill Cinsaut-Ruby Cabernet, Heerenhof Dry Red, Helderberg Cinsaut-Shiraz/ Vin Rouge, Huguenot Smooth Red, Inglewood Dry Red, Johnson & Jõrgensen Shiraz-Merlot, Kaapzicht Rouge de Kaap, Kango Claret, Ken Forrester Grenache-Shiraz, Klawer, Kumala Cinsaut-Pinotage/Ruby Cabernet-Merlot/**Cinsaut-Cabernet Franc/Cinsaut-Ruby Cabernet/ Merlot-Ruby Cabernet/Ruby Cabernet-Merlot**, **KWV Robert's Rock**

Shiraz-Malbec/Merlot-Cinsaut, La Cotte Claret/Grand Rouge, Landskroon Cinsaut-Shiraz, Louisenhof Perroquet Dry Red, Lutzville Robyn, **Makro Fairview Bin 422 Shiraz-Pinotage**, Malan Bros Rouge du Cap, Middelvlei Pinotage-Merlot, Montagu, Mount Claire Stellenbosch Mountain Red, **Mukuyu Symphony Pinotage-Merlot,** Naked Red, Nordale Vin Rouge, Oak Village Pinotage-Merlot, Overgaauw Pinotage-Cabernet Franc/Merlot-Touriga Naçional, Overmeer Selected Red, Paddagang Paddarotti/Paddajolais, Panarotti's Red, Pick 'n Pay No Name Dry Red, Rebel Dry Red, Rheboksskloof Dry Red, Riebeek Dry Red/**Pinotage-Tinta Barocca**, Romansrivier Vin Rood, Roodezandt Roodehuiswyn/Keizer's Creek, Rooiberg Selected Red, Rosenburg Grand Vin Rouge, **Ruitersvlei Mountainside Red, Sainsbury Cinsaut-Pinotage, Shoprite Oddbins Bin 179/Bin 41/Bin 151,** Simonsvlei Simonsrood, Spar Carnival Dry Red/Country Cellars Smooth Red, Spruitdrift Dry Red, Spur Buffalo Red, St. Elmo's, **Stellenzicht Shiraz-Grenache,** Swartland Dry Red 5 *l,* Tassenberg, Taverna Rouge, Tulbagh Claret, Uiterwyk, Van Loveren River Red, Vaughan Johnson Good Everyday Cape Red/Seriously Good Plonk, Villa Rossini Rosso, Vinipak Robertson Smooth Dry Red, Vlottenburg Reserve, Vredendal Gôiya G!aan, Welgemeend Amadé, Welmoed Rouge Royal, WhaleHaven Baleine Noir, Winelands Cinsaut-Tinta Barocca, Woolworths Selected Cape Red/Jug o' Red, Zomerlust Dry Red

PREMIER GRAND CRÛ: SA term for a wine-style—very dry, light-bodied usually a blend. NOT a "first great growth".
Autumn Harvest, Bellingham, Cellar Cask, Culemborg, Die Poort, Douglas Green, Douglas, Drostdyhof, Goudveld, Heerenhof, Huguenot, Jonkerskloof, Kellerprinz, Klawer, Landzicht, Langeberg Wonderfontein, Lutzville, Nederburg, Oranjerivier, Overmeer, Rebel, Rite, Rob Roy, Romansrivier, Rooiberg, Simonsvlei, Spar Carnival, Spruitdrift, Swartland/5 *l,* Tulbagh, Vaalharts, Vintners Choice, Vredendal Namaqua, Waboomsrivier, Weskus, **Woolworths Box Wines,** Zellerhof, Zonnebloem

PINOT GRIS
Berg & Brook, Fairview, Landskroon, L'Ormarins, Louisenhof Perroquet, Van Loveren

PINOT NOIR
Athlone, **Avontuur,** Backsberg (2), **Barefoot,** Bouchard Finlayson (5), Buitenverwachting, Cabrière, Claridge, De Trafford, Eikendal, Glen Carlou, Goedvertrouw, **Goudveld,** Hamilton Russell (2), Hoopenburg, Klein Constantia, **Makro Zevenwacht Premium Quality**, Meerlust/Reserve, Mukuyu Select, Muratie, **Neil Ellis,** Paul Cluver, **Simsberg, Twee Jonge Gezellen,** WhaleHaven

PINOTAGE
African Legend, Alphen, Altus, Altydgedacht, **Ashanti,** Athlone, **Avontuur Reserve**, **Babbling Brook,** Backsberg, **Badsberg,** Bay View, Beaumont (2), Bellingham (2), **Berg & Brook**/Savanha/Benguela Current, Bergsig, Beyerskloof, Blaauwklippen, Boland, Boplaas, **Botha,** Bottelary, Bovlei, Bredell, Cape Bay, **Cape Colours,** Cape Country, Cape Indaba, Cape Levant/Soleil, Cape River Isle, Cape Vintners, **Cederberg, Cheetah Valley, Cilmor,** Clos Malverne (2), Culemborg, Cullinan View, **Deetlefs,** Delheim, **De Meye, Devon Hill,** Die Krans, Diemersdal Estate/Export, Die Poort, Doc Craven, Douglas, Douglas Green, Drostdyhof, Du Toitskloof, **EagleVlei,** Eersterivier, **Eikestad,** Fairview/Cyril Back, Fleur du Cap, **Fort Simon,** Franschhoek **(2)**, **Goedvertrouw,** Goudini, Goudveld Soewenier, Goue Vallei, Grangehurst (2), Groot Constantia, Grooteberg, Helderberg,

Hermanusrivier, Hidden Valley, **Hoopenburg,** Huguenot, **Intaba,** Bredell Sinai Hill, Jacana (2), Jacobsdal, Kaapzicht, Kanonkop (2), **Kersfontein,** Klawervlei (**2**), Kleinbosch **(2),** Kleindal, **Klein Simonsvlei,** Koelenhof, Kumala Reserve, KWV/Cathedral Cellars, L'Avenir, Laborie, Laibach, Landskroon, Landzicht Rouge du Bois, Lanzerac, **La Petite Ferme,** L'Émigré, Libertas, Longridge, Louisenhof, **Louwshoek-Voorsorg Daschbosch,** Mamreweg, Meerendal, Middelvlei, Mooiuitsig, **Môreson Pinehurst,** Morgenhof, **Mount Rozier,** Mount Simon, Mouton Excelsior **(2)**, Mukuyu, Nederburg/P/Bin R172, Neethlingshof, Neil Ellis, Oak Village, Oranjerivier, **Overhex,** Paradyskloof, Perdeberg (2), **Pick 'n Pay, Remhoogte,** Rhebokskloof, **Riebeek,** Robertson, Romansrivier, Rooiberg, Sable View, Saxenburg, Sentinel, Simonsig, Simonsvlei (2), Slanghoek PR, **Somerbosch,** Southern Right, **Spice Route (2),** Spruitdrift, **Stapleford,** Stellenvale, Swartland (2), **Sylvanvale,** Trawal, Tulbagh, Uiterwyk (**2**), Villiersdorp Overberg, Vlottenburg, Vredenheim, Vriesenhof, Waboomsrivier, Wamakersvallei (2), Warwick, Wellington, Welmoed, Welvanpas, Wildekrans, Windmeul, Winelands, Woolworths/Reserve/Fireside Red/Festive Red, **Zanddrift,** Zevenwacht, Zonnebloem

PINOT BLANC

De Forellen, Hartenberg (Montagne), **Landskroon,** Mount Claire S'Bosch Mountain White, **Mukuyu Select,** Nederburg P/B D250

PONTAC

Hartenberg

CAPE "PORT"

Allesverloren, Ashton, **Axe Hill,** Beaumont, Bergsig, Blaauwklippen, Bloemendal, Boland, Boplaas (4), Bovlei, Bredell (**6**), Calitzdorp (2), Cape River Isle, Cogmans, De Wet, De Zoete Inval, Diamant, Die Krans (3), Die Poort, Domein Doornkraal, Douglas, Du Toitskloof, Franschhoek La Cotte, Glen Carlou, Goudveld, Goue Vallei, Government House, Groot Constantia, Grundheim Kannaland, Helderberg, Huguenot (2), Kango, Koelenhof, KWV (4)/**Cathedral Cellar**, L'Ormarins, Landskroon, Loopspruit Guinea Fowl, Louisenhof (**2**), **Louwshoek-Voorsorg Daschbosch, Makro Boplaas Bin 608, McGregor,** Monis (2), Mons Ruber, Mooituitsig (3), Morgenhof (2), **Mukuyu Vat 10,** Muratie, Overgaauw (2), **Paddagang,** Riebeek, Roodezandt, Rooiberg, Rudman's (3), **Rustenberg,** Simonsig, Simonsvlei (2), Slanghoek, **Stellenbosch Vineyards,** Stellenbosch Wines Direct, Swartland, Tulbagh, Vergenoegd, Villiersdorp (2), Vredendal, Waboomsrivier, Wamakersvallei, Wellington, Wonderfontein

RED DESSERT WINES

Boplaas, **Botha,** Bovlei Rooi Hanepoot, Clairvaux Rooi Jerepiko, Die Poort/Selected Release Jerepigo, Domein Doornkraal Kaptein/Pinta, Douglas, Fairview Sweet Red, Goue Vallei Rooi Jerepiko, Huguenot, Kango Rooi Jeropiko, Laborie Pineau de Laborie, Landzicht Jerepiko, Monis Moscato, Mons Ruber Cabernet Jerepigo/Elegantia, Mooiuitsig Marsala, Oranjerivier, Perdeberg Cinsaut Liqueur, Riebeek Red Jerepigo, Rooiberg Rooi Jerepiko, Simonsvlei Humbro, Slanghoek Rooi Jerepiko, Swartland Red Jerepigo, Vlottenburg Muscat d'Hambourg, Vredendal Namaqua Rooi Jerepigo, Weltevrede Muscat de Hambourg, Wonderfontein Jerepigo

RED MUSCADEL

Ashton, Boland, Bon Courage, Calitzdorp, Cogmans, De Leuwen Jagt, De Wet, Die Poort, Du Toitskloof, Grundheim, Jonkheer, Kango, Klawer, KWV Jerepigo, Landzicht, **Louiesenhof,** McGregor, **Mons Ruber,** Montagu, Mooiuitsig/Ruby Bonwin, Naked Soetes, Nordale, Nuy, Oranjerivier,

Ouderust, Overhex, Rietvallei, Robertson, Roodezandt, Rooiberg, Trawal, Van Loveren, Vredendal (2), Weltevrede/Oupa Se Wingerd, Wonderfontein

RHINE or WEISSER RIESLING

Amani, Backsberg, Blaauwklippen, Bon Courage, Buitenverwachting, Clairvaux, De Wetshof, Elephant Pass, Groot Constantia, Hartenberg, Inglewood, Jonkheer, Jordan, Kaapzicht, Klein Constantia, KWV, L'Ormarins, La Bri, Lievland, Long Mountain, Loopspruit Guinea Fowl, **Makro La Bri Bin 216,** McGregor, Morgenhof, Nederburg, Neethlingshof, Paul Cluver, Rhebokskloof, Rooiberg, Simonsig, **Slanghoek,** Spar Country Cellars Spruitdrift, **Stellenbosch Vineyards,** Thelema, Van Loveren, Villiera, Weltevrede, Zevenwacht, Zonnebloem

ROSÉ Dry

Berg & Brook Savanha, Bredasdorp, De Zoete Inval, Fairview, Goudveld, KWV, Mukuyu, Nederburg, Steenberg, Warwick

ROSÉ Off-dry Semi-sweet

Ashanti, Agulhas (Merwespont), Backsberg, Bellingham, Berg & Brook, Delheim, Dieu Donné, **Grünberger,** Kellerprinz Rosanne, Koelenhof, Kronendal, Lanzerac, **Landzicht, L'Avenir, Mukuyu Symphony,** Nederburg, Pick 'n Pay No Name, **Shoprite,** Swartland, Valley, Woolworths

RUBY CABERNET

Babbling Brook, Berg & Brook/Pierre Simond, Bredasdorp, Capelands, Clairvaux, Douglas, Drostdyhof, Fairseat, Goudini, **Hartswater,** Long Mountain, Louwshoek-Voorsorg Daschbosch, McGregor Village Red, Montestell, Oranjerivier/Bon Souvenir, Oude Wellington, Robertson (2), Rosevale, Stellenbosch Wines Direct, Table Peak, Waboomsrivier

SAUVIGNON BLANC (OAKED), sometimes called BLANC FUMÉ

Altydgedacht, Amani, **Ashanti,** Astonvale, Backsberg John Martin, Boplaas, Chamonix, **Delaire,** De Wetshof, De Zoete Inval Yvette, Delheim, Haute Provence, Jordan, Ken Forrester, L'Ormarins, La Motte, La Petite Ferme, **Makro Morgenhof Bin 212,** Morgenhof, Mulderbosch, Nederburg P/Bin D218/D234, **Newton Johnson, Rickety Bridge,** Ruitersvlei, Simonsig Vin Fumé, Spier Cellars IV Spears, Springfield Special Cuvée, Stapleford Private Cellar, Stellenzicht, Stone Wall, **TenFiftySix,** Verdun, Villiera, Woolworths

SAUVIGNON BLANC (UNWOODED)

African Legend, Alphen, Altus, Amani, Ashanti, Ashton, Astonvale, **Audacia, Avontuur/Reserve, Babbling Brook,** Backsberg/Hillside, **Badsberg, Bartho Eksteen,** Bay View, Beaumont, Bellingham, Berg & Brook/Savanha/Benguela Current/Pierre Simond, Bergsig, Blaauwklippen, Bloemendal, Boekenhoutskloof Porcupine Ridge, Boland, Bon Courage, Boplaas/Blanc de Blanc, Boschendal/Reserve, Bouchard Finlayson (2), Bovlei, Brampton, Bredasdorp, Buitenverwachting, **Cape Colours,** Cape Country, Cape Indaba, **Capell's Court, Cape Soleil,** Cederberg, **Cilmor,** Clairvaux, Cloete, Clos Malverne, Cogmans, Constantia Uitsig, Cordoba, Cullinan View, **Darling Cellars Groenekloof,** Delaire, Delheim, **De Meye,** Destinare, De Villiers, Devon Hill, De Wet, De Wetshof, **Die Krans,** Diemersdal Estate, Dieu Donné, **Domein Doornkraal,** Douglas Green, Drostdyhof, Du Toitskloof, Eersterivier, Eikendal, Elephant Pass, **Excelsior,** Fleur Du Cap, **Fort Simon,** Franschhoek La Cotte/Reserve, **Freedom Road,** Goede Hoop, Goedvertrouw, Goedverwacht, Goue Vallei, Graham Beck, Groot Constantia, Grooteberg, Hamilton Russell, Hartenberg, Haute Provence, Hazendal, Helderberg, Hermanusrivier, Hippo Creek, Hoopenburg, Inkawu, Jacana, Jonkheer, Jordan, Kaapzicht, Ken Forrester, Klawer, **Kleinbosch,** Klein Constantia, Kleindal, Kleine Zalze **(3)**, **Klein Simonsvlei,** Koelenhof, Kronendal, KWV/Cathedral Cellars, L'Émigré, **Le Moutonne,** L'Ormarins, La Bri, La Motte, La Petite Ferme, La Provence, Laborie/Granite Creek, Laibach, Landau du Val, Landskroon, Le Bonheur, Lemberg, L'Émigré Reserve, Lievland, Long Mountain, Longridge, Loopspruit Guinea Fowl, **Louwshoek-Voorsorg Daschbosch,** Lutzville, **Makro Neil Ellis Premium Quality**, **Malan Bros.,** Mamreweg, McGregor, Meerendal, Mont Rochelle/Petit Rochelle, **Mooiplaas,** Mooiuitsig, Môreson/**Pinehurst**, Morgenhof, **Morgenster,** Mount Simon, Mouton Excelsior, Mukuyu Select, Mulderbosch, Nederburg, Neethlingshof, Neil Ellis Elgin/Groenkloof, Nitida, Nuy, Oak Grove, Oak Village, Overgaauw, Overhex, Paddagang, Paul Cluver, **Pick 'n Pay (2)**, Plaisir De Merle, Rainbow Ridge, R de R-Fredericksburg, Rickety Bridge, Robertson, Roodezandt, Rooiberg, Rustenberg, Rylands Grove, Sable View, Saxenburg, Sentinel, Simonsig, Simonsvlei, **Simunye,** Somerbosch, Southern Right, Spar Country Cellars, **Spice Route,** Spier Cellars IV Spears, Springfield, Spruitdrift, Steenberg **(2)**, Stellenryck, Stellenzicht (2) Stony Brook, Swartland/Reserve, TenFiftySix, Tesco, Thelema, Tradouw, Tulbagh, Twee Jonge Gezellen, Two Oceans, Uiterwyk, Uitkyk, **Uva Mira,** Van Loveren, Van Ortloff, Van Zylshof, Vergelegen/Reserve, Villiera/Traditional Bush Vine, Vlottenburg, Von Ortloff, Vredendal **(2)**, Wamakersvallei, **Waterford,** Wellington, Welmoed/Reserve, Weltevrede, Welvanpas, WhaleHaven, Wildekrans, Windmeul, Woolworths/Constantia Reserve/**Premier**, **Zevenrivieren,** Zevenwacht, Zonnebloem (2)

SÉMILLON

Backsberg, Bergendal, Boekenhoutskloof, Boschendal, Constantia Uitsig (2), Deetlefs **(2)**, Delheim, Eikehof **(2)** Fairview, **Franschhoek Vineyards**, Hartenberg, Haute Provence, Klein Constantia, **Kleine Zalze,** La Bourgogne, La Cotte, Landau du Val, **Lutzville,** Rickety Bridge, **Savanha, Steenberg (2)**, Stellenzicht, Stonybrook,Villiersdorp, Zanddrift

SHIRAZ

African Legend, Allesverloren, Altydgedacht, Ashton, Astonvale, Athlone, Backsberg, Beaumont, Bellingham (2), Berg & Brook Savanha/Reserve, Bertrams, Blaauwklippen, Boekenhoutskloof, Bon Courage, Boschendal, Bovlei, Bredell, Cape Levant, **Capell's Court, Cape Soleil,** Carel Nel, **Cilmor, Cordoba, Darling Cellars,** Delheim, **De Meye,** Diemersdal Estate/Export, Du Toitskloof, Fairview/Reserve, Fleur du Cap, **Fort Simon, Franschhoek Vineyards, Goede Hoop, Graham Beck,** Groot Constantia, Grooteberg, Hartenberg, Hazendal, Helderberg, Jacana, **Kaapzicht, Kevin Arnold,** Klein Constantia, **Kleine Zalze,** KWV/**Cathedral Cellar**, La Motte, Landskroon, **La Petite Ferme,** Lemberg, L'Émigré, Lievland, **Longridge Bay View,** L'Ormarins, Louiesenhof, Meerendal, Middelvlei, Muratie, **Môreson/Pinehurst,** Mouton Excelsior, Nederburg, Neethlingshof, Nelson's Creek, **Nitida, Pick 'n Pay,** Rickety Bridge, Rooiberg, Rust en Vrede/Auction, Saxenburg, Sentinel, Simonsig/Reserve, Simonsvlei (2), Slanghoek, **Spice Route (2),** Stellenzicht, Stony Brook, Swartland, **Trawal,** Uitkyk, Vergenoegd, **Wellington,** Welmoed, Woolworths/Reserve, Zandvliet **(2)**, **Zevenrivieren, Zevenwacht,** Zonnebloem (2)

SPECIAL LATE HARVEST (often Gewürztraminer/Rhine riesling)

Ashton, Avontuur, Backsberg, Berg & Brook, Blaauwklippen, Bon Courage, Boplaas, Bovlei, Cape View (Kaapzicht), Cape Vintners, Cellar Reserve, Clairvaux (2), Delheim, Die Krans, Drostdyhof, Du Toitskloof, Eikendal, Fleur Du Cap, **Goudini,** Goue Vallei, Hartenberg, Hazendal, Huguenot,

Klawer, **Kleinbosch,** Koelenhof, L'Émigré, Loopspruit Guinea Fowl, Lutzville, Morgenhof, Nederburg (3), Neethlingshof, Oranjerivier, Overhex, Robertson, Roodezandt, Rooiberg, Ruitersvlei, **Shoprite,** Simonsig, Simonsvlei, Slanghoek, Spruitdrift, **Stellenbosch Vineyards,** Swartland, Thelema, Theuniskraal, Twee Jonge Gezellen (2), Trawal, Tulbagh, Van Loveren, Vlottenburg, Vredendal, Weltevrede, Zonnebloem

MÉTHODE CAP CLASSIQUE (Champenoise) WHITE
Ambeloui, Ashanti, Avontuur, Backsberg, Bon Courage, Boschendal (**3**), Buitenverwachting, Cuvée Cap by Mumm, Eikendal, Graham Beck (3), Helderberg, J C Le Roux (2), L'Ormarins, Laborie, Longridge, Louis Cauvin, **Makro Backsberg Cuvée Brut Bin 606,** Môreson, Morgenhof, Mukuyu (2), Mystery, Nederburg (2), Pick 'n Pay/Halves to Hogsheads Chapter 7, Pierre Jourdan (5), Pongrácz, Saxenburg, Simonsig (**2**), Stapleford, **TenFiftySix,** Twee Jonge Gezellen (2), Villiera (4), Woolworths (3), **Zanddrift,** Zandvliet

MÉTHODE CAP CLASSIQUE ROSÉ
Avontuur, **Graham Beck,** Louis Cauvin, Pierre Jourdan, Villiera, Woolworths

DRY WHITE SPARKLING (non MCC often carbonated)
Bellingham, Boland, **Botha,** Bovlei, Cape Country, Cinzano, Delaire, Die Poort, Du Toitskloof, Edward Snell, Eikendal, Goue Vallei, Haute Provence (**2**), Here XVII, J C Le Roux, KWV, La Cotte, Loopspruit Guinea Fowl, **Makro Mont d'Or (2),** Naked Truth, Nederburg (2), Paul Bonnay, Riebeek, Roodezandt, Rooiberg, Stapleford (2), Swartland, Van Loveren, Vredendal, Woolworths

OFF-DRY, SEMI-SWEET WHITE SPARKLING (non MCC)
Ashton, Autumn Harvest, **Badsberg,** Boland, Boplaas, Bovlei, Calitzdorp, Cape Country, Capenheimer, Carnival (2), Cinzano (2), Cogmans (2), Culemborg Diamanté, De Wet (2), Die Krans, Die Poort (3), Douglas Green, Edward Snell, Eikendal, Frère Jacques (2), Goudini, Goue Vallei, Grand Mousseux (3), Grand Provence, Grünberger, Huguenot, J C Le Roux, Jaq Canard (3), Jean Le Riche (2), Klawer, Koelenhof, KWV (2), La Cotte, Landzicht, Lutzville, McGregor, Merwida, **Montagu**, Naked Truth (2), Nederburg, Nuy, Overhex, Paarl Perlé, Panarotti's, Paul Bonnay (2), Rhebokskloof, Roodezandt, Rooiberg (2), Santino, Simonsvlei, Slanghoek, Spruitdrift, Spur, **Stapleford,** Swartland (2), Trawal, Tulbagh, Van Loveren, Villiersdorp, Vredendal (2), Vredenheim (2), Waboomsrivier, Woolworths (2)

DRY PINK SPARKLING (non MCC)
Boplaas, Laborie

OFF-DRY, SEMI-SWEET PINK SPARKLING (non MCC)
Bergsig, Bon Courage, Cold Duck, Culemborg Diamanté, Domein Doornkraal, Goue Vallei, Grand Mousseux, Huguenot, Klawer, KWV, Loopspruit, Rooiberg, Swartland, Vaalharts, Van Loveren, Waboomsrivier, Woolworths

SWEET RED SPARKLING
Boplaas, Cinzano, J C Le Roux, Paul Bonnay

SWEET RED
Avontuur Dolcetto, Cellar Cask Select Johannisberger

SYLVANER
Overgaauw

TINTA BAROCCA
Allesverloren, Die Krans, Rust en Vrede, Swartland

VIOGNIER
Fairview

WHITE DESSERT WINES
Bonnievale, Bredell Helderzicht, Cederberg Wit Jerepiko, Clairvaux Goue Jerepiko, Die Krans Heritage Collection White Jerepigo, Die Poort Wit/Golden/Raisin/Selected Release/Sweet Jerepigo, Domein Doornkraal/Korporaal/Majoor, Eersterivier Hanepoot Jerepigo, Goudveld Goue Nektar, Helderzicht Jerepigo, Huguenot Nagmaal/Jerepiko, **Jacaranda Jerepigo,** Kango Goue Jeropiko, Koelenhof Steen Jerepiko, **KWV Cavendish Cape White Jerepigo,** Landskroon Jerepigo Morio Muscat, Landzicht, Mons Ruber Bonitas, Muratie Amber, Oranjerivier Jerepigo St. Antonio/Jerepigo (sultana), Sedgwick's Old Brown, Ship, Swartland Wit Jerepiko, Weskus White Jerepiko, Wonderfontein Jerepigo

WHITE BLENDS: Dry (called Blanc de Blanc except where otherwise noted)
Astonvale Colombard-Sauvignon Blanc, Avontuur, Bay View Bay Blanc, Bergendal Bergenblanc, Blaauwklippen Sociable White, Boland Bon Vino, Bon Courage, Bonne Esperance Dry White, Boschendal/Pavillon Blanc/Petit Pavillon, **Botha,** Bouchard Finlayson Blanc de Mer, Buitenverwachting Buiten Blanc, Cape Vintry, Capelands Classic White/Sauvignon-Chenin Blanc, Cogmans, Constantia Uitsig Dry White, Culemborg, De Zoete Inval, Delheim Heerenwijn, Die Poort/Cape St. Blaize, **Domein Doornkraal Serenade/Steen-Sémillon**, Du Toitskloof (2), Edward Snell Dry White, Eersterivier Hanseret Edelblanc, Eikendal, Goue Vallei, Groot Constantia Blanc, Harewood Hill Colombard-Sauvignon Blanc, Hartenberg Bin 3, Haute Provence Fine White, Heerenblanc, Helderberg, Inglewood, Inkawu, Jonkheer, Klein Constantia, **Kleine Zalze Dry White, Kumala Sauvignon Blanc-Colombard**, La Bri Blanc de La Bri, La Cotte, Landskroon, Leidersburg Grand Cuvée Blanc, Lost Horizons Classic White, **Makro Stellenzicht Bin 223 Sauvignon Blanc/Chenin Blanc/Yellowwood Ridge Sémillon/Chenin Blanc,** Morgenhof Blanc de M, Mukuyu Meadows L'Etoile/**Symphony**, Naked White, Nuy Chant de Nuy, Oak Village Chenin Blanc-Colombard, Oom Tas, Opstal S/Blanc-Steen, Oudebos Dry White, Paddagang Paddadundee, Panarotti's Dry White, Pick 'n Pay, Rhebokskloof Harvest White, **Rickety Bridge Sauvignon Blanc-Chenin Blanc,** Robertson White, **Ruitersvlei Sauvignon Blanc-Chenin Blanc,** Slanghoek Riesling-Sémillon, Spar Carnival Dry White, Spar Country Cellars Dry White, Spier Cellars IV Spears Symphony, Spur Desert Moon, Steenberg Motif Blanc Sec, **Stellenbosch Vineyards Versus,** Stellenzicht Sauvignon Blanc-Chenin Blanc, St. Elmo's Dry White, Stormy Cape, Swartland, Table Peak, Twee Jonge Gezellen TJ 39, Trawal Classic Dry White, **Tulbagh,** Van Loveren, Vaughan Johnson's Sunday Best/Waterfront Collection Great White/Really Good White/Good Everyday Cape White/Seriously Good Plonk, Villiera, Vinipak Robertson Dry White, Vlottenburg, Vredendal Delicate/Namaqua Classic Dry White 5*l*/Tesco South African Dry White 5*l*, **Uitzicht Reyneke Chenin Blanc-Sauvignon Blanc,** Welmoed, Weltevrede, Weskus, Woolworths/Vin de Table/Spring Collection/Selected Cape White/Blanc de Blanc, Zevenwacht, Zomerlust, Zonnebloem

WHITE MUSCADEL
Ashton, Boland, Bon Courage, Boplaas, Calitzdorp, **Clairvaux,** Cogmans, De Wetshof, Die Krans, Die Poort, Goue Vallei, Graham Beck, Grundheim, **Hartswater**, Huguenot, Jonkheer, Kango, Klawer, Landzicht, Libertas, Loopspruit Guinea Fowl, McGregor, Mons Ruber/Regalis, Mooiuitsig (2), Nuy, Oranjerivier, Ouderust, Overhex, Roodezandt, Simonsvlei (2), Spruitdrift, Stellenzicht, Thelema, Trawal, Weltevrede, Wonderfontein

WHITE PORT
Boplaas, Domein Doornkraal, Douglas Green, Mons Ruber Bonitas Aridulus, Mooiuitsig, Oranjerivier, Wonderfontein

ZANTÉ
Domein Doornkraal Luitenant

ZINFANDEL
Blaauwklippen, Hartenberg

WINE STYLES

Blanc de Blancs *White wine made only from white grapes; also a Champagne term, when a sparkling wine is made only from white grapes/chardonnay.*

Blanc Fumé (or Fumé Blanc) *Dry white made of sauvignon blanc grapes, not necessarily finished in wood (nor smoked, smoky)!*

Blanc de Noir *A light wine (colour can range from off-white to pink or peach) made from red grapes.*

Cap Classique *See Méthode Cap Classique.*

Carbonated wines *Sparkling wines with carbon dioxide bubbles injected (as in fizzy soft drinks).*

Champagne *Sparkling wine. In South Africa "sparkling" is the correct description. Under an agreement with France, South Africa does not call its sparkling wines champagne, which properly is a geographic appellation describing French sparkling wines from the Champagne area.*

Charmat *See Sparkling Wine.*

Claret *Red wine from the Bordeaux region of France, now often misleadingly used as a generic term for lightish dry reds anywhere. Claret or claret-style in this guide infers that one or more of traditional Bordeaux varieties (always cabernet sauvignon, often with merlot, cabernet franc) feature in a wine.*

Crû *Meaning "growth" in French, or the vineyard responsible for the provenance of a wine, as in Grand Crû, denoting a great vineyard, or Crû Bourgeois, of lesser quality. (See Premier Grand Crû.)*

Cultivar *Grape variety (a contraction of "cultivated variety").*

Cuvée *French term for the blend of a wine.*

Demi-sec *Means half-dry, usually rather more sweet than dry. In South Africa can contain between 4 and 12 gms/l sugar.*

Dessert wine *A sweet wine, to accompany the last courses of a meal, but not necessarily only so; the French deploy their usual insouciance famously in drinking dessert Sauternes and Barsac at the start of a meal with pâté de foie gras.*

Dry to Sweet *See sweetness.*

Fortified *Wines increased in alcoholic strength by the addition of spirits, to 16% or more alcohol by volume.*

Grand Crû *Literally "great growth" but denoting, in South Africa at least, the producer's own subjective rating of a wine. Not an official rating.*

Jerepiko-Jeripigo *A fortified (usually with grape spirit) wine, red or white, very sweet, rich; fortification takes place before fermentation is completed—or sometimes before it's begun—thus retaining considerable unfermented grape flavours.*

Late Harvest *Sweet wine made from late-harvested and therefore sweeter grapes.*

Méthode Cap Classique *(MCC) South African term to describe sparkling wines made by the classic French "méthode Champenoise" (MC). The term was adopted unanimously by leading Cape sparkling wine growers, to distinguish their bubblies from those made by the tank or simple carbon dioxide injection (carbonated, see above) methods and to avoid French objections to usage of French wine terminology. A Cape MCC association has been formed.*

Noble Late Harvest *South African designation for intensely sweet desserts; must also exhibit a noble rot (botrytis) character from grapes infected by the botrytis fungus. Grapes must be harvested at 28 degrees Balling sugar or more. (Residual sugar in the wine must exceed 50 gms/l.)*

Nouveau *Term originated in Beaujolais for fruity young and light red, usually from gamay and made by the macération carbonique method. Bottled a few weeks after vintage to capture youthful, fresh flavour of fruit* *and yeasty fermentation.*

***Noble Rot** See Botrytis.*

***Old Cape style** Loose expression, denoting heavyish, quite pungent South African reds, usually from the period—mid-1980s—before new barrel oak maturation became more fashionable. A faintly musty, slightly leathery and stewed character pervades these wines, sometimes prized in the past but now generally considered to lack elegance and the complexity associated with oak "elevation". These wines were also referred to as "dikvoet"—heavy-footed—and were often heavy in alcohol, from either over-ripe grapes, or coarse in unripe tannin, from virus-infected, unripened grapes. High sulphur levels, badly-adjusted acids, capped malolactic fermentation, too-long skin contact, rough pressing were also common factors in producing clumsy, inelegant wines. A burned, tarry hardness was a noticeable—but again sometimes readily accepted—feature of these Old Cape style reds, including cabernets, shirazes and pinotages. Ones which featured cinsault (cinsaut) inclined toward a thinner sweet-sour sickliness.*

***Premier Grand Crû** Unlike in France, not an officially recognised rating in South Africa, simply a dry white.*

***Perlant, Perlé, Pétillant** Slightly sparkling, carbonated wine.*

***Punt** The concave shape or hollow in the base of some wine and sparkling wine bottles, traditionally so that deposits and crystals thrown by wines can collect there.*

***Rosé** Pinkish wine, either a blend of red and white grapes, or made only from red grapes, with skins removed quickly before the wine takes up too much red colouring.*

***Sparkling Wine** Bubbly, or "champagne", usually white but sometimes rosé and even red, given its effervescence by carbon dioxide—allowed to escape in the normal winemaking process. Sparkling wine is either made in the bottle, in which a secondary fermentation is induced (the true and expensive French **Méthode Champenoise** or in South Africa, Méthode Cap Classique) or by a process induced in a closed tank, called the **Charmat** or **Tank** method, after which the sparkling wine is bottled under pressure. More inexpensive sparkling wines are made simply by the injection of carbon dioxide which causes fizziness, as in soft drinks; this is simply **Carbonated** wine.*

***Special Late Harvest** A dessert wine, a South African designation. Minimum requirements are 20 gms/l of sugar and grapes must be harvested at a minimum of 22 degrees Balling sugar (quite normal for even dry wines).*

***Stein** Semi-sweet white style of wine, usually a blend and often confused with steen, a grape variety (chenin blanc), though most steins are made at least partly from steen grapes.*

***Sugar or sweetness in a wine** Extra-dry or bone-dry wines are below 2,5 gms/l in sugar content undetectable to the taster and a wine is dry up to 4 (legally). Taste buds will begin picking up a slight sweetness, or softness, in a wine—provided its acidity is not excessive—at about 5-6 gms/l, when it is still off-dry. But by about 8-9 gms/l, a definite sweetness can be noticed. However, an acidity of 8-9 gms can render a sweet wine fairly crisp even with a sugar content of 20 gms/l plus. The Noble Late Harvests reach up to a phenomenal 200 gms/l or more!*

***Sweetness** levels in wine: official classifications in South Africa.*

***Residual Sugar** in grams per litre for **Still Wines**:*

Extra dry: 2,5 gms/l and under.

Dry: 4 gms/l and under.

Semi-dry: 4-12 gms/l.

Semi-sweet: 4-30 gms/l.

Late Harvest: More than 20 gms/l, under 30 gms/l.

Special Late Harvest (SLH): No sweetness requirements in wine, but grapes must be harvested at 22 degrees Balling or more, i.e. ripe.

Sweet Natural (or Natural Sweet): More than 30 gms/l.
Noble Late Harvest (NLH): Over 50 gms/l, must have at least 30 gms/l sugar-free extract, grapes harvested at 28 degrees Balling or more.
In ***Sparkling Wines****:*
Extra Dry, Brut: 15 gms/l and under.
Dry: 15-35 gms/l.
Semi-sweet: 35-50 gms/l.
Sweet: More than 50 gms/l.
Doux *Sweet.*
Varietal Wine *Wine made from a single cultivar, or variety of grape. Must consist of 75% or more of the stated grape—BUT 85% or more if exported.*
Vintage *In South Africa used primarily to denote year of harvest. Not a substantive quality classification. (A "vintage" port in Europe means one from an officially declared great port grape year.)*

WINE TASTING

Short of a ready description? Here are a few frequently-used words, phrases, explanations; best used with the Aroma Wheel, which aims for more specific flavours and textures.

In the section on Grape Varieties, Reds and Whites, we list a few of the taste and fruit sensations most commonly associated with each of the main grape variety's wines.

Accessible, Approachable *a wine is not too hard, the flavours are friendly, easily recognised; the acids and alcohols don't put you off; the wine is ready to drink.*

Aftertaste *the lingering flavours and impressions of a wine—sometimes referred to as the* ***tail*** *or* ***end taste*** *or* ***finish****. A long tail is a good thing!* ***Persistence*** *is a good word for a long tail. SA wines have been criticised for coarse finishes.*

Attack *the first aromatic sensations—pungent, aggressive, tame, etc.*

Aroma *smells and flavours, first perceived in the* ***bouquet****, or* ***nose****.*

Austere *usually meaning, withdrawn, sometimes harsh, unyielding.*

Backbone *there's taste, weight, power—not a flabby, insipid wine.*

Baked *an over-ripe staleness, lack of freshness and fruity vitality, often associated with hot-climate wines.*

Balance *desirable attribute, when the wine's chief constituents—alcohol, acid, tannin, fruit—are in harmony, none overpowering, none lacking.*

Bead *bubbles in sparkling wine; fine bead, coarse bead etc., the former more desirable—and they shouldn't fizzle out too quickly, of course. See also Mousse.*

Bite *or* ***Grip*** *imparted by tannins and acids, giving a wine structure and staying power; but unacceptable (or unready) if overdone or verging on tannic bitterness.*

Body *fullness on the palate.*

Bottle-age *negative or positive, depending on context; usually used to describe maturing complexity in a bouquet which has lost its initial flush of youthful fruit; but can also mean a wine has acquired stale, empty, tired, even off odours as a result of time in bottle. Development of* ***secondary flavours*** *in some wines, notably fine chardonnays and most top quality reds, is highly prized, and the best one-word summary probably is* ***complexity****.*

Botrytis Cinerea *or noble rot (pourriture noble in French and edelfaule in German) is the result of a fungus denuding grapes of water and thus raising relative sugar content. With the berry's concentrated flavours and sweetness, winemakers can produce stunning dessert wines.*

Buttery *flavour and texture; rich, smooth, often associated with chardonnays, a rich, creamy saltiness—or citric freshness too.*

Brut *bone-dry—describing Champagnes and Cape sparkling wines.*

Classical *showing flavours, tastes, structure of the finest examples of European classics of Claret, Burgundy etc.; usually associated with balance, elegance, subtle; nothing coarse, blowsy, overdone, too obvious.*

Coarse *rough, too alcoholic,* ***clumsy, unbalanced****, acids too tart, oak too strong,* ***bitter, tannins*** *unripe.*

Complexity *strong recommendation, wine has several complementary flavours, is not* ***simple*** *or* ***one-dimensional****.*

Corked *wine is faulty if it is corked, or corky, meaning its flavours have been tainted by the cork; yeast, fungal and bacterial infections from the cork damage the wine. It smells of damp, mouldy bark in its worst stages—but sometimes it's barely detectable. In a restaurant, a corked wine should be rejected and returned immediately and producers are honour-bound to replace corked wine.*

Creamy *not literally creamy, of course; more a silky, buttery feel and texture.*

Crisp *tricky term, meaning fresh, or refreshing; or too clean, thin, tart.*

Dense *well-padded, rich, full, flavour-packed.*

Deposits or sediment *usually tasteless and harmless tartrates, acid crystals.*

Dried out *bereft of fruit, harder constituents remaining,* ***tired****.*

Earthy *usually positive, wine showing its origins from soil, minerally, damp leaves, mushrooms etc.*

Esters *scents and smells, usually generated by alcohols and acids in wine. A wine can be described as "estery" when these characteristics are prominent.*

Extract *expressed as "sugar-free" extract, or total extract (which will include some sugars). A reading of dry matter, or extract, that would be left in wine after suction, dehydration, leaching, etc. It is an indication of the "substance" of the wine. In a white, 18 gms/l would be low, light; anything much above 23 and a white has something to say. In reds, it should be higher. When it reaches about 30 and climbs, then the wine has full, packed flavours and will be mouth-filling, provided other constituents are present and in balance.*

Fat *big, full, ample in the mouth.*

Firm *as opposed to* ***Flabby****; compact, well-proportioned. Flabby would be too soft, inconsequential.*

Fleshy *very positive, meaning a wine is well-fleshed out with warm textures and grape flavours.*

Forward *rather than* ***shy****; advancing in age too, mature.*

Gravelly *with suggestions of minerally, earthy quality; also firm texture.*

Green *usually unripe, sour; sometimes simply youthful.*

Grip *often almost literally,* ***gripping****,* ***firm*** *on palate, in* ***finish****. Acid, tannin, alcohol are contributors.*

Herbaceous *as opposed to fruity; meaning grassy, hay-like, heathery—a general green-ness too.*

Hollow *empty of substance, flavours on palate,* ***dumb****,* ***retiring****.*

Hot *when the alcohol leaves a burning sensation in finish.*

Intensity, *also* ***concentration,*** *no flab, plenty of driving flavour.*

Lean, *thin, tinny and mean, lacking charm of ample fruit.*

Leesy; lees *are the taste-imparting dead yeast cells, rich, ripe (looking like custard) at the bottom of barrels, tanks; the longer the wine is "on its lees" the more richness and flavour it should absorb.*

Light *low in alcohol, light in body (and usually short on taste) made to capture a modern, health and weight-conscious market; a new trend in both reds and whites.*

Lively *with bounce, the mix of fruit and other flavours refreshing on the palate.*

Long, *with persistence and substance, flavours linger.*

Mousse *(French) froth or foam—see also "bead"—in sparkling wines, usually refers also to quality, size and effervescence of the bubbles.*

Mouth-feel, mouth-filling, *the texture, feel; racy, crispness (fine with appropriate dishes) or generous, smooth.* ***Filled out.***

Neutral, *what it says, neither here nor there.*

New World Wine style: *a loose term. Generally meant to embrace the accessible, bold and often uninhibitedly fruity and sometimes brazenly oak-influenced wines of America, Australia and elsewhere.* ***Old World style*** *advocates would perhaps say their favoured classic European wines were more subtle, complex, much less oaky, more varied and generally vinous, rather than brashly fruity. Many tasters with international experience would currently probably place South Africa's style, in the main, somewhere between these two.*

Palate *a.k.a flavour, taste, texture; discerned on the tongue (and by the olfactory bulb above the mouth and behind the nose).*

Perfumed *or* ***scented*** *with fragrances, fruity, flowery, animal etc.*

Porty *heavy, overdone—sometimes over-ripe, raisiny; a negative in unfortified wine.*

Rough *a bull-in-a-china-shop wine, or throat sand-papering quality.*

Sharp *all about acid, usually unbalanced; but occasionally sharpish, fresh wine is right for the occasion.*

Short *or* ***Quick*** *when it's attenuated, insubstantial, leaves little impression.* ***Simple****, little or no flavour spectrum to engage a drinker.*

Stalky *think of unripe, bitter stalks, stems.*

Stewed *over-ripe, cooked, soft, soggy fruit.*

Structure *a vague wine-tasting word, usually referring to acid, tannin and alcohol make-up; as in "it has the structure to age" and meaning these principal preservatives are in place. The flesh and fruit around the wine's structure provide additional flavours; acid and tannin—and even alcohol—also imparting flavour sensations of their own and contributing to "texture"—softness or hardness. A hard or too firmly "structured" wine will be unyielding, high acid, overly tannic or too brutally alcoholic, blocking out flavours and making for a rough rather than smooth-textured result.*

Supple *very desirable (not necessarily* ***subtle****), friendly, refined texture and flavours.*

Tannin *a vital preservative in wine, which derives from the grape skins. Tannin is necessary for a wine's longevity. A young wine's raw tannin gives it a youthful tanginess—not necessarily too harsh—but no red wine matures into a great one without some tannin, which itself undergoes change, combines with other substances and mellows. Tannin leaves a* ***Tannic*** *mouth-puckering dryness around the gums, gives "grip" to a wine. A wooded wine will also contain oak tannin. Tannins are said to be "hard" or "green" when unripe; "soft" or "ripe" tannins are much less harsh but give a necessary impression of weight and substance.*

Tension *when there's nervous fruity-acid play on the palate.*

Texture *the tactile "feel" in the mouth—hard, acidic, coarse and alcoholic; or, smooth, velvety, warm.*

Terpenes *strong-flavoured, floral compounds influencing the aromas of a number of grape varieties, especially Rhine riesling, gewürztraminer and the muscats; often demonstrated by a quite pungent resinous oiliness, accentuated by some years in bottle.*

Toasty *frequently used for barrel-fermented and aged wines, and after some years in bottle; a biscuity, toasty aspect develops to enrich a quality wine.*

Vegetal *grassy, leafy, herby—in contrast to fruity, flowery, oaky. Overdone, a no-no.*

Yeasty *rich, bread-like or bakery smells, often evident in barrel-fermented whites and sparkling wines made by méthode Champenoise where yeasts stay in contact with the wine some time after fermentation.*

WINE COURSES

Cape Wine Academy *The official education body for the SA wine industry headquartered in Stellenbosch and with a branch in Johannesburg and centres in Durban, Bloemfontein and Port Elizabeth. Runs theory and tasting courses at several levels, also examinations. Recently introduced a wine and food course, with wine service and sommelier courses to follow. The Principal is Christine Rudman. Stellenbosch: Tel: (021) 8087597/8. Fax: (021) 8864568; Johannesburg: Tel: (011) 7834585 Fax: (011) 8832356; Durban: Tel/fax: (031) 7051311; Pretoria: Tel: (012) 3331978; Bloemfontein: Tel: (051) 4355301, Fax: (051) 4355351; Port Elizabeth: Tel/fax: (041) 338889.*

Cape Wine Masters *The successful completion of tasting/theory examinations set since 1983 by the Cape Wine and Spirit Education Trust have qualified 34 wine aficionados for the CWM title. Their* ***Institute of Cape Wine Masters*** *holds seminars, charts trends, names a Wine Personality of the Year, etc. Chairman Christine Rudman is also Principal of the Cape Wine Academy—from 1995—succeeding Dame Phyllis Hands who co-founded the Academy in 1979. There are three Honorary Members of the Institute: Phyllis Hands, Dave Hughes and Colin Frith. Contact: Stellenbosch Tel: (021) 8087591 or Fax: (021) 8864568.*

WINEMAKING TERMS

A few quick reference explanations

Acid and Acidity *The fresh—or, in excess, sharp or sour—taste of wine. If the acidity is too low, in relation to a wine's other constituents (alcohol, sweetness etc.,) it can become dull, flat, flabby, lifeless. Too high, and the wine can be unpleasantly tart. In South Africa, winemakers are permitted to adjust acidity, either by adding tartaric acid—at any stage of the process before bottling—or by lowering the acid level with the use of calcium carbonate. In the laboratory, a wine's acids are expressed as* ***volatile*** *and* ***fixed****: the two making up its* ***Total Acid (TA).*** *Acids also function as preservatives. Youthful wines have a more pronounced acidity than mellowed, smoother, older wines. Acids in a wine can be masked—or covered—to some extent by sweetness, the sugar content. In dry white wine a total acid of 7 gms/l will make it tart; 6 gms/l is more balanced but by 5 gms/l the wine's liveliness can be dulled. In France and other European wine producing countries, they use sulphuric acid titration which lowers the result by 1,5 when compared with tartaric titration used in South Africa. Red wine—which does not require the freshness critical to white—usually has lower acidity but still may taste rough and unready due to the presence of other and heavier components such as tannins, usually absent or only marginally present, in whites, the exceptions being barrel-made whites which derive tannins from oak.*

Ascorbic Acid *Preservative in winemaking (and present naturally in grapes); Vitamin C. Recently in wider use in the Cape for white wines, not as an alternative to but in conjunction with sulphur dioxide. Said to keep wines fresher longer.*

Barrels *(barrel-aged; barrel-fermented)* ***Barrique*** *is a French word for barrel.* ***Vat*** *is a term generally used for larger (2 000-5 000 litre) wooden* *vessels. Barrels are generally 225-500 litre oak (but also redwood in California) casks. Wines are pumped into barrels to age, pick up oaky flavours, mature etc. When must, or fermenting must is put into barrels, the resulting wine is called* ***barrel-fermented****. (In the case of chardonnays, barrel-fermenting invariably produces more pronounced, distinctive, deep flavours. Whites merely barrel-aged are sometimes dominated, overwhelmed by the oaky flavours.)* ***New/Used*** *barrels: many flavours—spices, cinnamon, vanilla etc.,—contained in the oak staves are infused and diffused in the wine; new barrels obviously contain more such ingredients and "oak pickup" decreases with each filling. A used barrel is referred to as a* ***second-fill****, third-fill barrel, depending on how often it has been used. Most oak types used in South Africa come from French forests:* ***Tronçais, Nevers, Alliers, Limousin, Vosges, Jupille, Argonne*** *etc., and the different coopers e.g.* ***Dargaud & Jaegle, Taransaud, Demptos, Seguin-Moreau,*** *have their own adherents and reputations.* ***American (white) oak*** *(quercus alba) long known for its use in Spanish Rioja and Bourbon whisky, has a higher flavour profile, is sometimes shunned by those winemakers who want to retain vinosity and subtlety in their wines, though the more immediately obvious vanilla flavours of American oak have undoubted and immediate appeal to many wine drinkers.*

Blend *A wine made from two or more different grape varieties, or vintages, or vineyards. Some of the world's finest wines are blends.*

Chaptalisation *French term for the addition of sugar to grape must to raise the alcohol, and keeping properties, of a wine. Not permitted in South Africa. Legal in France, Germany, where they are not permitted to make the acid adjustments allowed in South Africa. Winemakers in both hemispheres bend the rules.*

Charmat *Method of making sparkling wine in a sealed tank (Cuvée Close) under pressure. Easier, cheaper than Méthode Champenoise manner of creating bubbles. See also Sparkling wine.*

Cold Stabilisation *Keeping a wine at about minus 4°C for a week or more to precipitate tartaric acid and "clean up" the wine, preventing later formation of (harmless) tartrate crystals in bottle. Some winemakers believe this process damages flavour and prefer not to cold stabilise.*

Dosage *The adjusted quantity of sugar, or level of sweetness in sparkling wines; in the case of bottle-fermented (méthode Champenoise, or MCC) added after the second fermentation. See Brut etc.*

Fermentation *The conversion of sugar in grapes into alcohol and carbon dioxide, a function of enzymes excreted by yeasts. Wild yeasts occur on the bloom of a grape berry, but in modern Cape winemaking cultured yeasts are added to secure the process. Beyond about 15% of alcohol, yeasts are overwhelmed and fermentation ceases, although it usually is stopped (for instance by cooling, filtration or the addition of alcohol) before this stage. Secondary or* ***malolactic*** *fermentation occurs when bacteria convert malic acids into lactic acids; this reduces the acidity of a wine, a normal and healthy process, specially in reds—provided of course it occurs before bottling.*

Filtering *Removes last impurities including yeast cells. Done excessively, can "thin" a wine. Some traditionalists, especially in France, go from barrel to bottle without cold-protein stabilisation or filtering. But trendy Californian wineries now boast of (and charge more for) "Unfiltered" pinot noir, for example. Cape cellars have begun to follow suit.*

Fining and Protein Stabilisation *Not to be confused with filtration, which means what it says. Fining is ridding wine of suspended particles by adding substances that attract and draw the particles from the wine. Gelatine, bentonite, and egg white are among those used to take out proteins which otherwise could cloud a wine after bottling.*

Free Run *After grapes have been de-stalked and crushed, juice runs freely* *(without pressing). This juice is the cleanest and some believe the purest, making fruitier wines.*

Lees *Spent yeast cells and other matter which form deposits and collect at the bottom of casks (or any containers) in winemaking. Yeast autolysis, or decomposition, can impart richness and flavour to a wine, sometimes referred to as* ***leesy****. The French attach great importance—in Champagne production, chardonnays etc—to leaving the wine in contact with the lees* (sur lie) *long enough for sufficient flavour uptake. Commercial wineries, concerned with "clean" wines often prefer not to take these risks—lees can also infect and degrade wine—and rack and filter wines clean soon after fermentation is completed.*

Macération Carbonique *Method of fermenting red wine without crushing grapes first. Whole clusters with stalks etc., put into closed vat. Fermentation occurs within the grape berries which then burst.*

Maturation *or ageing. Complexity, subtlety and mellowness come from maturation, after a young wine with harsh tannin is transformed into a mellow, smoother drink. Ageing properties are closely related to tannin and fixed acid content of a wine. A relatively full wine with tannin has lasting power. Lighter, almost tannin-free wines are drinkable sooner but will not reach the complexity of a great red. A number of Cape whites, especially chardonnays and Rhine rieslings, can last for years but most Cape whites are best drunk within a year to 18 months, before their youthful fruitiness is diminished.*

Méthode Champenoise *Classic method of making champagne by inducing secondary fermentation in the bottle and producing fine bubbles. As practised in Champagne. See also Sparkling wine and Méthode Cap Classique above.*

Oak Chips *of several kind of quercus, either placed in used barrels or stainless steel tanks, are used increasingly in Australia and South Africa, as are oak staves. Frowned on by some purists still, the "additives" are precisely those of a new barrel, far cheaper, more easily handled, often with indistinguishable results. See also: Barrels.*

Oak-matured*, See* ***Barrels.***

Oxidation *Change (usually for the worse) due to exposure to air, in whites often producing dark yellow or yellowish colour (called maderisation), altering, "ageing" the taste. Controlled aeration is used to introduce acceptable and desirable development in wine.*

pH *A chemical notation, used in winemaking and evaluation. The pH of a wine is its acidity—not in volume but by strength or degree. The reading provides a guide to a wine's keepability. The optimum pH in a wine is somewhere between 3,1 and 3,4—which significantly improves a wine's protection from bacterial spoilage, so permitting it to mature and develop if properly stored. Total Acid, expressed in volume—e.g. tartaric acid in gms/l—is a less reliable guide to longevity than pH, which is not subject to as much change or fluctuation since it is buffered by numerous other constituents. A pH of 7 is neutral, above is alkaline, below is acid. Cape growers have tended to harvest on the basis of pH, rather than sugar or sugar-acid ratios, but this now is a contentious matter. Many winemakers believe they can best determine a wine's quality by tasting the grapes. A wine's clarity and colour, overall quality and staying power are largely determined by pH.*

Reductive *Wine in an unevolved, unoxidised state is said to be "reductive"; usually with a tight, sometimes unyielding character. The absence of air (in a bottled wine) or the presence of substantial (anti-oxidant) sulphur dioxide levels, will inhibit both oxidation and reduction processes, which are linked and complementary. Controlled aeration, as in racking, or accidental exposure to air—with insufficient sulphur, carbon dioxide or nitrogen protection during winemaking—will* *determine the degree of oxidation and the loss of freshness in a wine. Over-oxidised wines are by definition faulty—flat, lifeless, stale; whites are more vulnerable than reds. Sulphur dioxide used judiciously, specially at bottling, provides an anti-oxidative control; over-use can "freeze" wine into a hard, reductive state, suppressing the (gradual) evolution and development which is obviously part of wine's progress to complexity with age.*

Racking *Drawing or pumping wine off from one cask or tank to another, to leave behind the deposit or lees.*

Skin contact *After crushing and de-stemming, white grapes may be left for a period with the juice, remaining "in contact" with skins (before being moved into the press, from which the grape juice is squeezed). The period of this skin contact varies from cellar to cellar—and some practise it not at all. A number of winemakers believe the colours and flavours in and under the grape skins should be maximised in this way; others believe extended contact can lead to coarseness, even bitterness. In red winemaking, the grape skins are usually fermented with the juice; some wineries practice* ***extended maceration*** *by leaving the skins (husks) for long periods after fermentation is complete (up to several weeks sometimes) to optimise colour, flavour and extract uptake. Opinions again differ, some believe the method risks producing coarse, rough, even volatile wines.*

Tartrates *Harmless crystals formed by tartaric acid precipitating in the bottle when it has not been cold stabilised. Particularly common in South African wines because of the high potassium content in our soils, and, because the public appears to be unready to accept a wine with crystals in it, usually avoided by using cold stabilisation.*

Volatile Acidity (VA) *That part of the acidity which can become volatile. A high reading indicates a wine is prone to spoilage. Recognised by a sharp, "hot", vinegary smell. In South Africa, wines must by law be below 1,2 gms of VA but in practice, the vast majority are well below 1 gm.*

Whole Bunch (or Cluster) Pressing *Some Cape cellars use this age-old process; whole bunches are placed directly in the press and squeezed, rather than currently conventional methods of* ***stemming*** *or* ***de-stalking*** *while crushing* ***before*** *pressing. Whole bunch pressing is said to yield fresher, cleaner must, and wine lower in polyphenols, which, in excess, tend to age wines faster and render them coarser.*

Wood-fermented/matured *Mainly French, American, Yugoslavian oak barrels are used in Cape cellars. Small barrels of new French oak in particular have transformed many local wines (chardonnay, sauvignon blanc) and a variety of reds. The complex and vast array of flavours from the wood, including cedar-vanilla flavours, add extra nuances to the must or wine and eventually have a mellowing effect. See also* ***Barrels****.*

Yeasts *Micro-organisms that excrete enzymes which convert or ferment sugar into alcohol. Naturally present in vineyards and on grapes but locally, wild yeasts are usually still doused with sulphur and cultured yeasts are inoculated. The wild yeasts in the Cape were generally thought unsuitable in the past, especially for white musts. Lately, a few growers have begun to experiment—with some excellent results—using natural v'yd yeasts, for both red and white wines.*

CAPE VINTAGES

South African vintage variations are relatively insignificant. Dry hot summers are the norm. Even when they aren't, as in 1996, the vastly different conditions in widely scattered growing areas—700 km. east to west—make any comments generalisations at best, unless confined to individual properties and their grape varieties. Also, most areas and estates plant a formidable mix of grapes ripening differently to stagger the harvest. The lack of uniformity goes further: soil types, new clones and climates within the same regions vary enormously. Vineyard practices themselves and wine-making techniques are changing so fundamentally from vintage to vintage and from winery to winery now that they are the important determinants of individual vintage quality variations in the more or less uniformly warm and dry Cape seasons. The comments below are therefore very general.

With very few exceptions, Cape dry whites should probably be consumed within a year.

1998 Hot, dry season marked by localised frost during October, heat-waves during January in some areas, causing an early, short harvest. Yield was down (below 1 000 million litres for the first time since 1995), grapes small but healthy. Fat, alcoholic wines generally: whites tend to lack flavour intensity; reds big, booming but flavoursome, excellent maturation potential. Undoubtedly a red-wine year.

1997 The coolest, longest season in several decades, certainly in the memory of still active winemakers; cabernets were harvested into May when these are usually gathered two months earlier. Establishments unprepared for the longer "hang time" picked too soon (tending to thinner, sourer wines); those who could wait often secured outstanding fruit. Virus infected vineyards were shown up much more dramatically, unable to infuse their fruit with any luscious ripeness, let alone opulence. A mixed year on balance; a number of wines—reds and whites—should outclass previous vintages but will take a little longer to open out, specially the reds.

1996 Cool season marked by several sets of late showers in many areas; but a record yield overall. Very average quality reds; below average quality from virus-infected vineyards. Patchy sauvignons and chardonnays, poor colombards, variable chenin blancs, good Cape rieslings and sémillons. Not a great year.

1995 The second consecutive very dry and hot vintage—and even lower yields in many varieties than in 1994. A very ripe year, for big but fairly concentrated reds in most coastal areas. Most dry whites should have been consumed by now.

Above-average red wine years:
1984, 1986, 1987, 1989, 1991 1992, 1994, 1995

The **1970s**: a rough rule of thumb, the even years were usually more favourable for reds. (Of only academic interest now, the uneven years, marginally cooler, favoured whites.) The best of the 1970s was undoubtedly **1974**; but it is rare to find any that have hung in. A few **1978s** are passable. Very little excitement elsewhere. Dry whites are all well past it now.

WINE ROUTES/TRUSTS/ASSOCIATIONS

Most of the Cape's wine areas have set up organisations to promote their own distinctive regional charms. Contact the following bodies for local information:

Calitzdorp Wine Route: Tel: (044) 2133314, Fax: 2133562.
Constantia Wine Route: Tel: (021) 7945128, Fax: 7941999.
Durbanville Wine Route: Tel: 083 310 1228.
Klein Karoo Wine Trust: Tel: (044) 2412562.
Olifants River Wine Trust: Tel/Fax: (0271) 33126.
Orange River Wine Trust: Tel: (054) 3324651, Fax: 3324408.
Paarl Wine Route: Tel: (021) 8723605, Fax: 8723841.
Robertson Valley Wine Route: Tel: (023) 6263167, Fax: 6261054.
Stellenbosch Wine Route: Tel: (021) 8864310, Fax: 8864330.
Swartland Wine Trust: Tel: (0224) 21134, Fax: 21750.
Tulbagh Wine Trust: Tel: (0236) 301001, Fax: 301358.
Vignerons de Franschhoek: Tel: (021) 8763062, Fax: (021) 8762768.
Wellington Wine Route: Tel: (021) 8734604, Fax: 8734607.
Worcester Winelands Ass.: Tel: (0231) 28710, Fax: 22294.

TOURS/INFORMATION

Vineyard Ventures *Tel: (021) 4348888, Fax: (021) 4349999, E-mail: vinven@iafrica.com. For specialised, small-group or private excursions Gillian Stoltzman and Glen Christie tailor trips to visitors' specs.*
The Capevine: *Annette Stals, Tel/Fax: (021) 9134580; (021) 9136611; Email: capevine@iafrica.com. Personal, tailor-made tours for individuals or groups combining all aspects of the winelands and surrounding areas.*
Window on Cape Wine: *Tour the whole of the winelands in ± an hour, in the convenience of the venue of your choice. Contact Meryl Weaver (021) 8891002 or Sandrine Sellmeyer Tel/Fax: (021) 8864549; Cell: 082 881 5488.*
Winelands of the Cape on Video: *Very professional armchair tour, includes. 28 top estates. Contact Sovereign Videos on Fax: (021) 4233056.*

ACCOMMODATION

The winelands offer anything from the grandest 5-star luxury to country inns, guest-houses, cottages and bed-and-breakfasts. Contact the information offices and/or publicity associations of the wine areas you plan visiting for brochures and local advice. Getaway and WINE magazine, are good sources of information. Highly recommended are the retreats listed in the "Portfolio" booklets: Portfolios of Country Places, Town and Country Retreats, Bed and Breakfast Retreats (phone (011) 8803414 or (0291) 43341 for more information on these).

Stellenbosch Publicity Association: Tel: (021) 8833584.
Franschhoek Publicity Association: Tel: (021) 8763603.
Paarl Publicity Association: Tel: (021) 8724842.
Helderberg Tourism Bureau: Tel: (021) 8514022.
Wellington Tourism Bureau: Tel: (021) 8734604.
Worcester Tourism Bureau: Tel: (0231) 71408.
Robertson Tourism Bureau: Tel: (02351) 4437.
Hermanus Tourism Bureau: Tel: (0283) 22629.
West Coast Tourism Bureau: Tel: (022) 7142088.
McGregor Publicity Association Tel: (02353) 954.

WINELANDS RESTAURANTS

Many cellars offer light lunches or picnics: look for a knife and fork symbol beside the individual entries in this guide. The restaurants featured below (recommended by locals) describe their own menus and attractions.

BREEDE RIVER VALLEY

Burchell's Restaurant, De Breede Estate (4 km from Worcester on the R43 Ceres Road; 2,5 km from the N1). Tel: 0231-25388. Bookings only for parties of ten or more. Lunch/dinner Mon-Sat; Sun lunch only. Enjoy spectacular views of the Hex River and Brandwacht Mountains while dining alfresco savouring imaginative modern style Cape cuisine, prepared with only the freshest local ingredients such as duck, trout and game. Housed in the 200-year-old cellar, a national monument, at one of the oldest homesteads in the area, the restaurant is hosted by Tim and Debbie Alcock who welcome you to savour specialities such as toasted feta and rocket salad; twice-roasted duck with spiced kumquats; quail with ginger and orange, and ostrich fillet with green peppercorns and Cape gooseberries. A carefully chosen selection of Breede River Valley wines adds the finishing touch to elegant yet relaxed dining at this picturesque country restaurant.

Mimosa Lodge, Church Street, Montagu. Tel: 0234-42351, Fax: 0234-42418. Open daily for breakfast 8.30-10, dinner. Booking essential. Non-smoking restaurant—guests may smoke in The Club or in the smoking lounge adjacent to the restaurant. A warm welcome awaits you in this historic house that has recently been renovated and restored to its former glory. This is a place to relax and enjoy the superb food created by owner/chef Andreas Küng. The table d'hôte changes daily and has its emphasis on fresh, local ingredients and home-baked treats. Game is one of the specialities, presented in many delicious ways. And dishes such as "con fungi" still show the European heritage that makes this place so special. Small, but fine wine list.

CONSTANTIA

Alphen, Alphen Drive. Tel: 021-7945011, Fax: 021-7945710. Lunch/dinner daily. At the gateway to the Constantia Valley, Alphen has been the home of Cape hospitality since the 18th century. In the Manor House restaurant chef Robert Pflaum creates tasty elegant dishes to complement the historic setting, with its gleaming antique furniture and pictures from the family collection. If you are looking for something less formal, try the Boer 'n Brit in the Jonkershuis. Here memorabilia from the time of the Boer War fill the walls. Enjoy a glass of wine from the Constantia Valley with your meal, seated in the warmth of the hearth fire or outside in the dappled shade of ancient oaks.

Buitenverwachting Restaurant, Klein Constantia Road. Tel: 021-7943522, Fax: 021-7941351. Lunch Tues-Fri; dinner Tues-Sat. Consistently rated among the top ten restaurants in the country and winner of the Business Day Restaurant Award, Buitenverwachting overlooks a vista of vineyards to the Constantiaberg. The menu changes daily. Sophisticated fare ranges from exotic continental dishes to traditional South African flavours, using only the finest seasonal produce sourced world-wide: prawns from Moçambique, venison from Namibia and selected cheeses from Europe. Award-winning wine list. Appointments and service match the exclusive ambience.

The Cellars, Hohenort Avenue. Tel: 021-7942137. Fax: 021-7942149. Breakfast/lunch/dinner daily. Cape Malay 7-9.30 pm. Nestled in the beautiful winelands of Constantia, you will find the enchanting and exquisitely beautiful grounds of the Cellars-Hohenort Hotel. A 5-star Relais & Chateaux establishment. The garden, known throughout the world for its beauty and lush green vegetation surrounds the two main buildings. The first of these is the cellar which boasts the **"Novelli at the Cellars"** restaurant. The kitchen is run by Michelin star-trained chef George Jardin. The menu offers the best in innovative, contemporary Continental cuisine with the emphasis on local products. This, together with the ambience, the attentive staff and sommelier Philippe Buttin, create an unequalled culinary "experience". The Novelli also boasts a wine list which has just won the prestigious Diners Club Platinum Award. For an equally unique experience, you will find the **Cape Malay Restaurant** situated in the Hohenort. For those who enjoy "real" Cape cuisine at its best, this is a must. Traditional boboties, curries and other Cape delights lovingly prepared by Martha Williams who has perfected these dishes over many years. For a "special" evening out, the choice is difficult, but always memorable!

Constantia Uitsig, Spaanschemat River Road. Tel: 021-7944480. Lunch/dinner Tues-Sat, dinner only Mon/Sun. Licensed. Booking essential. Nominated by Penta Publications as one of the Top Ten Restaurants in S.A. Overlooking the vineyards and mountains, serving Italian/Mediterranean cuisine. New restaurant "La Colombe" overlooks the swimming pool; manicured gardens. Serving traditional French Provençal cuisine with a Cape flavour.

The Jonkershuis, Groot Constantia Wine Estate, off Constantia Main Road. Tel: 021-7946255. Sun and Mon open 9-5; Tues-Sat 9 till late. Take time out to savour the tranquillity and "old-fashioned" friendly service in this charming corner of the Constantia winelands. Country breakfasts, fireside teas, lunch under the oaks and candlelit dinners. Cape country cooking rich in flavour. A delightful hideaway.

Parks, 114 Constantia Main Road. Tel: 021-7978202, Fax: 021-7978233. E-mail: goodfood@iafrica.com. Dinner Mon-Sat. New visitors and ever-growing numbers of regulars are assured of a warm welcome and professional service at Michael and Madeleine Olivier's popular Constantia restaurant. Guests dine in the rooms of the beautifully restored house, set in a pretty garden. The atmosphere is elegant but relaxed. Park's signature dishes—blackened fish and duck confit—are retained by popular demand. The daily chef's selection menu offers interesting and unusual dishes using fresh, seasonal ingredients. Desserts are scrumptious and while fresh fruits and sorbets always feature, the main emphasis here is, frankly, sinful. Both the food and the extensive wine list offer flair and quality at a fair price.

Peddlars-on-the-Bend, Spaanschemat Road. Tel: 021-7947747/50. Open daily from 11-11 (Pub), 12-11. (Rest.). Peddlars-on-the-Bend has become one of Cape Town's most popular destinations for locals and visitors. A warm country charm, a lovely garden setting under a huge oak tree and a reputation for quality service, make this a "must visit" venue. The menu offers generous (but reasonably priced) portions of wholesome country food: hearty casseroles in winter, good steaks, fresh linefish and tasty pastas. To complement the existing menu, a lighter lunch menu has recently been introduced. Peddlars is the Cape Argus/SAB Tavern of the Year for 1997. Award-winning wine list (Diners Club) showcasing the area, but venturing further afield too; includes some special buys from private cellars and auctions. Very popular, booking most advisable.

Steenberg Tel: 021-7132224; Fax: 021-7132221. Lunch/dinner daily. Constantia's newest eating-out spot in the original wine cellar of this old Cape farm, now a residential-golfing-wine estate. Food is high-quality informal; the freshest of ingredients and a menu that changes regularly. A small wine list, highlighting wines from Steenberg and the Constantia area, also offers the best from the New World. The mood is modern British in the Conran/Bibendum style: contemporary furniture, imported Italian lighting, white damask cloths to the ground. A stainless steel, mahogany and beechwood bar provides both a meeting place and delectable seafood delicacies like oysters—with champagne or local bubbly by the glass.

DURBANVILLE

De Oude Welgemoed, Kommissaris Street, Welgemoed. Tel: 021-9134962. Fax: 021-9132483. Lunch/dinner Mon-Fri; Sat dinner only. Tranquil restaurant in a 1670 homestead with walk-in private cellar where guests can choose their wines (reds dating back to 1960). Stylish, fresh country cuisine (making the most of garden produce), with a formal French influence. Run by David Grier of the Villiera wine family. Also bistro serving pizza/pasta.

FRANSCHHOEK

Ballon Rouge, 12 Reservoir Street. Tel: 021-8762651. Fax: 021-8763743. Breakfast, lunch 12-2.30 and dinner 7-10.30 pm. E-mail: info@ballon-rouge.co.za. A modern, family-owned and run, 60-cover restaurant, with conservatory, and attached terrace, Ballon Rouge features a "Brasserie" menu created by Chef Patron Rory Morgan, to complement fun-filled meal times, with regular live music entertainment on special occasions. The cuisine is "South African with a French flavour" and specialises in game, fresh seawater exotic fish, local salmon, grills and home-made pastas. Weekly specials and vegetarian dishes are always available and there is a fresh seafood "braai" on the terrace. An award-winning wine list, warm hospitality and efficient, friendly staff, complete the picture.

Chez Michel, Huguenot Road, opposite post office. Tel: 021-8762671. Lunch/dinner Tues-Sat. Sunday lunch. Licensed. Discover a small exclusive restaurant in Franschhoek. Great food and full of charm. "It's like dining out with good friends." Delicious local trout and the best of country cooking.

Haute Cabrière Restaurant, Franschhoek Pass. Tel: 021-8763688. Lunch daily; dinner in season (phone ahead to make sure). High up on the Franschhoek Pass with wonderful views over the pinot noir vineyards, this highly-rated restaurant offers a wonderfully different food and wine experience. Two unique winelands talents, cellar-master Achim von Arnim and chef-patron Matthew Gordon take the eating-out experience into a new dimension. It's a gastronomic adventure with a menu created to complement Haute Cabrière wines and Pierre Jourdan Cap Classiques. No starters or main courses just a variety of dishes in full and half portions to mix and match and pair with the wines—all available by the glass. Fresh fish daily, plump oysters, West Coast mussels and game are specialities. The salads—many grown on the restaurant's own farm, the Karoo lamb and home-made pasta are superb. The restaurant is situated over the cathedral-arched barrel maturation cellar.

La Maison de Chamonix, Uitkyk Street. Tel: 021-8762393. Lunch Wed-Mon; dinner Wed-Sun. A definitive winelands eating experience in a converted homestead with wrap-around views of the Franschhoek valley. The manor house menu, offering delicious French country-style dishes, is prepared with skill and care and enormous respect for superbly-sourced ingredients. Lighter meals and spit roasts available in the farm's original smithy.

La Petite Ferme, Pass Road. Tel: 021-8763016. Fax: 021-8763024. Lunch daily. Booking essential. Three generations of the Dendy Young family have been involved, and are now joined by cousin Nalabe Edgecumbe, to host the restaurant, as Mark nurtures his third vintage of award-winning wines which are featured on the wine list and are only available in the restaurant. Rainbow trout is de-boned & smoked on the farm, a house speciality continued along with Plum Crazy, made from home-grown Santa Rosa plums. The menu features unique recipes including dishes with a Malay influence, and the creative use of fresh local produce. A new addition to "The little farm" are three suites overlooking the vineyards from private verandahs with individual plunge-pools, stylishly decorated for the ultimate experience in tranquillity, privacy and warm hospitality.

Le Quartier Français, 16 Huguenot Road. Tel: 021-8762151, Fax: 021-8763105. Breakfast 7.30-10.30; lunch 12-2; dinner 7-10; light lunch 11-10 Mon-Sun. It's a year since the new look Le Quartier Français re-opened with its vibrant and colourful bar. The spacious, airy restaurant with its panoramic views of the mountains and gardens lends itself to the taste bud-tickling of chef Margot Janse and her team. Innovative dishes such as olive oil-poached salmon trout with a smoked salmon fritter, cucumber and seaweed are served in the restaurant. In the bar and on the terrace try the lamb burger with creamed avocado, marinated tomatoes and pickled cucumber on a toasted foccacia from 10-10 pm, complemented by an award-winning wine list featuring local wines. The 15 luxurious rooms have all been individually refurbished and the two suites now have their own private swimming pools and air-conditioning.

Monneaux, Franschhoek Country House, Main Road. Tel: 021-8763386. Fax: 021-8762744. Mon-Sun breakfast/lunch/dinner; 11 close. Experience the warm welcome of a country house combined with the best of cuisine and culinary conversation. Situated on the outskirts of the picturesque village of Franschhoek, is the charming Franschhoek Country House, the elegant Monneaux Restaurant and Wine Bar. The exciting modern French cuisine and superb local wines can be enjoyed at this once perfume-producing establishment. À la carte lunches are served in the tranquil gardens whilst dinner can be enjoyed in the understated dining room and enclosed verandah. A gastronomique experience!

Môreson Bread and Wine, Môreson Farm, Happy Valley Road, La Motte. Tel: 021-8763692, Fax: 021-8762348. Opening hours depend on the time of year: Mon-Sun 10-4; and in low season Wed-Sun 10-3. You will find this little gem in the heart of Franschhoek valley set on the Môreson-Marin Soleil wine farm. Le Quartier recently took over the management of the Bread & Wine Restaurant. The new menu boasts innovative alfresco meals devised by Margot Janse and lends itself to enjoying the fine wines of the Môreson farm. Guests can relax outside under the oaks and enjoy the best that Franschhoek has to offer.

Topsi and Company, 7 Reservoir St West. Tel/Fax: 021-8762952. Open daily except Tues from 12.30 lunch/5 pm dinner. Booking preferable. Unlicensed. In a luxuriant garden alongside a brook in Franschhoek, just off Huguenot Road, you will find this family-owned restaurant where fresh produce from the area is prepared with Topsi Venter's famous verve and style. Ambrosial soups, salads and vegetable dishes accompany daily specials such as leek cheesecake with a hazelnut dressing; port fillet marinated in beer; confit of duck with fruit salsa. Avid foodies will enjoy browsing through the cookery book collection and your dining experience is coloured by fine art on the walls and action emanating from the (nearly) open-plan kitchen.

GREYTON

Greyton Lodge, 46 Main Street. Tel: 028-2549876. Fax: 028-2549672. Breakfast/lunch/dinner daily (except Mon lunch). Revel in the historic soundings created by hospitable owners Philip and Sandra Engelen Antoneo; recently won the 1998 Chef of the Year at the Hermanus Food and Wine Festival. Emphasis is on refined country cooking, complemented by award winning wine lists for 96, 97 and 98. In summer, breakfast and lunch are served in the garden, while in winter dine by candlelight beside one of the cavernous log fires. Nailed to the ceiling in the Royal Bar are some 8 000 corks which only goes to show the popularity of this royal establishment.

GROOT-DRAKENSTEIN

Bien Donné Werf is the historical core of a research centre for the Cape fruit industry. Tel: 021-8741684/13. The **Petit Salon** restaurant, open daily from 10-5, offers tea and delicacies; meals combining regional cooking with fruit and herbs, served with local wines. Attractions include tours of the manor house (the farm dates back to 1691), the orchard and herb garden, a farm shop, guest-house and conference centre, plus workshops providing information on the fruit industry, with particular reference to Bien Donné. The tasting room presents fruit in every guise—from pure juice to wine, brandy and traditional mampoer.

Boschendal Restaurant, on the farm, off the R310. Tel: 021-8704274 Fax:: 021-8742137. Mon-Sun 8-4.30; lunch daily. Booking essential. Dress code: smart/casual (no jeans). Non-smoking restaurant—guests may smoke in the spacious reception area. Housed in the original cellar, the restaurant serves delicious buffet-style lunches. Heap your plate with expertly-prepared traditional Cape dishes, steaming roasts and local seafood specialities from tables groaning with tantalising treats (including sinful puds), complemented by fine Boschendal wines, including the Jean Le Long range, available only in this restaurant. Beautifully restored and well-appointed, this is an ideal place to settle back and savour the food, the ambience and the company. The manor house is a national monument and museum with fascinating artworks, Cecil Rhodes memorabilia, Kraak porcelain, furniture and displays.

Le Pique-Nique, Boschendal Wine Farm, off the R310. Tel: 021-8704274 Fax: 021-8742137. Mon-Sun 8-4.30 pm. Open November 1-April 30, weather permitting. Booking essential. Picnic baskets to be collected between 12.15-1.30. During the summer months Le Pique-Nique provides an ideal setting for an alfresco lunch. Collect a hamper filled with simple country fare from the gazebo and spread your picnic at tables in the shade of fragrant pine trees, or on the lawn beside a pond.

Le Café, Boschendal Wine Farm, off the R310. Open daily from 10-5. No bookings taken, enquiries 021-8704283. Tucked away in the original slave quarters, Le Café serves tasty light lunches and country teas. Enjoy warming Bobotie in the cosy restaurant in winter; in summer, relax outdoors with a glass of wine, a slice of quiche or a baguette and a salad under the dappled shade of ancient oaks.

HERMANUS

Burgundy, Market Square. Tel: 0283-22800. Fax: 0283-701204. Teas and lunch Mon-Sun 10-4.30. Dinner 7-close. The Burgundy restaurant with stunning views of Walker Bay is housed in the oldest building in Hermanus—now a national monument. Alfresco lunches are served in the garden and the menu offers a fusion of French and local cuisine and incomparable seafood. The wine list includes wines from the local wine estates. The Auberge Burgundy situated opposite the restaurant offers excellent accommodation on a bed & breakfast basis.

KUILS RIVER-STELLENBOSCH

Guinea Fowl, Polkadraai Rd, Kuils River. Tel: 021-9034308 Fax: 021-9038507. Lunch Wed-Mon, dinner Wed-Sat. Closed Tues. On the historic Saxenburg wine farm on the slopes of the Bottelary hills, with magnificent mountain and ocean views. The restaurant is now under the management of Gabi & Robert Christianus (of the famous Wagon Wheels in Paarl) who bring together a wonderful combination of European and Cape cuisine that is in harmony with the wines. Exceptional service is an important feature. In winer the warm log fire creates a wonderful ambience, in summer there's the terrace with spectacular views, perfect for that evening sundowner. Booking advisable, especially for dinner. The restaurant is also an ideal venue for private functions and weddings.

Hazendal Restaurant, Bottelary Road, Kuils River. Tel: 021-9035034/5, Fax: 021-9030057. Open for lunch Tues-Sun 12-2.30, Mon-Sun morning & afternoon teas. The intimate restaurant is situated between the original cellar that has now been renovated into the tasting centre and lounge area, and the new state-of-the-art cellar that was built in 1996. A lovely fireplace in the lounge area creates a warm welcome, and is a great area to relax after mealtimes. There is seating for approx. 50 people in the beautiful summer and winter courtyards, as well as the front stoep of the tasting centre, offering beautiful views of the surrounding mountain and hills. Hazendal offers lunch, wine tastings and afternoon teas. Meals are served from Tuesdays to Sundays. They vary from light fresh salads, hearty home-made soups and Russian blinis (reflecting the Russian involvement of the owner Dr. Mark Voloshin), to pasta and traditional Cape Malay dishes. There are seasonal dishes daily. Dessert and cakes are home-made and fresh bread is baked daily. The Estate caters for functions of up to 50 people seated, and 100 for cocktail functions. Attention to detail and excellent personalised service is guaranteed at all times.

Zevenwacht Country Restaurant, Zevenwacht Wine Estate, Langverwacht Road, Kuils River. Tel: 021-9035123. Fax: 021-9033373. Breakfast/lunch/dinner Mon-Sun. In a setting of unsurpassed tranquillity overlooking a lake housing the restaurant. Elegant country cuisine is served in a friendly, relaxed atmosphere. Quality picnic baskets also available in the gardens. Well-known Cape restaurateurs Keith Blake, John Jackson and Frank Mullineux operate all the venues for breakfast, lunch and dinner 7 days a week. A compulsory stop on the Cape Gourmet Trail.

De Weintafel Restaurant & Pub, Tel: 021-9061033. Lunch/dinner Tues-Sat, Sun lunch only. A new fun-restaurant at Zevenwacht Wine Estate offering Cape starters, seafood potjies, casseroles and other rustic, country fare. Housed in the old Langverwacht wine cellars, the restaurant has a charming setting and décor with a relaxed pub. Reasonably priced and friendly service combines to make a welcoming new addition to the Cape culinary scene.

McGREGOR

The Old Mill Lodge, Tel: 02353-841. Fax: 02353-941. Situated on the outskirts of McGregor, overlooking the village, with the Langeberg mountains in the background and the Lodge's small vineyard in the foreground—this spectacular view best enjoyed from the Lodge's dining room or front stoep. Full breakfasts and table d'hôte dinners (a three-course candle-lit affair with a set menu which changes daily—emphasis on seasonal and local produce) are served daily. Light lunches (open sandwiches on home-made bread or country style cheese platters) are served Monday to Saturday. Booking essential for dinner. 1997 & 1998 Diners Club Winelist Awards.

PAARL

Bosman's, Tel: 021-8632727. Open daily—all day at the five-star estate hotel, the Grande Roche, Plantasie Street. Tel: 021-8632727. Wind your way through the winelands and stop at Bosman's for light, elegant, informal lunches complemented by splendid wines from the superbly stocked cellar.

Bosman's is a world-class restaurant providing contemporary Cape gourmet cuisine in the refined atmosphere of a magnificent manor house. The Grande Roche has become a legend on the hospitality scene, winning a formidable array of awards and culinary accolades. Latest achievements include its selection as a World Wide Suburban Retreat in Andrew Harper's Hideaway Report and SATOUR's first Hotel of the Year award for its "incredible attention to detail, impeccable grounds, excellent food and superb levels of luxury". The first and only hotel-restaurant in Africa to achieve Relais Gourmand status, one of the world's highest Relais & Chateaux culinary appellations.

Laborie Restaurant and Wine House, off the R45 leading from the N1 into town, Taillefert Street. Tel: 021-8073095, Fax: 021-8073094. Lunch daily 12.30-2, dinner Tues-Sat 7.30-9. Laborie offers you only the best from the winelands of the Cape. Here you can experience the tranquil hospitality in the beautiful rural setting of KWV's wine estate, the traditional Old Cape atmosphere and dishes, as well as an à la carte menu and the inspiration of a special wine from the Paarl region. All this adds up to make it the ideal venue for lunch or dinner, while the value for money is an added bonus.

Mountain Shadows, Klein Drakenstein Road, Klein-Drakenstein. (On the N1, bypass Paarl and just before the tollgate turn left to Klein-Drakenstein. At the BP service station turn right, continue for 2 km and turn right again.) Tel: 021-8623192, Fax: 021-8626796. Breakfast/lunch/dinner daily from 7.00 am until late. Mountain Shadows is a superb Cape-Dutch manor house in the heart of the winelands, set against the dramatic backdrop of the Drakenstein mountains, only 7 km from Paarl. New owners Georges and Jean Gosselin offer tastefully decorated en-suite bedrooms furnished with antiques, each with private patio. All rooms are fully renovated and have TV, mini bars and safes. Enjoy noble wines and fine cuisine. Pursue the quieter pleasures, swimming, or enjoy a tour of the winelands.

Rhebokskloof Estate, Rhebokskloof Minor Road, Noorder-Paarl. Tel: 021-8638606, Fax: 021-8638906. Open Thurs-Mon 11.30 till late (teas/lunch/dinner); Tues 11.30-5.30 (teas/lunch). Closed Wed. Open on all public holidays. Located on the beautiful Rhebokskloof wine estate, Rhebokskloof restaurant is the ultimate venue for enjoying superb gourmet delights accompanied by the estate's award-winning wines in one of the best locations the winelands have to offer. Executive chef Stefan Achterfeld is renowned for creating continental cuisine using only the best, locally available fresh produce and is known for producing some interesting and extremely delightful culinary creations. Rhebokskloof is one of the few restaurants which is open every public holiday, including Christmas and New Year's Day.

Roggeland Country House, Roggeland Road, Dal Josafat Valley, Northern Paarl. Tel: 021-8682501. Lunch/dinner daily. Booking essential. Succumb to a celebration of the Cape's finest cuisine at this historic and exclusive country manor, acclaimed as the "preferred" choice of hotel in the Cape winelands (The New York Times—September 1996). Simplicity and variety is the key note of each gourmet course, delectably prepared by Chef Lee-Ann Wright using fresh regional produce accompanied by an excellent matching wine, resulting in its culinary delights continuously inspiring world-renowned gourmets and travel critics across the globe. Vegetarian meals are prepared by arrangement.

Wagon Wheels and Gabi's, 57 Lady Grey Street. Tel: 021-8725265. Lunch/dinner except Sun, Mon. Lunch only public holidays. Book ahead. Exceptional—this carnivores' paradise has no peers in the winelands for the consistency and quality of its prime focus—the simple, but extraordinary steak. Robert and Gabi Christianus, who have lost none of their Continental chic during years of residence in Paarl, seem to imbue everything they prepare with their own excellent taste. From those steaks (*****) to the accompanying, cracklingly crisp drifts of chips (the solid equivalent of this guide's new ☺ super-quafffer sign), the sophisticated garden salads—even the elegant onion rings!—this is a thoroughly relaxed gourmet meatery, rightly much-loved by locals, and regularly, much-admired by international wine visitors. Equally fine are the non-meat alternatives, which range around fresh, seasonal delicacies and locally-caught fish. Rustic, down-on-the-range décor is deceptive—look rather at next-door and interleading **Gabi's** Bar, with its sleek French café-bar ambience for the secrets of the Christianus style, and a pointer to a decidedly classy wine-list. (Yes, authentic Vintage Champagne can and does team deliciously with steak!) Immaculate espresso underlines the attention to every detail here. Also includes a warm reception for children, whom the Christianuses quite rightly welcome as the foodies of the future.

SIMONDIUM

Country Elephant, R45, Simondium. Tel: 021-8741355. Lunch daily (except Tues), dinner Mon, Wed-Sat. Booking advisable, for although a recent addition in the winelands, this delightfully relaxed restaurant in a renovated farmhouse—conveniently located about half way between Paarl and Franschhoek—has already built up a loyal following. Ambience is colourful and cuisine by chef Bernard Steyn (ex-The Bay penthouse suite) is a flavour-rich blend of French Provençal and Southern African dishes. A creative table d'hôte style menu, changing daily to make full use of seasonal local produce, is complemented by very reasonably priced wines from the area. Superb views of the Klein-Drakenstein mountains provide a dramatic setting for alfresco summer dining, while the cosy fire indoors is welcome in Cape winters.

SOMERSET WEST

Chez Michel, 41 Victoria Street. Tel:/Fax: 021-8516069. Open Tues-Fri lunch, 12-2; dinner 7-9.45. Dinner only Sat. Situated in a national monument, this old Cape-Dutch house with its warm atmosphere makes a delightful restaurant. Except for a brief interlude, Chez Michel has always been Swiss-owned and boasted a very good kitchen. The latest Swiss-Italian owner/chef, Reto Valentin is no exception; maintaining many traditional Swiss dishes like veal Zürich, Wiener Schnitzel and the unforgettable Rösti. Reto has also added Latin touches to his menu. A variety of meat and fish dishes accompanied by seasonal vegetables and teasing desserts to round off the meal.

De Voorkamer, Erinvale Estate Hotel, Lourensford Road. Tel: 021-8471166. Breakfast/lunch/teas/dinner daily. A restaurant with all the ingredients for a feast for the senses . . . delectable food . . . exquisite décor . . . gracious manor house atmosphere . . . beautiful country setting. It's part of the Erinvale Estate Hotel adjacent to the historic homes of Vergelegen and Fleur du Cap in the verdant Helderberg valley in Somerset West. Start the day with a hearty breakfast, discover the ever-changing luncheon menus, delight in elegant dinners—traditional Cape blended with classic Continental. Relax and enjoy drinks by the crackling winter fire in the Crag 'n Berg bar or take tea in the courtyard.

Die Ou Pastorie, 41 Lourens Street. Tel: 021-8522120, Fax: 021-8513710. Lunch/dinner Tues-Fri; dinner only Sat; lunch only Sun. Built in 1819, this former parsonage—which offers both elegant accommodation and superb cuisine—has established a reputation as one of the best restaurants in the Western Cape. The food is stylish and innovative, classically-based with modern individual flavour combinations. The emphasis is on fresh seasonal ingredients. The award-winning wine list and a well-varied menu set the stage for memorable and an unforgettable experience. Whether dining on the veranda in summer or in one of the interleading dining rooms—which are warmed by glowing fires in the winters, the elegant and tranquil surroundings are complemented with personal dedicated service.

Lady Phillips Restaurant, Vergelegen, Lourensford Road, Somerset West. Tel: 021-8471346. Fax: 021-8471608. Open 9.30-4 daily for teas/lunches, closed Good Friday, Workers' Day and Christmas Day. A delightful daytime venue, with open-air patio overlooking the Lourens River. Interior decorated with bright chintzes and filled with fresh flowers from the surrounding gardens. The small, innovative à la carte menu makes imaginative use of the large variety of herbs from the herb garden and salad ingredients from the farm, picked fresh daily. Country lunches, ranging from quiches to home-made gourmet pies and pastas, as well as continental dishes. Interesting vegetarian dishes are also a feature. During summer months, the nearby **Rose Terrace** is open for alfresco lunches of pâté, cheese platters, salads and baguettes.

L'Auberge du Paysan, off the R44 between Somerset West and Stellenbosch: into Winery Road; follow signs into Raithby Road. Tel:/Fax: 021-8422008. Lunch Tues-Sat; dinner Mon-Sat. Patron Frederick Thurmann's style and panache highlight the discreet charms of this chic French country restaurant, acknowledged to be amongst the finest in the country. The elegant appointments, décor and ambience complement the traditional French menu with specialities from Alsace, Burgundy and Provence. In summer sip pre-dinner cocktails on the patio, and in winter wine and dine in the romantic warmth of the open log fire. Sizzling escargots; lean, crispy roast duckling and the finest crème brûlee are the house specialities. In winter, oysters, venison and game birds, and in summer, crustaceans and fresh berries from Stellenbosch are seasonal delights. For the grand finale treat yourself to crêpes Suzette or sabayon prepared at your table. Superb wine list.

96 Winery Road, off the R44 between Somerset West and Stellenbosch. Tel: 021-8422020. Lunch/dinner Mon-Sat; lunch only Sun. Booking advisable. Well-known restaurateur Ken Forrester believes eating out should be fun. The result: a bright, buzzing, atmospheric venue in the winelands which is unsurprisingly immensely popular, a sort of foodie HQ for, in particular, local and international wine luminaries. Won a Perrier "SA" restaurant of the year award in a matter of months. Wooden furniture, enormous hearth and butternut walls hung with farm implements and the works of local artists contribute to a relaxed rural feel; windows offer views of the Helderberg. Food is fresh, colourful, zingily-flavoured country fare from chef Kathy Romer-Lee. A tastebud-revving, super-creative mix of Cape, Provençal and Eastern influences plus carnivore heaven: a platter of choice cuts of beef—from marbled steaks to succulently pink fillet—is presented for inspection, then cooked to individual specifications. Also delectable vegetables and decadent desserts (the chocolate torte is magnificent). Adventurous, excellent wine list.

Willowbrook Lodge, Morgenster Avenue, off Lourensford Road (1 km before Vergelegen and Erinvale Golf Estate). Tel: 021-8513759, Fax: 021-8514152. Lunch 12-2, dinner 7-10 Mon-Sun. Fully licensed. No children under 12. French owners Janik and Serge Olchanetzky preside over an intimate restaurant at this elegant country lodge which is a member of the prestigious Relais & Chateaux. It's a place where fresh flowers, antiques, works of art and paintings create a special backdrop to memorable cuisine and where warm hospitality, exceptional comfort and professional service await guests. French chef Alexandre Coupy offers delicious selections from a renowned à la carte menu which changes seasonally. His philosophy is simple: use the wonderful local resources such as springbok, ostrich and crayfish and make a tasty interpretation of French cuisine. *Bon Appètit.* Excellent small wine list.

STELLENBOSCH

De Cameron, 50 Plein St. Tel: 021-8833331. Licensed. Lunch/dinner daily, indoors or at pavement tables. Booking essential. A ristorante that buzzes like a good party day and night, winter and summer—when the vibrations spill out onto a shady pavement and the feeling of being in a warm corner of Italy intensifies. Longtime favourite of locals and international visitors alike. Really good, authentic, imaginative food—the finest, dewiest local produce given lashings of Mediterranean style, with particular reference to Napoli and Sardinia, youthful stamping grounds of proprietors Mario and Massimo, who re-visit annually to re-charge their palates. Naturally, the Italian dishes are excellent—everything from lamb (osso) bucco, to gnocchi, to pizza and pasta. But equally fine are the less specifically Italian offerings: great linefish, very serious steaks, marlin carpaccio with pickled Japanese ginger, luscious langoustines and plump Swakopmund oysters. Seasonal treats like green asparagus, wild mushrooms, local artichokes are handled with affection and pride. As is this warm, welcoming resaurant in general. Fine wine list, great espresso etc.

De Volkskombuis, Aan de Wagen Road, off Dorp Street. Tel: 021-8872121/8875239. Booking essential. Lunch Mon-Sun; dinner Mon-Sat. A traditional restaurant on the tree-lined banks of the Eerste River, specialising in Cape cooking, fresh fish and seafood dishes. There is also an innovative à la carte menu, and a set menu for Sunday lunch. Private functions catered for.

Doornbosch, Strand-Somerset West Road. Tel: 021-8875079 or 8866163. Lunch/dinner daily. A very exclusive restaurant in Stellenbosch set in a historic building. French-Moroccan accented dishes and finely prepared seasonal specialities. A vine-draped veranda for summer eating out, crackling fire in winter. Fine wine selection. You can also pop in—as locals do—for an espresso or glass of wine. Function facilities available.

Governor's Hall, Lanzerac Manor & Winery, Lanzerac Road. Tel: 021-8871132. Fax: 021-8872310. Open daily 12-4, 7-close. Set in the heart of a 300-year-old, 155 hectare wine estate on the outskirts of historic Stellenbosch, the Lanzerac Manor & Winery has long been a residence of choice for discerning travellers. Situated at the hotel is the Governor's Hall fine-dining restaurant, offering the traditional Lanzerac Cape Malay and cheese buffet during lunch, and an international à la carte menu at dinner. As a fitting end to the perfect meal, guests are invited to retire in the evenings to the elegant Craven Lounge with its authentic antiques, where champagne is served at a champagne bar, followed by coffee, cognacs and cigars.

Green Door, Delaire Wine Farm, Helshoogte (R310) Banhoek, Tel: 021-8851756, Fax: 021-8851270. Tues-Sun 12-3. Mondays in season. Booking essential. This small restaurant with its quirky Rooster theme, opened its doors on Delaire wine farm in December 1996. The Long Stoep has a panoramic view that stretches from sunrise to sunset! Cuisine is simple with a Californian (healthy) approach to its Cape cooking. The small menu changes regularly using only the best local fresh produce. Enjoy leisurely lunches in the shade of the pin oaks or, come winter time, gather around the hearth whilst savouring hearty soups and freshly baked breads. Picnics in season, weather permitting. Please book to avoid disappointment.

Le Pommier, Helshoogte Pass, Banhoek. Tel: 021-8851269. Open lunch/dinner Tues-Sat, lunch Sun. Closed Mon out of season. Booking essential. Nestled high up on the Helshoogte Pass overlooking the lush Banhoek Valley, this old converted farm shed offers not only spectacular views but a sense of timeless charm, warmth and personality. Like the mountains, forever suggesting different moods, Le Pommier offers cosy log fires in winter with snow-capped mountains in the distance, cool rolling greenery in the endless summer. The above combined with the personal service of your hosts, adds to an overall sense of well-being. Facilities include conference/ function centre, art gallery and guest-house.

Oom Samie se Winkel, 84 Dorp St. Old-Cape emporium (anything from velskoen to antiques), adjoins **Oom Samie's Wine Shop** (Tel: 021-8872612) where wines can be bought and dispatched world/country-wide. This little diningroom and wine garden are part of the charming and historic Oom Samie se Winkel. Simple wholesome snacks, teas, filter coffee and traditional lunches. Unpretentious and reasonable. The restaurant is fully licensed. Tel: 8873879.

Oude Libertas Restaurant, at the SFW Centre, off Adam Tas Road. Tel: 021-8087429 Fax: 021-8866908. Booking essential. Mon-Fri 8.30 till close; Sat 3 till close. In the heart of the winelands, this exclusive restaurant offfers the opportunity to get out of the hustle and bustle of the town centre and appreciate the natural beauty of the lovely surroundings. Gourmet cuisine, complemented by a choice of award-winning Zonnebloem and Nederburg wines. Whether at a table near the fireplace in winter or on the peaceful balcony with breathtaking views in summer, Oude Libertas is an ideal venue for a relaxed meal, business lunch or romantic dinner. Special services offered include an à la carte menu, private candlelight dinners for groups and special gourmet evenings.

Ralph's, 13 Andringa St. Tel: 021-8833532. Lunch Mon-Fri; dinner Mon-Sat. Licensed. Booking advisable. Cabaret on a plate, conceived by Ralph von Pletzen in his own image, with quirky menu descriptions to match. Deep-fried frogs' legs are titled Natural Born Swimmers! Tapas salad and raw marinated fresh fish are favourite starters, while Ralph's fillets (ostrich, venison and knockout beef) are famous. Daintier appetites should specify half portions.

Spier Jonkershuis, Spier Estate, R310, Lynedoch. Tel: 021-8091100 ext. 1127. Lunch 12.30-3.30, dinner from 7.30, Tues-Sat. Booking essential. The 150-year-old Spier Jonkershuis serves a traditional Cape Malay buffet including soup, farm breads, cold dishes, salads, bredies, curries. Malay specialities, Cape cheese and hot and cold desserts. The summer oak shaded terrace and the warm welcoming winter fires make this a favourite year-round venue. **Café Spier**, open 9.30-11.30 for breakfast, lunch 11.30-3.30. Offering local cuisine with farm style fare, serves sunrise breakfasts and light luncheons. There is hearty food and merriment galore for families and friends at **The Taphuis and Riverside Pub**. Open Mon-Sat 11-10.30; Sun 11-9.30. Relax and enjoy the ultimate winelands aflresco **Spier Picnic** or stop off at the **Spier Farmstall** and **Coffee Shop**.

The Vineleaf, Devon Valley Hotel, Devon Valley Rd. Tel: 021-8822012, Fax: 021-8822610. Open Mon-Sun breakfast/lunch/dinner. Booking essential. This historic hotel, a Stellenbosch landmark for 50 years, has been renovated and revitalised by new owners David and Lee Ann Nathan-Maister. The Vineleaf Restaurant now offers innovative Cape cuisine, with the freshest—and where possible—home-grown ingredients presented with originality and style. In summer sit on the patio and enjoy the incomparable views. In winter snuggle around a roaring log fire. Traditional Sunday lunches and cream teas are also a speciality! The award-winning wine list offers the full range of Devon Valley wines, together with a representative selection of the Cape's finest. After dinner savour a single malt whiskey—the hotel's selection of 60 is the largest in Africa!

The Wijnhuis, Upper Level, Dorpsmeent Centre, Cnr Church & Andringa Sts. Tel: 021-8877196. Fax: 021-8878078. Open Mon-Sun 9-12 pm. Closed Christmas Day & Good Friday. The Wijnhuis encompasses a restaurant, wine tasting centre, boutique wine shop and tourist information office.

Situated in the historic heart of Stellenbosch you will find the Dorpsmeent, a communal gathering place dating back to 1710 and within its walls a 600 square metre expanse dedicated to the region's finest and most celebrated wines. More than 45 wineries are represented. Their wines are displayed, sold, freighted and made available for tasting in the lounge. The Wijnhuis restaurant menu is Mediterranean and light with daily specials. The kitchen is managed by La Perla Restaurant (est. 1959). Wine-related and other events such as private functions and conferences are catered for.